Communication Yearbook 38

Communication Yearbook 38

Edited by
Elisia L. Cohen

Published Annually for the
International Communication Association

Routledge
Taylor & Francis Group
NEW YORK AND LONDON

First published 2014
by Routledge
711 Third Avenue, New York, etc

and by Routledge
2 Park Square, Milton Park, etc

Routledge is an imprint of the Taylor & Francis Group, an informa business

ISSN: 0147-4642
ISSN: 1556-7429

ISBN: 978-0-415-70931-6 (hbk)
ISBN: 978-1-315-85847-0 (ebk)

Typeset in Times
by Apex CoVantage, LLC

Printed and bound in the United States of America by
Edwards Brothers Malloy, Inc.

Contents

The International Communication Association

The International Communication Association (ICA) was formed in 1950, bringing together academics and other professionals whose interests focus on human communication. The Association maintains an active membership of more than 4,000 individuals, of whom some two thirds teach and conduct research in colleges, universities, and schools around the world. Other members are in government, law, medicine, and other professions. The wide professional and geographic distribution of the membership provides the basic strength of the ICA. The Association serves as a meeting ground for sharing research and useful dialogue about communication interests.

Through its divisions and interest groups, publications, annual conferences, and relations with other associations around the world, the ICA promotes the systemic study of communication theories, processes, and skills. In addition to *Communication Yearbook*, the Association publishes the *Journal of Communication*; *Human Communication Research*; *Communication Theory*; *Journal of Computer-Mediated Communication*; *Communication, Culture & Critique, A Guide to Publishing in Scholarly Communication Journals*; and the *ICA Newsletter.*

For additional information about the ICA and its activities, visit online at www.icahdq.org or contact Michael L. Haley, Executive Director, International Communication Association, 1500 21st Ave. NW, Washington, DC 20036 USA; phone 202–955–1444; fax 202–955–1448; email ica@icahdq.org.

Editors of the *Communication Yearbook* series:

Volumes 1 and 2, Brent D. Ruben
Volumes 3 and 4, Dan Nimmo
Volumes 5 and 6, Michael Burgoon
Volumes 7 and 8, Robert N. Bostrom
Volumes 9 and 10, Margaret L. McLaughlin
Volumes 11, 12, 13, and 14, James A. Anderson
Volumes 15, 16, and 17, Stanley A. Deetz
Volumes 18, 19, and 20, Brant R. Burleson
Volumes 21, 22, and 23, Michael E. Roloff
Volumes 24, 25, and 26, William B. Gudykunst
Volumes 27, 28, and 29, Pamela J. Kalbfleisch
Volumes 30, 31, 32, and 33, Christina S. Beck
Volumes 34, 35, and 36, Charles T. Salmon
Volume 37 and 38, Elisia L. Cohen

Philip Lodge
*Communication History Division
Chair*
Edinburgh Napier University

Laura Stein
*Communication Law & Policy
Division Chair*
University of Texas–Austin

Richard J. Doherty
*Environmental Communication
IG Chair*
University of Leeds

Miyase Christensen
*Ethnicity & Race in Communication
Division Chair*
Stockholm University; Royal
Institute of Technology (KTH)

Paula M Gardner
Feminist Scholarship Division Chair
OCAD University

James D. Ivory
Game Studies IG Chair
Virginia Tech

Travers Scott
*Gay, Lesbian, Bisexual &
Transgender IG Chair*
Clemson University

Adrienne Shaw
*Gay, Lesbian, Bisexual &
Transgender IG Chair*
Temple University

Rashmi Luthra
*Global Comm/Social Change
Div. Chair*
University of Michigan–Dearborn

Mohan Jyoti Dutta
*Health Communication Division
Chair*
National University of Singapore

Prabu David
Information Systems Division Chair
Washington State University

Brandi N. Frisby
*Instructional/Developmental
Division Chair*
University of Kentucky

Hee Sun Park
*Intercultural Communication
Division Chair*
Korea University

Howard Giles
*Intergroup Communication
IG Chair*
University of California–Santa
Barbara

Timothy R. Levine
*Interpersonal Communication
Division Chair*
Michigan State University

Stephanie L. Craft
Journalism Studies Division Chair
University of Illinois

Theresa R. Castor
*Language & Social Interaction
Division Chair*
University of Wisconsin–Parkside

Rene Weber
Mass Communication Division Chair
University of California–Santa
Barbara

Ted Zorn
*Organizational Communication
Division Chair*
Massey University

Amit Pinchevski
*Philosophy, Theory and Critique
Division Chair*
Hebrew University

Claes H. De Vreese
Political Communication Division Chair
University of Amsterdam

Jonathan Alan Gray
Popular Communication Division Chair
University of Wisconsin–Madison

Jennifer L. Bartlett
Public Relations Division Chair
Queensland University of
Technology

Jana Holsanova
*Visual Communication Studies
Division Chair*
Lund University

Michael L. Haley
Executive Director (ex-officio)
International Communication
Association

DIVISION CHAIRS

Erica L. Scharrer
*Children, Adolescents & the Media
Division Chair*
University of Massachusetts–
Amherst

Sahara Byrne
*Children, Adolescents & the Media
Division Vice-Chair*
Cornell University

Kwan Min Lee
*Communication & Technology
Division Chair*
University of Southern California

James A. Danowski
*Communication & Technology
Division Vice-Chair*
University of Illinois at Chicago

Philip Lodge
*Communication History Division
Chair*
Edinburgh Napier University

Richard K. Popp
*Communication History Division
Vice-Chair*
University of Wisconsin–Milwaukee

Laura Stein
*Communication Law & Policy
Division Chair*
University of Texas–Austin

Seamus Simpson
*Communication Law & Policy
Division Vice-Chair*
University of Salford

Miyase Christensen
*Ethnicity & Race in Communication
Division Chair*
Stockholm University; Royal
Institute of Technology (KTH)

Federico Subervi
*Ethnicity & Race in Communication
Division Vice-Chair*
Kent State University

Paula M Gardner
*Feminist Scholarship
Division Chair*
OCAD University

Natalia Rybas
*Feminist Scholarship Division Vice-
Chair*
Indiana University East

R. Lance Holbert
Mass Communication Division
Vice-Chair
The Ohio State University

Ted Zorn
Organizational Communication
Division Chair
Massey University

Craig R. Scott
Organizational Communication
Division Vice-Chair
Rutgers, the State University of
New Jersey

Keri Keilberg Stephens
Organizational Communication
Division Secretary
U of Texas–Austin

Amit Pinchevski
Philosophy, Theory and Critique
Division Chair
Hebrew University

Alison Hearn
Philosophy, Theory and Critique
Division Vice-Chair
University of Western Ontario

Claes H. De Vreese
Political Communication Division
Chair
University of Amsterdam

Jesper Stromback
Political Communication Division
Vice-Chair
Mid Sweden University

Jonathan Alan Gray
Popular Communication Division
Chair
University of Wisconsin–Madison

Melissa A. Click
Popular Communication Division
Vice-Chair
University of Missouri–Columbia

Jennifer L. Bartlett
Public Relations Division Chair
Queensland University of
Technology

Chiara Valentini
Public Relations Division
Vice-Chair
Aarhus University

Jana Holsanova
Visual Communication Studies
Division Chair
Lund University

Giorgia Aiello
Visual Communication Studies
Division Vice-Chair
University of Leeds

SPECIAL INTEREST GROUP CHAIRS

Richard J. Doherty
Environmental Communication
Interest Group Chair
University of Leeds

Merav Katz-Kimchi
Environmental Communication
Interest Group Vice-Chair
Tel Aviv University

James D. Ivory
Game Studies Interest Group
Chair
Virginia Tech

Nicholas David Bowman
Game Studies Interest Group
Vice-Chair
West Virginia University

Travers Scott
Gay, Lesbian, Bisexual &
Transgender Interest Group Chair
Clemson University

Adrienne Shaw
Gay, Lesbian, Bisexual &
Transgender Interest Group Chair
Temple University

Howard Giles
Intergroup Communication Interest
Group Chair
University of California–Santa Barbara

Janice Raup Krieger
Intergroup Communication Interest
Group Vice-Chair
The Ohio State University

Brandi N. Frisby	*University of Kentucky, USA*
Shiv Ganesh	*University of Waikato, New Zealand*
Howard Giles	*University of California–Santa Barbara, USA*
Nurit Guttman	*Tel Aviv University, Israel*
Nailah Hamdy	*The American University in Cairo, Egypt*
Nancy Grant Harrington	*University of Kentucky, USA*
Jenine Harris	*Washington University–Saint Louis, USA*
Jake Harwood	*University of Arizona, USA*
Magne Martin Haug	*Norwegian Business School, Norway*
Dale A. Herbeck	*Northeastern University, USA*
Evelyn Y. Ho	*University of San Francisco, USA*
Thomas A. Hollihan	*University of Southern California–Annenberg, USA*
Gregory G. Holyk	*Leiden University, Netherlands*
Liz Jones	*Griffith University, Australia*
Amy B. Jordan	*University of Pennsylvania, USA*
Joo-Young Jung	*International Christian University, Japan*
Jennifer A. Kam	*University of Illinois at Urbana–Champaign, USA*
Youna Kim	*The American University of Paris, France*
Yong Chan Kim	*Yonsei University, South Korea*
Robert L. Krizek	*Saint Louis University, USA*
Antonio C. La Pastina	*Texas A&M University, USA*
Annie Lang	*Indiana University, USA*
Robert LaRose	*Michigan State University, USA*
Michael Latzer	*University of Zurich, Switzerland*
Chin-Chuan Lee	*City University of Hong Kong, China*
Maria Len-Rios	*University of Missouri, USA*
Xigen Li	*City University of Hong Kong, China*
Maria Löblich	*Ludwig-Maximilians–Universität, Germany*
Robin Mansell	*London School of Economics and Political Science, UK*
Matthew M. Martin	*West Virginia University, USA*
Caryn Medved	*Baruch College, USA*
Rebecca Meisenbach	*University of Missouri, USA*
Monique Mitchell Turner	*George Washington University, USA*
Ananda Mitra	*Wake Forest University, USA*
Kang Namkoong	*University of Wisconsin–Madison, USA*
Philip M. Napoli	*Fordham University, USA*
Jeff Niederdeppe	*Cornell University, USA*
Seth M. Noar	*University of North Carolina at Chapel Hill, USA*
Mohammed Zin Nordin	*Universiti Pendidikan Sultan Idris, Malaysia*
Jon F. NussBaum	*Penn State University, USA*
Amy O'Connor	*North Dakota State University, USA*
Daniel J. O'Keefe	*Northwestern University, USA*
Mary Beth Oliver	*Pennsylvania State University, USA*
Edward Panetta	*University of Georgia, USA*

Hee Sun Park — Michigan State University, USA
Loretta Pecchioni — Louisiana State University, USA
Wei Peng — Michigan State University, USA
Marshall Scott Poole — University of Illinois at Urbana–Champaign, USA
Linda L. Putnam — University of California–Santa Barbara, USA
Jack Linchaun Qiu — Chinese University of Hong Kong, China
Brian L. Quick — University of Illinois at Urbana–Champaign, USA
Artemio Ramirez, Jr. — University of South Florida, USA
Rajiv N. Rimal — George Washington University, USA
Randall Rogan — Wake Forest University, USA
Michael Roloff — Northwestern University, USA
Dietram A. Scheufele — University of Wisconsin–Madison, USA
Allison M. Scott — University of Kentucky, USA
Deanna Sellnow — University of Kentucky, USA
Timothy Sellnow — University of Kentucky, USA
Michelle Shumate — University of Illinois at Urbana–Champaign, USA
Kami Silk — Michigan State University, USA
Aram Sinnreich — Rutgers University, USA
Sandi W. Smith — Michigan State University, USA
Jordan Soliz — University of Nebraska–Lincoln, USA
Lisa Sparks — Chapman University, USA
Krishnamurthy Sriramesh — Purdue University, USA
Laura Stafford — University of Kentucky, USA
Michael Stohl — University of California–Santa Barbara, USA
Jennifer Stromer-Galley — University of Albany, SUNY, USA
Ed Tan — University of Amsterdam, Netherlands
David Tewksbury — University of Illinois at Urbana–Champaign, USA
C. Erik Timmerman — University of Wisconsin–Milwaukee, USA
April R. Trees — Saint Louis University, USA
Mina Tsay-Vogel — Boston University, USA
Yariv Tsfati — University of Haifa, Israel
Sebastián Valenzuela — Pontificia Universidad Católica, Chile
Jens Vogelgesang — University of Hohenheim, Germany
Peter Vorderer — University of Mannheim, Germany
Ran Wei — University of South Carolina–Columbia, USA
Steve R. Wilson — Purdue University, USA
Werner Wirth — University of Zurich, Switzerland
Greg Wise — Arizona State University, USA
Saskia Witteborn — Chinese University of Hong Kong, China
Elaine Wittenberg-Lyles — University of Kentucky, USA
Y. Connie Yuan — Cornell University, USA
Xiaoquan Zhao — George Mason University, USA
Marc Ziegele — Johannes Gutenberg University Mainz, Germany

Ad Hoc Reviewers

Joshua B. Barbour	*Texas A&M University, USA*
Ambar Basu	*University of South Florida, USA*
Brenda L. Berkelaar	*University of Texas at Austin, USA*
Elizabeth L. Cohen	*West Virginia University, USA*
John D. H. Downing	*Southern Illinois University, USA*
Melanie Green	*University of North Carolina at Chapel Hill, USA*
Michael Hazen	*Wake Forest University, USA*
James K. Hertog	*University of Kentucky, USA*
Holley Wilkin	*Georgia State University, USA*
Katharine J. Head	*University of Kentucky, USA*
Marian Huhman	*University of Illinois at Urbana–Champaign, USA*
Nicholas T. Iannarino	*University of Kentucky, USA*
Bobi Ivanov	*University of Kentucky, USA*
Vikki S. Katz	*Rutgers, The State University of New Jersey, USA*
David M. Keating	*Michigan State University, USA*
Dan V. Kozlowski	*Saint Louis University, USA*
Janice L. Krieger	*The Ohio State University, USA*
Anthony M. Limperos	*University of Kentucky, USA*
Michelle McDowell	*Max Planck Institute for Human Development, Germany*
Michael Meffert	*Leiden University, Netherlands*
Joshua R. Pederson	*University of Iowa, USA*
Amber N. W. Raile	*Montana State University, USA*
Lance Rintamaki	*University of Buffalo, USA*
Patric Spence	*University of Kentucky, USA*
Zixue Tai	*University of Kentucky, USA*
Shari R. Veil	*University of Kentucky, USA*
Lynne Webb	*University of Arkansas, USA*
Erin Willis	*University of Memphis, USA*
Bianca Wolf	*University of Puget Sound, USA*

Editor's Introduction

Elisia L. Cohen

C ommunication theory generates practical insights about fundamental communication issues such as personal and intergroup conflict, media bias and representations of social order, the assimilation and dissemination of knowledge, and public protest and social control. The repeated study of these and other social problems from a communication perspective generates insights into how interpersonal, group, organizational, and mediated communication processes function and influence our social order. However, recent interdisciplinary efforts examining communication dilemmas in new social contexts are also generating novel insights into problems such as immigration and cultural brokering, problem solving and information seeking, health-care decision making, and the structure and function of narrative and information flow in large-scale social networks.

This volume of *Communication Yearbook* brings together essays on these and other innovative topics to offer new ways of thinking about how communication theories may accelerate the discipline's understanding of contemporary social phenomena. The chapters composing *Communication Yearbook 38* offer a glimpse of the ways the communication discipline may reengage in theory building, revalue and appraise communication mechanisms that underlie models of social choice and decision making, and deepen social scientific understanding of communication practices and social behavior.

The first section in *Communication Yearbook 38* identifies immigration challenges from a communication perspective. Chapter 1 in this volume begins with Jennifer A. Kam and Vanja Lazarevic outlining the challenges young immigrant family members experience as cultural brokers for parents. The authors explain both positive and negative consequences for the well-being of young brokers and family members and offer a theoretical model based in past research. In the second chapter, Vikki S. Katz examines the intersection between immigration research and communication research and demonstrates how the research on immigration can be used to develop and test communication theory. In addition, Katz explains how communication theory can contribute to our understanding of immigrant experiences.

The second section of *Communication Yearbook 38* includes essays that investigate communication patterns related to interpersonal and public "talk."

In Chapter 3, Jeong-Nam Kim and Arunima Krishna explain the situational theory of publics (STP) as a way to identify publics and their information behavior. Further, they also outline the extension of STP, the situational theory of problem solving (STOPS), to explain individual communication patterns and behaviors when problem solving. Next, Jordan Soliz and Howard Giles survey more than 40 years of research on communication accommodation theory (CAT) and provide a meta-analysis of quantitative studies using CAT. Although the essay focuses on how CAT was developed in the communication discipline, the findings of the meta-analysis point to new directions for research and the need for more standardization in how researchers assess a key variable, accommodation. In Chapter 5, Amy Janan Johnson, Dale Hample, and Ioana A. Cionea extend theorizing regarding interpersonal argumentation theory to offer a distinction between public- and personal-issue argumentation processes. The authors explain the importance of understanding individuals when analyzing both public and personal issues, how the episodes are interpreted and enacted, and implications for the outcomes of relationships. The next two chapters theorize the context and qualities of interpersonal talk in unsettled disciplinary terrain. In Chapter 6, Analisa Arroyo and Jake Harwood present a model for how talk about weight, or *fat talk*, influences individuals, relationships, and social identity. They propose that fat talk is not just an individual, psychological phenomena but rather a collective one that has implications for the individuals and society. At the same time, interpersonal conversations about weight and health challenge communication researchers to think about the intersection between behavioral and social science. In Chapter 7, Tina A. Coffelt and Loreen N. Olson examine research on how parents and children talk about sex and offer a new model to understand this type of sexual communication grounded in privacy management theory.

The third section of *Communication Yearbook 38* examines the complexities and effectiveness of theorizing difficult or problematic communication in health contexts. In Chapter 8, Allison M. Scott considers what effective communication at the end of life means and finds that little of the research in this area is grounded in communication theory. She identifies how communication scholars can contribute to this area of research in order to improve health-care decision making at the end of life. Next, Janice L. Krieger examines the complexities of cancer treatment decision-making processes. After reviewing previous literature and outlining both patient and family orientations toward decision making, Krieger proposes the DECIDE typology as a new way to theorize the decision-making process and to identify strategies for application in clinical practice. Finally, the last chapter in this section, Chapter 10, is a multidisciplinary research inquiry on communication and family caregivers, the adult children who take care of their aging parents. Nichole Egbert reviews how communication efforts focus on three common caregiver challenges: identity, attribution, and relationship.

Communication Yearbook 38 concludes with a variety of essays that cut into emerging areas of communication research. These essays identify how communication scholarship will address the 21st century information economy, globally networked communication media flow, and challenges within the academy. In "Net Neutrality and Communication Research: The Implications of Internet Infrastructure for the Public Sphere," Maria Löblich and Francesca Musiani consider how the underlying infrastructure of the Internet—the code that decides which pieces of information deserve priority—affects the neutrality of the net and, as a result, the public sphere. In Chapter 12, Ananda Mitra offers a framework for understanding the masses of data now available as a result of rapidly growing social media networks, such as Twitter and Facebook. Mitra proposes that these posts provide a "narb" or a narrative bit of a person's life. He offers a scheme for coding narbs and suggests how this type of research might prove useful in the future. Finally, in "Episodic, Network, and Inclusionary Mentoring: Taking a Communicative Perspective on Mentoring in the Workplace," a group of scholars led by Ziyu Long from Purdue University propose a research agenda for bridging mentoring and communication scholarship based on the communication-as-constitutive-of-organizing (CCO) approach. These scholars argue that viewing mentoring in this fashion illuminates research perspectives for mentoring and allows communication researchers to contribute to this area of study.

The scholarship represented in this volume reflects some of the breadth and diversity of problems we confront as communication scholars. These contributions reflect the manuscripts that were submitted to *Communication Yearbook 38*'s editorial board for peer review. Forty-nine partial and complete manuscripts were submitted to the editorial office for consideration in *Communication Yearbook 38*. Of these, 38 manuscripts were sent to at least three reviewers for peer review. After two or more reviewers accepted the manuscripts for publication, the essays selected for inclusion in this volume benefited from the constructive criticism offered by the reviewers and the editorial staff.

The resulting volume, including thirteen essays accepted from the peer review process, was shepherded into publication by my editorial assistants, Sarah Vos and Laura Young. These two PhD candidates provided timely correspondence with authors and were a critical source of reliable and accurate copyediting. Vos and Young edited final manuscript drafts, provided summaries of articles and critiques for my review, and assisted with compiling the final production package. I am grateful for their tireless work that benefits the readers of this volume.

I am fortunate to have outstanding colleagues in the Department of Communication at the University of Kentucky who continue to support my editorship. I particularly appreciate the timely advice of my friends and colleagues in helping me make tough decisions this year, including: J. Alison Bryant, Michael Cody, Glen Cameron, Lew Donahue, Brandi Frisby, Nancy Grant Harrington, Jenine Harris, Don Helme, Tom Hollihan, Amy Jordan, Rebecca Meisenbach, H. Dan O'Hair, Michelle Shumate, Cynthia Stohl, Jeff VanCleave, Shari Veil, and Elaine Wittenberg-Lyles. Finally, I thank my daughter, Addison Lydia, who inspires my daily communication theorizing and research. I know she will enjoy seeing her name in print.

Part I

Theorizing Immigration, Cultural Brokering, and Communication

CHAPTER CONTENTS

1 Communicating for One's Family

An Interdisciplinary Review of Language and Cultural Brokering in Immigrant Families

Jennifer A. Kam

University of Illinois at Urbana–Champaign

Vanja Lazarevic

Refugee Trauma and Resilience Center; Boston Children's Hospital and Harvard Medical School

Although language and cultural brokering is important for immigrant families, this behavior may have both positive and negative consequences for the well-being of young brokers and their family members. Few communication studies, however, have examined brokering in relation to the well-being of immigrant families, despite its prevalence in the United States and elsewhere. Thus, this chapter offers an interdisciplinary review of the brokering literature, identifies four primary perspectives on the well-being of young brokers, offers a unified theoretical model that represents past brokering research (while noting critical concerns that warrant future investigation), and concludes with implications for communication research.

In 2010, the U.S. Census Bureau reported that approximately 40 million foreign-born individuals resided in the United States, thereby comprising 13% of the nation's population (Grieco et al., 2012). Of the 40 million, 53% were born in Latin America, 28% in Asia, 12% in Europe, 4% in Africa, and 3% in other parts of the world. Such findings indicate that a substantial portion of the foreign-born population in the United States comes from countries where English is not the primary language. Consistent with this notion, 42% of the United States foreign-born population from Latin America, 22% of the foreign-born population from Asia, 12% from Europe, and 10% from Africa reported not speaking English "well" or "not at all" (Grieco et al., 2012). Navigating U.S. society, however, often depends on the degree to which individuals are familiar with the English language (Shin & Bruno, 2003). In immigrant families who live in the United States permanently or indefinitely, older family members often depend on younger members (e.g., preadolescents, adolescents, and emerging adults) to linguistically and culturally mediate for them when interacting with people from mainstream culture (Kam, 2011; McQuillan & Tse, 1995). Because younger family members participate in the U.S. education system almost daily, they acquire English-language skills and knowledge of mainstream culture more quickly than adults (Birman, 2006; Chao, 2006; Suárez-Orozco & Suárez-Orozco, 2001). Thus, younger members of immigrant families often serve as language and cultural brokers—individuals with little to no formal training who linguistically and culturally mediate for two or more parties (both of whom are from different cultural backgrounds). These brokers also may assume some authority in communicating on behalf of parents, other relatives, or the entire family (Kam, 2011; Tse, 1996).

Language and cultural brokering is a common experience among immigrant families in the United States (Morales & Hanson, 2005) and other countries (Cline, de Abreu, O'Dell, & Crafter, 2010; Degener, 2010). Across several studies (Hua & Costigan, 2012; Jones, Trickett, & Birman, 2012; Tse, 1995, 1996; Weisskirch & Alva, 2002), nearly all of the participating immigrant youth had engaged in a variety of language and cultural brokering. Such behavior included face-to-face interactions, phone conversations, e-mailing, letter writing, and explaining or responding to documents that family members received (Bauer, 2010; Jones & Trickett, 2005; Weisskirch, 2005). Language and cultural brokering requires younger family members to quickly understand and interpret more than one culture, carry out transactions that often require advanced vocabulary, participate in adult interactions, and make decisions that impact the family (Love & Buriel, 2007). Given such complex interactions, engaging in this behavior may have both positive and negative effects on the well-being of young brokers (Chao, 2006).

To date, the research on language and cultural brokering has yielded mixed results regarding the effects of this behavior on young members of immigrant families (Hua & Costigan, 2012; Morales & Hanson, 2005). As a result, four dominant perspectives on brokering have emerged. Figure 1.1 provides the conceptual models that summarize each perspective's corresponding assumption, which will be detailed later in this chapter. Briefly, however, the first two perspectives conceptualize language and cultural brokering as creating stress (see panel a of Figure 1.1) and prematurely imposing adult responsibilities on young brokers (see panel b of Figure 1.1), thereby highlighting the potentially problematic aspects of brokering (Mercado, 2003; Weisskirch & Alva, 2002). In contrast, two additional perspectives consider language and cultural brokering as a beneficial and "normal" way of contributing to immigrant family functioning that result in stronger parent–child relationships (see panel c of Figure 1.1), as well as enhanced cognitive and linguistic skills (see panel d of Figure 1.1) (Buriel, Perez, DeMent, Chavez, & Moran, 1998; Katz, 2014; Orellana, Dorner, & Pulido, 2003).

Although each perspective remains widely referenced in the literature, more research is needed to examine these four perspectives and to consider additional factors that may influence brokering's effects on the well-being of young immigrant family members. Instead of settling on one perspective over another, more recent research suggests that the outcomes of language and cultural brokering may depend on a number of complex factors such as

a) The Stress Perspective

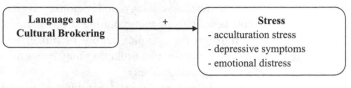

b) The Parentification Perspective

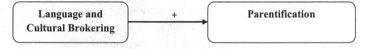

c) The Interdependent/Independent Scripts Perspective

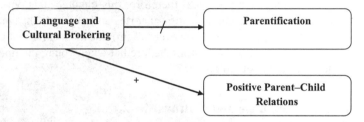

d) The Enhanced-Academic-Performance Perspective

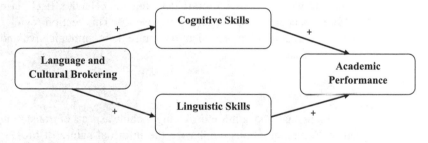

Figure 1.1 Conceptual models of the primary perspectives on brokering

Note: + indicates that brokering leads to experiencing this outcome; / indicates that brokering does not lead to experiencing this outcome.

how younger family members feel about brokering (Chao, 2006; Kam, 2011; Wu & Kim, 2009), the extent to which they perceive brokering as normative (Dorner, Orellana, & Jimenez, 2008; Kam & Lazarevic, 2013), their brokering efficacy (Kam & Lazarevic, 2013; Weisskirch, 2013), the type of relationship that they have with their parents (Lazarevic, 2012), and how researchers measure brokering (Kam, 2009). Language and cultural brokering, therefore, is a complex and multifaceted behavior that may lead to a variety of positive and negative outcomes, depending on the context. To date, much of the brokering literature, as well as the four perspectives, stem from the fields of education, human development and family studies, psychology, and sociology. Brokering research, however, also would benefit from incorporating a communication perspective, which can shed light on the complex nature of brokering and potentially elucidate the conditions under which brokering may be harmful or beneficial to the well-being of immigrant families.

Consequently, this chapter provides an interdisciplinary review of the brokering literature, identifies four primary perspectives on the well-being of young language and cultural brokers, offers a unified theoretical model that represents past brokering research (while noting critical concerns that warrant future investigation), and concludes with implications for communication research. Figure 1.2 provides a theoretical model of language and cultural brokering for immigrant youth, which we explicate in greater detail throughout this chapter. A brief inspection of this model, however, reveals that the brokering research largely lacks a communication presence; therefore, this chapter ends with a section that describes several communication theories and concepts that may contribute to brokering research. First, however, we provide an overview of the terms associated with brokering and factors that predict when young members of immigrant families are likely to broker.

Conceptualizing Language and Cultural Brokering

The definition of language and cultural brokering slightly varies across research, which is reflected in the many terms used to describe this behavior. Each term highlights different aspects of the brokering experience. This section reviews a number of terms and definitions intended to capture the communicative and relational facets of brokering.

Translating and Interpreting

All definitions of language and cultural brokering include aspects of translating and interpreting. Some definitions emphasize the informal nature of brokering, the decision-making role that brokers enact, the power dynamics between brokers and individuals who rely on them, and the familial contributions of brokers. When studying brokering, researchers (e.g., Dorner, Orellana, & Li-Grining, 2007; Jones, Trickett, & Birman, 2012; Kam, 2011) commonly use words such as *translating* or *interpreting* in their self-report measures. Distinctions, however, exist within the research community regarding the conceptualization of translators and interpreters. Translators are typically individuals who have undergone formal training and who attempt to use the word-for-word equivalence from one language to another (Valdés, 2003). In academic research, translating also refers to understanding and explaining written documents (Morales & Hanson, 2005). Interpretation often includes the oral form of translating, but it consists of deciding what cultural information to relay, thus making it less formal than translating (Valdés, 2003).

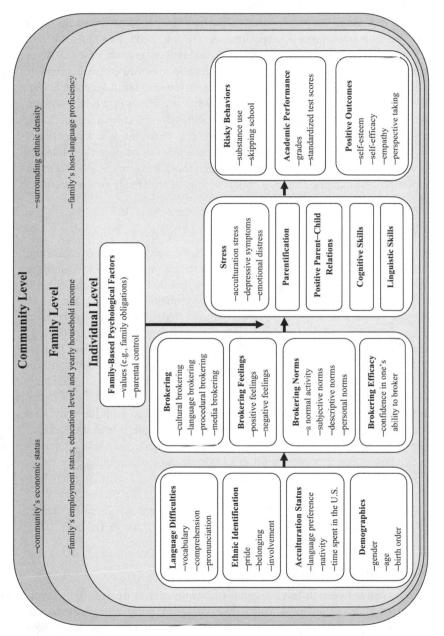

Figure 1.2 A theoretical model of brokering's effects on young members of immigrant families

Cultural Brokering

Similar to interpreting, cultural brokers may not translate messages word-for-word. Instead, they mediate and influence the content, and in so doing, brokers can affect the parties' perceptions of each other, their perceptions of the messages, and their subsequent actions (Jones & Trickett, 2005; McQuillan & Tse, 1995). Cultural brokering is not a neutral act, and brokers may alter the messages to benefit the family member, which may include preventing embarrassment or conflicts, or negotiating a better deal for the family member (Hall & Sham, 2007). Although past studies (e.g., Buriel et al., 1998; Kam, 2011) primarily focus on children of immigrant families, several researchers (e.g., Dorner et al., 2008; Katz, 2010; Villanueva & Buriel, 2010) note that brokering is a transactional process in which the parent and child work as a team to manage their interaction with individuals from mainstream culture. Thus, brokering involves a more complex process than the common understanding of translating or interpreting.

Language Brokering

The most commonly used term in the research community is language brokering, which focuses on linguistic translation and interpretation (Tse, 1995). Language brokering emphasizes the linguistic component, but de-emphasizes the cultural and interpersonal dynamics, as well as the decision-making processes that unfold during the interaction. Kam (2011) used the term "language brokering" because her measures focused on linguistically translating for family members (e.g., "How often do you translate for a family member?"), whereas Jones and Trickett (2005) used the term "culture brokering" to refer to youth who culturally (in addition to linguistically) mediate between their family members and individuals from the mainstream culture. This term, therefore, does not accurately represent the entire mediation process, where individuals act as both linguistic *and* cultural intermediaries. Past studies operationalizing language brokering tend to concentrate mainly on linguistic translations, asking participants how often they translated for different people, at different places, and with different documents (Buriel et al., 1998; Tse, 1995). When comparing the definitions of language brokering and culture brokering, they appear to address a similar process; however, the words *language* and *culture* draw attention to different aspects of brokering, with the latter focusing on a broader mediation process (Jones & Trickett, 2005).

Procedural Brokering

To distinguish between different aspects of brokering, Lazarevic (2012) developed the term "procedural brokering." Procedural brokering refers to mediation that extends beyond language but describes an educational process that enables immigrant family members to carry out activities in mainstream culture. An example of procedural brokering would be a child showing the parent how to shop online or teaching the parent how to pay their bills. Although it uses language as a means of communication, procedural brokering focuses on the process of teaching family members how to function in mainstream culture and educating family members about the cultural nuances of the mainstream. Thus, as language plays an important part in the mediation process, youth go beyond linguistic interpretations and employ their knowledge and skills to educate their family in interacting with members from mainstream culture.

Media Brokering

Related to procedural brokering, media brokering refers to children acting as intermediaries between their family members and media (e.g., television, newspapers, smartphones, social media; Katz, 2010). Media provide opportunities for learning about mainstream culture, for gaining access to local community resources, and for successfully maneuvering within the new environment (e.g., paying a bill online, applying for a job online, etc.). Katz revealed that children of immigrant families may interpret messages from a variety of mediated channels (e.g., answering machine, paper bills, cell phone). Thus, youth bridge the gap between their family and mainstream culture by interpreting media-based messages, which she refers to as media brokering.

In short, a review of the literature reveals that many overlapping terms exist to describe brokering. For the purposes of the current chapter, we use the terms "language" and "cultural brokering" because of their predominance in the brokering literature. Most of the studies in this area have used the term "language brokering" (cf. Trickett & Jones, 2007), and appropriately so because the literature has focused on exploring the most obvious form of brokering and the one that is more easily assessed—translating and interpreting. We view culture brokering as an umbrella term that encompasses many types of brokering including language brokering, procedural brokering, and media brokering, and we recommend using this term in the future. Nevertheless, to accurately represent how previous research on this topic has referred to and operationalized brokering, we rely on the terms "language" and "cultural brokering."

Language and Cultural Brokering as a Form of Interpersonal Communication

The research that has defined language and cultural brokering has primarily emerged from education, human development and family studies, psychology, and sociology. Explicating brokering, however, as a form of interpersonal communication can provide new ways of understanding brokering and its impact on immigrant families. Interpersonal communication is "a complex, situated social process in which people who have established a communicative relationship exchange messages in an effort to generate shared meanings and accomplish social goals" (Burleson, 2010, p. 151). Framing language and cultural brokering as a form of interpersonal communication is not intended to undermine prior conceptualizations; instead, it is meant to complement them.

Burleson's (2010) definition of interpersonal communication focuses our attention on key aspects of brokering that warrant further investigation and that may be of interest to researchers who study family communication, intercultural communication, health communication, and other forms of communication. In particular, by *complex process*, Burleson means that interpersonal communication involves numerous interdependent processes (e.g., message production, message processing, and interaction coordination) that occur simultaneously. For example, as youth engage in brokering, they may undergo the following process: receive information from the host culture in the form of verbal and nonverbal behaviors, assign meaning to the behaviors, determine how to make the behaviors comprehensible to their family member, and convey the information in a way that establishes shared meaning between both parties, all while managing this flow of information exchange across the entire course of the interaction. This emphasis on complex process highlights the need for longitudinal research on brokering that can provide further understanding of the flow of interactions that occur when brokering; however, prior research has largely been based on cross-sectional data.

Using the definition of interpersonal communication, brokering is a social, situated, and functional process. First, brokering is *social* because the interaction occurs between two or more parties. Thus far, and as will be evident throughout this chapter, past studies have chiefly relied on the brokers' perspective, but social processes emphasize the need to examine brokering also from family member's and mainstream culture's perspectives. Second, brokering is a *situated* social process, given the changing context that has an impact on communication exchanges (Burleson, 2010). Situational factors include, but are not limited to, the physical setting in which the brokering occurs (e.g., brokering at a hospital or a school or brokering over the phone), the relational setting (e.g., who requires brokering assistance, the relational quality between the broker and the involved parties), and the cultural setting (e.g., the involved parties' values, beliefs, norms, and social practices). Last, brokering is *functional* because of the multiple goals that each party has during the interaction. For example, brokers have to simultaneously manage three types of goals: relational goals (e.g., maintaining their parent–child or teacher–student relationship), instrumental goals (e.g., accurately interpreting the messages and ensuring that the involved parties have shared meaning), and identity goals (e.g., competently brokering to maintain one's self-esteem and self-concept). In sum, conceptualizing brokering as a form of interpersonal communication draws our attention to certain aspects of brokering and thus provides new directions for research.

Predictors of Brokering

Prior to delving deeper into explicating communication's contributions to our understanding of language and cultural brokering, we use the following section to lay a foundation for understanding brokering by identifying several of its predictors. The majority of young immigrant family members report brokering for their parents or other adults (Chao, 2006; Degener, 2010; McQuillan &

Tse, 1995; Tse, 1995). Various individual and contextual factors, however, may play a part in determining who within the family is designated or assumes the responsibility of brokering. For example, acculturation status, socioeconomic status, gender, age, and birth order are several of many factors that may increase the likelihood of brokering (Morales & Hanson, 2005).

Acculturation Status

Several acculturation-related factors are likely to influence the extent to which youth broker for their parents and other family members. In particular, acculturation includes cultural and psychological adjustments such as changes in economic and political customs and changes in individual attitudes, expectations, beliefs, values, and identity, which ensue when cultures come into contact (Berry, Phinney, Sam, & Vedder, 2006). Immigrant children often become more familiar with the host culture faster than their parents and other adults because of their immersion into mainstream society through schooling and frequent interactions with their peers (Birman & Trickett, 2001; Costigan & Dokis 2006; Sabatier & Berry, 2008). By having knowledge of mainstream culture, immigrant youth are often called on to broker.

Children's acculturation places them in a position to broker for their family, but the acculturation of immigrant parents also is an important factor (Chao, 2006; Martinez, McClure, & Eddy, 2009). Research has found that the less time parents have resided in the host country and the less proficient they are in their knowledge of the host language, the more frequently their children broker for them. These findings emerged in studies with immigrant youth and their families from various Asian (Chao, 2006; Trickett & Jones, 2007), Eastern European (Jones et al., 2012; Lazarevic, 2012), and Central American countries (Chao, 2006). These findings have implications for individuals working with immigrant families to devote special attention and resources to newly arrived immigrant families whose struggle with understanding the host culture is at its peak during the initial period after migration.

Socioeconomic Status

Immigrant families' socioeconomic status (SES) and its effect on their ability to navigate mainstream culture have often gone unexamined. SES, however, may predict brokering, as was indicated by a study with Eastern European (mainly Russian) immigrant parents and their children in the United States (Jones et al., 2012). For example, higher English-level proficiency was positively related to job prestige and employment, and as previously mentioned, families with higher English-level proficiency are less likely to require brokering. Instead, children brokered more for parents with lower status jobs, which in turn was related to higher levels of distress for the children (Jones et al., 2012). The findings indicate that immigrant families who experience lower SES and live in disadvantaged communities with limited resources tend to rely on their children to help them navigate mainstream culture.

Gender

In addition to parents' and children's acculturation, as well as their SES statuses, brokering is a gendered phenomenon. Although findings regarding gender and brokering remain mixed and inconclusive, there is some evidence that brokering tasks and responsibilities may vary by gender based on the cultural context of immigrant families. Specifically, in their study of first- and second-generation Latino American adolescents, Buriel et al. (1998) found that girls brokered more frequently than did boys. Similar trends emerged in studies with adolescents (Villanueva & Buriel, 2010) and children (Valenzuela, 1999) from Latino American immigrant families. To the contrary, a study with Mexican American first and second-generation adolescents found that boys reported translating more often for their parents than did girls (Weisskirch, 2007). Contrary to those findings, several studies found no gender differences in brokering (Hua & Costigan, 2012; Jones et al., 2012; Lazarevic, 2012; Love & Buriel, 2007). The variations in brokering may be due to the nature of certain activities (in regards to gender) in specific cultures, where girls are viewed as being more suitable than boys to provide detailed explanations and translate documents. The cultural traditions of immigrant families may play a role in determining whether girls or boys broker.

Age and Birth Order

Studies also explored the age of immigrant youth who broker, as well as their birth order. Many studies indicate that immigrant children begin brokering at a very young age, some as early as 8 or 9 years old (Tse, 1995). In general, research suggests that older children tend to broker more frequently than do younger children (Hua & Costigan, 2012; Valdés, Chavez, & Angelelli, 2003). In one qualitative study with nine Latina American adolescents (Villanueva & Buriel, 2010), first-born adolescent children reported a greater variety in the types of brokering settings and the types of brokered messages compared to middle- and last-born Latina adolescent children. Latina adolescents who had an older sister also reported that the older sister brokered more often. In contrast, a more recent study with 197 young-adult immigrants from Eastern Europe (Lazarevic, 2012) found no relation between birth order and brokering. Overall, however, few studies have considered age and birth order as predictors of brokering.

Four Perspectives on the Well-Being of Young Brokers

Over the last two decades, researchers primarily from education, human development and family studies, psychology, and sociology have investigated the consequences of brokering on the well-being of immigrant youth. Such research has focused largely on young brokers' mental health, academic performance, parent–child relationship, and tendency to engage in risky behaviors.

This inquiry has led to several dominant perspectives, some of which argue that brokering has harmful effects on youth while others argue that brokering has beneficial effects. Despite these dominant perspectives, few formal theoretical applications explain and justify these perspectives. Thus, this section describes each perspective, along with its corresponding theory that provides a rationale for the perspective.

Brokering as a Stressor (or a Strain)

One of the most common perspectives in the brokering literature, and the one that has garnered the greatest amount of empirical attention, is the stress perspective (see panel a of Figure 1.1). A cultural stressor is an adverse experience associated with racial/ethnic identity, immigration processes, and/or acculturation processes that leads to stress because of its undesirable, challenging, and at times, unwarranted nature (Agnew, 2001; Umaña-Taylor, Updegraff, & Gonzales-Backen, 2011). According to the stress perspective, linguistically and culturally mediating for family members creates a stressful environment for young brokers that may place them at risk for developing a number of poor mental health outcomes (e.g., acculturation stress, depressive symptoms, distress; Kam, 2011; Love & Buriel, 2007; Martinez et al., 2009).

More specifically, young brokers often interact in complex communicative situations in which they must draw upon their understanding of at least two cultures, make decisions that impact their family members' well-being, and ensure that the interaction proceeds smoothly. They also may find themselves in unfamiliar situations in which they must manage adult content that may extend beyond their cognitive and linguistic developmental stage (Acoach & Webb, 2004; Hall & Sham, 2007; Love & Buriel, 2007). Young brokers may experience a great deal of pressure and responsibility when managing different cultures to assist their family members (Weisskirch & Alva, 2002). In addition, family members may dominate brokers' time and energy, thereby preventing brokers from taking time for their own activities (e.g., completing schoolwork, participating in extracurricular activities, spending time with friends; McQuillan & Tse, 1995; Wu & Kim, 2009). With such pressures, youth may perceive brokering as stressful and burdensome (Love & Buriel, 2007; Weisskirch, 2005).

General strain theory perspective. To theoretically explicate why brokering may function as a stressor, we draw from general strain theory (GST; Agnew, 1992). Agnew's GST posits that when individuals experience strains (or stressors), they often develop negative psychological reactions such as anger, frustration, or sadness. Strains occur when individuals are subjected to adverse situations or experiences that are challenging, undesirable, and, at times, unwarranted (Agnew, 2001). Although individuals may find other ways to cope with their strain, GST focuses on strains that increase the likelihood of using unhealthy coping behaviors in the form of risky behaviors (e.g., substance use, theft, skipping school, and fighting; Agnew, 1992).

Individuals may be more likely to engage in unhealthy coping behaviors when their strain emerges from three particular sources (Agnew, 2001). First, the anticipated or actual inability to accomplish a goal is the classic source of strain. Agnew extended this conceptualization with GST to include two additional strain stimuli: the removal of a desired stimulus or the introduction of a negative stimulus (Broidy & Agnew, 1997). The strain that develops from these three sources is more likely to induce negative psychological reactions, and, in turn, individuals may attempt to reduce or escape from such negative psychological reactions by relying on unhealthy coping behaviors (e.g., substance use). As a result of strain, individuals may experience anger, anxiety, depression, distress, disappointment, and frustration; however, this list of negative psychological reactions is not exhaustive (Ellwanger, 2007).

Brokering as a strain.   When considering the application of GST to brokering, engaging in the behavior may become a strain based on the three ways that Agnew proposed with GST (Kam, 2011). For example, in some situations, brokers may lack knowledge and understanding of the content they interpret, thereby preventing them from fulfilling their goal of assisting a family member. Because brokering most often occurs among preadolescent and adolescent children, young brokers may experience greater anxiety, not knowing how adults may react to them as they enact adult responsibilities. Furthermore, at times, brokers may encounter negative experiences when brokering if they learn about a family member's sensitive information (e.g., a health problem). Finally, brokers' confidence (a positive stimulus) may decrease in situations in which the content is too advanced, thereby having a desired stimulus removed. These examples are several ways in which brokering can act as a strain. In such situations, the assumptions of GST would suggest that brokers may be at risk for developing negative psychological reactions and, in turn, may attempt to reduce or escape from such negative psychological reactions by using unhealthy coping behaviors (e.g., substance use and other delinquent behaviors; Kam & Lazarevic, 2013).

Empirical research on brokering as a strain (or a stressor).   The potentially stressful nature of brokering has been linked to a number of negative psychological outcomes such as acculturation stress, emotional distress, and depressive symptoms (Hall & Sham, 2007; Love & Buriel, 2007). For example, when the 5th grade students in Weisskirch and Alva's (2002) study did not perceive brokering as helping them learn their native language, they were more likely to experience higher levels of acculturation stress. Furthermore, the Mexican American sixth- to eighth-grade students in Kam's (2011) longitudinal study also reported increased acculturation stress the more often they brokered for their family members. Jones and Trickett (2005), in a study with 226 Russian American immigrant adolescent–mother dyads, also found that as the adolescents engaged in brokering more often, they were more likely to experience emotional distress. A study with Chinese adolescents in England found similar trends—adolescents reported feeling stressed, frustrated, and pressured to broker correctly for their parents (Hall & Sham, 2007). Lastly, in a survey study of 246 Mexican American adolescents, researchers found that brokering was associated with higher rates of depression (Love & Buriel, 2007). The aforementioned studies reveal that brokering may operate as a stressor, placing youth at risk for poor mental health outcomes (Jones & Trickett, 2005; Love & Buriel, 2007; Weisskirch & Alva, 2002).

Although past research (Weisskirch & Alva, 2002; Love & Buriel, 2007; Jones et al., 2012; Martinez et al., 2009) has established a relation between brokering and poor mental health outcomes, only a few studies have considered brokering's relation to risky behaviors. Chao (2006) found that brokering frequency was positively associated with internalizing behaviors (i.e., depression, anxiety, withdrawal) among Korean and Chinese adolescents in the United States but not among Mexican adolescents. In contrast, brokering frequency was positively associated with externalizing symptoms (i.e., aggression, delinquency, cheating) among Korean adolescents but not among Chinese or Mexican adolescents. Kam (2011) incorporated GST to examine a mediation model of brokering's indirect effects on 684 Mexican American adolescents' substance use and other risky behaviors. Based on longitudinal data, her study revealed that as Mexican American adolescents brokered for family more often, they were more likely to experience increased family-based acculturation stress (e.g., feeling upset with parents for not knowing U.S. customs) and, in turn, increased alcohol use and other risky behaviors (e.g., participating in a gang, skipping school, getting into physical altercations). In short, several studies on brokering provide evidence of its potentially stressful nature by linking this behavior to poor mental health outcomes and risky behaviors—such findings yield support for the stress perspective, which may be theoretically explicated by GST.

The stress perspective has garnered support from empirical research, but it is important to note that brokering only partially explains the stress that children of immigrant families may experience. For example, young members of immigrant families often carry out other responsibilities such as taking care of younger siblings, performing household chores, and running errands (Orellana, 2003; Villanueva & Buriel, 2010). Utilizing a sample of 27 Soviet Jewish adolescents in the United States, Vinokurov, Trickett, and Birman (2002) developed a measure of acculturative hassles related to school (e.g., discrimination at school), family (e.g., acculturation discrepancies between parents and youth), peers (e.g., experiencing difficulties establishing intercultural friendships and romantic relationships), and language (e.g., difficulties with language comprehension). Vinokurov et al. found that school hassles were related to a weaker sense of school membership, family hassles were related to lower levels of family satisfaction, peer hassles were related to loneliness, and language hassles were related to symptoms of depression, somatic distress, and performance anxiety. In addition, as previously mentioned, children in families with low SES broker more frequently, which may further contribute to their stress (Jones & Trickett, 2012). Thus, although previous research has provided evidence for the stress perspective, brokering only partially explains why some children of immigrant families experience stress.

Brokering's Negative Impact on Parent–Child Relationships

As a potential stressor, brokering also may negatively alter the relationship between youth and their parents (Umaña-Taylor, 2003). For example, in a study with first- and second-generation Vietnamese American adolescents, researchers found that when parents reported no family issues, adolescents reported that brokering contributed to family disagreements (Trickett & Jones, 2007). A study with Latino American adolescents found similar results. The study compared low-brokering and high-brokering families; the findings indicated that parents in low-brokering households reported greater parental effectiveness and lower internalizing behaviors of their brokering child compared to high-brokering households (Martinez et al., 2009). Last, a study with Eastern European immigrants in the United States found that brokering was related to higher levels of family conflict, which, in turn, was related to higher levels of depressive mood in immigrant youth (Lazarevic, 2012).

In addition to family conflict, the parentification perspective (also examined as a parent–child role reversal) suggests that young brokers adopt adult responsibilities that challenge expectations associated with their roles as children (see panel b of Figure 1.1; Oznobishin & Kurman, 2009). When brokering, youth often enter adult interactions; therefore, "the child's role in the traditional family hierarchy is shifted when the child assumes the power to communicate and to speak for the parent" (Weisskirch, 2005, p. 287). Consequently, this behavior can lead to parentification because brokering challenges the traditional power distribution between children and their parents (Mercado, 2003; Trickett & Jones, 2007; Weisskirch, 2005). Stemming from the clinical literature in family therapy, parentification refers to adults' functional or emotional reliance on a child to the point where such reliance risks obstructing the child's "normal" and appropriate developmental process (Castro, Jones, & Mirsalimi, 2004). Children prematurely assume adult responsibilities, sacrificing their own needs to benefit their family's needs (Stein, Rotheram-Borus, & Lester, 2007). Young brokers often interact in adult situations, handling adult content such as interpreting at medical appointments and parent–teacher conferences, or interpreting letters from banks and school report cards (Hall & Sham, 2007; Orellana et al., 2003). From the parentification perspective, parents' dependency on children to mediate in these types of adult situations may place youth at risk for negative outcomes (Trickett & Jones, 2007). Despite its popularity in the brokering literature, this perspective has lacked a theoretical explanation guiding its postulations. Role theory (Ashforth, 2001) elucidates brokering's potentially problematic effects on children through parentification.

Role theory perspective. Role theorists propose that throughout life, individuals have social roles that influence their actions. Roles refer to positions that individuals hold, as well as learned scripts and predictable patterns of behaviors that accompany each role (Biddle, 1986; Goldblatt & Eisikovits, 2005). Learning and enacting such behaviors appropriately and effectively constitutes role competence (Solomon, Surprenant, Czepiel, & Gutman, 1985). Roles are interdependent and stem from communicative interactions with others (Burnette, 1999). Expectations regarding a role are based on positions individuals hold within a social structure (Biddle, 1986; Solomon et al., 1985). Family members often establish some sort of hierarchical structure in which the role of a parent can only exist in correspondence to the role that a child assumes. At times, family members may have similar expectations regarding their roles, while at other times they may have contradictory expectations, which can result in conflict (e.g., pose competing demands; Biddle, 1986). Youth may experience challenges to their roles when brokering. From a Western perspective, children are typically expected to have less authority and power, and they are expected to allow their parents to lead in social interactions, particularly outside the home (Love & Buriel, 2007). If children, however, are the most skilled at linguistically and culturally interacting within mainstream culture, a role reversal may occur.

Empirical research on brokering as a source of parentification. Despite the previously held assumption that brokering places youth at risk for parentification, few studies have directly tested this link. One of the earlier studies that were conducted on brokering provided some evidence for parentification. In particular, the nine U.S. bilingual adults, who participated in brokering as children, described feeling like the adult in the family, making decisions regarding their siblings' school affairs, writing letters to school, signing notes, and contacting teachers without including or notifying their parents (McQuillan & Tse, 1995). Using quantitative data, Mercado (2003) found that brokering was positively related to parentification among her sample of 90 Latino American undergraduate students. Díaz-Lázaro (2002) did not directly measure parentification, but he found that brokering was not associated with Latino American adolescents' perceptions of how much their parents included them in family decisions or how much control they had over their parents' lives. Similarly, Oznobishin and Kurman (2009) did not directly test brokering in relation to parentification, but they found that former Soviet immigrants residing in Israel reported higher levels of child dominance than did Israeli-born college students. Using longitudinal data with 684 seventh- and eighth-grade Mexican American students, Kam (2011) found that brokering frequency was not significantly related to parentification, but feeling good about oneself when brokering was related to feeling more like an adult than a child in the family. In short, the limited empirical research on brokering in relation to parentification prevents one from making strong conclusions regarding the association, but Kam's (2011) study suggests that the parentification perspective may depend on the aspects of brokering that researchers examine.

Brokering's Positive Impact on Parent–Child Relationships

GST and role theory point to the potentially negative consequences of brokering, but Orellana, Dorner, and their colleagues (e.g., Orellana et al., 2003; Dorner et al., 2008) suggest that this behavior may actually be a "normal" way for young family members to contribute to the success of the family while maintaining appropriate, culturally based, adult–child roles. Although young brokers may be able to navigate within mainstream culture more competently than do their parents or other adult family members, Orellana and her colleagues, as well as Trickett and Jones (2007), propose that these young brokers continue to clearly perceive their parents and adult family members as authority figures. Using interviews with U.S. Latino adolescents and one of their parents, Katz (2010) found that even when youth brokered in adult situations, parents maintained authority. Orellana et al. (2003) also found that although children participated in family decisions, they did not make decisions on their own—that responsibility fell to their parents. Parents and their children worked together as a team to "take action for the family" (Orellan et al., 2003, p. 508). Thus, adults continued to maintain authority, power, and control, despite the intercession of the youth.

An independent/interdependent scripts perspective.   Although the Western perspective views adolescent development as a growth in independence from family, Dorner et al. (2008) suggest that immigrant families may emphasize both independence and interdependence (see panel c of Figure 1.1). From a Western perspective, adopting more responsibilities to assist the family may threaten children's "normal" development, forcing them to prematurely become more independent. Among certain ethnic groups, however, brokering may actually be a sign of interdependence as they complete tasks to assist others (Hua & Costigan, 2012). More recently, researchers have suggested that the perception of brokering as a source of parentification is based on a Western perspective of independence and interdependence that brokers may simultaneously balance independence and interdependence (Dorner et al., 2008; Villanueva & Buriel, 2010).

Examining brokering among children from independent/interdependent scripts leads scholars to different claims regarding the effects of this behavior. Research that supports this perspective would suggest that brokering does not result in parentification, but instead may enhance family functioning (Trickett & Jones, 2007). For instance, in their interviews with adult participants, who brokered as children, McQuillan and Tse (1995) discovered that these adults developed trusting relationships with their parents, possibly indicating that brokering enhances familial relationships. Similarly, Chao (2006) found that brokers reported higher levels of respect for their parents. Contrary to the predictions of role theory (e.g., parentification perspective) and GST, brokering may lead to positive outcomes when it is perceived as a "normal" way for children to assist their parents and other family members.

Empirical research on the interdependent/independent scripts perspective. Several studies found that young brokers perceived brokering as a "normal" way to help their families. A study with 37 youth in England found that those who brokered for their parents viewed their work as something they considered "normal" (Cline, Crafter, O'Dell, & de Abreu, 2011). A study with Turkish- and Arabic-speaking children in Germany found that most youth viewed their brokering as part of their life (Degener, 2010). In-home observations of Latino American early adolescents from immigrant families also revealed that brokering was perceived as "just normal" or "just something they do" (Orellana, 2003, p. 35). Interviews with bilingual adults, who brokered as children, indicated that even though they wrote school notes and made school-related decisions for their siblings without consulting their parents, they perceived their actions as a way to reduce their parents' daily burdens (McQuillan & Tse, 1995). Young brokers play an important and necessary role in their family's survival in the new environment, with Orellana, Dorner, and their colleagues suggesting that many immigrant families perceive such behaviors as "normal" and are not linked to parentification or stress (Dorner et al., 2008). The extent to which young brokers perceive the act as "normal," however, is likely to depend on their surrounding environment. When young brokers are among other youth who also broker, they may be more likely to perceive the behavior as "normal" (Kam & Lazarevic, 2013).

Immigrant families' perception of brokering as "normal" may explain why some researchers have found a connection between brokering and positive family dynamics. In particular, the common hardships and struggles experienced during migration may result in stronger family bonds (Love & Buriel, 2007). Brokering may increase family strength because the family shares a common goal of successfully navigating the new country. Studies find that immigrant youth who broker report feeling like they mattered to their parents (Hall & Sham, 2007; Wu & Kim, 2009) and that, overall, families expressed strong bonds with their child brokers (Morales, Yakushko, & Castro, 2012). Parents often praise their children and express gratitude for the work children do for the family. Thus, the independent/interdependent scripts perspective highlights some positive implications for brokering. Similarly, another theory that sheds light on the potentially favorable effects of brokering is rooted in the translation literature and focuses on the linguistic and cognitive benefits to engaging in brokering.

Brokering as a Cognitive, Linguistic, and Academic Enhancer

Additional benefits of brokering are the cognitive, linguistic, and academic improvements that immigrant youth may develop from engaging in complex linguistic and cultural tasks.

A translation-based-theory perspective. Based on three primary arguments, Buriel et al. (1998) theorized that through brokering, youth strengthen their cognitive and linguistic skills and, in turn, enhance their academic performance (see panel d Figure 1.1). Referencing Krashen's (1985) comprehensible input hypothesis, Buriel et al. (1998) suggested that brokers increase their cognitive processing and vocabulary level the longer they broker, meaning that an accumulation effect occurs. Because brokers participate in more advanced situations (i.e., medical, school, and other institutional contexts), they may develop linguistic and cognitive skills that are similar to those valued in an educational setting (Dorner et al., 2007). When brokering, youth also must undergo a complex mental process of identifying the vocabulary of the original message, understanding the meaning of the original message, adapting the message to match the other party's language, and evaluating whether their adjusted message sufficiently matches that party's language. During face-to-face interactions or on the telephone, brokers must quickly and spontaneously participate in this cognitive process, which may improve their cognitive and linguistic skills (McQuillan & Tse, 1995). Consequently, they may be more likely to perform better academically than non-brokering youth.

Empirical research on the academic-enhancement perspective.   De Ment et al. (2005) found from focus groups that Mexican, Chinese, and Vietnamese American college students thought brokering helped their later academic performance. Through interviews with 11 young adults (ages 18–25 years), who had brokered as children, researchers found that brokering helped the youth develop adult-level reasoning, increased their language acquisition, and enhanced their reading comprehension. In Tse's (1995) study involving 35 Latino students, 50% of the foreign-born participants and 22% of the U.S.-born participants reported that brokering helped them learn English, whereas 48% of U.S.-born participants and 12% of foreign-born participants thought that brokering helped them learn Spanish. Halgunseth (2003) reported that brokering helped increase the vocabulary level of U.S. immigrant youth, which had positive effects on their cognitive development. Similarly, Chinese British youth in Hall and Sham's (2007) study also reported improved English language and increased vocabulary as a result of brokering experiences. Finally, Dorner et al. (2007) found with longitudinal data from 280 U.S. fifth- and sixth-grade students that those who brokered extensively were more likely to score higher on their standardized reading comprehension test than students who brokered less extensively. Given such findings, it is possible that brokering enhances cognitive and linguistic skills, which, in turn, improves youths' academic performance. The findings, however, should be interpreted cautiously because participants' improvements stem from cross-sectional, self-reported data.

Distinguishing between Brokering Frequency, Feelings, Norms, and Efficacy

Thus far, this chapter has discussed brokering in terms of a communication behavior; however, it is important to note that more recent studies have distinguished between unique aspects of brokering, which may affect young brokers' well-being in distinct ways (Kam, 2011; Lazarevic, 2012). Prior research has chiefly focused on brokering frequency (Hua & Costigan, 2012; Jones et al.,

2012; Kam, 2011; Trickett & Jones, 2007; Weisskirch, 2007). Most immigrant children broker at some point in their lives (Tse, 1995); therefore, assessing frequency and its effects on youth's well-being is a vital aspect to investigate. Recent studies, however, have begun exploring the associations that brokering feelings, norms, and efficacy have with well-being, separate from only measuring brokering frequency (Kam & Lazarevic, 2013).

Brokering Feelings

Brokering feelings refer to positive (e.g., pride, enjoyment) and negative (e.g., embarrassment, nervousness) affective responses experienced when brokering (Buriel et al., 1998; Díaz-Lázaro, 2002). Although past studies (e.g., Tse, 1996; Weisskirch, 2006, 2007) have distinguished between positive and negative feelings, research considering the unique associations of positive and negative brokering feelings with mental, behavioral, and relational well-being remains limited. Young brokers' perceptions of this behavior, their feelings toward engaging in the act, and how they feel about themselves when participating in the act can have profound effects on their well-being. Consistent with this notion, Weisskirch (2007) reported that feeling embarrassed and nervous when brokering were positively associated with having problematic family relations for Mexican American adolescents. Similarly, a study with first-generation U.S. immigrant youth from Eastern Europe found that negative feelings toward brokering were associated with higher levels of family conflict, which was, in turn, associated with higher levels of depression for the brokers (Lazarevic, 2012). Furthermore, a study with Mexican American adolescents found that negative feelings toward brokering were associated with increased family-based acculturation stress, leading to increased alcohol use and other risky behaviors (Kam, 2011). Last, Kam and Lazarevic (2013) recently found that among 234 Latino American brokers, negative brokering feelings were related to increased depressive symptoms. In addition, feeling that brokering was a burden on one's time was related to increased family-based acculturation stress and, in turn, alcohol consumption. In this same study, brokering frequency was not significantly related to depressive symptoms, family-based acculturation stress, or the substance use outcomes when taking into account negative feelings, thereby indicating the importance of considering the multidimensional nature of brokering.

Although negative brokering feelings are likely to be problematic, positive feelings may be associated with enhanced well-being. For example, Weisskirch (2007) found a positive association between feeling proud of brokering and self-esteem. Feeling good about oneself when brokering means that youth are likely to feel more confident and proud of their skills, which, in turn, may enhance their self-esteem and self-worth. In her longitudinal study, Kam (2011) found that as Mexican American youth felt more positively toward brokering, they reported decreased cigarette use. To date, few studies have separated positive and negative feelings to determine how the two types of feelings are related to the well-being of young brokers. Nevertheless, the limited research that has been conducted on feelings provides evidence that negative feelings threaten the well-being of brokers (Wu & Kim, 2009). A number of factors may influence the types of feelings youth have when brokering, but several studies suggest that language difficulties and ethnic identification may be particularly important predictors.

Language difficulties.   One factor that may influence how young members of immigrant families feel toward brokering is their language comprehension. Based on qualitative data from nine Latina adolescent children in the United States, Villanueva and Buriel (2010) identified three types of linguistic challenges that made brokering difficult at times. Some Latina adolescents reported experiencing vocabulary problems, which referred to lacking knowledge of a word(s) that was used or needed during the brokering interaction. Participants also experienced comprehension problems that stemmed from a lack of understanding the context or interaction in a particular language. Pronunciation problems also emerged when participating Latina adolescents reported challenges to how they articulated a word to meet the linguistic expectations of the involved parties. Given the three types of language difficulties that emerged in Villanueva and Buriel's study, it is possible that experiencing vocabulary, comprehension, and pronunciation problems may produce more negative feelings toward brokering (e.g., feeling nervous or embarrassed about brokering) and weaker brokering efficacy (e.g., confidence in one's ability to successfully interpret). In contrast, as brokers experience fewer language difficulties, they are more likely to form positive brokering feelings.

Ethnic identification.   In addition to language difficulties, youth's ethnic identification may influence the types of feelings they have toward brokering. Ethnic identification refers to the degree to which individuals feel connected to their ethnic group and the culture associated with their ethnic group (Donthu & Cherian, 1992). Having a strong ethnic identification means being proud of one's ethnic group, feeling a sense of belonging to one's ethnic group, and engaging in the customs and traditions of one's ethnic group (Phinney, 1992). In contrast, Weisskirch and Alva (2002) found that some fifth-grade Latino American youth in their study, who did not strongly identify with their ethnic background, were embarrassed by their parents' limited English skills and familiarity with mainstream culture. Such embarrassment, in turn, may make youth less eager to broker and more likely to form negative brokering feelings. Since mainstream culture is often more highly regarded (Ajayi, 2006), youth who maintain a weak ethnic identification may be more likely to feel nervous and embarrassed when brokering.

Greater ethnic identification, then, is likely to be associated with more frequent brokering and more positive brokering feelings. Kam (2009) found that among a sample of Mexican American youth, ethnic pride and involvement were related to higher levels of brokering frequency, but lower levels of negative brokering feelings. Overall, ethnic identification appeared beneficial in its association with decreased negative brokering feelings. Similarly, Smith and Silva (2011) found in their meta-analysis that ethnic identification was positively related to a sense of well-being (e.g., self-esteem), and the authors suggested that maintaining a strong ethnic identity means that individuals are aware of the valuable and desirable aspects of their own ethnic group. Thus, it is possible that having a stronger ethnic identity is related to lower levels of negative brokering feelings because youth focus on the positive aspects of brokering. Given the complex nature of ethnic identification, however, further research must explore multiple dimensions of ethnic identification to determine whether certain ones are more beneficial than others.

Brokering Norms

Although limited research has been conducted on brokering norms, some youth may perceive brokering as a "normal" way to promote family success (Dorner et al., 2008; Orellana, 2003). To determine how brokering norms influence immigrant youth's well-being, Kam and Lazarevic (2013) used literature from the theory of planned behavior (Ajzen, 1991) to identify different norms: pro-language-brokering subjective, descriptive, and personal norms. They posited that as youth believe that important others (e.g., family, friends, people at school) think they should broker (i.e., subjective norms), that other kids (e.g., at school, in their neighborhood) broker (i.e., descriptive norms), and that they should broker for family (i.e., personal norms), they are more likely to perceive this behavior as a "normal" activity. As youth perceive brokering as normative, they may downplay any negative aspects of brokering and, in turn, be less likely to experience depressive symptoms and family-based acculturation stress. Kam and Lazarevic (2013) found that brokering descriptive norms protected against Latino American sixth- through eighth-grade students' adverse psychological and behavioral well-being.

Cultural values play an important part in determining the acceptable and expected work that youth do for their parents. Depending on the cultural context, brokering may be viewed as less burdensome by youth who grew up in cultures where such work is expected of them. For example, a study with second-generation Chinese American adolescents found that adolescents who were more Chinese oriented had a higher sense of family obligation, which was negatively associated with a sense of burden as brokers (Wu & Kim, 2009). Hua and Costigan (2012) tested the norm hypothesis by using measures of familial obligations. In their study, they unexpectedly found that for Chinese Canadian youth who maintained strong family obligations, brokering frequency was associated with poor psychological well-being. To explicate this finding that appears contrary to what other brokering researchers (e.g., Dorner et al., 2008; Orellana, 2003) posited, Hua and Costigan suggested that brokers who value family obligations may feel more psychological distress when brokering because they place greater importance on ensuring that the interaction between their family member and mainstream culture proceeds smoothly and successfully. A limited number of studies have examined the normative aspect of brokering, and thus far, prior research has resulted in mixed and unexpected findings. Examining the normative aspect of brokering is crucial to theory testing (e.g., interdependent/independent scripts vs. parentification perspective) and identifying potential protective factors for young brokers.

Brokering Efficacy

Self-efficacy refers to individuals' belief in their command over a certain behavior, such as their perceptions of how easy it is to carry out the behavior. Kam and Lazarevic (2013) posited that as youth felt confident and at ease about their brokering abilities, they would be less likely to experience depressive symptoms and family-based acculturation stress. Using longitudinal data from 234 Latino American sixth- through eighth-grade students, Kam and Lazarevic (2013) found that brokering efficacy attenuated the positive association between brokering for parents and family-based acculturation stress and, in turn, alcohol consumption. In addition, Wu and Kim (2009), as well as Weisskirch (2013), found that children who broker for their parents experience a sense of efficacy. Some young individuals reported that brokering helped them learn about their native culture and language and contributed to increased self-confidence in different social situations (Buriel et al., 1998; De Ment, Buriel, & Villanueva, 2005). Although few studies have examined brokering efficacy, the existing results suggest that this factor may be important for understanding the well-being of young brokers.

In sum, the knowledge that has been garnered on brokering frequency is valuable, but more research is needed to understand its nuances (e.g., feelings, norms, and efficacy) and how they operate to influence the well-being of young brokers. Brokering may have an impact on youth's well-being differently depending on various individual factors. For example, it is possible that different aspects of brokering interact with each other to affect the well-being of young immigrant family members, which Kam and Lazarevic (2013) recently found in their study. Nonetheless, scholars lack a clear understanding of the specific ways in which each aspect of brokering contributes to the overall well-being of youth from immigrant families; therefore, additional research is warranted to understand the complexities of brokering and its effects.

Avenues for Future Research

The research on brokering has drastically expanded in the past decade and has provided invaluable knowledge about the rich experiences of immigrant youth. Nevertheless, more research is warranted to understand the complexity of such experiences. This review of the brokering literature revealed four primary perspectives on brokering that have garnered support and some contradictory evidence; therefore, it is crucial for communication researchers to investigate why such inconsistencies exist. This section explores potential explanations for the mixed findings by identifying gaps in the literature. Conducting research to minimize these gaps may result in more consistent findings. This section also provides a background for a unified theoretical model. The theoretical model summarizes what we currently know about brokering and offers an approach for future research on this behavior.

By drawing from fields of communication, education, human development and family studies, psychology, and sociology, this chapter provided an integrative review of the literature on brokering. The review resulted in the development of a unified theoretical model that illustrates the brokering process from an interdisciplinary perspective (see Figure 1.2).

This theoretical model primarily focuses on the young brokers' perspective because prior research has largely taken an individual-level approach to studying this behavior. The theoretical model, however, acknowledges the importance of considering factors at the family and community levels. We also acknowledge that this model can be expanded to incorporate additional factors at different levels (e.g., free professional translation services available in the community, parents' perspective toward brokering, etc.) as well as more communication theory. Nevertheless, the theoretical model was developed to summarize past brokering research, as well as reveal current gaps in the literature. Thus, this section begins with an overview of the theoretical model and then highlights several directions for future research.

A Description of the Theoretical Model

First, this theoretical model identifies predictors of brokering (cultural, language, and procedural brokering), as well as predictors of brokering feelings, norms, and efficacy. For example, as immigrant youth experience language difficulties with vocabulary, comprehension, and pronunciation, they may be less likely to broker and more likely to develop negative brokering feelings, perceive brokering as a nonnormative behavior, and feel less efficacious about brokering. In contrast, as immigrant youth experience a greater sense of ethnic identification (e.g., pride, belonging, and involvement), they may be more likely to broker, form more positive feelings toward brokering, perceive brokering as normative, and feel efficacious about brokering. More acculturation toward mainstream culture may result in greater brokering frequency and efficacy because acculturated youth are likely to be more familiar with the English language and mainstream culture in general. Nevertheless, acculturation toward mainstream, in which brokering may not be perceived as normative, may result in more negative brokering feelings and perceptions of brokering as non-normative. Lastly, demographic variables such as gender, age, and birth order may predict the extent to which immigrant youth engage in brokering, as well as their feelings, norms, and efficacy. Identifying predictors of frequency, feelings, norms, and efficacy is crucial because there are components that can be promoted (e.g., ethnic identification) or decreased (e.g., language difficulties), which, in turn, can exhibit indirect effects on youth's well-being through brokering frequency, feelings, norms, and efficacy.

In addition to predicting brokering feelings, norms, and efficacy, the four primary perspectives led to the suggestion that these brokering components would indirectly affect immigrant youth's risky behaviors, academic performance, and positive psychological outcomes through stress, parentification, positive parent–child relations, cognitive skills, and linguistic skills. For example, having more positive feelings, perceiving brokering as normative, and feeling more efficacious about brokering are likely to be related to lower levels of stress and parentification, but higher levels of positive parent–child relations, cognitive skills, and linguistic skills. In turn, brokering youth may be less likely to engage in risky behaviors, but more likely to perform well academically and experience positive psychological outcomes. Nonetheless, the effects of brokering (which includes brokering frequency, feelings, norms, and efficacy) on stress, parentification, positive parent–child relations, as well as cognitive and linguistic skills may be dependent on a number of moderators such as the immigrant youth's family-based psychological factors (i.e., how they perceive their relationship with family members). The link between brokering frequency and stress may be weaker for youth who experience greater family obligations, but stronger for youth who report greater parental control. Last, this theoretical model extends beyond the individual level to incorporate family- and community-level factors that certainly play an important role, but require further elaboration in the future.

Environmental Resources at the Family and Community Levels

Although rarely considered, the environment can make the experience more or less challenging for brokers and their family members. Burleson's (2010) definition of interpersonal communication highlights the importance of the environment in affecting interactions. Jones et al. (2012) also argued for the importance of considering the surrounding environment and how it has an impact on brokers' experiences. When referring to the environment, Jones et al. focused on family and community factors, such as the family's employment status and English-language proficiency, as well as the ethnic density and economic conditions of the surrounding neighborhood. Their study with refugee adolescents from the former Soviet Union suggested that families with economic hardships (and we add low education level and yearly income) placed more pressure on their children to broker, which was related to family disagreement and emotional distress. Furthermore, youth who lived in ethnic enclaves brokered more for their parents than youth who lived in communities where there were not as many Russian families (Jones et al., 2012). To our knowledge, Jones et al. (2012) is the only study that examined family's environment in relation to brokering; thus, more research is required to understand how immigrant families and young brokers function in their larger community.

The Moderating Role of Family-Based Psychological Factors

To date, most of the studies on brokering have examined direct and indirect associations between brokering frequency and various outcomes, but Hua and Costigan (2012) recently emphasized the importance of considering moderators that attenuate or amplify the links between brokering and the well-being of immigrant families. They postulated that the relationship between brokering frequency and a variety of outcomes depends on young brokers' family-based psychological factors (e.g., family-obligation values and parental psychological control). Although Hua and Costigan (2012) did not find support for their hypothesized moderation with respect to family-obligation values, they found support for their posited moderation when considering parental psychological control. Moderators demonstrate the complexity of brokering and reveal that this behavior may function differently for young brokers because they are heterogeneous. Moreover, examining moderators is crucial to developing effective culturally grounded programs for immigrant families because the tailoring of messages may vary by different experiences.

Considering Prosocial Outcomes

The stress and parentification perspectives have focused our attention on the potential negative effects that brokering may have on the well-being of immigrant youth (Kam, 2011). In contrast, the interdependence/independence scripts and academic-enhancement perspectives highlight several positive outcomes that may emerge such as enhanced parent–child relationships, stronger cognitive and linguistic skills, and better academic performance. Orellana (2010), however, suggests that much of the research on brokering, including the first two perspectives, tend to frame brokering as problematic. Instead, Orellana calls for research that examines how brokering can lead to prosocial behaviors, as well as feelings such as "empathy, compassion, and perspective taking" (2010, p. 61). As brokers, youth assist their family members in succeeding in mainstream culture, which may make them more likely to help others. Consistent with this notion, de Guzman, Carlo, Brown, and Knight (2012) conducted focus groups with first- and second-generation Mexican American mothers and found several themes that represented prosocial behaviors (e.g., caring for siblings, participating in school programs to help others, brokering for nonfamily members, etc.). Such prosocial behaviors are likely to be highly correlated with brokering and may represent more positive effects of brokering.

Cross-Sectional and Longitudinal Data

Over the last two decades, cross-sectional studies have laid the groundwork for understanding brokering, but few studies have employed longitudinal designs (Hua & Costigan, 2012; Wu & Kim, 2009). Hence, brokering research would benefit from exploring how brokering frequency changes over time, what factors contribute to such change, and in what ways these changes affect the mental health of immigrant youth. Changes within the family, such as when a sibling leaves the home and another sibling begins brokering, and its effects both on the family dynamics, as well as on individual well-being, could be examined. Other valuable components of brokering, such as changes in the settings where youth broker, family's duration in the host environment, and changes experienced at the community level, could also be studied.

When investigating brokering's effects, future research also may consider developmental stages, capturing brokering from preadolescence to adulthood. For example, one research question is whether brokering predicts parentification for adult children or whether certain expectations of familial roles change over time, thereby decreasing the harmful effects of brokering. The risk may be more prevalent and problematic among early adolescents compared to young adult brokers. Last, researchers may examine if and how feelings about brokering change. On identifying factors that lead to change in feelings, these findings can inform culturally grounded programs intended to enhance the well-being of immigrant families. Messages can be tailored to address the factors that can be altered, with the goal of promoting well-being.

Measurement Concerns

When considering gaps within the brokering literature, one apparent limitation stems from inconsistencies across measures. Currently, brokering researchers have developed their own assessment tools and adapted measures according to their own needs. For example, a brokering scale developed by Tse (1995) and modified by Buriel et al. (1998) has often been used in various studies to assess brokering experiences of immigrants from different ethnic groups (Acoach & Webb, 2004; Lazarevic, 2012; Love & Buriel, 2007; Weisskirch & Alva, 2002). The scale is a valuable tool; however, it has often been modified to fit the needs of a research team, which prevents clear comparisons across samples. Lacking the necessary assessment, other researchers have developed their own survey items or instruments to assess brokering, but they often exclude measurement validation. Considering the diversity of experiences of immigrants from various backgrounds, it is understandable that one scale may not be adequate, but it would be useful to have established measures that could serve as the base for comparison. Although some efforts have been made to establish theoretically based measurement models that explain brokering (Wu & Kim, 2009), new scales must be developed, validated, and incorporated to fully represent brokering and its related processes and theories. Such consistency also may result in fewer mixed findings and may increase the ease of comparisons across studies.

Conceptualization Concerns

As already discussed, researchers have used different terms to explain brokering. The current chapter uses the terms "language" and "cultural brokering" to accurately represent past literature in this area. Cultural brokering, however, represents an umbrella term, which includes both language brokering and procedural brokering, and it does not emphasize one component over another. In addition, this definition of brokering strongly implies that brokers do more than mediate between two languages. When referring to both linguistic and cultural intermediaries, "cultural brokering" may be most appropriate. Nonetheless, when only referring to linguistically translating for a family member, "language brokering" may be the more appropriate term to use. Lastly, when assessing whether immigrant youth teach their family members about mainstream culture's values, norms, beliefs, and social practices, procedural brokering may be more suitable.

Heterogeneity among Immigrant Families

Although research on brokering has expanded in the past decade, much of what we know about brokering comes from research conducted in the United States with Latino youth (Acoach & Webb, 2004; Kam, 2011; Martinez et al., 2009; Villanueva & Buriel, 2010; Weisskirch, 2007). Immigrant youth, however, come from diverse backgrounds, and future studies should focus on exploring brokering among other ethnic groups, as well. Young immigrants from various ethnic/cultural backgrounds differ from one another by having a unique set of values and beliefs, and by emphasizing different aspects of their culture. Kim and Chao (2009) alluded to this when they found that native-language fluency was an important component of ethnic identity for second-generation Mexican adolescents, but not for second-generation Chinese adolescents. They suggested that the ethnic differences may attribute to varying perceptions of brokering as a normal activity. Further research must investigate whether brokering and its effects vary based on ethnicity/culture. If certain ethnic/cultural groups are at greater risk than others, culturally grounded prevention programs must take such differences into consideration. Perhaps certain groups that are more resilient utilize more effective coping strategies that can be taught to others.

Because most research on brokering has been conducted with immigrants in the United States, we know very little about experiences of immigrant youth and families in other countries. For example, an overview article indicates that much of the knowledge about brokering in the United Kingdom comes from small-scale studies or anecdotal evidence (Cline et al., 2010). Research in other countries is almost nonexistent (Antonini, 2010; Degener, 2010), which makes comparisons across international populations and settings challenging. Learning about the experiences of immigrant youth across the globe is crucial to understanding the processes that play a role in their development, and in establishing policies and practices that best serve this population.

Implications for Communication Research

The development of the unified theoretical model represents past research on brokering, but also offers avenues for future research. This model illustrates the limited presence of a communication perspective in studying brokering.

Nonetheless, several theories and concepts that are commonly utilized in communication research may enhance the unified theoretical model. Although many communication theories and concepts are applicable to language and cultural brokering, multiple goals theories, communal coping, and communication privacy management theory may be particularly useful in explicating brokering's impact on the well-being of immigrant families.

Multiple goals theories suggest that communication, whether intentional or unintentional, involves instrumental, identity, and relational goals that simultaneously exist and, at times, may conflict within and between the involved parties (Caughlin, 2010). Brokers, their family members, and members from the host culture all have multiple goals that influence their communicative exchanges (Guntzviller, 2013). For example, young brokers may have instrumental goals (e.g., trying to accurately interpret the information from two different cultures, helping their family members accomplish their goals), relational goals (e.g., exhibiting respect for their family members and members of the host culture, fulfilling both parties' expectations of them), and identity goals (e.g., being able to competently broker to maintain their own self-esteem and confidence, fulfilling their own self-expectations). Members of their family and of mainstream culture also have their own set of instrumental, relational, and identity goals. Thus, the brokering literature may benefit from exploring (a) the multiple goals of each party, (b) how different situations alter their goals, (c) how goals can conflict, (d) how the involved parties manage their conflicting and nonconflicting goals, and (e) how each party's goal management has an impact on its well-being.

In addition to utilizing multiple goals theories, brokering may be better understood from a communal coping perspective. Figure 1.2 reveals that most of the research on brokering involves individual-level processes, but more research is necessary to identify other influential factors at the family and community levels. Communal coping moves beyond individuals dealing with adversity, but instead considers coping as a joint effort between people. More specifically, communal coping involves two or more people who adopt ownership and responsibility of managing an adverse experience; therefore, they perceive the situation as their shared problem (Afifi, Hutchinson, & Krouse, 2006). Although brokering may not always be problematic, immigrant families and members of mainstream culture are faced with the challenge of establishing shared meaning when they come from different cultural backgrounds. Several studies (Dorner et al., 2008; Katz, 2010; Villanueva & Buriel, 2010) suggest that parents and children work together as a team when brokering, but thus far, few studies have explored this experience in detail. Researchers also may move beyond the family and examine whether and how the young broker, family member(s), *and* member(s) of the mainstream culture work together as a team during face-to-face interactions. Such teamwork may depend on a number of factors, such as how receptive the member of mainstream culture is to perceiving co-ownership of the problem and working with young brokers and their family. Because communal coping is defined by a sense of mutual responsibility, it is possible that all involved parties may not adopt this perspective. Nevertheless, future research may use communal coping to explore whether this type of coping occurs among immigrant families (and possibly members of the host culture) and the communication that each party uses to communally cope.

Another theory that is commonly used in the communication field and that may provide greater insight into brokering is communication privacy management (CPM) theory (Petronio, 2010). CPM focuses on the ways in which individuals use communication to manage their privacy based on their need for both openness and closedness (e.g., privacy). One of the primary concerns of the parentification perspective is not only that young brokers prematurely adopt adult responsibilities, but that they learn personal information intended only for adults. Moreover, if immigrant families adopt a communal coping perspective by working together as a team, they may be more likely to disclose private information to young brokers and include them in adult decision-making processes. Not only does CPM apply to young brokers gaining access to private information from adult family members, but young brokers also may have their own private information that they wish to disclose or withhold. Therefore, another primary concern in the brokering literature is the extent to which youth withhold negative information about their academic performance during parent–teacher conferences to prevent disciplinary action. If the teacher has concerns about the child's school performance, researchers and practitioners question whether the young broker will convey such information to his or her parent (Hall & Sham, 2007).

In short, this section provides several examples of ways in which communication researchers can contribute to our understanding of brokering and help identify factors that may have an impact on the well-being of young brokers and their family members. By explicating the ways in which brokering is a form of interpersonal communication, which can be examined using well-established communication theories and concepts, it is evident that brokering is a complex and nuanced experience that warrants more attention in the communication field.

Concluding Remarks

Language and cultural brokering remains a prevalent experience among immigrant families, and immigrant youth often begin brokering at a very early age (Martinez et al., 2009). Moreover, with the growing ethnic diversity in the United States and in other countries, brokering is an important process to study, given its implications for the well-being of immigrant families. To shed light on opportunities for future research, this chapter provided an interdisciplinary review of prior brokering research, examined four dominant perspectives on brokering's effects, used several theoretical frameworks as guiding rationales, developed a unified theoretical model to represent past brokering research, provided avenues for future research, and explored ways in which communication researchers can examine brokering. The number of studies on brokering has increased in the past decade. Many questions, however, remain, and more research (including more communication research) is needed to fully understand the diversity of experiences and the nuanced ways in which brokering affects the psychological, relational, and behavioral well-being of immigrant families.

Acknowledgments

The authors would like to express their deepest gratitude to John Caughlin, Robert Weisskirch, and the three reviewers for their feedback and suggestions regarding this chapter.

References

Acoach, C. L., & Webb, L. M. (2004). The influence of language brokering on Hispanic teenagers' acculturation, academic performance, and non-verbal decoding skills: A preliminary study. *The Howard Journal of Communications,15*(1), 1–19. doi:10.1080/10646170490275459

Afifi, T. D., Hutchinson, S., & Krouse, S. (2006). Toward a theoretical model of communal coping in postdivorce families and other naturally occurring groups. *Communication Theory, 16,* 378–409. doi:10.1111/j.1468–2885.2006.00275.x

Agnew, R. (1992). Foundation for a general strain theory of crime and delinquency. *Criminology, 30*(1), 47–87. doi:10.1111/j.1745–9125.1992.tb01093.x

Agnew, R. (2001). Building on the foundation of general strain theory: Specifying the types of strain most likely to lead to crime and delinquency. *Journal of Research in Crime and Delinquency, 38,* 319–361.

Ajayi, L. J. (2006). Multiple voices, multiple realities: Self-defined images of self among adolescent Hispanic English language learners. *Education, 126,* 468–480.

Ajzen, I. (1991). The theory of planned behavior. *Organizational Behavior and Human Decision Processes, 50,* 179–211.

Antonini, R. (2010). The study of child language brokering: Past, current and emerging research. *mediAzioni, 10,* 1–23. Retrieved from the mediAzioni website: http://mediazioni.sitlec.unibo.it

Ashforth, B. E. (2001). *Role transitions in organizational life: An identity-based perspective.* Mahwah, NJ: Erlbaum.

Bauer, E. (2010). Language brokering: Practicing active citizenship. *mediAzioni, 10,* 125–146. Retrieved from the mediAzioni website: http://mediazioni.sitlec.unibo.it

Berry, J. W., Phinney, J. S., Sam, D. L., & Vedder, P. (2006). Immigrant youth: Acculturation, identity, and adaptation. *Applied Psychology: An international Review, 55*(3), 303–332. doi:10.1111/j.1464–0597.2006.00256.x

Biddle, B. J. (1986). Recent developments in role theory. *Annual Review of Sociology, 12*(1), 67–92. doi:10.1146/annurev.so.12.080186.000435

Birman, D. (2006). Measurement of the "Acculturation gap" in immigrant families and implications for parent-child relationships. In M. H. Bornstein & L. R. Cote (Eds.), *Acculturation and parent-child relationships: Measurement and development* (pp. 113–134). Mahwah, NJ: Erlbaum.

Birman, D., & Trickett, E. J. (2001). Cultural transitions in first-generation immigrants: Acculturation of Soviet Jewish refugee adolescents and parents. *Journal of Cross-Cultural Psychology, 32*(4), 456–477.

Bourhis, R. Y. (1979). Language and ethnic interaction: A social psychological approach. In H. Giles & B. Saint-Jacques (Eds.), *Language and ethnic relations* (pp. 117–141). Oxford, England: Pergamon Press.

Broidy, L., & Agnew, R. (1997). Gender and crime: A general strain theory perspective. *Journal of Research in Crime and Delinquency, 34*(3), 275–306. doi:10.1177/0022427897034003001

Buriel, R., Perez, W., DeMent, T. L., Chavez, D. V., & Moran, V. R. (1998). The relationship of language brokering to academic performance, biculturalism, and self-efficacy among Latino adolescents. *Hispanic Journal of Behavioral Sciences, 20*(3), 283–297. doi:10.1177/07399863980203001

Burleson, B. R. (2010). The nature of interpersonal communication: A message-centered approach. In C. R. Berger, M. E. Roloff, & D. R. Roskos-Ewoldsen (Eds.), *The handbook of communication science* (pp. 145–164). Los Angeles, CA: Sage. doi:10.4135/9781412982818

Burnette, D. (1999). Social relationships of Latino grandparent caregivers: A role theory perspective. *The Gerontologist, 39,* 49–58.

Castro, D., M., Jones, R. A., & Mirsalimi, H. (2004). Parentification and the imposter phenomenon: An empirical investigation. *The American Journal of Family Therapy, 32*(3), 205–216. doi:10.1080/01926180490425676

Caughlin, J. P. (2010). A multiple goals theory of personal relationships: Conceptual integration and program overview. *Journal of Social and Personal Relationships, 27,* 824–848.

Chao, R. K. (2006). The prevalence and consequences of adolescents' language brokering for their immigrant parents. In M. H. Bornstein & L. R. Cote (Eds.), *Acculturation and parent-child relationships: Measurement and development* (pp. 271–296). Mahwah, NJ: Earlbaum.

Cline, T., Crafter, S., O'Dell, L., & de Abreu, G. (2011). Young people's representations of language brokering. *Journal of Multilingual and Multicultural Development, 32*(3), 207–220. doi:10.1080/01434632.2011.558901

Cline, T., de Abreu, G., O'Dell, L., & Crafter, S. (2010). Recent research on child language brokering in the United Kingdom. *mediAzioni, 10,* 105–124. Retrieved from the mediAzioni website: http://mediazioni.sitlec.unibo.it

Costigan, C. L., & Dokis, D. P. (2006). Relations between parent–child acculturation differences and adjustment with immigrant families. *Child Development, 77*(5), 1252–1267. doi:10.1111/j.1467–8624.2006.00932.x.

de Guzman, M.R.T., Carlo, G., Brown, J., & Knight, G. P. (2012). What does it mean to be prosocial? A cross-ethnic study of parental beliefs. *Psychology Developing Societies, 24,* 239–268. doi:10.1177/0971333611202400207

Degener, J. L. (2010). Sometimes my mother does not understand, then I need to translate'. Child and youth language brokering in Berlin-Neukölln (Germany). *mediAzioni, 10,* 346–367. Retrieved from the mediAzioni website: http://mediazioni.sitlec.unibo.it

DeMent, T. L., Buriel, R., & Villanueva, C. M. (2005). Children as language brokers: A narrative of recollection of college students. In R. Hoosain & F. Salili (Eds.), *Language in multicultural education* (pp. 255–272). Charlotte, NC: Information Age.

Díaz-Lázaro, C. M. (2002). *The effects of language brokering on perceptions of family authority structure, problem solving abilities, and parental locus of control in Latino adolescents and their parents* (Unpublished doctoral dissertation). State University of New York at Buffalo.

Donthu, N., & Cherian, J. (1992). Hispanic coupon usage: The impact of strong and weak ethnic identification. *Psychology & Marketing, 9,* 510–510.

Dorner, L. M., Orellana, M. F., & Jimenez, R. (2008). "It's one of those things that you do to help your family": Language brokering and the development of immigrant adolescents. *Journal of Adolescent Research, 23*(5), 515–543. doi:10.1177/0743558408317563

Dorner, L. M., Orellana, M. F., & Li-Grining, C. P. (2007). "I helped my mom," and it helped me: Translating the skills of language brokers into improved standardized test scores. *American Journal of Education, 113*(3), 451–478. doi:10.1086/512740

Ellwanger, S. J. (2007). Strain, attribution, and traffic delinquency among young drivers: Measuring and testing general strain theory in the context of driving. *Crime and Delinquency, 53*(4), 523–552. doi:10.1177/0011128706295991.

Goldblatt, H., & Eisikovits, Z. (2005). Role taking of youths in a family context: Adolescents exposed to interparental violence. *American Journal of Orthopsychiatry, 75*(4), 644–657. doi:10.1037/0002–9432.75.4.644

Grieco, E. M., Acosta, Y. D., de la Cruz, G. P., Gambino, C., Gryn, T., Larsen, L. J., Trevelyan, E. N., & Walters, N. P. (2012). *The foreign-born population in the United States: 2010.* (No. ACS19). Washington, DC: U.S. Census Bureau.

Guntzviller, L. M. (2013, November). *Testing multiple goals theory with low-income, mother-child Spanish-speakers: Language brokering interaction goals and relational satisfaction.* Paper presented at the annual convention of the National Communication Association, Washington DC.

Halgunseth, L. (2003). Language brokering: Positive developmental outcomes. In M. Coleman & L. Ganong (Eds.), *Points and counterpoints: Controversial relationship and family issues in the 21st century: An anthology* (pp. 154–157). Los Angeles, CA: Roxbury.

Hall, N., & Sham, S. (2007). Language brokering as young people's work: Evidence from Chinese adolescents in England. *Language and Education, 21*(1), 16–30. doi:10.2167/le645.0

Hua, J. M., & Costigan, C. L. (2012). The familial context of adolescent language brokering within immigrant Chinese families in Canada. *Journal of Youth and Adolescence, 41*(7), 894–906. doi:10.1007/s10964–011–9682–2

Jones, C. J., & Trickett, E. J. (2005). Immigrant adolescents behaving as culture brokers: A study of families from the former Soviet Union. *The Journal of Social Psychology, 145*(4), 405–427. doi:10.3200/SOCP.145.4.405–428

Jones, C. J., Trickett, E. J., & Birman, D. (2012). Determinants and consequences of child culture brokering in families from the former Soviet Union. *American Journal of Community Psychology, 50*(1–2), 189–196. doi:10.1007/s10464–012–9488–8

Kam, J. A. (2009). *Disentangling the effects of cultural brokering among Mexican-heritage youth* (Doctoral dissertation). The Pennsylvania State University, State College, PA.

Kam, J. A. (2011). The effects of language brokering frequency and feelings on Mexican-heritage youth's mental health and risky behaviors. *Journal of Communication, 61*(3), 455–475. doi:10.1111/j.1460–2466.2011.01552.x

Kam, J. A., & Lazarevic, V. (2013). The stressful (and not so stressful) nature of language brokering: Identifying when brokering functions as a cultural stress for Latino immigrant children in early adolescence. *Journal of Youth and Adolescence. Advanced online publication.* doi:10.1007/s10964-013-0061-z

Katz, V. S. (2010). How children of immigrants use media to connect their families to the community: The case of Latinos in South Los Angeles. *Journal of Children and Media, 4,* 298–315. doi:10.1080/17482798.2010.486136

Katz, V. S. (2014). Communication dynamics of immigrant integration. *Communication Yearbook 38,* pp. 39–68.

Kim, S. Y., & Chao, R. K. (2009). Heritage language fluency, ethnic identity, and school effort of immigrant Chinese and Mexican adolescents. *Cultural Diversity and Ethnic Minority Psychology, 15*(1), 27–37. doi:10.1037/a0013052

Krashen, S. D. (1985). *The input hypothesis: Issues and implications.* Harlow, England: Longman.

Lazarevic, V. (2012). *Effects of culture brokering on individual well-being and family dynamics in a sample of immigrant young adults from Eastern Europe* (Unpublished doctoral dissertation). University of Illinois, Urbana–Champaign.

Love, J. A., & Buriel, R. (2007). Language brokering, autonomy, parent-child bonding, biculturalism, and depression: A study of Mexican American adolescents from immigrant families. *Hispanic Journal of Behavioral Sciences, 29*(4), 472–491. doi:10. 1177/0739986307307229

Martinez, C. R., McClure, H. H., & Eddy, J. M. (2009). Language brokering contexts and behavioral and emotional adjustment among Latino parents and adolescents. *Journal of Early Adolescence, 29*(1), 71–98. doi:10.1177/0272431608324477

McQuillan, J., & Tse, L. (1995). Child language brokering in linguistic minority communities: Effects of cultural interaction, cognition and literacy. *Language and Education, 9*(3), 195–215. doi:10.1080/09500789509541413

Mercado, V. (2003). *Effects of language brokering on children of Latino immigrants* (Unpublished doctoral dissertation). Pace University, New York.

Morales, A., & Hanson, W. E. (2005). Language brokering: An integrative review of the literature. *Hispanic Journal of Behavioral Sciences, 27*(4), 471–503. doi:10.1177/0739986305281333

Morales, A., Yakushko, O. F., & Castro, A. J. (2012). Language brokering among Mexican-immigrant families in the Midwest: A multiple case study. *The Counseling Psychologist 40*(4), 520–553. doi:10.1177/0011000011417312

Orellana, M. F. (2003). Responsibilities of children in Latino immigrant homes. *New Directions for Youth Development, 100,* 25–39.

Orellana, M. F. (2010). From here to there: On the process of an ethnography of language brokering. *mediAzioni, 10.* Retrieved from the mediAzioni website: http://mediazioni.sitlec.unibo.it

Orellana, M. F., Dorner, L., & Pulido, L. (2003). Accessing assets: Immigrant youth's work as family translators or "para-phrasers." *Social Problems, 50*(4), 505–524. doi:10.1525/sp.2003.50.4.505

Oznobishin, O., & Kurman, J. (2009). Parent-child role reversal and psychological adjustment among immigrant youth in Israel. *Journal of Family Psychology, 23,* 405–415.

Petronio, S. (2010). Communication privacy management theory: What do we know about family privacy regulation? *Journal of Family Theory & Review, 2,* 175–196. doi:10.1111/j.1756-2589.2010.00052.x

Phinney, J. (1992). The multigroup ethnic identity measure: A new scale for use with adolescents and young adults from diverse groups. *Journal of Adolescent Research, 7,* 156–176.

Sabatier, C., & Berry, J. W. (2008). The role of family acculturation, parental style and perceived discrimination in the adaptation of second generation immigrant youth in

France and Canada. *European Journal of Developmental Psychology, 5*(2), 159–185. doi:10.1080/17405620701608739

Shin, H. B., & Bruno, R. (2003). *Language use and English-speaking ability: 2000.* Washington, DC: U.S. Census Bureau.

Smith, T. B., & Silva, L. (2011). Ethnic identity and personal well-being of people of color: A meta-analysis. *Journal of Counseling Psychology, 58,* 42-60. doi:10.1037/a0021528

Solomon, M. R., Surprenant, C., Czepiel, J.A., & Gutman, E.G. (1985). A role theory perspective on dyadic interactions: The service encounter. *Journal of Marketing, 49*(1), 99–111.

Stein, J. A., Rotheram-Borus, M. J., & Lester, P. (2007). Impact of parentification on long-term outcomes among children of parents with HIV/AIDS. *Family Process, 46*(3), 317–33. doi:10.1111/j.1545–5300.2007.00214.x

Suárez-Orozco, C. & Suárez-Orozco, M. (2001). Children of immigration. Cambridge, MA: Harvard University Press.

Trickett, E. J., & Jones, C. J. (2007). Adolescent culture brokering and family functioning: A study of families from Vietnam. *Cultural Diversity and Ethnic Minority Psychology, 13*(2), 143–150. doi:10.1037/1099–9809.13.2.143

Tse, L. (1995). Language brokering among Latino adolescents: Prevalence, attitudes, and school performance. *Hispanic Journal of Behavioral Sciences, 17*(2), 180–193. doi:10.1177/07399863950172003

Tse, L. (1996). Language brokering in linguistic minority communities: The case of Chinese- and Vietnamese-American students. *The Bilingual Research Journal, 20*(3–4), 485–498.

Umaña-Taylor, A. J. (2003). Language brokering as a stressor for immigrant children and their families. In M. Coleman & L. Ganong (Eds.), *Points & counterpoints: Controversial relationships and family issues in 21st century* (pp. 157–160). Los Angeles, CA: Roxbury.

Umaña-Taylor, A. J., Updegraff, K. A., & Gonzales-Backen, M. A. (2011). Mexican-origin adolescent mothers' stressors and psychosocial functioning: Examining ethnic identity affirmation and familism as moderators. *Journal of Youth and Adolescence, 40,* 140–157. doi:10.1007/s10964–010–9511-z

Valdés, G. (2003). *Expanding definitions of giftedness: The case of young interpreters from immigrant communities.* Mahwah, NJ: Erlbaum.

Valdés, G., Chavez, C., & Angelelli, C. (2003). A performance team: Young interpreters and their parents. In G. Valdés (Ed.), *Expanding definitions of giftedness: The case of young interpreters from immigrant countries* (pp. 63–97). Mahwah, NJ: Erlbaum.

Valenzuela, A. (1999). Gender roles and settlement activities among children and their immigrant families. *American Behavioral Scientist, 42*(4), 720–742. doi:10.1177/0002764299042004009

Villanueva, C. M., & Buriel, R. (2010). Speaking on behalf of others: A qualitative study of the perceptions and feelings of adolescent Latina language brokers. *Journal of Social Issues, 66*(1), 197–210. doi:10.1111/j.1540–4560.2009.01640.x

Vinokurov, A., Trickett, E. J., & Birman, D. (2002). Acculturative hassles and immigrant adolescents: A life domain assessment for Soviet Jewish refugees. *Journal of Social Psychology, 142*(4), 425–445. doi:10.1080/00224540209603910

Weisskirch, R. S. (2005). The relationship of language brokering to ethnic identity for Latino early adolescents. *Hispanic Journal of Behavioral Sciences, 27*(3), 286–299. doi:10.1177/0739986305277931

Weisskirch, R. S. (2007). Feelings about language brokering and family relations among Mexican American early adolescents. *Journal of Early Adolescence, 27*(4), 545–561. doi:10.1177/0272431607302935

Weisskirch, R. S. (2013). Family relationships, self-esteem, and self-efficacy among language brokering Mexican American emerging adults. *Journal of Child and Family Studies, 22,* 1147-1155. doi:10.1007/s10826-012-9678-x

Weisskirch, R. S., & Alva, S. (2002). Language brokering and the acculturation of Latino children. *Hispanic Journal of Behavioral Sciences, 24*(3), 369–378. doi:10.1177/0739986302024003007

Wu, N. H., & Kim, S. Y. (2009). Chinese American adolescents' perception of the language brokering experience as a sense of burden or a sense of efficacy. *Journal of Youth and Adolescence, 38*(5), 703–718. doi:10.1007/s10964–008–9379–3

CHAPTER CONTENTS

2 Communication Dynamics of Immigrant Integration

Vikki S. Katz

Rutgers University

Researchers across disciplines share an enduring interest in the social impacts of immigration. I review key intersections between communication and immigrant integration scholarship in order to demonstrate how communication research and theory can address gaps in the literature on immigrant integration. These applications also reveal how communication theories, when extended to the integration experiences of immigrants and their children, more robustly reflect the increasing diversity of our globalizing societies. The conclusion provides suggestions for future inquiry at the nexus of these fields.

The movement and settlement of peoples across international boundaries has long captured the attention of scholars across a range of disciplines. And rightly so. Migration deeply influences the social fabrics of the societies that receive these newcomers and those societies they leave behind. The political and social visibility of migration is belied by its relative rarity; the most comprehensive estimate is that international migrants account for 3% of the global population (International Organization for Migration, 2010). The social significance of migration is partly explained by who moves, because migrants are disproportionately highly skilled or are young and capable of physically challenging work. Sending countries therefore stand to lose valuable members of their workforces, while receiving countries stand to gain a great deal from their strengths (Carrington & Detragiache, 1999; Fischer, Martin, & Straubhaar, 1997).

Those who settle in the countries that they move to (as opposed to short-term or seasonal migrants) are usually referred to as *im*migrants, to emphasize that their entry into new national and social spaces has some level of permanence. Immigrants, as compared with temporary movers, are more likely to experience and cause change at various levels of social life. Portes (2010) described migration-related social change as "a hierarchy of 'micro-processes' affecting individuals and their immediate surroundings; 'meso-processes' affecting entire communities and regions; and 'macro-processes' affecting full societies and even the global system" (p. 1541). By leaving, immigrants prompt changes to their families and communities; in large enough numbers, their exits influence their country of origin as well (Fitzgerald, 2009). Likewise, moving to a new place involves changes for immigrants and their families, as well as for the community and country in which they reestablish their lives.

Researchers across a broad range of disciplines share an interest in under-standing the social impacts of immigration made manifest within and across various levels of analysis. This interest has been heavily weighted toward immigration's impact on countries of settlement (as opposed to places of ori-gin). In large part, this is because the social incorporation of immigrants and their children is a perennial concern in receiving societies.

The processes attending immigrant settlement have commonly been referred to as acculturation, assimilation, incorporation, and integration, and the spe-cific activities or outcomes each term describes vary among the researchers who use them (Schneider & Crul, 2010; Vermeulen, 2010). Although precise definitions differ and have been hotly contested, most agree that these pro-cesses involve incorporation into societal opportunity structures, such as higher education, and what Thomson and Crul (2007) called "broader and at times fuzzier concept[s]," such as expressions of identity and social forms of citizen-ship (p. 1025; Maira, 2002; Park, 2005; Zentella, 1997).

Scholars have long considered immigrants' movement and settlement expe-riences as being bound in their relationships. For example, ties to friends and family create "chain migration" between communities of origin and settle-ment so robust that even tighter immigration restrictions do not break the flows (Massey, Durand, & Malone, 2002). After arrival, social networks affect where immigrants work (Waldinger & Der-Martirosian, 2001), live (Zhou & Lee, 2013), and how they engage with local organizations and institutions (Kim & Ball-Rokeach, 2006a; Ramakrishnan & Bloemraad, 2008; Small, Jacobs, & Massengill, 2008). Immigrants' family relationships are recognized as being more influential still (Foner & Dreby, 2011). How immigrant families negotiate changes in their relationships and influence each other's community interac-tions deeply affects their individual and collective social trajectories (Foner, 2009; Louie, 2012; Park, 2002; Song, 1999; Valenzuela, 1999).

When immigrant integration is considered in this context—where inter-actions with family, friends, and other residents influence what immigrants and their children understand and experience in their everyday lives—social processes that are enduring interests for communication scholars are clearly implicated. Indeed, research and theory development in some areas of our discipline have been informed by a steady focus on immigrant populations. Communication accommodation theory, for example, has been applied to immigrants' experiences since its earliest usage approximately four decades ago, across social contexts ranging from health care interactions and police–citizen encounters, to perceptions of the relative status of ethnic/racial groups (Abrams & Giles, 2007; Giles, Linz, Bonilla, & Gomez, 2012; Street, 1991). Similarly, anxiety and uncertainty management theory (AUM) and its cor-relates in intercultural communication have guided research on interactions between immigrant and native-born individuals for many years (Gallagher, 2013; Gudykunst, 2005; Stephan, Stephan, & Gudykunst, 1999). However, attention to immigrants' experiences has been uneven across the discipline's subfields. For example, family and interpersonal communication theories have been minimally applied to immigrant populations. Immigrants' experiences provide rich opportunities to extend and refine these and other communication theories to better reflect the increasing diversity of our globalizing societies.

To address all the existing and potential points of convergence between communication and immigration theory and research would require (at least one) book-length treatment of the subject. I therefore circumscribe my focus to the intersections between research on immigrant family integration, outside and within the field of communication, to demonstrate how each can inform the other. I begin by providing an overview of the major themes and problems addressed in the broader literature surrounding segmented assimilation theory over the past 20 years. Wherever possible, I draw on international rather than U.S. examples and evidence. My goal here is to introduce readers not fully familiar with the immigration literature to this scholarly conversation.

Following this overview, I identify several gaps in this literature and communication research and theory that can address these lacunae. In the final sections, I suggest directions for future research and theory development at the intersections of communication and immigration scholarship. I begin by discussing a couple of prominent communication theories that have enjoyed increasing use in recent years to demonstrate how applying them to immigrant populations would address persistent gaps in the literature, as well as offer exciting opportunities to further refine these theories. I conclude with a call to action by identifying additional areas of convergence between communication and immigration research that would significantly advance both areas of inquiry.

Integration and Immigrant Families: An Introduction

The immigrant family has been studied both as a collective unit and as a primary site for negotiating individual-level change (see Foner & Dreby, 2011, for a comprehensive review). Although family relationships can provide respite from the stresses of migration and settlement, they can also be challenged by variations in members' abilities and desires to adapt to settlement country language and cultural practices (Durham, 2004; Maira, 2002; Song, 1999).

These intra-family differences have most often been studied by comparing the immigrant generation to their children. Gonzales (2011) recently argued that "for generations, the public school system has been the principal institution that educates and integrates children of immigrants in to the fabric of American society" (p. 603). Schooling serves this purpose in other immigrant-receiving societies as well (Crul & Schneider, 2010; Luthra, 2010). Gonzales (2011) goes on to note that "this assimilating experience is profoundly different from what most adult immigrants encounter" (pp. 603–604), especially if employed in sectors primarily occupied by immigrants of shared origin (Massey & Sànchez, 2010; Waldinger & Lichter, 2003). The combination of children's greater facilities to acquire language, combined with their higher likelihood of native-tongue phonology (Lippi-Green, 1997) and daily opportunities to engage with native-born schoolmates and teachers, has been used to explain why children's integration trajectories can differ from those of their immigrant parents (Louie, 2012; Stanton-Salazar, 2001).

Although the majority of researchers have found that children incorporate more easily than their parents (Gonzales, 2011; Louie, 2012; Zhou & Bankston, 1998), Telzer (2010) suggests that, under certain conditions, parents may incorporate more easily than their children. Differences between husbands' and wives' incorporation trajectories (Hirsch, 1999; Hondagneu-Sotelo, 1994, 2003; Pessar, 2003) and between siblings (Louie, 2012; Menjívar & Abrégo, 2009; Pyke, 2005) have also been found among different immigrant groups. Researchers have also noted variations in integration experiences at more macro-levels of analysis, including country of origin (Hein, 2006; Portes, Fernández-Kelly, & Haller, 2005, 2009), country of settlement (Schneider & Crul, 2010; Thomson & Crul, 2007), and community of settlement (Alba & Nee, 2003; Portes & Rumbaut, 2001, Zhou & Lee, 2013).

Building theory robust enough to explain variations within and across levels of analysis has been a complex ongoing project. The most dominant theory in this area for the last twenty years has been segmented assimilation theory (Schneider & Crul, 2010; Stepick & Stepick, 2010; Portes et al., 2009), a multilevel formulation that examines integration trajectories and outcomes for children of immigrants, in context of family- and community-level factors. Segmented assimilation theory reflects a commitment to accounting for multiple levels of influence on integration experiences. This orientation reflects a broader trend (Alba & Nee, 2003), because theoretical development has largely moved away from the linear and typological assimilation models that characterized earlier eras of scholarship (Gordan, 1964) to consider integration trajectories as ongoing processes without fixed endpoints.

Segmented Assimilation Theory

Segmented assimilation theory was first developed in the early 1990s as a reaction to researchers focusing almost exclusively on the experiences of the immigrant generation (Portes & Rumbaut, 1996; Portes & Zhou, 1993). Reflecting on the early stages of its development, Portes et al. (2009) note that:

> the reason for focusing attention on the children[1] was the realisation that the long-term effects of immigration on American society would be determined less by the first than by the second generation, and that the prognosis for this outcome was not as rosy as the dominant theories of the time would lead us to believe. (p. 1078)

In developing segmented assimilation theory, Portes, Rumbaut, and Zhou sought to explain divergences in the social trajectories of children of U.S. immigrants from those of the native born, as well as among children of immigrants with different origins (Portes et al., 2009; Portes & Rumbaut, 1996; Portes & Zhou, 1993). Segmented assimilation theory can apply to children of immigrants living anywhere; it has been adapted and applied in European contexts (Schneider & Crul, 2010; Vermuelen, 2010), and, to a lesser extent, in Australia (Brandon, 2008). The theory was, however, "developed specifically in reference to the U.S. children of immigrants who arrived after the Immigration and Nationality Act of 1965" (Stepick & Stepick, 2010, p. 1150). This landmark piece of legislation ended a series of restrictive immigration policies and opened the U.S. to newcomers from regions beyond Europe, notably Latin America, Asia, and, to a lesser extent, Africa.

In essence, segmented assimilation theory treats the second generation as the litmus test of family- and community-level influences on their social integration. Theorists also account for how more macro-level influences, which are unevenly distributed across immigrant groups (e.g., access to economic opportunity structures and experiences of racialization), are experienced and negotiated with the realms of family and community life. Family and community levels of analysis are the core of this theory, and each is discussed in more detail in the following sections.

Community-Level Influences

Segmented assimilation theorists attribute the reception immigrants are given to government, societal, and community-level influences. The government level includes formal policies[2] as well as labor market conditions; societal factors refer to the social discourses and attitudes related to immigration generally and to immigrants from certain countries in particular (Portes & Rumbaut, 1996; Portes et al., 2005, 2009). Governmental and societal influences are macro-level factors that immigrants usually experience indirectly, in that they are made manifest in the everyday interactions immigrants and their families have within their community of settlement.

The characteristics of settlement communities influence what immigrant families encounter in local spaces and the kinds of connections they can make to address their needs. Immigrants often settle in urban areas where people of their same origins have clustered.[3] These are the communities that segmented assimilation theories have primarily sought to understand. Also called "ethnic enclaves," these areas are often signified with unambiguously identifying names, such as Chinatown or Little Italy (Zhou & Lee, 2013). Immigrants in these areas can often address everyday needs and work in their native tongue (Light & Bonacich, 1991; Sanders & Nee, 1992; Waldinger & Lichter, 2003). These communities have distinctively ethnic infrastructures, including organizations and institutions that address immigrants' settlement concerns and their enduring interests in the places from which they came (Jones-Correa & de Graauw, 2013; Ramakrishnan & Bloemraad, 2008; Zhou & Lee, 2013). Ethnic media are often also prominent because these are primary markets for such publications (Matsaganis, Katz, & Ball-Rokeach, 2011).

Although living in ethnically concentrated areas can have advantages, urban neighborhoods often experience social conditions that Sampson and associates collectively termed "concentrated disadvantage," including high levels of poverty and un-/underemployment, limited and under-resourced local services, and high crime and school drop-out rates (Sampson, 2013; Sampson, Morenoff, & Gannon-Rowley, 2002). Segmented assimilation scholars initially contended that strong ties to an ethnic community helped shield families from these social challenges (Portes & Zhou, 1993; Portes & Rumbaut, 2001; Zhou & Bankston, 1998). More recently, scholars amended this claim, noting that these advantages are most likely enjoyed by immigrants with vertically integrated social networks (i.e., when middle-class, longer-settled immigrants share social networks with more newly arrived and less advantaged countrymen and -women). Such networks enable newcomers' access to a broad range of opportunities in and beyond their geographic community (Louie, 2004; Portes et al., 2009; Zhou, 2009).

Segmented assimilation theorists also consider living in a community with other immigrants who share their parents' values an enabling factor for maintaining traditional rules and parenting styles. Stepick and Stepick's (2010) review of the literature notes that the linkage between settlement community characteristics and family practices is one way that "communities can provide valuable resources [to families] even if they are not materially well off" (p. 1155). Stepick and Stepick note that family characteristics can also influence their settlement community; for example, parents' socioeconomic status largely determines the neighborhoods that children live in and, therefore, the quality of schools they attend. These factors contribute to children's educational and occupational attainment, two of the outcomes most commonly measured by segmented assimilation researchers (Portes & Fernàndez-Kelly, 2008).

Family-Level Influences

Segmented assimilation theorists have also stressed the importance of family-level factors since the earliest formulations of this approach (Portes & Zhou, 1993; Portes & Rumbaut, 1996). Specifically, they posit three potential integration trajectories, each of which associates individual outcomes with family- and community-level factors. The first trajectory is *consonant acculturation*, which occurs when parents and children adopt the settlement country's language and culture—while shedding ties to their language and culture of origin—at similar rates. The second is *selective acculturation*, when children and parents adopt the settlement country's language and culture at similar paces but also preserve ties to their culture and language of origin via connection to an ethnic community in the settlement country (Gibson, 1988; Zhou & Bankston, 1998). The final possibility is *dissonant acculturation,* which occurs when children acquire the settlement country language and culture more quickly than their parents and quickly shed their family's language and cultural practices in the process. Dissonant acculturation is associated with negative outcomes, including parent–child conflict and limited educational attainment (Portes & Rumbaut, 2001).

Although the frequency of consonant, selective, and dissonant acculturation trajectories has been debated (Portes et al., 2009[4]), researchers consistently report that dissonant acculturation is the least likely trajectory, from studies of Turkish immigrants in Germany (Luthra, 2010), to children of Brazilian immigrants in Japan (Takenoshita, Chitose, Ikegami, & Ishikawa, 2013). Drawing on data collected from 3,415 children of immigrants from China, Colombia, the Dominican Republic, Ecuador, the former Soviet Union, Hong Kong, Peru, Taiwan, and the West Indies who were raised in New York City, Waters and associates (2010) found that only 10% experienced dissonant acculturation. Twenty percent of respondents experienced consonant acculturation. Selective acculturation reflected the experiences of the remaining 70%, suggesting that parent–child negotiations of language and culture are the norm among immigrant families (Waters et al., 2010).

What remains largely unstudied is the nature of these family negotiations and what factors most influence integration outcomes. Segmented assimilation theorists have pointed to the importance of family structures by noting the positive influences that intact families and extended family involvement have on children's social trajectories and outcomes. Parenting practices—including holding high expectations of children, encouraging children's recognition and respect of their sacrifices, and direct intervention in and guidance of their children's activities—have also all received mention by segmented assimilation scholars (Portes & Fernàndez-Kelly, 2008; Portes & Rumbaut, 2001; Stepick & Stepick, 2010; Zhou & Bankston, 1998). However, these factors are often only mentioned in passing. When these concepts are included in data analyses, they are often operationalized in ways that fail to capture the dynamic nature of the processes they reflect—Portes and associates (2009) operationalized family structure as whether or not both parents lived in the home, for example. The limited attention that segmented assimilation theorists have paid to the actual family and community interactions that underlie their influence on integration trajectories remains a fundamental limitation of the theory's explanatory power.

Where Is Communication?

The dual emphases on family and community in segmented assimilation theory appear to clearly implicate communication processes. Although the connection seems intuitive, segmented assimilation scholars have paid surprisingly little attention to communication research and theory that could inform their understandings of these phenomena. The preceding review of segmented assimilation research reveals three important gaps that could be addressed by integrating communication research on these topics.

The first gap is the most basic: Segmented assimilation theory focuses squarely on second-generation integration trajectories rather than on those of all family members. Focusing solely on individual outcomes removes the relational aspects of immigrant integration that lie at the core of these experiences. In the next section, I describe some ways that communication scholars have theorized multidirectional family influence and how these theories can inform efforts to explain immigrant integration as a family project, rather than as an individual one. These perspectives capture the dynamic nature of family life and emphasize families' capacities for change, which aligns with segmented assimilation theory's emphasis on integration trajectories as ongoing processes, as opposed to more static typologies.

Having laid the groundwork for a more holistic, relational approach to social integration, the two sections that follow address gaps in the segmented assimilation literature at the family and community levels of analysis, respectively. In each, I draw on extant communication research to demonstrate how these findings could expand the explanatory power of segmented assimilation theory. At the family level, I assess what we know about everyday discursive practices in immigrant families—and specifically, about how these influence family members' connections to each other and their understandings of their settlement communities. At the community level, I address how communication theory and research can explain variations in immigrants' localized experiences by identifying linkages between family and community that mutually influence immigrants' integration trajectories.

Communication Perspectives on Immigrant Family Dynamics

The most obvious weakness in the structure of segmented assimilation theory is that the outcomes of interest are limited to the children. Despite the theory's emphasis on the family, children of immigrants are essentially treated as the dependent variable in an equation that accounts for family- and community-level factors. By failing to account for communication practices and activities within immigrant families, segmented assimilation theory essentially overlooks how children influence their parents' integration trajectories, as well as the intra-generational influences that siblings and parents have on each other.

Communication researchers have developed a number of theoretical orientations to understand communication in immigrant families as a dynamic process in which all members can influence each other. Family systems theory has been prominent among these, as it facilitates consideration of individual contributions, needs, and interests in context of the same from other family members (Galvin, Dickson, & Marrow, 2005; Olsen, 2000; Yerby, 1995). A family systems perspective is flexible, permitting consideration of both personal and collective motivations among family members, as well as possibilities for both cooperation and conflict. It also treats the family as a dynamic system, capable of both stability and change over time (McDevitt & Chaffee, 2002). I have applied family systems theory to the integration experiences of immigrant families and found that this framework provided both the necessary structure and flexibility to explain how family members interacted with each other at home and in community locations (Katz, 2014).

Multidirectional influence in these families has also been understood from other communication perspectives. Leeds-Hurwitz (2005) compiled a broad array of research on immigrant and ethnic minority families to explore how culture and identity are communicated across generations. Many authors in that volume (e.g., Haydari, 2005; Lum, 2005) either implied or discussed inter-cultural socialization experiences (language learning, cultural identification) not as top-down experiences but, rather, as reciprocal learning experiences between parents and children.

Harwood, Soliz, and Lin (2005) have argued that these family systems can also be understood from an intergroup perspective. Parent–child communication in immigrant families can be considered as intergroup communication because age, generation, language, and cultural differences may all become salient distinctions during interactions (see also Song, 1999). In some immigrant families, intergroup perspectives can also explain sibling communication. Pyke (2005) found that traditional (usually the eldest) siblings in U.S.-based Korean and Vietnamese immigrant families were tied to traditional communication channels and behaviors; they spent more time with parents and connecting with ethnic media, were more fluent in their parents' language, preferred traditional foods, and were more socially reserved. By comparison, their younger and more assimilated siblings spent more leisure time with friends and mainstream media, were less fluent in their parents' language, and were more openly affectionate.

Younger children in some of these families saw elder siblings as "genera-tional deserters" who sided with parents with regard to discipline and rules (Pyke, 2005). Conversely, elder children saw their "American" siblings as "black sheep" who did not show appropriate levels of family deference and loyalty. These intergroup differences could cause conflict, but Pyke (2005) also noted how they could enhance cooperation. Some siblings reported assum-ing complementary responsibilities in family-owned businesses that harnessed their respective linguistic and cultural skill sets; Song (1999) reported similar findings among Chinese immigrant families living and working in London.

What these theoretical orientations have in common is their emphasis on immigrant family communication as dynamic and capable of effecting change in all members. All of these orientations are able to account for fluidity in fam-ily interaction, in that the particulars of an experience can affect situational alignments within family subsystems. For example, siblings may band together to negotiate with parents in one instance but see their siblings as very different from themselves in another. Inherent in being able to account for coopera-tion and conflict is the notion that family members can negotiate individual and collective goals in ways that ultimately affect their integration trajectories, both separately and as a unit. All of these features speak directly to the core concerns of segmented assimilation theory but increase its explanatory power by accounting for the social integration experiences of all family members and how their experiences are tied together.

Communication Practices in Immigrant Families

Considering immigrant integration from these more holistic perspectives makes it possible to focus on families' everyday discursive practices and on how they influence what members learn and understand about the community and country in which they have settled. Given how central parents' and children's rates of linguistic and cultural change are to segmented assimilation theory, it is surprising how little attention has been paid to the actual interactions that influence and explain these rates of change.

Although immigrant families' discursive practices vary according to their particular needs and interests (Katz, 2014), there are common threads through these different practices. The preceding section already demonstrated that all family members can be engaged in these activities. The subsequent discussion emphasizes the roles children of immigrants often play in their families' connections with information and resources in their settlement communities. How parents and children engage each other in mutual learning activities also helps explain variations in their experiences of, and in, their local communities.

Although researchers have established that children affect how parents communicate, even as preverbal infants (Ochs & Schieffelin, 2001), immigration researchers have largely overlooked the active roles and contributions that children of immigrants make to families' settlement experiences. Only recently has scholarly interest in children's "brokering" burgeoned in North America, the U.K., and Europe (Cline, de Abreu, O'Dell, & Crafter, 2010; Kam, 2011; Kam & Lazarevic, 2014; Orellana, 2009; Park, 2002; Song, 1999, Valenzuela, 1999). Although definitions vary, in my own work I define brokering as the activities that children of immigrants engage in to facilitate their families' connections to and understandings of their local environments (Katz, 2010, 2014).

Children's brokering takes a number of forms. Most commonly, brokering has been studied in families in which children are the primary (or only) speakers of the host country's language. Although no representative studies specifically document how many children engage in brokering activities, U.S. Census data indicate that 61% of children of immigrants have at least one parent who reports difficulty speaking English (Urban Institute, 2009), a proportion that has steadily increased since the Census in 1990 (49%) and in 2000 (55%; Johnson, Kominski, Smith, & Tillman, 2005). Data collected in the United Kingdom, Germany, and Switzerland all indicate that children of immigrants routinely engage in these activities (Bischoff & Loutan, 2004; Cline et al., 2010; Cohen, Moran-Ellis, & Smaje, 1999; Meyer, Pawlack, & Kliche, 2010), although no representative data on these practices have been collected there either. These data do, however, suggest that having parents who need assistance navigating their adopted environments is the norm, rather than the exception, for many children of immigrants.

Children's brokering activities most often involve negotiating language, as children do when they enable a conversation between their parents and native-born individuals. Cultural brokering is often also intertwined into these interactions because child brokers engage at least two sets of cultural norms with regard to appropriate behavior and communication. Depending on where these interactions take place, child brokers may also have to negotiate the norms of an institutional culture (Katz, 2014). Finally, brokering activities often involve engaging media devices or content, ranging from making phone calls, to completing official documents, to enabling parents' Internet searches (Clark, 2012; Katz, 2014; Valenzuela, 1999). Child brokers may invoke their linguistic, cultural, and media-related skill sets separately or simultaneously, depending on the circumstances (Katz, 2010).

Children's brokering activities both influence and are influenced by interactions with other family members. The family needs that prompt children's brokering also engage families in collective communication practices that provide varying levels of support for brokering efforts. Children contribute their greater familiarity with the settlement country language and cultural norms, as well as with various media forms and content, to these family interactions. Parents contribute their adult understandings of how the world works and of what the family needs, as well as their greater proficiency with the mother tongue. Because parents and children come to these interactions as both learners and as more competent peers, these are opportunities for all family members to simultaneously support each other's and their own learning (Dorner, Orellana, & Li-Grining, 2007; Katz, 2014; Vygotsky, 1978).

These patterns in immigrant family interaction have been reported in studies on their experiences in health-care settings (Bischoff & Loutan, 2004; Cline et al., 2010), schools (Dorner et al., 2007; García-Sánchez & Orellana, 2006), family businesses (Park, 2002; Song, 1999), and parents' workplaces (Valenzuela, 1999). Political socialization processes in immigrant families provide a particularly rich example of these communication activities. McDevitt and Chaffee (2002) first proposed a "trickle up" model of family communication related to political socialization with evidence that child-initiated discussion of a civics curriculum prompted parents to seek information and to form opinions on related topics, in order to more competently engage in future discussions with their children. Building on McDevitt and Chaffee's work, Wong and Tseng (2008) examined these activities in immigrant families, differentiating between families in which both parents were immigrants and those in which one parent was an immigrant and the other was U.S. born.

Wong and Tseng (2008) found that parents' and children's reciprocal influence on each other's political socialization powerfully influenced how all family members understood and interacted with their political environments. In families with two immigrant parents, children played particularly critical roles in their parents' socialization to U.S. politics by addressing parents' questions about the U.S. political system and current issues, as well as by brokering government documents and political information for their parents. As such, children influenced what their parents knew about local and national politics in the settlement country. These learning experiences were not one-sided. Parents' interests and knowledge of settlement and home country politics also influenced their children's knowledge, attitudes, and behavior related to politics in both countries. As the authors expected, these influences were stronger among families where both parents were immigrants than in families where one parent was native-born. In both kinds of families, they argued, "political socialization consists of dynamic, relational processes which evolve over time" (p. 155), suggesting that parents and children continue to learn from each other over extended periods and that they contribute complementary strengths to these experiences.

The relationships between immigrant families' media connections and their settlement experiences have also received increased interest in recent years. The data suggest that immigrant families are more likely to make media connections together, as compared with native-born families. A representative survey of U.S. adolescents with parents from Central America, Mexico, the Dominican Republic, and China found that only 20% of respondents watched television "mainly alone" and that co-viewing was most likely to occur with family members (Louie, 2003). By contrast, a general study of U.S. teens during the same time period found that over one third of teens watched TV "mainly alone" and that co-viewing with friends was common (Rideout, Foehr, Roberts, & Brodie, 1999). Because media connections are implicated in children's brokering activities, these patterns are consistent with parents and children engaging with information resources together and pooling their resources to understand them. In my own research on children's brokering, Gabriela, a 12-year-old respondent, told me that she and her father watched the nightly news in English, and she would broker words he didn't understand. In return, Gabriela said, "He explains [what the news event means] to me" (Katz, 2010, p. 307). This example illustrates how Gabriela's command of English and her father's adult interpretations of that content allowed them to construct a shared understanding of local news that, over time, increased both of their familiarity with local events (Katz, 2010).

Elias and Lemish (2008, 2011) also found that media connections were embedded in immigrant family life, and, furthermore, that media connections were made strategically to support different goals. They found that media activities in Russian immigrant families living in Israel and Germany were often motivated by desires for internal or external integration. They defined internal integration as family members' desires to maintain family cohesion and shared cultural knowledge and values. These goals could motivate parents to select ethnic media to co-view with their children in order to support their native language development, for example (Elias & Lemish, 2011). Outward integration, on the other hand, involved media activities that supported integration into the settlement community; one of their teenaged respondents described watching a popular German television show as "homework" that supported her language learning (p. 1261; see also Elias, 2013).

Elias and Lemish's (2011) findings link family members' motivations to make media connections to different intended outcomes, which helps explain how media use can be connected to segmented assimilation trajectories. Dissonant acculturation trajectories may well be tied to family members' conflicts over media practices; Hargreaves and Mahdjoub (1997) reported that children of Maghrebi immigrants in France admitted to secretly repositioning the family satellite dish to receive more French stations, as opposed to the diasporic channels their parents preferred that they watch. Elias and Lemish (2008) also noted that media connections can serve internal and external motivations concurrently, which would support either consonant or selective acculturation depending on the kinds of media that parents and children used (Durham, 2004; Louie, 2003; Mayer, 2003; Matsaganis et al., 2011). Because families' media environments are intertwined with their everyday interactions with each other, their media activities may act as an amplifier for their acculturation trajectories. A deeper understanding of these relationships would contribute to the broader literature on children, families, and media and would directly inform segmented assimilation theory by identifying specific activities by which consonant, dissonant, and selective acculturation trajectories manifest over time.

Taken together, these findings suggest that immigrant families' discursive practices deeply influence what members understand about their settlement community and country. Interactions among immigrant family members at home are also dynamically related to interactions they have in their settlement community. I have found that immigrant families often enter the community as a unit and work together to understand their encounters in local healthcare institutions, schools, and social services, using strategies they developed in interactions at home (Katz, 2014). Families' experiences in their community were often preceded by discussions and media connections at home; by the same token, their community experiences also influenced subsequent family discussions and media engagement (Katz, 2014). Identifying the specific communication strategies that families develop and hone over time can therefore shed light on how the family and community levels of analysis in segmented assimilation theory are linked and how these links influence integration trajectories.

Community-Level Communication

Segmented assimilation theory posits that immigrants' contexts of reception are most influenced by the features of their settlement community, including the characteristics of local organizations and institutions, and the ethnic composition of the area (Zhou & Lee, 2013). But what explains variance in residents' local experiences, and how can that variance also be linked to family-level influences? Communication infrastructure theory (CIT) most directly addresses how immigrants' community interactions are tied to more micro-levels of interaction from a communication perspective (Wilkin, Katz, & Ball-Rokeach, 2009). Developed and refined by Ball-Rokeach and her Metamorphosis Project associates, CIT is a multilevel theoretical framework that explains the communication systems that residents experience in their predominantly immigrant and ethnic minority communities. The communication infrastructure is the communication system of a local community, capable of enabling or constraining residents' access to resources they need to achieve everyday goals. The communication infrastructure consists of two elements: the storytelling network and the communication action context (Ball-Rokeach, Kim, & Matei, 2001).

The storytelling network is a triangulated network consisting of residents' social networks, community organizations, and local media. Residents' social networks include family members, supported by ties with friends and other residents. Interactions in their social networks allow residents to share information resources that help them make decisions and address their needs, through the kinds of practices detailed in the preceding section. These social interactions can also be supported by residents' connections to local media and community organizations. CIT conceives of local media as meso-level actors, in that they can mediate and interpret events and content for residents that are tailored to their local environments and interests (Katz, Matsaganis, & Ball-Rokeach, 2012; Matsaganis et al., 2011). Community organizations are also considered meso-level actors, in that these collectives are arranged around shared interests and can be physical and discursive spaces for residents to engage each other about the local area (Ball-Rokeach et al., 2001; Wilson, 2002).

Research guided by CIT indicates that the integration of the storytelling network—meaning the degree to which residents' social networks, local media, and community organizations are dynamically engaged with each other—varies among communities, even geographically proximate ones with similar demographics (Kim, Jung, & Ball-Rokeach, 2006). Storytelling network integration helps explain why contexts of reception vary across immigrant settlement communities. An integrated storytelling network facilitates immigrant settlement by making it easier for residents to find out about and access local resources, because making connections to one storytelling network node (e.g., an active local organization) effectively facilitates access to the rest of the network (Matsaganis, 2007; Wilkin et al., 2009). Communities with less integrated storytelling networks are therefore often more challenging communication environments for immigrant families (Ball-Rokeach et al., 2001; Chen et al., 2012).

CIT also accounts for individual-level variance in the strength of residents' connections to the storytelling network within the same community. Residents' integration into the storytelling network—which, as described above, accounts for both micro-level (social networks) and meso-level connections (local media and community organizations)—have consequences for a wide range of individual outcomes. Researchers using CIT have reported that residents' integration into the storytelling network predicts levels of political participation, collective efficacy, and neighborhood belonging (Kim & Ball-Rokeach, 2006a, 2006b), knowledge about prevention and detection of breast cancer and diabetes (Kim, Moran, Wilkin, & Ball-Rokeach, 2011), perceived ease of receiving medical care (Wilkin & Ball-Rokeach, 2011), and emergency preparedness behaviors (Kim & Kang, 2010). Settling in a community where the communication infrastructure facilitates these kinds of connections can be particularly powerful enablers for immigrant families' integration trajectories.

Finally, CIT accounts for features of community environments that influence residents' connections to the storytelling network, collectively referred to as the communication action context (Ball-Rokeach et al., 2001). These factors include local social, economic, and physical features that segmented assimilation theorists have also identified as affecting immigrants' community experiences, but CIT considers these features as capable of constraining or facilitating the vitality of the storytelling network. For example, safe local parks where residents might congregate, quality health care so that residents need not travel outside the community for care, and well-maintained public transportation can all help facilitate residents' storytelling network integration. Conversely, communities where parks and public areas are unsafe, and local services are poor or scarce, can prompt residents' withdrawal from public life and constrain their engagement with the local area (Ball-Rokeach et al., 2001).

In essence, the linkages that CIT researchers have established between community-level features, residents' local activities and connections, and residents' outcomes explain how family- and community-level influences are linked with each other and affect the integration trajectories and outcomes with which segmented assimilation theory is primarily concerned. Families engage in discursive practices at home and in the community; these discussions draw on individual members' connections to storytelling network nodes and the news and information they glean from these connections. CIT not only explains linkages *between* levels of analysis but also how these influence individual and family experiences, such as health and well-being, work/life balance, and civic engagement (Loges, Ball-Rokeach, & Qiu, 2005; Kim et al., 2011; Kim & Ball-Rokeach, 2006b; Wilkin, 2013; Wilkin et al., 2009). The preceding discussion also demonstrates that CIT is able to account for variations *within* levels of analysis to explain why local engagement and outcomes vary among individuals and families living in the same community.

As such, CIT represents an important step toward meaningful intersections between communication and immigration research. CIT is not a communication theory that has been applied to research on immigrant integration nor is it a theory of immigrant integration that has been applied to communication research. Rather, CIT is a truly interdisciplinary theory, in that communication processes are the central mechanism for understanding how immigrants navigate their local communities—and how these communities are changed by the people who settle in them. CIT therefore represents meaningful advancement for research in both fields; furthermore, its compatibility with segmented assimilation theory demonstrates CIT's utility for scholars addressing integration-related questions across a range of disciplines.

Moving Forward: New Directions for Research on Communication and Immigration

The preceding sections demonstrate how communication research and theory can address gaps in the literature on immigrant integration. In this final section, I turn to the task of identifying additional points of convergence between these areas of inquiry. I begin by discussing two prominent areas of communication research that could be applied to immigrant populations. I use these two areas as examples of how such applications can address lingering questions about immigrant integration—and provide opportunities for researchers to broaden their understandings of the processes that communication theories seek to explain by exploring a greater diversity of individuals and families.

The preceding discussion centered on immigrant families living together in the settlement community. These families have received the most research attention, to date. However, not all families immigrate together; for certain groups, protracted separations between spouses, or between parents and children, are very common. These separations and (sometimes) reunifications have been studied among Filipino migrants to the United Kingdom and United States (Ehrenreich & Hochschild, 2004; Madianou & Miller, 2012; Parreñas, 2005), Central American migrants to the United States (Dreby, 2010; Menjívar & Abrégo, 2009), and Ukrainian and Ecuadorian parents in Spain (Leifsen & Tymczuk, 2012), among others. In recent years, the experiences of children who migrate to reunify with their parents after extended separations have garnered increased scholarly attention. I suggest that the considerable communication literature on stepfamily formation and resilience (see Afifi, 2008, for a review) could be fruitfully extended to understanding these reunification experiences.

Reunifying families are often also "mixed status" families, in which members' immigration status may include unauthorized residents, legal residents, and citizens (Dreby, 2012). These families face many difficulties, which have received considerable attention both from researchers and within public discourse (Donato & Armenta, 2011). However, how members manage this potentially deleterious secret, and, furthermore, how those management strategies affect their public interactions are not fully understood. I discuss how privacy management theory could be extended to explain these experiences.

Communication in Reunifying Families

Parents who immigrate without one or more of their children usually hope to send for them when they achieve financial stability. Families who realize these dreams are often surprised by how much conflict and anxiety result from such a long-awaited event. If children must enter the new country illegally, these reunifications may be tainted with trauma from the start.[5] Menjívar and Abrégo (2009) found that reunifications of Salvadoran and Guatemalan families in the United States were often fraught with serious challenges. Newly arrived children often harbored resentment about having been left behind—feelings that were exacerbated if parents had had more children after arriving in the United States. Differences among siblings were further attenuated by U.S.-born siblings having citizenship, whereas newly arrived elder siblings often lacked legal status and the considerable benefits associated with it. Although initial conflicts could be intense, Suárez-Orozco, Bang, and Kim's (2011) longitudinal study of adolescent immigrants revealed that their initial reports of conflict, anxiety, and depression abated with the 5 years following reunification, suggesting that these periods of family turmoil are usually transitional.

Although reunified families are not stepfamilies per se (though children do sometimes reunite with a parent who has a new spouse), the communication patterns and activities associated with stepfamilies are similar to those in reunifying immigrant families. Golish (2003) found that stepfamilies faced a core set of challenges, including ambiguity of parental roles, vying for resources, and building solidarity as a family unit. Menjívar and Abrégo's (2009) findings reveal the same: Parents are often unsure of how to parent children that they last cared for as infants, and children may grieve the loss of daily contact with grandparents or other relatives who were their primary caretakers. Children in stepfamilies vie for resources and are particularly sensitive to perceived favoritism (Golish, 2003); these same patterns are seen between newly arrived children and their U.S.-born siblings (Dreby, 2010). These dynamics, combined with unrealistic expectations—parents who thought children would fall gratefully into their arms and children who expected parents to somehow compensate for lost years—pose serious challenges for reunifying families trying to develop a sense of family solidarity.

While separated and reunifying immigrant families have been studied more broadly in recent years (Carling, Menjívar, & Schmalzbauer, 2012; Leifsen & Tymczuk, 2012; Suárez-Orozco et al., 2011), scholars have paid more attention to risk factors in these families than to identifying sources of resilience. This is similar to early scholarship on divorce and remarriage (Coleman, Ganong, & Fine, 2000). Research on communication in stepfamilies could guide scholars interested in understanding why some reunifying families manage these transitions more constructively than do others.

Afifi and Hamrick (2006) noted that in stepfamilies, "communication is an antecedent and consequence of coping, but is also a primary way in which family members cope with one another and generate meaning from their experiences" (p. 437). Hutchinson, Afifi, and Krause (2007) argued that family coping involves time spent on shared activities to create, maintain, and strengthen bonds. Practices that Golish (2003) identified as distinguishing strong stepfamilies from those having difficulties included spending time together as a family in shared space, communicating openly about conflict and engaging in family problem solving, establishing clear rules and boundaries, and having realistic expectations about how long family solidarity takes to develop. If these same communication practices are seen in more resilient reunifying families that would suggest that stepfamilies and reunifying families—and perhaps families experiencing other kinds of transitions—share important commonalities with each other.

Managing Privacy in Immigrant Families

Reunifying families are likely to be among the considerable proportion of immigrant families whose members hold different immigration statuses. Families that have least one member who lacks legal residency encounter considerable challenges related to privacy and disclosure of this family secret. Most disclosure research has focused on the privacy-disclosure dialectic in intimate relationships with family members, romantic partners, and friends (Afifi & Olson, 2005). In these contexts, disclosures have been understood as implying shifts in power, because the discloser becomes vulnerable to his or her confidante's response to that secret and has to trust the confidante not to share his or her secret with others (Petronio, 2002, 2010).

For mixed-status families, dilemmas related to disclosure are implied not only in their intimate relationships but in almost any interaction they have. Taking a sick child to an emergency room, for example, requires a complex calculation for an undocumented parent, who has to weigh that child's needs against the potential danger the family will face if their secret is involuntarily exposed in the process (Yoshikawa, 2011). Family members also face these dilemmas when deciding if service providers, health-care professionals, or teachers can be trusted when disclosure may provide access to desired support, services, and resources (Dreby, 2012; Gonzales, 2011). Because disclosure carries so much risk, unauthorized immigrants and their families are less likely to interact with local institutions than other low-income families (Gálvez, 2011; Yoshikawa, 2011). They are also less likely to develop relationships with longer settled and native-born neighbors. Yoshikawa (2011) found that the resulting isolation predicts significantly more depressive symptoms in mothers with unauthorized status than in their native-born counterparts; furthermore, these mothers' symptoms predicted lower cognitive skills in their children at 24 months.

Family privacy rules, then, seem central to how mixed-status families understand themselves and their relationships to their settlement communities (Petronio, 2010). The nature and severity of their family secret likely has a chilling effect on disclosure for all members, in keeping with Vangelisti and colleagues' findings about conditions under which family members may decide to disclose one another's secrets (Vangelisti & Caughlin, 1997; Vangelisti, Caughlin, & Timmerman, 2001). Privacy boundaries in mixed-status families tend to have extremely low permeability (Dreby, 2012; Gonzales, 2011; Petronio, 2002, 2010), which may help explain why members of these families are also less likely to make other kinds of disclosures, such as reporting domestic violence or crime victimization to law enforcement (Yoshikawa, 2011; Yoshioka, Gilbert, El-Bassel, & Baig-Amin, 2003).

Revealing one's immigration status can clearly have considerable costs, but Yoshikawa's (2011) results also suggest that disclosure can offer benefits and access to needed support and resources, in certain contexts. Determining when mixed-status family members feel that breaking their silence is warranted relates to current research on decisions to disclose potentially stigmatizing information (Derlega, Winstead, Greene, Serovich, & Elwood, 2004; Greene, Carpenter, Catona, & Magsamen-Conrad, 2013) or non-visible health conditions (Greene et al., 2012). Although immigration status is obviously not a health condition, it is often stigmatized in public discourse and media coverage (Santa Ana, 2002). Unauthorized immigration status is also popularly perceived as more "visible" in certain immigrant populations than in others

(Dreby, 2012; Portes et al., 2009), which may also affect disclosure decisions. Understanding how immigration status relates to family privacy norms and disclosure decisions would extend current research in these areas and help explain variations in how mixed-status families interact with their settlement communities.

Immigrant Families in the Broader Spectrum

These two suggestions for future research on immigrant families and their settlement experiences are meant to illustrate the rich opportunities at the intersection between communication research that does not currently focus on immigrant populations, on the one hand, and current research on immigrant integration that does not engage communication perspectives, on the other. Research conducted on either reunifying or mixed-status families would also have clear implications for segmented assimilation theory, since both imply the influence of structural variations (timing of migration and immigration status, respectively) on immigrant family members' interactions with each other and with their settlement communities.

For communication researchers, extending scholarship on resilience in step-families and on privacy management also has important implications for how immigrants' experiences should be contextualized within the broader research interests of the discipline. Rather than treating immigrant individuals and families as special or unique cases, we are best served by considering them within a wider spectrum of families' experiences. For example, immigrant families are hardly unique in having to negotiate closeness over geographic distances. Research on the affordances of information and communication technologies (ICTs) for fostering feelings of co-presence apply to families with a range of reasons for their extended separations; military families, for example, have received recent attention in this regard (Merolla, 2010; Theiss & Knobloch, 2011). Likewise, immigrants are not alone in trying to maintain distinctive cultural, religious, or ethnic identities, while also meaningfully engaging with a broader community (Galvin, 2007; Leeds-Hurwitz, 2005).

Communication researchers have and continue to seek out and examine the considerable dynamism and diversity within social relationships and families. Even a cursory examination of recent scholarship reveals efforts to understand communication in multiracial families, families with gay and lesbian parents, transgendered family members, and internationally adopted children, to give only a few examples (Docan-Morgan, 2010; Gartrell, Bos, Peyser, Deck, & Rodas, 2011; Harrigan, 2010; Lannutti, 2013; Norwood, 2012; Soliz, Ribarsky, Harrigan, & Tye-Williams, 2010; Soliz, Thorson, & Rittenour, 2009). The experiences of immigrant families should be considered as part of this ever-widening spectrum of research on communication in family life.

There is another reason for considering immigrants' experiences from this inclusive perspective. Immigrants and their children constitute large and growing proportions of many societies, some of which already have cities that are "majority minority" in composition (Alba & Nee, 2003). These trends are on the rise; currently, more than 20% of U.S.-born children have at least one immigrant parent, and Muslim immigrants and their children alone now account for 6% of the overall European population (Pew Forum on Religion and Public Life, 2011; Urban Institute, 2009). Given these changes, Schneider and Crul (2010) contended that "the notion of 'mainstream' (into which immigrants are supposed to assimilate) is not static . . . and implies processes of change on *both* sides" (p. 1144, emphasis in original). Therefore, understanding the social impacts of immigration, from micro- to macro-levels, requires considering not only how immigrants change in new environments but also how those environments are changed by their integration. This reality behooves communication scholars to include immigrants' experiences in their efforts to understand the communication processes across the general population—and, furthermore, to treat immigrants' experiences as a part of the larger story that communication research endeavors to tell, rather than as separate from a supposedly static societal majority or mainstream.

Expanding the Scope of Inquiry

I have focused on how communication can both contribute to research on immigrant integration and be enhanced by focusing on immigrants' settlement experiences and challenges. This is but a small slice of the intersections between communication and international migration research more broadly. For example, communication research on globalization can directly contribute to the burgeoning research on transnationalism, which is the study of supranational activity, identification, and connections immigrants maintain to both their country of origin and their country of settlement (Schiller, Basch, & Blanc, 1995). Transnationalism researchers consider it axiomatic that new communication technologies have made such practices easier than ever before (Levitt & Jaworsky, 2007), but few actually interrogate the relationship between transnational communication and these technological innovations (cf. Carling et al., 2012; Leifsen & Tymczuk, 2012; Madianou & Miller, 2012). For communication researchers, this is a natural intersection of interests.

Within the realm of applied communication research, focusing on immigrants provides a rich array of opportunities for scholars to address issues of concern to policy makers and stakeholders, in and outside the academy. Communication researchers routinely address structural factors that can enable or constrain communicative behavior and decision making. Unlike other disciplinary traditions, however, communication scholars do not limit their focus to structural factors, which are often difficult, expensive, or unlikely to change. The dynamic nature of communication suggests avenues for intervention that can be practical and cost-effective ways to effect change at various levels of analysis. For example, researchers using communication infrastructure theory have recently tested how leveraging existing communication capital can enable local residents and stakeholders to create changes that they deem important for their own community, which is itself an important indicator of immigrants' civic engagement (Chen et al., 2012).

From a disciplinary perspective, focusing on immigrants and their social integration presents opportunities for communication researchers to expand current research interests, to test and refine existing theories, and to increase the validity of findings by accounting for demographic change in many nations and urban centers, globally. The potential to deepen such research with meaningful cross-context or cross-national comparisons—such as those conducted by Livingstone and associates in their EU Kids Online projects over the last decade—is another potential avenue for growth (Hasebrink, Livingstone, & Haddon, 2008; Livingstone & Haddon, 2009). The preceding discussion also underscores the need for theoretical frameworks robust enough to account for and explain multiple levels of influence on immigrants' experiences and outcomes.

A growing number of communication scholars are working at the intersections of communication and immigration research and theory. As interest continues to build within the discipline, scholars' abilities to theoretically articulate communication's unique stake in conversations around topics related to immigration and international migration—within and across disciplinary boundaries—will be critical. This essay is intended as a contribution toward these deliberations and as encouragement for new and established researchers to consider how intersections between communication and migration research hold considerable promise for the future trajectories of the discipline.

Acknowledgments

The author thanks Elisia Cohen, Sarah Vos, and two anonymous reviewers for their assistance in developing this manuscript for publication. She is also grateful to Carmen Gonzalez and Matthew Matsaganis for their supportive, careful reads and patient discussions of many iterations of this work.

Notes

1. Segmented assimilation theorists have defined "children of immigrants" as having at least one parent born abroad (Stepick & Stepick, 2010). Children born in the settlement country are referred to as the second generation. Children born in the country of origin who migrate with their parents are considered part of the second generation if they start their formal schooling in the settlement country. Children of immigrants who enter the settlement country during adolescence are called the "1.5 generation," to signify that their socialization experiences have been split between countries of origin and settlement (Portes & Rumbaut, 2001).
2. Relevant policies include those related to immigration specifically but also economic, labor, and social policies.
3. Zhou (2009) noted that ethnic enclaves differ from immigrant neighborhoods, in which two or more ethnic groups share physical space but lead separate ethnic lives.
4. Portes et al. (2009) contend that because dissonant acculturation is associated with "school abandonment, unemployment, teenage childbearing, and arrest and

incarceration . . . even a minority experiencing these outcomes will have a significant impact in the cities and regions where it concentrates" (p. 1083).
5. Nazario (2013) reported that the U.S. Border Patrol apprehended 14,000 people
    younger than 18 years old in 2012, twice as many as in 2011. This figure does
    not account for an equal number of Mexican children who were immediately
    deported. The plights of "separated children" have also been documented in
    other countries, including Australia, Canada, and Ireland (Martin & Curran,
    2007; Mullaly, 2011).

References

Abrams, J. R., & Giles, H. (2007). Ethnic identity gratifications selection and avoidance
    by African Americans: A group vitality and social identity gratifications perspective.
    Media Psychology, *9*, 115–134. doi:10.1080/15213260709336805

Afifi, T. D. (2008). Communication in stepfamilies. In J. Pryor (Ed.), *International
    handbook of stepfamilies: Policy and practice in legal, research and clinical spheres*
    (pp. 299–320). Hoboken, NJ: Wiley.

Afifi, T. D., & Hamrick, K. (2006). Communication processes that promote risk and
    resilience in postdivorce families. In M. A. Fine & J. H. Harvey (Eds.), *Handbook of
    divorce and relationship dissolution* (pp. 435–456). Mahwah, NJ: Erlbaum.

Afifi, T. D., & Olson, L. (2005). The chilling effect in families and the pressure to
    conceal secrets. *Communication Monographs*, *72*, 192–216. doi:10.1080/036377
    50500111906

Alba, R., & Nee, V. (2003). *Remaking the American mainstream: Assimilation and con-
    temporary immigration*. Cambridge, MA: Harvard University Press.

Ball-Rokeach, S. J., Kim, Y.-C., & Matei, S. (2001). Storytelling neighborhood: Paths
    to belonging in diverse urban environments. *Communication Research*, *28*, 392–428.
    doi:10.1177/009365001028004003

Bischoff, A., & Loutan, L. (2004). Interpreting in Swiss hospitals. *Interpreting*, *6*, 181–204.

Brandon, P. (2008). The health risk behaviours and social connectedness of adolescents
    in immigrant families: Evidence from Australia. *International Migration*, *46*, 49–80.
    doi:10.1111/j.1468–2435.2008.00444.x

Carling, J., Menjívar, C., & Schmalzbauer, L. (2012). Central themes in the study of
    transnational parenthood. *Journal of Ethnic and Migration Studies*, *38*, 191–217.
    doi:10.1080/1369183X.2012.646417

Carrington, W. J., & Detragiache, E. (1999). How extensive is the brain drain? *Finance
    and Development*, *36*, 46–49.

Chen, N., Dong, F., Huang, J., Ball-Rokeach, S. J., Parks, M., & Huang, J. (2012).
    Building a new media platform for local storytelling and civic engagement in eth-
    nically diverse neighborhoods. *New Media & Society*, *14*, 931–950. doi:10.1177/
    1461444811435640

Clark, L. S. (2012). *The parent app: Understanding families in the digital age*. Oxford,
    England: Oxford University Press.

Cline, T., de Abreu, G., O'Dell, L., & Crafter, S. (2010). Recent research on child lan-
    guage brokering in the United Kingdom. *mediAzioni*, *10*. Retrieved from www.
    mediazioni.sitlec.unibo.it/index.php/no-10-special-issue-2010.html

Cohen, S., Moran-Ellis, J., & Smaje, C. (1999). Children as informal interpreters in GP
    consultations: Pragmatics and ideology. *Sociology of Health & Illness*, *21*, 163–186.
    doi:10.1111/1467–9566.00148

Coleman, M., Ganong, L., & Fine, M. (2000). Reinvestigating marriage: Another decade of progress. *Journal of Marriage and the Family, 62*, 1288–1307. doi:10.1111/j.1741-3737.2000.01288.x

Crul, M., & Schneider, J. (2010). Comparative integration context theory: Participation and belonging in new diverse European cities. *Ethnic and Racial Studies, 33*, 1249–1268. doi:10.1080/01419871003624068

Derlega, V. J., Winstead, B. A., Greene, K., Serovich, J., & Elwood, W. N. (2004). Reasons for HIV disclosure/nondisclosure in close relationships. *Journal of Social and Clinical Psychology, 23*, 747–767. doi:10.1521/jscp.23.6.747.54804

Docan-Morgan, S. (2010). Korean adoptees' retrospective reports of intrusive interactions: Exploring boundary management in adoptive families. *Journal of Family Communication, 10*, 137–157. doi:10.1080/15267431003699603

Donato, K. M., & Armenta, A. (2011). What we know about unauthorized migration. *Annual Review of Sociology, 37*, 529–543. doi:10.1146/annurev-soc-081309-150216

Dorner, L., Orellana, M., & Li-Grining, C. (2007). "I helped my mom" and it helped me: Translating the skills of language brokers into improved standardized test scores. *American Journal of Education, 113*, 451–478. doi:10.1086/512740

Dreby, J. (2010). *Divided by borders: Mexican migrants and their children.* Berkeley: University of California Press.

Dreby, J. (2012). The burden of deportation on children in Mexican immigrant families. *Journal of Marriage and Family, 74*, 829–845. doi:10.1111/j.1741-3737.2012.00989.x

Durham, M. (2004). Constructing the "new ethnicities": Media, sexuality and diaspora identity in the lives of South Asian immigrant girls. *Critical Studies in Media Communication, 21*, 140–161. doi:10.1080/07393180410001688047

Ehrenreich, B., & Hochschild, A. (Eds.). (2004). *Global women: Nannies, maids and sex workers in the new economy.* New York: Owl Books.

Elias, N. (2013). Immigrant children and media. In D. Lemish (Ed.), *The Routledge international handbook of children, adolescents and media* (pp. 336–343). New York: Routledge.

Elias, N., & Lemish, D. (2008). Media uses in immigrant families: Torn between "inward" and "outward" paths of integration. *The International Communication Gazette, 70*, 21–40. doi:10.1177/1748048507084576

Elias, N., & Lemish, D. (2011). Between three worlds: Host, homeland, and global media in the lives of Russian immigrant families in Israel and Germany. *Journal of Family Issues, 32*, 1245–1274. doi:10.1177/0192513X11400837

Fischer, P., Martin, R., & Straubhaar, T. (1997). Should I stay or should I go? In T. Hammar, G. Brochmann, K. Tamas, & T. Faist (Eds.), *International migration, immobility and development* (pp. 49–90). New York: Berg.

Fitzgerald, D. (2009). *A nation of emigrants: How Mexico manages its migration.* Berkeley: University of California Press.

Foner, N. (Ed.). (2009). *Across generations: Immigrant families in America.* New York: New York University Press.

Foner, N., & Dreby, J. (2011). Relations between the generations in immigrant families. *Annual Review of Sociology, 37*, 545–564. doi:10.1146/annurev-soc-081309-150030

Gallagher, H. C. (2013). Willingness to communicate and cross-cultural adaptation: L2 communication and acculturative stress as transaction. *Applied Linguistics, 34*, 53–73. doi:10.1093/applin/ams023

Gálvez, A. (2011). *Patient citizens, immigrant mothers: Mexican women, public prenatal care, and the birth-weight paradox.* New Brunswick, NJ: Rutgers University Press.

Galvin, K. M. (2007). "It's not all blarney: Intergenerational transmission of communication patterns in Irish American families." In P. Cooper, C. Calloway-Thomas, & C. Simonds (Eds.), *Intercultural communication* (pp. 172–192). Boston, MA: Allyn & Bacon.

Galvin, K., Dickson, F., & Marrow, S. (2005). Systems theory: Patterns and w(holes) in family communication. In D. O. Braithwaite & L. A. Baxter (Eds.), *Engaging theories in family communication* (pp. 309–324). Thousand Oaks, CA: Sage.

García-Sánchez, I., & Orellana, M. F. (2006). The construction of moral and social identities in immigrant children's narratives-in-translation. *Linguistics and Education, 17*, 209–239.

Gartrell, N., Bos, H., Peyser, H., Deck, A., & Rodas, C. (2011). Family characteristics, custody arrangements, and adolescent psychological well-being after lesbian mothers break up. *Family Relations, 60*, 572–585. doi:10.1111/j.1741–3729.2011.00667.x

Gibson, M. (1988). *Accommodation without assimilation: Sikh immigrants in an American high school.* Ithaca, NY: Cornell University Press.

Giles, H., Linz, D., Bonilla, D., & Gomez, M. L. (2012). Police stops of and interactions with Latino and White (non-Latino) drivers: Extensive policing and communication accommodation. *Communication Monographs, 79*, 407–427. doi:10.1080/0363775 1.2012.723815

Golish, T. D. (2003). Stepfamily communication strengths: Understanding the ties that bind. *Human Communication Research, 29*, 41–80. doi:10.1111/j.1468–2958.2003. tb00831.x

Gonzales, R. (2011). Learning to be illegal: Undocumented youth and shifting legal contexts in the transition to adulthood. *American Sociological Review, 76*, 603–604. doi:10.1177/0003122411411901

Gordan, M. (1964). *Assimilation in American life: The role of race, religion and national origins.* Oxford, England: Oxford University Press.

Greene, K., Carpenter, A., Catona, D., & Magsamen-Conrad, K. (2013). The Brief Disclosure Intervention (BDI): Facilitating African Americans' disclosure of HIV. *Journal of Communication, 63*, 138–158. doi:10.1111/jcom.12010

Greene, K., Magsamen-Conrad, K., Venetis, M. K., Checton, M. G., Bagdasarov, Z., & Banerjee, S. C. (2012). Assessing health diagnosis disclosure decisions in relationships: Testing the disclosure decision-making model. *Health Communication, 27*, 356–368. doi:10.1080/10410236.2011.586988

Gudykunst, W. (Ed.). (2005). *Theorizing about intercultural communication.* Thousand Oaks, CA: Sage.

Hargreaves, A., & Mahdjoub, D. (1997). Satellite television viewing among ethnic minorities in France. *European Journal of Communication, 12*, 459–477. doi:10.1177/ 0267323197012004002

Harrigan, M. M. (2010). Exploring the narrative process: An analysis of the adoption stories mothers tell their internationally adopted children. *Journal of Family Communication, 10*, 24–39. doi:10.1080/15267430903385875

Harwood, J., Soliz, J., & Lin, M.-C. (2005). Communication accommodation theory: An intergroup approach to family relationships. In D. O. Braithwaite and L. A. Baxter (Eds.), *Engaging theories in family communication* (pp. 19–34). Thousand Oaks, CA: Sage.

Hasebrink, U., Livingstone, S., & Haddon, L. (2008). Comparing children's online opportunities and risks across Europe: Cross-national comparisons for EU Kids Online. Retrieved from https://lirias.kuleuven.be/handle/123456789/200382

Haydari, N. (2005). (Re)defining Turkish identity across generations: Politics of home, nation, and identity. In W. Leeds-Hurwitz (Ed.), *From generation to generation: Maintaining cultural identity over time* (pp. 99–120). Cresskill, NJ: Hampton Press.

Hein, J. (2006). *Ethnic origins: The adaptation of Cambodian and Hmong refugees in four American cities.* New York: Russell Sage.

Hirsch, J. (1999). *A courtship after marriage: Sexuality and love in Mexican transnational families.* Berkeley: University of California Press.

Hondagneu-Sotelo, P. (1994). *Gendered transitions: Mexican experiences of immigration.* Berkeley: University of California Press.

Hondagneu-Sotelo, P. (Ed.). (2003). *Gender and U.S. immigration.* Berkeley: University of California Press.

Hutchinson, S. L., Afifi, T., & Krause, S. (2007). The family that plays together fares better: Examining the contribution of shared family time to family resilience following divorce. *Journal of Divorce & Remarriage, 46,* 21–48. doi:10.1300/J087v46n03_03

International Organization for Migration. (2010). *Global estimates and trends.* Retrieved from www.iom.int/cms/en/sites/iom/home/about-migration/facts—figures-1.html

Johnson, J. O., Kominski, R., Smith, K., & Tillman, P. (2005). *Changes in the lives of U.S. children: 1990–2000* (Working Paper No. 78, Population Division). Washington, D.C.: U.S. Census Bureau.

Jones-Correa, M., & de Graauw, E. (2013). Looking back to see ahead: Unanticipated changes in immigration from 1986 to the present and their implications for American politics today. *Annual Review of Political Science, 16,* 209–230. doi:10.1146/annurev-polisci-051211-164644

Kam, J. A. (2011). The effects of language brokering frequency and feelings on Mexican-heritage youth's mental health and risky behaviors. *Journal of Communication, 61,* 455–475. doi:10.1111/j.1460–2466.2011.01552.x

Kam, J. A., & Lazarevic, V. (2014). Communicating for one's family: An interdisciplinary review of language and cultural brokering in immigrant families. *Communication Yearbook 38,* 3–37.

Katz, V. S. (2010). How children use media to connect their families to the community: The case of Latinos in Los Angeles. *Journal of Children and Media 4*(3), 298–315. doi:10.1080/17482798.2010.486136

Katz, V. S. (2014). *Kids in the middle: How children of immigrants negotiate community interactions for their families.* New Brunswick, NJ: Rutgers University Press.

Katz, V. S., Matsaganis, M. D., & Ball-Rokeach, S. J. (2012). Broadband and ethnic media: Potential for opportunity and inclusion. *Journal of Information Policy, 2,* 79–102.

Kim, Y.-C., & Ball-Rokeach, S. J. (2006a). Civic engagement from a communication infrastructure perspective. *Communication Theory, 16,* 1–25. doi:10.1111/j.1468–2885.2006.00267.x

Kim, Y.-C., & Ball-Rokeach, S. J. (2006b). Community storytelling network, neighborhood context, and civic engagement: A multilevel approach. *Human Communication Research, 32,* 411–439. doi:10.1111/j.1468–2958.2006.00282.x

Kim, Y.-C., Jung, J.-Y., & Ball-Rokeach, S. J. (2006). Geo-ethnicity and civic engagement: A communication infrastructure perspective. *Political Communication, 23,* 421–441. doi:10.1080/10584600600976997

Kim, Y.-C., & Kang, J. (2010). Communication, neighborhood engagement, and household hurricane preparedness. *Disasters, 34,* 470–488. doi:10.1111/j.1467–7717.2009.01138.x

Kim, Y.-C., Moran, M., Wilkin, H. A., & Ball-Rokeach, S. J. (2011). Integrated connection to a neighborhood storytelling network (ICSN), education, and chronic disease knowledge among African Americans and Latinos in Los Angeles. *Journal of Health Communication, 16*, 393–415. doi:10.1080/10810730.2010.546483

Lannutti, P. J. (2013). Same-sex marriage and privacy management: Examining couples' communication with family members. *Journal of Family Communication, 13*, 60–75. doi:10.1080/15267431.2012.742088

Leeds-Hurwitz, W. (2005). *From generation to generation: Maintaining cultural identity over time.* Cresskill, NJ: Hampton Press.

Leifsen, E., & Tymczuk, A. (2012). Care at a distance: Ukrainian and Ecuadorian transnational parenthood from Spain. *Journal of Ethnic and Migration Studies, 38*, 219–236. doi:10.1080/1369183X.2012.646419

Levitt, P., & Jaworsky, B. N. (2007). Transnational migration studies: Past developments and future trends. *Annual Review of Sociology, 33*, 129–156. doi:10.1146/annurev.soc.33.040406.131816

Light, I. H., & Bonacich, E. (1991). *Immigrant entrepreneurs.* Berkeley: University of California Press.

Lippi-Green, R. (1997). *English with an accent: Language, ideology, and discrimination in the United States.* London, England: Routledge.

Livingstone, S., & Haddon, L. (Eds.). (2009). *Kids online: Opportunities and risks for children.* Bristol, England: Policy Press.

Loges, W. E., Ball-Rokeach, S. J., & Qiu, L. (2005, May). *Broken bonds at work, broken bonds at home: A theoretical connection.* Paper presented at the annual conference of the International Communication Association, New York.

Louie, J. (2003). Media in the lives of immigrant youth. *New Directions for Youth Development, 100*, 111–130. doi:10.1002/yd.66

Louie, V. (2004). *Compelled to excel: Immigration, education, and opportunity among Chinese Americans.* Palo Alto, CA: Stanford University Press.

Louie, V. (2012). *Keeping the immigrant bargain: The costs and rewards of success in America.* New York: Russell Sage Foundation.

Lum, C.M.K. (2005). Communicating Chinese heritage in America: A study of bicultural education across generations. In W. Leeds-Hurwitz (Ed.), *From generation to generation: Maintaining cultural identity over time* (pp. 75–98). Cresskill, NJ: Hampton Press.

Luthra, R. R. (2010). *Assimilation in a new context: Educational attainment of the immigrant second generation in Germany* (Institute for Social and Economic Research Working Paper Series, 2010–21). Colchester, England: University of Essex. Retrieved from www.iser.essex.ac.uk/people/rrluthra

Madianou, M., & Miller, D. (2012). *Migration and new media: Transnational families and new media.* London, England: Routledge.

Maira. S. (2002). *Desis in the house: Indian American youth culture in New York City.* Philadelphia, PA: Temple University Press.

Martin, F., & Curran, J. (2007). Separated children: A comparison of the treatment of separated child refugees entering Australia and Canada. *International Journal of Refugee Law, 19*, 440–470. doi:10.1093/ijrl/eem053

Massey, D. S., Durand, J., & Malone, N. J. (2002). *Beyond smoke and mirrors: Mexican immigration in an era of economic integration.* New York: Russell Sage.

Massey, D. S., & Sánchez, M. R. (2010). *Brokered boundaries: Creating immigrant identity in anti-immigrant times.* New York: Russell Sage Foundation.

Matsaganis, M. (2007). Neighborhood effects and the invisible motor of community change. In G. Burd, S. Drucker, & G. Gumpert (Eds.), *The urban communication reader* (pp. 73–103). Cresskill, NJ: Hampton Press.

Matsaganis, M. D., Katz, V. S., & Ball-Rokeach, S. J. (2011). *Understanding ethnic media: Producers, consumers and societies.* Thousand Oaks, CA: Sage.

Mayer, V. (2003). Living telenovelas/Telenovelizing life: Mexican-American girls' identities and transnational telenovelas. *Journal of Communication, 53,* 479–495. doi:10.1111/j.1460–2466.2003.tb02603.x

McDevitt, M., & Chaffee, S. (2002). From "top down" to "trickle up" influence: Revisiting assumptions about the family in political socialization. *Political Communication, 19,* 281–301. doi:10.1080/01957470290055501

Menjívar, C., & Abrégo, L. (2009). Parents and children across borders: Legal instability and intergenerational relations in Guatemalan and Salvadoran Families. In N. Foner (Ed.), *Across generations: Immigrant families in America* (pp. 160–189). New York: New York University Press.

Merolla, A. J. (2010). Relational maintenance during military deployment: Perspectives of wives of deployed U.S. soldiers. *Journal of Applied Communication Research, 38,* 4–26. doi:10.1080/00909880903483557

Meyer, B., Pawlack, B., & Kliche, O. (2010). Family interpreters in hospitals: Good reasons for bad practice? *mediAzioni, 10.* Retrieved from mediAzioni website: www. mediazioni.sitlec.unibo.it/index.php/no-10-special-issue-2010.html

Mullally, S. (2011). Separated children in Ireland: Responding to "terrible wrongs." *International Journal of Refugee Law, 23,* 632–655. doi:10.1093/ijrl/eer026

Nazario, S. (2013, April 10). Child migrants, alone in court. *New York Times.* Retrieved from www.nytimes.com/2013/04/11/opinion/give-lawyers-to-immigrant-children.html

Norwood, K. (2012). Transitioning meanings? Family members' communicative struggles surrounding transgender identity. *Journal of Family Communication, 12,* 75–92. doi:10.1080/15267431.2010.509283

Ochs, E., & Schieffelin, B. (2001). Language acquisition and socialization. In A. Duranti (Ed.), *Linguistic anthropology* (pp. 263–301). Malden, MA: Blackwell.

Olsen, D. (2000). Circumplex model of marital and family systems. *Journal of Family Therapy, 22,* 144–167. doi:10.1111/1467–6427.00144

Orellana, M. (2009). *Translating childhoods: Immigrant youth, language and culture.* New Brunswick, NJ: Rutgers University Press.

Park, L. (2002). Asian immigrant entrepreneurial children. In L. T. Võ & R. Bonus (Eds.), *Contemporary Asian American communities: Intersections and divergences* (pp. 161–177). Philadelphia, PA: Temple University Press.

Park, L. (2005). *Consuming citizenship: Children of Asian immigrant entrepreneurs.* Palo Alto, CA: Stanford University Press.

Parreñas, R. S. (2005). *Children of global migration: Transnational families and gendered woes.* Stanford, CA: Stanford University Press.

Pessar, P. (2003). Engendering migration studies: The case of new immigrants in the United States. In P. Hondagneu-Sotelo (Ed.), *Gender and U.S. immigration* (pp. 20–42). Berkeley: University of California Press.

Petronio, S. (2002). *Boundaries of privacy: Dialectics of disclosure.* Albany: State University of New York Press.

Petronio, S. (2010). Communication privacy management theory: What do we know about family privacy regulation? *Journal of Family Theory & Review, 2,* 175–196. doi:10.1111/j.1756–2589.2010.00052.x

Pew Forum on Religion and Public Life. (2011). *The future of the global Muslim population: Projections for 2010–2030.* Retrieved from www.pewforum.org/future-of-the-global-muslim-population-regional-europe.aspx#ftn36_rtn

Portes, A. (2010). Migration and social change: Some conceptual reflections. *Journal of Ethnic and Migration Studies, 36*, 1537–1563. doi:10.1080/1369183X.2010.489370

Portes, A., & Fernández-Kelly, P. (2008). No margin for error: Educational and occupational achievement among disadvantaged children of immigrants. *The Annals of the American Academy of Political and Social Science, 620*, 12–36. doi:10.1177/0002716208322577

Portes, A., Fernández-Kelly, P., & Haller, W. (2005). Segmented assimilation theory on the ground: The new second generation in early adulthood. *Ethnic and Racial Studies, 28*, 1000–1040. doi:10.1080/01419870500224117

Portes, A., Fernández-Kelly, P., & Haller, W. (2009). The adaptation of the immigrant second generation in America: A theoretical overview and recent evidence. *Journal of Ethnic and Migration Studies, 35*, 1077–1104. doi:10.1080/13691830903006127

Portes, A., & Rumbaut, R. (1996). *Immigrant America: A portrait.* Berkeley: University of California Press.

Portes, A., & Rumbaut, R. (2001). *Legacies: The story of the immigrant second generation.* Berkeley: University of California Press.

Portes, A., & Zhou, M. (1993). The new second generation: Segmented assimilation and its variants. *The Annals of the American Academy of Political and Social Science, 530*, 74–96. doi:10.1177/0002716293530001006

Pyke, K. (2005). "Generational deserters" and "black sheep": Acculturative differences among siblings in Asian immigrant families. *Journal of Family Issues, 26*, 491–517. doi:10.1177/0192513X04273578

Ramakrishnan, S. K., & Bloemraad, I. (2008). *Civic hopes and political realities: Immigrants, community organizations, and political engagement.* New York: Russell Sage.

Rideout, V., Foehr, U., Roberts, D., & Brodie, M. (1999). *Kids and media @ the new millennium.* Menlo Park, CA: Henry J. Kaiser Foundation.

Sampson, R. (2013). *Great American city: Chicago and the enduring neighborhood effect.* Cambridge, MA: Harvard University Press.

Sampson, R., Morenoff, J., & Gannon-Rowley, T. (2002). Assessing "neighborhood effects": Social processes and new directions in research. *Annual Review of Sociology, 28*, 443–478. doi:10.1146/annurev.soc.28.110601.141114

Sanders, J. M., & Nee, V. (1992). Problems in resolving the enclave economy debate. *American Sociological Review, 57*, 415–418.

Santa Ana, O. (2002). *Brown tide rising: Metaphors of Latinos in contemporary American public discourse.* Austin: University of Texas Press.

Schiller, N., Basch, L., & Blanc, C. (1995). From immigrant to transmigrant: Theorizing transnational migration. *Anthropological Quarterly, 68*, 48–63.

Schneider, J., & Crul, M. (2010). New insights into assimilation and integration theory. *Ethnic and Racial Studies, 33*, 1143–1148. doi:10.1080/01419871003777809

Small, M., Jacobs, E., & Massengill, R. (2008). Why organizational ties matter for neighborhood effects: A study of resource access through childcare centers. *Social Forces, 87*, 387–414. doi:10.1353/sof.0.0079

Soliz, J., Ribarsky, E., Harrigan, M. M., & Tye-Williams, S. (2010). Perceptions of communication with gay and lesbian family members: Predictors of relational satisfaction and implications for outgroup attitudes. *Communication Quarterly, 58*, 77–95. doi:10.1080/01463370903538622

Soliz, J., Thorson, A. R., & Rittenour, C. E. (2009). Communicative correlates of satisfaction, family identity, and group salience in multiracial/ethnic families. *Journal of Marriage and Family, 71,* 819–832. doi:10.1111/j.1741-3737.2009.00637.x

Song, M. (1999). *Helping out: Children's labor in ethnic businesses.* Philadelphia, PA: Temple University Press.

Stanton-Salazar, R. (2001). *Manufacturing hope and despair: The school and kin support networks of U.S.-Mexican youth.* New York: Teachers College Press.

Stephan, W. G., Stephan, C. W., & Gudykunst, W. B. (1999). Anxiety in intergroup relations: A comparison of anxiety/uncertainty management theory and integrated threat theory. *International Journal of Intercultural Relations, 23,* 613–628. doi:10.1016/S0147-1767(99)00012-7

Stepick, A., & Stepick, C. D. (2010). The complexities and confusions of segmented assimilation. *Ethnic and Racial Studies, 33,* 1149–1167. doi:10.1080/01419871003599518

Street, R. (1991). Accommodation in medical consultations. In H. Giles, J. Coupland, & N. Coupland (Eds.), *Contexts of accommodation: Developments in applied sociolinguistics* (pp. 131–156). Cambridge, UK: Cambridge University Press.

Suárez-Orozco, C., Bang, H. J., & Kim, H. Y. (2011). I felt like my heart was staying behind: Psychological implications of family separations and reunifications for immigrant youth. *Journal of Adolescent Research, 26,* 222–257. doi:10.1177/0743558410376830

Takenoshita, H., Chitose, Y., Ikegami, S., & Ishikawa, E. (2013). Segmented assimilation, transnationalism, and educational attainment of Brazilian migrant children in Japan. *International Migration.* Advanced online publication. doi:10.1111/imig.12057

Telzer, E. (2010). Expanding the acculturation gap-distress model: An integrative review of research. *Human Development, 53,* 313–340. doi:10.1159/000322476

Theiss, J. A., & Knobloch, L. K. (2011). Relational turbulence and the post-deployment transition: Self, partner, and relationship focused turbulence. *Communication Research.* Advanced online publication. doi:10.1177/0093650211429285

Thomson, M., & Crul, M. (2007). The second generation in Europe and the United States: How is the transatlantic debate relevant for further research on the European second generation? *Journal of Ethnic and Migration Studies, 33,* 1025–1041. doi:10.1080/13691830701541556

Urban Institute. (2009). *Children of immigrants.* Retrieved from http://datatool.urban.org/charts/datatool/pages.cfm

Valenzuela, A. (1999). Gender roles and settlement activities among children and their immigrant families. *American Behavioral Scientist, 42,* 720–742. doi:10.1177/0002764299042004009

Vangelisti, A. L., & Caughlin, J. P. (1997). Revealing family secrets: The influence of topic, function, and relationships. *Journal of Social and Personal Relationships, 14,* 679–705. doi:10.1177/0265407597145006

Vangelisti, A. L., Caughlin, J. P., & Timmerman, L. (2001). Criteria for revealing family secrets. *Communication Monographs, 68,* 1–17. doi:10.1080/03637750128052

Vermeulen, H. (2010). Segmented assimilation and cross-national comparative research on the integration of immigrants and their children. *Ethnic and Racial Studies, 33,* 1214–1230. doi:10.1080/01419871003615306

Vygotsky, L. (1978). *Mind in society: The development of higher psychological processes.* Cambridge, MA: Harvard University Press.

Waldinger, R., & Der-Martirosian, C. (2001). The immigrant niche: Pervasive, persistent, diverse. In R. Waldinger (Ed.), *Strangers at the gates: New immigrants in urban America* (pp. 228–271). Berkeley: University of California Press.

Waldinger, R., & Lichter, M. I. (2003). *How the other half works.* Berkeley: University of California Press.

Waters, M. C., Tran, V. C., Kasinitz, P., & Mollenkopf, J. H. (2010). Segmented assimilation revisited: Types of acculturation and socioeconomic mobility in young adulthood. *Ethnic and Racial Studies, 33,* 1168–1193. doi:10.1080/0141987100 3624076

Wilkin, H. A. (2013). Exploring the potential of communication infrastructure theory for informing efforts to reduce health disparities. *Journal of Communication, 63,* 181–200. doi:10.1111/jcom.12006

Wilkin, H. A., & Ball-Rokeach, S. J. (2011). Hard-to-reach? Using health access status as a way to more effectively target segments of the Latino audience. *Health Education Research, 26,* 239–253. doi:10.1093/her/cyq090

Wilkin, H. A., Katz, V. S., & Ball-Rokeach, S. J. (2009). The role of family interaction in new immigrant Latinos' civic engagement. *Journal of Communication, 59,* 387–406. doi:10.1111/j.1460–2466.2009.01421.x

Wilson, M. (2002, November). *Community organizations, communication infrastructure, and community.* Presented at the Annual Meeting of the National Communication Association, New Orleans, LA.

Wong, J., & Tseng, V. (2008). Political socialization in immigrant families: Challenging the top-down parental socialization models. *Journal of Ethnic and Migration Studies, 34,* 151–168. doi:10.1080/13691830701708742

Yerby, J. (1995). Family systems theory reconsidered: Integrating social construction theory and dialectical processes. *Communication Theory, 5,* 339–365. doi:10.1111/ j.1468–2885.1995.tb00114.x

Yoshikawa, H. (2011). *Immigrants raising citizens: Undocumented parents and their young children.* New York: Russell Sage Foundation.

Yoshioka, M. R., Gilbert, L., El-Bassel, N., & Baig-Amin, M. (2003). Social support and disclosure of abuse: Comparing South Asian, African American, and Hispanic battered women. *Journal of Family Violence, 18,* 171–180. doi:10.1023/A:1023568505682

Zentella, A. C. (1997). *Growing up bilingual: Puerto Rican children in New York.* Oxford: Blackwell Publishing.

Zhou, M. (2009). How neighborhoods matter for immigrant children: The formation of educational resources in Chinatown, Koreatown, and Pico Union, Los Angeles. *Journal of Ethnic and Migration, 35,* 1153–79. doi:10.1080/13691830903006168

Zhou, M., & Bankston III, C. (1998). *Growing up American: How Vietnamese children adapt to life in the United States.* New York: Russell Sage.

Zhou, M., & Lee, R. (2013). Transnationalism and community building: Chinese immigrant organizations in the United States. *The Annals of the American Academy of Political and Social Science, 647,* 22–49. doi:10.1177/0002716212472456

Part II

Theorizing Talk
Intrapersonal, Interpersonal, and Intergroup Communication

CHAPTER CONTENTS

3 Publics and Lay Informatics

A Review of the Situational Theory of Problem Solving

Jeong-Nam Kim

Purdue University

Arunima Krishna

Purdue University

The situational theory of publics (STP), one of the most popular public relations theories, provides a mechanism for the identification of publics and their information behaviors. The situational theory of problem solving (STOPS), an extension of the STP, is a more general theory of communication that looks at antecedents of individuals' communication and information behaviors in the process of problem solving. This chapter reviews and explicates the differences and similarities between the two theories, their respective intellectual origins, and the body of new research that is being and could be generated from the STOPS.

The situational theory of problem solving (STOPS; Kim, 2006; Kim & Grunig, 2011) is a communication theory that explains why and how an individual communicates during problematic life situations. The theory takes its conceptual roots from the situational theory of publics (STP; Grunig, 1966, 1968, 1997), which is well known as a theory of publics. STP explains active communication behavior (e.g., information seeking) as the central dependent variable and helps define and identify *a public* as a group of active communicators related to problematic situations.

Both situational theories take a distinct and explicit assumption on communication. According to situational theorists, communication is *a purposive behavior to cope with a problematic life situation* (Kim & Grunig, 2011). Historically, the situational theories are unique and rare in the field of communication in that they choose active communicative behaviors as the focal concept/phenomenon to be explained, whereas most communication theories before the 1970s explained the conditions and causes of attitudinal and behavioral changes among message receivers resulting from a message (Schramm, 1971).

In the 1960s, at the time the STP was constructed, the dominant theoretical paradigm of communication theories was "the symbolic, interpretive paradigm" (Kim, Hung-Baeseke, Yang, & Grunig, 2013, p. 201) wherein the focus was to understand how to create conditions (i.e., research on message-crafting strategies or message-channeling strategies) for the purpose of influencing audience attitudes and behaviors in ways that message senders desire. Most communication theories in the symbolic, interpretive paradigm assume that communication is what a message sender (source) does to message receivers (audience), and thus, the theories were grounded on the concepts of *attitude* (vs. *epistemic motivation*[1]) and *behavior* (vs. *communicative behaviors*). As a result, the theory and practice of communication have been more interested in developing symbolic strategies to influence what the audience thinks about and how to interpret what has happened for the audience, while rarely paying attention to the behavior of the message senders and the consequences of their behavior on the receivers' (audience's) life. In other words, if a communication effort brings about a change, it is almost always the resultant attitudes or behaviors of the receivers or of audiences that are studied, not that of the message sender. For this reason, communication theories have ordinarily been mostly "asymmetrical" (Grunig, 2003) and have been inclined toward "administrative research" (Chaffee, 1982), as a result of which these theories tend toward a "sender-bias" (Kim, 2006) and are tied to the "audience control" (vs. *audience autonomy*) paradigm (McQuail, 1997).

The situational theories present a departure from these communication theories, not in the least for the unique theoretical stance they take at their very core. In the theoretical view of the situational theories, communication is a *purposive* and *situational* human action. Communication should not be treated as a *constant* as is common in microeconomic theories of decision making. In brief, earlier decision-making theories have treated communication as free and given for individuals who face decision situations (i.e., the perfect knowledge assumption), and thus, an (economic) decision maker or an entrepreneur simply makes a choice that maximizes his or her utility/satisfaction. For instance, in a decision-to-buy situation, economic theory assumes that buyers have perfect information about all potential products that they could buy to serve their purpose, the prices of all such products, their uses, their availability, and so on and therefore make a decision based on their individual utility/satisfaction maximization. However, situational theorists have criticized the assumption of perfect knowledge; knowledge or information is neither free nor given in decision situations. Communicative behaviors, then, represent ways for decision makers to obtain the necessary information/knowledge for them to make a decision. Such efforts to obtain knowledge are bound to lead to varying results and to be treated as *a dependent variable* corresponding to one's subjective perception and motivation. In this vein, the situational theories have been constructed as a type of "teleological theory," that is, to explain when *communication needs* increase and decrease and thus set active communication as a dependent variable (e.g., information seeking).

From this critical reflection on the assumptions about knowledge and information, the situational theory of problem solving posits communication as an *epiphenomenal* characteristic of a human being who faces and deals with life problems—a parallel phenomenon simultaneously observable when one engages in problem solving (Kim, Grunig, & Ni, 2010). A problem solver who is motivated in problem solving will be likely to engage in communicative actions, where communicative actions may act as a coping mechanism in dealing with the problematic situation. In the situational theories, communicative action is "important because the individual can decide to act or not to act" about the faced indeterminacy (Carter, 1965, p. 203) and further provide means and resources to influence one's social contexts and individual conditions as adaptive and conducive to problem solving. According to situational theorists, therefore, communication is not something that message senders do to message receivers but something that people do to cope with problematic life situations (cf. sensemaking and the role of communication, Dervin, 1989; Weick, 1995).

It is rare in communication or in the field of behavioral, social sciences in general, for a theory to continue to evolve over decades to be a general theory (cf. Fishbein and Ajen's Theory of Reasoned Action and Theory of Planned Behavior).[2] The situational theory of problem solving is one of the few theories in the field of communication for which theorizing has continued for over 40 years by generations of scholars. In the present chapter, we provide a developmental overview of two generations of the situational theories. We review the shared theoretical premises and conceptual elements and sketch out how the situational theories have been developed to be a more general theory of human communication and how the phenomena of communicative actions (by communicative actors) have been connected to problem solving (by problem solvers) to evolve into the new theory, and we summarize current and new research based on the generalized situational theory.

Intellectual Origin of the Situational Theory

Shared and Distinct Assumptions in the Situational Theories

The situational theory of problem solving (STOPS) is a communication theory developed to explain how people's motivated communicative actions arise when they encounter problematic life situations. Kim (2006) theorized the STOPS as a continuation of its parent theory, the situational theory of publics (STP), which started from James E. Grunig's (1968) original situational theory about the role of information in human decision situations. The STP, as proposed by Grunig, forms the basis of a great deal of public relations research and practice today (for the role of the situational theories in constructing public relations theories and practice, see Grunig, 1997, 2003; Kim & Ni, 2010, 2013). STP builds on the concept of publics, defined by John Dewey (1927), as being issue groups that form around problems that people have recognized (Grunig, 1997), and provides measures for the identification and segmentation of these publics. While the two situational theories share common theoretical premises and assumptions, there are also some shifts in the conceptual frameworks and assumptions of the STOPS as compared to the STP. In this section we highlight the shared and differentiated assumptions in the two situational theories.

Communication research for audience control versus audience autonomy.   In the early 1960s, the most popular concepts in communication theories were rooted in attitudes or behavioral intention and based on the assumption of a passive audience (Power, Kubey, & Kiousis, 2002). The popularity of these concepts was due to the common understanding of communication as a tool for social influence and a symbolic strategy to influence or modify message receivers' attitudes or behaviors. Communication researchers and theorists looked for symbolic strategies and conditions that would favor the message senders' goals or interests. The underlying assumption was that communicating refers to effective messaging or channeling for the purpose of social influence in the minds and behaviors of passive-message receivers (an audience; Schramm, 1971). Not surprisingly, what changes audience receptivity was the key theoretical goals and research questions on which much communication research was based, and as a result, all such research was biased toward identifying the most effective and persuasive communication strategies. Such a research bias is called "administrative research" (Chaffee, 1982), which originated from "audience control" paradigm of communication research (McQauil, 1997).

In the midst of administrative research and the audience control paradigm in the 1960s, the situational theory stood out as one of the few theoretical frontiers distinct from most extant communication theories, along with the uses and gratification theory (Katz, Haas, & Gurevitch, 1973). In these audience autonomy theories, message receivers or audiences were considered active communicators who control their own (communicative) behaviors for the purpose of personal satisfaction or utility. More recently, in the 1990s, a new generation of information processing theories emerged that account for active communication behaviors.[3] These theories aim at understanding how and why people are active in search of some information at some time. Fundamentally, these theories considered the communication needs to increase as the given communicative acts provided a desired utility from communicative efforts. The change of the theoretical assumptions shifted the perspective from which communication was viewed—from communication being what a sender does to a receiver to communication being what a communicator (receiver) does for a self-serving purpose. Communication theories following the shifted paradigm of audience autonomy tend to be more *descriptive*—why, how, and when people communicate and do not communicate—rather than *prescriptive*—how communicative effectiveness can be improved for better message influence on the message recipients.

Communication as a constant versus a variable.   The earlier version of the situational theory in the 1960s criticized the then common assumption of *perfect knowledge* held by classical microeconomic theory. In the tradition of classical microeconomic theory, "perfect, continuous, costless intercommunication between all individual members of the society" is assumed (Knight, 1921, p. 78). As a result, decision makers, such as consumers or entrepreneurs, make an optimal choice that maximizes their satisfaction or utility based on the given free, perfect knowledge about decision choices (i.e., an idealistic decision situation wherein individuals possess all necessary and available information before making a choice). However, this assumption is fallacious, as the information available to decision makers is expensive and limited at best for effective and accurate decision making. Knight (1921) refuted the classical microeconomic theory in this vein and paved the way for neoclassical microeconomic theory and the concept of bounded rationality (Simon, 1956) that economic decision makers cannot maximize their utility or pleasure, instead they *satisfice*—make the best decision possible within the limited scope of information they are allowed in the given decision situation.

People frequently make decisions with imperfect knowledge or a lack of relevant information (Grunig, 1966). Under imperfect information/knowledge conditions, the risks of their choices and decisional consequences lead them to conduct a motivated search for more information to reduce risk and problematic consequences. In other words, people's informational efforts increase as their decisions imply higher risks and incur greater opportunity costs. Taking information as free and sufficient leads to information behaviors in decision situations to be assumed as *constant* (vs. a variable) at all times and result in a fallacious assumption that no decision situation ever needs communicative actions (Kim, 2006).

Resetting the troubling assumptions that knowledge is sufficient and free, James Grunig (1966) started to build a theory of decision making and information seeking with the new assumption of communication as *a purposeful action* related to the problems that one identifies. The situational theories make several conceptual transitions that distinguish them from other communication or decision-making theories. The situational theories posit first, that communication behaviors increase and decrease across people's problem-solving or decision situations, second, that communication should be conceptualized as *a variable*, especially a dependent variable, instead of *a constant* across situations, and third, that (de)motivators of communicative actions are likely to be influenced by situational perceptions, specifically as one's subjective perceptions of problem significance, connection, and obstacles in dealing with the problematic situations.

Communication for decision making versus problem solving.   The situational theory of publics problematized the common assumptions on communication (i.e., the sender-based view of communication and the perfect knowledge assumption) and made changes to incorporate constantly evolving human actions to cope with problematic life situations. It considered one's individuality and subjectivity of perception, cognition, and motivation as the factors that influence the resulting communicative behaviors across situations. Although the two situational theories share these assumptions of the communicator and communication situation, there is a difference in terms of conceptual frameworks on which they hinge.

The situational theory of publics originated from decision-making theory and the role of information in decision situations. Thus, the earliest version of theory was meant to describe what an economic man, that is, an imaginary, perfectly rational individual who seeks out maximum welfare/satisfaction when facing an economic decision, would do in decision situations. In contrast, the situational theory of problem solving has explicitly shifted the theory's focus from *decisional situations* (cf. battles) to *problematic situations* (cf. a war). The shift has important theoretical implications. For a decision maker (an economic actor) who makes a decision for his or her pleasure, profit, or utilities within the boundaries of constraints (i.e., satisficing), his or her communication behavior is most likely to seek out information regarding decisional choices. In contrast, for a problem solver (a social actor) who wants to solve a problem and cope with problematic consequences, his or her communicative behaviors will not only be to seek out information about the problem but also to select and give information about the problem. The shift in the conceptualization of an individual from a decision maker to a problem solver widens the scope of communication behaviors with which such an individual may engage.

The conceptual base we take in theorizing communicative behaviors will result in a qualitatively different view on the communicator, either as an isolated information seeker to make a satisficing decision, or a connected information seeker, selector, and giver trying to cope with problematic life situations. In other words, a problem solver frequently needs to produce and give information to others to draw attention, to reproduce similar problem conception, or to mobilize resources or support for a preferred way of problem solving, whereas a decision maker rarely does so.

Basics of the Situational Theory of Problem Solving: Key Elements and Assumptions

We cannot not communicate. Communication is like the air we inhale and exhale. Communicating is prevalent, commonplace, and inherent to human life. However, we rarely stop and think about why we engage in any given communicative behavior. For most of us communicating is taken for granted as part of being an intellectual living organism, an action for which thought is unnecessary. The human *experience of living* can almost never be separated from our conscious and unconscious *efforts of communicating*. Communicating is understood as reading, listening, talking, and writing regarding bits of knowledge or data crafted by self and others. The formal account of the ways that we communicate is an important but ambitious task. However, this review starts from the effect of problem recognition on two aspects of our communicating behaviors—*why we communicate* and *how we communicate*. In communication literature, these two basic questions are rarely asked, and few communication theories attempt to answer them.

Communication and problem solving.   The situational theories aim at answering two questions: Why and how do we communicate? The situational theories postulate that communication is epiphenomenal to the problem-solving process. Thus, it is necessary to define the key elements of "problem," "problem solving," and "communication," which are central to the theories. We first start with defining basic concepts related to problem solving and then formally define communication, data, knowledge, and information.

Defining problems and problem solving.   In the situational theory of problem solving, *problem recognition* is the prime mover that leads one into a problem-solving situation. The new situational theory defines *problem recognition* as the extent of a perceived discrepancy between what one expects and what one experiences, or the indeterminacy that breaks into one's automaticity in routine perceptual and cognitive processes (Kim & Grunig, 2011), and *problem solving* as one's behavioral, communicative, and cognitive efforts to narrow the discrepancy or indeterminacy.

Figure 3.1 illustrates the process by which a perceptual discrepancy leads to an interruption in one's routine and taxes one's cognitive efforts to construct a solution to the situation. The situational theory distinguishes between *a perceptual problem* (problem) and *cognitive problem* (metaproblem[4]). A perceptual problem results from a badness-of-fit between expectation and experience that may be easily and quickly resolved (narrowed) by a preconscious problem-solving effort, for example, one's unconscious processing of the sudden changes of traffic signs at crossroads. However, some perceptual problems cannot be resolved preconsciously and require cognitive action (a judgment phase following by an attention phase) on what should be done to narrow the perceived discrepancies—a cognitive problem following a perceptual problem. As one enters into a situation-related judgmental phase to decide what to do about the perceived gap or indeterminacy, one expends cognitive efforts to narrow the perceived discrepancy. This judgmental phase includes situational assessment, such as what caused the problem, how closely it is connected to one, how it can be approached, and what types of obstacles exist in the path of doing something about the indeterminacy.

The bottom of Figure 3.1 explains the epiphenomenal characteristic of communicative action. Problem solving in the illustration is defined as the narrowing of the discrepancy by any means at the disposal of the problem solver. It could be by physical, behavioral actions of modifying an experiential state (e.g., removing obstacles), or readjusting an expected state (e.g., lowering one's aspirations), or both. Although such efforts are present, the problem solver experiences heightened epistemic and communicative motivation to narrow the discrepant states. The motivation is epistemic to better understand the causes of the problem and how to deal with the problem, or to communicate

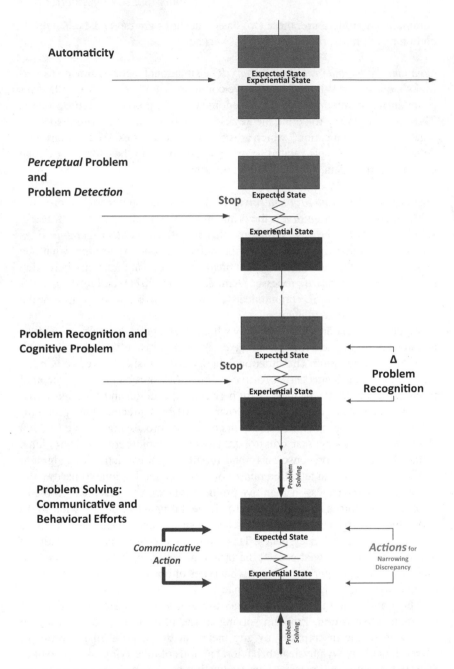

Figure 3.1 Metaphorical illustration of perceptual, cognitive, communicative, and behavioral process of problem solving

to influence or change the problem-causing conditions/contexts by mobilizing resources or bringing it to the attention of those who could provide the means to narrow the gap. However, it is also possible that some problem solving may not require much communicative effort if the given problem is routine, or is identical to one that the problem solver has dealt with previously. In such a case, the problem solver will need to apply and effectuate a ready-made solution (carried forward from a previously experienced problem) without expending much fresh communicative effort. Such a solution, that a problem solver carried forward from a previous problem, is what Grunig (1997) defined as the referent criterion. In this sense, communicative actions are not essential to the problem-solving process, but a side phenomenon of problem-solving efforts (epiphenomenal). Often, though, problem solving will take place simultaneously with communicative actions.

Defining communication, data, information, and knowledge. In situational theories, communication is defined as *a symbolic movement—a human action of moving words or symbols by a person within a life situation* (Carter, 1973; Kim, 2006). Communication is a behavior in itself (Grunig, 1976) that differs from other types of human behaviors (e.g., physical movement) in that a person (communicator) may use it to plan other behaviors but not necessarily translate it to those behaviors (e.g., a public threatens to sue a problem-causing entity but it does not act upon the threat). Notably, communicative behaviors in situational theories take various *action forms* such as learning, giving, and selecting, and various *content elements* such as facts, ideas, opinions, advice, and attitudes from one's knowledge store or cognitive efforts (Kim, 2006).

Situational theories distinguish between three similar concepts of content elements in communication: data, information, and knowledge. Shannon and Weaver (1949) defined information as anything that reduces entropy and uncertainty. However, Grunig (1968) criticized the definition as not being valid, albeit useful, because a valid definition of one concept should not be *what it does* but *what it is*. As a better alternative, Grunig advocated McDonough's (1963) definition, which distinguished the commonly used term *information* as having three components: *data* (unevaluated messages), *information* (data evaluated to apply in a specific problem situation), and *knowledge* (data evaluated for future use in general).

Situational theories take the position that only information and knowledge can reduce uncertainty in a judgmental situation (Grunig, 1968; Kim, 2006). Information comes from data that are judged to be specific and relevant to a given situation. In other words, all data could be candidates for information (or knowledge), but not all data becomes information unless they are available, judged relevant, and applicable to a specific problem-solving situation (Higgins, 1996; Kim, 2006).

A person (problem solver) who recognizes a problem explores a *sea of data* (i.e., the sea of unevaluated messages) inwardly and outwardly to palliate the perceived discrepancy. The more one is capable of narrowing the perceived discrepancy by *any* means, the shorter the situation (i.e., the psychological period of a problematic state). Typically, one initiates an internal search for knowledge that has relevance to the current problem. Knowledge carries over from prior situations or is improvised immediately upon problem recognition to apply to a similar kind of problems. This is "knowledge activation" (Higgins, 1996). When attempted knowledge activation is incomplete or when additional situation-specific data are necessary to construct an applicable referent criterion, one turns to an external source of knowledge (i.e., information seeking). This is *a knowledge action* (see Figure 3.2).

Situational theories distinguish between data, information, and knowledge so that information is the central concept in a problematic situation. Neither knowledge itself nor data themselves can be used without an evaluative process for the current specific problem state. Problem solvers judge it by their own subjective criteria, although their judgmental competencies vary. As illustrated in Figure 3.2, *knowledge* should first be *available* to the problem solver, and then the available knowledge is evaluated for its relevance and applicability to a given problem. Notably, knowledge can take any form, not only *factual or experiential* but also *affective or expectational content,* such as desired states or methods of problem solving. Whereas the former is more *situation-general* and could carry over across different but related problems, the latter is more *situation-specific* and is improvised at the time of a given problem situation. Yet, regardless of the type of knowledge, once the pieces of knowledge demonstrate sufficient relevance (i.e., judged usability) and applicability (a subjective cognitive effort influenced by individuality and situational desires), they become *information* to be applied to the current problem. Likewise, *data* from knowledge action should be available and situation specific and should be evaluated for its relevance and applicability to a given problem.

Once knowledge activation and knowledge action occur, problem solvers construct a new or revised referent criterion (T_{+1}). As is shown in the model toward the bottom of Figure 3.2, a new referent criterion (RC T_{+1}) earns its status by the combination of cognitive and communicative efforts between situation-general knowledge and situation-specific information in most cases. Using LEGO as an analogy, activated experiential, factual knowledge for a problem (cf. LEGO manual) cannot be directly applicable without situation-specific information (cf. LEGO Building Blocks) from a given problem-solving situation. Because the LEGO manual will guide or dictate what kind of LEGO block shapes are necessary, there should be high correlations between situation-general knowledge and situation-specific information (judged data as useful/applicable). For example, even the most experienced firefighter, who has a good situation-general knowledge of fire-fighting and safety, will need to inquire, search, and select data associated with the current problem-solving conditions/contexts (cf. bundling in expert problem solving in Gorman et al., 2001) that are unique to the given case,

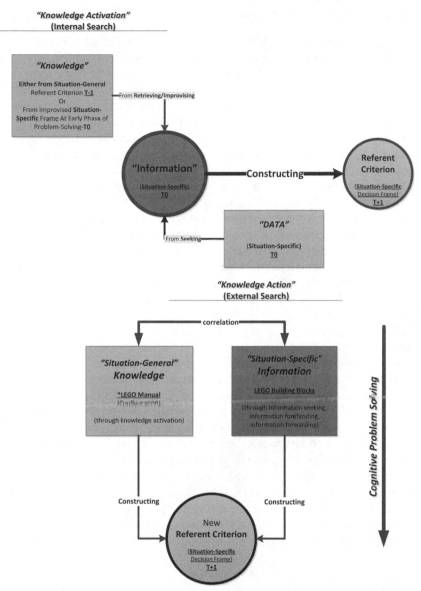

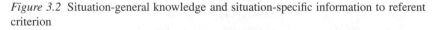

Figure 3.2 Situation-general knowledge and situation-specific information to referent criterion

such as wind direction, the people who are inside the burning building, and types of inflammatory causes. The communicative and cognitive efforts are called *cognitive problem solving* (Kim & Grunig, 2011) that will result in the construction of a new referent criterion; a detailed discussion is provided later.

Situational Theory of Problem Solving

Thus far, most theories on information seeking have viewed communicative behaviors as a means of decision making with the assumption that people require information when they are faced with making a decision. Potential information consumption increases when communicators become genuine decision makers (Grunig, 1968). Decision making as the eventual goal of communicative behaviors leaves little room for other types of communicative behaviors, such as information transmission, to be included in explanations of better decision making. However, with the shift in thinking about goals of communicative behaviors discussed in earlier sections, that is, from decision making as the goal of communication to problem solving as the conceptual base of communicative behaviors, the scope of communicative behaviors can thus be expanded. This section explicates the expansion in the scope of communicative behaviors, the communicative actions in problem solving, or CAPS, model.

As discussed earlier, communication research treats information acquisition as the most salient communicative behavior undertaken by an individual or a public. Several facets of human communication behaviors, such as information selection and information transmission have been underexplored or underused in research on publics (Ni & Kim, 2009).[5] Popular public relations theories, such as the situational theory of publics, visualize only information seeking and information attending as the dependent variable of public formation (Grunig, 1997). A review of extant literature on information behavior theories (Fisher, Erdelez, & McKechnie, 2005) revealed that this theoretical gap exists not just in research on publics, but also in other key areas of communication, as only 2 models of 70 detailed in the book tangentially conceptualized information transmission as a communication behavior (Kim, Grunig, & Ni, 2010). This limited view of communicative behaviors stems from the assumption that members of publics are economic actors looking to maximize their satisfaction rather than social actors who acquire, select, and transmit information within and outside of their social networks (Kim et al., 2010). Accordingly, the communicative actions in problem solving model has been proposed as a complementary theory to the STOPS to better represent the range of communicative behaviors that members of publics display.

CAPS

The previous section discussed the shift in goals of communication from that of decision making to problem solving. Although decision makers require only information acquisition to make a decision, problem solving is conceptualized as a broader and more inclusive construct. Problem solvers not only acquire information; they also feel the need to give information to others to stimulate the mobilization of resources. This allows for the inclusion of information transmission as a salient communicative behavior. Additionally, this shift allows for researchers to view members of publics as connected social actors who share, select, and acquire information to solve a problem rather than individualized decision makers. Accordingly, the CAPS model proposed by Kim, Grunig, and Ni (2010) presents a holistic view of the communicative actions of communicators during a problematic situation.

The CAPS model conceptualizes three distinct communicative behaviors displayed by problem solvers. These are *information selection, information transmission,* and *information acquisition.* Further, each of these three domains has a proactive and a reactive dimension, similar to the active and passive communicative behaviors in the original situational theory of publics. The sub-division of the three types of communicative behaviors into proactive and reactive dimensions is similar to Lippman's (1925) and Blumer's (1948) assertion that publics are composed of "both active and relatively passive elements" (Price, 1992, p. 31). Lippman (1925) viewed publics as composed of "actors" and "spectators," the former being active leaders in the publics' actions and the latter being passive followers of the actors' leadership. The dichotomous nature of members of publics' activeness has thus been captured in this model of communication by conceptualizing each domain (information selection, transmission, and acquisition) as having an active and a passive dimension. The active or the proactive dimension represents purposeful actions on the part of the individual to acquire, select, or transmit information. The passive or the reactive dimension applies to when a problem solver waits for others to initiate action (Kim et al., 2010). It is important to note that while passive problem solvers are more likely to display only passive communicative behaviors, active problem solvers display both high active communicative behaviors as well as high passive communicative behaviors, because problem solvers can come across information unintentionally irrespective of their activeness in problem solving.

The CAPS model therefore postulates that "the more one commits to problem solving, the more one *becomes acquisitive* of information pertaining to the problem, *selective* in dealing with information, and *transmissive* with the information" (Kim et al., 2010, p. 130). Each of the three dimensions is discussed in detail in the following.

Information acquisition: Information seeking and information attending. When an individual faces a problem for which he or she has no immediately applicable solution (Grunig, 1968), he or she is confronted by a *metaproblem.* In such cases, the problem solver will turn to external sources for information and engage in a communicative action referred to as information acquisition (Kim et al., 2010). The active (proactive) and passive (reactive) dimensions of information acquisition have been discussed in the original situational theory of publics as the dependent variables, information seeking, and information attending (Grunig, 1997). In general, as the problem solver becomes more active about the problem or the issue, he or she also engages in more information acquisition. An active problem solver is more likely to initiate a search for information—information seeking. A less active problem solver may remain passive and reactive in gaining information and may be content with acquiring such information that simply comes his or her way without effort—information attending (Kim et al., 2010). Information seeking is planned, in contrast to information attending, which is unplanned. However, although information seeking is unique to active problem solvers, both active and passive problem solvers could potentially engage in information attending because active problem solvers are equally likely to come across information unintentionally (Kim et al., 2010). Active problem solvers are therefore high in information seeking and attending, whereas passive problem solvers are high only in information attending.

Information selection: Information forefending and information permitting. Over time, problem solvers tend to develop preferences for certain types and sources of information (Case, 2007). This communicative behavior is referred to as information selection. Kim, Grunig, and Ni (2010) distinguished between two dimensions of information selection—information forefending and information permitting. These variables are distinct from information seeking and attending in that these are cognitive aspects of information use. Information forefending refers to the extent to which a problem solver rejects or does not acknowledge certain types of information or certain information sources. The problem solver evaluates a given piece of information and makes a judgment about its value and relevance to the problem at hand. The problem solver is therefore more systematic and specific in his or her pursuit of relevant information. Typically, the more active a problem solver is about a problem, and the longer that problem solver is entrenched in the problem, the more discriminatory he or she will become about the value and relevance of the information he or she receives.

In contrast, information permitting refers to a situation in which the problem solver accepts any information that he or she receives about the problem, with little regard for the value or relevance of the information *if it is related to the problem.* Information permitting is more driven by an "adding strategy" of information, whereas information forefending is driven by a "removing strategy"; one takes and gives some information *only if it is judged to be relevant to the problem* (Kim et al., 2010). The postulate of the CAPS model explains that those with weak situational perception (i.e., low problem and involvement recognition with high constraint recognition) will experience relatively lower motivation to solve the problem and therefore would tend to have a degree of "indifference" toward the information they deal with (i.e., they would not be motivated to engage in communicative actions).

However, information permitting should not be equated with *communicative inaction* from the lack of motivation. It is more of "diffidence" (vs. indifference), despite strong situational perception and high motivation, as one is developing a new referent criterion or subscribes to a yet-to-be complete referent criterion. Therefore, information permitting is still a type of selectivity a problem solver displays often *at an early phase of problem solving.* Such a problem solver tends to be *random, general,* and pursuing of *relations* in his/her search and selection for information and may accept and share even *marginally relevant* information as useful. In contrast, the presence of and one's stronger subscription to a referent criterion tends to associate with information forefending, often *at a later phase of problem solving.* Such a problem solver tends to be more *systematic, specific,* and pursuing of *subjective sense of relevance* in dealing with information to reduce information overload or information inconsistency.

Information transmission: Information forwarding and information sharing. The CAPS model envisions problem solvers not just as information consumers but also as providers of information. Members of publics engage in educating others about the issues and problems with which they are active. Such efforts have been captured in social movement theories (e.g., Ferre, 1992; Tarrow, 1998). In the CAPS model, a problem solver's efforts to communicate information to others, either by design or otherwise, are captured by information transmission (see Figure 3.3). The active (proactive) dimension of information transmission is information forwarding. Active problem solvers are eager to disseminate the information that they have to others, whether or not it has been solicited. Less active problem solvers, on the other hand, tend to share information only when asked, thus engaging in the passive or reactive form of information transmission, or information sharing.

Antecedents of Problem-Solving Communicative Action

The situational theory of publics identified three antecedents of public formation. These were problem recognition, level of involvement, and constraint recognition (Grunig, 1997). Earlier versions of the theory also included a fourth antecedent, the referent criterion, which was later dropped because it failed to predict the dependent variables of the theory. The STP, however, has been reconceptualized to become the situational theory of problem solving (STOPS), which redefines the antecedent variables of the STP and proposes the addition of a motivational variable, situational motivation. The referent criterion has also been reincorporated in the STOPS (Kim & Grunig, 2011).

Problem recognition. The definition of problem recognition put forth by STP was a state in which "people detect that something should be done about a situation and stop to think about what to do" (Grunig, 1997, p. 10). This definition has been modified in the STOPS to be "one's perception that something is missing and that there is no immediately applicable solution to it" (Kim & Grunig, 2011, p. 11). Problem recognition is conceptualized as a cognitive problem following a perceptual problem. A notable difference between the old and new definitions is that the "stop to think about what to do" part has been omitted from the new definition. This is because whether people think about a problem and how much they think about a problem is influenced by other perceptual factors.

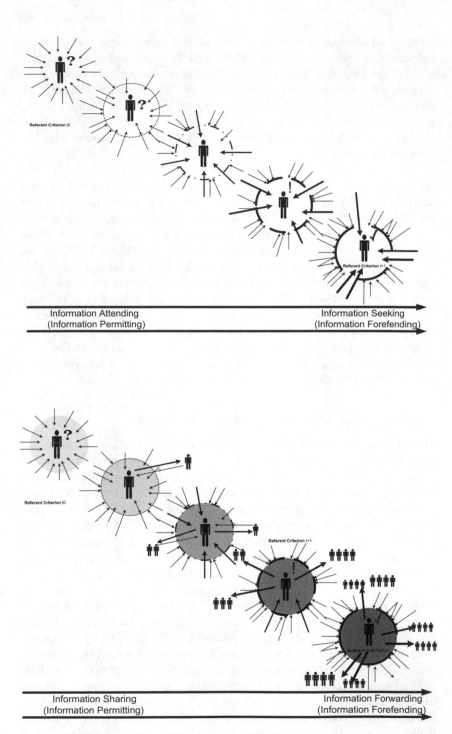

Figure 3.3 Domains of information behaviors by situational motivation in problem solving

Involvement recognition. Grunig (1997) conceived of level of involvement as an antecedent of public formation and defined it as "the extent to which people connect themselves with a situation" (p. 10). The magnitude and likelihood of people's communicative behaviors depends on their perceived closeness to the situation at hand. Although there may be an actual connection between an individual and a problematic situation, the individual will not act or think about it unless he or she can perceive his or her involvement with it. This distinction is important for the conceptualization of this variable because it shifts focus from actual connection to perceived connection. The STOPS therefore redefines level of involvement as involvement recognition—a perceived connection between the self and the problem (Kim & Grunig, 2011).

Constraint recognition. The concept of constraint recognition finds its roots in the restrictions of limited resources available to a decision maker (Grunig, 1968). The STP defines constraint recognition as a situation in which "people perceive that there are obstacles in a situation that limit their ability to do anything about the situation" (Grunig, 1997, p. 10). The STOPS retains this conceptualization of constraint recognition. This perceptual variable discourages communication even if the other perceptual variables are high (Ramanadhan & Viswanath, 2006). When problem solvers perceive barriers in their problem solving or limitations in their abilities to solve a problem, they are less likely to engage in communicative behaviors because they perceive these efforts to be of no avail (Kim & Grunig, 2011).

Referent criterion Referent criterion refers to any previously held knowledge or subjective judgmental system one activates or improvises at the time of the given problem-solving situation that influences the way in which one approaches problem solving (Kim & Grunig, 2011). In essence, it refers to an internal, cognitive search that one initiates that is related to the recognition of a problematic situation. A successful search results in "knowledge activation" (Higgins, 1996). One may also immediately improvise a new judging system related to the given problem situation. The referent criterion is more cognitive than perceptual and may include any decisional guidelines or inference rules from the problem solver's present interests and desires or previous problem-solving experiences. The presence of a referent criterion, that is *situation-general knowledge* (cf. LEGO manual), especially a strong one, is expected to lead to high communicative behaviors in taking, selecting, and giving information related to a given problem. In such cases, the referent criterion will become the cognitive framework or lens through which further *situation-specific information* (cf. LEGO building blocks) is sought, processed, transformed, and transmitted.

Situational motivation in problem solving. As discussed earlier, in redefining the concept of problem recognition, the STOPS omitted the "stop to think about it" aspect that was present in the STP's definition. This cognitive action is conceptualized as being an effect of problem recognition, other perceptual variables, and a motivation that was earlier treated as problem recognition itself (Kim & Grunig, 2011). Therefore, "situational motivation in problem solving represents the extent to which a person stops to think about, is curious about, or wants more understanding of a problem" (Kim & Grunig, 2011, p. 16). Such situational motivation is situation-specific and goal-specific in nature. As part of the STOPS, situational motivation sums up and mediates the effect of the three perceptual variables: problem recognition, involvement recognition, and constraint recognition.

The introduction of situational motivation in the STOPS holds practical implications for the successful execution of campaigns. The fact that motivation mediates the effect of all three perceptual variables means that practitioners could benefit by segmenting publics into groups with different levels of motivation and then devising strategies to increase motivation for each specific group.

Review of the Research Program from STOPS

That the STOPS is a theory of communication as well as a theory of public relations is demonstrated by the rich nature of emergent research that it has generated. The applications of the STOPS and CAPS models that have emerged so far cut across communication contexts. This section reviews some of the more prominent concepts and applications that have evolved from the STOPS and CAPS.

Examples of the Studies Using STOPS

One of the earliest applications of the STOPS has been in the area of long-term, controversial issues. Ni and Kim (2009) used the STOPS to propose a new taxonomy for the segmentation of chronic, prolonged publics. They segregated publics on long-term, controversial issues based on three factors: (a) history of problem solving, (b) the extent of activeness in problem solving, and (c) openness to approaches in problem solving. Based on these characteristics, they proposed eight types of subpublics that may form around a prolonged issue and validated their proposition by testing and identifying eight subpublics about a major, long-term environmental problem. The theoretical and practical implications posed by these eight subpublics are significant even more so because their application can be extended to various political, sociopolitical, environmental, and economic controversies and issues. The application of this new taxonomy of chronic publics proposed by Ni and Kim (2009) in the fields of political science (e.g., political controversy), health communication (e.g., environmental and health risk–related publics), and organizational communication (e.g., chronic publics about a crisis) is a promising direction for future research. Conceptually, Ni and Kim's typology is linked to the STOPS through the motivated information behaviors demonstrated by the various types of publics. For instance, the motivations displayed by *active* and *aware publics* and their attendant communicative actions differ over the period for which they have been active or aware about the issue.

Public segmentation, the method of classifying publics into categories for better strategic plan development, is a key tool that has emerged from the STOPS for public relations practitioners and theoreticians. Although methods for public segmentation have been in practice for several years (e.g., canonical correlations), most of these methods fail to be user-friendly. Kim (2011) proposed and demonstrated a simpler method of public segmentation: the summation method. The summation method uses three of the STOPS predictor variables by segmenting publics based on their self-reported levels of problem recognition, constraint recognition, and involvement recognition, providing public relations literature with a more intuitive and easy way of segmenting publics. This easy method of public segmentations allows public relations practitioners to choose their communication objectives with more accurate information about predicted information behaviors of various publics. In light of a recent study by Kim and Ni (2013b) in which the authors proposed the situational variables, problem recognition, constraint recognition, information seeking, forwarding, or forefending to be nonfinancial metrics of communication effectiveness, the accurate prediction of such behaviors becomes an important task for strategic planning of communication efforts. For example, a communication problem related to the environmental consequences of a new manufacturing site (i.e., public-initiated PR problem; Kim & Ni, 2013b) could be tracked by the decline in problem recognition and information seeking of the members of active publics as a result of public meetings or negotiating protective countermeasures. Whereas most strategic communication programs use attitudinal and behavioral measures to assess and track citizens' concerns about an issue, STOPS provides perceptual alternatives of problem recognition or information forwarding, which are the primary causes of collective actions in social networks. Likewise, organizational efforts for a communication problem to raise funds for higher education (i.e., *organization-initiated PR problem*; Kim & Ni, 2013b) can be more strategically planned and tracked by considering the situational variables (e.g., problem recognition, involvement recognition, constraint recognition) about the shortage of financial resources among alumni and faculty/staff, which may further trigger problem-solving motivation and communicative behaviors related to the problem (Kim & Ni, 2013b).

The six dependent variables of the STOPS (i.e., CAPS) have been successfully applied in employee communication. Kim and Rhee (2011) proposed three distinct communication behaviors displayed by an organization's employees. These communication behaviors include megaphoning, scouting, and microboundary spanning, each of which are predicted based on the organization-employee relationship perceived by the employee. For instance, an employee who perceives a positive relationship with the organization may be motivated to forward or share positive information with stakeholders outside of the organization positive *megaphoning*. When an employee voluntarily engages in information acquisition behaviors to forage for information relevant to the organization's goals and mission, and transmits that information to relevant people in the organization, the employee is said to engage in *scouting*. Thus, employees may act as voluntary bridges between the organization and its task and social environments, and engage in information seeking, selecting, and transmitting behaviors and acting as microboundary spanners. These new concepts were further tested in a crisis communication context to see whether an organization with a good relationship with employees would better cope with a corporate crisis with employees engaging in positive megaphoning and advocatory information behaviors (Mazzei, Kim, & Dell'Oro, 2012). In addition, employees' information scouting from their daily operations is strongly related to relationships and, further, the innovativeness of the hosting organization. A recent research showed that effective organizations have more employees engaging in scouting and entrepreneurship than in less-effective organizations (Park, 2013).

Health communication is another area that presents several opportunities for application of the CAPS and STOPS models. Together, the two theories have been applied to various health and risk communication contexts. For instance, Kim, Shen, and Morgan (2011) replicated the STOPS with publics about the shortage of organ donors and demonstrated the theoretical utility of the STOPS in predicting the communicative behaviors of publics through the CAPS model. In a major contribution to theory in public relations and risk communication, it was also recognized in this study that issues/problems of interest are often clustered and embedded within a network of problems and showed that recognition of an anchor issue could lead to higher levels of recognition of related issues in the minds of the original publics (Kim et al., 2011). Kim, Shen, and Morgan called this extension of recognition from one issue to a related issue the *problem chain recognition effect* (PCR effect). The recognition of the shortage of organ donors led to the same publics recognizing a related issue, the search for a cure for muscular atrophy using stem cell therapy. The problem chain recognition effect had far-reaching implications for research in risk and crisis communication. For instance, PCR effect may be used to predict whether publics about food crisis or food scare may also display high levels of recognition about a new food technology or a different food risk.

Another application of the STOPS and CAPS in the health communication context has been in *cybercoping*, coping with health issues by the communicative interactions among networked online publics (Kim & Lee, in press). Kim and Vibber (2012) defined cybercoping as information forwarding and information seeking through online social media to improve health problem-solving efforts and explained the boundary conditions (i.e., when it works and when it does not) of effective cybercoping among patients with serious illnesses such as HIV, lupus, cancer, and depression, and so on.

The two theories have also helped enhance our understanding of a special type of public: hot-issue publics (Aldoory & Grunig, 2012; Grunig, 1997). The STOPS and CAPS theories have been replicated for hot-issue publics, that is, short-term publics that arise out of the media coverage given to a controversial issue. In a recent study on a hot issue in Korea, the STOPS model was used to predict communicative actions of the publics, as well as to test the impact of cross-situational variables, such as technology optimism, risk perception, knowledge, and so on, on the perceptual variables and CAPS (Kim, Ni, Kim, & Kim, 2012).

The migration of municipal communication from a more traditional, one-sided, asymmetrical communication policy to building relationships with citizens has become an emergent research trend in the Web 2.0 era. Specifically, the factors motivating citizens' voluntary communicative actions on civic issues and resulting in civic knowledge were examined in an Italian context based on the STOPS framework (Lovari, Kim, Vibber, & Kim, 2011; Lovari, Martino, & Kim, 2012). The findings highlighted the importance of the role of lay-publics' information sharing and forwarding in the spread of political knowledge and civic participation in the new computer-mediated-communication (CMC) environment. Additionally, the communicative actions of constrained publics on sociopolitical issues may turn into online flaming. Kim and Kim (2009) modified STOPS to account for the situation-triggered flaming as a form of cyberactivism. The situational flaming model specified the perceptual conditions that trigger emotional reactions about problematic situations and the resulting information transmission in anonymous cyberspace. It extends STOPS into the CMC phenomenon of flaming and proposes some types of cyberviolence such as flaming to be a special case of public activism when their problem-solving efforts are frustrated by social barriers.

Kim and Ni (2011) also provided a theoretical account of how the CAPS model can be used to understand individual communicative actions and perceptions about foreign nations. The STOPS therefore has implications in the field of *sociological public diplomacy* through its application in the study of "soft power." As an extension of CAPS to communicative activism (e.g., negative megaphoning) among foreign publics, Vibber and Kim (in press) proposed a theoretical model that links and explains the nexus between social processes in the formation of national reputation and communicative activism among foreign publics. The STOPS and CAPS models have helped develop an understanding of how an individual experiences a foreign country, such as consumption of cultural products, and communication behaviors as well as how such experiences shape individual perceptions of goodwill or soft power toward that foreign country (Kim & Ni, 2011). In addition, CAPS also helped account for how members of diasporas experience a hosting country and how their influence flows through their communicative networks and information behaviors in their home country (Yun & Vibber, 2012).

Finally, a special issue of the *International Journal of Strategic Communication* (2012), which focused on strategic communication, showcased the variety of contexts within which the STOPS and CAPS models may be applied. The special issue began with a theoretical account of STOPS and CAPS and went on to present a series of studies demonstrating the application of the STOPS and CAPS models in varied fields such as tourism management, consumer research, marketing communication, public relations, internal communication, and public diplomacy. This issue of the *International Journal of Strategic Communication* focused on using the STOPS and CAPS frameworks to explain the role and values of relationships with strategic publics and stakeholders in a variety of contexts.

New Research Problems from STOPS[6]

The theoretical formulation of the STOPS looks closely at why and how one begins problem-solving efforts and what communicative characteristics the problem solver will show during the problem-solving process. In this concluding section, we introduce seven new research problems generated from STOPS as a conceptual framework, with regard to changes in information and communication environments, classical communication theories, and the emerging social communicative phenomena related to individual and collective problem solvers. This is not an exhaustive list of new research areas; it is only those problems that are intriguing and may have an impact on society and on individuals' research agendas.

Gossiping and the diffusion of innovation.   People gossip about almost anything. We consciously and unconsciously select topics and highlight some aspects of what has happened in our daily social and individual lives. Situational theorists define gossiping as another snapshot of communicative actions, often for trivial problems that may or may not have a high involvement to our lives (Kim & Grunig, in press). Yet, the mechanics of *when* and *how* people gossip can, in major part, be explained by STOPS. We recognize something as departing from our commonsensical expectations (i.e., problem recognition), which may increase the epistemic motivation of the recognized problem. As a result, we may seek and select some aspects of the event or problems and forward the information to or share it with neighboring communicators such as friends and family. In communication theory, research interests on the hows and whys of gossiping and the roles gossiping plays (cf. social grooming) are present. However, we still need a better understanding of the value of gossiping as an inadvertent vehicle for diffusion of innovation, social learning, or information trafficking. The need for more research has become greater as the new form of gossiping is in digital communication networks such as Twitter and Facebook. A theoretical explication for how and why gossiping occurs, which proposes a perceptual and motivational account of gossiping as a special type of an informal communicative action, seems promising. For example, network analysis research of gossiping (information trafficking) about the flow, social functioning, and differential patterns of diffusion of information across different types of social networks in conjunction with the situational theory's key variables will be an interesting theoretical research. Similarly, the primary vehicle of diffusion of innovation (Rogers, 2003) is informal information behaviors, such as gossiping, among individuals in socio-communicative networks. Further, the different patterns of adoption curves (e.g., J-Curve; Rogers, 2003) are explained by the number or ratios of information forwarders/sharers and information seekers/attenders in a diffusion network (Kim, 2006). Research using the situational variables (i.e., problem recognition and information behaviors) could provide another perspective to that most classical social theory, the diffusion of innovation.

Flaming and cyberactivism.   The STOPS starts from the premise that communicative actions arise for the purpose of coping with problematic life situations. Flaming is an anti-social and anti-normative behavior in an online setting, often including profanity aggression, and hostility, in computer-mediated communication environment (Denegri-Knott & Taylor, 2005). As seen in the recent research by Kim and Kim (2009), some types of flaming are not because of personal traits or sociopathic or psychopathological reasons but more driven by situational factors such as involvement and constraint recognition. The phenomenon of situational flaming has been conceptualized and examined as cyberactivism by problem solvers with aggressive digital communicative actions (Kim & Kim, 2009). It is necessary to investigate what social and contextual factors would influence one's likelihood of situational flaming. The situational theory of problem solving provides the theoretical building blocks to explain the situational conditions of flaming. As the problem, involvement, and constraint recognition increase, emotional residuals increase and thus emotion-focused coping through aggressive, abusive communicative action is likely. The new situation triggered model explains some online flaming is better understood as cyberactivism by frustrated problem-focused coping (Lazarus, 1993).

Yet, there are more questions that remain unanswered regarding the causes and strategies for reducing online flaming by angry publics. For example, one demanding research area is that of institutional/organizational strategies for dealing with angry publics to decrease their violent cyberactivism. The escalation of social conflict and group polarization in digital communication forums occur in major part because of flaming and counterflaming by a public and counterpublics in social controversies. The escalation of such social conflicts and their potential for resolution can and should be prevented by understanding the causes, processes, and consequences of flaming. The first step of this effort is to build theoretical accounts of flaming.

Lacuna publics and information forefending.   Group extremism has become a new social threat in the digital communication environment. Even traditional mass media are consumed through digital, computer-mediated channels (e.g., YouTube, news portals). Two major problems that increase social schisms are *Lacuna Publics and their motivated communicative actions.* Lacuna literally means a blank space or a missing part (*Merriam-Webster Dictionary,* 2013). We define *lacuna publics* as a subtype of an active public on a controversial issue that shows extreme attitudes but deficient knowledge and understanding about the issue. Lacuna publics tend to show directed and selective information seeking and giving (i.e., information forefending) about the issue, usually with high problem motivation and high information forefending. Because their epistemic motivation and problem-solving efforts are selective and lean heavily toward a preferred referent criterion, they are relatively more motivated and communicatively active, and their confidence or conviction to their preferred/ preoccupied position is stronger.

Lacuna publics rarely seek and share other viewpoints or factual information (i.e., affective information such as preference or personal opinions). Their presence and reproduction within social communicative networks is a major threat for informed social discussion in a controversy. The most significant and threatening aspects of lacuna publics is not the lack of interest or aspirations for problem solving, but the excessive conviction and the lack of tolerance about different ideas and stances in social problems. STOPS has the theoretical concepts and mechanisms to define and identify lacuna publics and how and why they arise and behave (e.g., presence and subscription to an affective, expectational referent criterion, directional epistemic motivation in problem solving, information forefending). This new research about the segmentation of lacuna publics and their behavioral distinctions offers promise in the new communicative environments.

PCR as an intrapersonal and interpersonal process.   PCR effect, as recognized by Kim, Shen, and Morgan (2011), refers to the perceptual contagiousness of similar types of individual and social problems that further trigger epistemic motivation and information behaviors. The embeddedness of a problem within a network of problems is a new direction for research, especially using the PCR effect. Quite a few communication problems can be explained by the PCR effect. For example, information campaigns to elicit problem recognitions by organ donors or citizens' recognition and voluntary adoption of environmental protective behaviors can be better approached if communicators understand the processes and mechanisms of PCR in a given network of problems. The research on the links between PCR effect and behavioral dimensions of individual problem solvers are key to mobilizing social support for collective problem solving from a salient issue to other related networks of similar issues.

The PCR effect was originally proposed and conceptualized as an *intrapersonal process of contagious problem recognition.* However, it is also possible and necessary to conceptualize the problem chain recognition effect as an *interpersonal process of contagious problem recognition,* that is, how the contextual talking of an individual's neighboring communicators (e.g., friends or family) for some problems (cf. gossiping) may trigger problem recognition for those problems in that individual. For example, recent research findings by the situational theorists provide evidence that as one is exposed more frequently to a "contextual conversation" about organ donation, one shows higher situational perceptions and a stronger epistemic and behavioral motivational tendency toward organ donation. Therefore, more research on the interpersonal PCR effect should be done to understand the process and consequences of how local, neighboring communicative actors ("focal communicants") provide contextual influence on problem recognition and problem motivation of others for various social problems or risks.

Cybercoping and collective effectuating of individual problems.   Traditionally, the health risks or health problems one experiences are attributed to an individual lifestyle and genetic conditions that require personal problem solving. However, individual health problems can be dealt with better if isolated problem solvers ideate and effectuate together (see Figure 3.4 for the different phases of problem solving). Recent studies of chronic health problem solvers have shown that collective effectuating through digital communicative networks is effective and rewarding for enhancing the manageability of chronic illnesses both psychologically and physically (Kim & DiTirro, 2013; Kim & Lee, in press; Kim & Vibber, 2012). Although it is necessary to avoid overconfidence in the new communicative technologies and their health consequences for chronic health problem solvers, more studies on the theory of problem solving and coping theories (Lazarus, 1993) will generate better understanding that could improve health communication policy for chronic patients.

Information forefending and information illiteracy.   Information literacy has arisen as a core research concept and an agendum for education and library/ information sciences. The almost free and infinite amount of data access through digital computing networks has reshaped the problem of problem solving from knowhow and knowwhere to selecthow and selectwhat problems. STOPS and the communicative action in problem solving models conceptually capture why and how individual problem solvers become selective in information seeking, attending, forwarding, and sharing, and when such selectivity becomes a problem for the problem solver. As discussed earlier in this chapter, STOPS differentiates between two types of referent criteria—factual, experiential versus affective, expectational—and two types of information forefending— communicative optimization or cognitive optimization.

In one type, the factual, experiential referent criterion and communicative optimization, a problem solver tends to forefend information without decreasing the effectiveness of problem-solving outcomes. However, in the latter type, the affective, expectational referent criterion (e.g., wishful/willful thinking) and cognitive and communicative optimization (e.g., search/give information fitting with one's desired/preferred way of problem solving), an individual tends to forefend information that may result in less-than-ideal problem-solving outcomes.

Situational theorists consider much of the information illiteracy in the digital communication environment to have been triggered and worsened by the subjective wishful or willful thinking of problem solvers and, further, by ascribing to affective, expectational referent criterion. For example, in the Google era,

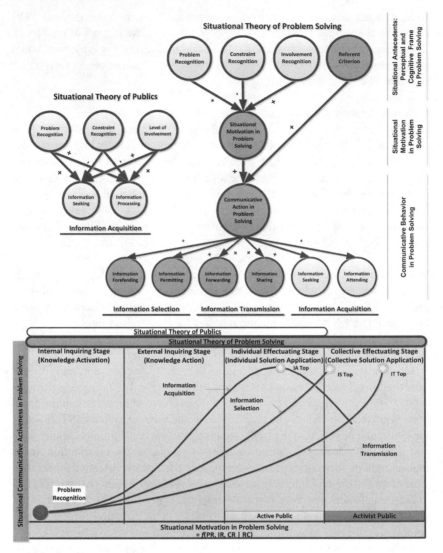

Figure 3.4 Conceptual summary of the situational theories

an information seeker will almost always find some type of confirmatory data as one consciously or unconsciously looks for some information consistent with preferred decisions/solutions/ways of thinking in the given problem situations. In fact, many public fears about or overconfidence in new scientific, technological advancements (e.g., Nano technology, Genetically Modified Organism (GMO) or Living Modified Organism (LMO), or health risks of new technology) may be related to information forefending and information illiteracy triggered by perceptual, cognitive, and motivational factors explained by the situational theory. Premature approval of and obstinate chronic resistance to new technology are both interesting areas of research using the situational theory of problem solving.

A more threatening problem seems to be that in digitalized, CMC conditions, less privileged, marginalized groups are more likely to fall into confirmatory traps and find it difficult to solve "information problems" (i.e., selecthow and selectwhat) during their problem solving. Specifically, some personal and situational factors can increase justificatory information forcfending for risky health behaviors. For instance, one's low eHealth literacy may activate and foster affective, expectational referent criterion that in turn may increase seeking and sharing of confirmatory health information. Therefore, it is important that more research be done to describe and prescribe how to solve information problems and information illiteracy in various problem-solving contexts.

Micro-information behaviors and macro-social and organizational consequences. The primary focus of the STOPS is on individual-level micro-communicative actions through perception and motivation that explain the individuality of thinking and behaving. Yet, individual behaviors can result in macro-consequences for society or organizations with which those individuals have relations.

As noted in the previous section on recent research, first, employees' information behavior from their routine activities could have major consequences for organizational effectiveness. Findings in recent studies of companies in the United States (Park, 2013) have shown that employees with good quality relationships with their hosting companies are highly likely to engage in "scouting" for strategic business information that brings innovation into a business and increases costs for rival companies. Stoffels (1994), a management information scientist, noted that two-thirds of strategic intelligence for organizations come from informal ways of communication. Park's (2013) recent study provides evidence for the observation that more effective organizations are more likely to have employees engaging in scouting and microboundary spanning than less effective organizations. This indicates that successful organizations benefit at the macro-level by their micro-actors' communicative actions. A new set of research questions also can be derived from the micro-information behaviors of employees pertaining to the compensation system, organizational culture, leadership types, and communication strategies in fostering and maintaining desirable information behaviors.

Further promising research directions in the area of internal and organizational communication include crisis communication management and the role of employees as sources of information for the organization (i.e., scouting) or as advocates for or adversaries against the organization (i.e., megaphoning). Another dimension of macro-consequences is that of information forefending, information forwarding and sharing by various strategic publics (e.g., consumer, ex-employees, activists) in and around organizations. For example, megaphoning (i.e., positive or negative) is also a commonly observed phenomenon among consumers who have experienced a company's products and services. Negative

megaphoning by angry publics either in on- or off-line communication channels are a source of reputation (i.e., the distribution of cognitive representations
about an organization, its products/service, or an individual; Grunig & Hung,
2002; Kim et al., 2013). Individuals who are passive but located in the vicinity
of some active communicators (i.e., megaphoners) are exposed to the content,
amount, and direction of the reputational information forwarded/shared by the
active communicators.

More importantly, as a result of the shift to digital information networks,
some negative accounts or testimonials will be stored almost forever as data
and may potentially be retrieved by information seekers repeatedly (Kim
et al., 2013). The formation and improvement of invisible corporate assets
such as reputation are determined by direct, experiential relationship holders,
that is, the strategic publics of an organization. An interesting area of research
would be the study of how the organization–public relationship perceived by
the strategic publics may manifest itself through positive (or negative) communicative behaviors by the strategic public, and through such behaviors, a
positive (or negative) reputation for the organization. Conceptual and empirical research is necessary to explicate the intertwined causal mechanisms
between organizational behaviors and public behaviors and the detailed links
between positive and negative megaphoning by consumers and other types of
active publics.

Conclusion

This review chapter looks at the paths that the two generations of the situational theory have taken to evolve into a more general communication theory of
human communicative behaviors in problematic life situations. Four decades
worth of theory-building effort is rarely found in the field of communication,
or in any behavioral, social scientific field. The most noteworthy contribution
of the situational theory of problem solving to the field of communication is
an epistemological turn, in that for theory to establish a bridge between two
important human natures—problem solving and communication. In constructing the theories, both generations of situational theorists took a unique stance
in their theoretical premise: communication as a purposive, coping mechanism
for problematic life situation.

The epistemological bridge of the two phenomena, problem solving and
communicative actions, tells communication theorists and researchers that
communicating can be usefully conceptualized as a special type of human
behavior for influencing problematic life situations and that purposeful communicative actions may or may not be effective or successful in solving one's
life problems. In this sense, the situational theory of problem solving is a teleological theory that aims at a better understanding of the link between problem
solving and communication, and a descriptive theory (vs. prescriptive theory)
to capture human communication phenomena, which may have the same cause
but may vary in their effects.

It is noteworthy that the situational theory of publics has provided the ground for building several influential prescriptive theories in public relations and organizational management to enhance communication with members of publics (i.e., a group of problem solvers) and create principles of effective and ethical organizational management and greater social good (e.g., the IABC Excellence Study; see Grunig, Ferrari, & França, 2009, for a review of the general theories of public relations based on the situational theory of publics). Just like its mother theory, the generalized STOPS and communicative actions has laid newer and broader ground for further theorizing in communication management in both constructing better communication practice (e.g., public segmentation) as well as newer communication theories related to communicative phenomena (e.g., megaphoning, scouting, problem chain recognition effect, and situation-triggered flaming).

As we deepen our migration into the digital, networked society, the theoretical values and power of STOPS have grown and show more promise. For example, in the era of digital media, the first wave of research interests was focused on word of mouth/buzzword/grapevine and communicator activities as an information prosumer (i.e., the changing trend of communicators producing and consuming information inseparably and simultaneously) hardly that has not been conceptualized as in audience research or mass mediated communication. We are not merely message takers. As we acquire new knowledge or information, we almost simultaneously transmit it while developing a taste for what is good or bad for making sense of and solving problematic situations.

However, communication literatures have rarely theorized such voluntary and simultaneous communicative behaviors of individuals as givers and producers of new information. We seem to be wary of giving theoretical names to the emerging changes in communicative actions. Since the situational theory of publics, several influential information processing models and theories have been proposed (e.g., Risk Information Seeking and Processing/Disruption Information Seeking and Processing, the Comprehensive Model of Information Seeking, the Theory of Motivational Information Management). Yet, most of the theories/models focus on information acquisition or information seeking but less the other aspects of communicative actions such as information transmission and information selection. There is still a marked paucity in the construction of general theories in recent years to capture and conceptualize all-encompassing aspects of communicative actions among users. In this vein, the new theoretical vocabularies, such as information forefending, information forwarding, or information attending, in the STOPS can help communication researchers and practitioners describe the changed behaviors of individuals who are communicative actors rather than passive audience, and help to explain why they display those communicative behaviors: because of motivated for problem solving and to cope with problematic life situations.

The renaming of the audience to (active) communicators spanning various dimensions and scopes of symbolic behaviors such as taking and giving of information goes beyond theoretical development. As noted earlier, in the past most theories and research in communication were constructed to serve the sender's interests—how to negotiate the meaning or to influence the audience's interpretation of what has happened through symbolic manipulation—instead of trying to serve mutual interests of both the sender and the receivers—how to negotiate behaviors that affect each other's interests through communicative interaction. The former is the symbolic, interpretive paradigm in communication management, and the latter is called the behavioral, strategic management paradigm (Grunig et al., 2009; Grunig & Kim, 2011; Kim, Bach, & Clelland, 2007). In the situational theories, especially in the theory of problem solving, the audience is conceptualized and understood as (a group of) problem solvers. The communication practices based on the situational theories may be very different from that of attitudinal theories because the theories do not conceive of the communicative partners as passive target audience but as active problem solvers.

In conclusion, the situational theorists hope that researchers and practitioners in communication identify more problems through the lens of the situational theory and construct more solutions for organizational communicators who deal with diverse communication problems as well as for individual communicators with various types of life and social problems.

Notes

1. Epistemic motivation refers to one's heightened cognitive interest to comprehend problematic situations one encounters. In the situational theory of problem solving, this refers to situational motivation in problem solving, defined as "a state of situation-specific cognitive and epistemic readiness to make problem-solving efforts—that is, to decrease the perceived discrepancy between the expected and experiential states" (Kim & Grunig, 2011, p. 132).
2. Another good example is risk information seeking and processing (RISP; Griffin, Dunwoody, & Neuwrith, 1999) and the recently added model, disruption information seeking and processing (DISP; Braun & Niederdeppe, 2012). RISP is an influential theory of information acquisition about risks specifying causal antecedents such as information sufficiency and self-efficacy. Braun and Niederdeppe (2012) proposed a new model, DISP, separated information sufficiency into self-relevant and risk-relevant information sufficiency, and added norm trumping as disruptive experience occurs.
3. Since the situational theory and the uses and gratification theory, some researchers have begun building information-processing theories by focusing on the personal and contextual conditions that increase/decrease information needs among individuals. For example, Johnson and Meischke (1993) proposed the comprehensive model of information seeking (CMIS) that identifies individual health related factors (e.g., demographics, salience) and information carrier factors (e.g., utility, editorial tone) as causal determinants of information seeking in health communication contexts. Another popular information-seeking theory that takes the view on active communicators is risk information seeking and processing (RISP; Griffin et al., 1999). By integrating social psychological theories such as self-efficacy (Bandura, 1986) and heuristic-systematic processing model (Chaiken, Liberman, & Eagley, 1989), RISP explains the varying information sufficiency influenced by perceived risk perception (e.g., severity, probability of risk) and its information seeking/processing potential.
4. Metaproblem refers to a problem about problem solving that requires cognitive labor to narrow the discrepancy between the experienced and expected states.

5. Although most information processing models focus on information acquisition (Case, 2007), there are a few exceptions. For instance, a recent theory proposed in interpersonal communication, theory of motivational information management (TMIM; Afifi & Weiner, 2004) has incorporated the motivational process of information provision.

6. Situational theorists have theorized certain cognitive aspects of problem solving (i.e., cognitive entrepreneurship in problem solving). These will be covered in detail in the forthcoming book on the situational theory of problem solving (Routledge).

References

Afifi, W. A., & Weiner, J. L. (2004). Toward a theory of motivated information management. *Communication Theory, 14,* 167–190. doi:10.1111/j.1468–2885.2004. tb00310.x

Aldoory, L., & Grunig, J. E. (2012). The rise and fall of hot-issue publics: Relationships that develop from media coverage of events and crises. *International Journal of Strategic Communication, 6,* 93–108. doi:10.1080/1553118X.2011.634866

Bandura, A. (1986). *Social foundations of thought and action.* Englewood Cliffs, NJ: Prentice Hall. doi:10.1002/9780470479216.corpsy0836

Blumer, H. (1948). Public opinion and public opinion polling. *American Sociological Review, 13,* 542–554.

Braun, J., & Niederdeppe, J. (2012). Disruption and identity maintenance in risk information seeking and processing. *Communication Theory, 22,* 138–162. doi:10.1111/j.1468–2885.2012.01402.x

Carter, R. F. (1965). Communication and affective relation. *Journalism Quarterly, 42,* 203–212.

Carter, R. F. (1973, August). *Communication as behavior.* Paper presented to the Theory and Methodology Division, Association for Education in Journalism, Fort Collins, CO.

Case, D. O. (2007). *Looking for information: A survey of research on information seeking, needs, and behavior* (2nd ed.). San Diego, CA: Academic Press.

Chaffee, S. H. (1982). Mass media and interpersonal channels: Competitive, convergent, or complementary? In G. Gumpert & R. Cathcart (Eds.), *Inter/Media: Interpersonal communication in a media world* (2nd ed., pp. 57–77). New York: Oxford University Press.

Chaiken, S., Liberman, A., & Eagley, A. H. (1989). Heuristic and systematic processing within and beyond the persuasion context. In J. S. Vleman & J. A. Bargh (Eds.), *Unintended thought* (pp. 212–252). New York: Guilford.

Denegri-Knott, J., & Taylor, J. (2005). The labeling game: A conceptual exploration of deviance on the Internet. *Social Science Computer Review, 23*(1), 93–107.

Dervin, B. (1989). Audience as listener and learner, teacher and confidante: The sensemaking approach. In R. E. Rice & C. K. Atkin (Eds.), *Public communication campaigns* (2nd ed., pp. 67–86). Newbury Park, CA: Sage.

Dewey, J. (1927). *The public and its problems.* Chicago, IL: Swallow.

Ferre, M. M. (1992). The political context of rationality: Rational choice theory and resource mobilization. In A. D. Morris & C. M. Mueller (Eds.), *Frontiers in social movement theory* (pp. 29–52). Binghamton: Yale University Press.

Fishbein, M., & Ajzen, I. (1975). *Belief, attitude, intention, and behavior: An introduction to theory and research.* Reading, MA: Addison-Wesley.

Fisher, K. E., Erdelez, S., & McKechnie, L. (2005). *Theories of information behavior.* Medford, NJ: Information Today.

Gorman, P., Ash, J., Lavelle, M., Lyman, J., Delcambre, L., Maier, D., . . . Bowers, S. (2001). Bundles in the wild: Managing information to solve problems and maintain situation awareness. *Library Trends, 49,* 266–289. doi:10.1109/ICDE.2001.914819

Griffin, R. J., Dunwoody, S., & Neuwirth, K. (1999). Proposed model of the relationship of risk information seeking and processing to the development of preventive behaviors. *Environmental Research Section A, 80,* S230–S245. doi:10.1006/enrs.1998.3940

Grunig, J. E. (1966). The role of information in economic decision making. *Journalism Monographs, 3.*

Grunig, J. E. (1968). *Information, entrepreneurship, and economic development: A study of the decision making processes of Colombian Latifundistas* (Unpublished doctoral dissertation). University of Wisconsin, Madison.

Grunig, J. E. (1976). Communication behaviors in decision and nondecision situations. *Journalism Quarterly, 53,* 232–263. doi:10.1177/107769907605300209

Grunig, J. E. (1997). A situational theory of publics: Conceptual history, recent challenges and new research. In D. Moss, T. MacManus, & D. Verčič (Eds.), *Public relations research: An international perspective* (pp. 3–46). London, England: International Thompson Business Press.

Grunig, J. E. (2003). Constructing public relations theory and practice. In B. Dervin & S. Chaffee, with L. Foreman-Wernet (Eds.), *Communication, another kind of horse race: Essays honoring Richard F. Carter* (pp. 85–115). Cresskill, NJ: Hampton Press.

Grunig, J. E., Ferrari, M. A., & França, F. (2009). *Relações públicas: Teoria, contexto e relacionamentos* [Public relations: Theory, context, and relationships]. São Paulo, Brazil: Difusao Editora.

Grunig, J. E., & Hung, C. R. (2002, March). *The effect of relationships on reputation and reputation on relationships: A cognitive, behavioral study.* Paper presented at the PRSA Educator's Academy 5th Annual International, Interdisciplinary Public Relations Research Conference, Miami, FL.

Grunig, J. E., & Kim, J.-N. (2011). Actions speak louder than words: How a strategic management approach to public relations can shape a company's brand and reputation through relationships. *Insight Train, 1,* 36–51.

Higgins, E. T. (1996). Knowledge activation, application, and salience. In E. T. Higgins & A. W. Kruglanski (Eds.), *Social psychology: Handbook of basic principles* (pp. 133–168). New York: Guilford.

Johnson, J. D., & Meischke, H. (1993). A comprehensive model of cancer-related information seeking applied to magazines. *Human Communication Research, 19,* 343–367. doi:10.1111/j.1468-2958.1993.tb00305.x

Katz, E., Haas, H., & Gurevitch, M. (1973). On the use of the mass media for important things. *American Sociological Review, 38,* 164–181.

Kim, J.-N. (2006). *Communicant activeness, cognitive entrepreneurship, and a situational theory of problem solving* (Unpublished doctoral dissertation). University of Maryland, College Park.

Kim, J.-N. (2011). Public segmentation using situational theory of problem solving: Illustrating summation method and testing segmented public profiles. *PRism, 8.* Retrieved from www.prismjournal.org/homepage.html

Kim, J.-N. (Ed.). (2012). Strategic values of relationships and the communicative actions of publics and stakeholders [Special issue]. *International Journal of Strategic Communication, 6(1).*

Kim, J.-N., Bach, S. B., & Clelland, I. J. (2007). Symbolic or behavioral management? Corporate reputation in high-emission industries. *Corporate Reputation Review, 10*(2), 77–98. doi:10.1057/palgrave.crr.1550042

Kim, J.-N., & DiTirro, L. (2013). Healthy communication: Cybercoping of mental and physical health problems and its health consequences. *Health Communication Research, 7,* 81–111.

Kim, J.-N., & Grunig, J. E. (2011). Problem solving and communicative action: A situational theory of problem solving. *Journal of Communication, 61,* 120–149. doi:10.1111/j.1460–2466.2010.01529.x

Kim, J.-N., & Grunig, J. E. (in press). *Situational theory of problem solving: Communicative, cognitive, and perceptive bases.* New York: Routledge.

Kim, J. N., Grunig, J. E., & Ni, L. (2010). Reconceptualizing the communicative action of publics: Acquisition, selection, and transmission of information in problematic situations. *International Journal of Strategic Communication, 4*(2), 126–154.

Kim, J.-N., Hung-Baesecke, C.-J., Yang, S-U., & Grunig, J. E. (2013). A strategic management approach to reputation, relationships, and publics: The research heritage of the Excellence Theory. In C. Carroll (Ed.), *Handbook of communication and corporate reputation* (pp. 197–212). New York: Wiley Blackwell.

Kim, J.-N., & Kim, J.-Y. (2009). *Mr. Hyde logged in: A theoretical account of situation-triggered flaming.* Chicago, IL: Korean American Communication Association, National Communication Association.

Kim, J.-N., & Lee, S. (in press). Communication and cybercoping: Coping with chronic illness through communicative action in online support networks. *Journal of Health Communication.*

Kim, J.-N., & Ni, L. (2010). Seeing the forest through the trees: The behavioral, strategic management paradigm in public relations and its future. In R. H. Heath (Ed.), *The SAGE handbook of public relations* (pp. 35–57). Thousand Oaks, CA: Sage.

Kim, J.-N., & Ni, L. (2011). The nexus between Hallyu and soft power: Cultural public diplomacy in the era of sociological globalism. In D. K. Kim & M. S. Kim (Eds.), *Hallyu: Influence of Korean popular culture in Asia and beyond* (pp. 131–154). Seoul, Korea: Seoul National University Press.

Kim, J.-N., & Ni, L. (2013a). Conceptualizing publics and constructing public relations theory: Situational theory of problem solving and its new research. In K. Sriramesh, A. Zerfass, & J.-N. Kim (Eds.), *Current trends and emerging topics in public relations and communication management* (pp. 126–142). New York: Routledge.

Kim, J.-N., & Ni, L. (2013b). Integrating formative and evaluative research in two types of public relations problems: A review of research programs within the strategic management approach. *Journal of Public Relations Research, 25,* 1–29. doi:10.108 0/1062726X.2012.723276

Kim, J.-N., Ni, L., Kim, S-H., & Kim, J. R. (2012). What makes people hot: Applying the situational theory of problem solving to hot-issue publics. *Journal of Public Relations Research, 24,* 144–164. doi:10.1080/1062726X.2012.626133

Kim, J.-N., & Rhee, Y. (2011). Strategic thinking about employee communication behavior (ECB) in public relations: Testing the models of megaphoning and scouting effects in Korea. *Journal of Public Relations Research, 23,* 243–268. doi:10.10 80/1062726X.2011.582204

Kim, J.-N., Shen, H., & Morgan, S. (2011). Information behaviors and problem chain recognition effect: Applying situational theory of problem solving in organ donation issues. *Health Communication, 26,* 171–184. doi:10.1080/10410236.2010.544282

Kim, J.-N., & Vibber, K. (2012). Networked sociability and cybercoping: The effects of enabled personal networks and enhanced health outcomes among chronic health problem solvers. In S. Duhé (Ed.), *New media and public relations* (2nd ed., pp. 218–229). New York City: Peter Lang.

Knight, F. H. (1921). *Risk, uncertainty, and profit*. Boston, MA: Hart, Schaffner & Marx.

Lacuna [Def. 1]. (n.d.). *Merriam-Webster Online*. In Merriam-Webster. Retrieved December 29, 2013, from www.merriam-webster.com/dictionary/lacuna

Lazarus, R. S. (1993). From psychological stress to the emotions: A history of changing outlooks. *Annual Reviews in Psychology, 44*, 1–21.

Lippmann, W. (1925). *The phantom public*. New York: Harcourt Brace Jovanovich.

Lovari, A., Kim, S., Vibber, K., & Kim, J-N. (2011). Digitisation's impacts on publics: Public knowledge and civic conversation. *PRism, 8*. Retrieved from www.prismjournal.org/homepage.html

Lovari, A., Martino, V., & Kim, J.-N. (2012). Citizens' relationships with a municipality and their communicative behaviors in negative civic issues. *International Journal of Strategic Communication, 6*, 17–33. doi:10.1080/1553118X.2011.634870

Mazzei, A., Kim, J.-N., & Dell'Oro, C. (2012). Strategic value of employee relationships and communicative actions: Overcoming corporate crisis with quality internal communication. *International Journal of Strategic Communication, 6*, 31–44. doi:1 0.1080/1553118X.2011.634869

McDonough, A. M. (1963). *Information economics and management systems*. New York: McGraw-Hill.

McQuail, D. (1997). *Audience analysis*. Thousand Oaks, CA: Sage.

Ni, L., & Kim, J.-N. (2009). Classifying publics: Communication behaviors and problem-solving characteristics in controversial issues. *International Journal of Strategic Communication, 3*, 1–25. doi:10.1080/15531180903221261

Park, S. (2013). *Employee relational antecedents and consequences: Scouting and intrapreneurship of employee publics and their strategic values in effective organizations* (Unpublished master's thesis). Purdue University, West Lafayette, IN.

Power, P., Kubey, R., & Kiousis, S. (2002). Audience activity and passivity: An historical taxonomy. *Communication Yearbook, 26*, 1–45.

Price, V. (1992). *Public opinion*. Newbury Park. CA: Sage.

Ramanadhan, S., & Viswanath, K. (2006). Health and the information nonseeker: A profile. *Health communication, 20*, 131–139. doi:10.1207/s15327027hc2002_4

Rogers, E. M. (2003). *Diffusion of innovations* (5th ed.). New York: Free Press.

Schramm, W. (1971). The nature of communication between humans. In W. Schramm & D. F. Roberts (Eds.), *The process and effects of mass communication* (Rev. ed., pp. 3–53). Urbana: University of Illinois Press.

Shannon, C. E., & Weaver, W. (1949). *The mathematical theory of communication*. Urbana: University of Illinois Press.

Simon, H. A. (1956). Rational choice and the structure of the environment. *Psychological Review, 63*, 129–138.

Stoffels, J. D. (1994). *Strategic issues management: A comprehensive guide to environmental scanning*. Oxford, OH: Pergamon.

Tarrow, S. (1998). *Power in movement: Social movements and contentious politics* (2nd ed.). Cambridge, England: Cambridge University Press.

Vibber, K., & Kim, J.-N. (in press). Communicative activism and sociological public diplomacy: Causes and consequences of positive and negative megaphoning of hosted foreign publics and their impacts on public diplomacy outcomes. In G. J. Golan, D. Kinsey, & S.-U. Yang (Eds.), *Handbook of strategic public diplomacy*. New York City: Peter Lang Publishing.

Weick, K. (1995). *Sensemaking in organization*. Thousand Oaks, CA: Sage.

Yun, S.-H., & Vibber, K. (2012). The strategic values and communicative actions of Chinese students for sociological Korean public diplomacy. *International Journal of Strategic Communication, 6*, 77–92. doi:10.1080/1553118X.2011.6348

CHAPTER CONTENTS

4 Relational and Identity Processes in Communication

A Contextual and Meta-Analytical Review of Communication Accommodation Theory

Jordan Soliz

University of Nebraska–Lincoln

Howard Giles

University of California–Santa Barbara

Communication Accommodation Theory (CAT) has served as a cross-disciplinary framework for understanding the adjustments individuals make to create, maintain, or decrease social distance in interactions. We provide a systematic review of CAT by examining 149 articles (1973–2010) to identify categories and trends in the contexts of inquiry, sample characteristics, and locus of assessment. Next, we summarize a meta-analysis of a subset of these articles ($k = 76$, $N = 18,382$) to identify effect sizes for specific behaviors (e.g., nonaccommodation, reluctant accommodation) and correlates of these behaviors (e.g., quality of contact, relational solidarity). Theoretical and methodological considerations are discussed.

Over the years, a number of theoretical frameworks have been developed for understanding how and why speakers adjust to each other's communicative styles (Shepard, Giles, & Le Poire, 2001; Street & Giles, 1982). Of these, communication accommodation theory (CAT) has attracted, arguably, the most cross-disciplinary, international research, including publications in multiple languages (Gallois & Giles, 1998; Giles & Ogay, 2006). It was developed in the 1970s (Giles, 1973; Giles, Taylor, & Bourhis, 1973) for predicting and explaining the adjustments individuals make to create, maintain, or decrease social distance in interaction, changes that are enacted for reasons that go beyond the mere exchange of referential information and emotions. Since those early days, CAT has been refined and elaborated a number of times to account for the dynamics of interpersonal and intergroup communication (Gallois & Giles, 1998; Giles, Willemyns, Gallois, & Anderson, 2007).

Originally a sociopsychological model exploring accent and bilingual shifts in interactions, CAT has now expanded into an "interdisciplinary model of relational and identity processes in communicative interaction" (Coupland &

Jaworski, 1997, pp. 241–242). It explores the different ways in which communicators accommodate, their motivations for doing so, and the consequences arising from these adjustments. Although language remains a central focus of the theory, discursive structures and nonverbal communication behaviors, as well as other communicative aspects of identity (such as dress and hairstyle), can also be understood from a CAT perspective (Coupland, Coupland, Giles, & Henwood, 1988; Giles & Wadleigh, 2008). Given the life of this theory and the various theoretical developments, we believe it is an appropriate time to subject CAT-based research to a systematic contextual review and an analysis of effects of accommodative behaviors with the purpose of identifying important conceptual, theoretical, and methodological considerations for future research. We first provide a brief history of the development and tenets of CAT, including some of the cumulatively unique features of this theory and the rationale and objectives for the analysis reported here.

Development and Basic Principles of CAT

CAT originated in the early 1970s as speech accommodation theory (Giles, 1973; Giles et al., 1973) with the goal of understanding shifts in speech styles particularly focusing on accents and dialects. In this early development, the theory introduced its core concepts of accommodation and two of these, *convergence* and *divergence*, are probably the most recognizable in this early stage of the theory. Convergence has been defined as a strategy whereby individuals adapt their communicative behaviors in such a way as to become more similar to their interlocutor's behavior. Typically, this is done to seek approval, affiliation, and/or interpersonal similarity as a manner of reducing social distance. As such, converging speakers are generally viewed more favorably than diverging and maintaining speakers and are perceived as more efficient and cooperative in their communications. Converging to a common linguistic style also improves the effectiveness of communication; this, in turn, has been associated with increased predictability of the other and, hence, lower uncertainty, interpersonal anxiety, and heightened mutual understanding (Gudykunst, 1995). Increasing similarity in communicative behavior such as speech rate increases both speakers' perceived attractiveness as well as their ability to gain addressees' compliance (Buller, LePoire, Aune, & Eloy, 1992). In addition, older adults who report that others generally accommodate them have higher self-esteem and life satisfaction than those who report that others do not generally accommodate them (Giles, McCann, Ota, & Noels, 2002). Among the different accommodative strategies that speakers use to achieve these relational and identity goals, convergence has been the most extensively studied and can be considered the historical core of CAT (Giles, 1973). Conversely, the strategy of divergence leads to an accentuation of speech and nonverbal differences between the self and the other. Often (but not always) the motive behind divergence is precisely the desire to emphasize distinctiveness from one's interlocutor, expressively highlighting contrasting group identities. A phenomenon similar to divergence is *maintenance*, in which a person persists in his or her original style, perhaps for reasons of authenticity or consistency, regardless of the communicative behavior of the interlocutor (Bourhis, 1979).

In the 1980s, the theory was applied to multiple contexts in order to examine differences in use and perceptions of accommodation between social groups (primarily focusing on age and ethnicity/culture). Coupland, Coupland, Giles, and Henwood (1988) elaborated on the theory to include multiple sociolinguistic encoding strategies as part of the repertoire of accommodative behaviors, including discourse (or topic) management and interpretability strategies. As such, the theory was now conceptualized as *communication* accommodation theory as it included an array of terms of a wide range of linguistic, paralinguistic (pitch, tempo), and nonverbal features (smiling, gazing) representing general levels of accommodative or nonaccommodative behaviors.

From this time on, researchers have developed and applied CAT to various contexts, resulting in a theory that attends to both interpersonal and intergroup dynamics of interactions by examining the association between accommodative behaviors and various relational and identity outcomes. The theory predicts that people may modify communication based on personal, idiosyncratic characteristics of a conversational partner. For example, knowing that a friend is very sensitive about certain political topics, one might avoid these in conversation. On the other hand, there are times when communication is influenced by social identities (race/ethnicity, religion, age, gender). In this way, we can make communication adjustments to show respect for or affiliation with the other's group in an attempt to transcend group boundaries. On other occasions, speakers may be strategically nonaccommodative (diverge) to demonstrate distinctiveness and, perhaps, pride in their social identity (Harwood & Giles, 2005). Oftentimes, such psycholinguistic distinctiveness is premised on communicative (self-)stereotypes an individual may have for the way his or her own group communicates, as well as corresponding (other) stereotypes attending the outgroup's perceived communicative attributes.

With this growth has come a complexity as various models and conceptualizations of accommodative behaviors have been introduced in the research to apply to various contexts (e.g., intergenerational, interethnic; Gallois, Ogay, & Giles, 2005). Across the studies and within these various contexts, scholars have used various labels and categories of CAT-based behaviors to assess how communication use is associated with interpersonal or intergroup attitudes, serves as a barometer of the level of social distance between interlocutors, or affects/reflects relational solidarity. For the purposes of this analysis, we have conceptualized these behaviors into four broad categories: accommodation, nonaccommodation, reluctant accommodation, and avoidant communication. The categories are based on previous taxonomies of accommodative behaviors and allow for investigation of both "traditional" (e.g., nonaccommodation) and relatively newer behaviors (e.g., avoidant communication) present in the empirical landscape of the theory. Within each of these categories, there are tactics that could (and should) be the subject of future scrutiny. However, these four broad categories provide a relatively parsimonious synthesis of behaviors in the CAT-based research.

Accommodation in the theory name is a more general term to represent various behaviors. However, within the empirical research and for the purposes of our analysis, *accommodation* refers to behaviors in which one or both of the individuals enact (or are perceived to enact) positive-oriented or conversationally appropriate behavior (e.g., appropriate topics of conversation) toward the other person. In research, this has been conceptualized as behaviors such as the aforementioned convergence, appropriate accommodation, and accommodative involvement. Central to this behavior is the notion that individuals have attuned their communication accurately to the needs and/or desires of the conversational partner. *Nonaccommodation* refers to behaviors typically categorized as underaccommodation in which individuals fail to attune their communication to others or overaccommodation in which individuals "overshoot" the needs or desires of a conversational partner. For instance, in the intergenerational context, underaccommodation is represented by painful self-disclosures (Coupland, Coupland, Giles, Henwood, & Wiemann, 1988), a problematic behavior in which young adults feel uncomfortable with older adults' disclosure of bereavement, health, feelings of isolation, and other more negatively valenced topics. Overaccommodation, on the other hand, has been highlighted by patronizing communication (slower, less complex speech) on the part of young adults based on negative age-based stereotypes of older adults. Not only is this a less satisfying behavior but continued exposure can also have negative effects on the older adult's self-concept and well-being (Ryan, Giles, Bartolucci, & Henwood, 1986). Because the empirical has investigated these behaviors at various levels of abstraction, we combine these into a general category of nonaccommodation for the current analysis.

Behaviors in which accommodation is based on norms of respect, obligation, and/or social hierarchies are categorized as *reluctant accommodation*. Although an individual may attune their conversational style to others, it is not done so as an attempt for relational closeness or affinity. Rather, this communication style is based on situation or cultural norms and is, therefore, not typically evaluated positively by the speaker. Finally, documented in certain encounters is *avoidant communication* (Ota, Giles, & Somera, 2007) in which interlocutors, moved unconsciously by negative stereotypes or, more overtly, by prior unfortunate experiences, wish to end the conversation as quickly as feasible and avoid future such interactions by withholding or constraining communication.

Given the extensive empirical work devoted to CAT and its appearance in encyclopedias and dictionaries across the social sciences, it has been the recipient of a variety of supportive intellectual evaluations in recent years (Griffin, 2009; Littlejohn, 1999). Likewise, multiple reviews of CAT have focused on the theoretical development (Gallois et al., 2005) and potential application of the theory across multiple contexts (Barker & Giles, 2003; Boggs & Giles, 1999; Harwood, Soliz, & Lin, 2006; Holland & Gentry, 1999). Although valuable, these reviews have been narrative in nature in that they are based on subjective assessments of the literature and empirical studies. Thus, the empirical work on CAT has not been subjected to a systematic assessment of contexts of inquiry and effect-size analysis of correlates of accommodative behavior. This type of analysis will allow us to integrate the statistical findings of the research to provide a quantitative assessment of accommodative behaviors (Allen, 2009), which is important for evaluation and/or refinement of theory (Ellis, 2010). In the following section, we outline our objectives of the current study.

Objectives of the Current Study and Research Questions

The first objective of this study is to summarize the various areas of inquiry for which CAT has been a guiding theoretical framework, including the methodological and conceptual trends that have developed over the years. As Griffin (2009) suggests, CAT's strength has been the development in the scope of behavior and focus of inquiry (purpose, context, correlates, intervening variables) as well as the cross-disciplinary utility of the research. However, we have yet to have a specific analysis of these contextual and disciplinary foci:

RQ 1: In what contexts has CAT-based research been applied?

Given the development of CAT, the linguistic and social underpinnings of the theory, and its multidisciplinary utility, it is not surprising that researchers have adopted a variety of empirical methods for assessing the phenomenon of interest. Although formulated as a traditional, logical-empirical framework, research has ranged from more qualitative research (Cretchley, Gallois, Chenery, & Smith, 2010) to various quantitative approaches. In the quantitative realm, many CAT-based studies have examined differences in levels or perceived levels of accommodative behaviors across various contexts (cultural groups, generational cohorts). Additionally, a great deal of research has been correlational in nature, by positioning accommodative behaviors as predictors/causes of certain outcomes, or accommodative behaviors as the outcomes themselves. Some of these outcomes or predictors have been individual or dyadic in nature (e.g., relational satisfaction), whereas others have more macro-level attributes (e.g., attitudes toward social groups). What is clear is that CAT-based research has focused on a variety of constructs associated with accommodative behaviors. In assessing the development and utility of CAT, it is important to identify the various constructs associated with accommodative behaviors. Thus, our second and primary objective in this review is to synthesize the results of the quantitative research. Our first step in addressing this objective is to identify variables that have been investigated as correlates (the outcomes and/or predictors) of accommodative behaviors in the empirical research. Foregrounded in our discussion on the development of CAT is the idea that specific accommodative behaviors are likely associated with specific relational or identity outcomes (e.g., convergence often associated with communication satisfaction). In fact, a feature of theory is that its testable propositions formalize relationships among motives for, forms of, and outcomes arising from accommodative strategies (Giles, Willemyns, et al., 2007). Thus, formulating a summary of the quantitative research requires synthesizing the effect sizes across salient correlates. As a first step in this, however, we must *identify* the correlates of CAT behaviors:

> **RQ 2:** What are the correlates of behaviors in CAT-based quantitative research?

The next step for our second objective is to address the *actual* strength of effect size in the research across various accommodative behaviors and the aforementioned correlates. As previously mentioned, reviews of CAT have been narrative in nature in that scholars have provided overviews of the development and tenets of the theory as well as key findings and opportunities or suggestions for future inquiries. Yet, in all of these, the empirical work has never been subjected to a meta-analytical review of the effect sizes. Thus, this type of analysis is a necessary next step in reviewing and evaluating CAT as it provides a metric (strength and variability of effect sizes) to evaluate the role of accommodative behaviors in our interactions, relational solidarity, and salient behavioral outcomes. In doing so, we can also identify future directions and methodological considerations for subsequent research. Given our conceptualization of the four categories of accommodative behavior, we are interested in general effects for each type of behavior as well as the effects specific to the correlates of these behaviors.

> **RQ 3:** What is the overall effect size of accommodation, nonaccommodation, reluctant accommodation, and avoidant communication across correlates in CAT-based empirical studies?

Finally, given the contextual scope of the research and the variability in methods, a meta-analytical approach allows us to identify potential methodological moderators of effect sizes. Identifying these moderators and potential effects will benefit the next stage of CAT scholarship, as researchers can control or, at minimum, address any factors that may confound the research findings. In this review, we focus on four specific moderators. *Locus of assessment* represents the nature of the inquiry in terms of the focal person of the inquiry (self vs. other ratings). *Nature of communication* refers to the evaluation of communication in terms of actual or perceived communication. *Sample type* refers to the makeup of the sample as there is variation given presumed convenience samples (undergraduate students) and perhaps more focused sampling (working professionals). *Research design* captures the difference, if any, between correlational and experimental designs.

> **RQ 4:** How, if at all, is the effect size across various accommodative behaviors moderated by (a) locus of assessment, (b) nature of communication, (c) sample type, or (d) research design?

Method

Literature Search

To locate articles to include in our analysis (as of December 2010), we searched the electronic databases PsycINFO, Communication and Mass Media Complete, and Academic Search Premier. Initially, we completed these searches using keywords (e.g., "communication accommodation theory," "overaccommodation") and names of scholars who are well known for their CAT-based research. From this initial search, we verified that any sources obtained were indeed CAT-based. Next, we cross-checked the results of our literature search with references in recent review chapters on CAT as well as our knowledge of the current research. After reviewing the literature, we excluded any articles that were solely narrative reviews resulting in 149 empirical articles (qualitative and quantitative) for our general analysis.

Coding Categories

For each article, we coded for basic information on study characteristics such as author, year of publication, publication source, type of analysis (quantitative vs. qualitative), and sample size (if applicable). In the following sections, we outline additional coding categories: contexts of inquiry (RQ 1), correlates (RQ 2) of CAT-based research, and methodological artifacts (RQ 4). For these categories, we went through a process akin to a constant-comparative method (Glaser & Strauss, 1967) by reviewing articles to develop an initial set of categories and refining these as the literature was reviewed. Next, with the assistance from a research assistant, approximately 10% of the relevant articles were reviewed to determine if final categories warranted revisions. After refining the categories, another research assistant unfamiliar with the goals of the study coded each of the categories across approximately 10% of the studies as a reliability check. In addition to calculating percent agreement, we calculated reliability coefficients using kappa that take into account chance agreement. As a whole, percent agreement ranged from 81.25% to 100% and the reliability coefficient ranged from .54 to 1.00 (avg. $\kappa = .80$), indicating acceptable to very high reliability. Central to the objective of this study, we also assessed an effect size for each study. We provide detailed information on each category in the following sections.

Contexts of inquiry.   One objective of this review was to identify and summarize the various contexts in which CAT has been applied. The final coding framework consists of ten categories (see Table 4.1). As the name suggests, *Culture/Ethnicity* (CE) refers to studies in which the focus was on variations in attitudes, perceptions, and behaviors of cultural/ethnic groups. This category also includes studies with an ethnolinguistic component. *Computer-Mediated Communication* (CMC) represents research on communication via various

Table 4.1 Categories for Contexts of Inquiry

Context of Inquiry	% of Research Overall (k = 149)	% of Research 2000–2010 (k = 80)
Culture/Ethnicity	40.94% (n = 61)	46.25% (n = 37)
Computer-Mediated Communication	4.70% (n = 7)	6.25% (n = 5)
Educational/ Instructional	4.70% (n = 7)	3.75% (n = 3)
Family	13.42% (n = 20)	23.75% (n = 19)
Gender/Sexual Identity	13.42% (n = 20)	11.25% (n = 9)
Health	12.75% (n = 19)	11.25% (n = 9)
Inter-(intra) generational	32.89% (n = 49)	33.75% (n = 27)
Legal	10.07% (n = 15)	15.00% (n = 12)
Media	4.03% (n = 6)	3.75% (n = 3)
Professional/ Organizational	12.08% (n = 18)	8.75% (n = 7)

Note: Percentage of research sums to more than 100% because studies could be categorized in multiple contexts.

communication technologies. Because of the span of the empirical research, we coded based on what could be considered communication technologies at the time of the study (e.g., answering machines in the early 1990s). Studies were coded as *Educational/Instructional* (EI) if there was a *specific* focus on the educational context or instructional (i.e., classroom) interactions. *Family* (F) refers to studies in which familial behavior or the family context was at the heart of the study. The category *Gender/Sexual Identity* (GSI) represents those studies focusing on gendered communication, gender differences, or sexual identity/ orientation. Although many studies have examined gender differences as part of the analysis, only those with specific hypotheses, research questions, or clear objectives (a priori designs/analysis) concerning gender or sexual identity were coded in this category. The category *Health* (H) corresponds with those studies in which health-related interactions were investigated and/or the study included a medical or health-related context. *Inter(intra)generational* (IG) refers to studies focusing on communication or attitudes between and, sometimes, within generations. *Legal* (L) includes those studies taking place in a legal context as well as policing and police–civilian interactions. The category *Media (M)* represents research focusing on mass media or effects of mass media. Finally, *Professional/Organizational* (PO) includes research centering on workplace interactions, other organizational settings, or those meant to simulate professional interactions (e.g., interviews).

These 10 contexts are not mutually exclusive (see Table 4.1). For instance, a study investigating accommodation in grandparent–grandchild relationships

Table 4.2 Correlates of Quantitative Studies (k = 76)

Category of Correlates and Examples (% of research)
Compliance (C): compliant actions, message agreement, persuasiveness (13.16%)
Communication Apprehension (CA): intergroup anxiety, communication anxiety (2.63%)
Convergence (CON): convergence/divergence, language adjustment, language choice (6.58%)
Credibility (CT): credibility, guilt/innocence, trust (19.74%)
Evaluation of Groups (EG): ingroup/outgroup attitudes, stereotyping, previous contact with outgroup, norms of evaluation (17.11%)
Evaluation of Individual (EI): sociability, attractiveness, general positive/negative valence, communication skills (21.05%)
Group Salience (GS): ingroup/outgroup identity (9.21%)
Personal Communication (PC): self-disclosure, communicative responsiveness (3.95%)
Power/Status (PS): power, social status, superiority (3.95%)
Quality of Contact (QC): communication satisfaction, immediacy, evaluation of conversation (34.21%)
Relational Solidarity (RS): relational satisfaction, closeness, common ingroup identity, intimacy (19.74%)
Well-Being (WB): self-esteem, life satisfaction, mental health (2.63%)

(Soliz & Harwood, 2006) would represent both the intergenerational and the family contexts. A few studies were not coded for one of the specific contexts as their assessment focused on general conversation or interactions void of one of the specific contexts (e.g., Aune & Kikuchi, 1993).

Correlates.   In addition to the contextual variability of CAT-based research, the second objective of this review included identifying constructs and variables put forth in the research as predictors or outcomes of accommodative behaviors. Obviously, these apply only to the studies that are quantitative in nature. Given the diversity in these variables, we followed techniques in other meta-analytical reports (Kite, Stockdale, Whitley, & Johnson, 2005; Schrodt, Witt, & Messersmith, 2008) and collapsed the variables into general categories of correlates. Categories and descriptions of the correlates are presented in Table 4.2.

Locus of assessment.   Each study was coded for the type of measurement based on the locus of assessment. Studies were coded for participant's assessment of their *own* behavior, assessment of *other's* behavior *directed toward them* (or a combination of both), or if they evaluated an actual or hypothesized interaction from a *third person* perspective. In this last category, participants rated features of the conversation or individuals in an actual or hypothetical conversation often in an experimental paradigm.

Nature of communication.   Studies in which participants were asked to reflect on past or general experiences in communicating with others were categorized as *perceived* communication in contrast to other studies in which individuals responded to *actual* communication (face-to-face, text, audio).

Sample.   Two categories were coded pertaining to the sample of the study. First, we coded the "origin" of the sample. In most cases, we coded for country of origin unless the researchers were clearly focusing on an ethnic/cultural group within a country. For instance, E. Jones, Gallois, Callan, and Barker (1995) sampled Australian students who had "Australian-born parents and grandparents" and "overseas students of Chinese ethnic background" (p. 440). In this case, the sample would be coded as both Australian and Chinese. We also coded for sample "type" as either *students, professionals, random population,* or a combination of the three.

Research design.   Each study was classified as a *correlational or* experimental design.

Effect size.   We calculated an effect size using the correlation coefficient r (for discussion of advantages of r, see Rosenthal & DiMatteo, 2001). In calculating our effect size, we followed recommended procedures for meta-analysis and made appropriate adjustments when possible (e.g., correlational corrections based on reliability coefficients; Hunter & Schmidt, 1990; Lipsey & Wilson, 2000). All effect size calculations and conversions to r were based on the best available data in the articles. In the very few cases when nonsignificant results were presented as "nonsignificant" without corresponding statistical information, we treated the effect size as zero (Lipsey & Wilson, 2000). In these cases, this creates a more conservative estimate of the overall effect size. However, we believe it was more appropriate than simply dropping the study or imputing values based on other effect sizes because, in these cases, the overall effect may be inflated and not representative of the actual effect size.

As qualitative studies cannot be assessed for effect sizes, 104 studies with quantitative data remained. Of these, 32 were not included in the effect size coding and subsequent analysis as these studies did not include enough information, the complexity of the analysis did not allow for calculation of an appropriate effect size based on the purpose of this review, or the data were presented in more than one published study and, thus, were only coded once in terms of the effect. Table 4.3 includes meta-analytical data for studies *included* in the effect size coding ($k = 76$). In the table, n refers to the sample size relevant to the calculated effect size. Typically, this is the same number as participants in the study. In some cases, this was different than the number of participants (e.g., analysis of pairs of participants).

Table 4.3 Meta-Analytical Data

Author(s)	Year	n	Overall Effect Size, r (k =76)	Specific Accommodative Behaviors			
				A, r (k =58)	NA, r (k =32)	RA, r (k =22)	AC, r (k =12)
Anderson, Harwood, & Hummert (Study 1)	2005	217	.620	.520			
Anderson, Harwood, & Hummert (Study 2)	2005	269	.455	.455			
Aune & Kikuchi	1993	286	.179	.179			
Barker	2007	400	.321		.321		
Barker, Choi, Giles, & Hajek	2008–2009	180	.418	.418			
Barker, Giles, Hajek, Ota, Noels, Lim, & Somera	2008	684	.417	.417			
Bilous & Krause	1988	60	.660	.660			
Bonnesen & Hummert	2002	127	.740		.740		
Brown, Giles, & Thakerar	1985	120	.230	.230			
Buller & Aune	1992	252	.237	.237			
Bunz & Campbell	2004	121	.280	.280			
Buzzanell, Burrell, Stafford, & Berkowitz	1996	129	.160	.160			
Cai, Giles, & Noels	1988	197	.224	.248	.220	.258	.173
Casasanto, Jasmin, & Casasanto	2010	62	.429	.429			
Chen & Cegala	1994	58	.356	.356			
Crook & Booth	1997	38	.378	.378			
Dixon, Schell, Giles, & Drogos	2008	191	.157	.157			
Dixon, Tredoux, Durrheim, & Foster	1994	129	.159	.159			
Dorjee, Giles, & Barker	2011	158	.390	.390			
Fowler & Soliz	2010	269	.344	.423	.107	.228	

(Continued)

Table 4.3 (Continued)

Author(s)	Year	n	Overall Effect Size, r (k=76)	Specific Accommodative Behaviors			
				A, r (k=58)	NA, r (k=32)	RA, r (k=22)	AC, r (k=12)
Fox & Giles	1996	149	.230		.230		
Gevorgyan	2010	96	.234	.234			
Giles, Ballard, & McCann	2002	393	.356		.372	.451	.246
Giles, Dailey, Sarkar, & Makoni	2007	232	.379			.196	.561
Giles, Fortman, Honeycutt, & Ota	2003	514	.299	.337	.26		
Giles, Fox, & Smith (Study 1)	1993	183	.168		.168		
Giles, Hajek, Stoitsova, & Choi	2010	399	.415			.380	.45
Giles, Liang, Noels, & McCann	2001	307	.228	.341	.226	.158	.186
Giles, Makoni, & Dailey	2005	336	.772			.806	.737
Giles, Noels, Williams, Ota, Lim, Ng, Ryan, & Somera	2003	731	.190	.190			
Giles, Ryan, & Anas	2008	240	.367	.240	.258	.606	.362
Giles, Taylor, & Bourhis	1973	80	.192	.192			
Giles & Williams	1994	252	.202		.202		
Hajek, Barker, Giles, Makoni, Pecchioni, Louw-Potgieter, & Myers	2006	363	.406	.406			
Hajek, Giles, Barker, Lin, Zhang, & Hummert	2008	682	.420	.420			
Hajek, Giles, Barker, Makoni,& Choi	2008	400	.356	.356			
Hajek, Villagren, & Wittenberg-Lyles	2007	112	.335	.335			
Harwood	2000	327	.487	.461	.534	.468	

Study	Year	N					
Harwood & Giles	1996	210	.161		.161		
Harwood, Giles, Fox, Ryan, & Williams	1993	222	.374	.374			
Harwood, Hewstone, Paolini, & Voci (Study 2)	2005	100	.518	.518			
Harwood, Raman & Hewstone	2006	198	.195	.234	.157		
Harwood, Ryan, Giles, & Tysoski	1997	162	.223		.223		
Hornsey & Gallois (Study 2)	1998	123	.130	.130			
Larsen, Martin, & Giles	1977	73	.255	.255			
Lin & Harwood	2003	208	.484	.533	.337	.582	
McCann, Cargile, Giles, & Cui	2004	554	.257	.242	.166	.413	.207
McCann, Dailey, Giles, & Ota	2005	137	.365			.303	.427
McCann & Giles	2006	348	.159	.134	.212	.130	
McCann & Giles	2007	267	.237	.108	.241	.361	
McCann, Ota, Giles, & Caraker	2003	341	.442	.264	.493	.545	.467
Myers, Giles, Reid, & Nabi	2008	112	.575	.575			
Namy, Nygaard, & Sauertieg	2002	64	.287	.287			
Noels, Giles, Cai, & Turay	1999	133	.271	.291	.283	.261	
Ota, Giles, & Somera	2007	509	.130	.130			
Pearce, Giles, Hájek, Barker, & Choi	2012	446	.377	.377			.248
Rittenour & Soliz	2009	190	.507		.507		
Robertson & Murachver	2003	43	.277	.277			
Ryan, Bourhis, & Knops	1991	186	.156		.156		
Ryan, Hamilton, & See	1994	151	.202		.202		
Ryan, Maclean, & Orange	1994	120	.276		.276		
Simard, Taylor, & Giles	1976	60	.524	.524			

(Continued)

Table 4.3 (Continued)

Author(s)	Year	n	Overall Effect Size, r (k=76)	Specific Accommodative Behaviors			
				A, r (k=58)	NA, r (k=32)	RA, r (k=22)	AC, r (k=12)
Speer, Denes, & Giles	2013	133	.771	.869	.720	.725	
Soliz & Harwood	2003	102	.284	.183	.375	.293	
Soliz & Harwood	2006	369	.241		.241		
Soliz, Ribarsky, Marko Harrigan, & Tye-Williams	2010	134	.320	.355		.285	
Soliz, Thorson, & Rittenour	2009	139	.357	.357			
Stoitsova, Choi, Giles, Barker, & Hajek	2009	138	.595	.595			
Street, Brady, & Putnam	1983	96	.479	.479			
Thomson (Study 1)	2006	72	.492	.492			
Thomson (Study 2)	2006	38	.525	.525			
Watson & Gallois	1998	134	.325	.325			
Williams & Garret	2002	490	.147	.168	.123	.128	.168
Williams & Giles	1996	126	.546	.560	.519	.560	
Williams, Ota, Giles, Pierson, Gallois, et al.	1997	1631	.114	.136	.076	.131	
Ytsma & Giles	1997	80	.171		.171		

Note: n = sample size for each study; k = number of studies included in the analysis; A = accommodation; NA = nonaccommodation; RA = reluctant accommodation; AC = avoidant communication.

Statistical Analysis

We followed established guidelines for effect size analysis (Allen, 2009; Ellis, 2010; Hunter & Schmidt, 1990; Lipsey & Wilson, 2000). First, we calculated a mean effect size across the studies using the inverse variance weight and a fixed-effects model to calculate a weighted average as our reported effect size. In presenting the effect size, we include a standard error (*SE*), 95% confidence intervals of the effect size (CI), number of studies (*k*), and sample size (*N* or *n*). Second, it is often the case that effect sizes vary across studies, and, in fact, variability in effect size is a stipulating condition to test for our potential methodological moderators (RQ 4). Thus, to test for homogeneity among the effect sizes, we computed a *Q* statistic with a significant *Q* indicating heterogeneity across the individual effects. Third, variability among effect sizes warrants a random effects analysis, and we computed a new effect that included a random effects variance component. Fourth, if there was significant heterogeneity across the studies, we calculated effect sizes for the four methodological artifacts to test for moderation: (a) locus of assessment, (b) nature of communication, (c) sample type, or (d) research design.

Prior to addressing RQ 3, in which we calculate the effects for the specific behaviors across various correlates, we computed an overall effect for each study. In doing so, we averaged any multiple effects in a study into one *overall* effect for the study as a reference and comparison point for individual behavioral effects (for recommended procedures, see Lipsey & Wilson, 2000). This step was performed to address the fact that studies often included various behaviors and outcomes (i.e., correlates). Collapsing across behaviors and outcomes accounts for interdependence among the various effect sizes in a study. Therefore, in presenting our results, we first provide a general *overall* effect size analysis as well as effect sizes for each of the four behaviors (accommodation, nonaccommodation, reluctant accommodation, avoidant communication) collapsed across the various correlates. Given that we were assessing effects across various types of behaviors and outcomes to provide this general assessment, effect sizes were converted to absolute values prior to calculating the overall effect size. As such, these initial effects are simply magnitudes of the effect size, and, thus, this initial reporting of results is limited in that it does not take into account support (or failure to support) theoretical tenets of the theory (e.g., perceived appropriate accommodation is associated with communication satisfaction). However, it is necessary to address interdependence of multiple effects in a study and allow for exploration of moderation effects given the inclusion of a large number of studies in each effect size calculation. To actually address RQ 3, we calculated and report separate effect sizes for each behavior across the correlates.

Results

Our first research question addressed the contexts of inquiry of CAT-based research. As indicated in Table 4.1 (representing all 149 studies), research focusing on cultural, ethnic, or ethnolinguistic factors (40.94%) as well as those focusing on the inter/intragenerational context (32.89%) make up a majority of the studies using CAT. This is not surprising considering the origins and early developmental trajectories of the theory. Although CAT is more than 40 years old, its interdisciplinary influence and utility is clearly evident. For instance, half (53.69%) of the studies have been published or completed since 2000. Although the two aforementioned categories still dominate the contexts in this span, there has been a notable increase in the proportion of research focusing on *family* and *legal* contexts. Further, a review of scholarly outlets demonstrate the scope of disciplinary focus as CAT has been published in 67 different journals spanning the communication, psychology, linguistic, sociology, organizational, marketing, medicine/health fields, and tourism fields, among others. Further, the "origin" of the sample represents more than 35 countries including ones in North America, Eastern and Western Europe, (South) East Asia, the Australiasia region, and Africa. In fact, more than 60% of the studies included samples outside of the United States. The geographic (and, thus, cultural) diversity of the samples supports the argument that CAT's emphasis on intergroup and interpersonal dimensions lends the theory to broad application as the tenets allow for consideration of macro-(cultural) and micro-(personal) aspects of interactions.

Two additional observations emerged from our analysis of the studies for this initial research question. First, although CAT is typically presented as a theory in the logical-empirical realm, there is considerable scholarship in which CAT is used as a theoretical and sensitizing framework for qualitative research. In fact, nearly 27% of the empirical articles we reviewed are qualitative inquiries or discourse analysis. Second, there is much variability in how accommodative behaviors are conceptualized and measured. We will return to these points in our discussion regarding considerations for future research.

Our second research question focused on the correlates of accommodative behavior in CAT-based research. As depicted in Table 4.2, we identified 12 general categories of correlates across the landscape of CAT research. Within these 12 categories, studies primarily focused on the role accommodative behaviors play in perceptions of *quality of contact, credibility,* general *evaluations of individuals* and *social groups,* and *relational solidarity.* Although not a correlate, a significant number of studies assessed *group differences* (e.g., age, culture) in use and/or perceptions of accommodative behaviors. This variable was present in 38.16% of the studies. We now focus on the effect-size analysis.

Overall Effect Size and General Effect Size for Specific Behaviors

Following the procedures outlined above, we found a significant, moderate overall effect size collapsed across behaviors and correlates, $r = .311$; $CI_{.95}$ [.296–.325], $SE = .007$, $k = 76$, $N = 18,382$. The sample of effect sizes was heterogenous, $Q = 416.820$, $p < .001$. The random effects analysis provides a similar mean effect with slightly larger confidence interval: $r = .335$, $CI_{.95}$ [.299–.371], $SE = .018$.

Given the heterogeneity across the sample, we examined the potential methodological moderating artifacts. There was a significant difference in effect sizes for locus of assessment, $Q = 101.870$, $p < .001$, suggesting it accounts for significant variability in the overall effect size: self ($r = .504$, $k = 7$, $n = 1,748$), other ($r = .363$, $k = 16$, $n = 4,673$), self and other ratings ($r = .253$, $k = 24$, $n = 8,366$), or third-person perspective ($r = .275$, $k = 29$, $n = 3,547$). We also investigated the type of sample as a potential point of variability among effect size. There was a significant difference in effect sizes when comparing solely student samples ($r = .321$, $k = 55$, $n = 14,156$) to samples that included professionals or participants from the general population ($r = .296$, $k = 21$, $n = 3,814$), $Q = 10.575$, $p < .01$. There was significant difference in effect sizes when comparing experimental and correlational designs, $Q = 6.492$, $p < .05$, with correlational designs ($r = .320$, $k = 48$, $n = 14,669$) demonstrating slightly larger effect sizes than experimental designs ($r = .273$, $k = 28$, $n = 3,713$). There was also a significant difference comparing studies that investigated actual communication ($r = .275$, $k = 33$, $n = 4,206$) versus perceived communication ($r = .321$, $k = 43$, $n = 14,176$), $Q = 6.731$, $p < .05$). In reviewing this analysis, the final two methodological artifacts—research design and nature of communication—are captured in the locus of assessment analysis as the third-person perspective accounts for nearly all of the experimental designs and those investigating actual communication as opposed to perceived communication. Due to space limitations and because locus of assessment provides more differentiation, as it includes four categories of methodological artifacts, we do not include separate effect decompositions for these two methodological variables in the remainder of the results. We now turn our attention to effect sizes for specific behaviors. Again, these should be interpreted with caution as they are collapsed across correlates and, thus, simply provide a general magnitude of effect.

Accommodation. There was a significant, moderate effect size, $r = .302$, $CI_{.95}$ [.28–.318], $SE = .008$, $k = 58$, $N = 14,306$. The sample of effect sizes was heterogenous, $Q = 301.282$, $p < .001$. Again, a random effects analysis demonstrates similar results: $r = .337$, $CI_{.95}$ [.297–.378], $SE = .021$. There was a significant difference in effect sizes for locus of assessment, $Q = 63.322$, $p < .001$: self ($r = .495$, $k = 3$, $n = 644$), other ($r = .374$, $k = 13$, $n = 3,762$), self/other ($r = .251$, $k = 23$, $n = 7,973$), and third-person perspective ($r = .306$, $k = 19$, $n = 1,927$). Variation was also found in effect sizes of the different sample types, $Q = 11.698$, $p < .001$: student ($r = .314$, $k = 43$, $n = 11,037$) and nonstudent ($r = .283$, $k = 15$, $n = 2,920$)

Nonaccommodation. For nonaccommodation, there was also a significant, moderate effect size, $r = .245$; $CI_{.95}$ [.224–.265], $SE = .01$, $k = 32$, $N = 9,357$. Test of homogeneity demonstrated variability among the sample: $Q = 206.923$, $p < .001$; random effects analysis: $r = .288$, $CI_{.95}$ [.232–.343], $SE = .028$. Locus of assessment again emerged as a significant source of variation: $Q = 22.268$,

$p < .001$: other ($r = .298$, $k = 4$, $n = 1,157$), self/other ($r = .259$, $k = 18$, $n = 6,580$), and third-person perspective ($r = .250$, $k = 10$, $n = 1,620$). Variation was also found in effect sizes of the different sample types, $Q = 7.566$, $p < .01$: student ($r = .226$, $k = 19$, $n = 6,457$) and nonstudent ($r = .287$, $k = 13$, $n = 2,900$).

Reluctant accommodation.   Again, there was a significant, moderate effect for reluctant accommodation, $r = .324$, $CI_{.95}$ [.301–.346], $SE = .012$, $k = 22$, $N = 7,304$. Test of homogeneity demonstrated variability among the sample: $Q = 281.77$, $p < .001$; random effects analysis: $r = .364$, $CI_{.95}$ [.276–.450], $SE = .044$. Significant variation was present for locus of assessment, $Q = 14.185$, $p < .001$: self ($r = .416$, $k = 5$, $n = 1,373$) and self/other ($r = .303$, $k = 17$, $n = 5,931$). However, there was no significant variation based on sample type, $Q = .339$, $p > .05$: nonstudent ($r = .313$, $k = 8$, $n = 2,077$) and student ($r = .328$, $k = 14$, $n = 5,227$).

Avoidant communication.   For avoidant communication, there was a significant, moderate effect, $r = .340$; $CI_{.95}$ [.308–.372], $SE = .016$, $k = 12$, $N = 3,759$; $Q = 116.445$, $p < .001$; random effects analysis: $r = .352$, $CI_{.95}$[.247–.458], $SE = .054$. There was significant variation for both locus of assessment, $Q = 72.084$, $p < .001$, and sample type, $Q = 19.19$, $p < .001$: self ($r = .558$, $k = 4$, $n = 1,104$), self/other ($r = .250$, $k = 8$, $n = 2655$), student ($r = .386$, $k = 8$, $n = 2,699$), and nonstudent ($r = .222$, $k = 4$, $n = 1,060$).

Effect Sizes for Correlates (RQ 3)

A main focus of the meta-analysis was to isolate specific effects of each correlate for the four types of behaviors as a way to assess effect sizes representing tenets of the theory. Results are presented in Table 4.4. Given the focus on the behavior and the specific correlate, this analysis is based on both the magnitude and direction of the individual effects in the study. We focused on correlates present in at least 10% of the studies used for the meta-analysis (see Table 4.2): compliance, credibility, evaluation of groups, evaluation of individuals, quality of contact, and relational solidarity. Effect sizes were calculated with higher scores representing more frequent or greater enactment of the behavior. Likewise, higher scores represent a more positive orientation for the correlate when applicable (e.g., higher scores on quality of communication indicate satisfaction with the interaction). Finally, we also included effect sizes for group difference. Results presented in Table 4.4 demonstrated that effect sizes ranged from small to large, although one nonsignificant effect emerged.

Discussion

Over the course of its lifespan and through various developmental trajectories, communication accommodation theory (CAT) has proved to be a broad-reaching theory offering a comprehensive explanation of the cognitive

Table 4.4 Meta-Analytical Data for Correlates and Group Difference

	C	CT	EG	EI	GD	QC	RS
Accommodation	.296	.592	.080	.340	.201	.446	.232
k	10	15	11	7	23	14	11
n	3,351	4,039	2,002	951	7,743	2,139	2,272
Nonaccommodation	—	—	−.133	−.206	.224	−.309	−.351
k	—	—	6	9	14	14	8
n	—	—	1,496	1,540	5,518	2,653	1,821
Reluctant Accommodation	—	—	−.166	—	.349	−.344	−.439
k	—	—	6	—	14	8	8
n	—	—	1,129	—	5,773	1,664	1,821
Avoidant Communication	—	—	−.07 (ns)	—	.359	−.500	—
k	—	—	3	—	11	3	—
n	—	—	760	—	3,527	768	—

Note: C = compliance; CT = credibility; EG = evaluation of groups; EI = evaluation of individuals; GD = group difference; QC = quality of contact; RS = relational solidarity. Unless indicated as nonsignificant (*ns*), all effect sizes are significant at $p < .01$. Effect sizes were calculated with higher scores representing a positive orientation for correlate when applicable (e.g., higher scores on QC indicate satisfaction with the interaction). Likewise, higher scores represent more frequent or greater enactment of behavior. For parsimony, we do not include results of random effects analysis or confidence intervals. Effect sizes are only provided for correlates that appeared in 10% or more of the studies.

antecedents and communicative variation in our interpersonal and intergroup interactions. Whereas other reviews have provided historical and in-depth overviews of the theory, the purpose of this analysis is to complete a systematic assessment of contexts, areas of inquiry, and overall effect size of accommodative behaviors. Our hope is that the information and findings provided here will serve as a resource and guide for scholars as they continue the application of CAT to various contexts.

Given the longevity and development of CAT, it is not surprising that this analysis confirmed the contextual diversity of the theory (RQ 1). Further, the methodological variety demonstrates the utility of CAT to guide studies from multiple methodological paradigms. Originally conceived in the logical-empirical tradition resulting in the various propositions put forth, we anticipated the large amount of quantitative CAT-based research. However, a substantial portion of the studies also used CAT as a sensitizing theory for qualitative, interpretive studies. In fact, we believe that is one of the interesting trajectories for future research as scholars find innovative ways to translate the tenets and propositions to a diverse methodological spectrum.

Our analysis of various correlates of the accommodative behaviors (RQ 3) indicate fairly robust effect sizes and demonstrate that the tenets of CAT are supported across the studies included in this review. First, there are direct relationships between accommodative behaviors and positive-oriented evaluations (quality of communication, relational solidarity) and outcomes (compliance, trust). Moreover, these effect sizes ranged from moderate to large effects based on conventional standards. Conversely, and in line with the tenets of CAT, there were negative relationships between nonaccommodation, reluctant accommodation, avoidant communication, and nearly all positive-oriented outcomes and evaluations. One trend evident in this analysis is the relatively smaller or nonsignificant effect sizes for evaluation of groups suggesting that, although features of an interaction may be associated with group-based evaluations, they are perhaps not as strong as those aspects of the individual or situation related to the specific context (quality of communication, evaluation of individual). In terms of effects for *group difference,* results demonstrate that uses and perceptions of accommodative behaviors are clearly dependent on attitudes and beliefs associate with social groups (e.g., cultural/ethnic groups, age groups).

The findings from this analysis and additional issues that emerged from the process of reviewing the literature pave the way for some methodological and theoretical considerations for the next iteration of CAT-based scholarship. We first discuss three general themes emerging from the analysis: heterogeneity of effect sizes, correlates and contexts of inquiry, and conceptualizing and operationalizing accommodation. Next, we discuss considerations for future research based on our assessment and reflection on the analysis and review of extant research. We conclude with a brief discussion of the limitations of this study, including how meta-analysis might be further incorporated into future reviews and development of CAT.

Heterogeneity of Effect Sizes

A benefit of an effect size analysis is that one can assess homogeneity of effects across research samples, and this is especially prudent for CAT-based inquiries given the diversity in samples across the studies. In this analysis, we primarily focused on two potential methodological artifacts that may be affecting the effect size of accommodative behaviors. The findings demonstrate that the locus of assessment and the type of sample may result in different effects of the accommodative behaviors (RQ 4). In general, studies that included solely self-ratings of behaviors demonstrated larger effect sizes. The comparative magnitude of other loci of assessment varied depending on the type of behavior (see Results section). As we discussed in the results sections, the locus of assessment also captured variation in two other methodological artifacts: research design and nature of communication. In general, correlational designs exhibit slightly larger effects than experimental designs. Likewise, studies assessing perceptions of communication demonstrate slightly larger effects than those assessing actual communication. Finally, variation exists in the type of sample used in the study in that, for the most part, samples that included nonstudent participants are likely to yield smaller (yet still moderate) effect sizes in overall behavior, although results suggest that this may depend on the specific type of behavior. In assessing nonaccommodation, for instance, the student samples have smaller effect sizes.

Obviously, these methodological artifacts are only some of myriad potential moderators for the effect size of accommodative behaviors. In fact, in our analyses of these moderators, there is still variation "leftover" (as indicated by a significant Q-statistic), signifying that there are other aspects of a sample that may have influenced accommodative effect sizes. For instance, research on intergenerational differences in enactment and perceptions of accommodation may be moderated by gender and/or ethnicity. Perhaps accommodation in patient–physician interactions is moderated by the country (and, thus, culture) of health care? These moderators not only may be characteristics of the sample (ethnicity/culture, gender, types of inquiries) but should also be theoretically derived factors (role/status of interlocutors, sociohistorical, or immediate context). Although the differences may be relatively small in some cases, the results of heterogeneity in our analysis provide rationale for researchers to investigate various moderating variables in their studies as a priori considerations in designing the study or post hoc analysis. Although investigating these moderators may be theoretically derived or exploratory in nature, the clear heterogeneity across samples in this analysis suggests this is an important step in further enhancing our understanding of the accommodative process.

In a similar vein, the results from analysis of specific correlates (RQ 3) suggests that effect sizes may vary based on predictor/outcome variables (correlates) or across different behaviors. For example, the effect for group difference is stronger when assessing reluctant accommodation compared to accommodation. As such, researchers may want to consider comparing effect sizes across various behaviors within a specific study with the goal of understanding factors that may differentiate the motivations, predictors, and outcomes of accommodative behaviors.

Correlates and Contexts of Inquiry

The findings from the current analysis of all of the empirical studies suggest that, although culture/ethnicity and inter- (or intra)generational contexts have historically been the primary domain of CAT research, the scope is broad and increasingly so in more recent years. For instance, CAT has been used more frequently to understand police–civilian interactions, health care, and family relationships. These are all areas which have received scholarly attention from other perspectives but for which CAT has been used to offer a novel framework. We believe there are also contexts in which CAT has not been applied (or minimally so) but could offer a useful theoretical perspective given the theory's joint interpersonal and intergroup focus. For instance, in the instructional context, CAT could be used to examine the motivation and relational or instructional outcomes (affect for learning, cognitive learning) associated with teacher–student (non)accommodation in and outside of the classroom, with a particular emphasis on the "teacher as instructor" versus "teacher as support provider" roles (A. Jones, 2008). Additionally, CAT has been rarely used to understand effects in mass and digital media in which a one-to-many communication mode creates interesting questions for the nature and effects of (non)accommodative behaviors in a networked society (Bell, 1991). Finally, in the relational realm, CAT can account for both idiosyncratic and group-based influences on our more personal interactions (Giles, 2008). Obviously, these are but a few of the possibilities, and we are encouraged by the heuristic value of the theory.

A similar argument can be made for the correlates in that research has been robust for some correlates and relatively sparse for others. For instance, as depicted in Table 4.2, we argue that our understanding of the relationship between accommodation and relational solidarity is more comprehensive than our understanding of the link between accommodation and communication apprehension. Further development of the theory and an enhanced understanding of accommodation are contingent on extending research into the underemphasized contexts and understudied correlates.

Conceptualizing and Operationalizing Accommodation

In the shift from speech accommodation theory to *communication* accommodation theory, the theory encompassed a wider range of communicative behaviors, and, over the years, scholars have continued this development by conceptualizing various types of behavior under the accommodative umbrella. As such, in our effect-size analysis, we addressed this variability by synthesizing and focusing on four broad behaviors (accommodation, nonaccommodation, reluctant accommodation, and avoidant accommodation). We believe the adaptability of the theory to various contexts is a strength of the theory. In reviewing the research, it is clear that the context of inquiry often shapes the conceptualization of accommodative behaviors—thus, the variability in how researchers are defining accommodative behaviors. Likewise, the complexity (or range) of behaviors examined varies across the studies. For instance, some studies will focus on a general assessment of accommodation, whereas others may assess multiple behaviors in a single study (accommodative involvement, reluctant accommodation, topic management, underaccommodation). Although this demonstrates the heuristic value of the theory, can this variability obfuscate the tenets of theory and/or the general premise of accommodation behaviors? In other words, what is accommodation? As scholars continue to progress with CAT scholarship, our hope is that there are always clear links to the foundational tenets and propositions of the theory ensuring a common theoretical understanding across the variations in conceptualizing accommodation.

Similarly, in our review, there was considerable variation in the operationalization of constructs. We view this as a strength as this variability serves as cross-validation of sorts on the overall understanding of accommodation through the multiple methods of assessment. However, we make two notes on this for future inquiries. First, it is likely that the manner in which we assess accommodation may influence the effect size in the study. For instance, there were aspects of our locus of assessment heterogeneity of effect size analysis that represents different methods of assessment (the category "third party" represents coding or rating of hypothesized or actual interactions, individuals, or outcomes). Thus, in designing and interpreting studies, researchers should consider how the operationalization of a construct may influence the overall results of the study. Second, although CAT scholars typically rely on previous research to formulate items and measures for the studies, there is no standard instrument for assessing accommodation. One reason for this is that the nature of the communication (and, thus, the items in the measures) may vary based on the context and population of inquiry. Therefore, we are not advocating for a "one-size-fits-all" measure in all cases. However, research might benefit by more standardization when possible.

Considerations for Future Research

In their 2005 overview of CAT, Gallois, Ogay, and Giles argued that many reviews of the theory were discursive in nature and did not put forth specific theoretical propositions. Given the breadth and scope of the theory, the authors distilled the various theories, models, and reviews to 11 propositions (see also Giles, Willemyns, et al., 2007). Depending on the focus of the specific research inquiry, not all studies can address each proposition. However, there are tenets of CAT that serve as strands throughout many of these propositions, and we encourage researchers to consider the following aspects of CAT as they continue to develop research programs aimed at identifying, understanding, and predicting behavior. First, as argued in previous reviews and evident in the contextual analysis, CAT is a theory of interpersonal and intergroup communication. Often, however, these orientations are falsely dichotomized, resulting in scholarship that focuses on one or the other, limiting our understanding of specific interactional episodes. With its emphasis on the macro (intergroup) and micro (interpersonal) factors, CAT provides not only a theory of human behavior but also a paradigm of understanding as it highlights the significance of collective identity in our interactions. As Harwood (2006) states, "we need to understand collective identities as a key aspect of human behavior, and we need to think about incorporating this higher-level sense of self into our communication research as a more routine issue" (p. 89). When possible, research should explicitly acknowledge the presence of both intergroup and interpersonal factors through the research questions and hypotheses put forth.

Second, some of the foundational tenets of CAT and the propositions laid out by Gallois et al. (2005) demonstrate the subjective nature of meaning between people in that original intentions of a speaker, actual behavior, and interpretation of a message may not always be in sync. An ideal research scenario, therefore, would be to investigate both interlocutors to examine motivation, intentions, and perceptions of communication as well as relevant outcomes. Whereas some of the "third person" assessments take this into account by having individuals rate aspects of conversations between dyads, we are at a point where methodological trends and advancements allow for investigation of reciprocity and interdependence in partners (Kenney, Kashy, & Cook, 2006). We also believe that CAT would benefit from more research using observational interaction analysis to investigate the sequential and communicative aspects of extended interactions.

Third, as scholars move forward with CAT research, we recommend continuing to focus on not only the identification and explanation of behaviors but also on understanding *motivations* for adjusting communication and explanations for the corresponding perceptions, evaluations, and outcomes because this represents a more comprehensive application of the theory. Motivations for accommodation may be an important ingredient in further understanding when and how accommodative behaviors influence or reflect communicative, relational, and identity outcomes. Although central to the theory, the motivations of accommodative behaviors are not always explicitly discussed in some of the literature. As such, future research should emphasize the nuances of the *why* and *how* of our (non)accommodative behaviors.

Finally, an important part of the CAT's future is not only continuing to investigate the association between accommodative behaviors to these outcomes, but to highlight the more applied outcomes of (non)accommodation. In much of the research, scholars have demonstrated the applied aspect in relating our communication to personal well-being and health outcomes. And more recent work has demonstrated the role of (non)accommodation in compliance (such as in policing), reduction of intergroup prejudice, and quality of patient–physician interaction. By highlighting or expanding the applied aspect of CAT, we can continue to address one of the more fundamental questions to both the theory and the communication discipline, in general: Why is communication important?

Limitations and Future Meta-Analysis

The current study used meta-analytical techniques to assess effect sizes across the spectrum of empirical work using CAT. Our analysis provides a more general assessment given the objectives of the study, and we believe the limitations of our study provide opportunities for future meta-analyses to guide and develop future studies. First, analysis should focus on specific behaviors within the broad categories of accommodative behaviors central to this study. For instance, nonaccommodation subsumes behaviors such as *under- and overaccommodation*. Given that growing body of research on specific aspects of nonaccommodation (Gasiorek, 2013), scholars may wish to examine the effects, outcomes, and potential moderators of specific behaviors to gain a more nuanced understanding of nonaccommodative communication that gets lost in more conceptual abstractions. Second, we believe there are opportunities to conduct context-specific meta-analysis. For instance, a great deal of CAT research has focused on intergenerational interactions. Although the research clearly demonstrates generational differences in perceptions and effects of accommodative behaviors, what is the actual magnitude of this effect? More important, what should we consider as potential moderating factors (e.g., culture, gender, assessment) to provide more precise insight into communication and intergenerational relations? Obviously, these types of questions can be applied to any context or methodological factor (e.g., origin of sample). In this capacity, a meta-analysis can uncover important areas and directions for research. Finally, future meta-analytical reviews on CAT could bring in behaviors outside of the CAT framework with conceptual similarities to better understand specific types of behaviors.

Acknowledgments

We would like to thank Colleen W. Colaner, Leslie R. Nelson, and Chad Wertley for their assistance with this manuscript. A previous version of this manuscript has been presented at the annual meeting of the International Communication Association.

References

*Indicates manuscript was used in contextual or meta-analysis.

*Al-Khatib, M. (1995). The impact of interlocutor sex on linguistic accommodation. A case study of Jordan radio phone-in programs. *Multilingua, 14*, 133–150. doi:10.1515/mult.1995.14.2.133

Allen, M. (2009). Meta-analysis. *Communication Monographs, 76*, 398–407. doi:10.1080/03637750903310386

*Anderson, K., Harwood, J., & Hummert, M. L. (2005). The grandparent-grandchild relationship: Implications for models of intergenerational communication. *Human Communication Research, 31*, 268–294. doi:10.1111/j.1468–2958.2005.tb00872.x

*Aritz, J., & Walker, R. C. (2010). Cognitive organization and identity maintenance in multicultural teams: A discourse analysis of decision-making meetings. *Journal of Business Communication, 47*, 20–41. doi:10.1177/0021943609340669

*Atkinson, K., & Coupland, N. (1988). Accommodation as ideology. *Language and Communication, 8*, 321–327. doi:10.1016.0271–5309(88)90025–0

*Aune, R. K., & Kikuchi, T. (1993). Effects of language intensity similarity on perceptions of credibility, relational attributions, and persuasion. *Journal of Language and Social Psychology, 12*, 224–238. doi:10.1177/0261927X93123004

*Ayoko, O. B., Hartel, C., & Callan, V. (2002). Resolving the puzzle of productive and destructive conflict in culturally heterogeneous workgroups: A communication accommodation theory approach. *International Journal of Conflict Management, 13*, 165–195. doi:10.1108/eb022873

*Azuma, S. (1997). Speech accommodation and Japanese emperor Hirohito. *Discourse and Society, 8*, 189–202. doi:10.1177/0957926597008002003

*Ball, P., Giles, H., Byrne, J., & Berechree, P. (1984). Situational constraints on the evaluative significance of speech accommodation: Some Australian data. *International Journal of the Sociology of Language, 46*, 115–129. doi:10.1177/0261927X970161001

*Barker, V. (2007). Young adults' reactions to grandparents painful self-disclosure: The influence of grandparent sex and overall motivations for communication. *International Journal of Aging and Human Development, 64*, 195–215. doi:10.2190/KTNU-0373–20W7–4781

*Barker, V., Choi, C., Giles, H., & Hajek, C. (2008–2009). Officer accommodation in police-civilian encounters: Reported compliance with police in Mongolia and the United States. *Mongolian Journal of International Affairs, 15–16,* 176–200. doi:10.5564/mjia.v0i15–16.35

Barker, V., & Giles, H. (2003). Integrating the communicative predicament and enhancement of aging models: The case of older Native Americans. *Health Communication, 15,* 255–275. doi:10.1207/S15327027HC1503_1

*Barker, V., Giles, H., Hajek, C., Ota, H., Noels, K., Lim, T-S., & Somera, L. (2008). Police-civilian interaction, compliance, accommodation, and trust in an intergroup context: International data. *Journal of International and Intercultural Communication, 1,* 93–112. doi:10.1080/17513050801891986

Bell, A. (1991). Audience accommodation and the mass media. In H. Giles, J. Coupland, & N. Coupland (Eds.), *Contexts of accommodation* (pp. 69–102). New York: Cambridge University Press.

*Bilaniuk, A. (2010). Language in the balance: The politics of non-accommodation on bilingual Ukrainian Russian television shows. *International Journal of the Sociology of Language, 201,* 105–133. doi:10.1515/ijsl.2010.006

*Bilous, F. R., & Krauss, R. M. (1988). Dominance and accommodation in the conversational behaviours of same- and mixed-gender dyads. *Language and Communication, 8,* 183–194. doi:10.1016/0271–5309(88)90016-X

Boggs, C., & Giles, H. (1999). "The canary in the cage": The nonaccommodation cycle in the gendered workplace. *International Journal of Applied Linguistics, 22,* 223–245. doi:10.1111/j.1473–4192.1999.tb00174.x

*Bonnesen, J. L., & Hummert, M. L. (2002). Painful self-disclosure of older adults in relation to aging stereotypes and perceived motivations. *Journal of Language and Social Psychology, 21,* 275–301. doi:10.1177/0261927X02021003004

Bourhis, R. Y. (1979). Language and ethnic interaction: A social psychological approach. In H. Giles & B. Saint-Jacques (Eds.), *Language and ethnic relations* (pp. 117–141). Oxford, England: Pergamon Press.

*Bourhis, R. Y. (1984). Cross-cultural communication in Montreal: Two field studies since Bill 101. *International Journal of the Sociology of Language, 46,* 33–48. doi:10.1515/ijsl.1984.46.33

*Bourhis, R. Y., & Giles, H. (1976). The language of cooperation in Wales: A field study. *Language Sciences, 42,* 13–16.

*Bourhis, R. Y., Roth, S., & MacQueen, G. (1989). Communication in the hospital setting: A survey of medical and everyday language use amongst patients, nurses and doctors. *Social Science and Medicine, 28,* 339–346. doi:10.1016/0277–9536(89)90035-X

*Bradac, J. J., Mulac, A., & House, A. (1988). Lexical diversity and magnitude of convergent versus divergent style shifting: Perceptual and evaluative consequences. *Language and Communication, 8,* 213–228. doi:10.1016/0271–5309(88)90019–5

*Brown, B. L., Giles, H., & Thakerar, J. N. (1985). Speaker evaluations as a function of speech rate, accent and context. *Language and Communication, 5,* 207–222. doi:10.1016/0271–5309(85)90011–4

*Buller, D. B., & Aune, R. K. (1992). The effects of speech rate similarity on compliance: Application of communication accommodation theory. *Western Journal of Communication, 56,* 37–53. doi:10.1080/10570319209374400

Buller, D. B., LePoire, B. A., Aune, R. K., & Eloy, S. V. (1992). Social perceptions as mediators of the effect of speech rate similarity on compliance. *Human Communication Research, 19,* 286–311. doi:10.1111/j.1468–2958.1992.tb00303.x

*Bunz, U., & Campbell, S. W. (2004). Politeness accommodation in electronic mail. *Communication Research Report, 21,* 11–25. doi:10.1080/08824090409359963

*Burt, S. M. (1994). Code choice in intercultural conversation: Speech accommodation theory and pragmatics. *Pragmatics, 4,* 535–559. doi:10.1177/13670069020060020401

*Buzzanell, P. M., Burrell, N. A., Stafford, S., & Berkowitz, S. (1996). When I call you up and you're not there: Application of communication accommodation theory to telephone answering machine messages. *Western Journal of Communication, 60,* 310–336. doi:10.1080/10570319609374552

*Cai, D., Giles, H., & Noels, K. (1988). Elderly perceptions of communication with older and younger adults in China: Implications for mental health. *Journal of Applied Communication Research, 26,* 32–51. doi:10.1080/00909889809365490

*Casasanto, L., Jasmin, K., & Casasanto, D. (2010). Virtually accommodating: Speech rate accommodation to a virtual interlocutor. In S. Ohlsson & R. Catrambone (Eds.), *Proceedings of the 32nd annual conference of the Cognitive Science Society* (pp. 127–132). Austin, TX: Cognitive Science Society.

*Chen, L., & Cegala, D. (1994). Topic management, shared knowledge, and accommo-dation: A study of communication adaptability. *Research on Language and Social Interaction, 27,* 389–417. doi:10.1207/s15327973rlsi2704_4

*Colley, A., & Todd, Z. (2002). Gender-linked differences in the style and content of e-mails to friends. *Journal of Language and Social Psychology, 21,* 380–392. doi:10.1177/026192702237955

*Collins, W. M. (2005). Codeswitching avoidance as a strategy for Mam (Maya) lin-guistic revitalization. *International Journal of American Linguistics, 73,* 239–276. doi:10.1086/497872

*Coupland, N. (1984). Accommodation at work: Some phonological data and their implications. *International Journal of the Sociology of Language, 46,* 49–70. doi:10.1515/ijsl.1984.46.49

*Coupland, J., Coupland, N., Giles, H., & Henwood, K. (1988). Accommodating the elderly: Invoking and extending a theory. *Language in Society, 17,* 1–41. doi:10.1017/S0047404500012574

*Coupland, J., Coupland, N., Giles, H., Henwood, K., & Wiemann, J. (1988). Elderly self-disclosure: Interactional and intergroup issues. *Language and Communication, 8,* 109–133. doi:10.1016/0271–5309(88)90010–9

Coupland, N., & Jaworski, A. (1997). Relevance, accommodation, and conversation. Modeling the social dimension of communication. *Multilingua, 16,* 235–258. doi:10.1515/mult.1997.16.2–3.233

*Cretchley, J., Gallois, C., Chenery, H., & Smith, A. (2010). Conversations between car-ers and people with schizophrenia: A qualitative analysis using Leximancer. *Quali-tative Health Research, 20,* 1611–1628. doi:10.1177/1049732310378297

*Crook, C. W., & Booth, R. (1997). Building rapport in electronic mail using accom-modation theory. *SAM Advanced Management Journal, 62,* 4–15. Retrieved from www.cob.tamucc.edu/sam/amj/Default.htm

*Dixon, J. A., Tredoux, C. G., Durrheim, K., & Foster, D. H. (1994). The role of speech accommodation and crime type in attribution of guilt. *The Journal of Social Psychol-ogy, 134,* 465–473. doi:10.1080/00224545.1994.9712197

*Dixon, T. L., Schell, T., Giles, H., & Drogos, K. (2008). The influence of race in police-civilian interactions: A content analysis of videotaped interactions taken during Cincinnati police traffic stops. *Journal of Communication, 58,* 530–549. doi:10.1111/j.1460–2466.2008.00398.x

*Dorjee, T., Giles, H., & Barker, V. (2011). Diasporic communication: Cultural deviance and accommodation among Tibetan exiles in India. *Journal of Multilingual and Multicultural Development, 32,* 343–359. doi:10.1080/01434632.2011.579130

*Ehala, M., & Uprus, T. (2008). The mechanism of substrate impact on superstrate: Assessing Uralic substrate in Germanic. *Linguistica Uralica, 2,* 81–96. doi:10.3176/lu.2008.2.01

Ellis, P. D. (2010). *The essential guide to effect sizes: Statistical power, meta-analysis, and the interpretation of research results.* Cambridge, England: Cambridge University Press.

*Ferguson, A., & Peterson, P. (2002). Intonation in partner accommodation for aphasia: A descriptive single case study. *Journal of Communication Disorders, 35,* 11–30. doi:10.1016/S0021–9924(01)00071–5

*Fitzpatrick, M. A., Mulac, A., & Dindia, K. (1995). Gender-preferential language use in spouse and stranger interaction. *Journal of Language and Social Psychology, 14,* 18–39. doi:10.1177/0261927X95141002

*Fowler, C. A., & Soliz, J. (2010). Responses of young adult grandchildren to grandparent's painful self-disclosures. *Journal of Language and Social Psychology, 29,* 75–100. doi:10.1177/0261927X09351680

*Fox, S. A., & Giles, H. (1996). Interability communication: Evaluating patronizing encounters. *Journal of Language and Social Psychology, 15,* 265–290. doi:10.1177/0261927X960153004

*Gallois, C., & Callan, V. J. (1988). Communication accommodation and the prototypical speaker: Predicting evaluations of status and solidarity. *Language and Communication, 8,* 271–283. doi:10.1016/0271–5309(88)90022–5

Gallois, C., & Giles, H. (1998). Accommodating mutual influence. In M. Palmer & G. A. Barnett (Eds.), *Mutual influence in interpersonal communication: Theory and research in cognition, affect, and behavior* (pp. 135–162). New York: Ablex.

Gallois, C., Ogay, T., & Giles, H. (2005) Communication Accommodation Theory: A look back and a look ahead. In W. B. Gudykunst (Ed.), *Theorizing about culture and communication* (pp. 121–148). Thousand Oaks, CA: Sage.

*Gardner, M. J., & Jones, E. (1999). Problematic communication in the workplace: Beliefs of superiors and subordinates. *International Journal of Applied Linguistics, 9,* 185–203. doi:10.1111/j.1473–4192.1999.tb00172.x

Gasiorek, J. (2013). "I was impolite to her because that's how she was to me": Perceptions of motive and young adults' communicative responses to underaccommodation. *Western Journal of Communication, 77,* 604–624. doi:10.1080/10570314.2013.778421

*Genesee, F., & Bourhis, R. Y. (1988). Evaluative reactions to language choice strategies: The role of sociostructural factors. *Language & Communication, 8,* 229–250. doi:10.1016/0271–5309(88)90020–1

*Gevorgyan, G. (2010). Does culture matter? Using accommodation, framing, and Hofstede theories to predict Chinese voters' perceptions and attitudes toward culturally oriented online political advertising. *China Media Research, 6,* 91–102.

Giles, H. (1973). Accent mobility: A model and some data. *Anthropological Linguistics, 15,* 87–105.

Giles, H. (2008). Communication accommodation theory. In L. A. Baxter & D. O. Braithwaite (Eds.), *Engaging theories of interpersonal communication* (pp. 162–274). Sage: Thousand Oaks, CA.

*Giles, H., Ballard, D., & McCann, R. M. (2002). Perceptions of intergenerational communication across cultures: An Italian case. *Perceptual and Motor Skills, 95,* 583–591.

Giles, H., Coupland, J., & Coupland. N. (Eds.). (1991). *The contexts of accommodation: Developments in applied sociolinguistics.* New York: Cambridge University Press.

*Giles, H., Dailey, R. M., Sarkar, J. M., & Makoni, S. (2007). Intergenerational communication beliefs across the lifespan: Comparative data from India. *Communication Reports, 20,* 75–89. doi:10.1080/08934210701643701

*Giles, H., Fortman, J., Honeycutt, J., & Ota, H. (2003). Future selves and others: A lifespan and cross-cultural perspective. *Communication Reports, 16,* 1–22. doi:10.1080/08934210309384486

*Giles, H., Fox, S., & Smith, E. (1993). Patronizing the elderly: Intergenerational evaluations. *Research in Language and Social Interaction, 26,* 129–149. doi:10.1207/s15327973rlsi2602_1

*Giles, H., Hajek, C., Stoitsova, T., & Choi, C. (2010). Intergenerational communication satisfaction and age estimates in Bulgaria and the USA. *Journal of Cross-Cultural Gerontology, 25,* 133–147. doi:10.1007/s10823–010–9114-x

*Giles, H., Liang, B., Noels, K., & McCann, R. M. (2001). Communicating across and within generations: Taiwanese, Chinese-Americans, and Euro-American perceptions of communication. *Journal of Asian Pacific Communication, 11,* 161–179. Retrieved from http://benjamins.com/#catalog/journals/japc

*Giles, H., Makoni, S., & Dailey, R. M. (2005). Intergenerational communication beliefs across the lifespan: Comparative data from West and South Africa. *Journal of Cross-Cultural Gerontology, 20,* 191–211.

Giles, H., McCann, R. M., Ota, H., & Noels, K. A. (2002). Challenging intergenerational stereotypes: Across eastern and western cultures. In M. S. Kaplan, N. Z. Henkin, & A. T. Kusano (Eds.), *Linking lifetimes: A global view of intergenerational exchange* (pp. 13–28). Honolulu, HI: University Press of America, Inc.

*Giles, H., Noels, K., Williams, A., Ota, H., Lim, T-S., Ng, S. H., . . . Somera, L. (2003). Intergenerational communication across cultures: Young people's perceptions of conversations with family elders, non-family elders, and same-age peers. *Journal of Cross-Cultural Gerontology, 18,* 1–30. doi:10.1023/A:1024854211638

Giles, H., & Ogay, T. (2006) Communication accommodation theory. In B. Whaley & W. Samter (Eds.), *Explaining communication: Contemporary theories and exemplars* (pp. 293–310). Mahwah, NJ: Erlbaum.

*Giles, H., Ryan, E. B., & Anas, A. P. (2008). Perceptions of intergenerational communication by young, middle-aged, and older adults in Canada. *Canadian Journal of Behavioral Science, 40,* 21–30. doi:10.1037/0008–400x.40.1.21

*Giles, H., Taylor, D. M., & Bourhis, R. Y. (1973). Towards a theory of interpersonal accommodation through speech: Some Canadian data. *Language in Society, 2,* 177–192. doi:10.1017/S0047404500000701

Giles, H., & Wadleigh, P. M. (2008). Accommodating nonverbally. In L. K. Guerrero, J. A. DeVito, & M. L. Hecht (Eds.), *The nonverbal communication reader: Classic and contemporary readings* (pp. 491–502). Prospect Heights, IL: Waveland Press.

Giles, H., Willemyns, M., Gallois, C., & Anderson, M. C. (2007). Accommodating a new frontier: The context of law enforcement. In K. Fiedler (Ed.), *Social communication* (pp. 129–162). New York: Psychology Press.

*Giles, H., & Williams, A. (1994). Patronizing the young: Forms and evaluations. *International Journal of Aging and Human Development, 39,* 33–53. doi:10.1017/S0047404500000701

*Giles, H., Zwang-Weismann, Y., & Hajek, C. (2004). Patronizing and policing elderly people. *Psychological Reports, 95,* 754–756. doi:10.2466/pr0.95.3.754–756

Glaser, B. G., & Strauss, A. L. (1967). *The discovery of grounded theory: Strategies for qualitative research.* Chicago, IL: Aldine.

*Gnisci, A. (2005). Sequential strategies of accommodation: A new method in courtroom. *British Journal of Social Psychology, 44,* 621–643. doi:10.1348/014466604X16363

*Gnisci, A., & Bakeman, R. (2007). Sequential accommodation of turn taking and turn length: A study of courtroom interaction. *Journal of Language and Social Psychology, 26,* 234–259. doi:10.1177/0261927X06303474

*Green, J. A. (2003). The writing on the stall: Gender and graffiti. *Journal of Language and Social Psychology, 22,* 282–296. doi:10.1177/0261927X03255380

*Gregory, S. W., Dagan, K., & Webster, S. (1997). Evaluating the relation of vocal accommodation in conversation partners' fundamental frequencies to perceptions of communication quality. *Journal of Nonverbal Behavior, 21,* 23–43. doi:10.1023/A:1024995717773

*Gregory, S. W., & Webster, S. (1996). A nonverbal signal in voices of interview partners effectively predicts communication accommodation and social status perceptions. *Journal of Personality and Social Psychology, 70,* 1231–1240. doi:10.1037//0022-3514.70.6.1231

Griffin, E. (2009). *A first look at communication theory.* Boston, MA: McGraw-Hill.

Gudykunst, W. B. (1995). Anxiety/uncertainty management theory: Current status. In R. Wiseman (Ed.), *Intercultural communication* (pp. 8–58). Thousand Oaks, CA: Sage.

*Haas, A., & Gregory, S. W. (2005). The impact of physical attractiveness on women's social status and interactional power. *Sociological Forum, 20,* 449–471. doi:10.1007/s11206–005–6597–2

*Hajek, C., Barker, V., Giles, H., Makoni, S., Pecchioni, L., Louw-Potgieter, J., & Myers, P. (2006). Communicative dynamics of police-civilian encounters: South African and American interethnic data. *Journal of Intercultural Communication Research, 35,* 161–182. doi:10.1080/17475750601026909

*Hajek, C., Giles, H., Barker, V., Lin, M.-C., Zhang, Y-B., & Hummert, M.-L. (2008). Expressed trust and compliance in police-civilian encounters: The role of communication accommodation in Chinese and American settings. *Chinese Journal of Communication, 2,* 168–180. doi:10.1080/17544750802287935

*Hajek, C., Giles, H., Barker, V., Makoni, S., & Choi, C. (2008). Reported compliance in police-civilian encounters: The roles of accommodation and trust in Zimbabwe and the United States. *Communicatio: South African Journal of Communication Theory and Research, 34,* 173–187. doi:10.1080/02500160802144660

*Hajek, C., Villagran, M., & Wittenberg-Lyles, E. (2007). The relationships among perceived physician accommodation, perceived outgroup typicality, and patient inclinations toward compliance. *Communication Research Reports, 24,* 293–302. doi:10.1080/08824090701624189

*Hannah, A., & Murachver, T. (1999). Gender and conversational style as predictors of conversational behavior. *Journal of Language and Social Psychology, 18,* 153–174. doi:10.1177/0261927X99018002002

*Harwood, J. (1998). Young adults' cognitive representations of intergenerational conversations. *Journal of Applied Communication Research, 26,* 13–31. doi:10.1080/00909889809365489

*Harwood, J. (2000). Communicative predictors of solidarity in the grandparent-grandchild relationship. *Journal of Social and Personal Relationships, 17,* 743–766. doi:10.1177/0265407500176003

Harwood, J. (2006). Social identity. In G. J. Shepherd, J. St. John, & T. Striphas (Eds.), *Communication as perspectives on theory* (pp. 84–90). Thousand Oaks, CA: Sage.

*Harwood, J., & Giles, H. (1993). Creating intergenerational distance: Language, communication and middle age. *Language Sciences, 15,* 1–24. doi:10.1016/0388–0001 (93)90003-B

*Harwood, J., & Giles, H. (1996). Reactions to older people being patronized: The role of response strategies and attributed thoughts. *Journal of Language and Social Psychology, 15,* 395–421. doi:10.1177/0261927X960154001

Harwood, J., & Giles, H. (Eds.). (2005). *Intergroup communication: Multiple perspectives.* New York: Peter Lang.

*Harwood, J., Giles, H., Fox, S., Ryan, E. B., & Williams, A. (1993). Patronizing young and elderly adults: Response strategies in a community setting. *Journal of Applied Communication Research, 21,* 211–226. doi:10.1177/0261927X07309513

*Harwood, J., Hewstone, M., Paolini, S., & Voci, A. (2005). Grandparent-grandchild contact and attitudes towards older adults: Moderator and mediator effects. *Personality and Social Psychology Bulletin, 31,* 393–406. doi:10.1177/0146167204271577

*Harwood, J., McKee, J., & Lin, M-C. (2000). Younger and older adults' schematic representations of intergenerational communication. *Communication Monographs, 67,* 20–41. doi:10.1080/03637750009376493

*Harwood, J., Raman, P., & Hewstone, M. (2006). The family and communication dynamics of group salience. *Journal of Family Communication, 6,* 181–200. doi:10.1207/s15327698jfc0603_2

*Harwood, J., Ryan, E. B., Giles, H., & Tysoski, S. (1997). Evaluations of patronizing speech and three response styles in a nonservice-providing context. *Journal of Applied Communication Research, 25,* 170–195. doi:10.1080/00909889709365475

Harwood, J., Soliz, J., & Lin, M. C. (2006). Communication accommodation theory. In D. O. Braithwaite & L. A. Baxter (Eds.), *Engaging theories of family communication* (pp. 19–34). Thousand Oaks, CA: Sage.

*Harwood, J., & Williams, A. (1998). Expectations for communication with positive and negative subtypes of older adults. *International Journal of Aging and Human Development, 47,* 11–33. www.baywood.com/authors/ia/ag.asp?id=0091–4150

*Heffernan, K. (2008). An investigation of diachronic change in communication accommodation. *Journal of Language and Social Psychology, 27,* 86–93. doi:10.1177/0261927X07309513

*Heinz, B. (2003). Backchannel responses as strategic responses in bilingual speakers' conversations. *Journal of Pragmatics, 35,* 1113–1132. doi:10.1016/S0378–2166(02)00190-X

*Hewett, D. G., Watson, B. M., Gallois, C., Ward, M., & Leggett, B. A. (2009). Intergroup communication between hospital doctors: Implications for quality of patient care. *Social Science and Medicine, 69,* 1732–1740. doi:10.1177/0261927X9801700303

*Hewett, D. G., Watson, B. M., Gallois, C., Ward, M., & Leggett, B. A. (2009). Communication in medical records: Intergroup language and patient care. *Journal of Language and Social Psychology, 28,* 119–138. doi:10.1177/0261927X08330612

*Hogg, M. A. (1985). Masculine and feminine speech in dyads and groups: A study of speech style and gender salience. *Journal of Language and Social Psychology, 4,* 99–112. doi:10.1177/0261927X9801700303

Holland, J., & Gentry, J. W. (1999). Ethnic consumer reaction to targeted marketing: A theory of intercultural accommodation. *Journal of Advertising, 28,* 63–77. Retrieved from www.journalofadvertising.org/

*Hornsey, M., & Gallois, C. (1998). The impact of interpersonal and intergroup communication accommodation on perceptions of Chinese students in Australia. *Journal of Language and Social Psychology, 17,* 323–347. doi:10.1177/0261927X9801700303

*Hummert, M. L. (1994). Physiognomic cues and the activation of stereotypes of the elderly in interaction. *International Journal of Aging and Human Development, 39,* 5–20. doi:10.2190/6EF6-P8PF-YP6F-VPY4

*Hummert, M. L., Shaner, J. L., Garstka, T. A., & Henry, C. (1998). Communication with older adults: The influence of age stereotypes, context, and communicator age. *Human Communication Research, 25,* 124–151. doi:10.1111/j.1468–2958.1998. tb00439.x

Hunter, J. E., & Schmidt, F. L. (1990). *Methods of meta-analysis: Correcting error and bias in research findings.* Newbury Park, CA: Sage.

Johnson, B. T., & Eagly, A. H. (2000). Quantitative synthesis of social psychological research. In H. T. Reis & C. M. Judd (Eds.), *Handbook of research methods in social and personality psychology* (pp. 496–528). Cambridge, England: Cambridge University Press.

Jones, A. C. (2008). The effects of out-of-class support on student satisfaction and motivation to learn. *Communication Education, 57,* 373–388. doi:10.1080/03634520 801968830

*Jones, E., Gallois, C., Barker, M., & Callan, V. (1994). Evaluations of interactions between students and academic staff. *Journal of Language and Social Psychology, 13,* 158–191. doi:10.1177/0261927X94132004

*Jones, E., Gallois, C., Callan, V., & Barker, M. (1995). Language and power in an academic context: The effects of status, ethnicity, and sex. *Journal of Language and Social Psychology, 14,* 435–461. doi:10.1177/0261927X99018002001

*Jones, E., Gallois, C., Callan, V., & Barker, M. (1999) Strategies of accommodation: Development of a coding system for conversational interaction. *Journal of Language and Social Psychology, 18,* 123–151. doi:10.1177/0261927X99018002001

*Jones, L., Woodhouse, D., & Rowe, J. (2007). Effective nurse parent communication: A study of parents' perceptions in the NICU environment. *Patient Education and Counseling, 69,* 206–212. doi:10.1016/j.pec.2007.08.014

Kenny, D. A., Kashy, D. A., & Cook, W. L. (2006). *Dyadic data analysis.* New York: Guilford.

Kite, M. E., Stockdale, G. D., Whitley, B. E., Jr., & Johnson, B. T. (2005). Attitudes toward older and younger adults: An updated meta-analysis. *Journal of Social Issues, 61,* 241–266. doi:10.1111/j.1540–4560.2005.00404.x

*Koslow, S., Shamdasani, P. M., & Touchstone, E. E. (1994). Exploring language effects in ethnic advertising: A sociolinguistic perspective. *Journal of Consumer Research, 20,* 575–585. doi:10.1086/209371

*Ladegaard, H. J. (2009). Pragmatic cooperation revisited: Resistance and non-cooperation as a discursive strategy in asymmetrical discourses. *Journal of Pragmatics, 41,* 649–666. doi:10.1016/j.pragma.2008.09.021

*Larsen, K., Martin, H., & Giles, H. (1977). Anticipated social cost and interpersonal accommodation. *Human Communication Research, 3,* 303–308. doi:10.1111/j.1468-2958.1977.tb00533.x

*Le Poire, B. A., Ota, H., & Hajek, C. (1997). Self-disclosure responses to stigmatizing disclosures: Communicating with gays and potentially HIV+ individuals. *Journal of Language and Social Psychology, 16,* 159–190. doi:10.1177/0261927X970162003

*Levin, H., & Lin, T. (1988). An accommodation witness. *Language and Communication, 8,* 195–198. doi:10.1016/0271-5309(88)90017-1

*Li, H. Z. (2001). Cooperative and intrusive interruptions in inter- and intracultural dyadic discourse. *Journal of Language and Social Psychology, 20,* 259–284. doi:10.1177/0261927X01020003001

*Li, H. Z. (2006). Backchannel responses as misleading feedback in intercultural discourse. *Journal of Intercultural Communication Research, 35,* 99–116. doi:10.1080/17475750600909253

†Lin, M-C., & Harwood, J. (2003). Predictors of grandparent-grandchild relational solidarity in Taiwan. *Journal of Social and Personal Relationships, 20,* 537–563. doi:10.1177/02654075030204006

Lipsey, M. W., & Wilson, D. B. (2000). *Practical meta-analysis.* Thousand Oaks, CA: Sage.

Littlejohn, S. W. (1999). *Theories of human communication* (6th ed.). Belmont, CA: Wadsworth.

*Marlow, M. L., & Giles, H. (2008). "Who you tink You, talkin Propah?": Pidgin demarginalized. *Journal of Multicultural Discourse, 3,* 53–68. doi:10.2167/md060.0

*Mazer, J. P., & Hunt, S. K. (2008). "Cool" communication in the classroom: A preliminary examination of student perceptions of instructor use of positive slang. *Qualitative Research Reports in Communication, 9,* 20–28. doi:10.1080/17459430802400316

*McCann, R. M., Cargile, A., Giles, H., & Cui, B. T. (2004). Communication ambivalence towards elders: Data from North Vietnam, South Vietnam, and the USA. *Journal of Cross-Cultural Gerontology, 19,* 275–297. doi:10.1023/B:JCCG.0000044685.45304.ca

*McCann, R. M., Dailey, R. M., Giles, H., & Ota, H. (2005). Beliefs about intergenerational communication across the lifespan: Middle age and the roles of age stereotyping and respect norms. *Communication Studies, 56,* 293–311. doi:10.1080/10510970500319286

*McCann, R. M., & Giles, H. (2006). Communication with people of different ages in the workplace: Thai and American data. *Human Communication Research, 32,* 74–108. doi:10.1023/B:JCCG.0000044685.45304.ca

*McCann, R. M., & Giles, H. (2007). Age-differentiated communication in organizations: Perspective from Thailand and the United States. *Communication Research Reports, 24,* 1–12. doi:10.1080/08824090601120841

*McCann, R. M., Ota, H., Giles, H., & Caraker, R. (2003). Accommodation and nonaccommodation across the lifespan: Perspectives from Thailand, Japan, and the United States of America. *Communication Reports, 16,* 1–23. doi:10.1080/08934210309384492

*McRoberts, G. W., & Best, C. T. (1997). Accommodation in mean f_0 during mother–infant and father–infant vocal interactions: A longitudinal case study. *Journal of Child Language, 24*, 719–736.

*Melton, A. K., & Shadden, B. B. (2005). Linguistic accommodations to older adults in the community: The role of communication disorders and partner motivation. *International Journal of Speech-Language Pathology, 7*, 233–244. doi:10.1080/14417040500337039

*Moon, S., & Nelson, M. R. (2008). Exploring the influence of media exposure and cultural values on Korean immigrants' advertising evaluations. *International Journal of Advertising, 27*, 299–330. doi:10.2501/S0265048708080281

*Myers, P., Giles, H., Reid S. A., & Nabi, R. (2008). Law enforcement encounters: The effects of officer accommodativeness and crime severity on interpersonal attributions are mediated by intergroup sensitivity. *Communication Studies, 59*, 1–15. doi:10.1080/10510970802467361

*Myers-Scotton, C. (1988). Self-enhancing codeswitching as interactional power. *Language and Communication, 8*, 199–211. doi:10.1016/0271–5309(88)90024–9

*Namy, L. L., Nygaard, L. C., & Sauerteig, D. (2002). Gender differences in vocal accommodation: The role of perception. *Journal of Language and Social Psychology, 21*, 422–432. doi:10.1177/026192702237958

*Ng, S. H. (2007). From language acculturation to communication acculturation: Address orientations and communication brokering in conversations. *Journal of Language and Social Psychology, 26*, 75–90. doi:10.1177/0261927X06296471

*Ng, S. H., & Anping He, J. (2004). Codeswitching in tri-generational family conversations among Chinese immigrants in New Zealand. *Journal of Language and Social Psychology, 23*, 28–48. doi:10.1177/0261927X03260807

*Noels, K., Giles, H., Cai, D., & Turay, L. (1999). Intergenerational communication and health in the United States and the People's Republic of China. *South Pacific Journal of Psychology, 10*, 120–134.

*Ota, J., Giles, H., & Somera, L. P. (2007). Beliefs about intra- and intergenerational communication in Japan, the Philippines, and the United States: Implication for older adults' subjective well being. *Communication Studies, 58*, 173–188. doi:10.1080/10510970701341139

*Pearce, K., Giles, H., Hajek, C., Barker, V., & Choi, C. (2012). The roles of communication and trust in reported compliance with police in Armenia and the United States. *The Armenian Review, 53*, 39–62.

*Platt, J., & Weber, H. (1984). Speech convergence miscarried: An investigation into inappropriate accommodation strategies. *International Journal of the Sociology of Language, 46*, 131–146. doi:10.1515/ijsl.1984.46.131

*Prince, E. F. (1988). Accommodation theory and dialect shift: A case study from Yiddish. *Language and Communication, 8*, 307–320. doi:10.1016/0271–5309(88)90024–9

*Rajadurai, J. (2007). Sociolinguistic perspectives on variation in not-native varieties of English. *Multilingua, 26*, 409–426. doi:10.1515/MULTI.2007.019

*Rajadurai, J. (2007). Outgroup phonological markers and the negotiation of identity. *International Journal of Multilingualism, 4*, 282–299. doi:10.2167/ijm069.0

*Rittenour, C. E., & Soliz, J. (2009). Communicative and relational dimensions of shared family identity and relational intentions in mother-in-law/daughter-in-law relationships: Developing a conceptual model for mother-in-law/daughter-in-law research. *Western Journal of Communication, 73*, 67–90. doi:10.1080/10570310802636334

*Robertson, K., & Murachver, T. (2003). Children's speech accommodation to gendered language styles. *Journal of Language and Social Psychology, 22,* 321–333. doi:10.1177/0261927X06292991

Rosenthal, R., & DiMatteo, M. R. (2001). Meta-analysis: Recent developments in quantitative methods for literature reviews. *Annual Review of Psychology, 52,* 59–82. doi:10.1146/annurev.psych.52.1.59

*Ross, S., & Shortreed, I. M. (1990). Japanese foreigner talk: Convergence or divergence? *Journal of Asian Pacific Communication, 1,* 135–145.

*Ryan, E. B., Bourhis, R. Y., & Knops, U. (1991). Evaluative perceptions of patronizing speech addressed to elders. *Psychology and Aging, 6,* 442–450. doi:10.1037//0882–7974.6.3.442

Ryan, E. B., Giles, H., Bartolucci, G., & Henwood, K. (1986). Psycholinguistics and social psychological components of communication be and with the elderly. *Language and Communication, 6,* 1–24. Retrieved from http://dx.doi.org/10.1016/0271-5309(86)90002-9

*Ryan, E. B., Hamilton, J. M., & See, S. K. (1994). Patronizing the old: How do younger and older adults respond to baby talk in the nursing home? *International Journal of Aging and Human Development, 39,* 21–32. doi:10.2190/M52C-M2D2-R6C2–3PBM

*Ryan, E. B., MacLean, M. & Orange, J. B. (1994). Inappropriate accommodation in communication to elders: Inferences about nonverbal correlates. *International Journal of Aging and Human Development, 39,* 273–291. doi:10.2190/M52C-M2D2-R6C2–3PBM

*Sandel, T. L., Chao, W., & Liang, C. (2006). Language shift and language accommodation across family generations in Taiwan. *Journal of Multilingual and Multicultural Development, 27,* 126–147. doi:10.2190/M52C-M2D2-R6C2–3PBM

Schrodt, P., Witt, P. L., & Messersmith, A. (2008). A meta-analytical review of family communication patterns and their associations with information processing, behavioral, and psychosocial outcomes. *Communication Monographs, 75,* 248–269. doi:10.1080/03637750802256318

Shepard, C., Giles, H., & LePoire, B. (2001). Communication accommodation theory. In W. P. Robinson & H. Giles (Eds.), *The new handbook of language and social psychology* (pp. 33–56). Chichester, England: Wiley.

*Simard, L., Taylor, D. M., & Giles, H. (1976). Attribution processes and interpersonal accommodation in a bilingual setting. *Language and Speech, 19,* 374–387. doi:10.1177/002383097601900408

*Soliz, J. (2007). Communicative predictors of a shared family identity: Comparison of grandchildren's perceptions of family-of-origin grandparents and stepgrandparents. *Journal of Family Communication, 7,* 177–194. doi:10.1080/1369681032000132582

*Soliz, J., & Harwood, J. (2003). Perceptions of communication in a family relationship and the reduction of intergroup prejudice. *Journal of Applied Communication Research, 31,* 320–345. doi:10.1080/1369681032000132582

*Soliz, J., & Harwood, J. (2006). Shared family identity, age salience, and intergroup contact: Investigation of the grandparent-grandchild relationship. *Communication Monographs, 73,* 87–107. doi:10.1080/1369681032000132582

*Soliz, J., Ribarsky, E., Harrigan, M. M., & Tye-Williams, S. (2010). Family communication with gay and lesbian family members: Implications for relational satisfaction and outgroup attitudes. *Communication Quarterly, 58,* 77–95. doi:10.1080/1369681032000132582

*Soliz, J., Thorson, A., & Rittenour, C. E. (2009). Communicative correlates of satisfaction, family identity, and group salience in multiracial/ethnic families. *Journal of Marriage and Family, 71,* 819–832. doi:10.1111/j.1741-3737.2009. 00637.x

*Sparks, B. (1994). Communicative aspects of the service encounter. *Journal of Hospitality & Tourism Research, 17,* 39–50. doi:10.1177/109634809401700205

*Speer, R., Giles, H., & Denes, A. (2013). Investigating stepparent-stepchild interactions: The role of communication accommodation. *Journal of Family Communication,* 13, 218–241. doi:10.1080/15267431.2013.768248

*Stoitsova, T., Choi, C., Giles, H., Barker, V., & Hajek, C. (2009). Reported compliance in police-civilian encounters: The roles of accommodation and trust in Bulgaria and the United States. *Journal of Psychological Research, 1,* 99–116.

*Street, R. L., Jr., Brady, R. M., & Putnam, W. B. (1983). The influence of speech rate stereotypes and rate similarity on listeners' evaluations of speakers. *Journal of Language and Social Psychology, 2,* 37–56. doi:10.1177/0261927X8300 200103

Street, R. L., Jr., & Giles, H. (1982). Speech accommodation theory: A social cognitive model of speech behavior. In M. Roloff & C. R. Berger (Eds.), *Social cognition and communication* (pp. 193–226). Beverly Hills, CA: Sage.

*Thomson, R. (2006). The effect of topic discussion and gendered language in computer-mediated communication discussion. *Journal of Language and Social Psychology, 25,* 167–178. doi:10.1177/0261927X06286452

*Thomson, R., Murachver, T., & Green, J. (2001). Where is the gender in gendered language? *Psychological Science, 12,* 171–175. doi:10.1111/1467–9280.00329

*Tien, C. (2009). Conflict and accommodation in classroom codeswitching in Taiwan. *International Journal of Bilingual Education and Bilingualism, 12,* 173–192. doi:10.1080/13670050802153160

*Van Den Berg, M. E. (1988). Long term accommodation of (ethno)linguistic groups toward a societal language norm. *Language and Communication, 8,* 251–269. doi:10.1016/0271–5309(88)90021–3

*Watson, B., & Gallois, C. (1998). Nurturing communication by health professional toward patients: A communication accommodation theory approach. *Health Communication, 10,* 343–355. doi:10.1207/s15327027hc1004_3

*Willemyns, M., & Gallois, C. (1997). Accent accommodation in the job interview. *Journal of Language and Social Psychology, 16,* 3–22. doi:10.1177/0261927X970161001

*Willemyns, M., Gallois, C., & Callan, V. J. (2003). Trust me, I'm your boss: Trust and power in supervisor-supervisee communication. *International Journal of Human Resources Management, 14,* 117–127. doi:10.1111/1467–9481.00014

*Williams, A., & Garrett, P. (2002). Communication evaluations across the life span: From adolescent storm and stress to elder aches and pains. *Journal of Language and Social Psychology, 21,* 101–126. doi:10.1111/1467–9481.00014

*Williams, A., & Giles, H. (1996). Intergenerational conversations young adults' retrospective accounts. *Human Communication Research, 23,* 220–250. doi:10.1111/ j.1468–2958.1996.tb00393.x

*Williams, A., Ota, H., Giles, H., Pierson, H. D., Gallois, C., Ng, S. H., . . . Harwood, J. (1997). Young people's beliefs about intergenerational communication: An

initial cross-cultural comparison. *Communication Research, 24,* 370–393. doi:10. 1177/009365097024004003

*Yaeger-Dror, M. (1988). The influence of changing group vitality on convergence toward a dominant linguistic norm: An Israeli example. *Language and Communication, 8,* 285–305. doi:10.1016/0271–5309(88)90023–7

*Ytsma, J., & Giles, H. (1997). Reactions to patronizing talk: Some Dutch data. *Journal of Sociolinguistics, 1,* 259–268. doi:10.1111/1467–9481.00014

CHAPTER CONTENTS

5 Understanding Argumentation in Interpersonal Communication

The Implications of Distinguishing Between Public and Personal Topics

Amy Janan Johnson

University of Oklahoma

Dale Hample

University of Maryland

Ioana A. Cionea

University of Oklahoma

In this chapter, we review an important distinction in interpersonal argumentation between public-issue arguments and personal-issue arguments. Public-issue arguments focus on concerns outside an interpersonal dyad, whereas personal-issue arguments focus on issues tied closely to an interpersonal relationship. These two types of interpersonal arguments differ in terms of who argues about these topics, how argumentative episodes are interpreted and enacted, and the stakes that the arguments have for relational outcomes. This distinction is argued to be consequential for several areas of communication research including persuasion, conflict, relational communication, political deliberation, and public argument.

Social science research in argumentation and conflict often proceeds by exposing participants to a communication stimulus and asking them to converse about it or respond to various instruments in light of it. In this chapter, we discuss a feature of those stimuli that has often gone unnoticed: whether the argument's topic concerns public or personal matters. In other words, are the two conversational partners arguing about issues that pertain directly to their relationship (e.g., child care) or issues that are not directly relevant to their relationship (e.g., capital punishment)?

The focus on personal or public *issues* should not be confused with the distinction that scholars make between public, technical, and personal argument *spheres*. Goodnight's (1982) distinction among argument spheres delineated spheres as the natural homes and origins for certain topics and their associated deliberations. The personal sphere is characterized by conversations that occur between arguers who share an interpersonal relationship (Dimock, 2009) and whose consequences are relevant for the two people involved in the argument (Goodnight, 1987; Zarefsky, 2012). Zarefsky (2012) explained that arguing in the personal sphere required a preexisting relationship between arguers and that the standard for evaluating the argument was based on the effect it had on the arguers' relationship. The technical sphere is characterized by discourse presented to experts in a certain field, such as scientific debates about the effects of climate change or fracking. Finally, the public sphere is a forum in which issues pertinent to an entire community are discussed by designated spokespeople and in which arguments are judged based on more rigid standards than in the other two spheres (Goodnight, 1982). For example, social movements discourse, campaigns against the war, and public activism about topics of interest to our society may be issues discussed in the public sphere. Zarefsky (2012) summarized by stating that, as the number of people affected by the argument increases, we gradually move from the personal sphere (fewest number of people affected), to the technical, and finally to the public sphere (greatest number of people affected).

This chapter is about different topics of argument that are all located within the personal sphere. Related arguments might also appear in the public or technical spheres, but that is not our main concern here because our focus is mainly on what happens within interpersonal relationships. We use the terms *personal-issue arguments* and *public-issue arguments* to distinguish between topics about which people argue in the personal sphere and not the other spheres. We argue that researchers should pay attention to which sort of topics they analyze because of the methodological and theoretical implications of the public/personal issue distinction, and most of the attention in this chapter will focus on these implications. Our general conclusion is that interpersonal communication scholars can benefit from distinguishing between the two types of arguments given the different behaviors and consequences arguing about each type produces. Paying attention to this distinction not only enhances our understanding of the nuances of arguing in interpersonal relationships but also helps explain one of the situational influences that affect interpersonal exchanges and, potentially, overall communicative behavior among people.

First, we discuss the distinction between the two types of arguments and further differentiate it from related distinctions, such as Goodnight's (1982) argument spheres and Newell and Stutman's (1988) distinction between disagreements over ideas and disagreements over behaviors. Second, we discuss three main differences between public-issue and personal-issue arguments that current research has highlighted and explain why these differences are consequential for those who study interpersonal communication. We then supply examples of how the public/personal distinction is relevant to current research in persuasion, conflict, and relational communication and connect the distinction we make with the broader fields of political deliberation and public argument. Finally, we offer conclusions and future research directions.

Argument Episodes and the Public/
Personal Argument Distinction

By "argument" we mean an exchange of reasons in the face of actual or possible disagreement, not a hostile shouting match (Hample, 2005; Jackson & Jacobs, 1980; O'Keefe, 1977). When considering interpersonal arguing, O'Keefe (1977) distinguished between two concepts. On one hand, *argument*₁ consists of "a kind of utterance or communicative act" (O'Keefe, 1977, p. 121). These are statements supported by reasons, and we would expect to see them in any sphere of argument. On the other hand, an interaction with at least one other person involving a disagreement is designated *argument*₂ (O'Keefe, 1977). An argument₁ is something people make, whereas an argument₂ is something people have. In this chapter, public- and personal-issue arguments always refer to dialogic arguments; they involve having an argument with an interpersonal partner.

The distinction between public-issue arguments and personal-issue arguments is relatively straightforward. In any setting, either sort of topic can be discussed by two intimates, so the context in which the argument occurs has no definitive connection to whether the topic is a personal or public one. For example, a husband and wife may be overheard arguing in a restaurant or appearing on a reality show, but that does not make their argument one about a public topic. Similarly, they can privately talk together about whom to vote for, but the topic remains a public one. For us, the issue at hand determines the argument's category, along with the fact that it occurs in an interpersonal relationship between the two individuals arguing. A public topic is one that is not connected directly to the interpersonal relationship. In other words, the argument topic is not inherently related to the day-to-day interaction or relational definition that characterizes the connection between the two arguers. Rather, a public-issue argument relates to concerns outside of the interpersonal dyad. Sample topics are political matters, prospects for good weather, and sports.[1] A personal topic, in contrast, is one that raises matters bearing directly on the nature or conduct of the arguers' relationship. Sample topics include whose turn it is to cook, whether the arguers' children are being properly disciplined, and whether one person owes the other a favor. So, if the husband and wife at the restaurant were discussing their child-rearing practices, the argument would be a personal-issue one, despite the fact that it occurs in a public setting. If they were discussing which baseball team is likely to win the World Series, their argument would be a public-issue one even if it occurs in a private conversation. Although we are making a distinction between public and personal *topics*, both of this couple's arguments would belong in the personal *sphere* due to their pertaining to the individual needs of the two arguers, without ramifications to other areas (Zarefsky, 2012).

In public-issue arguments, any potential behavioral implications of the arguments (e.g., voting behavior) are not very closely related to the dyad's day-to-day functioning. Public-issue arguments may help individuals increase their argumentative skill (Rancer & Infante, 1985), and lack of resolution does not *necessarily* have negative effects (Newell & Stutman, 1988). Compared to arguments on public topics, differences in personal-issue arguments cannot be as easily left unsettled without harmful effects. However, even with personal-issue matters, there is variability in the relational stakes or the costs and benefits of arguing (Singer, 1974). For example, Zietlow and Sillars (1988) found that married couples considered irritability and lack of communication as their most salient personal argument topics and disagreements about leisure time and household responsibilities as the least important.

Our distinction between argument types is different from the one previously made by Newell and Stutman (1988) who distinguished between two types of argument$_2$, disagreements over behaviors and disagreements over ideas. They gave the example of a married couple discussing welfare as a disagreement over ideas, which would satisfy our definition of public-issue arguments. Their example of a disagreement over behaviors consisted of two brothers arguing over one borrowing the car without permission, which is a personal-issue argument topic. Newell and Stutman (1988) claimed that disagreements over ideas can be "pursued just for the fun of it" (p. 271), whereas disagreements over behaviors focus on the interdependence of the two individuals. These latter disagreements "make a difference" because they concern interference with one person's goals (Newell & Stutman, 1988, p. 271). The defining characteristic of the argument types discussed in this chapter, however, is related to whether the issue is focused on some aspect within the arguing party's relationship (personal) or outside of the relationship (public). Either type of argument could focus on ideas, behaviors, or both. For example, public-issue arguments could be about ideas or behaviors (e.g., capitalism or whether people should publically protest when they are upset with their government), and so can personal-issue arguments (e.g., what constitutes marital fidelity for a couple or whether to invite another couple to dinner). So, the public/personal and idea/behavior pairs are associated, but not identical. We consider that the public/personal distinction is more immediately interesting because it is founded in the ongoing character of the interpersonal relationship in which the arguments appear.

Although we focus on research concerning the personal sphere in this chapter, it is important to note that not all arguments about personal issues or public issues remain strictly confined to the personal sphere. Sometimes what is originally discussed in the personal sphere (be it a public-issue or personal-issue argument) extends beyond this realm to become a matter of public interest. In fact, we might suppose that many public issues originate in private discussions; obvious historical examples would include gay marriage, women's voting rights, abortion, the government's right to tax individuals' property, and who should take care of the elderly. For example, Murray (2012) argued that Cindy Sheehan's rhetoric protesting the war in Iraq originated in grief, a private emotion caused by the death of her son. This grief became the catalyst for a public debate regarding the war in Iraq because it went beyond the "boundaries between the public and personal spheres" (Murray, 2012, p. 3). In other words, the argument transcended Sheehan's private life to become an issue of interest to a whole community. Similarly, public sphere matters may seep into private life. For example, Cindy Sheehan and her husband separated due to conflict concerning her public role (Murray, 2012).

Perhaps we have devoted too much space to overlaps and possible exceptions. In fact, coders have little difficulty making the public/personal distinction reliably (A. Johnson & Hall, 2001). We do not claim, of course, that this is the only distinction that can be made between argument topics. Workplace topics (Cionea & Hample, 2013; Hample & Irions, 2013; Hample, Paglieri, & Na, 2012) are also important and different in terms of their characteristics and outcomes from public-issue and personal-issue arguments. Close relationships are also not the only context in which such arguments occur. For instance, Cionea and Hample (2013) reported that colleagues in the workplace argued about personal-issue topics as well. Certainly, the distinction extends beyond the realm of close relationships, although the vast majority of research has only analyzed it in this interpersonal context.

The next section summarizes existing research on this argument distinction by discussing three consequential differences between public-issue and personal-issue arguments: (a) they differ in terms of who argues about these topics, (b) they differ in how the argumentative episodes are interpreted and enacted, and (c) they differ in terms of the stakes the arguments have for the relationships that give rise to them. Therefore, this distinction is meaningful in order to understand fully how individuals engage in arguments in their interpersonal relationships.

Three Key Differences Between Public-Issue and Personal-Issue Arguments

Who Argues About Each Sort of Topic

Although most previous work on argumentation in interpersonal relationships has focused on personal-issue arguments, both public-issue and personal-issue arguments commonly occur in family relationships, friendships, and romantic relationships and hence both need to be examined to understand argumentation in these contexts. Previous research has illustrated that individuals report arguing about both public- and personal-issue arguments with their romantic partners, friends, and family members (A. Johnson, 1999a, 2000, 2002, 2009). In an early study (A. Johnson, 1999a), 35 students kept diaries of their interpersonal arguments for 3 weeks. A total of 127 arguments were listed: 20% public-issue arguments and 80% personal-issue arguments. Cionea and Hample (2013) found the same was true in serial arguments: People argue repeatedly about personal-issue topics more than about public-issue topics. So, people tend to address more personal-issue topics in their everyday arguments.

A. Johnson (2009) found that undergraduates were most likely to report arguing with a friend for both personal- and public-issue arguments, followed by romantic partners, and family members. However, the percentage of friends was higher in the public argument condition (66% of public-issue arguments, 41% of personal-issue arguments). An earlier study (A. Johnson, 2002) found slightly different results, with friends being the most likely interpersonal partner for public-issue arguments and romantic partners for personal-issue arguments. In addition, several studies have suggested that males or male–male dyads are more likely to engage in public-issue arguments (e.g., A. Johnson, 1999a). It seems that some kinds of people may *invite* certain sorts of topics (e.g., male friends argue about sports given the nature of the relationship between them), and some kinds of people may *require* certain types of topics (e.g., romantic partners argue about household chores given the likelihood of occurrence of such a topic in their relationship).

So what factors predict what type of argument topic people engage in? Although many possible predispositions may relate to whether individuals are more attracted to public-issue or personal-issue arguments, prior research has focused mainly on the predictive ability of argumentativeness (Infante & Rancer, 1982) and verbal aggressiveness (Infante & Wigley, 1986). Both argumentativeness and verbal aggressiveness affect whether people will involve themselves in an argument, but these two predispositions point people toward different sorts of engagement (Rancer & Avtgis, 2006). People high in argumentativeness tend to focus on the other person's evidence, reasons, and standpoint, whereas people high in verbal aggressiveness tend to attack the other person's self-concept (Infante & Wigley, 1986).

Overall, the research related to argument type illustrates that argumentativeness is more relevant to public-issue arguments, but verbal aggressiveness is more important for personal-issue arguments. A. Johnson (2000) found that one's own argumentativeness predicted how often one reported arguing about public- and personal-issue argument topics with a friend. The perception of a friend's verbal aggressiveness was positively related to how often an individual argued about personal-issue argument topics with that friend. A. Johnson, Becker, Wigley, Haigh, and Craig (2007) examined whether argument type affected the relationship between trait measures of argumentativeness and verbal aggressiveness and reported levels of these two variables during a particular argument episode. They found that individuals reported higher levels of argumentativeness when considering public-issue arguments rather than personal-issue arguments, with individuals reporting a greater tendency to approach and a lower tendency to avoid the public-issue argument. They also found that individuals reported higher levels of verbal aggressiveness when arguing about personal-issue topics as compared to public-issue topics. This pattern was particularly strong among women. These personality traits (argumentativeness and verbal aggressiveness) can be understood as behavioral thresholds. A highly argumentative person, for instance, needs little incentive to argue, but someone lower in argumentativeness needs to perceive more urgency or potential benefit in order to engage. For example, A. Johnson (1999b) found that friendship dyads composed of two people low in argumentativeness reported arguing about public issues significantly less than did friendship dyads composed of other combinations of argumentativeness levels. This finding is consistent with the results of Levine and Boster (1996), who examined the argumentativeness composition of stranger dyads. Similarly, verbal aggressiveness levels also indicate how much stimulus is needed for a person to insult or harass another person. The conclusion of these studies is that one's level of argumentativeness and verbal aggressiveness affects one's engagement in each particular type of argument topic.

One of the main purposes of research on argumentativeness and verbal aggressiveness is to teach individuals to argue constructively in their every-day lives (Infante & Rancer, 1996; Rancer & Avtgis, 2006). As the situational factor of argument topic type is related to reported argumentativeness and ver-bal aggressiveness levels, examining the relationship between these variables extends the literature in an important way: It helps determine how to encour-age constructive communication in both types of arguments. Argumentation scholars who wish to encourage constructive argumentation in interpersonal relationships could start by teaching people to argue about public-issue topics due to their lower levels of involvement. This is the tactic adopted by Kuhn (2005) when she "scaffolds" a sequence of arguing skills for children. Accord-ing to Kuhn (2005), for those with little arguing experience, arguing is often a competitive endeavor, in which one aims to win the argument. In such circum-stances, arguing about personal issues can damage the relationship because such arguments are emotional, have the potential to hurt feelings, and generate conflict that is more personalized for the two arguers. Teaching people to argue about less involving public issues would permit an initial focus on reasoning and evidence.

Nevertheless, encouraging constructive arguing in personal-issue argu-ments should be the ultimate goal because these are the arguments with the most consequential pragmatic outcomes, as we will show. Moving to personal matters would then require other-orientation and facework to be scaffolded onto the earlier skills. People do appear to be more careful in their engage-ments over personal-issue argument topics. Richards and Cionea (in press) found that when people argued about personal-issue topics they thought more carefully about the effects such arguments had on their relationship, compared to public-issue topics. This tendency was also illustrated by the findings that respondents were more willing to approach and less likely to avoid public-issue arguments than personal-issue arguments (A. Johnson et al., 2007). Because verbal aggressiveness has been found to be more relevant to personal-issue arguments than argumentativeness, and the difference between high and low argumentatives is mitigated in personal-issue arguments compared to public-issue arguments (A. Johnson et al., 2007), researchers should focus on how to encourage argumentative behavior in personal-issue arguments in particular. So, learning to argue about public-issue topics can teach dialogical argumenta-tion (Kuhn, 2005) and the skills necessary for constructive arguing, which can then be transferred to issues that are more relevant to the interpersonal dyad, and ensure a more constructive discussion of those issues than in the absence of argumentation skills (cf. Infante, Chandler, & Rudd, 1989).

Other important factors might also influence how individuals argue about certain public issues. For instance, the amount of coverage a topic receives in the news should affect whether individuals argue about certain public-issue argument topics. Examples include the presidential election of 2000 that led to debates in both public and personal settings. Another example is gay marriage, which is currently a prominent topic in the media. People are likely to talk most about the public-issue topics that have the greatest salience to them, and media coverage could be one way that such salience is increased. So, for some topics, individual differences in media consumption or need for cognition (Cohen, Stotland, & Wolfe, 1955) might predict the incidence of public-issue arguments. People may also differ in their depth of commitment on certain public-issue arguments. For instance, people may be more or less wedded to their particular view on an issue; some may be more open to changing their opinions, whereas others may resist persuasion attempts. Such individual differences could be related to argumentativeness (Infante & Rancer, 1982) but also to other variables, such as dogmatism (Boster & Levine, 1988) or persuasibility (Linton & Graham, 1959). All of these matters (e.g., the salience of the public issue discussed, media consumption, open-mindedness, and so forth) are yet untouched in the research tradition reviewed here and may be promising questions for future research.

To summarize, different sorts of people are drawn toward or repelled by each argument type. Whether people engage in public-issue or personal-issue arguments is related to their individual predispositions, at least in terms of argumentativeness and verbal aggressiveness. It is also related to whom one is communicating with (e.g., friend, romantic partner) and to one's own and the other's biological sex. Future research should examine other trait variables that might predict arguing about each type of topic. The next section discusses a second difference between public-issue and personal-issue arguments: that argument type predicts how people interpret and enact argumentative episodes that occur in their interpersonal relationships.

How Argument Episodes Are Enacted and Interpreted

Public-issue and personal-issue arguments differ in terms of how they are performed and understood. We believe this difference exists because the degree of engagement that individuals experience while enacting each type of argument is different. We discuss Singer's (1974) explorations of the concept of engagement-involvement to explain this difference and then use that frame to discuss prior research that has investigated the differences in enacting and interpreting public-issue and personal-issue arguments.

Singer's notion of engagement-involvement.   Singer (1974) and her colleagues encountered what must have seemed at first an annoying result in their psychophysiological laboratories. They found that participants' responses were not well connected with the sort of stimulus in the study (e.g., stress) or the sorts of respondents (e.g., hypertensive patients). Instead, the relationship between the participant and the experimenter was sometimes determinate in explaining people's cardiovascular and endocrine responses. Involvement with one's experimenter predicted blood pressure, even though measures of affect types and levels did not. Singer proposed that these and many similar results could be explained by a concept she labeled *engagement-involvement,* which she defined as follows: "Engagement-involvement . . . is that central phenomenon which suggests a person is locking into, actually investing in a transaction, in its internal and external aspects" (Singer, 1974, pp. 1–2).

The connection between this idea and our topical distinction is that we believe personal topics are more engaging, in that people "lock into" them more, and "invest" themselves more in arguments on those matters. For example, personal topics have been found to be more ego-involving (A. Johnson, 2002) and to appear more realistic (Warner & Hample, 2008) than do public ones. This is not to say that exceptions from this rule do not exist. Some people become vested in public-issue argument topics because they are important matters to their own personhood, their values, and their beliefs. For example, consider those who have dedicated their lives to fighting a particular piece of legislation or policy. A person who is homosexual may take a personal-issue argument further and become involved in public support for gay marriage, marches, and testimonies before legislative bodies, and so on. But, in general, people are more concerned with issues immediately affecting their everyday relationships; not everyone ends up being an activist. The next section presents research evidence that illustrates how individuals engage and interpret public-issue and personal-issue arguments in different ways.

Argument engagement.   We believe that personal topics produce different sorts of transactions than public ones. Transactional phenomena, such as affect toward the experimenter and comfort in the room, were important in explaining engagement involvement in an interaction (Singer, 1974). Thus, engagement-involvement is caused by features of the situation (Miller, Cody, & McLaughlin, 1994), and these features notably include the people involved and the topic of the interaction (Hample, 2005). We believe, as Singer (1974) does, that the topic of a particular argument and the relationship between the individuals arguing are distinct considerations, but we also believe that they can modify one another. For example, an accusation of slovenliness has different meanings when it originates from a stranger or a spouse.

Singer (1974) began her analysis by suggesting that every person has a default level of engagement, what she called a preferred style of engagement-involvement. Work on need for cognition has a similar premise (Cohen et al., 1955). Particular interactional episodes can raise or lower a person's engagement. "These short-term changes in engagement-involvement are shown both in outward behavior with other persons, events, and surroundings and in the level of responsiveness to inner states, memories, and ideas" (Singer, 1974, p. 1). Responsiveness to an argumentative interaction can be displayed by the level of scrutiny arguments received as well as by the interactional presence an arguer exhibits or perceives (e.g., Burgoon et al., 2002). Higher than normal engagement can be pleasurable or punishing, and these affective responses during face-to-face arguments are beginning to be documented (e.g., Hample, Thompson-Hayes, Wallenfelsz, Wallenfelsz, & Knapp, 2005). Disengagement—lower than normal levels of involvement—is also implied by this formulation, and here connections to research on relational apathy, loneliness, and depression are clear (Berger & Bell, 1988; Segrin, 2000; Singer, 1974).

The different argument topics have been shown to predict whether one chooses to engage in an argument. Several authors (Cionea, Hample, & Paglieri, 2011; Hample et al., 2012; Paglieri, 2009; Paglieri & Castelfranchi, 2010; Richards & Cionea, in press) have theorized that people consider the costs and benefits of arguing prior to engaging in an argument. Singer (1974) explained that every transaction proceeds from participants' levels of engagement-involvement and, therefore, that people consider the costs and benefits of transacting. The idea here is that the excess of benefits over costs must meet an individual's threshold, or engagement will not take place. Public and personal issues have been shown to have systematically different levels and types of costs and benefits.

To explore this issue, Hample et al. (2012), Cionea et al. (2011), Richards and Cionea (in press), and Hample and Irions (2013) used a similar design in which they exposed participants to a topical stimulus, either public or personal, that invited interpersonal argument. They asked participants to provide estimates of costs and benefits, and then used those estimates to predict intention to engage in arguing. In Hample et al. (2012), engagement in public topic arguments was predicted the most strongly by a participant's estimate that he or she would win the argument, and less by the expectation that the argument would be civil and appropriate. Engagement in personal topic arguments was predicted by the estimate that the participant would win the argument, and less strongly by the perception that such an argument would be appropriate and beneficial.

Cionea et al. (2011) studied public topics and found that argument engagement was predicted by the likelihood of winning, the perceived appropriateness of arguing, and the expected level of civility in the argument. Richards and Cionea (in press) found that engagement in the public topic differed from engagement in the personal topic in that the benefit of engaging was predicted by effort and likelihood of winning the argument when the topic was a public one, and by effort, resolvability of the issue, and the overall civility of the argument when the topic was a personal one. In addition, when the argument was about a personal issue, people considered not only the probability that an outcome would occur, but also the value they placed on that outcome, which was not the case for arguments about public issues. Hample and Irions (2013) replicated the common finding that likelihood of winning and perceived appropriateness were generally important to engagement on any sort of topic. These were the only significant predictors of engagement on public topics, but personal issue engagement was also sensitive to expected effort, other's reasonableness, possible rewards, and how strongly one was invited to engage. Taken all together, these results illustrate Singer's (1974) claim that costs and benefits are predictive of whether a transaction will take place, in this case whether individuals were willing to argue about these issues. Different costs and benefits were consequential for public-issue and personal-issue arguments.

In addition to deciding to engage in an argument, individuals can choose to edit what they would say in an argumentative encounter, and argument-topic type has been shown to make a difference in this endeavor as well. Hample and Dallinger (2002) illustrated that situational features systematically affected the way arguers edited their messages, although all the studies summarized in Hample and Dallinger focused only on personal topics. However, in Warner and Hample (2008), respondents reported their editorial decisions concerning particular arguments twice, once on a public topic and once on a personal one. Respondents were provided with lists of phrases they might say during the argument and were asked to either endorse or indicate why the message would be suppressed. Of the eight substantive editorial criteria, topic type produced significant differences on five. Personal topics led to less endorsement, more use of principled objections (e.g., "this is too negative to use"), more concern for harm to relationship, more attention to the truth of what was being argued, and less concern for relevance than public topics did. In short, when considering a personal topic, people reported that they were generally more careful about what they were willing to say. In particular, they were more sensitive to the relationship and the consequences of exaggerating or lying. They were more willing to say irrelevant things and move off topic, perhaps because they had more concern for the relationship than the argument, compared to people considering public topics.

To explore argument enactment, A. Johnson, Brown, and Wittenberg (2005) used Canary's (1989) coding instrument to explore whether public-issue and personal-issue argument episodes differed in observable argument structure. They had 45 friendship dyads discuss each type of topic for 5 minutes. People engaging in public-issue arguments used significantly more challenges; people engaging in personal-issue arguments used significantly more acknowledgements, indicating recognition of another's point but not agreement. Perhaps in the public-issue arguments, attacking the other's views on the issue was more acceptable because these issues were not as relevant for the particular friendship, lowering the stakes for aggressive challenges. Because the personal-issue arguments were more relevant to the actual friendship, individuals may have sought to show solidarity by acknowledging each other's views, but may have illustrated reluctance to actually agree with the other person because this agreement might have led to calls for behavioral change.

In summary, whether and why individuals engage in interpersonal arguments, what editing process they utilize, and how they enact an argument, all related to whether one was considering a public-issue or personal-issue argument. The next section applies this distinction to the examination of how individuals interpret an argument.

Argument interpretation and sensemaking.   Our reading of Singer (1974) suggests that one's level of involvement-engagement is an element of sensemaking; that is, a situation actually has different meanings for a highly involved person versus a person who is indifferent to what is going on. We have been suggesting that personal topics are more involving. According to the various dual processing persuasion models (e.g., Petty & Cacioppo, 1986), this closer involvement should lead to more scrutiny and intricate sensemaking of the arguments themselves. For example, Hample, Jones, and Averbeck (2009) showed that most fallacies are harmless: In focused conversation, people most often ignore, reject, or repair fallacious arguments. However, the type of interpersonal argument presented moderates this tendency to ignore fallacies. To explore this phenomenon, Hample, Sells, and Inclán Velázquez (2009) asked respondents to read two vignettes, one on a personal topic and one on a public one. Each vignette reported conversation turns, and the last turn expressed one of six fallacies. Respondents rated each final turn regarding its appropriateness, effectiveness, soundness, and playfulness. If there were no difference in terms of the scrutiny public and personal topics produce, one would expect the ratings to be essentially equivalent. However, fallacious arguments on personal subjects were rated as less appropriate, less effective, and less sound as compared to fallacious arguments on public topics. For ordinarily sound arguments, Hample, Warner, and Norton (2006) reported the reverse: Arguments on personal topics were consistently rated as more appropriate, effective, and sound than arguments on public topics. The presence of fallacies—which should trigger critical reactions only under conditions of high scrutiny—seems to be the key. This finding suggests that participants naturally found themselves attending more closely to argument quality when the topics were personal.

In addition, individuals have been shown to exhibit different beliefs about public-issue and personal-issue arguments (A. Johnson, 2002), which also illustrates that they interpret and make sense of these arguments differently. Individuals believe that public-issue arguments are higher in enjoyment and opportunities to enhance one's self-concept, whereas personal-issue arguments are higher in pragmatic outcomes and ego-involvement (A. Johnson, 2002). A. Johnson, Kelley, Liu, and Averbeck (2012) showed that these same beliefs about interpersonal arguments predicted stress and stress-related symptoms experienced after the argument. As previous research on argument beliefs (Rancer, Baukus, & Infante, 1985; Rancer, Kosberg, & Baukus, 1992) has had a goal of helping individuals argue more effectively, taking both types of arguments into account when considering the pragmatic implications of this research is important.

Making sense of an argument involves applying self to the interaction. The apparent content of the exchange is understood in terms of one's beliefs about that type of argument and one's own general orientations. Topic type affects level of scrutiny, beliefs about the episode, and affective reactions. All of these are involved in sensemaking, and so a full account of what people think they are doing when they argue needs to take argument topic type into consideration. The next section discusses a third important difference between public-issue and personal-issue arguments: the different stakes or consequences each argument type has for one's interpersonal relationship.

The Stakes/Consequences of Each Argument Topic Type

When examining arguments that individuals have in their interpersonal relationships, it is important to consider that these two types of arguments differ in their relational stakes. Although this may seem definitional (after all, one issue type is called personal because it involves relational conduct or definition), only our taken-for-granted assumptions that personal lives are more important than public lives (i.e., are more involving) make the personal stakes automatically seem to be higher. For a contrasting case, consider a workaholic. He or she might occasionally say that family comes first, but the truth is, family almost never does. For such a person, the most involving topics would be those at work. For a relationally impaired Internet game addict, the most involving matters might include World of Warcraft. So higher involvement in personal-issue arguments is an empirical matter, not a definitional one.

Several studies have examined variables that relate to the types of stakes that an argument has for the arguing dyad, such as relational satisfaction. A. Johnson (1999b) found that, for both public-issue and personal-issue arguments, the frequency of arguing about these issues was negatively related to friendship satisfaction. This is not the usual result in studies of serial arguments in romantic relationships in which frequency and satisfaction were not associated (e.g., K. Johnson & Roloff, 1998), although some researchers have found a negative association between argument frequency and satisfaction (e.g., Lloyd, 1987). Villagran, A. Johnson, Villagran, and Wittenberg (2001) found that argument topic type and resolution interacted such that the resolvability of the argument had a stronger relationship with friendship satisfaction in the personal-issue argument than in the public-issue argument. Resolvability has a strong positive association with relational satisfaction, even in studies where the frequency effect does not appear (e.g., K. Johnson & Roloff, 1998). A. Johnson, Averbeck, Kelley, and Liu (2011) found that in the case of serial arguments, type of argument and perceived resolvability interacted to predict relational harm from the argument. In conditions of high resolvability, there was little difference in perceived relational harm between public- and personal-issue arguments, but in conditions of low resolvability, personal-issue arguments were perceived as more harmful. Therefore, to fully understand how variables such as perceived resolvability affect the stakes of an interpersonal argument, argument-topic type should be taken into account.

Research examining the functions that arguments play in interpersonal relationships (A. Johnson, 2009) has supported the view that personal-issue arguments have higher stakes for the interpersonal dyad. A. Johnson (2009) found that the reasons for which these arguments were enacted in interpersonal relationships differed. Public-issue arguments were perceived as functioning more often to gain or give knowledge to the other person, to pass the time in an enjoyable fashion, or to express one's views to the other. Personal-issue arguments were perceived to function more often to portray the self in a positive light or to solve behavioral incompatibilities.

Although the most general conclusion regarding argument stakes is that arguments about personal topics will be more enmeshing, public-issue matters can also have important consequences for the relationship under some conditions, although the exploration of these conditions is only now under way. Consider the case in which the position one takes on a public issue is perceived as implying something about the person's character or values. If someone is against the death penalty, this position on a public issue may be perceived as indicative of the value one places on human life or what one believes about justice, and these perceptions might affect whether one wants to develop a relationship with that person. Public and personal matters may collide, as they did when Cindy Sheehan separated from her husband because of their disagreements about her public profile (Murray, 2012). If individuals sacrifice their personal lives to engage in activism within the public sphere, this engagement would be expected to affect their interpersonal relationships. We explore this matter further at the end of this chapter.

Although a public topic is defined as external to the dyad, individuals may believe that attitudes about these topics may predict behavior within the relationship. Aron and Aron (1986) have defined closeness as the perceived overlap of the two individuals' selves, which implies that disagreeing on an issue closely tied to one's values may lead to deterioration of the relationship. For example, A. Johnson, Averbeck, Kelley, and Liu (2010) found that in public-issue serial arguments, perceived resolvability of both public-issue and personal-issue arguments was more important when it involved a high value-relevant topic. Future research should specifically examine this potentially important subset of cases involving high-stakes public-issue arguments.

In summary, we have highlighted three overarching differences regarding the distinction between personal-issue and public-issue arguments that summarize the existing literature on this topic: (a) Individuals differ in how likely they are to argue about each topic with their interpersonal partners. This distinction might be of particular interest to those interpersonal communication scholars who focus on everyday talk and how we actually enact our personal relationships. (b) People differ in how they enact and interpret public-issue and personal-issue arguments. This line of research might be especially relevant to those communication scholars who are interested in factors that predict our communication choices in interpersonal relationships. Finally, (c) public-issue and personal-issue arguments differ in terms of the stakes they have for interpersonal relationships. These findings are relevant to those interpersonal communication scholars who focus on what factors predict particular relationship-specific outcome variables, such as relational satisfaction.

In what follows, we elaborate on specific implications of this distinction for several areas of study within communication research, including interpersonal (persuasion, conflict, and relational communication), political (political deliberation and public argument), and other broad areas of communication research. Rather than an exhaustive description of all possible relevant applications of the concept of argument type, the following section's goal is to illustrate that the argument distinction has heuristic value for many areas of communication.

Applicability of Argument Topic Type to Other Areas of Research

Type of argument should relate to how one seeks to persuade or influence others, how one resolves conflict, and how arguing relates to other communication in our relationships. This section illustrates how the argument distinction may apply in these areas and thus provides further evidence for argument topic type's potential importance. It also suggests future research directions for scholars in these particular areas. More general future directions for research are presented in a later section of this chapter.

Persuasion

Personal-issue arguments' ties to our relationships affect how we respond to persuasive attempts in these arguments and the persuasive attempts that we implement. For example, as we have shown, individuals attend more closely to personal-issue arguments (Hample et al., 2009), as suggested by dual processing models (e.g., Petty & Cacioppo, 1986). This greater amount of central processing in these arguments may indicate that persuasion functions differently in the case of public-issue and personal-issue arguments. Individuals are also more careful about what they say in personal-issue arguments (Warner & Hample, 2008), meaning they edit their arguments more cautiously. This result suggests people may present different persuasive messages when trying to persuade someone about a personal-issue topic (e.g., immediate condom use) as compared to a public-issues topic (e.g., voting behavior). Finally, different compliance gaining strategies or influence attempts may be used depending on the topic at hand. For example, several typologies of compliance-seeking strategies have focused on how people try to make others comply with their requests in different situations (e.g., Marwell & Schmitt, 1967; Schenck-Hamlin, Wiseman, & Georgacarakos, 1982). It may be useful to analyze whether such strategies are affected by whether the topic is a personal-issue or a public-issue one.

Second, consider balance theory. Newcomb (1953) argued that people could cope with a lack of similarity in attitudes by changing their own attitude toward the other person or the other object, by changing the other's attitude toward the self or the object, or by perceiving the other's attitude toward the self or the object as different from reality. Our distinction between personal-issue and public-issue arguments suggests that the urgency (or lack thereof) for engaging in these coping behaviors depends on the stakes of the particular argument for the interpersonal dyad. Personal-issue arguments have higher stakes than public-issue arguments, so the former would involve more urgency to cope with dissimilarities than the latter. This may be the reason why agreeing to disagree (i.e., accepting imbalance) is a more likely outcome for public-issue arguments (A. Johnson & Hall, 2001), in which persuasion to one's point of view is not needed. Agreeing to disagree may not often be a viable option in personal-issue arguments because attitude dissimilarity in these cases may hinder a dyad's functioning. Some dissimilarities are tolerable (and may even improve the relationship), but too many dissimilarities may indicate the partners are incompatible. Thus, one would expect a more forceful need to change certain attitudes about a personal-issue topic in order to maintain a relationship.

Persuasion researchers can use the distinction between personal issues and public issues to refine explanations about attitude change, compliance gaining, and influence attempts. For example, if personal-issue arguments are more involving for a dyad than public-issue arguments, does this mean that attitude change processes function differently depending on the topic of argument? Does changing a partner's attitude about household chores require more arguments, better arguments, more baring of the arguer's self, or more appeals, as compared to changing his/her attitude about the death penalty? This point also suggests a potential avenue for research into persuasive message quality. For example, the two types of arguments may invite or require different persuasive messages, and these messages may differ in persuasiveness.

Conflict

Many issues that have traditionally been examined under the conflict framework are relevant to the type of argument distinction. For example, research has examined "taboo topics" among romantic partners (Roloff & Ifert, 1998), where individuals stop discussing certain areas of conflict in their relationships. Which type of argument topic is more likely to become taboo in an interpersonal relationship: public-issue arguments because of their potential tie to values or personal-issue arguments because of their higher involvement levels? The work reviewed here on argument engagement is relevant, but it did not move to the pointed examination of never-to-be-engaged topics, as in Roloff and Ifert's (1998) work. The public/personal topic distinction could further inform research on the causes of conflict and conflict avoidance in relationships.

The distinction between personal-issue and public-issue arguments may also be helpful in explaining conflict outcomes. For example, a classic study was Vuchinich's (1990) exploration of naturally occurring conflicts around the dinner table. This research found that most argumentative episodes ended without resolution. Type of argument should influence which arguments end without resolution (with public-issue arguments being more likely) and may affect which conflict topics may begin again later, to become serial arguments. Individuals may be more likely to engage in standoffs (where no agreement is reached) in public-issue arguments. Only 9% of the conflicts in Vuchinich's (1990) research ended in compromise. Individuals should have more incentive to work toward compromise in personal-issue arguments.

Gayle, Preiss, and Allen (2002) discussed research on conflict strategies (Blake & Mouton, 1964) that suggested that one's choice of strategies was related to the balance between one's concern for self and one's concern for other (Thomas, 1988). The literature related to type of argument suggests that there is a third concern relevant to how we engage in conflict: concern for the relationship (A. Johnson, 2002; A. Johnson et al., 2011). Whether a conflict is tied to the interpersonal relationship affects how and whether we approach it (with implications for conflict avoidance literatures; A. Johnson et al., 2007) and how we enact it (with implications for conflict "styles" or conflict behavior literatures; A. Johnson et al., 2005). The conflict styles model (Blake & Mouton, 1964) is based on "the underlying assumption that individuals develop fairly stable preferences for certain conflict strategies regardless of situations or topics" (Gayle et al., 2002, p. 348). However, the literature covered in this chapter does not support such a view but instead argues that to divorce a conflict from its situation (relationship) and type of argument (topic) causes a loss of predictive power.

Relational Communication

The distinction between argument topics is also useful for studying relational communication. Arguing about personal-issues versus public-issues may be connected to relationship development as outlined by social penetration theory (Altman & Taylor, 1973). It is likely that public-issues arguments are more prevalent in incipient stages of a relationship, when self-disclosure is low and people usually discuss general topics, or in superficial relationships, such as those with strangers or acquaintances. Personal-issues arguments are likely more prevalent in deeper stages of social penetration when the relationship between arguers has progressed. As Altman and Haythorn (1965) noted, as the depth of self-disclosure increases in a relationship, intimacy increases, and the topics approached by people change from nonintimate to intimate—in other words, from public to personal. The public/personal distinction could be used as an indicator or corollary of social penetration and self-disclosure in interpersonal relationships.

Argument topic is also relevant to levels of closeness in an interpersonal relationship. Disagreements on an issue closely tied to one's self may threaten closeness between partners. For most people, personal-issue arguments are more closely connected to one's self than are public-issue arguments, so disagreements about such issues may lead to the deterioration of the relation-ship. Public-issue argument topics closely tied to values, however, should be an exception to this rule. Arguments about personal issues are also more closely connected to taking conflict personally (Hample, Dallinger, & Fofano, 1995; Hample, Dallinger, & Nelson, 1994) because they involve more aspects of the self than arguments about public issues.

In addition, argument topic may also affect individual interpersonal behavior while communicating in relationships. Successful arguments about personal issues may require more empathy, more active listening, more positiv-ity, and more constructive communication given that such arguments are more involving and have a more serious impact on the relationship, as compared to public-issue arguments. Personal-issue arguments' close connection with the relationship between the two people makes them more likely to evoke more intense emotions (both positive and negative) than do public-issue arguments. However, a person may be more cooperative, willing to compromise or to let go of his or her position, when it comes to personal-issue arguments as compared to public-issue arguments because of the value placed on the relationship with the other party.

Political Deliberation

The distinction between personal-issue arguments and public-issue arguments may also aid scholars interested in political deliberation. According to Eve-land, Morey, and Hutchens (2011), current research on political deliberation has ignored the interpersonal processes at work in much informal political con-versation. They claimed that instead of only focusing on individuals as citizens when considering deliberation, "there should be a greater emphasis on indi-viduals functioning as communicators in relationships" (Eveland et al., 2011, p. 1082). Although political issues are only one type of public-issue arguments, considering the literature on public-issue arguments suggests many aspects of the interpersonal relationship that are relevant to political deliberation.

Eveland et al. (2011) defined informal political conversation as "interper-sonal and small-group interactions about the broad topic of politics that take place outside of formal deliberation settings" (p. 1083). This type of talk is casual, carried out freely, and much less formal than the type of deliberation that occurs in the public sphere. However, Kim and Kim (2008) claimed that this type of talk is still important because it helps individuals prepare and gain skills needed to argue effectively within the public sphere. In addition, they claimed that such talk helps individuals to learn what their interests are and helps them "construct the concept of the sociopolitical self in their daily lives" (Kim & Kim, 2008, p. 58). Eveland et al. (2011) also suggested that scholars interested in informal political communication should focus on how people actually talk about these issues in their everyday lives and should explore what argument structures exist when engaging in these conversations. Research on public-issue arguments can give a sense of some of these issues. For instance,

A. Johnson et al. (2005) found that individuals engaging in public-issue arguments engaged in more challenges, whereas those engaged in personal-issue arguments engaged in more acknowledgments.

Wyatt, Katz, and Kim (2000) found that individuals engaging in informal political communication felt free to talk about political issues and reported talking about these issues most commonly at work and at home. Thus, the work on political deliberation emphasizes the importance of casual talk about political issues in interpersonal relationships. Eveland et al. (2011) found that when queried as to why they discussed politics with their conversation partners, people reported "noncivic" motivations, such as passing the time or developing an interesting argument, more commonly than forming an opinion or persuading the other, more traditional foci for political deliberation research. These results dovetail well with the work on argument functions by A. Johnson (2009) who found that people reported public-issue arguments fulfilled the functions of gaining or giving knowledge, passing the time, and expressing one's views.

Although the political deliberation literature focuses more on preparing individuals to participate in argument in the public sphere and the line of research discussed in this chapter focuses more on the stakes and effects of these arguments for interpersonal relationships, both lines of research are relevant to each other. For instance, Eveland et al. (2011) claimed that the effects of political conversations may depend on interpersonal factors. The research on public-issue arguments shows many of the variables that are important, including the type of relationship (A. Johnson, 1999), the argumentativeness and verbal aggressiveness levels of the individuals (A. Johnson et al., 2007), and the value relevance of the topic (A. Johnson et al., 2011). Hence, conjoining these two lines of thought should permit us to see how private political talk projects upward to the social level and how public sphere deliberation can focus downward to affect individual conversations and relationships.

Public Argument

Overall, the research in this chapter has focused on how individuals argue within the personal sphere (Goodnight, 1982). As such, both public-issue and personal-issue arguments have a more informal structure and their stakes tend to be limited to the interpersonal relationship, rather than having consequences that extend beyond the personal and technical spheres, as argument in the public sphere tends to have. However, another interesting area for future research that we have alluded to in this chapter relates to how arguing in the public sphere affects interpersonal relationships. There are many individuals whose beliefs and values lead them to engaging in arguments within the public sphere, whether it involves protesting the death penalty or blocking a church group from picketing a soldier's funeral. For example, Duncan's (1999) study of feminist activists illustrates several connections between women's interior lives and their public activism. Thus, engagement within the public sphere can also affect interpersonal relationships. The distinction between argument types has not yet examined the possibility of influences from another argument sphere.

Although the distinction between personal and public topics is clear, both conceptually and empirically, readers may have noticed that we are intrigued by close cases, circumstances in which an argument seems to partake of both social and private characters. We have mentioned Cindy Sheehan's case at several points, and her social place as an activist about what began for her as a personal matter (her grief over her son's death in Iraq). In fact, activism seems generally to confuse things (naturally, few of our respondents seemed to be activists and so this problem did not really assert itself in the research program). Some activists dedicate their lives to a public cause, and it comes to dominate their personal relationships as well. Public and personal issues blur for these people. For example, McAdam (1989) studied more than 300 people who applied to work in the 1964 Mississippi Summer Freedom project; more than 200 did work there, although 100 were accepted but did not participate. Among the many differences between participants and nonparticipants, several are interesting from our point of view: Participants had a greater number of other activists in their social networks, were less likely to have had children or jobs in the 1960s, belonged to more political organizations, were more likely to be "leftist" in political orientation, and were more likely to endorse this survey item: "My participation in social movements affected my choice of mate(s)." Although participants and nonparticipants were equally likely to be married in the 1960s, 20 years later, participants were 20% to 30% less likely than nonparticipants to be married. McAdam speculated that the activists' marriages might have been especially vulnerable to political instability. Private matters were obviously quite strongly influenced by public issues for these activists. For more mainstream political figures, public participation can also conflict with private life. In her study of 1972 delegates (many of whom held office) to presidential nominating conventions, Sapiro (1982) found public/personal role conflicts for both men and women, but her analysis suggested this was a more concerted problem for women than for men.

Certain topics are theorized to be clearly personal or public, just as certain arguments obviously take place in the public, personal, or technical spheres. Here, however, we have noticed some systematic confusion that occurs when people are not as argumentatively tidy as our theories expect. A very private set of feelings propelled Cindy Sheehan into a public life in which she expressed them (Murray, 2012); the same can be said of many prominent religious leaders, as another example. Public commitments to racial equality affected activists' personal relationships (McAdam, 1989). When special circumstances occur, such as activism or the public expression of self-defining values, our distinction does not lie neatly next to Goodnight's (1982), and we find a wonderful intricacy of public and personal connections. Micro-politics become large-scale deliberation, and macro-politics become resources for friendship, romance, and divorce. These matters remain to be worked out and represent an interesting intersection for interpersonal and rhetorical scholars.

Other Types of Communication

Personal issues look inward to the relationship and public issues look outside it. This pattern appears in other areas of study as well. For example, Simons (1970) pointed out that social movements have internal and external rhetorics: extreme, emotional, motivating internal messages for the movement's members (i.e., similar to personal-issue discourse) and moderate, thoughtful, invitational rhetoric addressed to the public audience (i.e., similar to public-issue discourse). Organizations can also have different tones when they speak to their internal (personal-issues) and external (public-issues) audiences (McPhee & Zaug, 2008). For example, the employee handbook might be legalistic, cold, and insistent, whereas the public relations messages might be good-humored and open-minded. Small groups can have a different character when directed inward than outward, even to the extent of having different leaders for external task and internal emotional work (Bales, 1958). Members of different cultures distinguish in their communication with in-groups and out-groups (Chen, 2002; Suzuki, 1998; Triandis, 1995). We do not propose that the same patterns we found for interpersonal relationships will repeat on those other institutional or cultural levels, but it does appear that the sort of topical distinction we are discussing could be systematically explored throughout the messaged world.

Conclusion and Future Directions for Research

This chapter claims that how individuals argue about public issues or personal issues in their interpersonal relationships is an important distinction. It provides a framework for understanding this distinction, summarizes the existing literature on this topic, and suggests implications for researchers who focus on interpersonal communication, political communication, and public argument.

In general, personal-issue argument topics stimulate different understandings of the argumentative episode, different reactions to it, and different editorial behavior in choosing what to say than do public-issue argument topics. Overall, we believe this chapter shows that the distinction between public-issue and personal-issue arguments adds a new dimension to research on interpersonal argument. It provides an explanatory mechanism for why research in which participants are exposed to communication stimuli that involve arguing about a particular topic may produce different results. As such, both types of arguments need to be examined and compared to fully understand arguments in interpersonal contexts. Beyond the direct applicability to social science research in argumentation, conflict, persuasion, and interpersonal communication, we also argue that the public/personal topic distinction can inform several other areas of communication research, with potential for interdisciplinary studies that permit us to understand the complex phenomenon of arguing in our everyday public or private lives.

So where does the distinction of argument types go from here? In what follows, we highlight several general directions for future research (although we have also dispersed more specific directions for future research throughout this chapter). First, we suggest that the research community should examine how arguments evolve in interpersonal relationships. For example, a public topic (e.g., abortion or politics) may suddenly become personal if one person is considering an abortion or a run for public office. In such cases, these topics should function much more like personal-issue arguments because of their direct behavioral implications for the interpersonal dyad, but individuals may integrate information from public life (e.g., whether they define themselves as traditional or feminist) to support their positions in the interpersonal argument. Examining public issues that become personal would also allow one to explore time order issues such as the following: How does a public topic become personal? Is it related to changes in involvement that the arguers have in the topic? Can a personal topic change to a public one? For example, if two romantic partners regard a topic as "taboo" as it relates to their relationship (Roloff & Ifert, 1998), can they instead talk about it in a more general manner as if it did not relate to their relationship? Also, a personal argument might become a public argument for onlookers who perceive someone else's personal argument as a public one for them to discuss.

Second, studies on argument topics thus far have focused mainly on an arguing dyad in an interpersonal relationship. However, the argument topic distinction could also be relevant to larger groups, different contexts, and argument spheres. For example, a friendship group could also argue about public or personal issues. Individuals in organizations argue about public or personal topics as Cionea and Hample (2013) found. An interesting topic for future research could involve examining how arguments about public topics affect the relationship between coworkers or how personal-issue arguments between coworkers affect the work environment for others.

A third line of future research could focus on emotional and physiological reactions to each argument type. If people are more involved in personal-issue arguments, this involvement might be reflected in the emotional reactions and physiological changes they experience during either a public-issue or a personal-issue argument. Such physiological changes could relate to the consequences of each argument for the interpersonal relationship. For example, Gottman (1994) suggested that men were likely to experience greater physiological arousal during conflict than women were, which led men to stonewall or avoid the conflict. Whether this tendency is more apparent in public-issue or personal-issue arguments and the implications for the arguing dyad's relationship are important areas that could be explored.

A fourth improvement for our knowledge base would be to move beyond college students. Married partners could be examined. Another possibility is to examine engaged couples to see how disagreements on public-issue and personal-issue argument topics might relate to decisions to marry. For example, if people have different beliefs about a public-issue argument topic, such as politics or abortion, do they discuss this topic before they marry, or do they declare it "taboo" (Roloff & Ifert, 1998)? We have already seen how important these matters are for activists; where is the default level of agreement on public issues for less involved couples? Examining public-issue and personal-issue arguments in their ordinary settings could add to this line of research as most of the reviewed studies have focused on arguments conducted in the laboratory setting (e.g., A. Johnson, 2000), scenarios (e.g., Villagran et al. 2001), or recall of naturally occurring arguments (e.g., A. Johnson, 2002; A. Johnson et al., 2007). Such research could be patterned after Vuchinich's (1987) focus on family conflict around the dinner table where naturally occurring interaction was observed.

Another area of future research would involve examining public-issue and personal-issue arguments that occur in channels other than face-to-face. Previous research has examined arguments over computer-mediated channels but has focused on strangers or zero-history groups (e.g., Ellis & Maoz, 2007; Lemus, Seibold, Flanagin, & Metzger, 2004; Stewart, Setlock, & Fussell, 2007) rather than on intimates. O'Sullivan (2000) found that individuals decided what channels to use to communicate messages based on how face-threatening the message was perceived. Very possibly, the higher stakes of personal topics could be decisive in their choice of a communication medium. If an argument topic becomes a serial or repeated argument for an interpersonal dyad, they might even switch back and forth between different communication channels based on how the argument heats up and simmers down (Trapp & Hoff, 1985). How people choose which channel to use for an interpersonal argument episode (both public issue and personal issue) is a needed topic for future research and would help us to further understand how interpersonal relationships are enacted in the current multimedia environment.

Ultimately, the public/personal distinction asks us to reconsider the role of arguing in our lives. People lead lives that are both personal and public. Their personal lives are at home or in the company of those they love or like. Their public lives are prototypically in the voting booth but are also experienced whenever they focus thought outside their home: How should other people's children be educated? What should be done about the homeless? What sort of person would join the Tea Party or Occupy Wall Street? Should the Red Sox trade players from their minor league clubs for another frontline starting pitcher? In many respects, both lives are worked out through arguments.

Not all of our talk is argumentative but quite a bit of it is. Our relationships are, and are created in, interpersonal exchanges. What we have suggested here is that the way we work through interpersonal exchanges (i.e., how we argue about different types of topics) is important to our relationships (both our intimate and more distanced ones). It affects how they are constituted, maintained, and enacted, and it affects our overall communicative behavior. Furthermore, our approach to arguing affects how we communicate as part of our groups, communities, and society. The public/personal distinction highlights how, why, and when our communication engages us as arguers in our private or public lives.

Note

1. Argument topic has been used as a proxy measure for argument topic type in most research examining public-issue and personal-issue arguments. Given the definitions of public-issue and personal-issue arguments and face validity, topics taken from prior research (Canary, Brossmann, Brossmann, & Weger, 1995; Canary, Weger, & Stafford, 1991; A. Johnson, 2002; Legge & Rawlins, 1992; Levine & Boster, 1996) have been designated as public or personal: (a) Public-issue argument topics include the death penalty, abortion, the environment, drug legalization, racial prejudice, sex discrimination, sexual orientation discrimination, religion, gun control, drug testing, military spending, animal experimentation, surrogate mothering, foreign product restriction, sports, movies, etiquette/manners, race discrimination, and politics. (b) Personal-issue argument topics include conflicts over a romantic partner, leisure time, other friends, household chores, roommate problems, hurt feelings, money/bills, trust/jealousy, showing consideration, apartment space, broken plans, using other's possessions, giving advice, and doing favors.

References

Altman, I., & Haythorn, W. W. (1965). Interpersonal exchange in isolation. *Sociometry, 28*, 411–426. Retrieved from http://dx.doi.org/10.2307/2785992

Altman, I., & Taylor, D. (1973). *Social penetration: The development of interpersonal relationships*. New York: Holt.

Aron, A., & Aron, E. (1986). *Love as the expansion of self: Understanding attraction and satisfaction*. New York: Hemisphere.

Bales, R. F. (1958). Task roles and social roles in problem-solving groups. In E. E. Maccoby, T. M. Newcomb, & E. L. Hartley (Eds.), *Readings in social psychology* (pp. 437–447). New York: Holt, Rinehart & Winston.

Berger, C. R., & Bell, R. A. (1988). Plans and the initiation of social relationships. *Human Communication Research, 15*, 217–235. doi:10.1111/j.1468–2958.1988. tb00182.x

Blake, R. R., & Mouton, J. S. (1964). *The managerial grid*. Houston, TX: Gulf.

Boster, F. J., & Levine, T. (1988). Individual differences in compliance message selection: The effects of verbal aggressiveness, argumentativeness, dogmatism, and negativism. *Communication Research Reports, 5*, 114–119. Retrieved from http://dx.doi.org/10.1080/08824098809359811

Burgoon, J. K., Bonito, J. A., Ramirez, A., Jr., Dunbar, N. E., Kim, K., & Fischer, J. (2002). Testing the interactivity principle: Effects of mediation, propinquity, and verbal and nonverbal modalities in interpersonal interaction. *Journal of Communication, 52*, 657–677. doi:10.1111/j.1460–2466.2002.tb02567.x

Canary, D. J. (1989). *Manual for coding conversational arguments* (Unpublished manuscript). Pennsylvania State University, State College, PA.

Canary, D. J., Brossmann, J. E., Brossmann, B. G., & Weger, H., Jr. (1995). Toward a theory of minimally rational argument. Analyses of episode-specific effects of argument structures. *Communication Monographs, 62*, 183–212. doi:10.1080/03637759509376357

Canary, D. J., Weger, H., Jr., & Stafford, L. (1991). Couples' argument sequences and their associations with relational characteristics. *Western Journal of Speech Communication, 55*, 159–179. doi:10.1080/10570319109374377

Chen, L. (2002). Communication in intercultural relationships. In W. B. Gudykunst & B. Mody (Eds.), *Handbook of international and intercultural communication* (2nd ed., pp. 241–258). Thousand Oaks, CA: Sage.

Cionea, I. A., & Hample, D. (2013, August). *Serial argument topics*. Paper presented at the biannual meeting of the NCA/AFA Argumentation Conference, Alta, UT.

Cionea, I. A., Hample, D., & Paglieri, F. (2011). A test of the argument engagement model in Romania. In F. Zenker (Ed.), *Argumentation: Cognition and community: Proceedings of the 9th international conference of the Ontario Society for the Study of Argumentation* [CD-ROM]. Windsor, Ontario, Canada.

Cohen, A., Stotland, E., & Wolfe, D. (1955). An experimental investigation of need for cognition. *Journal of Abnormal and Social Psychology, 51*, 291–294. doi:10.1037/h0042761

Dimock, J. (2009). Putting the argument back in the spheres of argument. In S. Jacobs (Ed.), *Concerning argument: Proceedings of the 15th SCA/AFA conference on argumentation* (pp. 184–191). Washington, DC: National Communication Association.

Duncan, L. E. (1999). Motivation for collective action: Group consciousness as mediator of personality, life experiences, and women's rights activism. *Political Psychology, 20*, 611–635. doi:10.1111/0162-895X.00159

Ellis, D. G., & Maoz, I. (2007). Online argument between Israeli Jews and Palestinians. *Human Communication Research, 33*, 291–309. doi:10.1111/j.14682958.2007.00300.x

Eveland, W. P., Morey, A. C., & Hutchens, M. J. (2011). Beyond deliberation: New directions for the study of informal political conversation from a communication perspective. *Journal of Communication, 61*, 1082–1103. doi:10.1111/j.1460-2466.2011.01598.x

Gayle, B. M., Preiss, R. W., & Allen, M. (2002). A meta-analytic interpretation of intimate and nonintimate interpersonal conflict. In M. Allen, R. W. Preiss, B. M. Gayle, & N. Burrell (Eds.), *Interpersonal communication research: Advances through meta-analysis* (pp. 345–368). Mahwah, NJ: Erlbaum.

Goodnight, G. T. (1982). The personal, technical, and public spheres of argument: A speculative inquiry into the art of public deliberation. *Journal of the American Forensic Association, 18*(4), 214–227.

Goodnight, G. T. (1987). Public discourse. *Critical Studies in Mass Communication, 4*, 428–432. doi:10.1080/15295038709360154

Gottman, J. M. (1994). *What predicts divorce? The relationship between marital processes and marital outcomes*. Hillsdale, NJ: Erlbaum.

Hample, D. (2005). *Arguing: Exchanging reasons face to face*. Mahwah, NJ: Erlbaum.

Hample, D., & Dallinger, J. M. (2002). The effects of situation on the use or suppression of possible compliance gaining appeals. In M. Allen, R. Preiss, B. Gayle, & N. Burrell (Eds.), *Interpersonal communication research: Advances through meta-analysis* (pp. 187–209). Mahwah, NJ: Erlbaum.

Hample, D., Dallinger, J. M., & Fofano, J. (1995). Perceiving and predicting the tendency to personalize arguments. In S. Jackson (Ed.), *Argumentation and values: Proceedings of the 9th SCA/AFA conference on argumentation* (pp. 434–438). Annandale, VA: Speech Communication Association.

Hample, D., Dallinger, J. M., & Nelson, G. K. (1994). Aggressive and passive arguing behaviors, and their relationship to taking conflict personally. In F. H. van Eemeren, R. Grootendorst, J. A. Blair, & C. A. Willard (Eds.), *Proceedings of the third ISSA conference on argumentation: Vol. 3. Reconstruction and application* (pp. 238–250). Amsterdam, the Netherlands: SicSat.

Hample, D., & Irions, A. (2013, August). *Argument engagement under invitational versus demanding conditions*. Paper presented at the biannual meeting of the NCA/AFA Argumentation Conference, Alta, UT.

Hample, D., Jones, A. K., & Averbeck, J. M. (2009). The rationality engine: How do arguers deal spontaneously with fallacies? In S. Jacobs (Ed.), *Concerning argument: Proceedings of the 15th NCA/AFA conference on argumentation* (pp. 307–317). Washington, DC: National Communication Association.

Hample, D., Paglieri, F., & Na, L. (2012). The costs and benefits of arguing: Predicting the decision whether to engage or not. In F. H. van Eemeren & B. Garssen (Eds.), *Topical themes in argumentation theory: Twenty exploratory studies* (pp. 307–322). New York: Springer. doi:10.1007/978–94–007–4041–9_20

Hample, D., Sells, A., & Inclán Velázquez, A. L. (2009). The effects of topic type and personalization of conflict on assessments of fallacies. *Communication Reports, 22,* 74–88. doi:10.1080/08934210903008935

Hample, D., Thompson-Hayes, M., Wallenfelsz, K., Wallenfelsz, P., & Knapp, C. (2005). Face-to-face arguing is an emotional experience: Triangulating methodologies and early findings. *Argumentation and Advocacy, 42*(2), 74–93.

Hample, D., Warner, B., & Norton, H. (2006). The effects of arguing expectations and predispositions on perceptions of argument quality and playfulness. *Argumentation and Advocacy, 43*(1), 1–13.

Infante, D. A., Chandler, T. A., & Rudd, J. E. (1989). Test of an argumentative skill deficiency model of interspousal violence. *Communication Monographs, 56,* 163–177. doi:10.1080/03637758909390257

Infante, D. A., & Rancer, A. S. (1982). A conceptualization and measure of argumentativeness. *Journal of Personality Assessment, 46,* 72–80. doi:10.1207/s15327752jpa4601_13

Infante, D. A., & Rancer, A. S. (1996). Argumentativeness and verbal aggressiveness: A review of recent theory and research. *Communication Yearbook, 19,* 320–351.

Infante, D. A., & Wigley, C. J., III. (1986). Verbal aggressiveness: An interpersonal model and measure. *Communication Monographs, 53,* 61–69. doi:10.1080/036377 58609376126

Jackson, S., & Jacobs, S. (1980). Structure of conversational argument: Pragmatic bases for the enthymeme. *Quarterly Journal of Speech, 66,* 251–265. doi:10.1080/00335638009383524

Johnson, A. J. (1999a, February). *Public-issue versus personal-issue arguments: Examining arguments concerning public issues in interpersonal relationships.* Paper presented at the annual meeting of the Western States Communication Association, Vancouver, British Columbia, Canada.

Johnson, A. J. (1999b). *Public-issue versus personal-issue arguments: Examining arguments concerning public issues in friendships* (Unpublished doctoral dissertation). Michigan State University, East Lansing, MI.

Johnson, A. J. (2000, June). *Public-issue versus personal-issue arguments: Factors which affect public-issue arguments in friendships.* Paper presented at the annual meeting of the International Communication Association, Acapulco, Mexico.

Johnson, A. J. (2002). Beliefs about arguing: A comparison of public-issue and personal-issue arguments. *Communication Reports, 15,* 99–112. doi:10.1080/0893421 0209367757

Johnson, A. J. (2009). A functional approach to interpersonal argument. Differences between public- and personal-issue arguments. *Communication Reports, 22,* 13–28. doi:10.1080/08934210902798528

Johnson, A. J., Averbeck, J. M., Kelley, K. M., & Liu, S. (2010). Serial arguments and argument type: Comparing serial arguments about public and personal issue argument topics. In D. S. Gouran (Ed.), *The functions of argument and social context: Selected papers from the 16th biennial conference on argumentation* (pp. 211–218). Washington, DC: National Communication Association.

Johnson, A. J., Averbeck, J. M., Kelley, K. M., & Liu, S. (2011). When serial arguments predict harm: Examining the influences of argument function, perceived resolvability, and argumentativeness. *Argumentation and Advocacy, 47*(4), 214–217.

Johnson, A. J., Becker, J.A.H., Wigley, S., Haigh, M. M., & Craig, E. A. (2007). Reported argumentativeness and verbal aggressiveness levels: The influence of type of argument. *Communication Studies, 58*, 189–205. doi:10.1080/10510970701341154

Johnson, A. J., Brown, K., & Wittenberg, E. M. (2005). Type of argument and argument composition. In C. A. Willard (Ed.), *Critical problems in argumentation: Proceedings of the 13th NCA/AFA conference on argumentation* (pp. 577–586). Washington, DC: National Communication Association.

Johnson, A. J., & Hall, H. T. (2001, May). *Public-issue and personal-issue arguments: Validating a distinction between interpersonal argument topics.* Paper presented at the annual meeting of the International Communication Association, Washington, DC.

Johnson, A. J., Kelley, K., Liu, S., & Averbeck, J. (2012, November). *Family serial arguments: Beliefs about the argument and perceived stress from the argument.* Paper presented at the annual meeting of the National Communication Association, Orlando, FL.

Johnson, K. L., & Roloff, M. E. (1998). Serial arguing and relational quality: Determinants and consequences of perceived resolvability. *Communication Research, 25*, 327–343. doi:10.1177/009365098025003004

Kim, J., & Kim, E. J. (2008). Theorizing dialogic deliberation: Everyday political talk as communicative action and dialogue. *Communication Theory, 18*, 51–70. doi:10.1111/j.1468–2885.2007.00313.x

Kuhn, D. (2005). *Education for thinking.* Cambridge, MA: Harvard University Press.

Legge, N. J., & Rawlins, W. K. (1992). Managing disputes in young adult friendships: Modes of convenience, cooperation, and commitment. *Western Journal of Communication, 56*, 226–247. doi:10.1080/10570319209374415

Lemus, D. R., Seibold, D. R., Flanagin, A. J., & Metzger, M. J. (2004). Argument and decision making in computer-mediated groups. *Journal of Communication, 54*, 302–320. doi:10.1111/j.1460–2466.2004.tb02630.x

Levine, T. R., & Boster, F. J. (1996). The impact of self and others' argumentativeness on talk about controversial issues. *Communication Quarterly, 44*, 345–358. doi:10.1080/01463379609370022

Linton, H., & Graham, E. (1959). Personality correlates of persuasibility. In C. I. Hovland & J. L. Irving (Eds.), *Personality and persuasibility* (pp. 69–101). Oxford, England: Yale University Press.

Lloyd, S. A. (1987). Conflict in premarital relationships: Differential perceptions in males and females. *Family Relations, 36*, 290–294. doi:10.2307/583542

Marwell, G., & Schmitt, D. R. (1967). Dimensions of compliance-gaining behavior: An empirical analysis. *Sociometry, 30*, 350–364. Retrieved from http://dx.doi.org/10.2307/2786181

McAdam, D. (1989). The biographical consequences of activism. *American Sociological Review, 54*, 744–760. doi:10.1080/03637758909390257

McPhee, R. D., & Zaug, P. (2008). The communicative constitution of organizations: A framework for explanation. In L. L. Putnam & A. M. Nicotera (Eds.), *Building theories of organizations: Centering organizational communication* (pp. 21–48). New York: Routledge.

Miller, L. C., Cody, M. J., & McLaughlin, M. L. (1994). Situations and goals as funda-
mental constructs in interpersonal communication research. In M. L. Knapp & G. R.
Miller (Eds.), *Handbook of interpersonal communication* (2nd ed., pp. 162–198).
Thousand Oaks, CA: Sage.

Murray, B. (2012). For what noble cause: Cindy Sheehan and the politics of grief in
public spheres of argument. *Argumentation and Advocacy, 49*(1), 1–15.

Newcomb, T. M. (1953). An approach to the study of communicative acts. P*sychologi-
cal Bulletin, 60*, 393–404. doi:10.1037/h0063098

Newell, S. E., & Stutman, R. K. (1988). The social confrontation episode. *Communication Monographs, 55*, 266–285. doi:10.1080/03637758809376172

O'Keefe, D. J. (1977). Two concepts of argument. *Journal of the American Forensic
Association, 13*(3), 121–128.

O'Sullivan, P. (2000). What you don't know won't hurt me: Impression management
functions of communication channels in relationships. *Human Communication
Research, 26*, 403–431. doi:10.1111/j.1468–2958.2000.tb00763.x

Paglieri, F. (2009). Ruinous arguments: Escalation of disagreement and the dangers of
arguing. In J. Ritola (Ed.), *Argument cultures: Proceedings of 8th international conference of the Ontario Society for the Study of Argumentation* [CD-ROM]. Windsor,
Ontario, Canada.

Paglieri, F., & Castelfranchi, C. (2010). Why argue? Towards a cost-benefit analysis of
argumentation. *Argument & Computation, 1*, 71–91. doi:10.1080/19462160903494584

Petty, R. E., & Cacioppo, J. T. (1986). *Communication and persuasion: Central and
peripheral routes to attitude change.* New York: Springer-Verlag.

Rancer, A. S., & Avtgis, T. A. (2006). *Argumentative and aggressive communication.*
Thousand Oaks, CA: Sage.

Rancer, A. S., Baukus, R. A., & Infante, D. A. (1985). Relations between argumentativeness and belief structures about arguing. *Communication Education, 34*, 37–47.
doi:10.1080/03634528509378581

Rancer, A. S., & Infante, D. (1985). Relations between motivation to argue and the argumentativeness of adversaries. *Communication Quarterly, 33*, 209–218. doi:10.1080/
01463378509369599

Rancer, A. S., Kosberg, R. L., & Baukus, R. A. (1992). Beliefs about arguing as predictors
of trait argumentativeness: Implications for training in argument and conflict management. *Communication Education, 41*, 375–387. doi:10.1080/03634529209378899

Richards, A. S., & Cionea, I. A. (in press). Extending the argument engagement model:
Expected utility and interacting traits as predictors of the intent to argue with friends.
Journal of Argumentation in Context.

Roloff, M. E., & Ifert, D. E. (1998). Antecedents and consequences of explicit agreements to declare a topic taboo in dating relationships. *Personal Relationships, 5*,
191–206. doi:10.1111/j.1475–6811.1998.tb00167.x

Sapiro, V. (1982). Private costs of public commitments or public costs of private commitments? Family roles versus political ambition. *American Journal of Political Science, 26*, 265–279. doi:10.2307/2111039

Schenck-Hamlin, W. J., Wiseman, R. L., & Georgacarakos, G. N. (1982). A model of
properties of compliance-gaining strategies. *Communication Quarterly, 30*, 92–100.
Retrieved from http://dx.doi.org/10.1080/01463378209369434

Segrin, C. (2000). Social skills deficits associated with depression. *Clinical Psychology
Review, 20*, 379–403. doi:10.1016/s0272–7358(98)00104–4

Simons, H. W. (1970). Requirements, problems, and strategies: A theory of persuasion for social movements. *Quarterly Journal of Speech, 56*, 1–11. doi:10.1080/00335 637009382977

Singer, M. T. (1974). Presidential address—Engagement-involvement: A central phenomenon in psychophysiological research. *Psychosomatic Medicine, 36*, 1–17.

Stewart, C. O., Setlock, L. D., & Fussell, S. R. (2007). Conversational argumentation in decision making: Chinese and U.S. participants in face-to-face and instant-messaging interactions. *Discourse Processes, 44*, 113–139. doi:10.1080/01638530701498994

Suzuki, S. (1998). In-group and out-group communication patterns in international organizations: Implications for social identity theory. *Communication Research, 25*, 154–182. doi:10.1177/009365098025002002

Thomas, K. W. (1988). The conflict handling modes: Toward more precise theory. *Management Communication Quarterly, 1*, 430–436. doi:10.1177/0893318988001003009

Trapp, R., & Hoff, N. (1985). A model of serial argument in interpersonal relationships. *Journal of the American Forensic Association, 22*(1), 1–11.

Triandis, H. (1995). *Individualism and collectivism: New directions in social psychology*. Boulder, CO: Westview Press.

Villagran, P., Johnson, A. J., Villagran, M. M., & Wittenberg, E. (2001, November). *Arguing in interpersonal relationships: The effect of argument type, resolution, and verbal aggressiveness*. Paper presented at the annual meeting of the National Communication Association, Atlanta, GA.

Vuchinich, S. (1990). The sequential organization of closing in verbal family conflict. In A. D. Grimshaw (Ed.), *Conflict talk: Sociolinguistic investigations of arguments in conversations* (pp. 118–138). Cambridge, England: Cambridge University Press.

Warner, B., & Hample, D. (2008, May). *Argument engagement, argumentativeness, verbal aggressiveness, topic type, and argument realism: Their effects on editorial choices*. Paper presented at the annual meeting of the International Communication Association, Montreal, Quebec.

Wyatt, R. O., Katz, E., & Kim, J. (2000). Bridging the spheres: Political and personal conversation in public and private spheres. *Journal of Communication, 50*, 71–92. doi:10.1111/j.1460–2466.2000.tb02834.x

Zarefsky, D. (2012). Goodnight's "speculative inquiry" in its intellectual context. *Argumentation and Advocacy, 48*(2), 211–215.

Zietlow, P. H., & Sillars, A. L. (1988). Life-stage differences in communication during marital conflicts. *Journal of Social and Personal Relationships, 5*, 223–245. doi:10.1177/026540758800500206

CHAPTER CONTENTS

6 Theorizing Fat Talk

Intrapersonal, Interpersonal, and Intergroup Communication About Groups

Analisa Arroyo

University of Georgia

Jake Harwood

University of Arizona

Women frequently reference weight in their talk (e.g., "I'm so fat"). This chapter reviews the literature on weight-related communication—*fat talk*—and presents a conceptual model describing the antecedents and consequences of engaging in communicative interactions about weight at the individual, relational, and social identity levels. Our model expands previous understandings by proposing that fat talk needs to be understood as a psychological, interpersonal, and collective phenomenon. By investigating and acknowledging the causes, consequences, and processes of fat talk, we anticipate potential in altering individuals' and society's ideas, expectations, and discourse about the ideal body image.

The disproportionate value placed on personal attractiveness, particularly for women, result in a sociocultural pressure to fit that ideal (Thompson, Heinberg, Altabe, & Tantleff-Dunn, 1999; Tiggemann, 2012). Messages and pressures from the media, family, and peers have made women's bodies an important component of how they evaluate themselves and others and focus particularly on weight as an important component of attractiveness (Harrison, Taylor, & Marske, 2006; McCabe & Ricciardelli, 2001; Tiggemann, Polivy, & Hargreaves, 2009). These messages promote sociocultural pressures and standards and serve to construct an environment of weightist discourse. Weightist messages influence individuals' self-perceptions, with women across the life span being dissatisfied with their bodies, having negative beliefs about their own physical attraction, and striving to fit the idealized body image (Cahill & Mussap, 2007; Durkin & Paxton, 2002; Harrison & Hefner, 2006). Consequently, concern and anxiety about appearance is linked to many questionable physical health activities (e.g., unhealthy dieting and supplement use, clinical eating disorders, cosmetic surgery, extreme exercising) and mental health issues such as depression, anxiety, sexual dissatisfaction, and low self-esteem (Davison & McCabe, 2005; Delinsky, 2012; Tantleff-Dunn & Linder, 2012; Weiderman, 2012).

Because women's bodies are tied to their sense of self and self-worth and because of concerns and dissatisfaction with their bodies, women's communication often focuses on appearance-related issues (Martz, Petroff, Curtin, & Bazzini, 2009; Nichter, 2000). In this chapter, we focus particularly on research concerning communication about weight. In doing so, we (a) discuss *fat talk* as a ritualized and problematic behavior among women; (b) discuss social identity and social categorization of people into groups and the varying levels of categorization; (c) discuss weight as a categorical system that is frequently communicated about and that carries stigma; and (d) present a conceptual model that explicates the connections between communication, category systems, and outcomes at three levels of categorization (personal, relational, social group). The conceptual model puts forth possible antecedents and consequences of communication about weight, specifically exploring what motivates women to engage in fat talk and what the consequences of fat talk may be.

Fat Talk

Brief references to "feeling fat" or "needing to drop a few pounds" are frequent in women's casual conversation; indeed, interpersonally disparaging oneself is a normative practice among women (Martz et al., 2009; Nichter, 2000). Such references are known as *fat talk*: ritualistic conversation about one's own and others' bodies (e.g., "I'm so fat!" "No you're not. I'm the one who is fat!"). These comments are defined as "speaking *negatively* about one's body" (Britton, Martz, Bazzini, Curtin, & LeaShomb, 2006, p. 247, emphasis added) and involve "explicit *negative* self-statements, physical appearance complaints, and weight management tips" (Martz et al., 2009, p. 34, emphasis added). Thus, fat talk conversations can include negatively valenced comments about one's own weight, shape, or diet; what one's eating and exercise habits should be; fears of becoming out of shape or overweight, how one's eating and exercise habits compare to others'; and other people's shape and appearance (Nichter, 2000; Ousley, Cordero, & White, 2008).

Fat talk conversations take place among women more than men (Martz et al., 2009; Payne, Martz, Tompkins, Petroff, & Farrow, 2010), occur across all ages (ranging from adolescence into adulthood; Nichter, 2000, Stice, Maxfield, & Wells, 2003), and occur among women who suffer from eating disorders, who are normal weight, and who are overweight (Martz et al., 2009; Nichter, 2000; Stice et al., 2003). Individuals with eating disorders engage in fat talk more frequently than others (at least once a day; Ousley et al., 2008); however, individuals who do not have eating disorders also frequently make fat talk comments (Ousley et al., 2008; Salk & Engeln-Maddox, 2011). Nearly all college women (93%) report engaging in fat talk, with about a third of them stating that fat talk is frequent or very frequent (Salk & Engeln-Maddox, 2011). Further, women report that *normal weight* women are the most frequent participants in fat talk (Nichter, 2000; Nichter & Vuckovic, 1994).

Research exploring the social and interpersonal conditions in which fat talk occurs shows that fat talk is a normative and expected behavior (Britton et al., 2006; Tompkins, Martz, Rocheleau, & Bazzini, 2009). Women conform to peer norms and engage in fat talk to "fit in" (Britton et al., 2006; Nichter, 2000; Tucker, Martz, Curtin, & Bazzini, 2007). Women report feeling pressure to make negative comments about themselves more than positive or self-accepting comments (Martz et al., 2009); those who do not conform to this norm are perceived to "think they are better than" their peers (Nichter, 2000). Alas, engaging in these normative interactions is problematic because of the negative nature of the talk (Martz et al., 2009)—the specific tone and content of fat talk messages perpetuate negative self-perceptions (e.g., "I'm so fat," "My ass is huge"). For instance, Gapinski, Brownell, and LaFrance (2003) found that women experience exacerbated self-objectification after hearing another person make fat talk comments, and Arroyo and Harwood (2012) found that the act of making fat talk comments predicts negative health outcomes.

As in Arroyo and Harwood's (2012) communication perspective on fat talk, this chapter frames fat talk as a collaborative process in which weight- and appearance-related issues are shared among women. We propose that fat talk informs women's understandings of their bodies; it is the means by which women construct, come to terms with, and fall victim to societal ideas about the meaning of weight. Moreover, we propose that making evaluative and disparaging comments about oneself falls in line with objectification theory's central premise that women communicatively treat their bodies as objects that should be evaluated (Fredrickson & Roberts, 1997). Fat talk is a behavioral manifestation of body ideals and evaluation; that is, fat talk is a means of self-objectification (Arroyo & Harwood, 2012). As such, this chapter discusses the implications of sending and receiving weight-related messages for our selves, our relationships, and the social groups to which we belong. We incorporate an identity perspective to the understanding of fat talk because how individuals feel about themselves and the groups they belong to are expressed and enacted in their communication (Hecht, 1993).

Social Identity and Categorization

Social identity theory (Tajfel & Turner, 1986) is the dominant theoretical perspective on psychological processes surrounding group identifications. The theory states that individuals understand their social worlds in terms of categories; they categorize themselves into some of the categories (ingroups with which they identify) and categorize others either as fellow ingroup members or as outgroup members—members of different categories. These identifications serve as the basis for social comparisons by which individuals aim to increase positive distinctiveness: the perception that the ingroup is both different from and better than the outgroup on some valued dimension.

Self-categorization theory (Turner, Hogg, Oakes, Reicher, & Wetherell, 1987) builds on social identity theory and explains the cognitive processes by which specific groups gain salience and importance at certain moments. Specifically, the theory suggests that specific identities become active as a result of accessibility and fit. Accessibility can be situational or context specific; for example, trying on a swimsuit or wedding dress may make a person's weight and body shape identities more salient. Accessibility can also be chronic, such that, for some people, their weight group membership is important in most areas of their lives (e.g., people with eating disorders). Fit can occur as a function of existing stereotypes and ongoing activity. For instance, seeing an overweight person eating an ice cream would make weight salient because of perceived fit between their weight and stereotypes of gluttony. Seeing two families on a beach—one all skinny and the other one all overweight—would likewise raise the salience of weight given both the physical clustering by weight and its particular visibility in a beach setting.

Social identity theory and self-categorization theory both argue that categorization processes operate at different levels of abstraction ranging from the individual to the collective: Depending on accessibility and fit, individuals categorize others and the self into group-level categories (e.g., fat/thin, old/young, Black/White) or as unique individuals (e.g., Angel, Elizabeth). Categorizations of self correspond to *identity*—the specific conceptualization of self that is operating in a given context. When individuals categorize themselves and those around them as individuals and operate in terms of personal identities, their ensuing judgments and behaviors will be at the *individual level*. At this level, individuals are operating in terms of their own unique attributes and roles. At other times, relationships may be most central. Individuals will categorize others and themselves in terms of relational identities (e.g., family member, girlfriend), and ensuing judgments and behaviors will operate at the *relational level*. At a higher level of abstraction, individuals may operate in terms of social groups (e.g., Republican, Democrat, woman, man), and those broader categorizations will drive behavior at the *social identity level* (Turner et al., 1987). As this chapter develops, we will describe further the ways in which levels of self-categorizations affect interpersonal communicative processes surrounding weight and the implications for individual-level outcomes, relational processes, and group-based phenomena. In making this connection, we integrate Hecht's (1993) communication theory of identity and build on the foundational work of Giles, who pioneered the integration of intergroup and interpersonal principles (Giles, 2012; Giles, Coupland, & Coupland, 1991; Giles, Reid & Harwood, 2010).

Communication and Identity

Communication is a significant part of the categorization process: Individuals talk about others and themselves in terms of categories, and those discussions contribute to the elaboration and reification of the category systems (Giles, Reid, & Harwood, 2010). For instance, labeling someone as "fat" invokes social norms to which that person might feel obliged to conform and stereotypes concerning the individual's abilities and characteristics (e.g., being lazy). Hecht's (1993) communication theory of identity adds to psychological theories of identity and categorization by specifying mutual influences between identity and communication and the interpenetration of different identity levels. Hecht and colleagues (Hecht, Collier, & Ribeau; 1993; Hecht, Jackson, & Ribeau, 2003) conceptualize identity *as* communication, as opposed to seeing identity and communication as unidirectional influences on one another. Thus, Hecht's (1993) communication theory of identity is a useful foundation for this chapter because our model will argue that, through communication and identity, individuals have different attitudes about and motivations for engaging in communication about their weight.

Hecht (1993) says that there are several loci of identity: (a) Personal identity refers to individuals' self-concepts or self-images; (b) enacted identity refers to individuals' performed or expressed identity—people enact and exchange their identities through communication; (c) relational identity refers to how individuals develop their identities based on how others view them, through relationships with others or through identification with the relationship; and (d) communal identity refers to how a collective group of individuals define their identity. Hecht's identity frames mirror the levels of identities from social identity and social categorization theory, further supporting the role that each plays in understanding social and personal behaviors. Although similar to the previously discussed layers of identity, Hecht's (1993) approach brings communication more centrally into this arena by reminding us that communication is not merely a product of psychological categorization processes but rather that identity is fundamentally formed, reformed, and manifested at all of these levels *in* communication (Hecht, Jackson, & Pitts, 2005).

Although we build heavily from the work of Hecht and Giles (among others), our chapter offers some significant advances. First, we delve more deeply and specifically into the area of weight as a significant personal and social identity concern—one that has received relatively little attention from scholars concerned with communication and identity. Second, we present a more formal model of connections between communication, identity, and other important social constructs (e.g., attitudes). While we endorse the idea of communication and identity as being intertwined and "interpenetrated" (Hecht, 1993), we lean toward separating the intrapersonal and interpersonal components of identity and communication. In this sense, our work is probably more similar to work by Giles, for instance, in the intergenerational arena (Giles, Williams & Coupland, 1990).

Categorizing Bodies in Terms of Weight

Weight is particularly interesting in the context of a chapter examining the construction and communication of category systems. First, weight is continuous, and people move gradually along the underlying continuum. However, specific regions on the continuum are treated as static categories in many contexts (e.g., people with certain body types are "fat"). Hence, we suspect that communicative processes "police" the boundaries between constructed categories on the continuum (Giles & Reid, 2005). Second, some regions of the continua are associated with prejudice (e.g., obesity, disordered eating). This prejudice manifests in attitudes about other people, as well as attitudes about *self* when self shows signs of gaining/losing "too much" weight. Third, weight is associated with multibillion-dollar industries designed to avoid, defer, or conceal stigmatized physical signs (ABC News, 2012; Marketdata Enterprises Inc., 2011). The cosmetics, cosmetic surgery, and diet product industries consume massive economic activity and (via advertising) function to perpetuate stigmas concerning weight. Fourth, weight has legitimate health issues associated with it—obesity is increasingly understood to represent significant health risks to individuals (Centers for Disease Control and Prevention, 2012; Flegal, Carroll, Ogden, & Curtin, 2010). However, and echoing our point about prejudice, the health issues associated with weight have perhaps come to overshadow other important aspects of group membership. One driving idea behind this chapter is that weight and appearance are phenomena about which we *talk* quite a bit—in contrast perhaps to categories such as race or disability, which appear to be less convenient fodder for conversation. As such, weight as a category and frequent topic of conversation make it a particularly important issue that needs to be understood in terms of a *communication* process that interacts with other attitudinal and motivational processes.

Communicating Weight Identity

In order to present a model by which we explain the causes and consequences of weight-related communication, it is important to discuss and differentiate comments people make about their bodies. In this section, we review the small literature on actual talk related to weight, organized within a preliminary typology of fat talk based on the literature and some of our own data. Our data involved 138 participants (age = 18–70+ years old) completing open-ended responses about the comments they hear and say about age and weight. Each participant separately provided three examples of comments that they both *say* and *hear* about weight; thus, a total of 828 comments were provided. To capture the central topics, themes, and structures of fat talk, the responses were analyzed and categorized by the two authors by consistent themes and topics. We used a grounded theory approach (Glaser & Strauss, 1967), although our approach was also informed by our knowledge of the literature on weight-related communication. Our examination of these responses led us to the preliminary typology in Table 6.1.

We focus particularly on how communication can be understood on three levels of identity discussed in the earlier section on categorization (personal, relational, social group). However, we do not believe it is productive to treat communication as only working on one level of identity at any point in time. Any specific message might be used at any level and a message driven by

Table 6.1 A Preliminary Typology and Examples of Fat Talk

Type	Fat Talk Example
Routinized talk	*Gotta shed those holiday pounds; one more won't make any difference.*
Truisms, aphorisms, etc.	*You are what you eat; the freshman 15.*
Self-identifying with a group or stage	*I'm overweight; I'm 120 pounds.*
Evaluating self	*It's so depressing I can't drop five pounds; I shouldn't eat this.*
Accounts (justifications/ rationalizations)	*It's genetic; I can't start a diet until after the holidays.*
Describing change	*I lost 8 pounds since you last saw me! You're looking very svelte.*
Seeking feedback	*Do I look fat in this? Do you see how much weight I've gained?*
Evaluating interlocutor	*Are you pregnant? You're so skinny.*
Talking about other people	*She really shed the baby weight quickly; that guy doesn't need a dessert!*
We-talk	*We've got more to love; fat and proud!*
Talking about groups as abstractions	*Fat people are so funny; obesity is a social crisis.*
Expression of fears	*I'd hate myself if I got fat.*
Discussing coping/ mobility strategies	*Try the Atkins diet! A balanced diet and exercise . . .*

motivations at one level may have implications at other levels of identity. Hecht et al.'s (2005) presentation of the communication theory of identity acknowledges the interpenetration of layers of identity with layers sometimes complementing and sometimes contradicting one another. Language use is sufficiently unpredictable, multifunctional, and contextually variable that most comments might be driven by motivations at any level (or all three). Nonetheless, some regularities occur in fat talk and relate in reliable (if not definitive) ways to the levels of identity; we mention those as appropriate. Next, we briefly describe the thirteen types of fat talk comments in our typology while simultaneously reviewing the literature in this area.

Fat talk is *routinized talk*. As with other forms of phatic talk (Laver, 1975), routinized references to weight build on shared understandings and establish common ground for moving a conversation along. Fat talk comments occur habitually, at least in some peer groups, and individuals become comfortable conversing in this manner (Nichter & Vuckovic, 1994). Thus, weight, although stigmatized in its own way, also provides shared ground with which "everyone" struggles and can relate. At times, we suspect forms of this talk are relatively mindless, involving minimal conscious reflection about weight status, similar to the manner in which phatic "How are you?" inquiries typically involve little intrinsic curiosity as to actual well-being.

Routinized talk is related to the *truisms and aphorisms* we have about weight (e.g., "you are what you eat"). They are flexible in nature, being used to describe or refer to self, or for more general social discourse. For instance, the "Freshman 15" refers to the amount of pounds purportedly gained during the first year of college (Brown, 2008). Despite research debunking this "fact" (Butler, Black, Blue, & Greteback, 2004), such truisms retain cultural power through media and interpersonal discourse and can influence expectations and fears about weight.

People sometimes make *self-identifying* comments about their weight. Simply stating "I'm fat" serves multiple functions. This phrase can be used to provide an outlet for negative emotions (e.g., expressing that one is stressed or depressed; an intrapersonal process), to seek and provide feedback (e.g., hoping to hear confirmations from peers that one really is *not* fat; an interpersonal process), and establish a group identity (e.g., if a response is elicited to mitigate discomfort and build group solidarity; a social identity process; Nichter, 2000).

Evaluating self in terms of weight can derive from emotional expression motivations or can be a response to actual-ideal discrepancies. Fat talk can reveal a person's dissatisfaction and preoccupation with weight, as well as initiate sense making concerning the type of person s/he is. Normal weight and anorexic women alike make comments about wanting to be thinner—"oh my gosh, look at my stomach sticking out," "there's something wrong with me" (Chesters, 1994, p. 451). Such negative comments directly tap into self-worth and can have negative effects on self-perceptions. In other cases, people make self-accepting comments; one of Smith-Jackson, Reel, and Thackeray's (2011) respondents reported, "I get in my bra and underwear and I stand and look at the mirror for like 20 minutes . . . I say, 'This is who I am. Nothing is changing. This is me'" (p. 339). Such statements express and organize individual level cognitions and self-categorizations concerning one's body. The effects of these statements depend substantially on their valence and whether they are framed as claiming or ceding control (e.g., "wishing" to be thinner or weight-related guilt versus self-acceptance; Jolanki, 2008).

Our talk sometimes serves to explain or justify ourselves (*accounts/ justifications*). Weight itself is sometimes a phenomenon in need of explanation: People need (or feel the need) to account for and explain their weight ("It's a hormone thing"). Nichter (2000) notes that fat talk is used to relieve guilt or provide a justification when eating certain foods: Saying "Look how big of a pig I am" before eating a large meal can be seen as an apology and explanation for overindulging.

People sometimes make comments about how they have escaped from or have worked hard to avoid stigmatized aspects of weight. Comments *describing change* may serve cathartic personal and relational functions as they are other-directed and emphasize positive or (less commonly) negative changes. Salk and Engeln-Maddox (2011) found that weight talk often elicits responses that suggest taking action together to lose weight (e.g., "Do you want to go to the gym together?" "We should diet together!"). Such comments emphasize the malleability of weight and enhance self-efficacy in weight loss (Crandall, Nierman, & Helb, 2009). Descriptions of change undermine the groupness of weight-specific identities, acknowledging the slippery nature of the boundaries between skinny and fat.

When we are uncertain, we may ask others to (dis)confirm our beliefs about self (*seeking feedback*). At the personal level, people engage in these conversations as a way to seek social validation and to uphold their self-view (Swann, 1983). One reason for asking "Does this make me look fat?" is to hear confirmations from others that one really is not fat (Nichter, 2000). However, seeking feedback typically occurs within relationships, and the relational stakes may be higher than the personal stakes. A wife asking a husband, "Does this make my butt look big?" presents herself and her husband with a communicative situation that could have negative relational consequences. In this area, fat talk research has strong links to well-mined areas of interpersonal and relational communication such as social support and social influence, particularly insofar as relational partners reinforce and support one another's (un)healthy behaviors and cognitions.

As a complement to seeking feedback, we often must provide feedback to the other as well (*evaluating interlocutor*). Most such communication is positive, including denial ("Shut up! No you're not!") and direct compliments ("You look fantastic!"; O'Dougherty, Schmitz, Hearst, Covelli, & Kurzer, 2011; Salk & Engeln-Maddox, 2011). These comments reflect personal and relational aspects of fat talk, but evaluating the interlocutor can also implicate the intergroup level as well by making explicit which group the person fits into (the ingroup, the fatties, or the outgroup, the skinnies).

Much of the empirical literature on weight-related talk has focused on presentations and evaluations of self—probably reflecting an underlying interest in how people existentially cope with their own weight. But sometimes individuals evaluate people who are not present (*talking about other people*). Evaluations of other people's weight and appearances are reported to be the most frequent fat talk comments (e.g., "Look how much weight she gained. She looks terrible!"; Ousley et al., 2008). Evaluative comments serve as a means of social comparison (e.g., "Look how skinny she is, and I am so fat"), and also can emphasize group solidarity, providing an avenue for friends, partners, and groups to strengthen their closeness by emphasizing shared beliefs and opinions (Foster, 2004; Leaper & Holliday, 1995). Although talking about third parties is virtually absent from the fat talk literature, third parties constitute exemplars of categories; we suspect that this form of talk does interesting work in constructing and maintaining categorical boundaries concerning weight.

We-talk offers the paradigm case of a social-identity-level communication phenomenon. "We" includes others who share a categorization with the speaker—all skinny people, all fat people. Thus, we-talk is a communicative pronouncement of group membership that carries at a minimum a message of not being alone (collective membership) and can carry a message of pride (building group solidarity). On the pathological end of this, Borzekowski, Schenk, Wilson, and Peebles (2010) examine discourse in pro-ana (pro-anorexia) websites.

They provide a number of examples indicating a collective identity among the individuals on these sites that reflects both ingroup pride and support and outgroup denigration (e.g., "It is not us who is at fault; they kill their bodies with fats and grease but we give our bodies nothing at all, so, you see, we really are the purest of the pure nothing but skin and bones"). Such comments reveal an awareness of stereotypes, as well as a sense of solidarity with others who fall victim to the stereotypes. Such talk challenges established negative ideas related to anorexia and builds shared social identity. Similarly, Nichter (2000) reports that saying "I'm so fat" can be used to establish group identity among adolescent girls; by making this comment, a response from a peer is elicited to mitigate the discomfort a person feels, consequently building group solidarity by sharing positive comments. This solidarity can serve as a means of certainty for those involved, signifying that the people involved are supportive and that the group is cohesive. By being a part of this group, people become certain with which group they should identify with in terms of weight.

Sometimes fat talk involves *talking about groups as abstractions*: groups and group-related phenomena become topics of conversation independent of a specific person. Such talk may reflect general social concerns (e.g., current discussions of obesity as a societal problem). It may also be an attempt to place a personal experience within a broader social context. Weightist jokes would fit comfortably in this category, as well as more explicit prejudicial statements. All such forms of talk emphasize ingroup versus outgroup identities and elaborate on intergroup relations.

Discussing coping/mobility and *expression of fears* both capture dimensions of fat talk as social identity processes. As described earlier, the fact that individuals currently inhabit an unstigmatized region of the continua (e.g., skinny) does not mean that they will not one day inhabit the stigmatized region (fat). Hence, weight offers a unique space for talk about moving *between* categories and apprehension about future possible category membership. People with eating disorders regularly express fears about becoming overweight (Ousley et al., 2008). This fear is grounded in the physical but also the social aspects of weight (e.g., friendships and romantic relationships; Crandall et al., 2009): fear of fatness is an aspect of Crandall's (1994) anti-fat attitudes measure. Discussions of coping/mobility strategies deserve considerably more attention, given their close theoretical ties to Tajfel and Turner's (1986) suggestions concerning how stigmatized group members cope with their low status. Trying to move out of a group (lose weight: "I've got to shed some pounds"), creatively interpreting group membership ("We have more to love"), and even engaging in social competition ("Fat Pride!") are communicatively constructed options that merit attention by communication scholars.

It is important to note that our typology is not meant to be an exhaustive list; we are certain that other forms of fat talk occur. These types of talk are neither mutually exclusive nor easily distinguishable; at times a single utterance will invoke multiple forms of reference to weight with specific ensuing effects. Our goal in presenting this typology is simply to illustrate as much diversity as we find in our data and the empirical literature and to begin a discussion of the variety of functions served by this talk at various levels of identity.

A Model of the Determinants and Consequences of Fat Talk

We have presented weight as a category and as an identity system and have discussed the ways in which individuals communicatively express and construct their weight at different levels of identity. We now present a conceptual model of the antecedents and consequences of engaging in fat talk. The model in Figure 6.1 portrays the process by which daily communication propagates and resists sociocultural pressures to be (or appear to be) thin and attractive. As is clear from the bar spanning the top of the model, the entire theoretical process is seen to be occurring in a context of a society that emphasizes a narrow definition of physical attractiveness, resulting in sociocultural pressures related to objectification. In a society that objectifies women's bodies, women learn to self-objectify (i.e., treat their bodies as objects that should be evaluated; Fredrickson & Roberts, 1997). In this instance, engaging in fat talk is a behavioral manifestation of self-objectification (Arroyo & Harwood, 2012). Therefore, in the context of sociocultural pressure and objectification, the general model (see the bolded, second row in Figure 6.1) predicts that identity influences the salient attitude objects in a situation, which in turn shape motivations for engaging in fat talk; such fat talk comments are then predicted to be associated with both positive and negative outcomes.

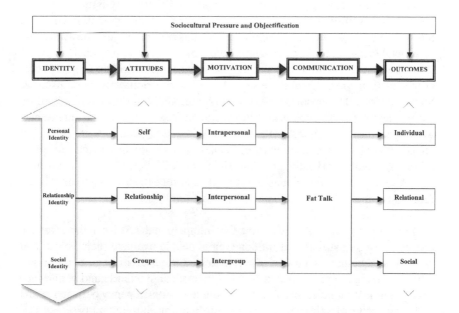

Figure 6.1 Schematic model of the determinants and consequences of fat talk

The reasons why people self-categorize at one level rather than another were discussed earlier and are specified in greater detail in the self-categorization literature (Turner et al., 1987). As this is a continuum, the levels of identity are not mutually exclusive. For example, self-esteem (the intrapersonal level) may influence one to seek social validation (the interpersonal level). The following sections, however, separate the levels for clarity. In addition, scholarship in this area typically assumes some level of consistency across levels of identity (Turner et al., 1987). People acting at the intrapersonal level will typically operate at that level in terms of identities, attributions, behaviors, and the like; when operating at the group level, all aspects of cognition and behavior will be predominantly driven by group-level identifications (Drury & Reicher, 1999). We integrate our typology into the following sections, but we further discuss the communication aspect of the model after discussing the other elements at the three levels of identity.

Personal Identity: The Intrapersonal Level

The intrapersonal level is associated with affective and cognitive features of the individual and their relation to the causes and consequences of fat talk.

Personal identity.   At the personal level, weight identity is concerned with the centrality of weight to self-concept: the extent to which people's weight factors into "who they are" as individuals and how they look. Centrality is influenced by personal factors and both local and sociocultural contexts (Settles, 2004). Some people will be chronically more concerned with body issues in understanding the self. For example, weight is more central to individuals who internalize society's thin ideal. Internalization is more than just the awareness of societal ideals (e.g., "in our society, fat people are regarded as unattractive"); it is an adoption of the thin ideal as one's own personal ideal (e.g., "photographs of thin women make me wish I were thin;" Heinberg, Thompson, & Stormer, 1995; Thompson et al., 1999). Additionally, all individuals will be more concerned with such issues in specific contexts (e.g., trying on clothes, wearing swimsuits; Gapinski et al., 2003). When these identities are salient on an individual level, social comparisons can occur to evaluate self and seek positive self-perceptions (Festinger, 1954; Helgeson & Taylor, 1993). When weight is more central to the individual, the subsequent processes leading to fat talk are more likely to emerge and to serve individual level functions.

Attitudes toward self.   Attitudes at the intrapersonal level are the affective and cognitive constructs that influence how people evaluate their bodies and relate to individuals' degree of (dis)like toward themselves (e.g., body dissatisfaction). People are motivated to meet their ideal standards and experience disappointment and dissatisfaction when there is a discrepancy between actual and ideal views of self (i.e., the actual attributes an individual possesses versus the attributes an individual hopes to possess; Higgins, 1987). If people internalize physical ideals that are different from the attributes that they actually possess, they will experience body dissatisfaction (Jacobi & Cash, 1994). People who are dissatisfied with their bodies or suffering from eating disorders make more weight-related comments (Arroyo & Harwood, 2012; Ousley et al., 2008); thus, the model presumes that negative attitudes toward one's body leads to intrapersonal motivations for engaging in fat talk. It is important to note here that research has not yet explored whether more positive self-views are related to more positive weight-related comments. However, future work would benefit from exploring the possibility that individuals with higher body satisfaction not only make fewer fat talk comments but may also express more positive forms of weight-related communication.

Intrapersonal motivations. At the intrapersonal level, fat talk is driven by a need to express thoughts and feelings about oneself or by perceived threats to face (Brown & Levinson, 1978). When individuals feel objectified, they accept observers' perspectives of their bodies, they treat their bodies as objects that should be evaluated, and they place a substantial amount of pressure on their appearance (Fredrickson & Roberts, 1997). This can be threatening to an individual and create dissatisfaction, given that most people do not conform to the homogenous images shown in the media. Such dissatisfaction might motivate people to make self-evaluative comments about their bodies as a way of expressing body-related emotions, coping with dissatisfaction, and making attributions for weight (or associated phenomena such as related health deficits; Gapinski et al., 2003, Nichter, 2000). Among its various functions, fat talk is used to provide an outlet for negative emotions as well as to account for specific behaviors (especially eating; i.e., accounts/justifications). Other research notes a cathartic motivation may drive some self-focused talk (Coupland, Coupland, Giles, Henwood, & Wiemann, 1988); thus, intrapersonal motivations involve drawing attention to and alleviating pressure and shame felt about self.

Individual outcomes. Individual outcomes center on affective and cognitive evaluations of one's body and the consequences of those evaluations. A number of the self-attitude constructs previously mentioned could be reiterated here (e.g., actual-ideal self-discrepancy, social comparison, self-objectification), but we are particularly concerned with the generalization of body evaluation measures into broader mental health concerns (e.g., depressive symptomatology, low self-esteem; Cahill & Mussap, 2007; Davison & McCabe, 2005). Engaging in fat talk can exacerbate depressive effects related to weight to the extent that the talk (a) heightens salience of weight, (b) emphasizes negative outcomes, and (c) de-emphasizes personal control (Arroyo & Harwood, 2012). These elements are common in fat talk (Nichter, 2000). Such talk raises the salience of weight and appearance as an issue, it universally views fat as bad, and it externalizes locus of control emphasizing helplessness, hopelessness, and an inability to deal with weight (Beck, 1974). In extreme cases, people develop eating disorders to cope with weight-related pressures. The cosmetics and cosmetic surgery industries, of course, feed on and exacerbate these insecurities (Lirola & Chovanec, 2012). We also suspect that those industries supply much of the language that individuals then adopt in their everyday conversations about appearance-related concerns. Thus, fat talk is part of a broader sociocultural discourse of appearance-related objectification.

Relationship Identity: The Interpersonal Level

The interpersonal level is associated with interdependent relationships and communication, allowing understanding of the dynamic and collaborative interpersonal processes of fat talk.

Relationship identity.   Relationships are cultures unto themselves, composed of traditions, rituals, and symbols that are unique to those involved (Baxter, 1987). These symbols represent what is expected and valued in the relationship and allow people to test whether they share similar perceptions of the relationship (Oring, 1984). Body issues are more central in some relationships than others—for instance, weight issues might be more salient when couples work out together or when they have developed a culture of discussing diet (Burke, Randall, Corkery, Young, & Butler, 2012; Franks et al., 2012). Similarly, all relationships will fluctuate in terms of the relative importance of weight. For example, when a wife gains weight in pregnancy, weight will become more central in the relational identity. As this happens, more weight-related talk would be expected in the relationship and the other relationship-level processes in the model will gain importance.

Attitudes toward relationship.   Evaluation of one's own weight, one's partner's weight, or partners' joint weight can all occur in the relational context. For instance, a man might be satisfied with his weight at the individual level, but at the relational level, he might understand that his wife is dissatisfied with his weight. This issue can unite or divide couples (Ledyard & Morrison, 2008); partners who do not match one's "ideal" reduce relational quality (Campbell, Simpson, Kashy, & Fletcher, 2001). Additionally, individuals' (dis)satisfaction with their bodies affects the process of fat talk at the relational level. People who are unhappy with their bodies make more fat talk comments (and it might also be the case that people who are satisfied make more constructive and confident remarks). These comments may be about self or about the partner in response to the partner's self-disparaging comments. At this level, individuals who are happy with their bodies may provide support to another about how to be more comfortable with one's body or how to reach a goal (Dailey, Romo, & Thompson, 2011). As such, when weight becomes relationally salient, interpersonal motivations for engaging in fat talk will be salient.

Interpersonal motivations.   Motivated to uphold their self-views, people engage in relational fat talk to seek social validation from others (i.e., to validate their own self-impression through others' responses; Swann, 1983). One reason for saying "I'm so fat" is to hear confirmations from others that one really is not fat (i.e., feedback seeking; Nichter, 2000). Moreover, people might engage in fat talk as a way to manage others' impressions of them (Nichter, 2000) by accommodating their communication to match the tone and content of their partners (Giles et al., 1991). If a woman claims unhappiness with her weight, and a friend does not reciprocate the expression of discontent, the failure to reciprocate may be seen as rude (Nichter, 2000). People may feel obliged to engage in fat talk as part of a dyadic ritual—to maintain the relationship by making the partner feel good ("you look great" or "I like your curves," i.e., routinized talk). Likewise, the tone of fat talk is reciprocated: If another woman speaks negatively about her body, a female friend is more likely to also speak unfavorably about her own body (Tucker et al., 2007). Thus, seeking social validation, managing impressions, and reciprocity are underlying motivations for engaging in fat talk at the interpersonal level.

Relational outcomes. Nichter (2000) emphasizes the idea that fat talk interactions are pervasive in friendship circles and that these interactions function to maintain relational solidarity. We predict higher relational quality when relationships feature disclosure about weight issues (Altman & Taylor, 1987) to the extent that such disclosure reveals insecurities or uncertainties and yields support and comfort (e.g., "you're not fat;" "you look great," i.e., evaluating the interlocutor). Of course, fat talk is not useful if the recipient is not helpful in providing feedback and support (Barbee, Derlega, Sherburne, & Grimshaw, 1998). Moreover, too much and too negative disclosure is often perceived negatively (Cozby, 1973) and can have negative relational consequences (Greene, Derlega, & Mathews, 2006). Although the literature tends to emphasize positive interdependence, negative interdependence is also possible—fat talk might reinforce an overweight couple's eating habits and lack of control, and they might mutually support continuation of unhealthy practices.

Fat talk dynamics within relationships might also result in behavior change, as social influence and social support can be important mechanisms for encouraging people to engage in health-related behaviors. Couples influence the healthy and unhealthy behaviors of their partners (Homish & Leonard, 2008), including eating and exercise habits (Gruber, 2008). Engaging in fat talk might heighten partners' awareness of body issues, causing them to share ideas about coping with sociocultural pressures. In fact, communication with close others that both accepts them for who they are and challenges them to enact healthy behaviors is most effective in promoting healthy behavior (Dailey, Romo, & Thompson, 2011). The fat talk literature is practically mute on positive forms of fat talk, but supportive communication about weight does occur. Dailey and colleagues (2010, 2011) have examined weight management messages received from significant others. Their research indicates that significant others frequently make reassuring comments ("You're much slimmer than you seem to think. I don't think you see yourself as you really are"), comments of encouragement/mutual participation ("Well keep on trying and even if you don't lose weight, the exercise will help you in the long run"), and comments including advice/information ("You know you should be running at least twice a week and eating healthier"). More positive forms of fat talk can be beneficial to the well-being for the individuals involved; for example, women with greater support have better dietary practices and are more willing to seek regular medical exams (Jackson, 2006).

Although the intrapersonal level predicts negative consequences for engaging in fat talk (due to the largely negative affective and cognitive aspects of it), the interpersonal level predicts that positive health-related habits might increase. Although these two processes can happen simultaneously at different levels, encouraging and promoting such health behaviors (i.e., the interpersonal level) may result in a change in how one views weight (i.e., intrapersonal level).

Social Identity: The Intergroup Level

The intergroup level is based on broad social group–related attitudes, beliefs, and stereotypes that contribute to the process of engaging in fat talk—weight-related prejudice, for instance.

Social identity.   People's self-concepts come in part from the social groups they belong to—*social identity* in social identity theory terms (Tajfel & Turner, 1986). People categorize themselves and others in terms of weight and operate as members of these categories. They identify with others who are similar in terms of weight, behave in ways that they perceive as typical of those groups, and hold less positive attitudes about those who are different on these dimensions. Such group processes are more likely to occur when these categories have chronic accessibility to the individual (i.e., one regularly evaluates self and others in terms of weight) and when the categories are relevant to the situation (e.g., a weight-watcher's meeting, a visit to the gym; Turner et al., 1987).

Attitudes toward group.   Attitudes at the intergroup level refer primarily to prejudicial feelings and sociocultural stereotypes about weight groups. Stereotypes influence people's perceptions, attitudes, and behaviors toward people or groups, as well as perceptions of how well people fit into certain social groups (Cuddy & Fiske, 2002). Most (though not all) stereotypes and attitudes toward fat people are negative (Crandall, 1994): Fat people are thought to be lazy, sloppy, and lacking in self-discipline (Puhl & Brownell, 2001). Negative attitudes form at early ages (Cramer & Steinwert, 1998) and can be applied to oneself when one self-categorizes into a stigmatized group (O'Brien & Hummert, 2006). When fat talk is driven by attitudinal factors at the group level, intergroup motivations will be the primary drive behind engaging in fat talk.

Intergroup motivations. At the intergroup level, people are motivated to do fat talk as a way of building solidarity within their social groups or managing actual or perceived social group memberships (i.e., we-talk). Fat talk can reduce uncertainty about where one "fits" on the continua of weight, whether it be celebrating being in a favored group or commiserating and creatively finding sources of value and solidarity in a less favored identity (Hogg, 2000). Because people are motivated to reduce uncertainty because it is unpleasant (Berger & Calabrese, 1975), they can do so by identifying with certain groups; group membership brings structure and order to the world and provides norms and behavioral guidelines for group members (Hogg, 2000). Vorauer (2006) argues that individuals attempting to reduce uncertainty may seek information about what valued others (e.g., friends, family) think about them. Such conversations provide feedback that helps reduce uncertainty about which weight group someone can claim membership in. Likewise, fat talk at the group level can be a source of sharing about group-relevant experiences, and hence can contribute to a building of shared ingroup identity ("We're both fat!"). Motivational factors at the intergroup level then are predicted to result in comments that involve coming to terms with social identity level concerns: the delineation of group boundaries, self-categorization into relevant groups, and establishing shared identities with others.

Social identity outcomes. Engaging in social identity motivated conversations about weight is predicted to heighten the salience of weight categorizations. These conversations allow people to distance themselves from groups they do not want to belong to and reduce uncertainty about self- and other-group identification. If people are not satisfied with their weight-related social identities, they can deal with those identities in three ways (as predicted by social identity theory; Tajfel & Turner, 1986). First, they can engage in *social mobility* (i.e., identify with or act in accordance with the more valued groups): People who are unhappy with their weight may choose to exercise and diet as a way to lose weight or deny their weight and self-categorize into a slimmer group (including via communication). Interestingly, talk about leaving the group could serve as a source of group identification for the chronically overweight. Among this group, actually leaving the group is probably not viewed as a realistic option. But the act of discussing leaving the group and how to do so (diet, exercise, surgery, etc.) may be something similar to an identity-serving fantasy theme among group members (Rossel, 1981).

Second, people can engage in *social creativity* by redefining the categorical or dimensional bases for the intergroup comparisons they are engaged in. In this case, those who are overweight might emphasize positive aspects of gaining weight. For example, many African American adolescent girls (who are typically more comfortable with a heavier weight than are White and Latino girls; Grabe & Hyde, 2006) associate beauty with personality characteristics and report that boys prefer them to have curves (Nichter, 2000). Fat talk may serve explicit social creativity functions in maintaining a positive attitude towards a stigmatized group membership ("Curves are sexy!").

Third, people can engage in *social competition* by seeking to change stigmatized attitudes about weight. Certain aspects of we-talk from the typology would likely reinforce or precipitate this outcome. If people find and express pride in their group memberships, they will tend to pursue positive images of their group and to fight against prejudice. For instance, the National Association to Advance Fat Acceptance (NAAFA) is a non-profit civil rights organization whose goal is to build equality and end size discrimination through advocacy, education, and support (NAAFA, 2012).

Communication

Language varies contextually and is multifunctional. In this section, we discuss how the familiar comment "I'm so fat" operates at the three levels just outlined. We illustrate that it is not useful to treat communication as only working on one level of identity—any specific message might be used at any level and have consequences at other levels of identity.

At the intrapersonal level, "I'm so fat" could serve cathartic needs of expressing an emotion or concern and might ease body-related concerns at least in the short term. At the same time, many of the forms of fat talk observed in the literature appear to manage intrapersonal concerns by releasing personal control and emphasizing "wishing" and "fearing" ("This is going to make me so fat;" "I can't believe I ate so much"). Such comments seem likely to result in outcomes of regret and guilt with associated negative and distorted self-perceptions (e.g., depression, loss of control; Arroyo & Harwood, 2012). Nonetheless, they may be functional in the immediate sense in that they absolve the self of direct responsibility for the body.

At the interpersonal level, "I'm so fat" may be intended as a relational gambit to test the partner (Will he or she comfort me?) or as an attempt to move both parties toward a healthier lifestyle (Maybe he or she will suggest we work out together). Fat talk thus reduces uncertainty about relational-level processes and enhances the relationship. Because of the interdependent nature of communication and relationships, this level may offer the most potential for positive weight-related communication—through interacting and expressing "I'm so fat" to another, individuals can be both supported ("Stop worrying; your body looks great") and challenged ("Let's eat less and start a workout routine") to move toward a more healthy lifestyle and sense of self (Dailey et al., 2010).

At the intergroup level, "I'm so fat" would be said as part of a drive to negotiate solidarity within a social group or to reduce uncertainty about what group someone belongs to. At this level, the comment might be intended to solicit reciprocation in a group of overweight people and build a sense of acceptance and solidarity ("We're all fat and that's OK"). Alternatively, it could be a boundary test to see whether one is perceived by others as belonging to that category ("No way—she is fat; you're just fine"), thus soliciting clarification both on the position of (negotiated) category boundaries and on one's position relative to those boundaries.

Further Complexities of the Model

Fat Talk Across the Levels

As noted earlier, the effects of fat talk may occur across levels, which is a complexity of the model. For instance, fat talk driven by interpersonal motivations might have effects at the intergroup or intrapersonal level that are unanticipated and unintended. Such effects may not always be consistent in terms of valence, and at times, they may clearly be ironic. Harwood (2007) notes that certain forms of talk may be effective strategies at an individual level but may have negative consequences at the social-identity level. For instance, asking someone, "Did you lose weight? You look great!" establishes a positive social comparison for the individual and might yield positive self-esteem. However, the message's framing carries with it an implicit (yet clear) statement that being heavier is unattractive and that members of the "fat" group have negative characteristics. Hence, the same statement carries positive intrapersonal connotations but a negative social-identity message. If the latter are internalized, the message is "I look great now, but I did not before, so I cannot regain the weight." Such messages lead to fear and negative intrapersonal outcomes. As such, fat talk serves positive and negative functions simultaneously, both within and across levels.

Self-categorization theory (Turner et al., 1987) offers the best resources for tapping levels of identity and identifying avenues for examining these effects. To fully understand these effects, we need to use self-categorization theory methods to assess the level of identity that people are operating on as they enter a conversation. By doing so and then examining effects on relevant attitudes (e.g., body satisfaction, relational satisfaction) and motivations (e.g., desire for thinness, relational maintenance, boundary uncertainty) at all three levels, it will be possible to empirically disentangle the functions and outcomes of specific fat talk behaviors across levels within our model.

Fat Talk Typology

We presented a typology of different types of fat talk comments that may occur at the intrapersonal, interpersonal, and intergroup levels. It is important to note again that this typology is preliminary. Based on our data and on the current fat talk literature, we have presented fat talk comments as, among others, routinized talk (Nichter & Vuckovic, 1994), self-evaluative comments (Engeln-Maddox, Salk, & Miller, 2012), seeking feedback (Swann, 1983), and group solidarity (Nichter, 2000). We understand that such a typology may miss the nuances and the breadth of fat talk. Particularly, it is important to note that more positive types of talk likely occur (e.g., "I look great today"; "I'm so happy I've lost 5 pounds"), but our data did not capture that, and the literature focuses almost exclusively on negative talk. We also did not encapsulate the various responses to fat talk from others, wherein such responses may influence the outcomes of fat talk and weight-related comments (Dailey et al., 2010). Future research would benefit from in-depth analyses and validation of the typology, as well as exploring other types of fat talk not captured here.

Individual Differences

We examine three sources of individual differences: race/ethnicity, gender, and weight-related differences. First, individuals' racial/ethnic backgrounds play a central role in weight issues because different ethnicities do not conform to sociocultural pressures in the same ways. White women, compared to their non-White counterparts, are less satisfied with their bodies (Wildes, Emery, & Simons, 2001). African American women have higher body satisfaction than women of other ethnic groups (Grabe & Hyde, 2006), perhaps because African American women do not compare themselves to women of other ethnic groups and are more likely to define physical attractiveness in terms of body shape and style rather than size (Frisby, 2004; Poran, 2006). Results on Latinos' body satisfaction have been mixed (Barry & Grilo, 2002; McComb & Clopton, 2002). In Latino cultures, full-figured bodies are perceived as healthy and of high status (Gil-Kashiwabara, 2002); however conforming to the traditional feminine gender role (including body image) is also emphasized (Avila & Avila, 1995). Such contradictory expectations may help explain these inconclusive results. Although not much work has been done on Asian Americans, women in this group tend to endorse the same sociocultural standards of beauty as White women do (Evans & McConnell, 2003). They show heightened dissatisfaction when it comes to race-specific body parts (e.g., eyes; Mintz & Kashubeck, 1999). Cultural variation therefore clearly influences attitudes and beliefs about bodies and weight. Within our model, these concerns would fall into the sociocultural context outlined at the top of the model. As work progresses, research should consider race/ethnicity as a critical variable, particularly insofar as similar forms of fat talk serve different functions and have different effects across cultural groups. By examining cultural variation in fat talk, we may discover new ways of talking about weight that yield different, and perhaps more positive, consequences for the participants in those conversations.

Second, although objectification and pressure to fit the ideal body image affect men (Grieve & Helmick, 2008; Wiseman & Moradi, 2010), the appearance-related pressures faced by women are probably stronger (Tiggemann et al., 2009). Compared to men, women are more likely to learn from the media to view their bodies from external perspectives (McKinley & Hyde, 1996): Media portrayals of idealized women influence women's body image more than men's (Fredrickson & Roberts, 1997). These images permeate the normative discontent experienced by women about their bodies (McKinley & Hyde, 1996; Rodin, Silberstein, & Striegel-Moore, 1984). Our model was developed based on a literature that focuses on women, but men also report hearing and engaging in fat talk (Martz et al., 2009). However, men and women feel different pressures to engage in comments about their appearance. Women feel pressure to say negative things about themselves, while men feel pressure to say self-accepting things (Martz et al., 2009). Additionally, women and men receive different messages about what is ideal: Women are pressured to be thin, whereas men feel pressure to be muscular (Thompson et al. 1999). Inherently, then, comments about one's ideal differ based on gender, and future examinations of the model should incorporate those differences.

Third, individual differences in terms of weight identity and actual weight affect the process of fat talk. For example, people with high weight centrality may interpret and evaluate their bodies more harshly than people for whom weight is less central to self. This should be moderated by valence of identity: Someone with a negative identity and high weight centrality might interpret sociocultural pressures as threats to self; someone with a positive identity and high weight centrality might find that such pressures serve as motivation for self-improvement. Actual weight should also moderate this effect, such that there will be differences between people with high and low body mass indexes (BMI) in terms of what is said and how it is interpreted. "I'm so fat" will clearly elicit differing responses when one is undeniably fat compared to when one is skinny.

Mass Media and Interpersonal Fat Talk

Productive investigations of the intersections between mediated and interpersonal communication in this arena are warranted. The media are aggressive purveyors of sociocultural norms in regard to women's bodies (Fredrickson & Roberts, 1997), as women are inundated with media messages and images of the thin (and young and beautiful) ideal (Field et al., 2001; Levine & Harrison, 2003; Tiggemann, 2005). Because the media serve as a cultural indicator of beauty and attractiveness, many women strive for and compare themselves to idealized media images (Harrison, 2001; Knobloch-Westerwick & Romero, 2011). This creates a pervasive pressure to be thin in our society and results in many women feeling dissatisfaction about their body shape, size, and appearance (i.e., normative discontent; Rodin et al., 1984). Given that some forms of fat talk perpetuate negative self-perceptions, we should explore how systematic, repetitive patterns of ideal body representations presented in the media contribute to such interpersonal behavior. Also, future research should examine the extent to which interpersonal weight-related discourses in our typology are derived from the media. The media might stimulate envious fat talk, for instance, by portraying idealized celebrities (e.g., "She's so beautiful; I wish I was as skinny as her").

Theoretical Expansions: Beyond Weight

We have focused here on fat talk, which we suggest is a type of group-related talk. However, we see avenues for research and theorizing on other group memberships, in particular similar processes surrounding talk about age and age groups. Age is similar to weight in important ways as a category system: (a) Age is a continuum along which people move gradually and smoothly, wherein specific regions on the continuum are associated with prejudice (e.g., being "elderly"), and (b) there are also legitimate health issues associated with age (i.e., old age carries with it increased risk of chronic health problems), which have become almost inseparable from the broader categorization. Further, (c) age and weight both relate in fundamental ways to our bodies, the ways in which our bodies change, and the identity management issues that come along with such changes. They are both intimately tied into issues of appearance, cultural standards of attractiveness, and the relative value that we place on one body over another. Interestingly, (d) age- and weight-related stigmas also appear to be intertwined in the empirical literature: People who are more concerned about the losses associated with aging experience also more body-weight perception problems (Gupta & Schork, 1993; Lewis & Cachelin, 2001). Weight and age are also (e) both things that we frequently talk about (Coupland, Coupland, Giles, & Henwood, 1991).

Although this chapter focuses on fat talk, age-related talk shares some underlying determinants such as concern for appearance. Weight- and age-related concerns are associated with negative perceptions of oneself, so the processes in the model should function similarly for age-related talk as for fat talk. Thus, the use of the term *body talk,* which generalizes across areas of body concern, would be appropriate as we expand the model. Objectification theory states that people treat their bodies as objects based on sociocultural pressures. From this perspective, people's bodies are a point of concern, and communication attempts to make sense of specific body perception problems. With self-objectification at its basis, people's body talk perpetuates sociocultural pressures and fosters unreal expectations of the ideal body image.

At another level of abstraction, our model suggests value in examining how people talk about groups and their own group memberships. Here we are following Sutton's (2010) claim that "language is not just *at* the heart, but *is* the beating heart of intergroup relations" (p. 115). If we want to get to the heart of group relations in any context, examining the details of talk about those groups is essential. So, for instance, gender is a persistent source of talk in society and a staple for stand-up comedians. Identifying the resources on which people draw in talking about gender groups, the common themes of such talk, and the outcomes would help extend the model presented to broader intergroup relations. In contrast to age and weight, gender identities are (with exceptions) relatively fixed and dichotomous; the extent to which differences between gender talk and fat talk can be explained by the different underlying categorical structures could lead toward powerful theoretical frameworks. The contested nature of gender also brings to light the difficulties in delineating between talk that is explicitly about gender and talk that is gendered in more implicit ways (e.g., via power implications and sexual stratification; Speer, 2005). Similar arguments could be developed for the interest in examining talk about race, culture, disability, or religion. For instance, research on race (Trawalter & Richeson, 2008) and age (Henwood, Giles, Coupland, & Coupland, 1993) suggests that talking about groups in intergroup contexts is more comfortable for low-status group members (African Americans, older adults) than for high-status group members (Whites, young adults). Further examination of such phenomenon will help us understand the scope conditions for some of the processes described in our model. We see tremendous potential in understanding how group-related talk may differentially affect individual and collective outcomes in complex ways, well beyond the context of fat talk.

Conclusion

We have presented a conceptual model of the determinants and consequences of fat talk. We present this as a conceptual (not testable) model—the elements in the model represent classes of variables, not operationalizable concepts. Although testing the entire model is not possible, we hope that the model presented inspires empirical examination. We have made suggestions for specific variables within categories, so the variables emerging from the broad categories can be examined in the form of "micro" models developed from our macro model. We endorse symbolic interactionist and social constructionist views (e.g., Blumer, 1969; Goffman, 1963) that "humans, in concert with one another, create symbolic worlds and how these worlds, in turn, shape behavior" (LaRossa & Reitzes, 1993, p. 136). It is through communication that we understand, express, and construct the meaning of weight for ourselves, our relationships, and our groups. Only by understanding more about the identity-level processes that lead to types of talk and their outcomes will we get closer to understanding precisely how weight is constructed socially.

This chapter suggests that engaging in conversations about weight perpetuates sociocultural pressures about an ideal image for both women and men and that these pressures influence people to engage in more fat talk. We note that fat talk is serving intrapersonal, interpersonal, and intergroup functions for those involved in the conversations, and we outline the different identities, attitudes, motivations, and outcomes associated with fat talk at those three levels. Using our typology, we illustrated the diversity in how people talk about weight, and the intricate ways in which such talk intersects with levels of identities. By investigating and acknowledging the causes, consequences, and processes of fat talk and other body-related talk, there is potential to change individuals' and society's ideas, expectations, and communication about the ideal body image and to increase individual and societal acceptance and appreciation of diverse bodies.

References

ABC News (2012, May 12). *100 million dieters, $20 billion: the weight-loss industry by the numbers.* Retrieved from http://abcnews.go.com/Health/100-million-dieters-20-billion-weight-loss-industry/story?id=16297197#.UMgb1qWpfWE

Altman, I., & Taylor, D. (1987). Communication in interpersonal relationships: Social penetration theory. In M. E. Roloff & G. R. Miller (Eds.), *Interpersonal processes: New directions in communication research* (pp. 257–277). Newbury Park, CA: Sage.

Arroyo, A., & Harwood, J. (2012). Exploring the causes and consequences of engaging in fat talk. *Journal of Applied Communication Research, 40,* 167–187. doi:10.1080/00909882.2012.654500

Avila, D. L., & Avila A. L. (1995). Mexican-Americans. In N. A. Vacc & S. B. DeVaney (Eds.), *Experiencing and counseling multicultural and diverse populations* (3rd ed., pp. 119–146). Philadelphia, PA: Accelerated Development.

Barbee, A. P., Derlega, V. J., Sherburne, S. P., & Grimshaw, A. (1998). Helpful and unhelpful forms of support for HIV-positive individuals. In V. J. Derlega & A. P. Barbee (Eds.), *HIV and social interaction* (pp. 83–105). Thousand Oaks, CA: Sage.

Barry, D. T., & Grilo, C. M. (2002). Eating and body image disturbances in adolescent psychiatric inpatients: Gender and ethnicity patterns. *International Journal of Eating Disorders, 32,* 335–343. doi:10.1002/eat.10082

Baxter, L. A. (1987). Symbols of relationship identity in relationship cultures. *Journal of Social and Personal Relationships, 4,* 261–280. doi:10.1177/026540758700400302

Beck, A. T. (1974). The development of depression: A cognitive model. In R. Friedman & M. Katz (Eds.), *Psychology of depression: Contemporary theory and research* (pp. 3–20). Washington, DC: Winston-Wiley.

Berger, C. R., & Calabrese, R. (1975). Some explorations in initial interaction and beyond: Toward a developmental theory of interpersonal communication. *Human Communication Research, 1,* 99–112. doi:10.1111/j.1468–2958.1975.tb00258.x

Blumer, H. (1962). Society as symbolic interaction. In A. M. Rose (Ed.), *Human behavior and social process: An interactionist approach* (pp. 179–192). Boston, MA: Houghton-Mifflin.

Borzekowski, D. L. G., Schenk, S., Wilson, J. L., & Peebles, R. (2010). e-Ana and e-Mia: A content analysis of pro–eating disorder web sites. *American Journal of Public Health, 100,* 1526–1534. doi:10.2105/AJPH.2009.172700

Britton, L. E., Martz, D. M., Bazzini, D. G., Curtin, L. A., & LeaShomb, A. (2006). Fat talk and self-presentation of body image: Is there a social norm for women to self-degrade? *Body Image, 3,* 247–354. doi:10.1016/j.bodyim.2006.05.006

Brown, C. (2008). The information trail of the "Freshman 15": A systematic review of a health myth within the research and popular literature. *Health Information Libraries Journal, 25,* 1–12. doi:10.1111/j.1471–1842.2007.00762.x

Brown, P., & Levinson, S. (1978). *Politeness: Some universals in language use.* Cambridge, England: Cambridge University Press.

Burke, T. J., Randall, A. K., Corkery, S. A., Young, V. J., & Butler, E. A. (2012). "You're going to eat that?" Relationship processes and conflict among mixed-weight couples. *Journal of Social & Personal Relationships, 29,* 1109–1130. doi:10.1177/0265407512451199

Butler, S. M., Black, D. R., Blue, C. L., & Greteback, R. J. (2004). Change in diet, physical activity, and body weight in female college freshman. *American Journal of Health Behavior, 28,* 24–32. doi:10.5993/AJHB.28.1.3

Cahill, S., & Mussap, A. J. (2007). Emotional reactions following exposure to idealized bodies predict unhealthy body change attitudes and behaviors in women and men. *Journal of Psychosomatic Research, 62,* 631–639. doi:10.1016/j.jpsychores.2006.11.001

Campbell, L., Simpson, J. A., Kashy, D. A., & Fletcher, G.J.O. (2001). Ideal standards, the self, and flexibility of ideals in close relationships. *Personality & Social Psychology Bulletin, 27,* 447–462. doi:10.1177/0146167201274006

Centers for Disease Control and Prevention. (2012). *Adult obesity facts.* Retrieved from www.cdc.gov/obesity/data/adult.html

Chesters, L. (1994). Women's talk: Food, weight and body image. *Feminism & Psychology, 4,* 449–457. doi:10.1177/0959353594043017

Cozby, P. C. (1973). Self-disclosure: A literature review. *Psychological Bulletin, 79,* 73–91. doi:10.1037/h0033950

Coupland, J., Coupland, N., Giles, H., & Henwood, K. (1991). Formulating age: Dimensions of age identity in elderly talk. *Discourse Processes, 14,* 87–106. doi:10.1080/01638539109544776

Coupland, N., Coupland, J., Giles, H., Henwood, K., & Wiemann, J. (1988). Elderly self-disclosure: Interactional and intergroup issues. *Language & Communication, 8,* 109–133. doi:10.1016/0271–5309(88)90010–9

Cramer, R., & Steinwert, T. (1998). Thin is good, fat is bad: How early does it begin? *Journal of Applied Developmental Psychology, 19,* 429–451. doi:10.1016/S0193–3973(99)80049–5

Crandall, C. S. (1994). Prejudice against fat people: Ideology and self-interest. *Journal of Personality and Social Psychology, 66,* 882–894. doi:10.1037/0022–3514.66.5.882

Crandall, C. S., Nierman, A., & Helb, M. (2009). Anti-fat prejudice. In T. D. Nelson (Ed.), *Handbook of prejudice, stereotyping, and discrimination* (pp. 469–487). New York: Psychology Press.

Cuddy, A.J.C., & Fiske, S. T. (2002). Doddering, but dear: Process, content, and function in stereotyping of older persons. In T. Nelson (Ed.), *Ageism: Stereotyping and prejudice against older persons* (pp. 3–26). Cambridge, MA: MIT Press.

Dailey, R. M., Romo, L. K., & McCracken, A. A. (2010). Messages about weight management: An examination of how acceptance and challenge are related to message effectiveness. *Western Journal of Communication, 74,* 457–483. doi:10.1080/1057 0314.2010.512279

Dailey, R. M., Romo, L. K., & Thompson, C. M. (2011). Confirmation in couples' communication about weight management: An analysis of how both partners contribute to individuals' health behaviors and conversational outcomes. *Human Communication Research, 37,* 553–582. doi:10.1111/j.1468–2958.2011.01414.x

Davison, T. E., & McCabe, M. P. (2005). Relationships between men's and women's body image and their psychological, social, and sexual functioning. *Sex Roles, 52,* 463–475. doi:10.1007/s11199–005–3712-z

Delinsky, S. S. (2012). Body image and anorexia nervosa. In T. F. Cash & L. Smolak (Eds.), *Body image: A handbook of science, reactive and prevention* (2nd ed., pp. 179–287). New York: Guilford.

Drury, J., & Reicher, S. (1999). The intergroup dynamics of collective empowerment: Substantiating the social identity model. *Group Processes and Intergroup Relations, 2,* 381–402. doi:10.1177/1368430299024005

Durkin, S. J., & Paxton, S. J. (2002). Predictors of vulnerability to reduced body satisfaction and psychological well-being in response to exposure to idealized female media images in adolescent girls. *Journal of Psychosomatic Research, 53,* 995–1005.

Engeln-Maddox, R., Salk, R. H., & Miller, S. A. (2012). Assessing women's negative commentary on their own bodies: A psychometric investigation of the Negative Body Talk Scale. *Psychology of Women Quarterly, 36,* 162–178. doi:10.1177/0361684312441593

Evans, P. C., & McConnell, A. R. (2003). Do racial minorities respond in the same way to mainstream beauty standards? Social comparison processes in Asian, Black, and White women. *Self and Identity, 2,* 153–167.

Festinger, G. (1954). A theory of social comparison processes. *Human Relations, 7,* 117–140. doi:10.1177/001872675400700202

Field, A. E., Camargo, C. A., Taylor, C. B., Berkey, C. S., Roberts, S. B., & Colditz, G. A. (2001). Peer, parent, and media influences in the development of weight concerns and frequent dieting among preadolescent and adolescent girls and boys. *Pediatrics, 107,* 54–60. doi:10.1542/peds.107.1.54

Flegal, K. M., Carroll, M. D., Ogden, C. L., & Curtin, L. R. (2010). Prevalence and trends in obesity among US adults, 1999–2008. *The Journal of the American Medical Association, 303,* 235–241. doi:10.1001/jama.2009.2014

Foster, E. K. (2004). Research on gossip: Taxonomy, methods, and future directions. *Review of General Psychology,* 8, 78–99. doi:10.1037/1089–2680.8.2.78

Franks, M. M., Shields, C. G., Lim, E., Sands, L. P., Mobley, S., & Boushey, C. J. (2012). I will if you will: Similarity in married partners' readiness to change health risk behaviors. *Health Education & Behavior, 39,* 324–331. doi:10.1177/1090198111402824

Fredrickson, B. L., & Roberts, T. (1997). Objectification theory: Toward understanding women's lived experiences and mental health risks. *Psychology of Women Quarterly, 21,* 173–206. doi:10.1111/j.1471–6402.1997.tb00108.

Frisby, C. M. (2004). Does race matter? Effects of idealized images on African American women's perceptions of body esteem. *Journal of Black Studies, 34,* 323–347. doi:10.1177/0021934703258989

Gapinski, K. D., Brownell, K. D., & LaFrance, M. (2003). Body objectification and "fat talk": Effects on emotion, motivation, and cognitive performance. *Sex Roles, 48,* 377–388.

Gil-Kashiwabara, E. (2002). Body image disturbance and disordered eating in African American and Latina women. In L. H. Collins, M. R. Dunlap, & J. C. Chrisler (Eds.), *Charting a new course for feminist psychology* (pp. 282–206). New York: Praeger/Greenwood.

Giles, H. (Ed.). (2012). *The handbook of intergroup communication.* New York: Routledge.

Giles, H., Coupland, J., & Coupland, N. (1991). Accommodation theory: Communication, context, and consequence. In H. Giles, J. Coupland, & N. Coupland (Eds.), *Contexts of accommodation: Developments in applied sociolinguistics* (pp. 1–58). New York: Cambridge University Press.

Giles, H., & Reid, S. (2005). Ageism across the lifespan: Towards a self-categorization model of ageing. *Journal of Social Issues, 61,* 389–404. doi:10.1111/j.1540–4560.2005.00412.x

Giles, H., Reid, S. A., & Harwood, J. (Eds.). (2010). *The dynamics of intergroup communication.* New York: Peter Lang.

Giles, H., Williams, A., & Coupland, N. (1990). Communication, health and the elderly: Frameworks, agenda and a model. In H. Giles, N. Coupland, & J. Wiemann (Eds.), *Communication, health and the elderly* (Fulbright Colloquium Series 8, pp. 1–28). New York: St. Martin's Press.

Glaser, B. G., & Strauss, A. (1967). *Discovery of grounded theory: Strategies for qualitative research.* Mill Valley, CA: Sociology Press.

Goffman, E. (1963). *Stigma: Notes on the management of spoiled identity.* Englewood Cliffs, NJ: Prentice-Hall.

Grabe, S., & Hyde, J. S. (2006). Ethnicity and body dissatisfaction among women in the United States: A meta-analysis. *Psychological Bulletin, 132,* 622–640. doi:10.1037/0033–2909.132.4.622

Greene, K., Derlega, V., & Mathews, A. (2006). Self-disclosure in personal relationships. In A. L. Vangelisti & D. Perlman (Eds.), *Cambridge handbook of personal relationships* (pp. 409–428). Cambridge, England: Cambridge University Press.

Grieve, R., & Helmick, A. (2008). The influence of men's self-objectification on the drive for muscularity. *International Journal of Men's Health, 7,* 288–298.

Gruber, K. J. (2008). Social support for exercise and dietary habits among college students. *Adolescence, 43,* 557–575.

Gupta, M. A., & Schork, N. J. (1993). Aging related concerns and body image: Possible future implications for eating disorders. *International Journal of Eating Disorders, 14,* 481–486.

Harrison, K. (2001). Ourselves, our bodies: Thin-ideal media, self-discrepancies, and eating disorder symptomatology in adolescents. *Journal of Social and Clinical Psychology, 20,* 289–323. doi:10.1521/jscp.20.3.289.22303

Harrison, K., & Hefner, V. (2006). Media exposure, current and future body ideals, and disordered eating among preadolescent girls: A longitudinal panel study. *Journal of Youth and Adolescence, 35,* 153–163. doi:10.1007/s10964–005–9008–3

Harrison, K., Taylor, L. D., & Marske, A. L. (2006). Women's and men's eating behavior following exposure to ideal-body images and text. *Communication Research, 33,* 507–529. doi:10.1177/0093650206293247

Harwood, J. (2007). *Understanding communication and aging: Developing knowledge and awareness.* Thousand Oaks, CA: Sage.

Hecht, M. L. (1993). 2002—A research odyssey: Toward the development of a communication theory of identity. *Communication Monographs, 60,* 76–82. doi:10.1080/03637759309376297

Hecht, M. L., Collier, M. J., &, & Ribeau, S. (1993). *African American communication: Ethnic identity and cultural interpretations.* Newbury Park, CA: Sage.

Hecht, M. L., Jackson II, R. L., & Pitts, M. J. (2005). Culture: Intersections of intergroup and identity theories. In J. Harwood & H. Giles (Eds.), *Intergroup communication: Multiple perspectives* (pp. 21–42). New York: Peter Lang.

Hecht, M. L., Jackson, R. L., & Ribeau, S. (2003). *African American communication: Exploring identity and culture* (2nd edition). Mahwah, NJ: Erlbaum.

Heinberg, L. J., Thompson, J. K., & Stormer, S. (1995). Development and validation of the Sociocultural Attitudes Towards Appearance Questionnaire. *International Journal of Eating Disorders, 17,* 81–89. doi:10.1002/1098–108X(199501)17:1<81::AID-EAT2260170111>3.0.CO;2-Y

Helgeson, V. S., & Taylor, S. E. (1993). Social comparisons and adjustment among cardiac patients. *Journal of Applied Social Psychology, 23,* 1171–1195.

Henwood, K., Giles, H., Coupland, N., & Coupland, J. (1993). Stereotyping and affect in discourse: Interpreting the meaning of elderly painful self-disclosure. In D. M. Mackie & D. L. Hamilton (Eds.), *Affect, cognition, and stereotyping* (pp. 269–296). San Diego, CA: Academic Press.

Higgins, E. T. (1987). Self-discrepancy: A theory relating self and affect. *Psychological Review, 94*, 319–304. doi:10.1037//0033–295X.94.3.319

Hogg, M. A. (2000). Subjective uncertainty reduction through self-categorization: A motivational theory of social identity processes. *European Review of Social Psychology, 11*, 223–255. doi:10.1080/14792772043000040

Homish, G. G., & Leonard, K. E. (2008). Spousal influence on general health behaviors in a community sample. *American Journal of Health Behavior, 32*, 754–763. doi:10.5993/AJHB.32.6.19

Jackson, T. (2006). Relationships between close social support and health practices within community samples of American women and men. *Journal of Psychology, 140*, 229–246. doi:10.3200/JRLP.140.3.229–246

Jacobi, L., & Cash, T. F. (1994). In pursuit of the perfect appearance: Discrepancies among self-ideal percepts of multiple physical attributes. *Journal of Applied Social Psychology, 24*, 379–396. doi:10.1111/j.1559–1816.1994.tb00588.x

Jolanki, O. (2008). Discussing responsibility and ways of influencing health. *International Journal of Ageing and Later Life, 3*, 45–76. doi:10.3384/ijal.1652–8670. 083145

Knobloch-Westerwick, S., & Romero, J. P. (2011). Body ideals in the media: Perceived attainability and social comparison choices. *Media Psychology, 14*, 27–48. doi:10.1 080/15213269.2010.547833

LaRossa, R., & Reitzes, D.C. (1993). Symbolic interactionism and family studies. In P. G. Boss, W. J. Doherty, R. LaRossa, W. R. Schumm, & S. K. Steinmetz (Eds.), *Sourcebook of family theories and methods: A contextual approach* (pp. 135–163). New York: Plenum.

Laver, J. (1975). Communicative functions of phatic communion. In A. Kendon, R. Harris, & M. Key (Eds.), *The organisation of behaviour in face-to-face interaction* (pp. 215–238). The Hague, the Netherlands: Mouton.

Leaper, C., & Holliday, H. (1995). Gossip in same-gender and cross-gender friends' conversations. *Personal Relationships, 2*, 237–246.

Ledyard, M. L., & Morrison, N. C. (2008). The meaning of weight in marriage: A phenomenological investigation of relational factors involved in obesity. *Journal of Couple & Relationship Therapy, 7*, 230–247. doi:10.1080/15332690802 237946

Levine, M. P., & Harrison, K. (2003). Media's role in the perpetuation and prevention of negative body image and disordered eating. In J. K. Thompson (Ed.), *Handbook of eating disorders and obesity* (pp. 695–717). New York: Wiley.

Lewis, D., & Cachelin, F. M. (2001). Body image, body dissatisfaction, and eating attitudes in midlife and elderly women. *Eating Disorders: The Journal of Treatment & Prevention, 9*, 29–39. doi:10.1080/106402601300187713

Lirola, M. M., & Chovanec, J. (2012). The dream of a perfect body come true: Multimodality in cosmetic surgery advertising. *Discourse & Society, 23*, 487–507. doi:10.1177/0957926512452970

Marketdata Enterprises Inc. (2011). *The U.S. Weight Loss & Diet Control Market (11th Edition)*. Retrieved from www.marketresearch.com/Marketdata-Enterprises-Inc-v416/Weight-Loss-Diet-Control-11th-6314539/

Martz, D. M., Petroff, A. B., Curtin, L., & Bazzini, D. G. (2009). Gender differences in fat talk among American adults: Results from the psychology of size survey. *Sex Roles, 61*, 34–41. doi:10.1007/s11199–009–9587–7

McCabe, M. P., & Ricciardelli, L. A. (2001). Parent, peer, and media influences on body image and strategies to both increase and decrease body size among adolescent boys and girls. *Adolescence, 36,* 225–240.

McComb, J. R., & Clopton, J. (2002). Explanatory variance in bulimia nervosa. *Women and Health, 36,* 115–123. doi:10.1300/J013v36n04_09

McKinley, N., & Hyde, J. (1996). The Objectified Body Consciousness scale: Development and validation. *Psychology of Women Quarterly, 20,* 181–215. doi:10.1111/j.1471–6402.1996.tb00467.x

Mintz, L. B., & Kashubeck, S. (1999). Body image and disordered eating among Asian American and Caucasian college students. *Psychology of Women Quarterly, 23,* 781–796. doi:10.1111/j.1471–6402.1999.tb00397.x

National Association to Advance Fat Acceptance. (2012). Retrieved from www.naafa online.com/dev2/

Nichter, M. (2000). *Fat talk.* Cambridge, MA: Harvard University Press.

Nichter, M., & Vuckovic, N. (1994). Fat talk: Body image among adolescent girls. In N. Sault (Ed.), *Many mirrors: Body image and social relations* (pp. 109–131). New Brunswick, NJ: Rutgers University Press.

O'Brien, L. T., & Hummert, M. L. (2006). Memory performance of late middle–aged adults: Contrasting self–stereotyping and stereotype threat accounts of assimilation to age stereotypes. *Social Cognition, 24,* 338–358. doi:10.1521/soco.2006.24.3.338

O'Dougherty, M., Schmitz, K. H., Hearst, M. O., Covelli, M., & Kurzer, M. S. (2011). Dual conversations: Body talk among young women and their social contacts. *Qualitative Health Research, 21,* 1191–1204. doi:10.1177/1049732311405804

Oring, E. (1984). Dyadic traditions. *Journal of Folklore Research, 21,* 19–28.

Ousley, L., Cordero, E. D., & White, S. (2008). Fat talk among college students: How undergraduates communicate regarding food and body weight, shape and appearance. *Eating Disorders, 16,* 73–84. doi:10.1080/10640260701773546

Payne, L., Martz, D., Tompkins, K. B., Petroff, A., & Farrow, C. (2010). Fat talk in the United Kingdom and the United States. *Sex Role, 65,* 557–565. doi:10.1007/s11199–010–9881–4

Poran, M. (2006). The politics of protection: Body image, social pressures, and the misrepresentation of young Black women. *Sex Roles, 55,* 739–755. doi:10.1007/s11199–006–9129–5

Puhl, R., & Brownell, K. D. (2001). Bias, discrimination and obesity. *Obesity Research, 9,* 788–805. doi:10.1038/oby.2001.108

Rodin, J., Silberstein, L., & Striegel-Moore, R. (1984). Women and weight: A normative discontent. *Nebraska Symposium on Motivation, 32,* 267–307.

Rossel, R. D. (1981). Word play: Metaphor and humor in the small group. *Small Group Research, 12,* 116–136. doi:10.1177/104649648101200109

Salk, R. H., & Engeln-Maddox, R. (2011). "If you're fat, then I'm humungous!": Frequency, content, and impact of fat talk among college women. *Psychology of Women Quarterly, 35,* 18–35. doi:10.1177/0361684310384107

Settles, I. H. (2004). When multiple identities interfere: The role of identity centrality. *Personality and Social Psychology Bulletin, 30,* 487–500. doi:10.1177/0146167203261885

Smith-Jackson, T., Reel, J. J., & Thackeray, R. (2011). Coping with "bad body image days": Strategies from first-year young adult college women. *Body Image, 8,* 335–342. doi:10.1016/j.bodyim.2011.05.002

Speer, S. (2005). *Gender talk: Feminism, discourse, and conversation analysis.* New York: Routledge.

Stice, E., Maxfield, J., & Wells, T. (2003). Adverse effects of social pressure to be thin on young women: An experimental investigation of the effects of "fat talk." *International Journal of Eating Disorders, 34,* 108–117. doi:10.1002/eat.10171

Sutton, R. (2010). The creative power of language in social cognition and intergroup relations. In H. Giles, S. Reid, & J. Harwood (Eds.), *The dynamics of intergroup communication* (pp. 105–116). New York: Peter Lang.

Swann, W. B., Jr. (1983). Self-verification: Bringing social reality into harmony with the self. In J. Suls & A. G. Greenwald (Eds.), *Social psychological perspectives on the self* (Vol. 2, pp. 33–66). Hillsdale, NJ: Erlbaum.

Tajfel, H., & Turner, J. C. (1986). The social identity theory of intergroup behavior. In W. G. Austin & S. Worchel (Eds.), *Psychology of intergroup relations* (pp. 7–24). Chicago, IL: Nelson-Hall.

Tantleff-Dunn, S., & Linder, D. M. (2012). Body image and social functioning. In T. F. Cash & L. Smolak (Eds.), *Body image: A handbook of science, reactive and prevention* (2nd ed., pp. 263–270). New York: Guilford.

Thompson, J. K., Heinberg, L. J., Altabe, M., & Tantleff-Dunn, S. (1999). *Exacting beauty: Theory, assessment, and treatment of body image disturbance.* Washington DC: APA.

Tiggemann, M. (2005). Television and adolescent body image: The role of program content and viewing motivation. *Journal of Social and Clinical Psychology, 24,* 361–381. doi:10.1521/jscp.24.3.361.65623

Tiggemann, M. (2012). Sociocultural perspectives on human appearance and body image. In T. F. Cash & L. Smolak (Eds.), *Body image: A handbook of science, reactive and prevention* (2nd ed., pp. 12–19). New York: Guilford.

Tiggemann, M., Polivy, J., & Hargreaves, D. (2009). The processing of thin ideals in fashion magazines: A source of social comparison or fantasy? *Journal of Social and Clinical Psychology, 28,* 73–93. doi:10.1521/jscp.2009.28.1.73

Tompkins, K. B., Martz, D., Rocheleau, C., & Bazzini, D. (2009). Social likeability, conformity, and body talk: Does fat talk have a normative rival in female body image conversations? *Body Image, 6,* 292–298. doi:10.1016/j.bodyim.2009.07.005

Trawalter, S., & Richeson, J. A. (2008). Let's talk about race, baby! When Whites' and Blacks' interracial contact experiences diverge. *Journal of Experimental Social Psychology, 44,* 1214–1217. doi:10.1016/j.jesp.2008.03.013

Tucker, K. L., Martz, D. M., Curtin, L. A., & Bazzini, D. G. (2007). Examining "fat talk" experimentally in a female dyad: How are women influences by another woman's body presentation style? *Body Image, 4,* 157–164. doi:10.1016/j.bodyim.2006.12.005

Turner, J. C., Hogg, M. A., Oakes, P. J., Reicher, S. D., & Wetherell, M. (1987). *Rediscovering the social group: A self-categorization theory.?* Oxford, England: Basil Blackwell.

Vorauer, J. (2006). An information search model of evaluative concerns in intergroup interaction. *Psychological Review, 113,* 862–886.

Weiderman, M. W. (2012). Body image and sexual functioning. In T. F. Cash & L. Smolak (Eds.), *Body image: A handbook of science, reactive and prevention* (2nd ed., pp. 271–278). New York: Guilford.

Wildes, J., Emery, R., & Simons, A. (2001). The roles of ethnicity and culture in the development of eating disturbance and body dissatisfaction: A meta-analytic review. *Clinical Psychology Review, 21,* 521–551. doi:10.1016/S0272–7358(99)00071–9

Wiseman, M. C., & Moradi, B. (2010). Body image and eating disorder symptoms in sexual minority men: A test and extension of objectification theory. *Journal of Counseling Psychology, 57,* 154–166. doi:10.1037/a0018937

CHAPTER CONTENTS

7 No More Birds and Bees

A Process Approach to Parent–Child Sexual Communication

Tina A. Coffelt

Iowa State University

Loreen N. Olson

University of North Carolina–Greensboro

In this chapter, we present conjoined models of parent–child sexual communication. These models rely on communication privacy management theory to show how sexual information is contained within individual privacy boundaries and shared when a question is asked. Information is revealed in little bits and pieces over the course of a child's development. Privacy boundary permeability opens, and the circumference of privacy boundaries expands over time. During a specific interaction, parents and children regulate how much information they share. These models apply to parent–child relationships where sexual communication is accomplished, recognizing that many parents and children never or rarely talk about sex.

Adolescent sexual behaviors and health statistics have been tracked for many years by identifying trends, problematic areas, and improvements in sexual health. Problem areas of teenage pregnancy, sexually transmitted diseases (STDs) and/or sexually transmitted infections (STIs), or HIV/ AIDS concern members of society because of the physical, relational, and economic consequences to adolescents, their families, partners, and communities. This tracking has recently shown that between 1991 and 2011, the number of adolescents in the United States ever having sexual intercourse declined, condom use increased, and unprotected sex declined (Centers for Disease Control [CDC], 2012a). Although these trends indicate improvements in adolescent sexual behavior, the data continue to underscore problematic areas. For example, in the United States, half of all new STD cases are reported by 15- to 24-year-old youth (CDC, 2012b), and 20% of those diagnosed with HIV/AIDS in 2009 were between the ages of 13 to 24 (CDC, 2011). Additionally, 40% of high school students did not use a condom and nearly 13% used no form of STD/STI protection or birth control during their last intercourse episode (CDC, 2012b). Thus, finding intervention and educational strategies to support adolescents during the initiation of their sexual lives remains an important undertaking.

Communication from parents provides one source of influence on the sexual behaviors of adolescents (e.g., Clawson & Reese-Weber, 2003; Fox & Inazu,

1980; Jaccard & Dittus, 1991; Karofsky, Zeng, & Kosorok, 2000; McKay, 2003). Parents are often deferred to as the primary socialization agent for their children (Christopher & Roosa, 1991; Rollins & Thomas, 1979; Stafford, 2004), and their communication with adolescents has been studied more than any other parental influence, such as values, socioeconomic status, parental marital status, or ethnicity, on adolescent sexual behavior (Meschke, Bartholomae, & Zentall, 2000). Rosenthal, Feldman, and Edwards (1998) summarized beliefs about the role of parents by writing, "It has always been assumed that parents should play a pivotal role in the sex education of their children because of their primary role in preparing young people for adult life and because sexuality brings with it questions of values and morality" (p. 727).

Although evidence shows that the topic of sex is an important one for parents to discuss with their children, the topic plagues many relationships because it aligns with the qualities of a taboo topic, such as being unpleasant to discuss (Baxter & Wilmot, 1985). In addition, sex is discussed relatively infrequently within families (Jaccard, Dittus, & Gordon, 2000; Warren & Neer, 1986). Adults report difficulty and discomfort communicating about sex with each other (Meschke et al., 2000); therefore, it is not surprising that parent–child discussions on the topic would also present challenges. Some of the difficulty may be due, in part, to the adolescent phase of child development when adolescents continue to depend on parents while simultaneously establishing independence on the path to adulthood. The awkwardness associated with sexual information coupled with the communication changes between adolescents and parents complicates parent–child sexual communication (PCSC).

Researchers have embraced this line of inquiry for decades for several reasons and with varying results. The goal of many studies has been to show that PCSC influences teens' sexual behaviors such as delaying sexual activity, using contraception, minimizing sexual STDs/STIs, and/or reducing teenage pregnancy. To that end, results from studies show mixed results, ranging from those that have found no correlation, to positive correlation, or negative correlation between PCSC and teens' sexual behaviors. For example, Fisher (1988) found no relationship between the extent of PCSC and premarital sex as reported by college students. By contrast, Clawson and Reese-Weber (2003) found that as the extent of sexual communication increased with fathers or mothers, the age of first intercourse decreased and the number of sexual partners increased. However, Karofsky and colleagues' (2000) sample of 12 to 21 year olds reported that the extent of sexual communication with parents was lower among nonvirgins than among virgins. Thus, it seems as if common research designs that measure sexual topics discussed and the frequency of discussion do not provide enough information to understand how communication influences sexual behavior.

In addition, this vast body of work privileges variable-analytic research methods, underutilizes process in theory building, and treats communication as a unidirectional flow of information from parent to child. Communication scholars have much to contribute to this area of research because of the unique ways the discipline conceptualizes interaction. For example, a communication-as-process approach recognizes the dynamic way information exchange happens over time, the dyadic nature of interaction, and the mutual influence between two parties. Drawing from these strengths of the communication discipline, we propose two conjoined models of PCSC that are rooted in relevant literature and empirical findings.

Teleological Process Models of Parent–Child Sexual Communication

The heuristic models advanced in this chapter illustrate the process of sexual communication in parent–child relationships, likely very close relationships, and shift the research stance from a solitary, parental monologue to a series of dyadic interactions prompted by either a parent or a child. Two points need emphasis at the outset: (a) The term *child* is used rather than *adolescent* because the models employ a life-span approach, recognizing the advent of conversations when children are young and continue into the emerging adult years, and (b) the models apply to relationships where PCSC is accomplished, rather than relationships that do not talk about sex. For purposes of this chapter, an initial definition of *accomplished PCSC* refers to verbal conversations about sex where a parent and child agree they discussed a sexual topic. Certainly many parents and children avoid the topic of sex. Pistella and Bonati (1999) reported 20% of their sample of 249 late adolescent females indicated they never talked to a parent about sex. King and Lorusso (1997) also found that 59.4% of their sample of undergraduate students reported never having a meaningful conversation about sex with a parent. These models may benefit children and parents such as these by steering them toward a new approach to PCSC.

Further, the models must involve change, reflect time, contain events, and demonstrate interrelationships among events to satisfy the criteria for process (Poole, 2012). More specifically, the models adopt a teleological perspective (Poole, 2012) because they seek the achievement of goals and implement a series of communication events where each event leaves the parent–child dyad receptive to future interaction. The goals of social interaction vary with each parent–child relationship, yet likely encompass instrumental, relational, and/or identity goals (Wilson & Feng, 2007). The models further satisfy the characteristics of a teleological model because the path toward goal accomplishment varies for each parent–child dyad. No predetermined actions are required at a given period or age of the child in these models.

The models also depict sexual information as emerging from multiple parent–child conversations about sex over time and offer contra-evidence to the static birds-and-the-bees, onetime conversation. The models showcase conversations that begin before adolescence, often prompted by a child's question, and answered appropriately by a parent. In this way, children receive relevant sexual information and come to see their parents as sources of sexual information. Questions arising in the future by either a parent or a child spark other conversations. During a given interaction, the parent or child releases only relevant information, a notion called incremental disclosures, which offers a new perspective on PCSC not found in the literature. Additionally, the models recognize the influence of children on their parents' communication. A few clues permeate the literature that hint at children's communication characteristics. However, these clues, combined with other pieces of data taken from several studies, have yet to coalesce into a presentation of the process of sexual communication. Relying on the suppositions of communication privacy management (CPM) theory (Petronio, 2002) and integrating empirical data (i.e., Coffelt, 2008, 2010), the models highlight the process of sexual communication and move researchers toward a richer understanding of how sexual communication operates within parent–child dyads.

To be clear, these models illustrate the accomplishment of sexual communication in parent–child relationships, rather than silence on or avoidance of the topic. Indeed, these models do not reflect the process of absolute concealment of sexual information, which arguably conveys communicative value and is an area for continued examination. Additionally, studies have shown that adolescents make fewer disclosures to their parents during adolescence (Noller & Bagi, 1985), avoid topics (Mazur & Hubbard, 2004), or withdraw (Caughlin & Malis, 2004). However, the extant research shows that many parents and children discuss sex to some extent (e.g., Heisler, 2005; Rosenthal & Feldman, 1999). Pistella and Bonati's (1999) study found that more than 70% of teens indicated sexual communication had occurred with a parent, but only 20% said it was comfortable and easy to discuss. Thus, it is important to recognize the communicative challenges attached to sexual information and remain open to the possibility that discussing sex can be accomplished.

These models are situated within an interpretive, socially constructed paradigm (Burrell & Morgan, 1979) where parents and children co-create their patterns of interaction with no predetermined, cause–effect relationship between sexual disclosures and behavioral or relational outcomes. Rather, the models convey the process of sexual communication as experienced by mothers and daughters, with additional support from the literature. The linear appearance of these models reflects the need to simplify a complex series of interactions for explanatory reasons. The process, in reality, is much less tidy, and complications to the process abound. For example, children's emotional or biological forces could modify the process. Further, parents, experience transitions to different partners or different jobs that interfere with their attention to sexual conversations.

In this chapter, we prepare the reader for the models by summarizing extant literature, much of which resides in the disciplines of family studies, education, psychology, or health care, then point out several overarching assumptions made across these studies, and finally introduce two models as a way to shift scholars' ways of thinking about sexual communication as they advance research in this area. The first model shows the overall pattern of PCSC as

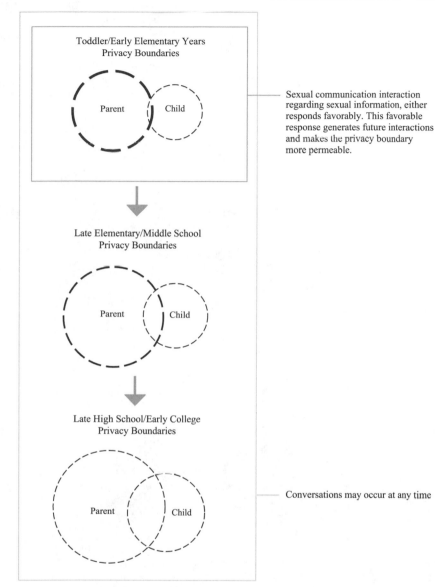

Toddler/Early Elementary Years
Privacy Boundaries

Parent   Child

Sexual communication interaction
regarding sexual information, either
responds favorably. This favorable
response generates future interactions
and makes the privacy boundary
more permeable.

Late Elementary/Middle School
Privacy Boundaries

Parent   Child

Late High School/Early College
Privacy Boundaries

Parent   Child

Conversations may occur at any time

Figure 7.1 Shifting parent–child privacy boundaries around sexual information

seen in Figure 7.1, Shifting Parent–Child Privacy Boundaries around Sexual
Information. Then, Figure 7.2, sexual communication interaction model in
parent–child relationships, explains the flow of information during a specific
communication event. After, the defining qualities of a process and a teleological process model are synthesized with the suppositions of these models.

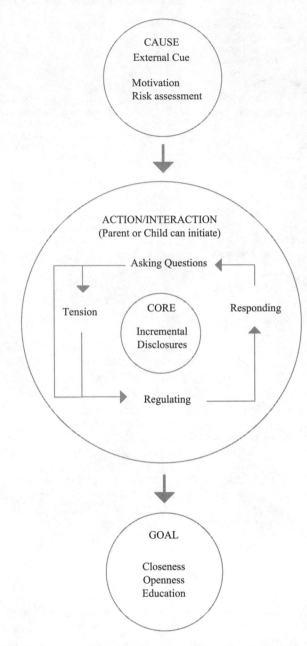

Figure 7.2 Sexual communication interaction model in parent–child relationships

Parent–Child Sexual Communication Research

Dimensions of Talk

A wide research net cast over several disciplines captures many articles that describe aspects of PCSC. This research organizes around five "dimensions" designated as "(1) extent of communication, (2) content of the communication, (3) timing of the communication, (4) general family environment, and (5) style in which information is conveyed" (Jaccard, Dittus, & Gordon, 1998, p. 247). These aspects of PCSC impart numerous findings.

First, researchers described the content of sexual conversations and associated or predicted sexual behaviors stemming from them (see Table 7.1). Most researchers listed several a priori topics and then asked respondents to indicate the frequency with which each topic was discussed. The topics selected vary across studies but generally fall within one of four factors: development and societal concerns, sexual safety, experiencing sex, and solitary sexual activity (Rosenthal & Feldman, 1999).

Second, the extent of communication garnered attention from researchers because "the channels must be opened sufficiently in order for sex discussion to become an effective part of a family's communication agenda" (Warren & Neer, 1986, p. 91). The extent of sexual communication has been ascertained by asking parents, adolescents, or emerging adults to report on a Likert-type scale the extent to which a given topic (as introduced previously) has been discussed. The extent of communication alone provides interesting descriptions about the nature of PCSC and reinforces the notion that control over sexual information is quite diverse across families.

Third, parents struggle to determine the appropriate time to discuss issues of sexuality with their children. Some researchers recommended that parents talk with children around age 12 (Jaccard & Dittus, 1991) or no later than age 16 to have the greatest impact (Warren & Neer, 1986). Others argued for talking with children *on time*, which means prior to first intercourse, rather than *off time*, which occurs after first intercourse (Clawson & Reese-Weber, 2003). Measuring the timing of sexual communication infers that interactions on the topic occur once. However, Beckett and colleagues (2010) showed that conversations happened at three key periods and the topics at each moment differed, which suggests that multiple conversations may occur at various points in a child's life.

Fourth, the general family environment, or "overall quality of the relationship between parent and teen" (Jaccard et al., 1998, p. 247), has been studied in connection with adolescent sex behaviors and relational qualities. As noted earlier, discrepancies in findings amplify the challenges of examining the family environment and its impact on sexual behaviors.

Fifth, the style of communication refers to the manner in which sexual information is communicated (Jaccard et al., 1998). Several approaches have examined the style of parents' communication such as information seeking,

Table 7.1 Examples of Studies Measuring Sexual Topics

	Crosby et al. (2001)	DiIorio et al. (1999)	Fisher (1986)	Hutchinson & Cooney (1998)	Jaccard et al. (2000)	Jordan et al. (2000)	Rosenthal & Feldman (1999)
Developmental and Societal Concerns							
Pregnancy	X	X	X				X
Fertilization			X	X		X	
Intercourse	X	X	X				
Menstruation		X	X	X		X	X
Homosexuality			X			X	X
Not having sex		X		X		X	X
Sexual Safety							
STDs/AIDS	X	X	X	X	X	X	X
Birth control		X	X	X		X	X
Abortion			X			X	X
Prostitution			X			X	
Using a condom	X	X		X		X	X
Solitary Sexual Activity							
Masturbation						X	X
Wet dreams		X					X
Experiencing Sex							
Dating and sex behavior		X				X	X
Getting a bad reputation					X		
Regretting not waiting					X		
Boy/girlfriend losing respect					X		

Topic					
Dangers of many sex partners	X				
Managing unwanted pressures	X	X		X	
Sexual desire	X				
Sexual satisfaction	X				
Different types of sex	X				
Sexual abuse incl. rape		X			
Talking about sexual needs	X	X			
Other					
Religious morals/sinful			X		
Upset mother/father			X		
Mother/father punish			X		
Consequences of pregnancy		X	X		X
Decision to have a baby			X		
Friends think about sex				X	X
Parents think about sex					X
Choice of partner				X	
Marriage/divorce		X			
Media pressures		X			
Pornography		X			

Note: An "other" category lists topics that do not fall into one of these four categories.

turn taking, comfort, or openness/closedness. Rosenthal and colleagues (1998) set out to describe communication style in an interview study of 30 mothers. They found that mothers approached the topic with the communication styles of avoidant, reactive, opportunistic, child-initiated, or mutually interactive. The research on style of communication taps into the *how* of communication, rather than the *what*, which moves the research from description toward process. Absent from this line of research, however, is the communication style of children, such as their approachability or receptivity, and how that has an impact on accomplishing sexual communication within parent–child relationships.

In sum, the literature on PCSC focuses on content, extent, timing, family environment, and style. These approaches have been useful to describe conversations about sex and underscore communication's importance to child sexual development. The findings from this collective body of work lay groundwork for future advancements. However, future research must overcome some limitations found in this body of work.

Limitations of Parent–Child Sexual Communication Literature

Theory-building needs process.   Theory organizes and summarizes knowledge obtained from data, aids in understanding observations, or provides a "heuristic sensitizing device" (Braithwaite & Baxter, 2006, p. 11). Theory building in a post-positivist paradigm relies on cause and effect relationships or associations between variables. Within the PCSC literature, several researchers have asked parents or adolescents/emerging adults to respond to how often pre-selected topics have been discussed and then correlated or regressed these data on behavioral outcomes such as engaged in sexual activity (Fisher, 1988; Jaccard, Dittus, & Gordon, 1996; Karofsky et al., 2000; Wight, Williamson, & Henderson, 2005), or used a condom (Wight et al., 2005) or other contraception (Jaccard et al., 1996; Rodgers, 1999). The data gleaned with this approach have been useful to measure sexual communication—number of sexual topics, the frequency of their discussion, the timing of the disclosures—and multiple variables that associate with it, its predictors, or its outcomes. However, scholars have yet to present a process model or heuristic device to show process or changes over time, to see how sexual communication evolves as parent–child relationships change.

Through an interpretive paradigm, the experiences of parents and their offspring with sexual information replace a priori dimensions of talk. Pluhar and Kuriloff (2004) concur that "relatively few studies have looked at how communication occurs, i.e., communication process" (p. 304). The importance of understanding process was articulated by Poole, McPhee, and Canary (2002):

> Ideally, a narrative explanation provides an account of how and why a sequence of events typically unfolds that is sufficiently flexible to encompass a range of observed cases, yet sufficiently powerful to help the researcher discern the operation of the generative mechanism in a multitude of particularized sequences. (p. 29)

Samples.   Convenience samples of emerging adults inform a considerable amount of research on PCSC, which presents issues of generalizability to adolescents when college students are asked to provide retrospective accounts of interactions with their parents. Although samples of emerging adults can be problematic, there are some benefits to including their voices as well. For example, emerging adults can recall events that unfolded over time, which is essential to seeing the process of PCSC. Research with 13-year-olds, for example, tells scholars what is known about 13-year-olds, which has value for that period of adolescence but not when looking at the overall process. In studies linking PCSC to sexual behaviors, it is helpful to include samples of emerging adults in order to measure the occurrence of virginity loss, STDs/STIs, or pregnancy. Thus, the perspectives of emerging adults reveal their understanding of all the PCSC they have encountered and their experiences with sexual activity as soon as they have transitioned out of adolescence as possible. Process models proposed in this chapter are strengthened by reviewing research findings reported by both adolescents and emerging adults. Sampling frames of parents also contribute to this body of literature. Information about the samples is included in this chapter to clarify whose perspective the findings were based on.

Unitary and unidirectional treatment of communication.   Another limitation with the extant literature is the central, omnipotent role of the parent who is the sole conveyer of sexual information. The preoccupation with the content of parents' disclosures, their communication styles, or their values and beliefs negates the presence of children and their influence on an interaction. Some emerging adults described their communication with their mother as "one way" (Dennis & Wood, 2012, p. 210), so it is not surprising that much of the research would follow suit. Further, parents and 14- to 17-year-old adolescents as well as college students often disagree about whether sexual communication occurred (Jaccard et al., 1998; King & Larusso, 1997); therefore, it seems important to examine sexual communication from the perspectives of parents and children.

The crux of this issue centers on the understanding of interpersonal communication. Those outside the communication discipline often restrict their definition of communication to content or amount, as described earlier, and as sent by a parent. However, interpersonal communication is "a complex, situated social process in which people who have established a communicative relationship exchange messages in an effort to generate shared meanings and accomplish social goals" (Burleson, 2010, p. 151). Through a communication lens, scholars recognize the dyad, the importance of the context, the exchange of information, and the mutual influence each interactant incites from the other. Indeed, the communication styles of children—their receptivity, curiosity, hostility, or openness—impede or spark conversations about sex. Furthermore, regardless of who starts a conversation, the interaction likely involves turn taking and a few iterations of information flowing back and forth. A few researchers make these points (e.g., Pistella & Bonati, 1999), and yet they have not made the child's communication the focal point. A process approach to sexual communication must account for the presence of children, the initiation of interaction by children, and the reciprocity of information.

In brief, PCSC is believed to be important and has been the focus of many studies (more than 90 according to DiIorio, Pluhar, & Belcher, 2003). No meta-analysis has been conducted to the knowledge of the authors, although Wright (2009) reduced an initial search of 296 articles on PCSC down to 49 on father–child sexual communication for a review and synthesis. Further, Miller and Moore (1990) published a review of research conducted in the 1980s on parental communication and adolescent pregnancy. These are the closest attempts, yet neither is a formal, statistical meta-analysis. A thorough literature review of these studies shows the propensity for scholars to describe the content of sexual disclosures and the extent to which sexual topics were discussed. Some work on the style of parental communication and the family communication environment shows the qualitative aspects of parent–child interaction. At this juncture, a bricolage would benefit the academic community interested in this topic to combine information and overcome the limitations of the research. Specifically, (a) theorizing needs an understanding of process; (b) a process approach needs to include samples of emerging adults, adolescents, and parents; and (c) children's influence during interaction needs attention. To over-come these deficits, two conjoined process models are presented that describe PCSC, relying on the suppositions of CPM (Petronio, 2002) as the theoretical framework.

Parent–Child Sexual Communication and CPM

CPM (Petronio, 2002) sets the theoretical tone because it is a theory about private information and the process by which it is managed. The test for CPM is whether or not educational sexual information qualifies as private information. Warren (1995) established definitions for sexual communication by differentiating between sex education and sexual communication in which education "implies the valuation of a teaching model of information transfer, where senders seek to add knowledge to receivers' frames of reference about biological reproduction, sexuality and sexual intercourse, and birth control" (pp. 173–174), and communication "implies the valuation of a co-creation of meaning about sexual beliefs, attitudes, values, and/or behavior" (p. 173). For example, discussing birth control could be an educational topic about different methods or a private concept when a mother discloses her choice for contraception.

CPM permits educational sexual information to qualify as private within familial relationships because family members control and regulate the dissemination of the information. Petronio described sexual information as "proprietary family information" (personal communication, July 2007). The way educational sexual information is discussed in the family becomes a private issue because how parents and children discuss these public aspects of sex are personal, private conversations. These conversations are informed by public knowledge, yet private talks in the ways parents and children approach the topics. While the educational aspects of sexual information pervade the public arena, the topics are enacted at the individual level. Further, discussions about sex, whether educational or not, are more likely when children perceive their parents as trustworthy (Guilamo-Ramos, Jaccard, Dittus, & Bouris, 2006). Trust can be earned by keeping information confidential, which is an important concept in CPM (Petronio, 2010). Parents protect their children from sexual information and regulate, to the best of their ability, when to release it (Byers & Sears, 2012). Parents experience pressure to talk about sex earlier than they would prefer (Geasler, Dannison, & Edlund, 1995), showing the constraints they experience on their privacy boundaries. This parental control exemplifies the need to manage sexual information in family relationships, and the tenets of CPM inform the practices parents and children undergo to regulate sexual information.

CPM uses a boundary metaphor to explain the process individuals go through to manage and control private information as they move information across a privacy boundary from the inner self to an outer, shared space (Petronio, 2002). As such, CPM leads the models toward a process approach to understanding sexual communication. Additionally, the privacy rule foundations of CPM discuss the rules individuals use when they contemplate revealing or concealing private information. These rules "tangibly show the way people regulate and therefore coordinate their privacy boundaries with others" (Petronio, 2002, p. 37). Rules about revealing information are believed to vary not only by relationship type, such as families, but also by the specific topic (Dailey & Palomares, 2004). The diversity across families can be understood by considering how parents and children create privacy boundaries around sexual information and establish rules about revealing or concealing the information.

The theory makes a unique contribution to this analysis because of its dual emphasis on information and process. The focus of the theory is on private information, the unique characteristics of revealing or concealing the information, and the management of information during interaction. The models presented here apply to one topic of information, illustrate the ways this information is concealed and/or revealed over time, and elucidate the nuances of revealing sexual information during a specific conversation.

Shifting Parent–Child Privacy Boundaries Around Sexual Information

The basic sequence of a teleological model includes several activities or stages that lead toward achieving a goal (Poole, 2012). The first model adheres to this sequence by looking at multiple interactions over time, each leading toward the accomplishment of sexual communication between a parent and child. This model contains three major components, which are pulled from CPM—information, privacy boundaries, and time—to explain the basic sequence and the process of change.

Sexual information is the first component and refers to the content or subject matter of the information discussed by the parent and child. In Figure 7.1, sexual information is represented by the space within each circle. CPM's supposition of private information defines privacy as "the feeling that one has the right to own private information" (Petronio, 2002, p. 6) or "perceive[ing] it as belonging to them" (Caughlin & Petronio, 2004, p. 381). Applied to the current context of sexual information, such disclosures might include demonstrating how to use a condom, explaining the advantages/disadvantages of birth control, or sharing one's age at first intercourse.

A discussion of private information must also distinguish between secrets and topic avoidance because the two bodies of literature are related to sexual information yet qualitatively different. Guerrero and Afifi (1995b) clarified that there is a difference between topic avoidance and secrets. Secrets imply that information is hidden and unknown to others and often contains negative information (Vangelisti, 1994), whereas topics that are avoided may be known to another, positive or negative, or are not discussed with another (Guerrero & Afifi, 1995b). The literature on sexual topics shows that the content of sexual information often includes reproduction, pregnancy, menstruation, or birth control, among others. This information is not secretive information because it can be found in public spheres such as the sex education curriculum in schools (Kirby, 2002), the Internet, health pamphlets, or magazines. Further, college students reported obtaining sexual information during adolescence from sources other than or in addition to their parents (Daugherty & Burger, 1984; Gephard, 1977; Spanier, 1977). Therefore, parents likely know sexual information, whereas children increase their sexual knowledge as they develop.

The failure to communicate about sexual information is, as Guerrero and Afifi (1995a) found, a result of topic avoidance, rather than an attempt to conceal personal, secretive information. However, if personal information such as pregnancy, an STD or an STI, or rape were the content of a conversation, then the secrets literature would be more appropriate than topic avoidance research. The public–private distinction with sexual information has not been addressed in the studies on sexual topics and the extent they have been discussed in parent–child relationships. Thus, the models presented here encompass all sexual information, both public and private. Within the parent–child dyad, even public or educational information mimics private information because disclosing indicates to "other" that I know, want to know, or want to share this information in our relationship. Many parents know their children know sexual information and children know their parents know about sex, yet each avoids conversations with the other because of discomfort or embarrassment. However, when the parent or child introduces the information into their relationship, they relinquish an individual claim to it and elect to share information within a collective boundary (Petronio, 2002).

The second component of the model is the privacy boundary each person constructs around sexual information. Privacy boundaries are shown on Figure 7.1 by circles that encompass sexual information. Privacy boundaries vary in permeability, ranging from thin and open, allowing substantial information to cross, to thick and viscous, thereby limiting the flow of information (Petronio,

2002). As sexual information is revealed to the other, the privacy boundaries expand to make room for the newly acquired sexual information held within a collective boundary (Petronio, 2002). Parents and children own the remaining information held within their respective privacy boundary. Ownership denotes control of the information and the ability to regulate its passage across the privacy boundary. In one study, mothers were able to distinguish which sexual information they had already discussed or intended to discuss with their adolescents, indicating their control over dissemination (Byers & Sears, 2012). Co-ownership of information in a collective boundary brings new challenges to parents and children as they rely on each other to refrain from boundary leakage, which means giving the information to another person without permission (Petronio, 2002). Thus, there are several considerations when revealing information, relinquishing control, and trusting the information with someone else.

The privacy boundaries are further depicted by the width of the boundary and breaks in the boundary. A thicker privacy boundary is more impenetrable than a thinner boundary, and the openings reflect the porosity of the boundary. More openings allow a greater flow of information to pass through whereas fewer openings permit less information to pass. The data upon which the models are based (Coffelt, 2008) showed that mothers' privacy boundaries started as open to some extent when children were young. For sexual communication to be accomplished, mothers recognized the need to release some sexual information, particularly when young children asked questions about body parts or where babies come from, for example. The model shows a few fractures in the parents' privacy boundaries to depict disclosures through which little information passes. The models suggest that young children have fairly open privacy boundaries as they randomly ask questions with little inhibition. When these early communication events received a receptive response, parents validated the child's curiosity and showed acceptance of questions on sexual topics. This tempered openness accomplished the momentary goal and generated new information for the child.

Disclosures may diminish guilt or shame associated with sexual curiosity and solidify relational trust. Certainly, the perception of comfort with sexual topics in a confidant is positively associated with sexual self-disclosures (Herold & Way, 1988). The models further suggest that as children age and their sexual curiosity crescendos, they approach parents with increasingly permeable privacy boundaries. These boundaries contain resistance because the privacy boundaries are not removed altogether. Rather, children regulate their questions and comments to their parents and test their parents' comfort with sexual information. For parents who want to share sexual information with their children, they open their privacy boundaries, as well, allowing additional sexual information to pass. Parents identified various sexual topics they intended to talk to their children about and the ages at which they intended to discuss the topic (Koblinsky & Atkinson, 1982). Ages to discuss topics ranged from 3 or 4 to discuss body differences and 11 or 12 to discuss petting, contraception, or homosexuality. The sharing of information allows the collective privacy boundary to increase in size. The circumference of the child's privacy boundary increases, and new information enters. The acceptance and reciprocity present with each communication event permits future interactions. Indeed, multiple communication events may transpire as sexual information is often revealed briefly and randomly with fragmented disclosures (Dennis & Wood, 2012).

The process of change is most pronounced when a parent or child regulates the passage of information through the privacy boundary, which requires fluctuation in permeability or openness (Kirkman, Rosenthal, & Feldman, 2005) and an expansion in the circumference of the privacy boundary. Each event relies on the success of a previous interaction. When parents judge their children for sexual curiosity or dictate sexual behaviors, children may begin to turn away, discontinue conversation, and restrict their privacy boundaries. However, when parents accept their children's curiosity and open their privacy boundaries by sharing sexual information, their children receive the information and enlarge their privacy boundaries.

Time, the third component of the model, is depicted by the box around the whole process. Time represents the entire lifespan of child development, recognizing that sexual communication begins earlier than adolescence. Meschke and colleagues (2000) noted a need to extend PCSC research beyond adolescence. These models align with this claim while also arguing for inclusion of early childhood, as well. Thus, the parent–child dyads are depicted on the model at three periods—toddler/elementary years, late elementary/middle school, and late high school/emerging adulthood—because these moments represent key transitional phases in the lives of children, which prompt surges in sexual conversations. However, these conversations could happen at any time during the development of the child. Lefkowitz and Stoppa (2006) suggest that parents should "seize opportune moments" rather than plan formal conversations (p. 49). The models contend that conversations emerge in conversation when the child is ready, rather than relying on specific ages to determine when parents should reveal particular topics. A social constructionist perspective reinforces this approach by stipulating the emergent nature of conversations and the co-constructed meaning that parents and children develop for their management of sexual information.

Throughout the process, interactions between parents and children are impacted by privacy rule development criteria. The criteria, as set forth in CPM, inform the planning and coordination individuals undergo prior to or when revealing private information (Petronio, 2002). Mothers of preschool-age children identified their intentions for managing sexual information years before their children reached adolescence (Koblinsky & Atkinson, 1982), demonstrating the forethought that goes into rule development. Additionally, mothers of adolescents refined these intentions by indicating specific topics they expected to talk to their child about, such as the birth process and menstruation, body differences, reproduction, sexual morals, venereal disease, contraception, intercourse, and rape/sexual offenses, among others. Neither children nor adolescents nor emerging adults have been asked about their intentions to discuss sexuality with parents, which would complement the literature.

Knowledge of rule development helps understand the differences between parents and children who reveal sexual information to each other and those who do not and deepens understanding about the process of initiating conversations about sex. These criteria are culture, gender, context, motivation for revealing or concealing, and the risk-benefit ratio. An introduction to each criterion follows, accompanied by relevant literature that may inform the actual rules that guide family members when discussing sex.

Culture. Cultures have distinct norms about revealing private information at societal, familial, and individual levels. Western culture has particular ideologies about sexuality that guide the treatment of sexual information in interpersonal relationships. Reiss (1981) described how the history of sexuality arrived on the 20th century with "strong guilt, secrecy, and psychological qualms woven into its basic fabric" (p. 278). Thus, it is not surprising that so many people remain challenged to discuss this topic. However, there are those who accomplish discourse on this topic, and the models presented here align with the experiences of those who talk about sex in their parent–child relationships.

Co-cultures within the United States are believed to have different rules about communication. However, co-cultural differences may have little impact when the topic is sex. Barber (1994) asserts that cross-cultural similarity is unique to the topic of sexual behavior because there were no significant differences about parent–adolescent disagreements over sexual behavior in his study among Black, Hispanic, and White parents. But several examples illustrate that co-cultural differences may exist. For example, sexual communication messages by Muslim mothers were limited to two messages: "Sexuality is an endowment from God," and "Virginity until marriage is important and the key to successful new marital relationships" (Orgocka, 2004, p. 265). Asian Americans reported much less sexual communication than Black, White, or Latino samples (Kim & Ward, 2007), and Hispanic mothers reported that social mobility was their primary motivator to talk to their daughters about refraining from or delaying sex (McKee & Karasz, 2006). Comparisons between African American and Latina mothers showed that African American mothers emphasized pregnancy and STD prevention, whereas Latina mothers were concerned with preventing sexual contact (O'Sullivan, Meyer-Bahlburg, & Watkins, 2001).

These findings suggest that the content of sexual discussions and motivations to discuss sex differ across co-cultures in the United States. However, the process by which families accomplish sexual discourse may be similar. Future research on families' privacy rules from different cultural perspectives would inform this aspect of the models.

Gender. The next rule development criterion is gender. The PCSC literature shows marked differences between fathers and mothers and between daughters and sons. Mothers overwhelmingly engage in much of the communication about sex with their children. Further, daughters receive more information than do sons, and they hear different information than sons (e.g., DiIorio, Kelley, & Hockenberry-Eaton, 1999; Fisher, 1988). For example, 13- to 15-year-old males received 4 strong messages out of a possible 12 from their parents: (a) There are negative consequences to pregnancy before marriage (58.7%), (b) sexual relations express love (31.7%), (c) it is easy for petting to lead to intercourse (20.8%), and (d) nice people do not have sex before marriage (20.4%; Darling & Hicks, 1982). For females of the same age, the topics were, in rank order: (a) the negative consequences of pregnancy (61.0%), (b) nice people do not have sex before marriage (43.8%), (c) petting too easily leads to intercourse (35.7%), and (d) sex is a good way to reflect love for someone (34.2%). Although the topics discussed most frequently with males and females were the same, the percentages of males and females who heard each topic differed. Other evidence shows that conversations about sex between mothers and 11- to 14-year-old daughters contained more words than did conversations with sons of the same age (Lefkowitz, Kahlbaugh, & Sigman, 1996). In another study, the top three topics of discussion between mothers and adolescent males were STDs/AIDS, using a condom, and sexual intercourse, whereas the topics with females were menstrual cycle, dating and sex behavior, and STDs/AIDS (DiIorio et al., 1999). In brief, many studies reinforce gendered differences that accompany sexual conversations.

The models presented here apply to mothers or fathers, daughters or sons. The empirical data upon which the models are derived come from mothers and daughters. Some of these mothers and daughters believed that sexual information should remain within same-sex parent–child relationships, whereas some mothers and daughters did not (Coffelt, 2008). However, mothers' propensity to engage in these conversations more than fathers and the differences between information shared with sons and daughters signals a need for continued research on the processing of sexual information within designated, gendered family relationships. Gender seems to have an impact on rule development by relegating sexual conversations to mothers instead of fathers and limiting sexual conversations to same-sex family relationships. This is not to say that other families do not deviate from these norms, but rather to say that research findings show strong tendencies in these ways.

Motivation.   The third criterion for rule development influencing parent–child sexual communication is the motivation of the sender to reveal private information. The primary motivating factor of researchers has been to show that parental communication influences adolescents' sexual behaviors to keep them from having sex that may result in pregnancy, HIV/AIDS, or STDs/STIs (e.g., Clawson & Reese-Weber, 2003; Jaccard & Dittus, 1991; Miller, Benson, & Galbraith, 2001; Rosenthal, Senserrick, & Feldman, 2001). Jaccard, Dodge, and Dittus (2002) assert their view as "We believe that parents should assume responsibility for the information that their children have about sex and birth control" (p. 22). But are parents motivated to talk with their adolescents for the same reason that researchers believe? Of parents, 15% to 20% believe it is permissible for their adolescent to engage in intercourse under certain conditions (Jaccard & Dittus, 1991). Furthermore, what motivates children to talk with their parents?

CPM identifies three types of motivation used to develop privacy rules—expressive needs, self-knowledge, or self-defense (Petronio, 2002). Expressive needs motivate individuals to disclose when they have a desire to share their thoughts or feelings. Self-knowledge needs are those in which revealers want to know more about themselves and use self-disclosure to obtain feedback from listeners. Self-defense needs are motivations that guide non-disclosure because the risks associated with revealing seem too great.

The empirical findings on which these models are based failed to show alignment with these three types of motivation. Instead, mothers identified sexual health and safety, abstinence, contraception, and relational health as reasons to reveal sexual information to their daughters, and daughters were motivated to talk to their mothers to get accurate information from a trustworthy and valued source (Coffelt, 2008). In another study, Guerrero and Afifi (1995a) identified social inappropriateness, self- and relationship protection, and parental unresponsiveness as the motivations 17 to 24 year olds reported to guard private information. Additionally, children may avoid the topic of sex with their mothers because of privacy or self-protection needs, as reported by 13 to 22 year olds (Golish & Caughlin, 2002), and therefore leave their own sexual information within a privacy boundary.

However, when parents are receptive, informal, and composed when talking about sex, adolescents report feeling less embarrassment and discomfort (Afifi, Joseph, & Aldeis, 2008). Several motivating factors have been identified to reveal and conceal sexual information in parent–child relationships. Specific rules that could emanate from these findings include talking about sex when children need self-knowledge about bodies or relationships or when children want to feel connected to parents and ask for advice. Certainly, more research would propel this aspect of the process of sexual communication in necessary directions.

Context. The contextual criteria for privacy disclosures include the social environment and the physical setting (Petronio, 2002). Family structure stands as an appropriate social environment for the context of PCSC. To that end, family structure affects adolescent sexual behaviors (Wight et al., 2006) and privacy management differently in intact, single parent, and blended families. For example, Golish and Caughlin (2002) found that the motivation to avoid topics was significantly different for biological parents and stepparents. Afifi (2003) found that boundary management in stepfamilies is characterized by feelings of being caught, enmeshed boundaries, and a revealing/concealing dialectical tension, among others. Although rule development was not the focus of these studies, the findings show that family structure brings about differences in privacy management and must be considered. For example, the models may be most applicable in parent–child relationships that are uniquely close, such as children of divorce and the custodial parent (Coleman, Fine, Ganong, Downs, & Pauk, 2001). Further, the arguments of these models may be suspended during significant transitions, such as divorce or death of a parent, when privacy rules are renegotiated (Petronio, 2000).

The physical setting may have some impact on PCSC, as well. Mothers who reported being open with their daughters about sex indicated they talked with their daughters in the car, the kitchen, or in front of the TV (Pluhar & Kuriloff, 2004; Rosenthal et al., 1998). Considering the discomfort with the topic, a car makes sense because the forward sitting position of the driver and passenger limit eye contact and diminish some of the discomfort accompanying this topic. In all three physical spaces, the preoccupation with another activity may buffer the experience of awkwardness. Therefore, families might develop implicit rules that sex is discussed in the car or in front of the TV, among other contextual rules.

Risk-Benefit Ratio.   The risk-benefit ratio leads to understanding the differences between parents who proceed to have conversations about sex and those who do not. Communicating with a child about sex has risks such as tuning out a parent (Pluhar & Kuriloff, 2004) or being evaluated negatively by the adolescent (Feldman & Rosenthal, 2000). However, there are some benefits of sexual communication such as closeness (Pluhar & Kuriloff, 2004) or fewer sexual risk behaviors during adolescence (Jaccard et al., 1996; Koesten, Miller, & Hummert, 2001; Miller, Forehand, & Kotchick, 1999). Using a CPM lens, the level of risk is evaluated while deciding whether to reveal or conceal private information. Three levels of risk, according to CPM, are high, moderate, or low (Petronio, 2002). Petronio (2002) defines high-risk information as that which causes "shame, threat or severe embarrassment" (p. 67), whereas moderate-risk information involves that which is "uncomfortable, troublesome, or aggravating" (p. 69). The views about sexual information are important in order to assess the risk that parents and children associate with sexual information. When asked about risks and benefits of talking about sex, mothers who participated in the study upon which these models are based thought giving too much information was a risk, showing their concerns about regulating the amount of information their daughters received (Coffelt, 2008). The daughters identified fear of judgment and fear of boundary leakage to their fathers as risks of talking to their moms.

A second consideration of the risk-benefit ratio criterion is the type of risk. Petronio (2002) identifies types of risk as security, stigma, face, relational, or role. Managing the disclosure of private information is guided by considering the type of risk and the benefits or costs the disclosure may impart. No known studies have asked parents or children to describe the type of risks or benefits they associate with sexual communication and how the type of risk guides their decision to reveal or conceal sexual information. However, Afifi and Steuber (2009) found that as the risk of telling a secret increases the willingness to reveal information decreases. Thus, it seems as if individuals establish rules that they will talk about sexual issues when the benefits outweigh the risks or when they evaluate the level of risk as low, regardless of the type of risk. However, parents might be willing to take relational risks for the sake of their children's health and wellness. Children might be willing to risk saving face if they have an STD, knowing the relational benefits may be sacrificed. This criterion should be included with the other rule development criteria to recognize its impact and to inform research.

In sum, the first model illustrates the gestalt of PCSC in which parents and children maintain individual privacy boundaries around sexual information, reveal sexual information incrementally over time, and generate opportunities for future interaction based on the openness during a current communication event. Rule development criteria of culture, gender, context, motivation, and the risk-benefit ratio guide parents and children in their decisions about revealing information. As the child matures, the circumference of the child's privacy boundary expands as new sexual information enters the boundary during each communication event. The child's privacy boundary is fairly open when very young and gradually expands as communication events unfold and parents and children share information with each other. In addition to expanding privacy boundaries, boundary permeability opens as well. When children view their parents as a trusted confidant (Petronio, Reeder, Hecht, & Ros-Mendoza, 1996), they are comfortable approaching parents for more information or discussion. Parents' privacy boundaries broaden when children ask questions or disclose information about personal experiences, thereby giving parents new information about their children.

Revealing sexual information creates a collective privacy boundary, which contains co-owned sexual information. The collective privacy boundary also expands over time when the parent and child reveal more information to each other. Each communication event paves the way for a future interaction when new information may be revealed. When parents and children interact in ways that build trust, they reinforce their receptivity to sexual discussions and leave the door open for future interactions. The first model shows the communication process as it evolves over time and depicts the changes in privacy boundaries as disclosures occur. However, part of the process occurs with each interaction. The box around Early Childhood on the first model serves as the linchpin between it and a second model called the sexual communication interaction model in parent–child relationships (Interaction Model). The Interaction Model provides a microscopic view of a specific communication event.

Sexual Communication Interaction Model in Parent–Child Relationships

The interaction model displays the process of revealing sexual information during a specific communication event by highlighting three components called cause, action/interaction, and goal. The interaction model includes both the parent and child, calling attention to the dyadic nature of communication. The sequence of interaction begins with either the parent or the child.

The model begins with the causal component, which shows the influences that prompt a specific interaction. Specifically, an external cue leads a parent or child to communicate on a sexual topic. The data upon which these models are based showed a strong propensity for conversations to begin because of an external cue such as a movie, book, or statements made by siblings or peers (Coffelt, 2008). Further, Petronio (2010) noted that a shift in privacy boundaries results from some catalyst. Here, the privacy rule criteria of motivation and risk assessment weigh into this decision about initiating a conversation. When motivation is high and/or risk is moderate to low, parents or children are more likely to ask a question and reveal their curiosity about a given topic. Each communication event builds on the interaction before it. When parents and children respond with openness, comfort, or acceptance, they convey their willingness to interact when the subject matter of the conversation is sex (Afifi et al., 2008; Kirkman et al., 2005). Hence, the parent or the child reduces the risk or embarrassment associated with sexual topics and reinforces willingness to communicate in the future.

As the model shows, the action/interaction component unfolds after the external cue is perceived and the motivation and risk are assessed. Broadly, the interaction follows a sequence of asking a question, experiencing tension by some, regulating the disclosure, responding, and repeating the cycle. At the core of the interaction rests the concept of incremental disclosures, a strategy used by victims of child sexual abuse (Petronio et al., 1996) and by individuals when revealing a secret (Afifi & Steuber, 2009). The mothers who participated in the study upon which these models are based said they released sexual information to their children in little bits and pieces (Coffelt, 2008), which shows a different context for the application of incremental disclosures. In this way, sexual information is fragmented into small portions and only that which directly relates to a question flows through the privacy boundary. The fragments left behind linger inside the privacy boundary until a future inquiry calls one forth. Indeed, parents reported talking with children in Grades K through 8 and increased the sexual communication as their children got older (Byers, Sears, & Weaver, 2008). Elaboration on each component of the action/interaction segment of the model follows.

First, the interaction begins with the parent or child asking a question. Mothers who participated in the study upon which these models are derived reported that much of their sexual communication was initiated by a daughter's question (Coffelt, 2008). Similarly, some mothers talk about sex with their children only after a question has been asked (Rosenthal et al., 1998). Parents and children lack information about the other's possession of sexual information, and asking questions is an ideal rhetorical tool to supplement a lack of information (Fiengo, 2007). In brief, asking questions advances a unique approach to initiating PCSC.

Second, the next phase of the action/interaction sequence for some is the experience of tension, which may be dialectical in nature. Petronio (2002,

2010) asserts that CPM is a dialectical theory as communicators feel the tug between wanting to reveal information and simultaneously desiring to conceal the information within the privacy boundary. As Kirkman and colleagues (2005) suggested, parents may feel a contradiction in their desire to discuss sex and avoid the topic. Children may also experience this contradiction when they want to get information from a trusted source but also want to protect their sexual thoughts or experiences.

Parents and children often experience a tension between revealing and concealing or openness and closedness (Baxter & Montgomery, 1996). As children mature, parents may privilege the pole of openness, contributing to the expansion of their children's privacy boundaries. Petronio (2002) asserts that privacy boundaries expand from childhood, to adolescence, to adulthood. The dialectical tension of autonomy-connectedness may also explain how some family members have been able to talk about sex during a time when adolescents, in particular, establish independence (Baxter & Montgomery, 1996; Petronio, 2002). For mother-daughter relationships, in particular, the tug to remain connected while establishing autonomy is a lifetime tension (Miller-Day, 2004). Applied to this model, for example, children who are asked if they know how to use a condom might want to confirm this information to reassure a parent and, at the same time, want to conceal the information so the parent does not conclude that the child is sexually active.

On the second path between asking questions and regulation, no tension appears because the data upon which these models are contrived showed that some mothers and their daughters experience no tension when talking about sex as they believe talking about sex is natural (Coffelt, 2010). Whether tension is experienced or not, individuals proceed to share information and regulate the amount of sexual information they disclose.

Regulation, the third moment in the action/interaction sequence, is a fundamental aspect of CPM (Petronio, 2002) because it shows the control individuals have over the information they possess. Individuals decide how much information to convey and how much to retain. Consider, for example, a 3-year-old child who asks, "Mommy, how did that baby get in your tummy?" and Mommy replies with a broad answer such as "The miracle of birth" or "This is what happens when parents love each other." Mom has vastly more knowledge about reproduction, yet holds nearly all of the information within her privacy boundary until a future time. However, she wants to establish comfort with this topic between her and her child, so she opens her privacy boundary slightly to provide a modest answer. Information is released based on how permeable the privacy boundaries are. The maturity level of the child also affects parents' openness (Kirkman et al., 2005). Again, as one communication event is completed, the privacy boundaries become more porous, permitting new information to flow in the future.

Fourth, the action/interaction sequence advances to a response. The response is the moment when the confidant replies to the question. As this information infiltrates the privacy boundary of another, the circumference of the privacy boundary stretches. Finally, this iteration has the potential to repeat. The privacy rule criteria of culture, context, gender, motivation, and the risk-benefit ratio influence the decision and keep the conversation going. Or, at some point, the sequence ends or the topic shifts, which discontinues the flow of sexual information.

The final component of the model shows goals of a specific interaction that could be attained, using closeness, openness, and/or education as exemplars. The goals depicted on the model represent those specifically shared by the mothers and daughters interviewed for the original conceptualization of the models. Research further supports specific goals of PCSC. For example, as parents and 14- to 17-year-old adolescents increased the number of sexual topics they discussed, they reported higher relationship satisfaction (Jaccard et al., 2000). Additionally, college women who reported engaging in only one risky behavior during high school described their family communication cultures as having trust, comfort in talking to parents about a number of topics, and openness to negotiate rules (Koesten et al., 2001). By contrast, college women who engaged in at least four risky behaviors in high school believed they had limited opportunities for discussion or negotiation, described a lack of trust and openness in their families, and were not comfortable talking to their parents. These findings suggest that openness and closeness are associated with PCSC. However, a close relationship does not influence whether parents and adolescents will talk about sex (Afifi et al., 2008), even though the perception of openness in the family communication environment led to a stronger belief that regular sexual discussions occurred (Booth-Butterfield & Sidelinger, 1998; White, Wright, & Barnes, 1995).

Parents or children may want to demonstrate or reinforce their relational closeness by incorporating sexual discourse into their conversations. Parents likely want to promote closeness in the parent–child relationship because adolescents who experience less closeness get more sexual information from their peers than from parents (Whitbeck, Conger, & Kao, 1993). Education may be a goal, as well, as parents may want to impart sexual education information and children might educate their parents about trendy sexual behaviors. These goals are illustrative because there could be any number of goals, such as behavior modification, agreement to go on the birth control pill, or support after a sexual encounter, for example.

In brief, the interaction model zooms in on one communication event, which occurs multiple times over the course of a child's life. These events enlarge the privacy boundaries of children as they obtain new sexual information. Parents' privacy boundaries may expand to some extent if their children share personal, sexual experiences of which the parents were not aware. If positive goals are attained, future interactions on the subject could occur with more ease. Relying on questions and the use of incremental disclosures minimizes risk and vulnerability because small amounts of information are processed with each interaction, rather than an attempt at sharing substantial amounts of sexual information in one sitting. With this long-term, intermittent approach, parents and children can build comfort and openness with each other.

Synthesis

These two visual depictions advance a teleological process model of sexual communication between parents and children. When proposing a teleological model, Poole (2012) submitted four conditions to satisfy: (a) "a singular entity" that "works to maintain coherence and consensus," (b) a goal or end state, (c) "a set of functional prerequisites for attaining the goal, and the activities undertaken by the entity should attempt to address them," and (d) "discernible stages which differ in form and function" (p. 393).

The models proposed in this chapter satisfy these requirements as captured in Table 7.2. First, the parent–child dyad serves as the singular entity that works to maintain its relationship while managing sexual information. Second, the goals of interactions between parents and children could include instrumental, relational, and/or identity goals (Wilson & Feng, 2007). Third, prerequisites for goal attainment include privacy boundaries, possessing sexual information, and the rule development criteria. The activities undertaken include asking questions in response to an external cue and making incremental disclosures in response to the questions. Fourth, stages differ in form and function, as noted by changes in privacy boundaries. Specifically, privacy boundaries become more permeable as time passes and more information is capable of passing through. Further, the circumference of the privacy boundary expands when new information is obtained, and new collective boundaries form where information known to both parent and child is contained. Stages are discernible not by age of children, but by surges in sexual communication in response to external

Table 7.2 Conditions for a Teleological Model

Poole's Conditions for a Teleological Model	Satisfaction of These Conditions
An individual or group that acts as a singular entity and works to maintain coherence and consensus	A parent–child interaction serves as the singular entity; the dyad works to maintain its relationship.
A goal or end state	The dyad seeks the reciprocity of sexual information, relational openness, and/or education, for example.
A set of functional prerequisites for attaining the goal; the activities undertaken by the entity should attempt to address them	Prerequisites include privacy boundaries, possessing sexual information, and criteria for regulating privacy boundaries; activities undertaken include asking questions in response to an external cue, and incremental disclosures to respond to the questions.
Discernible stages that differ in form and function	As time passes, privacy boundaries become more permeable and expand in circumference as they allow more sexual information to pass through; co-owned privacy boundary forms that contains information shared by both parent and child.

cues. These surges are unique to each parent–child relationship based, in large part, on the sexual curiosity and development of the child.

The models answer the call for a process approach to the study of sexual communication (Pluhar & Kuriloff, 2004) because they demonstrate how sexual information is revealed in small increments over time as well as during a specific interaction. Each conversation commences with a question that is prompted by an external cue. Sexual information passes through permeable privacy boundaries. Disclosures may be preceded by tension for some parents or children as they evaluate the risks and benefits of revealing sexual information. Regardless of tension, disclosures are made yet are regulated such that some information is revealed while other information remains inside the privacy boundary. The passage of information during one interaction may result in positive qualities, which prepares the parent and the child for future interactions.

Parents and children reveal some information at each interaction event while also concealing information. These conversations leave openings in the relationship so that future questions or needs for information can be met with openness and more disclosures. Over time, parents could retrace the conversations about sex with children and see how one interaction built from the last, connecting multiple discussions into a cohesive knowledge base about sexual health and relating. Each parent–child relationship navigates the trajectory through sexual information in a distinct path unique to the relationship, reinforcing the teleological nature of the process models. Specific topics should not necessarily be addressed at a particular age in family relationships. Rather, parents monitor their children's activities and interactions to gauge appropriate times to begin a communication event. Similarly, children observe an environmental cue that serves as the catalyst to ask parents for information.

The models show that parents' and children's privacy boundaries around sexual information converge and increase in their interconnectedness over time. This assumption contradicts other research that shows adolescents renegotiate boundaries during adolescence such that there is more separation in the parent-adolescent relationship, particularly as adolescents struggle to develop their identity (Blieszner, 1994; Erikson, 1968) and gain independence from their parents (Bell, 1967). The models most likely operate in very close parent–child relationships. The interconnectedness between parents and children necessary for these models to apply may resemble enmeshed relationships (Olson, Russell, & Sprenkle, 1989) because they need very high closeness and trust to achieve communication on this difficult topic of sex.

These models acknowledge the role of children, which is critical as researchers proceed to study sexual communication in family relationships. In the past, researchers seemed to approach sexual communication as if a parent gave information to a child (e.g., Jaccard et al., 2002). However, these models suggest that children have agency and exercise their curiosity because they ask questions and initiate communication. Children's privacy boundaries expand only by gaining more information. Therefore, they ask questions in order to obtain sexual information. They also respond to parents' inquiries and reveal information incrementally to their parents.

Another unique attribute of these models is the inclusion of time. Sexual communication changes as children develop, and the models illuminate the ways in which these changes may occur. Events such as pregnancy, the onset of puberty, statements by peers, or dating, among others, trigger sexual communication events. These contextual aspects support Petronio's (2002) claim that life circumstances require changes in boundary management. Indeed, more sexual information is revealed to children as they age, regardless of the source.

Professionals who promote public health in the area of adolescent sexual activity could apply these models in at least three ways. First, designing messages that discuss the risks and benefits of talking about sex could help alleviate fears, circumvent myths or stereotypes that restrict sexual communication, or promote relational goals that can result from sexual communication. Statistics about teenage sexual behaviors seem to be the dominant message and persuasive strategy used in public health campaigns or by educators. Resource providers could also share the risks and benefits of sexual communication. Recall Petronio's (2002) description of high, moderate, or low risks that are juxtaposed with benefits to decide whether to reveal information. Parents and children may have new insights when they understand each other's perceived risks, such as children's fear of punishment or parents' concerns of being tuned out. Further, parents, in particular, may come to understand that some children may perceive the risks of sharing sexual information as too high.

Second, adolescents could be encouraged to participate in conversations with their parents. Promoting emotional closeness and obtaining accurate information are two motivational factors that could influence adolescents to talk with their parents about sex. Such a discussion would also need to emphasize the risks they take in making disclosures and evaluating those risks with their parents. The models show that although the co-owned privacy boundary expands, each person retains sexual information within his or her individual privacy boundary. Indeed, in some situations, openness may lead to negative relational outcomes and withholding may be beneficial (Goldsmith, Miller, & Caughlin, 2007).

Third, the suggestion to communicate with young children about sex could extend many training and education programs. Because some children ask questions on sexual topics long before adolescence begins, parents could benefit from the experiences of others who respond positively when children ask questions. Such an approach could be used to help families who struggle with bringing sexual information into their conversations. Further, anyone who conducts interventions could use these models to help parents, teachers, health-care providers, or children approach sexual conversations in new ways.

The models present two additional possibilities. First, they prompt additional questions for future research. For example, what would the models look like in parent–child relationships in which no sexual communication occurred? What events prompt a cessation of sexual discourse after it has been introduced into the relationship? How do biological, physiological, or emotional changes in child development alter the experience of parents and children when they talk about sex? These questions suspend the descriptive research approaches and propel the PCSC literature into relational qualities. Second, the models provide a discussion point for other contexts/topics such as romantic couple discussions about sex or parents and children talking about other risky behaviors such as alcohol, drugs, or smoking. The models advocate multiple conversations during the course of a child's life. They emphasize the mutual influence of parents and children, and they suggest that sharing information incrementally may help parents and children achieve relational and behavioral goals. Other applications may expand the utility of these models.

The models introduced in this chapter integrate literature and empirical findings from several disciplines to present a process approach to sexual communication in parent–child relationships. These models rely on the tenets of CPM theory (Petronio, 2002) to explain the flow of sexual information through privacy boundaries erected around sexual information. Using incremental disclosures to regulate the passage of information, parents or children reveal sexual information during interaction while constricting the flow of other sexual information. Taken together, these models recognize the co-presence of parent and child. The accomplishment of sexual communication is a reality for some in our society, and their experiences benefit those who are motivated to talk with a parent or child about sex.

Acknowledgments

This chapter is a revision and update of the first author's dissertation at the University of Missouri under the direction of Loreen N. Olson (chair), Debbie S. Dougherty, Jon A. Hess, Mark A. Fine, and Mary-Jeanette Smythe, committee members. The authors acknowledge Sandra Petronio for her input on earlier versions of this paper and Jessie Fullerton for her graphic design work. A version of this chapter was presented to the National Communication Association in San Diego, California, November 2009.

References

Afifi, T. D. (2003). "Feeling caught" in stepfamilies: Managing boundary turbulence through appropriate communication privacy rules. *Journal of Social and Personal Relationships, 20*, 729–755. doi:10.1177/0265407503206002

Afifi, T. D., Joseph, A., & Aldeis, D. (2008). Why can't we just talk about it? An observational study of parents' and adolescents' conversations about sex. *Journal of Adolescent Research, 23*, 689–721. doi:10.1177/0743558408323841

Afifi, T. D., & Steuber, K. (2009). The revelation risk model (RRM): Factors that predict the revelation of secrets and the strategies used to reveal them. *Communication Monographs, 76*, 144–176. doi:10.1080/03637750902828412

Barber, B. K. (1994). Cultural, family, and personal contexts of parent-adolescent conflict. *Journal of Marriage and the Family, 56*, 375–386. Retrieved from www.jstor.org/stable/353106

Baxter, L. A., & Montgomery, B. M. (1996). *Relating: Dialogues & dialectics.* New York: Guilford.

Baxter, L. A., & Wilmot, W. W. (1985). Taboo topics in close relationships. *Journal of Social and Personal Relationships, 2,* 253–269. doi:10.1177/0265407585023002

Beckett, M. K., Elliott, M. N., Martino, S., Kanouse, D. E., Corona, R., Klein, D. J., & Schuster, M. A. (2010). Timing of parent and child communication about sexuality relative to children's sexual behaviors. *Pediatrics, 125,* 34–42. doi:10.1542/peds.2009–0806

Bell, R. R. (1967). *Marriage and family interaction.* Homewood, IL: Dorsey Press.

Blieszner, R. (1994). Close relationships over time. In A. Weber & J. Harvey (Eds.), *Perspectives on close relationships* (pp. 1–17). Boston, MA: Allyn and Bacon.

Booth-Butterfield, M., & Sidelinger, R. (1998). The influence of family communication on the college-aged child: Openness, attitudes and actions about sex and alcohol. *Communication Quarterly, 46,* 295–308. doi:10.1080/01463379809370103

Braithwaite, D. O., & Baxter, L. A. (2006). *Engaging theories in family communication: Multiple perspectives.* Thousand Oaks, CA: Sage.

Burleson, B. R. (2010). The nature of interpersonal communication: A message-centered approach. In C. R. Berger, M. E. Roloff, & D. R. Roskos-Ewoldsen (Eds.), *The handbook of communication science* (pp. 145–163). Thousand Oaks, CA: Sage.

Burrell, G., & Morgan, G. (1979). *Sociological paradigms and organizational analysis.* Portsmouth, NH: Heineman.

Byers, E. S., & Sears, H. A. (2012). Mothers who do and do not intend to discuss sexual health with their young adolescents. *Family Relations, 61,* 851–863. doi:10.1111/j.17413729.2012.00740.x

Byers, E. S., Sears, H. A., & Weaver, A. D. (2008). Parents' reports of sexual communication with children in kindergarten to grade 8. *Journal of Marriage and Family, 70,* 86–96. doi:10.1111/j.1741–3737.2007.00463.x

Caughlin, J. P., & Malis, R. S. (2004). Demand/withdraw communication between parents and adolescents as a correlate of relational satisfaction. *Communication Reports, 17,* 59–71. doi:10.1080/08934210409389376

Caughlin, J. P., & Petronio, S. (2004). Privacy in families. In A. L. Vangelisti (Ed.), *Handbook of family communication* (pp. 379–412). Mahwah, NJ: Erlbaum.

Centers for Disease Control (2011). HIV among youth [Fact sheet]. Retrieved from www.cdc.gov/ hiv/youth/pdf/youth.pdf

Centers for Disease Control (2012a). Trends in the prevalence of sexual behaviors and HIV testing national NYRBS: 1991–2011. Retrieved from www.cdc.gov/healthyyouth/yrbs/pdf/us_sexual_trend_yrbs.pdf

Centers for Disease Control (2012b). Youth risk behavior surveillance–United States, 2011. *MMWR, 61,* 1–45. Retrieved from www.cdc.gov/mmwr/pdf/ss/ss6104.pdf

Christopher, F. S., & Roosa, M. W. (1991). Factors affecting sexual decisions in the premarital relationships of adolescents and young adults. In K. McKinney and S. Sprecher (Eds.), *Sexuality in close relationships* (pp. 111–133). Hillsdale, NJ: Erlbaum.

Clawson, C. L., & Reese-Weber, M. (2003). The amount and timing of parent-adolescent sexual communication as predictors of late adolescent sexual risk-taking behaviors. *The Journal of Sex Research, 40,* 256–265. doi:10.1080/00224490309552190

Coffelt, T. A. (2008)."*Little bits and pieces": The process of revealing sexual information in close mother-daughter relationships* (Doctoral dissertation). Retrieved from ProQuest. (304518108.)

Coffelt, T. A. (2010). Is sexual communication challenging between mothers and daughters? *Journal of Family Communication, 10,* 116–130. doi:10.1080/15267431003595496

Coleman, M., Fine, M. A., Ganong, L. H., Downs, K., & Pauk, N. (2001). When you're not the Brady Bunch: Identifying perceived conflicts and resolution strategies in step-families. *Personal Relationships*, *8*, 55–73. doi:10.1111/j.1475–6811.2001.tb00028.x

Crosby, R. A., DiClemente, R. J., Wingood, G. M., Sionean, C., Cobb, B. K., Harrington, K., . . . & Oh, M. K. (2001). Correlates of using dual methods for sexually transmitted diseases and pregnancy prevention among high-risk African-American female teens. *Journal of Adolescent Health*, *28*, 410–414. doi:http://dx.doi.org/10.1016/S1054–139X(00)00210-X

Dailey, R. M., & Palomares, N. A. (2004). Strategic topic avoidance: An investigation of topic avoidance frequency, strategies used, and relational correlates. *Communication Monographs*, *71*, 471–496. doi:10.1080/0363452042000307443

Darling, C. A., & Hicks, M. W. (1982). Parental influence on adolescent sexuality: Implications for parents as educators. *Journal of Youth and Adolescence*, *11*, 231–245. doi:10.1007/BF01537469

Daugherty, L. R., & Burger, J. M. (1984). The influence of parents, church, and peers on the sexual attitudes and behaviors of college students. *Archives of Sexual Behavior*, *13*, 351–359. doi:10.1007/BF01541907

Dennis, A. C., & Wood, J. T. (2012). "We're not going to have this conversation, but you get it": Black mother-daughter communication about sexual relations. *Women's Studies in Communication*, *35*, 204–223. doi:10.1080/07491409.2012.724525

DiIorio, C., Kelley, M., & Hockenberry-Eaton, M. (1999). Communication about sexual issues: Mothers, fathers, and friends. *Journal of Adolescent Health*, *24*, 181–189. Retrieved from www.jahonline.org/article/S1054–139X%2898%2900115–3/fulltext

DiIorio, C., Pluhar, E., & Belcher, L. (2003). A review of the literature on parent-child communication about sexuality: 1980–2002. *Journal of HIV/AIDS Prevention & Education for Children & Adolescents*, *5*, 7–32. doi:10.1300/J129v05n03_02

Erikson, E. E. (1968). *Identity: Youth, and crisis.* New York: Norton.

Feldman, S. S., & Rosenthal, D. A. (2000). The effect of communication characteristics on family members' perceptions of parents as sex educators. *Journal of Research on Adolescence*, *10*, 119–150. Retrieved from http://onlinelibrary.wiley.com/journal/10.1111/%28ISSN%291532–7795

Fiengo, R. (2007). *Asking questions: Using meaningful structures to imply ignorance.* New York: Oxford University Press.

Fisher, T. D. (1986). An exploratory study of parent-child communication about sex and the sexual attitudes of early, middle, and late adolescents. *The Journal of Genetic Psychology*, *147*, 543–557. doi:10.1080/00221325.1986.9914529

Fisher, T. D. (1988). The relationship between parent-child communication about sexuality and college students' sexual behavior and attitudes as a function of parental proximity. *The Journal of Sex Research*, *24*, 305–311. doi:10.1080/00224498809551429

Fox, G. L., & Inazu, J. K. (1980). Patterns and outcomes of mother-daughter communication about sexuality. *Journal of Social Issues*, *36*, 7–29. doi:10.1111/j.15404560.1980.tb01896.x

Geasler, M. J., Dannison, L. L., & Edlund, C. J. (1995). Sexuality education of young children: Parental concerns. *Family Relations*, *44*, 184–188. doi:10.2307/584807

Gephard, P. (1977). The acquisition of basic sex information. *Journal of Sex Research*, *13*, 148–184. doi:10.1080/00224497709550972

Goldsmith, D. J., Miller, L. E., & Caughlin, J. P. (2007). Openness and avoidance in couples communicating about cancer. *Communication Yearbook*, *37*, 62–115.

Golish, T. D., & Caughlin, J. P. (2002). "I'd rather not talk about it": Adolescents' and young adults' use of topic avoidance in stepfamilies. *Journal of Applied Communication Research, 30*, 78–106. doi:10.1080/00909880216574

Guerrero, L. K., & Afifi, W. A. (1995a). What parents don't know: Topic avoidance in parent-child relationships. In T. J. Socha & G. H. Stamp (Eds.), *Parents, children, and communication: Frontiers of theory and research* (pp. 219–245). Mahwah, NJ: Erlbaum.

Guerrero, L. K., & Afifi, W. A. (1995b). Some things are better left unsaid: Topic avoidance in family relationships. *Communication Quarterly, 43*, 276–296. doi:10.1080/01463379509369977

Guilamo-Ramos, V., Jaccard, J., Dittus, P., & Bouris, A. M. (2006). Parental expertise, trustworthiness, and accessibility: Parent-adolescent communication and adolescent risk behavior. *Journal of Marriage and Family, 68*, 1229–1246. doi:10.1111/j.17413737.2006.00325.x

Heisler, J. M. (2005). Family communication about sex: Parents and college-aged offspring recall discussion topics, satisfaction, and parental involvement. *Journal of Family Communication, 5*, 295–312. doi:10.1207/s15327698jfc0504_4

Herold, E. S., & Way, L. (1988). Sexual self-disclosure among university women. *The Journal of Sex Research, 24*, 1–14. doi:10.1080/00224498809551394

Hutchinson, M. K., & Cooney, T. M. (1998). Patterns of parent-teen sexual risk communication: Implications for intervention. *Family Relations, 47*, 185–194. doi:www.jstor.org/stable/585623

Jaccard, J., & Dittus, P. (1991). *Parent-teen communication: Toward the prevention of unintended pregnancies.* New York: Springer-Verlag.

Jaccard, J., Dittus, P. J., & Gordon, V. V. (1996). Maternal correlates of adolescent sexual and contraceptive behavior. *Family Planning Perspectives, 28*, 159–165. Retrieved from www.jstor.org/stable/2136192

Jaccard, J., Dittus, P. J., & Gordon, V. V. (1998). Parent-adolescent congruency in reports of adolescent sexual behavior and in communications about sexual behavior. *Child Development, 69*, 247–261. doi:10.1111/j.1467–8624.1998.tb06146.x

Jaccard, J., Dittus, P. J., & Gordon, V. V. (2000). Parent-teen communication about premarital sex: Factors associated with the extent of communication. *Journal of Adolescent Research, 15*, 187–208. doi:10.1177/0743558400152001

Jaccard, J., Dodge, T., & Dittus, P. (2002). Parent-adolescent communication about sex and birth control: A conceptual framework. *New Directions for Child and Adolescent Development, 97*, 9–41. doi:10.1002/cd.48

Karofsky, P. S., Zeng, L., & Kosorok, M. R. (2000). Relationship between adolescent-parental communication and initiation of first intercourse by adolescents. *Journal of Adolescent Health, 28*, 41–45. Retrieved from www.jahonline.org/search/quick

Kim, J. L., & Ward, L. M. (2007). Silence speaks volumes: Parental sexual communication among Asian American emerging adults. *Journal of Adolescent Research, 22*, 3–31. doi:10.1177/0743558406294916

King, B. M., & Lorusso, J. (1997). Discussions in the home about sex: Different recollections by parents and children. *Journal of Sex & Marital Therapy, 23*, 52–60. doi:10.1080/00926239708404417

Kirby, D. (2002). The impact of schools and school programs upon adolescent sexual behavior. *The Journal of Sex Research, 39*, 27–33. doi:10.1080/00224490209552116

Kirkman, M., Rosenthal, D. A., & Feldman, S. S. (2005). Being open with your mouth shut: The meaning of 'openness' in family communication about sexuality. *Sex Education, 4*, 49–66. doi:10.1080/1468181042000301885

Koblinsky, S., & Atkinson, J. (1982). Parental plans for children's sex education. *Family Relations, 31*, 29–35. Retrieved from www.jahonline.org/

Koesten, J., Miller, K. I., & Hummert, M. L. (2001). Family communication, self-efficacy, and white female adolescents' risk behavior. *The Journal of Family Communication, 2*, 7–27. doi:10.1207/S15327698JFC0201_3

Lefkowitz, E. S., Kahlbaugh, P. E., & Sigman, M. D. (1996). Turn-taking in mother-adolescent conversations about sexuality and conflict. *Journal of Youth and Adolescence, 25*, 307–321. doi:10.1007/BF01537387

Lefkowitz, E. S., & Stoppa, T. M. (2006). Positive sexual communication and socialization in the parent-adolescent context. *New Directions for Child & Adolescent Development, 112*, 39–55. doi:10.1002/cd.161

Mazur, M. A., & Hubbard, A.S.E. (2004). "Is there something I should know?": Topic avoidant responses in parent-adolescent communication. *Communication Reports, 17*, 27–37. doi:10.1080/08934210409389371

Meschke, L. L., Bartholomae, S., & Zentall, S. R. (2000). Adolescent sexuality and parent-adolescent processes: Promoting healthy teen choices. *Family Relations, 49*, 143–154. doi:10.1111/j.1741–3729.2000.00143.x

McKay, S. (2003). Adolescent risk behaviors and communication research: Current directions. *Journal of Language and Social Psychology, 22*, 74–82. doi:10.1177/0261927X02280058

McKee, M. D., & Karasz, A. (2006). "You have to give her that confidence": Conversations about sex in Hispanic, mother-daughter dyads. *Journal of Adolescent Research, 21*, 158–184. doi:10.1177/0743558405285493

Miller, B.C., Benson, B., & Galbraith, K. A. (2001). Family relationships and adolescent pregnancy risk: A research synthesis. *Developmental Review, 21*, 1–38. Retrieved from http://dx.doi.org/10.1006/drev.2000.0513

Miller, K. S., Forehand, R., & Kotchick, B. A. (1999). Adolescent sexual behavior in two ethnic minority samples: The role of family variables. *Journal of Marriage and the Family, 61*, 85–98. Retrieved from www.jstor.org/stable/353885

Miller, B.C., & Moore, K. A. (1990). Adolescent sexual behavior, pregnancy, and parenting: Research through the 1980s. *Journal of Marriage and Family, 52*, 1025–1044. Retrieved from www.jstor.org/stable/353317

Miller-Day, M. A. (2004). *Communication among grandmothers, mothers, and adult daughters: A qualitative study of maternal relationships.* Mahwah, NJ: Erlbaum.

Noller, P., & Bagi, S. (1985). Parent-adolescent communication. *Journal of Adolescence, 8*, 125–144. Retrieved from http://dx.doi.org.proxy.lib.iastate.edu/10.1016/S01401971(85)80042–7

O'Sullivan, L. F., Meyer-Bahlburg, H. F. L., & Watkins, B. X. (2001). Mother-daughter communication about sex among urban African American and Latino families. *Journal of Adolescent Research, 16*, 269–292. Retrieved from http://jar.sagepub.com/

Olson, D. H., Russell, C. S., & Sprenkle, D. H. (1989). *Circumplex model: Systemic assessment and treatment of families.* New York: Haworth.

Orgocka, A. (2004). Perceptions of communication and education about sexuality among Muslim immigrant girls in the US. *Sex Education, 4*, 255–271. doi:10.1080/1468181042000243349

Petronio, S. (2000). The boundaries of privacy: Praxis of everyday life. In S. Petronio (Ed.), *Balancing the secrets of private disclosures* (pp. 37–49). Mahwah, NJ: Erlbaum.

Petronio, S. (2002). *Boundaries of privacy: Dialectics of disclosure.* New York: State University of New York Press.

Petronio, S. (2010). Communication privacy management theory: What do we know about family privacy regulation? *Journal of Family Theory & Review*, 2, 175–196. doi:10.1111/j.1756–2589.2010.00052.x

Petronio, S., Reeder, H. M., Hecht, M., & Ros-Mendoza, T. M. (1996). Disclosure of sexual abuse by children and adolescents. *Journal of Applied Communication Research*, 24, 181–199. doi:10.1080/00909889609365450

Pistella, C.L.Y., & Bonati, F. A. (1999). Adolescent women's recommendations for enhanced parent-adolescent communication about sexual behavior. *Child and Adolescent Social Work Journal*, 16, 305–315. Retrieved from www.springerlink.com/content/104690/

Pluhar, E. I., & Kuriloff, P. (2004). What really matters in family communication about sexuality? A qualitative analysis of affect and style among African American mothers and adolescent daughters. *Sex Education*, 4, 303–321. doi:10.1080/1468181042000243376

Poole, M. S. (2012). On the study of process in communication research. *Communication Yearbook*, 36, 371–409.

Poole, M. S., McPhee, R. D., & Canary, D. J. (2002). Hypothesis testing and modeling perspectives on inquiry. In M. L. Knapp & J. A. Daly (Eds.), *Handbook of interpersonal communication* (pp. 23–72). Thousand Oaks, CA: Sage.

Reiss, I. L. (1981). Some observations on ideology and sexuality in America. *Journal of Marriage and the Family*, 43, 271–283. Retrieved from www.jstor.org/stable/351379

Rodgers, K. B. (1999). Parenting processes related to sexual risk-taking behaviors of adolescent males and females. *Journal of Marriage and the Family*, 61, 99–109. Retrieved from www.jstor.org/stable/i215039

Rollins, B.C., & Thomas, D.C. (1979). Parental support, power, and control techniques in the socialization of children. In W. R. Burr, R. Hill, F. I. Nye, & I. L. Reiss (Eds.), *Contemporary theories about the family* (pp. 317–364). New York: Free Press.

Rosenthal, D., Senserrick, T., & Feldman, S. (2001). A typology approach to describing parents as communicators about sexuality. *Archives of Sexual Behavior*, 30, 463–482. doi:10.1023/A:1010235116609

Rosenthal, D. A., & Feldman, S. S. (1999). The importance of importance: Adolescents' perceptions of parental communication about sexuality. *Journal of Adolescence*, 22, 835–851. doi:10.1111/j.1741–3729.2000.00143.x

Rosenthal, D. A., Feldman, S. S., & Edwards, D. (1998). Mum's the word: Mothers' perspectives on communication about sexuality with adolescents. *Journal of Adolescence*, 21, 727–743. doi:10.1111/j.1741–3729.2000.00143.x

Spanier, G. B. (1977). Sources of sex information and premarital sexual behavior. *The Journal of Sex Research*, 13, 73–89. doi:10.1080/00224497709550964

Stafford, L. (2004). Communication competencies and sociocultural priorities of middle childhood. In A. L. Vangelisti (Ed.), *Handbook of family communication* (pp. 311–332). Mahwah, NJ: Erlbaum.

Vangelisti, A. L. (1994). Family secrets: Forms, functions and correlates. *Journal of Social and Personal Relationships*, 11, 113–135. doi:10.1177/0265407594111007

Warren, C. (1995). Parent-child communication about sex. In T. J. Socha & G. H. Stamp (Eds.), *Parents, children, and communication: Frontiers of theory and research* (pp. 173–201). Mahwah, NJ: Erlbaum.

Warren, C., & Neer, M. (1986). Family sex communication orientation. *Journal of Applied Communication Research*, 14, 86–107. doi:10.1080/00909888609360307

Whitbeck, L., Conger, R., & Kao, M. (1993). The influence of parental support, depressed affect, and peers on the sexual behaviors of adolescent girls. *Journal of Family Issues*, *14*, 261–278. doi:10.1177/019251393014002006

White, C. P., Wright, D. W., & Barnes, H. L. (1995). Correlates of parent-child communication about specific sexual topics: A study of rural parents with school-aged children. *Personal Relationships*, *2*, 327–343. doi:10.1111/j.1475–6811.1995.tb00096.x

Wight, D., Williamson, L., & Henderson, M. (2005). Parental influences on young people's sexual behaviour: A longitudinal analysis. *Journal of Adolescence*, *29*, 473–494. Retrieved from http://dx.doi.org.proxy.lib.iastate.edu/10.1016/j.adolescence.2005.08.007

Wilson, S. R., & Feng, H. (2007). Interaction goals and message production: Conceptual and methodological developments. In D. Roskos-Ewoldsen & J. Monahan (Eds.), *Communication and social cognition* (pp. 71–96). Mahwah, NJ: Lawrence Erlbaum.

Wright, P. J. (2009). Father-child sexual communication in the United States: A review and synthesis. *Journal of Family Communication*, *9*, 233–250. doi:10.1080/15267430903221880

Part III

Theorizing Communication in Health Contexts

CHAPTER CONTENTS

8 Communication About End-of-Life Health Decisions

Allison M. Scott

University of Kentucky

Most end-of-life research assumes that effective communication is critical to the delivery of high-quality end-of-life health care, but less is known about what constitutes effective end-of-life communication. In this review, I synthesize literature on improving advance directive completion, physician training, and family communication about end-of-life issues. I demonstrate how this work has produced mixed results about what makes end-of-life communication more or less effective because this research has remarkably little grounding in a communication perspective. I conclude by arguing that communication scholars, especially those utilizing a multiple goals approach, are well positioned to take end-of-life research in new directions that will improve end-of-life practice.

Rapid advances in nutrition, medicine, and technology have given people more choices than ever before about their health at the end of life. However, the same medical advances that have made countless end-of-life choices available have not necessarily improved the process of end-of-life decision making. Reviews of the state of end-of-life health care have revealed substantial inadequacies in the quality of care most people receive. Pain is inconsistently assessed and poorly controlled, leading to needless physical suffering (SUPPORT Principal Investigators, 1995). Physicians face greater legal risk for doing too little than for doing too much, leading to the implementation of costly life-sustaining treatments when there is little chance of improving the patient's condition but every chance of intensifying the patient's distress (Field & Cassel, 1997). Nearly half of family members of patients receiving end-of-life care experience anxiety or depression that is consistent with post-traumatic stress disorder (Lautrette et al., 2007). In short, the state of end-of-life care in the United States is a "public health crisis" (Byock, 2012, p. 5).

Recognizing the urgent need to improve health care at the end of life, government health agencies and private foundations, scholars and practitioners alike have called for a focus on communication as the key to improving end-of-life practice. The result has been a proliferation of interdisciplinary investigations on how people talk about end-of-life health decisions. Overall, this work confirms that communication is a critical aspect of providing high-quality end-of-life care. When communication about end-of-life issues is poor, dying patients are more likely to receive treatment that is inconsistent with their wishes, which incurs immense physical, psychosocial, and financial cost (DeFanti, 2010). Ahrens, Yancey, and Kollef (2003) estimate that unnecessary or unwanted end-of-life medical treatment costs approximately $80 billion per year. In addition, poor end-of-life communication can compromise quality of life for patients and their family members (Tilden, Tolle, Nelson, & Fields, 2001) and lead to burnout among physicians (Jackson et al., 2008). By contrast, effective end-of-life communication leads to lower levels of patient anxiety and depression (Pautex, Herrmann, & Zulian, 2008), fewer physician errors (Slort et al., 2012), and less stress among family members (Wright et al., 2008). Not only can skillful communication aid patients and their families in pragmatically and meaningfully dealing with death (McQuellon & Cowan, 2000), but it is also possible that hospital costs could be reduced by up to 43% by adopting better end-of-life communication practices (Byock, 2012).

In this chapter, I synthesize findings from research focusing on communication as the key to improving the quality of end-of-life care. This body of work has remarkably little grounding in a communication perspective and thus has produced mixed results about what makes communication more or less effective in the context of end-of-life health care. The use of unsophisticated conceptualizations and operationalizations of communication in end-of-life research have led to a wealth of discrepant findings that are difficult to interpret. I argue that to make sense of the available literature on end-of-life decision making, we must study end-of-life communication from a distinctly communicative perspective. I present a multiple goals approach as one communication perspective that is well suited to serve as the basis for empirically furthering our understanding of how to optimize the end-of-life decision making process.

Formal and Informal Communication About End-of-Life Health Decisions

Research predicated on communication as the linchpin for improving the quality of end-of-life practice has taken three distinct directions, focusing on improving completion of advance directives, improving communication training for physicians, and improving communication with family members (particularly surrogate decision makers) about end-of-life issues. The research in each of these areas has not produced clear evidence for the effectiveness of communication in improving end-of-life care, likely because end-of-life communication has largely been studied by those outside the communication discipline.

End-of-Life Documentation

An advance directive is a written or oral statement of a person's wishes concerning future medical care issued when the person is capable of making such decisions in anticipation of a time when he or she may not possess decision-making capacity (Silveira, Kim, & Langa, 2010). Advance directives include a number of legal documents, such as living wills (which provide instructions for end-of-life medical treatment), do not resuscitate orders (which indicate a person's desire to forego cardiopulmonary resuscitation or intubation in the event that the person's heart or breathing stops), and durable power of attorney for health care (which legally authorizes another person to act on an individual's behalf in making health decisions).

Advance directives gained traction in the 1990s as an important tool for improving end-of-life care and were often presented by medical institutions and the media as the "cure all for all that ails end-of-life medical decision making" (Ditto, 2009, p. 215). Efforts were focused largely on increasing completion rates, and these efforts were met with some success. The Pew Research Center (2006) reports that the number of Americans who have executed an advance directive increased from 12% in 1990 to 29% in 2006, although estimates still vary widely, ranging from 15% (Cardenas-Turanzas, Gaeta, Ashoori, Price, & Nates, 2011) to 70% (Teno, Gruneir, Schwartz, Nanda, & Wetle, 2007). The focus on increasing completion rates led researchers to discover a host of factors that affect whether a person completes an advance directive. In general, people are less likely to complete an advance directive if they are younger (Lingler et al., 2008), less educated (Lingler et al., 2008), not White (Degenholtz, Arnold, Meisel, & Lave, 2002; Rich, Gruber-Baldini, Quinn, & Zimmerman, 2009), of lower socioeconomic status (Tarzian, Neal, & O'Neil, 2005), or less health literate (Volandes et al., 2008). People are more likely to complete an advance directive if they are concerned about protecting family members from burden, disagreement, or guilt (Seymour, Gott, Bellamy, Ahmedzai, & Clark, 2004).

The focus on increasing completion rates is based on the assumption that advance directives improve the quality of end-of-life practice, and there is some evidence to support this assumption. Advance directives are associated with lower levels of patient depression and anxiety (Pautex et al., 2008), smoother transition from acute to palliative care (Travis, Loving, McClanahan, & Bernard, 2001), lower use of artificial nutrition and respiration (Teno et al., 2007), less frequent utilization of cardiopulmonary resuscitation (Lahn, Friedman, Bijur, Haughey, & Gallagher, 2001), and lower family distress concerning the decision to withdraw life-sustaining support (Tilden et al., 2001).

However, improvement in rates of completion for advance directives does not always correspond to improvement in end-of-life care. In fact, there is evidence that having an advance directive does not affect a patient's psychosocial or health outcomes or reduce the use of hospital resources (Teno et al., 1997; Wenger et al., 2000; Yoo, Nakagawa, & Kim, 2012). For instance, in a randomized controlled trial intervention in which patients were offered advance directives, there were no significant differences between the intervention group and control group on any patient outcomes (i.e., cognitive function, satisfaction, psychological well-being, health-related quality of life), the receipt of life-sustaining treatments (i.e., cardiopulmonary resuscitation, mechanical ventilation, artificial nutrition and hydration), or the cost of care in the last month of life, which averaged $19,502 for patients in the intervention group, compared to $19,700 for patients in the control group (Schneiderman,

Kronick, Kaplan, Anderson, & Langer, 1992). More recently, in a matched pairs, case-control study at the M. D. Anderson Cancer Center, researchers found no significant difference between patients with and without advance directives in the decision to initiate life-sustaining treatment, including mechanical ventilation (44% vs. 42%, respectively), cardiopulmonary resuscitation (7% vs. 12%, respectively), or dialysis (3% vs. 7%, respectively); in addition, hospital survival rates did not differ significantly among patients with (56%) and without (59%) an advance directive (Wallace, Martin, Shaw, & Price, 2001).

Researchers and practitioners have offered a number of possible explanations for the disappointing performance of advance directives. First, advance directives are not always practical. Implementation can be difficult due to logistical problems, such as misplaced, invalid, or inconsistent documentation (Freeborne, Lynn, & Desbiens, 2000). Some estimates suggest that as few as 14% of doctors are even aware of their patients' end-of-life documented preferences (DesHarnais, Carter, Hennessy, Kurent, & Carter, 2007).

Second, people's end-of-life preferences and values can be affected by various factors that change over time and across contexts (Fagerlin, Ditto, Hawkins, Schneider, & Smucker, 2002). For example, a person's desire for life-sustaining treatment tends to decrease if the person experiences a decline in quality of life (Danis, Garrett, Harris, & Patrick, 1994) or is admitted to a hospital (Ditto, Jacobson, Smucker, Danks, & Fagerlin, 2006). Moreover, many people may not even realize their preferences have changed. Gready et al. (2000) assessed actual and perceived changes in individuals' end-of-life preferences over a 2-year period and found that the stability of preferences was 75%, but only 20% of individuals correctly recognized that their preferences had changed. These results are consistent with research showing that people make systematic errors in predicting how they will react in future illness (Jansen, Stiggelbout, Nooij, Noordijk, & Kievit, 2000), and such forecasting errors can make advance directives an unreliable tool for end-of-life decision making.

But perhaps the most compelling reason for the inefficacy of advance directives is the typically poor quality of the formal communication about end-of-life issues. Most advance directives often are too general or too specific to usefully affect end-of-life care. Some documents focus on recording a person's overall end-of-life goals and values but fail to capture important nuances in the person's preferences (e.g., Aging With Dignity, 2013). Other advance directive protocols are too specific in documenting treatment preferences (e.g., Physician Orders for Life-Sustaining Treatment, 2013), which is not always helpful since no one can possibly anticipate all possible end-of-life choices, and thus the advance directives ultimately may not apply to a person's actual situation. Winter, Parks, and Diamond (2010) compared individuals' end-of-life preferences for treatment as recorded in standard living will documents with their preferences recorded in six specific end-of-life scenarios and found no significant correlation between the two records of preferences in five out of the six scenarios. This mismatch between documented and actual end-of-life situations can force physicians and family members to interpret out-of-context preferences (Seymour et al., 2004) and call into question whether the advance directive ethically and legally meets the standard criteria for informed refusal of treatment (Shaw, 2012).

To summarize, advance directives can be a useful tool in communicating about end-of-life goals, but they are blunt tools at best. It is likely that improving rates of advance directive completion does not also improve end-of-life practice because the quality of the documents is poor. Some researchers have argued that advance directives are only helpful to the extent that they occur in concert with conversations about end-of-life health decisions (Janssen, Engelberg, Wouters, & Curtis, 2012) and that perhaps the greatest value of advance directives is that they stimulate discussion about end-of-life issues (Fagerlin et al., 2002). Informal end-of-life communication can occur over time through a series of conversations (Black et al., 2009), thus accounting for changing preferences. Informal conversations also afford the opportunity to negotiate important nuances in people's preferences and thus may more consistently and favorably affect end-of-life care than advance directives. Consequently, considerable research has focused on communication as the key to improving end-of-life care by examining patients' conversations with their physicians.

Conversations With Physicians About End-of-Life Health Decisions

Communication between patients and their physicians is an obvious aspect of end-of-life health care, and typically the goals of such talk include delivering a diagnosis or prognosis, making choices about specific treatment options, and assessing and managing pain or other symptoms (Cartwright et al., 2007). Considerable research demonstrates the value of effective physician/patient end-of-life discussion. In their longitudinal, multi-institutional study funded by the National Institute of Mental Health and the National Cancer Institute, B. Zhang et al. (2009) found that for patients who reported having an end-of-life conversation with their doctor, the average cost of care in the last week of life was $1,876, compared to $2,917 for patients who had not discussed end-of-life issues with their doctor. Effective end-of-life communication between physicians and patients is also related to less physical (B. Zhang et al., 2009) and psychological (Wentlandt et al., 2012) stress for patients, lower rates of emotional burnout among physicians who care for patients at the end of life (Jackson et al., 2008), and higher quality of life for family members of patients (Wright et al., 2008).

Several reports indicate that only one-third of patients have talked about some aspect of end-of-life care with their physicians (Furman, Head, Lazor, Casper, & Ritchie, 2006; Wenger et al., 2001; Wright et al., 2008). In their study of 196 patients in intensive care units, Rady and Johnson (2004) found that not a single patient had discussed non-curative end-of-life care as a possible treatment. There are a number of reasons that end-of-life conversations between patients and doctors do not occur more frequently. Logistical barriers to end-of-life talk include time constraints (Fine, Reid, Shengelia, &

Adelman, 2010), lack of clarity about which physician is responsible for initiating end-of-life discussion (Larson & Tobin, 2000; Levin, Moreno, Silvester, & Kissane, 2010), and the absence of a clear precipitating event (such as a terminal diagnosis) to prompt the conversation (Schonfeld, Stevens, Lampman, & Lyons, 2012). Doctors also report emotional barriers to engaging in end-of-life conversations with their patients, including feelings of uncertainty (Deep, Green, Griffith, & Wilson, 2007), discomfort with death (Chittenden, Clark, & Pantilat, 2006), fear of taking away hope or causing pain (Hickman, 2002), or anticipation of disagreement (Morrison, 1998).

Moreover, even when patient/physician conversations about end-of-life decisions do occur, there is a tendency for such talk to go poorly. For instance, Deep, Griffith, and Wilson (2008b) interviewed 28 dyads of physicians and patients following a discussion regarding preferences for resuscitation and found that in 21% of the dyads, the physician and the patient reported different decision outcomes, including dyads in which patients who did not want resuscitation lacked a do not resuscitate order and dyads in which patients did not even recall having the conversation. Many physicians present value-laden medical choices in a scripted, impersonal, and procedure-focused manner (Deep, Griffith, & Wilson, 2008a). Doctors also tend to dominate end-of-life conversations and to focus on medical or technical aspects of end-of-life care while ignoring more emotional or quality of life issues (Fine et al., 2010; Trice & Prigerson, 2009). Patients' and family members' unfamiliarity with end-of-life terminology can result in misunderstanding a doctor's explanation about diagnosis and care options (Biola et al., 2007; Limerick, 2002). Nearly a third of the families interviewed in Abbott, Sago, Breen, Abernethy, and Tulsky (2001) reported unprofessional behavior during conversations with doctors, citing examples of feeling pressure to hasten a loved one's death because doctors mentioned the need for the dying patient's bed, or feeling distressed because doctors initiated discussion of do not resuscitate orders at the bedside of a ventilated patient who could hear but could not respond to the conversation.

Poor provider/patient communication about end-of-life care can be costly. B. Zhang et al. (2009) estimate that if the rate of patients who discuss end-of-life issues with physicians were increased to just 50%, more than $76 million could be saved annually. In addition, lack of communication between doctors and patients results in more aggressive and medically futile treatments in a person's final days, which can exacerbate the patient's suffering and complicate the family members' experience of grief (J. Goldsmith, Wittenberg-Lyles, Ragan, & Nussbaum, 2011). These cost considerations have prompted a call for efforts to improve the frequency and the quality of end-of-life communication between physicians and their patients through medical training in end-of-life communication skills (Field & Cassel, 1997).

The priority (and, in some cases, the accreditation requirement) of instruction in how to communicate with patients at the end of life has led to the development of a number of communication training programs. The most prominent such program is the SPIKES curriculum, a script-based protocol for sharing bad news with patients. According to the SPIKES model, a doctor should arrange an appropriate *setting* for the end-of-life conversation, assess the patient's *perception* of the illness and treatment, obtain the patient's *invitation* to disclose information, share *knowledge* about the diagnosis or prognosis, address the patient's *emotions* by expressing empathy, and develop a *strategy* for the next steps of care (Baile et al., 2000).

Evaluations of the SPIKES curriculum have produced mixed results. Back et al. (2007) conducted a pretest/posttest training workshop and found that after receiving instruction based on the SPIKES protocol, physicians demonstrated improved skill in checking patient perception, securing patient invitation to disclose, relaying information, and empathizing with patient emotion. In a prospective controlled intervention, Alexander, Keitz, Sloane, and Tulsky (2006) found that doctors who received the SPIKES communication training were rated as more skillful in delivering information and responding to patient emotion than were doctors in the control group, but they found no difference between the intervention and control groups in terms of general communication skills. McFarland and Rhoades (2006) compared pretest and posttest assessments of physician end-of-life communication after the physicians participated in a communication skills training retreat and found that although physicians perceived that the instruction would improve their communication with patients in the future, there was no significant improvement in reported communication skills. Similarly, Bonnaud-Antignac, Campion, Pottier, and Supiot (2010) examined external evaluations of physician communication after the physicians were instructed in the SPIKES curriculum and found that few physicians were able to effectively adapt their communication to patient knowledge and emotions.

The mixed evaluation of the SPIKES protocol is likely due, at least in part, to its relatively unsophisticated conceptualization and measurement of communication. The SPIKES model has received criticism from communication scholars for "conceptualizing communication as mechanistic and formulaic rather than as a complex, non-scripted process that requires constant adaptation" (J. Goldsmith et al., 2011, p. 447). Physician training in end-of-life communication has been based largely on the assumptions that physicians can plan a scripted end-of-life discussion, that end-of-life communication involves the physician/patient dyad, and that end-of-life conversations focus on information (Eggly et al., 2006). As Wittenberg-Lyles and her colleagues (Wittenberg-Lyles, Goldsmith, Sanchez-Reilly, & Ragan, 2008) have argued, however, these assumptions are mistaken. The complexity of end-of-life decisions is more successfully navigated with adaptive rather than scripted communication strategies. End-of-life decisions are typically made in the context of the family, and thus, a patient's family members are key participants in end-of-life discussions (Wittenberg-Lyles, Goldsmith, & Ragan, 2010). The quality of a doctor's end-of-life communication is more usefully explained in terms of goal achievement rather than in terms of information exchange. In fact, medical students report that they are less interested in being trained in what information to share with patients at the end of life and more interested in learning *how* to convey certain information (Wittenberg-Lyles, Goldsmith, Ragan, & Sanchez-Reilly, 2010).

The faulty assumptions and deficient outcomes of current end-of-life communication training for physicians led Wittenberg-Lyles and her colleagues (Wittenberg-Lyles, Goldsmith, Ferrell, & Ragan, 2013) to develop the COMFORT training initiative. Rather than taking a linear approach to scripted information giving, the COMFORT model outlines core communication competencies that equip physicians to engage in person-centered, goal-directed dialogue with patients and their families. The skills identified in the COMFORT curriculum include *communicating* with verbal clarity and nonverbal immediacy, being aware of a patient's and family's *orientation* to health decisions based on their health literacy, maintaining *mindfulness* by being physically and emotionally present in interaction, recognizing that a patient's *family* represents the unit of care, engaging in *ongoing* discussion of care, *reiterating* the same messages in different ways to facilitate understanding, and coordinating with other members of the health care *team* to provide consistent care (Villagran, Goldsmith, Wittenberg-Lyles, & Baldwin, 2010). The effectiveness of the COMFORT initiative has yet to be fully evaluated, but initial results are promising. Wittenberg-Lyles, Goldsmith, Richardson, Hallett, and Clark (2013) assessed the COMFORT training program among practical nurses using a pretest/posttest design and found that the instruction resulted in improved self-reported end-of-life communication skills. Further research is needed to determine whether the training influences actual communication performance among physicians.

In sum, improving physician communication is important but not sufficient in improving the quality of end-of-life health care. Both the frequency and the quality of physicians' end-of-life communication are less than optimal, and training efforts have not been consistently successful in improving communication skill (primarily because they have not conceptualized communication well). Consequently, researchers have also focused on family conversations about end-of-life health decisions as a key point of leverage in improving the quality of end-of-life practice.

Conversations With Family Members About End-of-Life Health Decisions

One reason family involvement in end-of-life health care is so important is simply that people are more likely to talk with family members than with doctors about end-of-life decisions. According to the Pew Research Center (2006), 69% of married people have discussed end-of-life issues with their spouse, and among those with living parents, 57% have talked with their mothers and 48% have talked with their fathers about end-of-life care. The importance of family talk about end-of-life issues is further underscored by considerable evidence that family communication has the potential to improve or to complicate the end-of-life experience. Effective family end-of-life discussion can lead to lower rates of depression and anxiety in patients (Weiner & Roth, 2006) and is associated with lower risk of posttraumatic stress disorder and lower rates of clinical depression and anxiety in family members (Lautrette et al., 2007). Poor communication can increase the risk of implementing life-sustaining treatment against the patient's wishes (Parks et al., 2011) and lead to lower quality of life for patients and their family members (Siminoff, Rose, Zhang, & Zyzanski, 2006). Ineffective end-of-life communication in families also results in longer hospital stays for patients and in significantly higher end-of-life care cost (Ahrens et al., 2003).

Perhaps the greatest importance of family communication about end-of-life decisions is derived from the family's role in surrogate decision making. In order for a person to effectively participate in making end-of-life choices, the person must possess the capacity to make informed decisions. Most scholars and practitioners agree that to be capable of making an end-of-life choice, an individual must understand evidence relevant to the choice, must rationally manipulate relevant information to provide reasons for the choice, and must appreciate the consequences of the choice (Christensen, Haroun, Schneiderman, & Jeste, 1995; Drane, 1984). End-of-life health decisions are often made when a person's health is deteriorating, and this deterioration can come at the expense of the person's decision-making capacity (Sessums, Zembrzuska, & Jackson, 2011). For this reason, many individuals are not able to make their own choices at the end of life. In fact, between 70% and 80% of people are unable to make some or all of their own end-of-life health decisions (American Psychological Association Working Group on Assisted Suicide and End-of-Life Decisions, 2000).

When a person's decision-making capacity is impaired, a proxy, or a surrogate decision maker, often assumes responsibility for making choices on the person's behalf (Sulmasy & Snyder, 2010). Substituted judgment, the standard for proxy decision making recommended by bioethicists, involves faithfully representing the incapacitated individual by making the treatment choices the individual would have made (President's Commission for the Study of Ethical Problems in Medicine and Biomedical and Behavioral Research, 1983). Family members are usually best positioned to know and advocate for a patient's end-of-life preferences (Brock, 1992), which is likely why most people (as many as 90%) designate a family member as their proxy decision maker (Carr & Khodyakov, 2007). However, decision-making surrogacy usually entails a great deal of emotional anguish and interpersonal conflict as family members struggle to discern an appropriate course of action (Ditto, 2009; Givens, Lopez, Mazor, & Mitchell, 2012). Even when a patient's end-of-life preferences have been recorded, surrogate decision making can be fraught with a great deal of uncertainty (Lopez & Guarino, 2011).

The obvious purpose of designating a surrogate decision maker is to ensure that a patient's end-of-life goals of care are followed. But overwhelming evidence demonstrates that, in fact, concordance between a patient's end-of-life wishes and a proxy's anticipation of those wishes is no better than chance.

Although reported rates of concordance vary somewhat, most estimates fall between 40% and 70% (e.g., Fagerlin, Ditto, Danks, Houts, & Smucker, 2001; Sharma et al., 2011; Suhl, Simons, Reedy, & Garrick, 1994). These estimates are consistent with a meta-analysis of 16 studies of patient/proxy concordance, which found that surrogates predict patient end-of-life preferences with 68% accuracy overall (Shalowitz, Garrett-Mayer, & Wendler, 2006).

Several explanations for surrogate inaccuracy have been offered. One possible reason for low concordance is projection bias, which occurs when the proxy assumes the patient has preferences similar to the proxy (Fagerlin et al., 2001; Moorman, Hauser, & Carr, 2009). Low concordance may also be explained in part by the tendency for surrogates to make decisions with an overtreatment bias, which leads them to overestimate the patient's desire for life-sustaining treatment or to underestimate the negative impact of treatment on the patient's quality of life (Ayalon, Bachner, Dwolatzky, & Heinik, 2012; Ditto et al., 2001). Individual and family factors may also impact concordance, with evidence that higher levels of family conflict yield lower rates of concordance (Parks et al., 2011), and surrogates with insecure attachment orientations (i.e., anxious, avoidant) are less accurate in predicting a family member's end-of-life wishes (Turan, Goldstein, Garber, & Carstensen, 2011).

Some researchers have hypothesized that rates of concordance will be higher if the patient and surrogate discuss end-of-life decisions. But mounting evidence indicates that having a conversation about end-of-life wishes does not significantly increase proxy accuracy. Ditto et al. (2001) implemented an intervention that facilitated discussion between individuals and their surrogates about end-of-life scenarios and values, and their finding that the intervention produced no improvement in the prediction accuracy of surrogates demonstrated the "unequivocal . . . ineffectiveness of . . . patient-surrogate discussion to improve the accuracy of surrogate substituted judgment" (p. 426). By contrast, Barrio-Cantalejo et al. (2009) compared pairs of patients and proxies who received an intervention with control group pairs and found significantly higher concordance rates among the intervention pairs who had engaged in an end-of-life discussion than among the control pairs who had not engaged in a facilitated discussion about end-of-life preferences. However, Hines et al. (2001) found that having more conversations about end-of-life issues was associated with higher surrogate-reported confidence in their understanding of patient end-of-life preferences, but the number of conversations was unrelated to surrogate prediction of patient preferences concerning specific treatments or general values. As part of the Wisconsin Longitudinal Study, Moorman et al. (2009) examined a sample of 2,750 married couples (5,500 individuals) and found that spouses who had talked about their end-of-life preferences did not differ in concordance from those who had not discussed end-of-life preferences.

Taken together, these results demonstrate that having a conversation about end-of-life decisions with family members does not necessarily improve end-of-life practice. However, it is likely that simply talking about end-of-life choices does not appear to matter because many people who talk about end-of-life issues do so poorly. For example, Hines et al. (2001) found that family members who had had at least five conversations about end-of-life care still had not discussed important issues, such as preferences for tube feedings, cardiopulmonary resuscitation, or dialysis. Families also may talk in ways that perpetuate unwarranted optimism about a family member's condition to protect themselves and their loved ones from painful conversations, leading to the initiation of unnecessary or unwanted life-sustaining treatment (A. Zhang & Siminoff, 2003). The profundity of end-of-life choices makes end-of-life decision making ripe for conflict, even in well-functioning families (King & Quill, 2006), and increasing the frequency of communication when conflict is unresolved can inappropriately prolong the dying process (Swigart, Lidz, Butterworth, & Arnold, 1996; Winter & Parks, 2008).

A guiding assumption for a great deal of research focused on end-of-life communication in families has been that increasing the incidence or frequency of discussion will improve end-of-life care outcomes. As the findings from this body of work demonstrate, however, this guiding assumption is fundamentally flawed. More communication does not necessarily yield better communication. Any beneficial outcome of discussing end-of-life issues likely depends on the quality of that discussion. However, what counts as high-quality communication in the context of family conversations about end-of-life health decisions is not well understood. It is clear that certain kinds of messages hold particular importance at the end of life, but little is known about how such messages yield positive or negative effects. For instance, messages about personal identity can affirm individuals' positive qualities, and acknowledging difficult relationship issues provides an opportunity for reconciliation (Keeley, 2007). Everyday family communication, such as small talk and routine interactions, can provide comfort as well as a sense of normalcy at the end of life (Keeley & Baldwin, 2012). These categories represent people's interpretation and evaluation of certain messages, but the categories do not indicate the discursive features that elicited the interpretation. Without information about why certain messages are evaluated as favorable or unfavorable, it is unclear what kind of talk is best suited for successfully engaging in end-of-life conversation in families.

Furthermore, a common recommendation is to "be open" in family conversations about end-of-life issues (e.g., Babcock & Robinson, 2011; Kramer, Kavanaugh, Trentham-Dietz, Walsh, & Yonker, 2010; Levin et al., 2010; Norris et al., 2007; Wittenberg-Lyles, Goldsmith, & Ragan, 2011). "Being open," however, can mean different things. D. Goldsmith and Domann (2013) interviewed patients who had experienced a cardiac event and their partners and found that some participants were open by talking regularly and unrestrainedly about a variety of issues, some were open by having a onetime "big talk" in which the partners acknowledged mortality and reaffirmed their love but then did not discuss health issues again, and still others reported being open by focusing on medical information and decision making rather than personal or relational implications of the patient's cardiac health. Several participants reported being open because their conversations were marked by a lack of constraint (although they did not necessarily discuss unconstrained topics), whereas others perceived themselves to be open because the family members knew each other well, and so even though they did not necessarily discuss health issues, they were confident in one another's familiarity with their thoughts and feelings. Caughlin, Mikucki-Enyart, Middleton, Stone, and Brown (2011) interviewed adult children whose parents had died of lung cancer and found that families commonly endorsed the value of open communication about the parent's health while also engaging in closed communication. Some participants reported "being open while avoiding" (Caughlin et al., 2011, p. 423), which involved claiming openness while also engaging in avoidance, yet they did not interpret their avoidant communication as contradictory to their articulated value of open communication. Collectively, these findings demonstrate that there are many different ways to "be open," but it is not yet clear whether some ways of being open are better than others in the context of family communication about end-of-life health.

Some evidence indicates that framing conversations around goals for end-of-life care makes for more effective family communication (Tulsky, 2005). For example, Detering, Hancock, Reade, and Silvester (2010) conducted a randomized, controlled trial that facilitated discussion between patients and their families about the patient's goals for end-of-life care by reflecting on how the patient's values and beliefs shaped their choices about end-of-life health care. Compared to the control group, the wishes of patients in the intervention group were significantly more likely to be known and followed, patients and family members in the intervention group reported significantly higher levels of satisfaction, and family members of patients who had died in the intervention group experienced significantly fewer symptoms of post-traumatic stress and lower rates of depression and anxiety. The researchers concluded that focusing on patient goals for care rather than systematically considering specific treatments for particular circumstances was the key to the effectiveness of the family discussion. Kirchhoff, Hammes, Kehl, Briggs, and Brown (2010) also conducted a randomized, controlled trial that focused on clarifying goals in end-of-life conversations between patients and their family members. Families in the intervention group specifically discussed the patient's goals for end-of-life care, experiences that have affected the patient's goals for future medical decision making, and the need for engaging in future discussions as situations and preferences change. Kirchhoff et al. (2010) found that family surrogates in the intervention group demonstrated significantly better understanding of patient preferences for treatment than did family surrogates in the control group. In a prospective, observational study, Lamba, Murphy, McVicker, Smith, and Mosenthal (2012) collected outside ratings of the quality of family conversations about goals of end-of-life care and found that better family discussion resulted in significantly higher incidence and timing of do not resuscitate orders, higher rates of life support withdrawal, and shorter length of stay in the intensive care unit by an average of 3 days. Results from these three interventions suggest that conceptualizing and measuring family communication in terms of goals for end-of-life health care leads to a consistent pattern of associations between family communication and end-of-life care outcomes.

In short, family communication holds a great deal of potential for improving end-of-life health care, but this potential likely lies in the quality, not the quantity, of family talk. Not surprisingly, when research has quantitatively assessed family communication, few associations between communication and end-of-life outcomes are found. However, when research has accounted for the quality of family talk, a much clearer picture emerges of the connection between effective family discussion and better end-of-life outcomes.

Summary

The multimillion-dollar Study to Understand Prognoses and Preferences for Outcomes and Risks of Treatment (SUPPORT) funded by the Robert Wood Johnson Foundation aptly illustrates a fundamental flaw of extant end-of-life communication research. The investigation, which enrolled more than 9,000 participants and consisted of a 2-year, prospective, observational study followed by a 2-year, controlled, clinical trial, assessed end-of-life health care at five sites and found substantial inadequacies in the quality of care most people received (SUPPORT Principal Investigators, 1995). For instance, 53% of doctors were unaware of their patient's preference to avoid cardiopulmonary resuscitation, 49% of patients who indicated a desire to avoid cardiopulmonary resuscitation did not have a do not resuscitate order written, and 50% of patients experienced moderate to severe pain in the last 3 days of life (SUPPORT Principal Investigators, 1995). To improve the quality of end-of-life practice, the SUPPORT researchers implemented an intervention that focused on increasing the frequency of end-of-life conversations among patients, their families, and physicians. But the intervention failed. There was no improvement in physician awareness of patient end-of-life documentation, in the incidence or timing of do not resuscitate orders, or in the amount of pain patients experienced in their final days (SUPPORT Principal Investigators, 1995).

The failure of the SUPPORT intervention (and others like it) is, at least in part, the result of researchers trying to understand communicative phenomena without attending to communicative processes. Previous research on end-of-life communication has largely considered whether patients have documented their preferences or discussed them with their physicians or families, but not whether certain qualities of end-of-life communication matter. The findings from this literature suggest that furthering our understanding of how communication can improve end-of-life care requires a shift from focusing on quantity of talk to focusing on quality of talk. Taking a communication perspective on end-of-life decision making allows us to examine not only the frequency and type of talk, but also what is said, how it is said, and the meanings and assessments typically attributed to particular ways of saying things. I present a multiple goals perspective as a distinctly communicative framework that provides a useful means of conceptualizing and operationalizing what counts as high-quality communication about end-of-life decisions.

A Multiple Goals Perspective on End-of-Life Decision Making

A multiple goals approach is one communication perspective that could prove particularly useful for conducting and interpreting research on end-of-life communication. A multiple goals perspective focuses on identifying features of talk that differentiate more from less skillful discussion in particular contexts, and thus the perspective could be fruitfully employed to conceptualize and evaluate what counts as better or worse communication about end-of-life decisions. Here I present the theoretical principles of the multiple goals perspective, including a discussion of salient goals in end-of-life contexts, I detail some of the methodological implications of conducting end-of-life research from a multiple goals perspective, and I discuss how the perspective can be applied in end-of-life medical practice.

Multiple Goals Theoretical Perspective

Many communication scholars agree that communication frequently is aimed at addressing goals. The conceptualization of communication as goal-oriented has led to the development of several multiple goals theories (for a review, see Wilson & Feng, 2007) which share a number of common assumptions that are relevant to explaining end-of-life communication. First, a multiple goals theoretical perspective assumes that communication is purposeful and that people typically try to accomplish multiple purposes simultaneously in an interaction (Caughlin, 2010). Although countless idiosyncratic interaction goals are possible, certain types of goals are relevant across situations, including task, identity, and relational goals (Clark & Delia, 1979).

A great deal of research has identified commonly salient task goals in end-of-life decision making. An obvious task goal in end-of-life situations is making decisions about treatments. People face a litany of life-sustaining treatments to consent to or refuse, withdraw from or continue, such as cardiopulmonary resuscitation, mechanical ventilation, tube feeding, artificial hydration, dialysis, chemotherapy, and antibiotics. People also face choices about legal documentation (e.g., selecting a person to hold the durable power of attorney for health care, completing a living will, requesting a do not resuscitate order), type of care (e.g., continuing with illness-directed curative care or transitioning to comfort-focused palliative care), and place of care (e.g., hospital, nursing home, hospice, home). In addition to making decisions about these options, other possible task goals of end-of-life communication include exchanging information (Trice & Prigerson, 2009; Wittenberg-Lyles, 2005), managing pain and symptoms (Downey, Engelberg, Curtis, Lafferty, & Patrick, 2009; Singer, Martin, & Kelner, 1999; Steinhauser et al., 2000), providing support to a dying patient or to the patient's family members (Considine & Miller, 2010), influencing a patient's health decision (D. Goldsmith, Lindholm, & Bute, 2006), and preserving a sense of hope (Back et al., 2008; Thompson, 2011).

A number of identity-related goals are also relevant in end-of-life communication. Perhaps the overriding identity goal is to preserve an individual's autonomy by respecting the individual's right to refuse any medical treatments and to choose legitimate and available medical treatments (Byock, 2012). The goal of preserving patient autonomy is privileged in bioethics (Menikoff, 2001) and legislation (Patient Self-Determination Act, 1990), and the value placed on communication in end-of-life care by scholars and practitioners is predicated on the assumption that better communication will enable physicians and families to better honor a patient's end-of-life wishes. Other salient identity goals in end-of-life conversations may include maintaining a sense of dignity (Chochinov, 2002; Natan, Garfinkel, & Shachar, 2010), being treated as a whole person (Steinhauser et al., 2000), maintaining independence (Moorman, 2011a), negotiating new roles or the loss of roles (Boquet, Oliver, Wittenberg-Lyles, Doorenbos, & Demiris, 2011; Quin et al., 2012), being a good doctor (Karasz, Dyche, & Selwyn, 2003), being a good patient (Proulx & Jacelon, 2004), or being a good family member (Hinds et al., 2012).

Relational goals are also normatively relevant in end-of-life communication. Being with family and strengthening relationships with loved ones is consistently ranked as an important goal in end-of-life talk (Downey et al., 2009; Singer et al., 1999). The end of life is a time when people typically want to achieve a sense of relational completion (Steinhauser et al., 2000), reconcile any broken relationships (Byock, 1997), and extend or receive needed forgiveness (Exline, Prince-Paul, Root, Peereboom, & Worthington, 2012). In addition, individuals may pursue the goal of feeling understood (Moorman, 2011b), having someone listen (Natan et al., 2010), maintaining trust in the physician (Melhado & Bushy, 2011; Seymour et al., 2004), or relieving burden on family members (Singer et al., 1999; Winter & Parks, 2012).

A second assumption of a multiple goals theoretical perspective is that the various relevant goals in an interaction can be potentially conflicting. The pursuit of one goal may constrain or prevent the pursuit of another goal in a conversation. In complex situations, variations in goals (and variations in how those goals are pursued) become meaningful because relevant goals are greater in number, more inconsistent with each other, and more difficult to achieve than in less complex situations (O'Keefe & Delia, 1982). Making end-of-life decisions represents a particularly complex communicative situation in which the actions that help achieve one goal may compete with actions that accomplish other relevant goals. For example, Thompson (2011) has identified the tension between the simultaneous goals of being open and preserving hope in end-of-life discussion. Some family members may want to talk frankly about the details of a patient's terminal diagnosis, while other family members may not want to hear details that could take away their sense of hope. The goal of showing support for a spouse's decision to forego mechanical ventilation may run contrary to the goal of showing how much the spouse's survival is valued.

A physician may want to persuade a patient to not refuse artificial hydration, but may be worried that doing so will undermine the patient's sense of autonomy. Parents who wish to designate one of their adult children as their surrogate decision maker may be concerned that doing so will place undue strain on the designated child or hurt the feelings of their other children. The cross-purposes of pertinent goals can leave people feeling that they have to choose among bad options (e.g., undermine their identity or relational goals or give up making the choice they want), which is why discussing end-of-life decisions can be so challenging.

According to a multiple goals perspective, the quality of communication depends on how well the various interaction goals are attained without ignoring or undermining other salient goals. Skillful communication achieves the primary interaction task (e.g., making an end-of-life decision) while also successfully managing what the conversations mean for identities and relationships (D. Goldsmith, 2001, 2004). In previous work, we have found remarkable variation in how family members manage multiple relevant goals in end-of-life discussions and demonstrated how some ways of managing competing goals are more skillful than others. In Scott and Caughlin (2012), we conducted a discourse analysis of end-of-life conversations between 121 pairs of older adults and their adult children and found that the ways in which certain goals were accomplished had implications for how other goals were pursued. Some parents expressed their desire to not be a burden to their child by affirming the importance of maintaining close family relationships, whereas other parents expressed their desire to not burden their child by implying that their relationship may not be strong enough to support the burden of family caregiving. In addition, some participants used relational affirmation to avoid talking about end-of-life choices (e.g., implying that discussion was unnecessary because they knew they would agree on everything), whereas other participants avoided the conversation by explicitly refusing to talk with the other person about certain topics. These examples illustrate how individuals can achieve one goal in concert with or at the expense of other pertinent goals, and communication that attends to multiple relevant goals is more sophisticated than communication that does not.

An important implication of the assumption that communication is skillful to the extent it attends to the various relevant goals is that goal attention is not only a means to account for how people produce messages, but goals also provide a way to evaluate communication quality (D. Goldsmith, 2004). Most research utilizing a multiple goals framework has focused on how goals shape the way a person communicates (Berger, 2005; Wilson & Feng, 2007). However, a multiple goals perspective also accounts for how people make sense of communication (Caughlin, 2010). For example, a physician giving advice to a patient about whom to designate as a proxy decision maker for end-of-life choices could be interpreted as offering helpful expertise, invading privacy, or fulfilling a professional duty. Depending on these interpretations, the communication may be effective or ineffective, which is why well-intentioned messages do not always translate into favorable conversational outcomes (D. Goldsmith et al., 2006). This means that a multiple goals perspective provides a theoretical framework for connecting communication quality to end-of-life outcomes by means of perceived goals.

Multiple Goals Methodological Approach

In addition to providing a means of conceptualizing communication quality in end-of-life research, a multiple goals perspective also entails a number of implications for the methodology of end-of-life investigations. On the whole, communication has been poorly measured in extant end-of-life research, and a multiple goals approach suggests several ways of improving the assessment of communication, including examining actual interaction, evaluating the quality of communication based on attention to multiple goals, and accounting for enacted as well as perceived goal attention.

First, it is critical to examine actual end-of-life conversations between patients, their family members, and physicians. A great deal of end-of-life research has utilized counts of conversations, self-report surveys asking participants to indicate the extent to which they agree with abstract, global statements about communication, or responses to hypothetical scenarios to assess communication. Such methods do not reveal the effectiveness of actual end-of-life communication. For instance, most work on end-of-life communication between doctors and patients has evaluated communication skill using doctor self-report (Eggly et al., 2006), which may not be an accurate barometer of the skillfulness of communication. In a 5-year, multisite, randomized trial, Dickson, Engelberg, Back, Ford, and Curtis (2012) collected reports on physician end-of-life communication skill during an end-of-life conversation with patients and their families from the physicians themselves, their patients, the patients' family members, and outside clinical evaluators. They found no significant associations between physician reports of communication skill and the reports from patients or families. The one significant association between reports from physicians and reports from outside evaluators was in the opposite direction (i.e., higher ratings of skill from physicians were related to lower ratings of skill from evaluators). Recall that Deep et al. (2008b) found that in one out of five cases, patients and physicians, referencing the same end-of-life conversation, reported that different decisions were made regarding the patient's care. Without looking at the actual conversation, little can be learned about how people in the same discussion can reach such different conclusions. The different interpretations of what happens during and as a result of an end-of-life discussion points to the need to examine the discussion itself.

Using counts of conversations, self-report, and hypothetical scenarios to study communication often reveals what participants value in talk or how participants make decontextualized interpretations of talk rather than how they actually talk about end-of-life health choices. Furthermore, the results from these methods can be difficult to interpret because they do not tap the value-laden meanings people assign to the idea of "communication." For example, end-of-life researchers frequently ask participants to report how many times they have talked about end-of-life decisions with a family member. If an individual considers any comment about an end-of-life issue to constitute a conversation, the reported number may be very high, but if another person considers only a "big talk" about end-of-life issues to count as a conversation, the reported number may be much lower, even if the person has casually discussed end-of-life issues more frequently. Thus, two individuals may talk with family members about end-of-life issues with comparable frequency, but their reports may differ drastically depending on what they count as "communication." This is exactly what Libbus and Russell (1995) found when they asked 30 individuals and their surrogate decision makers to report how many end-of-life conversations they had had with each other, and nearly half of the pairs disagreed about whether such a conversation had even taken place. Instead of assuming that most behaviors have an inherent meaning or impact, a multiple goals approach sensitizes researchers to the fact that meaning in communication is bound by context. The same behavior can be constructive or destructive, depending on the context of the interaction, and so the only way to account for variation in meaning (as well as variation in relevant outcomes) is to examine participants' construction and interpretation of messages in the context of actual conversations.

Actual end-of-life conversations can be studied in a number of ways. Researchers can observe and record naturally occurring discussions between patients and their physicians during medical appointments (e.g., Wittenberg-Lyles, Oliver et al., 2010). Researchers can also examine elicited conversations between individuals and their family members in naturalistic settings where the talk is prompted by a conversational task (e.g., Scott & Caughlin, 2012). Discussions elicited as part of a conversational task represent a particularly advantageous method for studying actual end-of-life conversations because elicited conversations retain many qualities of realism accorded to naturally occurring conversations but provide a way to study interactions that rarely occur naturally, such as end-of-life discussions (McLaughlin, 1984).

Second, a multiple goals perspective provides a sophisticated means of assessing communication quality. The overwhelming majority of studies on end-of-life communication consider whether or how often people have talked about end-of-life issues, but not whether certain characteristics of that talk matter. For example, in their communication-focused study, Wright et al. (2008) measured communication as a dichotomous construct, asking participants if they had had a conversation about end-of-life issues with their physician and coding their answers as "yes" or "no." Barrio-Cantelejo et al. (2009) likewise measured communication in terms of whether a conversation had taken place. Although significant associations were found in each of these studies, the findings are likely a crude gloss on how communication affects end-of-life care.

Moreover, recall that the SUPPORT study (1995), as well as Ditto et al. (2001), Hines et al. (2001), and Moorman et al. (2009) all quantitatively assessed communication and (not surprisingly) found no associations between having had a conversation about end-of-life preferences and relevant outcomes. In their systematic review of studies of physician empathy in end-of-life settings, Lelorain, Brédart, Dolbeault, and Sultan (2012) found that doctors' empathy was related to higher patient satisfaction and lower patient distress when the measure was patient-reported, but when the measure involved coding systems, no clear pattern of associations emerged, likely because the coding systems used in the reviewed studies focused on the frequency of empathic statements (e.g., proportion of affective utterances, tally of emotional words). These rudimentary measurements of communication do not consider that the way people talk about end-of-life decisions matters as much as that people talk about end-of-life decisions.

Communication scholars working from a multiple goals perspective can enrich the end-of-life literature by identifying the discursive features that differentiate more from less skillful communication in end-of-life contexts. Although a multiple goals perspective does not imply that it is possible to compose a catalog of effective and ineffective communication strategies, it is useful to explain variation in conversational outcomes by identifying specific discursive resources that people more or less successfully draw upon in managing multiple purposes within particular contexts (D. Goldsmith, 2004). For example, politeness can indicate the extent to which identity goals are addressed in interaction. Politeness is a discursive means of addressing other people's face, which is the self-image a person tries to project in interaction with others (Brown & Levinson, 1987). In general, individuals want others to show regard for their positive face (i.e., approval of the self-image they enact) as well as for their negative face (i.e., respect for their freedom from imposition; Brown & Levinson, 1987). Talking about end-of-life health decisions can render these identity concerns particularly vulnerable, and thus assessing how well a person balances attention to positive and negative face with other goals may provide one means of evaluating the quality of communication about end-of-life decisions.

Relational maintenance, which involves keeping a relationship in a desired condition (Dindia, 2003), provides a second potential means of assessing how well multiple goals are managed in interaction. Relational maintenance can take a number of forms, including positivity, openness, assurances, sharing tasks, and small talk (Dainton & Stafford, 1993). Perhaps the most salient aspect of relational maintenance from a multiple goals perspective is the intentionality of maintenance strategies. Strategic relational maintenance occurs when a person enacts conscious, intentional behavior with the goal of maintaining the relationship, whereas routine relational maintenance occurs when a person's actions are not necessarily intended to maintain the relationship but nevertheless accomplish that relational goal (Dainton & Stafford, 1993). The same relational maintenance behavior could be invoked in strategic or routine ways with different implications. For example, in talking about end-of-life decisions, showing relational assurance intentionally could imply that the person thinks the relationship is in need of such assurance (especially if relational assurance is not the primary goal of the interaction, such as in end-of-life decision making). Communicating relational assurance through routine means could imply that the person values the relationship but does not think that the end-of-life conversation places the relationship at risk of needing assurance. Thus, routine relational assurance may be a discursive feature that differentiates more from less sophisticated end-of-life communication.

A task-related discursive feature that may usefully indicate communication skill in end-of-life contexts is the degree to which decision making is explicitly or implicitly marked by elaboration. In the context of end-of-life decision making, elaboration is the process of providing contextual information to explain the reasoning behind end-of-life decisions (Scott & Caughlin, 2012). In discussing their end-of-life care, individuals can elaborate on their specific choices by providing hypothetical or real-life scenarios that illustrate what kind of treatment they would or would not want, explaining the contextual factors that affect why they would want a certain treatment in some cases but not others, or detailing the conditions under which their end-of-life preferences might change. By contrast, implicit decision making involves making a choice through more off-record means (Sillars & Kalbfleisch, 1989), which is associated with poorer outcomes (e.g., lower rates of concordance) in the context of end-of-life decision making (Pecchioni, 2001). Individuals may try to avoid explicitly discussing end-of-life decisions by instead talking about, for example, how well they know one another and therefore trust one another to make end-of-life decisions on each person's behalf (Pecchioni, 2001). Politeness, relational maintenance, and elaboration are just three examples of discursive features that previous research suggests may be particularly salient in end-of-life decision making and thus may be useful for assessing communicative success in end-of-life contexts.

A third methodological implication of a multiple goals perspective is that it is important to assess not just enacted goal attention by means of discursive resources, but it is also important to consider perceived goal attention in end-of-life conversations. People's inferences about their own goals and the goals of others often shape the interpretation, and thus the impact, of communication. Perceptions of avoidance, for example, affect the outcomes of that avoidance (Caughlin & Afifi, 2004; Donovan-Kicken & Caughlin, 2010). Within families, avoiding discussions of death could mean different things, depending on perceived goals. If a person perceives that a family member is avoiding discussion of end-of-life issues to protect other family members from a distressing conversation or to maintain optimism, the impact of that avoidance is likely different than if the perceived reason for avoidance is that the family member does not believe the family relationship is strong enough to warrant such a discussion or that the family member is in denial about what is really happening.

The notion that the impact of communication is moderated by perceptions of goals is a departure from most models of interaction, which tend to assume a more simplistic relationship between communication and its outcomes (Caughlin, 2010). Instead, a multiple goals perspective implies that discrepancies between enacted and perceived goal attention are possible (if not likely) and worth considering in communication research (D. Goldsmith, 2004). For instance, there is evidence that perceived avoidance and enacted avoidance function differently in end-of-life conversations. In Scott and Caughlin (2011), we examined actual conversations between family members about end-of-life health decisions and found that perceived avoidance (reported by participants) but not enacted avoidance (as assessed by outside raters) was associated with lower levels of participant-reported hopefulness. Furthermore, we found that perceived avoidance and enacted avoidance interacted to predict participants' sense of decision-making efficacy. These findings suggest that fully understanding the connection between end-of-life communication and its impact probably requires accounting for both actual goal attention as well as perceptions of goal attention.

Multiple Goals in Practice

In addition to informing theoretical and methodological choices in research, a multiple goals perspective can also be applied to end-of-life clinical practice. One of the main forums for facilitating end-of-life communication among patients, their family members, and physicians is the family meeting (J. Goldsmith et al., 2011). Family meetings (also termed family conferences) about end-of-life medical care have recently gained traction in end-of-life practice as a more formal opportunity for members of the interdisciplinary health care team to talk with a patient and all members of the patient's family who wish to participate. These meetings have proven to be an effective means of negotiating end-of-life decisions, promoting interdisciplinary coordination; increasing patient, family, and staff satisfaction; and reducing resource utilization (Billings, 2011; Fineberg, Kawashima, & Asch, 2011). Family meetings are frequently framed in terms of information exchange (e.g., Hudson, Thomas, Quinn, & Aranda, 2009; Wittenberg-Lyles, Oliver et al., 2010), and indeed, educating patients and family members about a patient's health and treatment options, resolving discrepancies in information from multiple providers, and giving patients and family members the chance to ask questions are common (and worthwhile) purposes of family meetings.

However, in addition to promoting the exchange of information, family meetings are also forums for providing emotional support, mediating among family members in conflict, and eliciting patient and family goals of care and making those goals the basis of decisions about end-of-life medical treatment (Billings, 2011; Byock, 2012). In fact, a multiple goals approach would suggest that, in addition to explicitly establishing health-related goals of care, it may also be helpful to make identity-related and relationship-related goals just as explicit (Weissman, Quill, & Arnold, 2010). Utilizing the existing communication mechanism of the family meeting and reframing it in terms of goal attention is one way that a multiple goals approach can be applied to improve end-of-life practice.

Another practical implication of a multiple goals perspective concerns the language used to describe end-of-life choices. In contexts where technology advances rapidly, such as end-of-life medical care, language often develops haphazardly and reflects early experiences, which eventually can lead to a discrepancy between the use of a treatment option and evidence of its efficacy (Brauner, 2010). Take the case of orders to forego artificial nutrition or hydration, for example. Family members of patients can be reluctant to adopt such orders because they wrongly interpret them to mean "no care." However, employing the newly proposed "comfort feeding only" order reframes the end-of-life choice in terms of what is done for the patient rather than what is not done (Palecek et al., 2010). Similarly, the phrase "do not resuscitate" can have negative connotations for many people (Venneman, Narnor-Harris, Perish, & Hamilton, 2008), leading some practitioners to call for using instead the phrase "allow natural death," which avoids the false care/no care dichotomy entailed in the language of current orders to forego resuscitation (Levin et al., 2010). The change in wording makes a difference, as Venneman et al. (2008) found when they examined endorsement rates for different medical orders and discovered that orders labeled "allow natural death" were significantly more likely to be endorsed by laypeople as well as individuals with medical training than orders labeled "do not resuscitate." However, replacing "do not resuscitate" with "allow natural death" may not necessarily improve the precision of end-of-life language given that the treatments implied by both terms are not equivalent (Chen & Youngner, 2008). A do not resuscitate order prohibits cardiopulmonary resuscitation but still allows other life-sustaining treatments to be implemented, whereas an allow natural death order implies that no life-sustaining treatments should be initiated. Clearly, there is still a need to further refine the language used to describe end-of-life medical treatments, but labeling end-of-life terminology in terms of goals of care (rather than the non-goals of care) can frame end-of-life talk in a way that is more consistent with a person's end-of-life care goals and thereby shape the actual decisions that patients and their families make.

Summary

Again, the fallout of the SUPPORT study is an apt illustration of the value of grounding end-of-life research in a multiple goals perspective. When the SUPPORT initiative failed (SUPPORT Principal Investigators, 1995), researchers conducted a close review of the intervention and offered several possible explanations for its ineffectiveness, including that practice patterns and social expectations exert too strong an influence in shaping patients' decision making to be overcome by an individual-level intervention (Lynn et al., 2000). They concluded that targeting patient-level decision making is not the most effective strategy for improving end-of-life care and recommended that efforts instead be directed toward system-level innovation in routine practices.

Although it is likely that system-level intervention offers a powerful opportunity for improving end-of-life care, a multiple goals perspective suggests that the SUPPORT researchers are perhaps too quick to dismiss the potential of patient-level or family-level interventions. Interpreting the available end-of-life literature from a communication perspective offers an alternative explanation for the null findings of the SUPPORT intervention and others like it: The absence of significant associations between communication and end-of-life outcomes is likely due to unsophisticated treatments of communication. By conceptualizing, measuring, and applying communication in terms of attention to interaction goals, a multiple goals perspective shifts the focus from improving how often patients, families, and physicians talk about end-of-life health to improving how well patients, families, and physicians talk about end-of-life health. By focusing on improving how well people talk about end-of-life decisions, an individual-level intervention informed by a multiple goals perspective could afford powerful leverage for changing end-of-life health care for the better.

Conclusion

End-of-life health care is a high-stakes context in which communication is routinely a matter of life or death. The research reviewed here demonstrates the centrality of communication to successful end-of-life decision making. The research also consistently demonstrates that communication has not been studied well thus far in end-of-life research. The call for improving end-of-life communication as a means of improving end-of-life care has been answered with investigations of formal and informal communication about end-of-life health choices that have assessed communication poorly and thus have produced inconsistent findings about what makes communication more or less effective in improving end-of-life health care.

What we need is to study end-of-life communication from a communication perspective. A multiple goals approach enables us to do just that. The theoretical, methodological, and practical implications of a multiple goals perspective for end-of-life research have the potential to provide valuable insight into the connection between end-of-life communication and end-of-life outcomes. Communication scholars are best positioned to conceptualize, measure, and apply communication in end-of-life research. Improving the actual conversations that people have about end-of-life health decisions represents one possible means of solidifying the valuable contribution communication researchers can make in facilitating sound end-of-life decision making and the delivery of high-quality end-of-life health care. My hope is that communication scholars will seize the valuable opportunity presented in end-of-life research to substantively improve one of the most challenging and profound experiences people can face.

Acknowledgments

The author would like to thank John Caughlin for his helpful feedback on this manuscript.

References

Abbott, K. H., Sago, J. G., Breen, C. M., Abernethy, A. P., & Tulsky, J. A. (2001). Families looking back: One year after discussion of withdrawal or withholding of life-sustaining support. *Critical Care Medicine*, *29*, 197–201. doi:10.1097/00003246–200101000–00040

Aging With Dignity. (2013). Five Wishes. Retrieved from www.agingwithdignity.org/five-wishes.php

Ahrens, T., Yancey, V., & Kollef, M. (2003). Improving family communication at the end of life: Implications for length of stay in the intensive care unit and resource use. *American Journal of Critical Care*, *12*, 317–324.

Alexander, S. C., Keitz, S. A., Sloane, R., & Tulsky, J. A. (2006). A controlled trial of a short course to improve residents' communication with patients at the end of life. *Academic Medicine*, *81*, 1008–1012. doi:10.1097/01.ACM.0000242580.83851.ad

American Psychological Association, Working Group on Assisted Suicide and End-of-Life Decisions. (2000). *Report of the APA Working Group on Assisted Suicide and End-of-Life Decisions.* Retrieved from www.apa.org/pubs/info/reports/aseol-full.pdf

Ayalon, L., Bachner, Y. G., Dwolatzky, T., & Heinik, J. (2012). Preferences for end-of-life treatment: Concordance between older adults with dementia or mild cognitive impairment and their spouses. *International Psychogeriatrics*, *24*, 1798–1804. doi:10.1017/S1041610212000877

Babcock, C. W., & Robinson, L. E. (2011). A novel approach to hospital palliative care: An expanded role for counselors. *Journal of Palliative Medicine*, *14*, 493–500. doi:10.1089/jpm.2010.0432

Back, A. L., Anderson, W. G., Bunch, L., Marr, L. A., Wallace, J. A., Yang, H. B., & Arnold, R. M. (2008). Communication about cancer near the end of life. *Cancer*, *113*, 1897–1910. doi:10.1002/cncr.23653

Back, A. L., Arnold, R. M., Baile, W. F., Fryer-Edwards, K. A., Alexander, S. C., Barley, G. E., . . . Tulsky, J. A. (2007). Efficacy of communication skills training for giving bad news and discussing transitions to palliative care. *Archives of Internal Medicine*, *167*, 453–460. doi:10.1001/archinte.167.5.453

Baile, W., Buckman, R., Lenzi, R., Blober, G., Beale, E., & Kudelka, A. (2000). SPIKES—a six step protocol for delivering bad news: Application to the patient with cancer. *Oncologist*, *5*, 302–311. doi:10.1634/theoncologist.5–4-302

Barrio-Cantalejo, I., Molina-Ruiz, A., Simón-Lorda, P., Cámara-Medina, C., López, I. T., del Águila, M. M. R., . . . Bailón-Gómez, R. M. (2009). Advance directives and proxies' predictions about patients' treatment preferences. *Nursing Ethics*, *16*, 93–109. doi:10.1177/0969733008097995

Berger, C. R. (2005). Interpersonal communication: Theoretical perspectives, future prospects. *Journal of Communication*, *55*, 415–447. doi:10.1111/j.1460–2466.2005.tb02680.x

Billings, J. A. (2011). The end-of-life family meeting in intensive care part I: Indications, outcomes, and family needs. *Journal of Palliative Medicine*, *14*, 1042–1050. doi:10.1089/jpm.2011.0038

Biola, H., Sloane, P. D., Williams, C. S., Daaleman, T. P., Williams, S. W., & Zimmerman, S. (2007). Physician communication with family caregivers of long-term care residents at the end of life. *Journal of the American Geriatrics Society, 55*, 846–856. doi:10.1111/j.1532–5415.2007.01179.x

Black, B. S., Fogarty, L. A., Phillips, H., Finucane, T., Loreck, D. J., Baker, A., . . . Rabins, P. V. (2009). Surrogate decision makers' understanding of dementia patients' prior wishes for end-of-life care. *Journal of Aging and Health, 21*, 627–650. doi:10.1177/0898264309333316

Bonnaud-Antignac, A., Campion, L., Pottier, P., & Supiot, S. (2010). Videotaped simulated interviews to improve medical students' skills in disclosing a diagnosis of cancer. *Psycho-Oncology, 9*, 975–981. doi:10.1002/pon.1649

Boquet, J. R., Oliver, D. P., Wittenberg-Lyles, E., Doorenbos, A. Z., & Demiris, G. (2011). Taking care of a dying grandparent: Case studies of grandchildren in the hospice caregiver role. *American Journal of Hospice and Palliative Medicine, 28*, 564–568. doi:10.1177/1049909111405644

Brauner, D. J. (2010). Reconsidering default medicine. *Journal of the American Geriatrics Society, 58*, 599–601. doi:10.1111/j.1532–5415.2010.02743.x

Brock, D. W. (1992). What is the moral basis of the authority of family members to act as surrogates for incompetent patients? *Journal of Clinical Ethics, 3*, 121–123.

Brown, P., & Levinson, S. C. (1987). *Politeness: Some universals in language usage.* New York: Cambridge University Press.

Byock, I. (1997). *Dying well: Peace and possibilities at the end of life.* New York: Riverhead Books.

Byock, I. (2012). *A physician's quest to transform care through the end of life: The best care possible.* New York: Penguin Group.

Cardenas-Turanzas, M., Gaeta, S., Ashoori, A., Price, K. J., & Nates, J. L. (2011). Demographic and clinical determinants of having do not resuscitate orders in the intensive care unit of a comprehensive cancer center. *Journal of Palliative Medicine, 14*, 45–50. doi:10.1089/jpm.2010.0165

Carr, D., & Khodyakov, D. (2007). Health care proxies: Whom do young old adults choose and why? *Journal of Health and Social Behavior, 48*, 180–194. doi:10.1177/002214650704800206

Cartwright, C., Onwuteaka-Philipsen, B. D., Williams, G., Faisst, K., Mortier, F., Nilstun, T., . . . Miccinesi, G. (2007). Physician discussions with terminally ill patients: A cross-national comparison. *Palliative Medicine, 21*, 295–303. doi:10.1177/0269216307079063

Caughlin, J. P. (2010). A multiple goals theory perspective of personal relationships: Conceptual integration and program overview. *Journal of Social and Personal Relationships, 27*, 824–848. doi:10.1177/0265407510373262

Caughlin, J. P., & Afifi, T. D. (2004). When is topic avoidance unsatisfying? Examining moderators of the association between avoidance and satisfaction. *Human Communication Research, 30*, 479–513. doi:10.1093/hcr/30.4.479

Caughlin, J. P., Mikucki-Enyart, S. L., Middleton, A. V., Stone, A. M., & Brown, L. E. (2011). Being open without talking about it: A rhetorical/normative approach to understanding topic avoidance in families after a lung cancer diagnosis. *Communication Monographs, 78*, 409–436. doi:10.1080/03637751.2011.618141

Chen, Y.-Y., & Youngner, S. J. (2008). "Allow natural death" is not equivalent to "do not resuscitate": A response. *Journal of Medical Ethics, 34*, 887–888. doi:10.1136/jme.2008.024570

Chittenden, E. H., Clark, S. T., & Pantilat, S. Z. (2006). Discussing resuscitation preferences with patients: Challenges and rewards. *Journal of Hospital Medicine, 1,* 231–240. doi:10.1002/jhm.110

Chochinov, H. M. (2002). Dignity-conserving care: A new model for palliative care: Helping the patient feel valued. *Journal of the American Medical Association, 287,* 2253–2260. doi:10.1001/jama.287.17.2253

Christensen, K., Haroun, A., Schneiderman, L. J., & Jeste, D. V. (1995). Decision-making capacity for informed consent in the older population. *Bulletin of the American Academy of Psychiatry and the Law, 23,* 353–365.

Clark, R. A., & Delia, J. G. (1979). *Topoi* and rhetorical competence. *Quarterly Journal of Speech, 65,* 187–206. doi:10.1080/00335637909383470

Considine, J. M., & Miller, K. (2010). The dialectics of care: Communicative choices at the end of life. *Health Communication, 25,* 165–174. doi:10.1080/10410230903544951

Dainton, M., & Stafford, L. (1993). Routine maintenance behaviors: A comparison of relationship type, partner similarity, and sex differences. *Journal of Social and Personal Relationships, 10,* 255–271. doi:10.1177/026540759301000206

Danis, M., Garrett, J., Harris, R., & Patrick, D. L. (1994). Stability of choices about life-sustaining treatments. *Annals of Internal Medicine, 120,* 567–573.

Deep, K. S., Green, S. F., Griffith, C. H., & Wilson, J. F. (2007). Medical residents' perspectives on discussions of advanced directives: Can prior experience affect how they approach patients? *Journal of Palliative Medicine, 10,* 712–720. doi:10.1089/jpm.2006.0220

Deep, K. S., Griffith, C. H., & Wilson, J. F. (2008a). Communication and decision making about life-sustaining treatment: Examining the experiences of resident physicians and seriously-ill hospitalized patients. *Journal of General Internal Medicine, 23,* 1877–1882. doi:10.1007/s11606–008–0779–6

Deep, K. S., Griffith, C. H., & Wilson, J. F. (2008b). Discussing preferences for cardiopulmonary resuscitation: What do resident physicians and their hospitalized patients think was decided? *Patient Education and Counseling, 72,* 20–25. doi:10.1016/j.pec.2008.10.017

DeFanti, T. R. (2010). Changing the cultural view and coverage of end-of-life care. *American Journal of Hospice and Palliative Medicine, 27,* 365–368. doi:10.1177/1049909110361732

Degenholtz, H. B., Arnold, R. A., Meisel, A., & Lave, J. R., (2002). Persistence of racial/ethnic disparities in advance care plan documents among nursing home residents. *Journal of the American Geriatrics Society, 50,* 378–381. doi:10.1046/j.1532–5415.2002.50073.x

DesHarnais, S., Carter, R. E., Hennessy, W., Kurent, J. E., & Carter, C. (2007). Lack of concordance between physician and patient: Reports on end-of-life care discussions. *Journal of Palliative Medicine, 10,* 728–740. doi:10.1089/jpm.2006.2543

Detering, K. M., Hancock, A. D., Reade, M. C., & Silvester, W. (2010). The impact of advance care planning on end of life care in elderly patients: Randomised controlled trial. *British Medical Journal, 340,* c1345. doi:1136/bmj.c1345

Dickson, R. P., Engelberg, R. A., Back, A. L., Ford, D. W., & Curtis, J. R. (2012). Internal medicine trainee self-assessments of end-of-life communication skills do not predict assessments of patients, families, or clinician-evaluators. *Journal of Palliative Medicine, 15,* 418–426. doi:10.1089/jpm.2011.0386

Dindia, K. (2003). Definitions and perspectives on relational maintenance communication. In D. J. Canary & M. Dainton (Eds.), *Maintaining relationships through communication: Relational, contextual, and cultural variations* (pp. 1–28). Mahwah, NJ: Erlbaum.

Ditto, P. H. (2009). What would Terri want? In J. L. Werth & D. Blevins (Eds.), *Decision making near the end of life: Issues, developments, and future directions* (pp. 209–229). New York: Routledge.

Ditto, P. H., Danks, J. H., Smucker, W. D., Bookwala, J., Coppola, K. M., Dresser, R., . . . Zyzanski, S. (2001). Advance directives as acts of communication: A randomized controlled trial. *Archives of Internal Medicine, 161*, 421–430. doi:10.1001/archinte.161.3.421

Ditto, P. H., Jacobson, J. A., Smucker, W. D., Danks, J. H., & Fagerlin, A. (2006). Context changes choices: A prospective study of the effects of hospitalization on life-sustaining treatment preferences. *Medical Decision-Making, 26*, 313–322. doi:10.1177/0272989X06290494

Donovan-Kicken, E., & Caughlin, J. P. (2010). A multiple goals perspective on topic avoidance and relationship satisfaction in the context of breast cancer. *Communication Monographs, 77*, 231–256. doi:10.1080/03637751003758219

Downey, L., Engelberg, R. A., Curtis, J. R., Lafferty, W. E., & Patrick, D. L. (2009). Shared priorities for the end-of-life period. *Journal of Pain and Symptom Management, 37*, 175–188. doi:10.1016/j.jpainsymman.2008.02.012

Drane, J. F. (1984). Competency to give an informed consent: A model for making clinical assessments. *Journal of the American Medical Association, 252*, 925–927. doi:10.1001/jama.252.7.925

Eggly, S., Penner, L. A., Greene, M., Harper, F. W., Ruckdeschel, J. C., & Albrecht, T. L. (2006). Information seeking during "bad news" oncology interactions: Question asking by patients and their companions. *Social Science and Medicine, 63*, 2974–2985. doi:10.1016/j.socscimed.2006.07.012

Exline, J. J., Prince-Paul, M., Root, B. L., Peereboom, K. S., & Worthington, E. L., Jr. (2012). Forgiveness, depressive symptoms, and communication at the end of life: A study with family members of hospice patients. *Journal of Palliative Medicine, 15*, 1113–1119. doi:10.1089/jpm.2012.0138

Fagerlin, A., Ditto, P. H., Danks, J. H., Houts, R. M., & Smucker, W. D. (2001). Projection in surrogate decisions about life-sustaining medical treatments. *Health Psychology, 20*, 166–175. doi:10.1037/0278–6133.20.3.166

Fagerlin, A., Ditto, P. H., Hawkins, N. A., Schneider, C. E., & Smucker, W. D. (2002). The use of advance directives in end-of-life decision making. *American Behavioral Scientist, 46*, 268–283. doi:10.1177/000276402236678

Field, M. J., & Cassel, C. K. (Eds.). (1997). *Approaching death: Improving care at the end of life*. Washington, DC: National Academy Press.

Fine, E., Reid, M. C., Shengelia, R., & Adelman, R. D. (2010). Directly observed patient-physician discussions in palliative and end-of-life care: A systematic review of the literature. *Journal of Palliative Medicine, 13*, 595–603. doi:10.1089/jpm.2009.0388

Fineberg, I. C., Kawashima, M., & Asch, S. M. (2011). Communication with families facing life-threatening illness: A research-based model for family conferences. *Journal of Palliative Medicine, 14*, 421–427. doi:10.1089/jpm.2010.0436

Freeborne, N., Lynn, J., & Desbiens, N. A. (2000). Insights about dying from the SUPPORT project. *Journal of the American Geriatric Society, 48*, S199–S205.

Furman, C. D., Head, B., Lazor, B., Casper, B., & Ritchie, C. S. (2006). Evaluation of an educational intervention to encourage advance directive discussions between medicine residents and patients. *Journal of Palliative Medicine*, 9, 964–967. doi:10.1089/jpm.2006.9.964

Givens, J. L., Lopez, R. P., Mazor, K. M., & Mitchell, S. L. (2012). Sources of stress for family members of nursing home residents with advanced dementia. *Alzheimer Disease and Associated Disorders*, 26, 254–259. doi:10.1097/WAD.0b013e31823899e4

Goldsmith, D. J. (2001). A normative approach to the study of uncertainty and communication. *Journal of Communication*, 51, 514–533. doi:10.1111/j.1460–2466.2001. tb02894.x

Goldsmith, D. J. (2004). *Communicating social support*. New York: Cambridge University Press.

Goldsmith, D. J., & Domann, K. (2013). The meanings of "open communication" among couples coping with a cardiac event. *Journal of Communication*, 63, 266–286. doi:10.1111/jcom.12021

Goldsmith, D. J., Lindholm, K. A., & Bute, J. J. (2006). Dilemmas of talking about lifestyle changes among couples coping with a cardiac event. *Social Science and Medicine*, 63, 2079–2090. doi:10.1016/j.socscimed.2006.05.005

Goldsmith, J., Wittenberg-Lyles, E., Ragan, S., & Nussbaum, J. F. (2011). Life span and end-of-life health communication. In T. L. Thompson, R. Parrott, & J. F. Nussbaum (Eds.), *The Routledge handbook of health communication* (2nd ed., pp. 441–454). New York: Routledge.

Gready, R. M., Ditto, P. H., Danks, J. H., Coppola, K. M., Lockhart, L. K., & Smucker, W. D. (2000). Actual and perceived stability of preferences for life-sustaining treatment. *Journal of Clinical Ethics*, 11, 334–346.

Hickman, S. E. (2002). Improving communication near the end of life. *American Behavioral Scientist*, 46, 252–267. doi:10.1177/000276402236677

Hinds, P. S., Oakes, L. L., Hicks, J., Powell, B., Srivastava, D. K., Baker, J. N., . . . Furman, W. L. (2012). Parent-clinician communication intervention during end-of-life decision making for children with incurable cancer. *Journal of Palliative Medicine*, 15, 916–922. doi:10.1089/jpm.2012.0006

Hines, S. C., Glover, J. J., Babrow, A. S., Holley, J. L., Badzek, L. A., & Moss, A. H. (2001). Improving advance care planning by accommodating family preferences. *Journal of Palliative Medicine*, 4, 481–489. doi:10.1089/109662101753381629

Hudson, P., Thomas, T., Quinn, K., & Aranda, S. (2009). Family meetings in palliative care: Are they effective? *Palliative Medicine*, 23, 150–157. doi:10.1177/0269216308099960

Jackson, V. A., Mack, J., Matsuyama, R., Lakoma, M. D., Sullivan, A.M., Arnold, R. M., . . . Block, S. D. (2008). A qualitative study of oncologists' approaches to end-of-life care. *Journal of Palliative Medicine*, 11, 893–906. doi:10.1089/jpm.2007.2480

Jansen, S.J.T., Stiggelbout, A. M., Nooij, M. A., Noordijk, E. M., & Kievit, J. (2000). Response shift in quality of life measurement in early-stage breast cancer patients undergoing radiotherapy. *Quality of Life Research*, 9, 603–615. doi:10.1023/A:1008928617014

Janssen, D.J.A., Engelberg, R. A., Wouters, E.F.M., & Curtis, J. R. (2012). Advance care planning for patients with COPD: Past, present and future. *Patient Education and Counseling*, 86, 19–24. doi:10.1016/j.pec.1011.01.007

Karasz, A., Dyche, L., & Selwyn, P. (2003). Physicians' experiences of caring for late-stage HIV patients in the post-HAART era: Challenges and adaptations. *Social Science and Medicine*, 57, 1609–1620. doi:10.1016/S0277–9536(03)00013–3

Keeley, M. P. (2007). "Turning toward death together": The functions of messages during final conversations in close relationships. *Journal of Social and Personal Relationships, 24,* 225–253. doi:10.1177/0265407507075412

Keeley, M., & Baldwin, P. (2012). Final conversations, phase 2: Children and everyday communication. *Journal of Loss and Trauma, 17,* 376–387. doi:10.1002/pon.3107

King, D. A., & Quill, T. (2006). Working with families in palliative care: One size does not fit all. *Journal of Palliative Medicine, 9,* 704–715. doi:10.1089/jpm.2006.9.704

Kirchhoff, K. T., Hammes, B. J., & Kehl, K. A., Briggs, L. A., & Brown, R. L. (2010). Effect of a disease-specific planning intervention on surrogate understanding of patient goals for future medical treatment. *Journal of the American Geriatrics Society, 58,* 1233–1240. doi:10.1111/j.1532–5415.2010.02760.x

Kramer, B. J., Kavanaugh, M., Trentham-Dietz, A., Walsh, M., & Yonker, J. A. (2010). Predictors of family conflict at the end of life: The experience of spouses and adult children of persons with lung cancer. *The Gerontologist, 50,* 215–225. doi:10.1093/geront/gnp121

Lahn M., Friedman, B., Bijur, P., Haughey, M., & Gallagher, E. J. (2001). Advance directives in skilled nursing facility residents transferred to emergency departments. *Academic Emergency Medicine, 8,* 1158–1162. doi:10.1111/j.1553–2712.2001.tb01133.x

Lamba, S., Murphy, P., McVicker, S., Smith, J. H., & Mosenthal, A. C. (2012). Changing end-of-life care practice for liver transplant service patients: Structured palliative care intervention in the surgical intensive care unit. *Journal of Pain and Symptom Management, 44,* 508–519. doi:10.1016/j/jpainsymman.2011.10.018

Larson, D. G., & Tobin, D. R. (2000). End-of-life conversations: Evolving practice and theory. *Journal of the American Medical Association, 284,* 1573–1578. doi:10.1001/jama.284.12.1573

Lautrette, A., Darmon, M., Megarbane, B., Joly, L. M., Chevret, S., Adrie, C., . . . Azoulay, E. (2007). A communication strategy and brochure for relatives of patients dying in the ICU. *New England Journal of Medicine, 356,* 469–478. doi:10.1056/NEJMoa063446

Lelorain, S., Brédart, A., Dolbeault, S., & Sultan, S. (2012). A systematic review of the associations between empathy measures and patient outcomes in cancer care. *Psycho-Oncology, 21,* 1255–1264. doi:10.1002/pon

Levin, T. T., Moreno, B., Silvester, W., & Kissane, D. W. (2010). End-of-life communication in the intensive care unit. *General Hospital Psychiatry, 32,* 433–442. doi:10.1016/j.genhosppsych.2010.04.007

Libbus, K. M., & Russell, C. (1995). Congruence of decisions between patients and their potential surrogates about life-sustaining therapies. *IMAGE: Journal of Nursing Scholarship, 2,* 135–140. doi:10.1111/j.1547–5069.1995.tb00837.x

Limerick, M. (2002). Communicating with surrogate decision-makers in end-of-life situations: Substitutive descriptive language for the healthcare provider. *American Journal of Hospice and Palliative Care, 19,* 376–380. doi:10.1177/104990910201900606

Lingler, J. H., Hirschman, K. B., Garand, L., Dew, M. A., Becker, J. T., Schulz, R., & DeKosky, S. T. (2008). Frequency and correlates of advance planning among cognitively impaired older adults. *American Journal of Geriatric Psychiatry, 16,* 643–649. doi:10.1097/JGP.0b013e31816b7324

Lopez, R. P., & Guarino, A. J. (2011). Uncertainty and decision making for residents with dementia. *Clinical Nursing Research, 20,* 228–240. doi:10.1177/1054773811405521

Lynn, J., Arkes, H. R., Stevens, M., Cohn, F., Koenig, B., Fox, E., . . . Tsevat, J. (2000). Rethinking fundamental assumptions: SUPPORT's implications for future reform. *Journal of the American Geriatrics Society, 48*, S214–S221.

McFarland, K. F., & Rhoades, D. R. (2006). End-of-life care: A retreat format for residents. *Journal of Palliative Medicine, 9*, 82–89. doi:10.1089/jpm.2006.9.82

McLaughlin, M. L. (1984). *Conversation: How talk is organized.* Beverly Hills, CA: Sage.

McQuellon, R. P., & Cowan, M. A. (2000). Turning toward death together: Conversation in mortal time. *American Journal of Hospice and Palliative Care, 17*, 312–318. doi:10.1177/104990910001700508

Melhado, L., & Bushy, A. (2011). Exploring uncertainty in advance care planning in African Americans: Does low health literacy influence decision making preferences at end of life. *American Journal of Hospice and Palliative Medicine, 28*, 495–500. doi:10.1177/1049909110398005

Menikoff, J. (2001). *Law and bioethics: An introduction.* Washington, DC: Georgetown University Press.

Moorman, S. M. (2011a). Older adults' preferences for independent or delegated end-of-life medical decision making. *Journal of Aging and Health, 23*, 135–157. doi:10.1177/0898264310385114

Moorman, S. M., (2011b). The importance of feeling understood in marital conversations about end-of-life health care. *Journal of Social and Personal Relationships, 28*, 100–116. doi:10.1177/0265407510386137

Moorman, S. M., Hauser, R. M., & Carr, D. (2009). Do older adults know their spouses' end-of-life treatment preferences? *Research on Aging, 31*, 463–491. doi:10.1177/0164027509333683

Morrison, M. F. (1998). Obstacles to doctor-patient communication at the end of life. In M. D. Steinberg & S. J. Youngner (Eds.), *End-of-life decisions: A psychosocial perspective* (pp. 109–136). Washington, DC: American Psychiatric Press.

Natan, M. B., Garfinkel, D., & Shachar, I. (2010). End-of-life needs as perceived by terminally ill older adult patients, family and staff. *European Journal of Oncology Nursing, 14*, 299–303. doi:10.1016/j.ejon.2010.05.002

Norris, K., Merriman, M. P., Curtis, J. R., Asp, C., Tuholske, L., & Byock, I. R. (2007). Next of kin perspectives on the experience of end-of-life care in a community setting. *Journal of Palliative Medicine, 10*, 1101–1115. doi:10.1089/jpm.2006.2546

O'Keefe, B. J., & Delia, J. G. (1982). Impression formation and message production. In M. E. Roloff & C. R. Berger (Eds.), *Social cognition and communication* (pp. 33–72). Beverly Hills, CA: Sage.

Palecek, E. J., Teno, J. M., Casarett, D. J., Hanson, L. C., Rhodes, R. L., & Mitchell, S. L. (2010). Comfort feeding only: A proposal to bring clarity to decision-making regarding difficulty with eating for persons with advanced dementia. *Journal of the American Geriatrics Society, 58*, 580–584. doi:10.1111/j.1532–5415.2010.02740.x

Parks, S. M., Winter, L., Santana, A. J., Parker, B., Diamond, J. J., Rose, M., & Myers, R. E. (2011). Family factors in end-of-life decision-making: Family conflict and proxy relationship. *Journal of Palliative Medicine, 14*, 179–184. doi:10.1089/jpm.2010.0353

Patient Self-Determination Act, U.S. P.L. 101–508 (1990). Washington, DC: US Code.

Pautex, S., Herrmann, F. R., & Zulian, G. B. (2008). Role of advance directives in palliative care units: A prospective study. *Palliative Medicine, 22*, 835–841. doi:10.1177/0269216308094336

Pecchioni, L. L. (2001). Implicit decision-making in family caregiving. *Journal of Social and Personal Relationships, 18*, 219–237. doi:10.1177/0265407501182004

Pew Research Center for the People and the Press. (2006). *Strong public support for right to die: More Americans discussing—and planning—end-of-life treatment.* Retrieved from www.people-press.org/2006/01/05/strong-public-support-for-right-to-die/

Physician Orders for Life-Sustaining Treatment. (2013). Retrieved from www.cdph.ca.gov/programs/LnC/Documents/MDS30-ApprovedPOLSTForm.pdf

President's Commission for the Study of Ethical Problems in Medicine and Biomedical and Behavioral Research. (1983). *Deciding to forego life-sustaining treatment: Ethical, medical, and legal issues in treatment decisions.* Washington, DC: Author. Retrieved from http://bioethics.georgetown.edu/pcbe/reports/past_commissions/deciding_to_forego_tx.pdf

Proulx, K., & Jacelon, C. (2004). Dying with dignity: The good patient versus the good death. *American Journal of Hospice and Palliative Medicine, 21*, 116–120. doi:10.1177/104990910402100209

Quin, J. R., Schmitt, M., Baggs, J. G., Norton, S. A., Dombeck, M. T., & Sellers, C. R. (2012). Family members' informal roles in end-of-life decision making in adult intensive care units. *American Journal of Critical Care, 21*, 43–51. doi:10.4037/ajcc2012520

Rady, M. Y., & Johnson, D. J. (2004). Admission to intensive care unit at the end-of-life: Is it an informed decision? *Palliative Medicine, 18*, 705–711. doi:10.1191/0269216304pm959oa

Rich, S. E., Gruber-Baldini, A. L., Quinn, C. C., & Zimmerman, S. I. (2009). Discussion as a factor in racial disparity in advance directive completion at nursing home admission. *Journal of the American Geriatrics Society, 57*, 146–152. doi:10.1111/j.1532-5415.2008.02090.x

Schneiderman, L. J., Kronick, R., Kaplan, R. M., Anderson, J. P., & Langer, R. D. (1992). Effects of offering advance directives on medical treatments and costs. *Annals of Internal Medicine, 117*, 599–606.

Schonfeld, T. L., Stevens, E. A., Lampman, M. A., & Lyons, W. L. (2012). Assessing challenges in end-of-life conversations with elderly patients with multiple comorbidities. *American Journal of Hospice and Palliative Medicine, 29*, 260–267. doi:10.1177/1049909111418778

Scott, A. M. & Caughlin, J. P. (2011, November). *Enacted and perceived goal attention in family conversations about end-of-life decisions.* Paper presented at the annual convention of the National Communication Association, New Orleans, LA.

Scott, A. M., & Caughlin, J. P. (2012). Managing multiple goals in family discourse about end-of-life health decisions. *Research on Aging, 34*, 670–691. doi:10.1177/0164027512446942

Sessums, L. L., Zembrzuska, H., & Jackson, J. L. (2011). Does this patient have medical decision-making capacity? *Journal of the American Medical Association, 306*, 420–427. doi:10.1001/jama.2011.1023

Seymour, J., Gott, M., Bellamy, G., Ahmedzai, S. H., & Clark, D. (2004). Planning for the end of life: The views of older people about advance care statements. *Social Science and Medicine, 59*, 57–68. doi:10.1016/j.socscimed.2003.10.005

Shalowitz, D. I., Garrett-Mayer, E., & Wendler, D. (2006). The accuracy of surrogate decision makers. *Archives of Internal Medicine, 166*, 493–497. doi:10.1001/archinte.166.5.493

Sharma, R. K., Hughes, M. T., Nolan, M. T., Tudor, C., Kub, J., Terry, P. B., & Sulmasy, D. P. (2011). Family understanding of seriously-ill patient preferences for family involvement in healthcare decision making. *Journal of General Internal Medicine*, *26*, 881–886. doi:10.1007/s11606–011–1717–6

Shaw, D. (2012). A direct advance on advance directives. *Bioethics*, *26*, 267–274. doi:10.1111/j.1467–8519.2010.01853.x

Sillars, A. L., & Kalbfleisch, P. J. (1989). Implicit and explicit decision-making styles in couples. In D. Brinberg & J. Jaccard (Eds.), *Dyadic decision making* (pp. 179–215). New York: Springer.

Silveira, M. J., Kim, S.Y.H., & Langa, K. M. (2010). Advance directives and outcomes of surrogate decision making before death. *The New England Journal of Medicine*, *362*, 1211–1218. doi:10.1056/NEJMsa0907901

Siminoff, L. A., Rose, J. H., Zhang, A., & Zyzanski, S. J. (2006). Measuring discord in treatment decision-making: Progress toward development of a cancer communication and decision-making assessment tool. *Psycho-Oncology*, *15*, 528–540. doi:10.1002/pon.989

Singer, P. A., Martin, D. K., & Kelner, M. (1999). Quality end-of-life care: Patients' perspectives. *Journal of the American Medical Association*, *281*, 263–268. doi:10.1001/jama.281.2.163

Slort, W., Schweitzer, B.P.M., Blankenstein, A. H., Abarshi, E. A., Riphagen, I. I., Echteld, M.A., . . . Deliens, L. (2012). Perceived barriers and facilitators for general practitioner-patient communication in palliative care: A systematic review. *Palliative Medicine*, *25*, 613–629. doi:10.1177/0269216310395987

Steinhauser, K. E., Christakis, N. A., Clipp, E. C., McNeilly, M., McIntyre, L., & Tulsky, J. A. (2000). Factors considered important at the end of life by patients, family, physicians, and other care providers. *Journal of the American Medical Association*, *284*, 2476–2482. doi:10.1001/jama.284.19.2476

Suhl, J., Simons, P., Reedy, T., & Garrick, T. (1994). Myth of substituted judgment: Surrogate decision making regarding life support is unreliable. *Archives of Internal Medicine*, *154*, 90–96. doi:10.1001/archinte.154.1.90

Sulmasy, D. P., & Snyder, L. (2010). Substituted interests and best judgments: An integrated model of surrogate decision making. *Journal of the American Medical Association*, *304*, 1946–1947. doi:10.1001/jama.2010.1595

SUPPORT Principal Investigators. (1995). A controlled trial to improve care for seriously ill hospitalized patients: The Study to Understand Prognoses and Preferences for Outcomes and Risks of Treatments (SUPPORT). *Journal of the American Medical Association*, *274*, 1591–1598. doi:10.1001/jama.1995.03530200027032

Swigart, V., Lidz, C., Butterworth, V., & Arnold, A. (1996). Letting go: Family willingness to forgo life support. *Heart and Lung*, *25*, 483–494. doi:10.1016/S0147–9563(96)80051–3

Tarzian, A. J., Neal, M. T., & O'Neil, J. A. (2005). Attitudes, experiences, and beliefs affecting end-of-life decision-making among homeless individuals. *Journal of Palliative Medicine*, *8*, 36–48. doi:10.1089/jpm.2005.8.36

Teno, J. M., Gruneir, A., Schwartz, Z., Nanda, A., & Wetle, T. (2007). Association between advance directives and quality of end-of-life care: A national study. *Journal of the American Geriatrics Society*, *55*, 189–194. doi:10.1111/j.1532–5415.2007.01045.x

Teno, J., Lynn, J., Wenger, N., Phillips, R. S., Murphy, D. P., Connors, A. F., Jr., . . . Knaus, W. A. (1997). Advance directives for seriously ill hospitalized patients: Effectiveness with the Patient Self-Determination Act and the SUPPORT intervention. *Journal of the American Geriatrics Society, 45*, 500–507.

Thompson, T. (2011). Hope and the act of informed dialogue: A delicate balance at end of life. *Journal of Language and Social Psychology, 30*, 177–192. doi:10.1177/0261927X10397150

Tilden, V. P., Tolle, S. W., Nelson, C. A., & Fields, J. (2001). Family decision-making to withdraw life-sustaining treatments from hospitalized patients. *Nursing Research, 50*, 105–115. doi:10.1097/00006199-200103000-00006

Travis, S. S., Loving, G. L., McClanahan, L., & Bernard, M. A. (2001). Hospitalization patterns and palliation in the last year of life among residents in long-term care. *The Gerontologist, 41*, 153–160. doi:10.1093/geront/41.2.153

Trice, E. D., & Prigerson, H. G. (2009). Communication in end-stage cancer: Review of the literature and future research. *Journal of Health Communication, 14*, 95–108. doi:10.1080/10810730902806786

Tulsky, J. A. (2005). Beyond advance directives: Importance of communication skills at the end of life. *Journal of the American Medical Association, 294*, 359–65. doi:10.1001/jama.294.3.359

Turan, B., Goldstein, M. K., Garber, A. M., & Carstensen, L. J. (2011). Knowing loved ones' end-of-life health care wishes: Attachment security predicts caregivers' accuracy. *Health Psychology, 30*, 814–818. doi:10.1037/a0025664

Venneman, S. S., Narnor-Harris, P., Perish, M., & Hamilton, M. (2008). "Allow natural death" versus "do not resuscitate": Three words that can change a life. *Journal of Medical Ethics, 34*, 2–6. doi:10.1136/jme.2006.018317

Villagran, M., Goldsmith, J., Wittenberg-Lyles, E., & Baldwin, P. (2010). Creating COMFORT: A communication-based model for breaking bad news. *Communication Education, 59*, 220–234. doi:10.1080/03634521003624031

Volandes, A. E., Paasche-Orlow, M., Gillick, M. R., Cook, E. F., Shaykevich, S., Abbo, E. D., & Lehmann, L. (2008). Health literacy not race predicts end-of-life care preferences. *Journal of Palliative Medicine, 11*, 754–762. doi:10.1089/jpm.2007.0224

Wallace, S. K., Martin, C. G., Shaw, A. D., & Price, K. J. (2001). Influence of an advance directive on the initiation of life support technology in critically ill cancer patients. *Critical Care Medicine, 29*, 2294–2298. doi:10.1097/00003246-200112000-00010

Weiner, J. S., & Roth, J. (2006). Avoiding iatrogenic harm to patient and family while discussing goals of care near the end of life. *Journal of Palliative Medicine, 9*, 451–463. doi:10.1089/jpm.2006.9.451

Weissman, D. E., Quill, T. E., & Arnold, R. M. (2010). The family meeting: End-of-life goal setting and future planning. *Journal of Palliative Medicine, 13*, 462–463. doi:10.1089/jpm.2010.9846

Wenger, N. S., Kanouse, D. E., Collins, R. L., Liu, H., Schuster, M. A., Gifford, A. L., . . . Shapiro, M. F. (2001). End-of-life discussions and preferences among persons with HIV. *Journal of the American Medical Association, 285*, 2880–2887. doi:10.1001/jama.285.22.2880

Wenger, N. S., Phillips, R. S., Teno, J. M., Oye, R. K., Dawson, N. V., Liu, H., . . . Lynn, J. (2000). Physician understanding of patient resuscitation preferences: Insights and clinical implications. *Journal of the American Geriatrics Society, 48*, S44–S51.

Wentlandt, K., Burman, D., Swami, N., Hales, S., Rydall, A., Rodin, G., . . . Zimmerman, C. (2012). Preparation for the end of life in patients with advanced cancer and association with communication with professional caregivers. *Psycho-Oncology, 21,* 868–876. doi:10.1002/pon.1995

Wilson, S. R., & Feng, H. (2007). Interaction goals and message production: Conceptual and methodological developments. In D. R. Roskos-Ewoldsen & J. L. Monahan (Eds.), *Communication and social cognition: Theories and methods* (pp. 71–95). Mahwah, NJ: Erlbaum.

Winter, L., & Parks, S. M. (2008). Family discord and proxy decision makers' end-of-life treatment decisions. *Journal of Palliative Medicine, 11,* 1109–1114. doi:10.1089/jpm.2008.0039

Winter, L., & Parks, S. M. (2012). The reluctance to burden others as a value in end-of-life decision making: A source of inaccuracy in substituted judgment. *Journal of Health Psychology, 17,* 179–188. doi:10.1177/1359105311414956

Winter, L., Parks, S. M., & Diamond, J. J. (2010). Ask a different question, get a different answer: Why living wills are poor guides to care preferences at the end of life. *Journal of Palliative Medicine, 13,* 567–572. doi:10.1089/jpm.2009.0311

Wittenberg-Lyles, E. (2005). Information sharing in interdisciplinary team meetings: An evaluation of hospice goals. *Qualitative Health Research, 15,* 1377–1391. doi:10.1177/1049732305282857

Wittenberg-Lyles, E., Goldsmith, J., Ferrell, B., & Ragan, S. L. (2013). *Communication in palliative nursing.* New York: Oxford University Press.

Wittenberg-Lyles, E., Goldsmith, J., & Ragan, S. (2010). The COMFORT Initiative: Palliative nursing and the centrality of communication. *Journal of Hospice and Palliative Nursing, 12,* 282–292. doi:10.1097/NJH.0b013e3181ebb45e

Wittenberg-Lyles, E., Goldsmith, J., & Ragan, S. (2011). The shift to early palliative care: A typology of illness journeys and the role of nursing. *Clinical Journal of Oncology Nursing, 15,* 304–310. doi:10.1188/11.CJON.304–310

Wittenberg-Lyles, E., Goldsmith, J., Ragan, S., & Sanchez-Reilly, S. (2010). Medical students' views and ideas about palliative care communication training. *American Journal of Hospice and Palliative Medicine, 27,* 38–49. doi:10.1177/1049909109347327

Wittenberg-Lyles, E., Goldsmith, J., Richardson, B., Hallett, J. S., & Clark, R. (2013). The practical nurse: A case for COMFORT communication training. *American Journal of Hospice and Palliative Medicine, 30,* 162–166. doi:10.1177/1049909112446848

Wittenberg-Lyles, E., Goldsmith, J., Sanchez-Reilly, S., & Ragan, S. (2008). Communication a terminal prognosis in a palliative care setting: Deficiencies in current communication training protocols. *Social Science and Medicine, 66,* 2356–2365. doi:10.1016/j.socscimed.2008.01.042

Wittenberg-Lyles, E., Oliver, D. P., Demiris, G., & Baldwin, P. (2010). The ACTive Intervention in hospice interdisciplinary team meetings: Exploring family caregiver and hospice team communication. *Journal of Computer-Mediated Communication, 15,* 465–481. doi:10.1111/j.1083–6101.2010.01502.x

Wright, A. A., Zhang, B., Ray, A., Mack, J. W., Trice, E., Balboni, T., . . . Prigerson, H. G. (2008). Associations between end-of-life discussions, patient mental health, medical care near death, and caregiver bereavement adjustment. *Journal of the American Medical Association, 300,* 1665–1673. doi:10.1001/jama.300.14.1665

Yoo, J. W., Nakagawa, S., & Kim, S. (2012). Integrative palliative care, advance directives, and hospital outcomes of critically ill older adults. *American Journal of Hospice and Palliative Medicine, 29,* 655–662. doi:10.1177/1049909111435813

Zhang, A. Y., & Siminoff, L. A. (2003). Silence and cancer: Why do families and patients fail to communicate? *Health Communication, 15,* 415–429. doi:10.1207/ S15327027HC1504_03

Zhang, B., Wright, A. A., Huskamp, H. A., Nilsson, M. E., Maciejewski, M. L., Earle, C. C., . . . Prigerson, H. G., (2009). Health care costs in the last week of life: Associations with end of life conversations. *Archives of Internal Medicine, 169,* 480–488. doi:10.1001/archinternmed.2008.587

CHAPTER CONTENTS

9 Family Communication About Cancer Treatment Decision Making

A Description of the DECIDE Typology

Janice L. Krieger

The Ohio State University

This chapter reviews key theoretical perspectives on treatment decision making, examines situation and relational influences on the treatment decision-making process, reviews models of patient and family participation in treatment decision making, and proposes a typology for understanding the different ways in which families negotiate treatment decisions. The typology suggests new insights for theorizing decision-making processes related to cancer treatment and offers strategies for integrating the typology into clinical practice in order to improve medical and psychosocial outcomes for patients and their families.

Cancer is the second leading of cause of death in the United States, with approximately 1,500 people dying from cancer each day (Jemal, Siegel, Xu, & Ward, 2010; National Center for Health Statistics, 2012). Given the serious consequences associated with cancer, most individuals are overwhelmed with emotion when they are diagnosed. Despite the emotional difficulties associated with coming to terms with one's illness, patients must often make rapid decisions about what type of treatment to pursue. The complexity of decision making, particularly under time pressure, has rendered the topic of treatment decision making of great interest to scholars in both social and medical sciences.

Current approaches for mapping patient involvement in clinical decision making have focused almost exclusively on the relationship between patients and their health care providers (Charles & DeMaio, 1993; Elwyn, Edwards, & Kinnersley, 1999; Emanuel & Emanuel, 1992). Although health care providers are important sources of health information and social influence, there is growing evidence that other members of a patient's social network also shape the decision-making process. Recent studies find that patients frequently discuss treatment options with significant others when deciding what medical treatments to pursue (Chouliara, Kearney, Stott, Molassiotis, & Miller, 2004; Schumacher et al., 2008; Weber, Haunani Solomon, & Meyer, 2013). Further, spouses, children, and extended family members have all been identified by patients as a significant source of influence during the treatment decision-making process (Avis, Smith, Link, Hortobagyi, & Rivera, 2006; Mills et al., 2006; Schoenberg, Peters, & Drew, 2003).

The process by which family members influence important health care decisions is understudied. However, available evidence suggests that family conversations about medical decision making can spark serious interpersonal conflict (Pitts, Raup-Krieger, Kundrat, & Nussbaum, 2009; Speice et al., 2000). The presence of family conflict associated with medical decision making is of clinical importance because it can reduce patient adherence to their treatment regime (DiMatteo, 2004) and increase strain on patients and family caregivers (Scharlach, Li, & Dalvi, 2006).

The purpose of the current chapter is to extend the literature on communication and health decision making by identifying the interpersonal processes that influence how cancer clinical trial treatment decisions are made and how those processes might influence decision-making outcomes. In doing so, it fulfills a need for theorizing that extends beyond the physician-patient dyad to fill theoretical gaps in knowledge about the process by which family members become involved in patient care (Charles, Gafni, & Whelan, 1997; Epstein, 2013; Siminoff, Rose, Zhang, & Zyzanski, 2006). Specifically, the chapter describes current models of medical decisions, reviews research on the influences of family on medical decision making, and proposes the Family DECIDE (*Deter*minants of *Clinical Decision*-Making) typology that describes how patient and family goals for patient autonomy or patient interdependence yields different family decision-making styles.

Theoretical Models of Cancer Treatment Decision-Making Processes

Theoretical models of cancer treatment decision-making processes center on the role of cognition for making particular choices. In many cases, the focus on cognition has resulted in decision making being conceptualized as a "whole mind" or individual-level process (Epstein, 2013, p. 200). Within individual psychological perspectives, current theorizing tends to focus on either micro- or macro-cognitive approaches. Micro-cognitive approaches are built on rational reasoning (value analytic), such as in classical decision-making (CDM) theory. Macro-cognitive approaches focus on intuitive "thinking," a prime example of which is naturalistic decision-making (NDM) theories. More recently, there has been a shift in the decision-making literature in considering the merits of "shared mind" or distributive cognition for understanding the process of mutual influence in clinical treatment decision making (Epstein, 2013). The following section provides a brief synopsis of each of these three theoretical traditions.

Whole Mind: Analytic and Intuitive Decision Making

Whole-mind perspectives on decision making focus on the patient in isolation. As such, they include both value-analytic and intuitive decision-making theories. The most well-known value-analytic approach to treatment decision making is classical decision theory (CDT). CDT defines decision making as a choice among a range of available alternatives. The focus is on explaining the circumstances under which one behavioral alternative will be perceived as superior to others, and thus, chosen (Beach, 1993). The decision-making process begins with the decision maker screening a set of possible behavioral choices for their compatibility with his or her decision standards. Decision standards are the minimum requirements that a particular choice must meet in order to be considered. These requirements include factors such as whether a given option contributes to the enhancement of the decision maker's future and is compatible with his or her goals, morals, values, and beliefs. After screening, the decision maker evaluates the remaining options and makes a choice. If no options survive the screening process, the decision maker must search for new options or reevaluate the decision standards. If one option remains, it is the default choice. If multiple options remain, a choice must be made.

The primary application of classical decision theory in the cancer context is the decision-analytic approach. The decision-analytic approach focuses less on the screening process and more on how people identify potential alternatives and how they quantify the costs and benefits of alternative courses of action (McNutt, 2004). In this approach, major medical decisions involve ascertaining the probability of a potential clinical event and the relative worth (or utility) of that outcome. For example, a patient with cancer in the leg must evaluate the probabilities associated with available treatment options (McNutt, 1989). Having the leg amputated is likely to be associated with a reduced risk of surgical death and cancer recurrence as compared to limb-sparing surgery. Based on these probabilities, the patient would be expected to decide to amputate the leg. However, if the patient perceived the utility of being an amputee as equivalent to death, he or she would be expected to opt for the limb-sparing surgery.

The analytical approach that underlies classic decision making has been the focus of much critique. The chief criticism is that this approach lacks external validity because people rarely make decisions by identifying all possible courses of action and mathematically calculating the probabilities and the expected utility of each option (Klein, 2008; Lipshitz, Klein, Orasanu, & Salas, 2001). Often, people rely on heuristic rather than analytical strategies, thus leading to decisions that deviate from optimal judgments as defined by expected utility theory. These critiques led to the development of theory based on observations of the decision-making strategies used by individuals in their natural environment.

The move toward naturalistic decision making emerged out of recognition that in real-life decision-making scenarios, individuals lack the motivation and ability to identify and evaluate all possible behavioral options (Klein, 2008). Attention is a scarce resource, and it is impossible to allocate all of our attention to each of our various daily decisions. Whereas classical decision making focuses on identifying and analyzing potential courses of action in order to make a selection, naturalistic decision making focuses on how people use their experiences to commit to courses of action (Lipshitz et al., 2001). Specifically, naturalistic decision making conceptualizes the selection process as based on matching rather than on choice.

Naturalistic decision-making (NDM) theories stipulate that when faced with a decision, people use past experience to categorize situations. These categories or schemas are associated with a particular course of action (analogous to the idea of a script) and serve as the basis for the decision. In other words, the decision is based on a process of matching the category of the decision to past experiences that yielded acceptable results. Matching a possible course of action, even if it is the first one that comes to mind, with a decision that is expected to yield acceptable outcomes eliminates the need for an individual to identify all possible courses of action. Also, the focus is on making an acceptable, not necessarily optimal, decision, and relies on intuitive (or a blend of analytical and intuitive) strategies. From an evolutionary perspective, the processes involved in NDM are highly adaptive (Lipshitz et al., 2001).

NDM approaches are particularly appropriate for situations requiring a decision that are associated with ambiguity, uncertainty, the need for timeliness, competing goals, contextual norms, the involvement of multiple individuals, or significant consequences for the decision maker. Although these criteria can apply to a variety of decision-making contexts, such as military commanders in battle or airline pilots in crises, they are exceedingly common in health care. Many health decisions, such as the decision about what type of cancer treatment to pursue, are associated with some degree of ambiguity and uncertainty, a time frame, and competition with other goals; are governed by contextual norms; involve multiple players; and are associated with significant consequences. For this reason, NDM approaches are commonly applied to the decision-making behaviors of nurses and physicians (Bogner & Klein, 1997; Cader, Campbell, & Watson, 2005). However, NDM may have the potential to contribute to understanding of lay, as well as expert, health decision making. For example, a study of breast cancer treatment decisions revealed that some patients presented with the treatment options of mastectomy or lumpectomy with radiation for breast cancer report being immediately drawn to one treatment option as compared to another (Pierce, 1993). For these women, their intuitive or "gut level" attraction to one option enabled them to make their treatment decision quickly and without conflict.

There are inherent limitations of both the classical decision-making theories and naturalistic decision-making theories. One limitation is that both approaches make the assumption that the decision maker is aware of the opportunity for selection. In some health situations, the opportunity for selection is obvious, such as when a patient must decide between two possible therapies for treating an illness. In other cases, it may be less clear. From a classical decision-making perspective, a recommended behavior may fail to meet a decision standard on screening, thus eliminating the opportunity for a decision. From a naturalistic decision-making perspective, a lack of relevant experience may prevent individuals from recognizing the opportunity for choice in the context; thus, they may not attend to cues indicating a selection opportunity. Another critique is that cognitive processes such as problem recognition, deliberation, and decision making in the clinical context often include more than one individual (Epstein, 2013). This has led to efforts to understand how decision making occurs in circumstances where there is cognitive overlap among the individuals involved, a process known as distributed cognition.

Shared Mind: Distributed Cognition and Decision Making

Shared mind refers to the idea that cognitive and affective schemas can be distributed across two or more people (Epstein & Street, 2011). In the field of communication, distributive cognition has been explored in the domains of negotiation and group decision making for years (Fisher, 1970; Gouran & Hirokawa, 1983; Janis, 1972; Roloff & Van Swol, 2007). However, these ideas have only recently been assimilated in theorizing on clinical decision making (Epstein, 2013; Epstein & Gramling, 2012; Epstein & Street, 2011). Essentially, a shared-mind perspective acknowledges that the entirety of clinical treatment decision making is more than the sum of its individual or "whole mind" parts because distributed cognition should result in the emergence of new ideas and perspectives that any one individual involved in the decision-making process could not arrive to on his or her own (Epstein, 2013).

Communication is central to shared cognition, and as such, the growing interest in applying these ideas in health contexts signals the increasing importance of understanding interpersonal communication processes in the realm of health care. Communication can be thought of as a process through which shared cognition occurs, as well as an outcome or product of shared cognition (Roloff & Van Swol, 2007). Conceptualizing communication as a process through which shared cognition develops means that the exchange of verbal and nonverbal messages over time can result in cohesion. Cohesion refers to overlap in the cognitions and emotions of two or more individuals regarding a given situation. There must be some degree of cohesion in order for effective treatment decision making to occur (Epstein, 2013). For example, a provider who considers "watch and wait" as the preferred treatment plan for certain types of prostate cancer will likely have a difficult time achieving cohesion with a patient who has a biomedical mental model of treatment that associates surviving cancer with immediate excising of the tumor and aggressive chemotherapy. Alternatively, the same provider will likely have an easier time achieving cohesion with a patient with a more holistic mental model centered on achieving balance with regard to risks and benefits of medical intervention.

Conceptualizing communication as an outcome or product draws on the idea that the degree of cohesion among individuals will shape the type and extent of messages exchanged. According to Roloff and Van Swoll (2007), shared mental models "improve and facilitate communication once they are formed" (p. 175). To illustrate, if a patient expresses a preference for a given treatment that a provider also views as being optimal, the treatment negotiation process will likely contain fewer discussions of the benefits of a given treatment because both the patient and provider share similar views. Conversely, if a patient wishes to pursue a particular treatment that his or her spouse views as unnecessarily risky, the lack of cohesion between the couple may produce numerous conversations on a range of topics that may or may not yield a mutually satisfactory resolution.

To summarize, theoretical approaches for conceptualizing the role of communication in clinical treatment decision making vary widely. As a result, health communication theory and research need to be explicit about the assumptions underlying how decision making is negotiated. Whole-mind approaches, represented by CDT and NDM, represent two common, yet diverse approaches for conceptualizing cognitive and affective factors that influence how individuals *independently* arrive at treatment decisions. Alternatively, a shared-mind approach is based on the premise that individuals rarely make important treatment decisions completely autonomously. Instead, people interact with others on both cognitive and emotional levels, leading to the creation of shared mental models. The theoretical move from whole mind to shared mind conceptualizations of decision making holds tremendous promise for understanding the process through which family members become involved in treatment decision making (Epstein & Street, 2011). However, given this interest is relatively new, it is important to identify areas where these ideas might alter traditional perspectives on conceptualizing communication and treatment decision making. To this end, the following section identifies key situation and relational features that may inform transactional approaches.

Situational Features Influencing Communication and Cancer Treatment Decision Making

Although much health communication research is concerned with understanding how people make decisions about their health, the most commonly utilized theories and models do not specify how situational features influence communication and decision-making processes (e.g., Ajzen & Fishbein, 1980). Understanding how such features influence decision making is useful because it encourages theoretical predictions to be grounded in an understanding of real-world conditions. Next, the situational features that influence individual and collective cancer treatment decision making are reviewed. Situational features include the different levels at which cancer treatment decision making occurs (i.e., macro to micro), how features of various clinical contexts constrain or support participation in cancer treatment decision making, the stages involved in cancer treatment decision making, and common models for classifying patient involvement in decision making related to cancer treatments.

Levels and Contexts of Cancer Decision Making

The broad term *health decision making* encompasses three subdomains: macro level, service level and treatment level (Charles & DeMaio, 1993). Macro-level health decision making refers to the process of creating public health policies and distributing resources in a defined political entity (e.g., nation, state) that influence cancer care. Service-level health decision making refers to the allocation of resources on a local level, such as what type of cancer care is rendered, where, how, and by whom within a given health care system. Treatment-level health decision making refers to the manner in which particular types of cancer treatment services are selected for individual patients. These three subdomains are interrelated; a patient is unlikely to receive a treatment if such a treatment is not supported by public health policy or is not available within a given health care organization. Nonetheless, the particular issues that influence each type of decision making are distinct. The focus herein is on the factors that influence treatment-level decision making.

The clinical contexts in which treatment decision-making occurs are situated along a continuum ranging from emergency care, acute illnesses, and long-term monitoring of chronic disease to palliative care (Charles et al., 1997). The extent of patient involvement will vary according to the availability of reasonable medical choices available in each context. For example, although a patient with a gunshot wound to the abdomen and unstable vital signs retains the right to refuse treatment, the only reasonable medical treatment in this circumstance is for the patient to undergo emergency surgery (Whitney, McGuire, & McCullough, 2004). In this scenario, patient participation in treatment decision making will likely be limited to providing informed consent to receive the recommended treatment. Conversely, a woman who has been diagnosed with early stage breast cancer will likely have the opportunity to choose a lumpectomy rather than a mastectomy and whether to receive adjuvant chemotherapy and/or radiation after surgery (Charles et al., 1997). In this context, the patient would be expected to play a much more active role in the treatment decision-making process. Next, the extent to which a patient is involved in each step of the decision-making process is examined by reviewing the stages of clinical treatment decision making.

Stages of Clinical Treatment Decision Making

Another focus of the decision-making literature has been to articulate the sequential stages, or *decisional processes*, involved in shared decision making as being distinct from the *decisional outcome* or the chosen alternative (Whitney et al., 2008). The decision-making process has been articulated as having as few as three (Lown, Clark, & Hanson, 2009) and as many as seven stages (Whitney et al., 2008). All classification schemes share some common phases of the decision-making process. The first stage is typically described as *awareness* of an opportunity to make a behavioral selection. This involves information sharing that a decision can (or must) be made and presenting available treatment options and their associated risks and benefits (Lown et al., 2009; Whitney et al., 2008). Another stage is *deliberation*. In deliberation, the patient and the provider have to agree on how the decision is going to be made (Lown et al., 2009). This stage includes eliciting patient values and preferences (e.g., how much information the patient wishes to receive and his or her desired level of participation in decision making) and comparing the treatment options resulting in one being identified as superior (Lown et al., 2009; Whitney et al., 2008). This latter component in which one of the involved parties (physician, patient, or a third party) proposes one option as being superior to the others is referred to as *decisional priority* (Whitney et al., 2008).

The final stage is *behavioral selection*, in which the patient and provider agree on the decision and take steps to implement the choice (Lown et al., 2009; Whitney et al., 2008). From an ethical perspective, patients' (or their surrogates) retain *decisional authority,* which is the moral, legal, or practical right to accept or reject the proposed decision (Whitney et al., 2008). However, some patients' and their surrogates delegate decisional authority to the provider. Lown and colleagues (2009) propose an additional stage, which is *renegotiation* of the decision. The idea of renegotiation emphasizes the idea that clinical treatment decision making may not always be a linear process and that a given decision can be revisited and potentially reversed. For example, one of the patients in the Lown et al. study described the process of renegotiating treatment with his physician as follows:

> I . . . [made] a decision that my doctor absolutely hated. And, I think, the best thing he did was actually expressed that. He said, "Today you are saying no. Can we agree to talk about it tomorrow?" And I said, "Well, we can agree to talk about it an hour from now, two hours from now, a day from now, but it's not going to change my mind." Well, surprisingly I changed my mind. (2009, p. 168)

Thus far, this section has discussed specificity in defining clinical decision making with regard to the levels, contexts, and stages of treatment decision making. In addition to knowing the level at which a decision is being made, the context in which it is being made, and the stages involved, it is essential to explicate how individuals interact to arrive at a decision. The role of interpersonal interaction in decision making is the focus of models of interaction in clinical treatment decision making.

Models of Interaction in Clinical Treatment Decision Making

Models of clinical interaction are frequently referred to in the literature as models of participation (e.g., Charles & DeMaio, 1993). The term *participation* is used to refer to the degree to which the patient's communication behaviors signal engagement in the clinical interaction. Patients perceived to be too low on participation may be characterized as "passive" (e.g., Zhang & Siminoff, 2003), while patients perceived to be too high on participation may be characterized as "consumers" (e.g., Reeder, 1972). The term *interaction* is used in the current chapter to reflect the reality that provider–patient communication is transactional (Siminoff & Step, 2005). This means that patients and providers engage in a process of mutual influence such that patients are more engaged when providers encourage his or her input, and providers provide more information to patients that are highly engaged (Cegala & Post, 2009; Cegala, Street, & Clinch, 2007; Street, Gordon, Ward, Krupat, & Kravitz, 2005; Street, Voigt, Geyer, Manning, & Swanson, 1995).

Given the importance of the patient–provider relationship, much effort has been dedicated to identifying the processes by which providers and patients arrive at treatment decisions. There are many different classifications of provider–patient interaction in treatment decision making. The focus of existing typologies is how physicians and patients negotiate the rights and responsibilities of treatment decision making along dimensions such as goals of provider–patient interaction, degree of information exchange, provider obligations, patient values, and patient autonomy (Charles & DeMaio, 1993; Elwyn et al., 1999; Emanuel & Emanuel, 1992). The three dominant models or levels for understanding the extent to which patients participate in treatment decision making include paternalistic, informative/consumerist, and shared decision making.

Paternalistic model. The paternalistic model, also referred to as the consultation model, refers to provider–patient interaction driven by the goal of maximizing the physical health of the patient (Emanuel & Emanuel, 1992). To achieve this goal, the role of the provider is to use his or her skills to correctly diagnose the patient, identify the treatment expected to ameliorate the condition, and provide the patient with selected information that encourages the patient to consent to a particular treatment. In cases where there are two or more potential treatment options, patients may be given an opportunity to express their wishes, but there is no guarantee that those wishes will be taken into account when the health care provider makes the final decision (Charles & DeMaio, 1993). Patients have little to no autonomy in the decision-making process, and patient involvement is limited to informed consent to the recommended treatment (Charles et al., 1997).

Informative model. If paternalism is at one end of the patient involvement continuum, the informative model lies at the other end. Also known as *consumerist* or *dominant lay control* model, the goal of provider–patient interaction in the informative paradigm is for the provider to transfer all relevant medical knowledge of the illness, available treatment options, and associated risks and benefits so that the patient can select the option that aligns most closely with his or her values (Beisecker & Beisecker, 1993; Emanuel & Emanuel, 1992). As the metaphor of patient-as-consumer implies, the medical relationship is recast with the provider fulfilling a "seller" role and the patient enacting a "buyer" role. As such, patients possess a high level of autonomy in the decision-making process (Charles & DeMaio, 1993). Just as the paternalistic model does not account for the patient in the physician's decision-making process, the informed decision-making model does not truly include the physician in the patient's decision making (Charles et al., 1997).

Shared decision-making model.   The shared decision-making model, also called partnership, lies between the paternalistic and informative models in that power is redistributed in the clinical interaction such that both providers and patients share information relevant to the selection of an appropriate course of action (Charles & DeMaio, 1993). The idea is that a health-care provider shares technical information about health, the patient shares values and preferences, and an agreement is reached on either the decision to be made (e.g., deciding to do something or nothing) or the process by which the decision will be made (e.g., agreeing that the patient, provider, or a third party will maintain decisional authority). The shared decision-making approach aims to achieve health care choices that are agreed upon by patients and their practitioners (for a review of shared decision making, see Makoul & Clayman, 2006; Stacey, Légaré, Pouliot, Kryworuchko, & Dunn, 2010). The key features of shared decision-making interactions include recognition that a decision can be made, knowledge transfer and exchange, expression of values or preferences, deliberation, achieving consensus regarding a course of action, and implementing the decision (Stacey et al., 2010).

Although shared decision making is currently considered the best approach, there are still limitations associated with this paradigm. One limitation is the lack of clarity or consistency in conceptually defining shared decision making (Charles et al., 1997; Stacey et al., 2010). Scholars have been quick to point out that the shared decision-making model is not a panacea for solving the ethical dilemmas inherent in the negotiation of treatment decision making between patients and providers (Charles et al., 1997; Charles, Gafni, & Whelan, 1999). Specifically, information sharing is not the same as shared decision making; thus, in order for shared decision making to occur, both patients and clinicians need to share information as well as decision-making rights and responsibilities. At the same time, it is difficult to specify how people share decision-making responsibilities when only one person can maintain decisional authority. For this reason, Charles and colleagues (1997, 1999) have argued that shared decision making refers to the treatment decision-making *process* as being shared, rather than the decision itself.

Another critique of shared decision making is that it is sometimes conflated with the concept of informed consent (Whitney et al., 2004). Informed consent addresses legal and ethical requirements that patients understand the risks and benefits of treatments associated with a high degree of risk (Whitney et al., 2004). The informed consent process is likely to vary depending on the availability of alternatives. When there is only one reasonable treatment choice, informed consent is an educational process, not an aid in decision making because it is assumed that a "rational" patient will opt for the medically appropriate treatment (Whitney et al., 2004). Decisions involving medical uncertainty due to the availability of more than one reasonable treatment choice, such as the decision about whether to have a mastectomy or lumpectomy plus radiation for early stage breast cancer, are most appropriate for shared decision making. The informed consent process can help facilitate a conversation between providers and patients about the benefits and risks of each treatment.

The final critique is that shared decision making is conceptualized as a process that occurs between a physician and patient. This does not reflect the realities of practice, in that patients may see multiple health-care providers and involve family or friends in the decision-making process (Charles et al., 1997). Indeed, the primary health-care provider's opinion is not the only one that a patient is likely to consider when weighing the benefits and risks of particular treatment options (Avis et al., 2006; Chouliaraet al., 2004; Schoenberg et al., 2003). One study of the decision-making strategies of early stage breast cancer survivors found that patients valued the support of their family, but the involvement of family members in decision making was associated with familial conflict (Hilton, 1994). A meta-analysis of patients who are accompanied to medical visits found that approximately one-third of patients preferred their physician to be the primary decision maker, another third preferred to make the decision themselves in consultation with the physician and companion, and the other third preferred that all parties (i.e., physician, patient, and companion) have equal influence in the decision-making process (Laidsaar-Powell et al., 2013).

It can be concluded that many patients are likely to seek out and consider the advice of nonmedical personnel, such as family, friends, coworkers, and neighbors, in deciding what treatments to pursue. In some cases, patients may even desire to cede their decision-making rights and responsibilities to their loved ones (Kapp, 1991). High levels of involvement by family members in cancer decision making alters the idea of shared decision making as a challenge undertaken by a provider–patient dyad to something more akin to group decision making. The following section explores these ideas in more detail by exploring the influence of close relationships on cancer treatment decision making.

Relational Influences on Cancer Treatment Decision Making

Family members are frequently shown to be an important source of social influence on patient cancer treatment decision making, however, explanations as to how and why families influence treatment outcomes are often overlooked (Avis et al., 2006; Mills et al., 2006). There are multiple models of how individuals exert mutual influence leading to specific outcomes, such as cancer treatment decision making. The following review focuses on contributions of literature demonstrating how social norms influence the types of health decisions that people make and how family communication about treatment decisions can be influenced by a variety of goals, such as maximizing both physical and relational well-being, and it ends with a focus on the management of potentially conflicting goals within the family associated with the decision-making process.

Social Norms

One way close relations exert social influence on health decision making is through descriptive and injunctive norms (Lapinski & Rimal, 2005). Normative messages influence decision making in a variety of health contexts, including cancer detection and treatment (Egbert & Parrott, 2001; Elek, Miller-Day, & Hecht, 2006; Rimal & Real, 2005; Sieverding, Matterne, & Ciccarello, 2010). For example, one study found that women are more willing to use adjuvant chemotherapy in breast cancer treatment when exposed to messages stating that the practice is popular (Zikmund-Fisher, Windschitl, Exe, & Ubel, 2011). Applying these findings outside of the message design context, it would be expected that a woman with family and close friends who have been treated with adjuvant chemotherapy following breast cancer surgery may be more likely to be in favor of pursuing this type of treatment. Even if a patient lacks any vicarious experience with cancer treatment, the treatment choices he or she makes will likely be influenced to some extent by injunctive norms, or their perceptions of what family members think they should do.

The cancer treatment decision-making literature lends support to the importance of injunctive norms in the cancer treatment decision-making context. One study using a sample of breast, colorectal, lung, and prostate patients drawn from a cancer registry found that 43% reported that family members influenced their treatment decisions (Walsh et al., 2010). Another investigation conducted with a sample of breast cancer patients found that 71% of participants reported that family members provided some type of support related to their treatment decision (Arora, Finney Rutten, Gustafson, Moser, & Hawkins, 2007). Certain individuals in the network are more significant than others, with studies reporting that the perceived wishes of an individual's spouse and adult children tend to be more influential than those of other relatives (Hauke, Reiter-Theil, Hoster, Hiddemann, & Winkler, 2011; Laidsaar-Powell et al., 2013). The influence of injunctive norms and decision making demonstrates that concerns about relational, as well as medical, well-being can influence medical treatment decisions. The ways in which the co-occurrence of medical and relational concerns influence interactions in the decision-making process can be articulated more specifically via a multiple goals perspective.

Multiple Goals

Goals are states that individuals desire to attain or maintain, and people use messages to achieve desired states during interaction (Wilson & Feng, 2007). There are various theories that address the pursuit of multiple goals in human communication, but the commonalities among them yield general principles that are useful for understanding relational influences in the cancer treatment decision process (Caughlin, 2010). One commonality is the assumption that communication is purposeful. In other words, people create messages to achieve specific ends regardless of whether they are consciously aware of those goals. For example, a cancer patient might be motivated to disclose to her spouse the details of her treatment options to maintain relational closeness during a health crisis.

Another common principle is that people pursue multiple goals simultaneously in communicative situations. The patient in the previous example might be motivated to disclose to her spouse the details of her treatment options in an effort to receive assistance with the decision in addition to achieving the relational goal of closeness. Third, people enter communicative situations with competing goals. The spouse in this situation may simultaneously want to share his opinion about what treatment would be safest and most effective in an effort to protect the health of his wife but may also be motivated to avoid sharing an opinion because he anticipates feeling guilty if his preferred treatment option would fail. Finally, people make subjective evaluations of their partner's goals in a conversation. For example, if the husband is silent or changes the subject after his wife expresses a desire to pursue a particular course of treatment, the patient will evaluate the meaning of his silence. She may interpret his reaction as a lack of support for her decision and/or that he is being rude or dismissive. Both outcomes are potentially detrimental to both the patient's physical and emotional well-being.

There are a variety of potential interaction goals that could be relevant to conversations about cancer and even cancer treatment in particular (for a review, see Caughlin, 2010). However, one overarching goal identified in the patient participation literature is the extent to which individuals pursue their optimal level of involvement in a treatment decision. As previously discussed, what a patient considers optimal involvement might vary from person to person. While one individual might prefer to assume all rights and responsibilities associated with decision making (i.e., informative model), another might prefer to share those rights and responsibilities or give them over to someone else. This represents a continuum in a patient's preference for autonomous or interdependent decision making. Just as patients pursue goals related to autonomy or interdependence in health decision making with providers, they also do so with family members. Family members also range as to whether they desire to promote patient autonomy in treatment decision making versus fostering interdependence as a means of influencing the decision-making outcome. Congruent with a multiple goals perspective, it is assumed that patients and family members pursue their desired level of involvement along with other goals that may or may not compete with their decisional involvement goals and that individuals will make assessments regarding the decisional involvement goals of other family members during interactions. In order to contribute to the theoretical conceptualizations of how this process evolves, the following section elaborates on autonomy and interdependence in the context of cancer treatment decisions.

Patient Autonomy Versus Interdependence

The term *autonomy* is commonly used in the patient-participation literature, but is rarely explicitly defined (Charles et al., 1997). As a result, patient participation in physician–patient interactions is conceptualized in a number of different ways, including desiring information about one's illness and treatment choices, participating actively in the decision-making process, and assuming complete control over decision making (Brashers, Haas, & Neidig, 1999; Chewning et al., 2012; Sutherland, Llewellyn-Thomas, Lockwood, Tritchler, & Till, 1989). A core theme across approaches is that patient autonomy is an individual right (Entwistle, Carter, Cribb, & McCaffery, 2010).

What is less commonly addressed are the perceived responsibilities associated with this right. For example, some patients may feel burdened by the responsibilities associated with being the sole decision maker (Kapp, 1991). In an effort to be relieved of this burden, some patients delegate their decision-making power to a health-care provider. Thus, what many consider to be paternalism may actually be patients exercising their decisional authority by putting someone else in charge of the decision (Charles et al., 1997). In other words, delegating decisional authority can be considered a form of autonomy because the individual is exercising his or her right to self-determination by deciding to abdicate the responsibilities associated with a given decision (Sutherland et al., 1989). This approach to decision making is sometimes labeled *shared autonomy* (Cicirelli, 1992). However, the distinction between personally assuming the rights and responsibilities of decision making and delegating the same to another person is theoretically useful. For the purposes of the current chapter, *patient autonomy* is defined as pursuing goals associated with the patient personally assuming all rights and responsibilities associated with decisional authority.

Another term for shared autonomy is interdependence (Pecchioni & Nussbaum, 2000). *Patient interdependence* is defined herein as patient or family goals of distributing some portion (including all) of the rights and responsibilities associated with decisional authority to others. A preference for interdependence in decision making can extend to individuals other than a physician, such as family members. There are several important reasons why patients may want to share the rights and responsibilities of decision making. One is that shared decision making can minimize family burden because it reduces tension or guilt that may result from family disagreement (Kapp, 1991). Some individuals may also feel that it is unethical not to include family members in decision making if they will bear burdens (i.e., emotional, financial, or physical) as a result of the medical decision that is made. In this way, patients and families may conceptualize decision making as a fairness issue.

Distributing the rights and responsibilities associated with decisional authority among the network assumes that family members will be providing some level of decisional support to the patient. Drawing on Goldsmith's (2004) typology of enacted social support, decisional support refers to the communicative behaviors that people use to help each other with treatment decisions. The process of providing decisional support may result in family members fulfilling particular roles, such as information gatherer, coach, advisor, advocate, and support provider (Charles et al., 1997). Although some studies find decisional support by network members as having uniformly positive outcomes, others indicate their involvement can create significant conflict during the decision-making process and after the decision has been made (Hauke et al., 2011; Hilton, 1994; Speice et al., 2000; Zhang & Siminoff, 2003). Involving third parties in medical decisions can result in patients feeling "left out" of the decision or that family members are exchanging information with providers "behind their back" (Speice et al., 2000). Conflict can also occur when the family disagrees with a patient's treatment decision. Relatives disagree with patients about what treatments to pursue about a third of the time (Hauke et al., 2011). Zhang and Siminoff (2003) find that disagreements occur in response to decisions about routine treatment, discontinuation of curative treatment, and hospice care. Others have found that disagreements tend to be in the direction of relatives preferring more aggressive treatment than the patient and physician (Hauke et al., 2011).

Some scholars have hypothesized that the extent or type of decision-making support a patient receives is positively related to the severity of the patient's illness (Sekimoto et al., 2004; Walsh et al., 2010). Conceptually, it would be expected that as a patient becomes physically, mentally, or emotionally less able to engage in decision making, she or he would desire greater family involvement in decision making (Sekimoto et al., 2004). However, some studies find that the very sick are less able to access decision-making support (Walsh et al., 2010), while others find no evidence of a relationship between illness severity and the likelihood of receiving decision-making support from family members (Hauke et al., 2011).

To summarize, previous research has found perceived injunctive norms to be influential in the decision-making process. One reason that injunctive norms are so powerful is because patients have relational, as well medical, goals related to clinical decisions. One type of relational goal is negotiating the degree of autonomy or interdependence a patient has in the decision-making process. The following section describes a new typology drawing on interaction goals for patient autonomy or interdependence that can be used to understand decision-making processes and outcomes, including patient and family goals for interaction, expectations regarding decisional authority, and satisfaction with family interactions stemming from the decision-making process.

The Family DECIDE Typology

The purpose of the Family *De*terminants of *Cli*nical *De*cisions (DECIDE) Typology is to articulate the decision-making goals of patients and their family members as related to serious clinical treatment decisions. The focus is on patient and family preferences for a decision-making style that emphasizes patient autonomy or patient interdependence. This approach is designed to help answer several key questions related to the influence of interpersonal communication on health decision making. One question is how patients arrive at their treatment decisions. Health care providers are commonly perplexed by the decision-making patterns of patients (McNutt, 2004). For example, a patient may make decisions that a provider finds medically unreasonable because his or her social network felt it was best. Understanding a patient's orientation toward the decision-making process as well as the orientation of the family can provide insight on how particular decisions are made and on how decisional priority and authority are distributed.

It is also expected that the proposed typology will provide insight into the relational implications of decision making, such as how particular message strategies can be used to enhance, maintain, or weaken ties with others (Goldsmith, Miller, & Caughlin, 2008). In some cases, individuals may use an interdependent decision-making style to promote connectedness between themselves and their loved ones (Baxter & Montgomery, 1996; Montgomery & Baxter, 1998). In other cases, a patient may seek a particular decision-making style that enables them to establish autonomy. For example, a patient who is deciding whether or not to participate in a randomized cancer clinical treatment trial may ask family members for input and advice on the decision in order to enhance relational goals such as being open and creating closeness. Alternatively, this individual may make the decision to not seek input from family members in order to maintain a sense of control in a context often associated with feelings of helplessness.

In short, the typology considers the extent to which patients desire the treatment decision-making process to be more autonomous or interdependent as well as whether the family desires the decision-making process to be more autonomous or interdependent. Further, patient and family preferences for autonomy and interdependence are conceptualized as opposite ends on a continuum that can be plotted using a Cartesian coordinate system (see Figure 9.1).

The *y*-axis represents a patient orientation toward decisional autonomy or interdependence and the *x*-axis represents the degree to which a family seeks to promote patient autonomy or interdependence. This configuration, moving

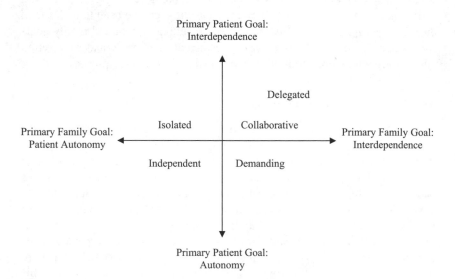

Figure 9.1 Typology of family decision-making styles

clockwise from the bottom left, yields five potential decision-making styles: independent, isolated, collaborative, delegated, and demanding.

Independent

Patients with an independent decision-making style—the first of the five styles in the typology—have a goal of maintaining autonomy in the treatment decision process, and the patient's family strives to facilitate this autonomy. A patient's desire for autonomy may result in various behavioral outcomes. One way patients may pursue autonomy is by not disclosing to family members that there is a decision-making opportunity. In other cases, patients may disclose the opportunity to make a decision out of obligation but attempt to do so in ways that express that they do not expect or desire decisional involvement from the family. It is likely that patients desiring high levels of autonomy may prefer to attend appointments alone in order to control whether and how information is shared. Alternatively, if another individual is present when treatment options are discussed, the patient may directly or indirectly establish boundaries around the information management and decision-making process.

Family members who are aware of a patient's opportunity to make a treatment decision are considered to be promoting autonomy when they refrain from direct and indirect attempts to influence the decision-making process or outcome. Family members may have different motivations for promoting patient autonomy. One motivation is a disinterest or fear in sharing in the responsibilities of decision making. For instance, a family member may be overwhelmed by the patient's diagnosis and not have a clear sense of what option would be best to pursue. In this case, that family member may prefer that the patient make the decision autonomously and thus avoid the potential guilt that could result from giving the patient advice that proves to be incorrect. Another motivation is the perception that the patient does not desire decisional support. A family member may wait for explicit or implicit cues that his or her input is desired and, in the absence of those cues, may refrain from comment. There may also be pragmatic reasons why families prefer the patient to maintain an autonomous style. For example, the family may be too busy with work or other commitments to participate in decision making. It is expected that when patients and family members achieve cohesion with regard to their preferences regarding autonomy and interdependence that the patient and family will be more satisfied with both the decision-making process and the outcome.

Isolated

The second decision-making style—isolated—refers to families in which patients desire an interdependent decision-making style but the family desires the patient to make the treatment decision autonomously. The isolated decision-making style is characterized by patient attempts to garner decisional support from her family while family members either ignore or rebuff these attempts.

Patients may directly request decisional support, such as asking for opinions about which treatment option would be best to pursue. Importantly, such requests may be framed as drawing on the individual's medical knowledge, which may be more likely if the family member has received some level of medical training or relational knowledge, such as which treatment option would be most consistent with the patient's values. Patients may also indirectly request decisional support, such as expressing feelings of being overwhelmed by the decision or wishing someone would tell them what to do.

Although the reasons why family members might prefer the patient maintain an autonomous decision-making style are the same as in the independent decision-making style, the relational implications are likely to be quite different. If a patient is directly or indirectly requesting advice that a family member cannot or does not wish to give, he or she is likely to resort to several strategies. One strategy is for the family member to directly explain to the patient that he cannot or will not share in the responsibilities of decision making. Given the high potential for face threat associated with this approach, family members are likely to opt for alternative strategies. One alternate strategy is to avoid discussing topics related to treatment with the patient. Family members may strategically reduce the amount of time spent communicating with the patient, ignore patient attempts to initiate a conversation about treatment options, or change the subject when the topic is pursued. The lack of cohesion in the preferred treatment decision-making styles between the patient and the family is expected to result in greater distress for the patient and reduced satisfaction with the decision-making process and the outcome for both the patient and family as compared to the independent decision-making style.

Collaborative and Delegated

The collaborative decision-making style refers to patients and families who seek an interdependent decision-making style. Put another way, the patient invites family members to share in the rights and responsibilities associated with the decision-making process and family members are willing to do so. Importantly, patients and family members may negotiate different degrees of collaboration in decision making from full-and-equal say to more conditional input. In other words, some patients may desire family members to provide all levels of decisional support, while others may want select types of support. For example, some patients may desire family members to gather information about the treatment decision, such as seeking information from outside resources (e.g., Internet searches), recording results of tests and information conveyed in appointments, or contacting health-care providers to request information on the patient's behalf (Speice et al., 2000). Some patients may desire family members to have a coaching role in which they remind patients to ask questions during appointments or function as an advisor that provides opinions on their merits of the treatment choices, including assuming decisional priority (i.e., providing an opinion on which treatment decision is best).

The fourth style is a subcategory of collaborative decision making titled "delegated" because the patient gives over the rights and responsibilities of decision making to someone else. In delegated decision making, patients solicit and receive more extreme forms of decisional support. This can range from a durable power of attorney to situations in which the patient maintains (at least theoretically) the cognitive ability to make medical decisions but chooses to grant this to another individual. Because the patient and family are concordant in their decision-making preferences, collaborative and delegated family decision-making styles are predicted to be associated with a higher degree of patient adjustment and family satisfaction with decision making than the isolated decision-making style, but they are similar to the independent decision-making style.

Demanding

The final type of decision making in the typology is the demanding decision-making style. This style describes situations in which the patient desires to make autonomous decisions, but the family desires a more interdependent style. The demanding decision-making model is expected to be most common in situations where a patient informs his or her family of a particular decisional opportunity out of duty, and family members attempt to provide various forms of decisional support unsolicited. Regardless of whether family members are unaware or unconcerned that decisional support is unwanted, this style of decision making describes situations in which family members wrestle with the patient to share in the rights and responsibilities associated with the treatment decision. Like the isolated decision-making style, demanding family styles are predicted to result in lower patient and family satisfaction with decisional outcomes as compared to the independent and collaborative styles.

Embracing Complexity in Mapping Decision-Making Styles

The DECIDE typology captures a portion of the complexity associated with how patients manage different close relationships in the process of treatment decision making. However, it would be overly simplistic to posit that the decision making of a particular patient and his or her family will be perfectly captured by one of these styles across family members and across time. Patients have different goals for interactions with various members of their family based on their relational roles and prior experiences in the relationship. In other words, the degree to which a patient desires autonomy or interdependence in decision making might vary depending on the particular relationship. To illustrate, a family in which a patient asks her husband explicitly for advice but he responds by ignoring the request would be considered to have an isolated decision-making style. At the same time, that patient may negotiate an independent decision-making style with her adult children if she informs them of her decision rather than soliciting their advice and the adult children abide by the decision-making boundaries she has established. In addition, the way the patient and his or her family members view the decision-making process may change over time. For example, family members may pursue the goal of patient autonomy until the patient makes a decision they perceive as being harmful. At that point, the family members may desire a greater role in the decision-making process. Similarly, a patient may initially desire high interdependence in the decision-making process but move toward greater autonomy in decision making if particular events cause her to feel that she has begun to lose too much control over the process.

Implications and Conclusion

The current chapter synthesizes diverse literature from medicine, public health, and communication on cancer treatment decision making for the purpose of expanding theoretical perspectives on the role of family communication in cancer treatment decision making. In so doing, it answers the call for a more comprehensive approach to understanding the factors that influence health decision making (Stokols, Allen, & Bellingham, 1996) and addresses the need for theoretical work that addresses the process by which family members become involved in patient care (Charles et al., 1999; Epstein, 2013; Siminoff et al., 2006). Although theoretical conceptualizations of the role of the family in influencing cancer treatment decision making are still in their infancy, there is substantial evidence that family members can be active participants in the process (Lown et al., 2009; Speice et al., 2000). The goal of theory development should be to avoid conceptualizing the influence of the family as either simply present or absent but rather seek to explore the complexities of relational dynamics that shape interactions among individuals with a shared connection and ultimately alter the decision-making process (Siminoff et al., 2006).

Although there are many potential ways to theorize the role of family in treatment-level decision making, the current chapter proposes a typology that focuses on patient and family goals related to fostering patient autonomy or interdependence in the context of cancer decision making. This approach is a departure from whole mind theoretical traditions that conceptualize treatment decision making as an isolated, individual pursuit. Instead, it embraces a shared-mind perspective in which the focus is the extent to which patients and their family members create shared mental models for how the treatment decision-making process will unfold. It is predicted that greatest physical and relational benefits will be achieved when patients and their family members conceive of the decision-making process similarly. For example, if both a patient and her family view the cancer treatment decision-making process from a perspective that prioritizes patient autonomy, family conflict regarding the negotiation of rights and responsibilities of decision making will be unlikely. Conversely, a lack of a shared mental model regarding the decision-making process has the potential to generate patient distress and family conflict. A patient who desires a more interdependent decision-making style may feel abandoned or overwhelmed if family members desire him or her to have a more autonomous decision-making style. Similarly, patients who wish to maintain a high degree of autonomy may feel coerced or bullied by family members who desire to share in the rights and responsibilities of decision making.

The introduction of this typology has meaningful implications for future research on clinical decision making. One implication is that current descriptions of the stages of clinical decision making should be expanded to address the complexity of various types of family involvement (Lown et al., 2009; Whitney et al., 2008). Whereas current typologies focus on the negotiation of treatment decision making exclusively within the patient–provider dyad, the current chapter suggests that there may be additional stages wherein treatment decisions are also negotiated with the family. A potentially useful direction for future research is to explore whether the stages of clinical decision making between patients and family members mirror those identified for patients and providers or whether they diverge in theoretically meaningful ways. Furthermore, it would be helpful to identify how different family decision-making styles alter specific stages in the process. For example, it is unknown the extent to which the deliberation process within families is one that is implicit or explicitly negotiated.

Another implication is furthering the development of decision-making theories that move beyond an exclusive focus on cognitive indicators of health behaviors and incorporate interaction variables as predictors of decisional outcomes. Theoretical accounts that include perceptions of social norms (e.g., theory of reasoned action and theory of planned behavior) provide some insight into the relational influence of health behaviors. However, these theories could benefit from a greater appreciation for how people manage multiple goals in health-related contexts (e.g., Caughlin et al., 2009) as well as the negotiation of goals specifically related to the decision-making process (e.g., seeking autonomy or interdependence).

A theoretical move toward specifying the goals underlying the decision-making process could help health communication research better address decision making in diverse situational and cultural contexts. One example of a situational context that might influence the decision-making process is the extent to which individuals in the family are influenced by a patient's diagnosis or treatment decision. If family members are serving as caregivers or helping to pay for medical treatment, they may feel entitled to know all relevant information and have a say in treatment decisions (Muula & Mfutso-Bengo, 2004). For this reason, a patient diagnosed with a severe disease may be more concerned with social norms (e.g., what decisions his or her caregivers prefer) as compared to personal attitudes than may someone for whom loved ones will not be affected by the illness or treatment decision. Similarly, examining these constructs across cultural contexts may enrich understanding how autonomy and interdependence are negotiated within different environments. For example, some scholars have argued that it is unclear how patient autonomy should be conceptualized in collectivist cultural environments, particularly when cultural norms for decision making conflict with standards of medical practice such as patient confidentiality and individual informed consent (Muula & Mfutso-Bengo, 2004).

It is expected that the proposed typology will also have practical implications, such as inciting the development of interventions that will help patients and families negotiate the decision-making process. Currently, treatment decision making is frequently conceptualized as occurring at the patient level. As a result, interventions to improve health decision making or patient involvement in clinical interactions are targeted exclusively to the patient. Although such interventions are extremely valuable, it is worth evaluating whether patients are truly making their treatment decisions independently. As the typology presented in this chapter demonstrates, many patients desire the involvement of their loved ones in their medical decisions, ranging from offering opinions to taking full responsibility for the decision (e.g., the delegated style).

If families are influencing medical decisions, there are important ethical implications of developing and disseminating patient-focused health education and intervention efforts and an exclusive focus on individual informed consent (particularly related to delegated decision-making styles). As such, this typology could serve as the basis of measures that can help rapidly assess the decision-making orientation of patients and their family caregivers. There are two potential applications of the results. One is that patients and families that do not report a high degree of cohesion in their decision-making orientation can be identified, monitored, and potentially referred to other services (e.g., social worker) for remediation if family conflict is causing excessive stress on the patient.

In addition, the DECIDE typology can serve as a starting point for clinical interventions that provide interpersonal communication training for patients and family members regarding how to negotiate decision making in stressful situations. Such interventions may help family members feel more efficacious about providing decisional support as well as improving the quality of their support. In turn, patients may feel less distress as a result of the participation of family members in a decision (when so desired), and family-level educational efforts may help reduce conflict associated with decision making.

In conclusion, many current theoretical perspectives of health decision-making processes focus on individual processes, while empirical evidence continues to mount demonstrating the importance of interpersonal interaction on cancer treatment decisions. This disconnect is stymieing theoretical advancements as well as improved standards for clinical practice. Increased research on patient and family goals for autonomy and interdependence and application of the DECIDE typology can enrich theoretical perspectives on social influence processes as well contribute to the improved physical and relational health of patients.

Acknowledgments

This research was supported by the Appalachia Community Cancer Network 5U01CA114622 (PI: Dignan). The author would like to thank Angela Palmer-Wackerly, Phokeng Dailey, Jessica Krok, and the three anonymous reviewers for their contributions to the development of this manuscript.

References

Ajzen, I., & Fishbein, M. (1980). *Understanding attitudes and predicting social behavior.* Englewood Cliffs, NJ: Prentice Hall.

Arora, N. K., Finney Rutten, L. J., Gustafson, D. H., Moser, R., & Hawkins, R. P. (2007). Perceived helpfulness and impact of social support provided by family, friends, and health care providers to women newly diagnosed with breast cancer. *Psycho-Oncology, 16*, 474–486. doi:10.1002/pon.1084

Avis, N. E., Smith, K. W., Link, C. L., Hortobagyi, G. N., & Rivera, E. (2006). Factors associated with participation in breast cancer treatment clinical trials. *Journal of Clinical Oncology, 24*, 1860–1867. doi:10.1200/JCO.2005.03.8976

Baxter, L. A., & Montgomery, B. M. (Eds.). (1996). *Relating: Dialogues and dialectics.* New York: Guilford.

Beach, L. R. (1993). Broadening the definition of decision making: The role of pre-choice screening of options. *Psychological Science, 4*, 215–220. doi:10.1111/j.1467-9280.1993.tb00264.x

Beisecker, A. E., & Beisecker, T. D. (1993). Using metaphors to characterize doctor-patient relationships: Paternalism versus consumerism. *Health Communication, 5*, 41–58.

Bogner, M. S., & Klein, G. (1997). Naturalistic decision making in health care. In G. Klein & C. E. Zsambok (Eds.), *Naturalistic decision making* (pp. 61–69). Mahwah, NJ: Erlbaum.

Brashers, D. E., Haas, S. M., & Neidig, J. L. (1999). The patient self-advocacy scale: Measuring patient involvement in health care decision-making interactions. *Health Communication, 11*, 97–121. doi:10.1207/s15327027hc1102_1

Cader, R., Campbell, S., & Watson, D. (2005). Cognitive continuum theory in nursing decision-making. *Journal of Advanced Nursing, 49*, 397–405. doi:10.1111/j.1365-2648.2004.03303.x

Caughlin, J. P. (2010). A multiple goals theory of personal relationships: Conceptual integration and program overview. *Journal of Social & Personal Relationships, 27*, 824–848. doi:10.1177/0265407510373262

Caughlin, J. P., Bute, J. J., Donovan-Kicken, E., Kosenko, K. A., Ramey, M. E., & Brashers, D. E. (2009). Do message features influence reactions to HIV disclosures? A multiple-goals perspective. *Health Communication, 24*, 270–283. doi:10.1080/10410230902806070.

Cegala, D. J., & Post, D. M. (2009). The impact of patients' participation on physicians' patient-centered communication. *Patient Education and Counseling, 77*, 202–208. doi:10.1016/j.pec.2009.03.025

Cegala, D. J., Street, R. L., & Clinch, C. R. (2007). The impact of patient participation on physicians' information provision during a primary care medical interview. *Health Communication, 21*, 177–185. doi:10.1080/10410230701307824

Charles, C., & DeMaio, S. (1993). Lay participation in health care decision making: A conceptual framework. *Journal of Health Politics, Policy and Law, 18,* 881–904.

Charles, C., Gafni, A., & Whelan, T. (1997). Shared decision-making in the medical encounter: What does it mean? (Or it takes at least two to tango). *Social Science & Medicine, 44,* 681–692.

Charles, C., Gafni, A., & Whelan, T. (1999). Decision-making in the physician–patient encounter: Revisiting the shared treatment decision-making model. *Social Science & Medicine, 49,* 651–661.

Chewning, B., Bylund, C. L., Shah, B., Arora, N. K., Gueguen, J. A., & Makoul, G. (2012). Patient preferences for shared decisions: A systematic review. *Patient Education and Counseling, 86,* 9–18. doi:10.1016/j.pec.2011.02.004

Chouliara, Z., Kearney, N., Stott, D., Molassiotis, A., & Miller, M. (2004). Perceptions of older people with cancer of information, decision making and treatment: A systematic review of selected literature. *Annals of Oncology, 15,* 1596–1602. doi:10.1093/annonc/mdh423

Cicirelli, V. G. (1992). *Family caregiving: Autonomous and paternalistic decision making.* Newbury Park, CA: Sage.

DiMatteo, M. R. (2004). Social support and patient adherence to medical treatment. *Health Psychology, 23,* 207–218.

Egbert, N., & Parrott, R. (2001). Self-efficacy and rural women's performance of breast and cervical cancer detection practices. *Journal of Health Communication, 6,* 219–233.

Elek, E., Miller-Day, M., & Hecht, M. L. (2006). Influences of personal, injunctive, and descriptive norms on early adolescent substance use. *Journal of Drug Issues, 36,* 147–172. doi:10.1177/002204260603600107

Elwyn, G., Edwards, A., & Kinnersley, P. (1999). Shared decision-making in primary care: The neglected second half of the consultation. *The British Journal of General Practice, 49,* 477–482.

Emanuel, E. J., & Emanuel, L. L. (1992). Four models of the physician-patient relationship. *JAMA: The Journal of the American Medical Association, 267,* 2221–2226.

Entwistle, V. A., Carter, S. M., Cribb, A., & McCaffery, K. (2010). Supporting patient autonomy: The importance of clinician-patient relationships. *Journal of General Internal Medicine, 25,* 741–745. doi:10.1007/s11606–010–1292–2

Epstein, R. M. (2013). Whole mind and shared mind in clinical decision-making. *Patient Education and Counseling, 90,* 200–206. doi:10.1016/j.pec.2012.06.035

Epstein, R. M., & Gramling, R. E. (2012). What is shared in shared decision making? Complex decisions when the evidence is unclear. *Medical Care Research and Review, 70,* 94S–112S. doi:10.1177/1077558712459216

Epstein, R. M., & Street, R. L. (2011). Shared mind: Communication, decision making, and autonomy in serious illness. *Annals of Family Medicine, 9,* 454–461. doi:10.1370/afm.1301

Fisher, B. A. (1970). Decision emergence: Phases in group decision-making. *Speech Monographs, 37,* 53–66. doi:10.1080/03637757009375649

Goldsmith, D. J. (2004). *Communicating social support.* Cambridge, England: Cambridge University Press.

Goldsmith, D. J., Miller, L. E., & Caughlin, J. P. (2008). Openness and avoidance in couples communication about cancer. *Communication Yearbook, 31,* 62–115.

Gouran, D. S., & Hirokawa, R. Y. (1983). The role of communication in decision-making groups: A functional perspective. In M. S. Mander (Ed.), *Communications in transition* (pp. 168–185). New York: Praeger.

Hauke, D., Reiter-Theil, S., Hoster, E., Hiddemann, W., & Winkler, E. C. (2011). The role of relatives in decisions concerning life-prolonging treatment in patients with end-stage malignant disorders: Informants, advocates or surrogate decision-makers? *Annals of Oncology, 22,* 2667–2674. doi:10.1093/annonc/mdr019

Hilton, B. A. (1994). Family decision-making processes about early stage breast cancer treatment. *Canadian Oncology Nursing Journal, 4,* 9–16.

Janis, I. L. (1972). *Victims of groupthink: A psychological study of foreign policy decisions and fiascoes.* Boston, MA: Houghton, Mifflin.

Jemal, A., Siegel, R., Xu, J., & Ward, E. (2010). Cancer statistics, 2010. *CA: A Cancer Journal for Clinicians, 60,* 277–300. doi:10.3322/caac.20073

Kapp, M. B. (1991). Health care decision making by the elderly: I get by with a little help from my family. *The Gerontologist, 31,* 619–623. doi:10.1093/geront/31.5.619

Klein, G. (2008). Naturalistic decision making. *Human Factors: The Journal of the Human Factors and Ergonomics Society, 50,* 456–460. doi:10.1518/00187200 8X288385

Laidsaar-Powell, R. C., Butow, P. N., Bu, S., Charles, C., Gafni, A., Lam, W.W.T., . . . Juraskova, I. (2013). Physician-patient-companion communication and decision making: A systematic review of triadic medical consultations. *Patient Education and Counseling, 91,* 3–13. doi:10.1016/j.pec.2012.11.007

Lapinski, M. K., & Rimal, R. N. (2005). An explication of social norms. *Communication Theory, 15,* 127–147. doi:10.1111/j.1468–2885.2005.tb00329.x

Lipshitz, R., Klein, G., Orasanu, J., & Salas, E. (2001). Taking stock of naturalistic decision making. *Journal of Behavioral Decision Making, 14,* 331–352. doi:10.1002/bdm.381

Lown, B. A., Clark, W. D., & Hanson, J. L. (2009). Mutual influence in shared decision making: A collaborative study of patients and physicians. *Health Expectations, 12,* 160–174. doi:10.1111/j.1369–7625.2008.00525.x

Makoul, G., & Clayman, M. L. (2006). An integrative model of shared decision making in medical encounters. *Patient Education and Counseling, 60,* 301–312. doi:10.1016/j.pec.2005.06.010

McNutt, R. A. (1989). Measuring patient preferences for health outcomes: A decision analytic approach. *Patient Education and Counseling, 13,* 271–279.

McNutt, R. A. (2004). Shared medical decision making: Problems, process, progress. *JAMA: The Journal of the American Medical Association, 292,* 2516–2518. doi:10.1001/jama.292.20.2516

Mills, E. J., Seely, D., Rachlis, B., Griffith, L., Wu, P., Wilson, K., . . . Wright, J. R. (2006). Barriers to participation in clinical trials of cancer: A meta-analysis and systematic review of patient-reported factors. *The Lancet Oncology, 7,* 141–148. doi:10.1016/S1470–2045(06)70576–9

Montgomery, B. M., & Baxter, L. A. (1998). *Dialectical approaches to studying personal relationships.* Mahwah, NJ: Erlbaum.

Muula, A. S., & Mfutso-Bengo, J. M. (2004). Important but neglected ethical and cultural considerations in the fight against HIV/AIDS in Malawi. *Nursing Ethics, 11,* 479–488.

National Center for Health Statistics. (2012). *Health, United States, 2011: With special feature on socioeconomic status and health.* Hyattsville, MD: US Government Printing Office.

Pecchioni, L. L., & Nussbaum, J. F. (2000). The influence of autonomy and paternalism on communicative behaviors in mother-daughter relationships prior to dependency. *Health Communication, 12,* 317–338. doi:10.1207/S15327027HC1204_1

Pierce, P. F. (1993). Deciding on breast cancer treatment: A description of decision behavior. *Nursing Research, 42,* 22–28.

Pitts, M. J., Raup-Krieger, J. L., Kundrat, A. L., & Nussbaum, J. F. (2009). Mapping the processes and patterns of family organ donation discussions: Conversational styles and strategies in live discourse. *Health Communication, 24,* 413–425. doi:10.1080/10410230903023469

Reeder, L. G. (1972). The patient-client as a consumer: Some observations on the changing professional-client relationship. *Journal of Health and Social Behavior, 13,* 406–412. doi:10.2307/2136833

Rimal, R. N., & Real, K. (2005). How behaviors are influenced by perceived norms a test of the theory of normative social behavior. *Communication Research, 32,* 389–414. doi:10.1177/0093650205275385

Roloff, M., & Van Swol, L. M. (2007). Shared cognition and communication within group decision making and negotiation. In D. R. Roskos-Ewoldsen & L. Monahan (Eds.), *Communication and social cognition: Theories and methods* (pp. 171–195). Mahwah, NJ: Erlbaum.

Scharlach, A., Li, W., & Dalvi, T. B. (2006). Family conflict as a mediator of caregiver strain. *Family Relations, 55,* 625–635. doi:10.1111/j.1741–3729.2006.00431.x

Schoenberg, N. E., Peters, J. C., & Drew, E. M. (2003). Unraveling the mysteries of timing: Women's perceptions about time to treatment for cardiac symptoms. *Social Science & Medicine, 56,* 271–284. doi:10.1016/S0277–9536(02)00026–6

Schumacher, K. L., Stewart, B. J., Archbold, P. G., Caparro, M., Mutale, F., & Agrawal, S. (2008). Effects of caregiving demand, mutuality, and preparedness on family caregiver outcomes during cancer treatment. *Oncology Nursing Forum, 35,* 49–56. doi:10.1188/08.ONF.49–56

Sekimoto, M., Asai, A., Ohnishi, M., Nishigaki, E., Fukui, T., Shimbo, T., & Imanaka, Y. (2004). Patients' preferences for involvement in treatment decision making in Japan. *BMC Family Practice, 5,* n.p. doi:10.1186/1471–2296–5-1

Sieverding, M., Matterne, U., & Ciccarello, L. (2010). What role do social norms play in the context of men's cancer screening intention and behavior? Application of an extended theory of planned behavior. *Health Psychology, 29,* 72–81. doi:10.1037/a0016941

Siminoff, L. A., Rose, J. H., Zhang, A., & Zyzanski, S. J. (2006). Measuring discord in treatment decision-making; progress toward development of a cancer communication and decision-making assessment tool. *Psycho-Oncology, 15,* 528–540.

Siminoff, L. A., & Step, M. M. (2005). A communication model of shared decision making: Accounting for cancer treatment decisions. *Health Psychology, 24,* S99–S105. doi:10.1037/0278–6133.24.4.S99

Speice, J., Harkness, J., Laneri, H., Frankel, R., Roter, D., Kornblith, A. B., . . . Holland, J. C. (2000). Involving family members in cancer care: Focus group considerations of patients and oncological providers. *Psycho-Oncology, 9,* 101–112.

Stacey, D., Légaré, F., Pouliot, S., Kryworuchko, J., & Dunn, S. (2010). Shared decision making models to inform an interprofessional perspective on decision making: A theory analysis. *Patient Education and Counseling, 80,* 164–172. doi:10.1016/j.pec.2009.10.015

Stokols, D., Allen, J., & Bellingham, R. L. (1996). The social ecology of health promotion: Implications for research and practice. *American Journal of Health Promotion, 10,* 247–251.

Street, R. L., Gordon, H. S., Ward, M. M., Krupat, E., & Kravitz, R. L. (2005). Patient participation in medical consultations: Why some patients are more involved than others. *Medical Care, 43*, 960–969. doi:10.2307/4640903

Street, R. L., Voigt, B., Geyer, C., Manning, T., & Swanson, G. P. (1995). Increasing patient involvement in choosing treatment for early breast cancer. *Cancer, 76*, 2275–2285. doi:10.1002/1097–0142(19951201)76:11<2275::AID-CNCR2820761115>3.0.CO;2-S

Sutherland, H. J., Llewellyn-Thomas, H. A., Lockwood, G. A., Tritchler, D. L., & Till, J. E. (1989). Cancer patients: Their desire for information and participation in treatment decisions. *Journal of the Royal Society of Medicine, 82*, 260–263.

Walsh, M. C., Trentham-Dietz, A., Schroepfer, T. A., Reding, D. J., Campbell, B., Foote, M. L., . . . Cleary, J. F. (2010). Cancer information sources used by patients to inform and influence treatment decisions. *Journal of Health Communication, 15*, 445–463. doi:10.1080/10810731003753109

Weber, K. M., Haunani Solomon, D., & Meyer, B.J.F. (2013). A qualitative study of breast cancer treatment decisions: Evidence for five decision-making styles. *Health Communication, 28*, 408–421. doi:10.1080/10410236.2012.713775

Whitney, S. N., Holmes-Rovner, M., Brody, H., Schneider, C., McCullough, L. B., Volk, R. J., & McGuire, A. L. (2008). Beyond shared decision making: An expanded typology of medical decisions. *Medical Decision Making, 28*, 699–705. doi:10.1177/0272989X08318465

Whitney, S. N., McGuire, A. L., & McCullough, L. B. (2004). A typology of shared decision making, informed consent, and simple consent. *Annals of Internal Medicine, 140*, 54–59.

Wilson, S. R., & Feng, H. (2007). Interaction goals and message production: Conceptual and methodological developments. In D. R. Roskos-Ewoldsen and L. Monahan (Eds.), *Communication and social cognition: Theories and methods* (pp. 71–96). Mahwah, NJ: Erlbaum.

Zhang, A. Y., & Siminoff, L. A. (2003). The role of the family in treatment decision making by patients with cancer. *Oncology Nursing Forum, 30*, 1022–1028. doi:10.1188/03.ONF.1022–1028

Zikmund-Fisher, B. J., Windschitl, P. D., Exe, N., & Ubel, P. A. (2011). "I'll do what they did": Social norm information and cancer treatment decisions. *Patient Education and Counseling, 85*, 225–229. doi:10.1016/j.pec.2011.01.031

CHAPTER CONTENTS

10 Integrating Intergenerational Family Caregiving Challenges Across Discipline and Culture

Identity, Attribution, and Relationship

Nichole Egbert

Kent State University

In the past few decades, worldwide increases in chronic illness and life expectancies have drastically amplified the burden experienced by family caregivers. As a result of their many responsibilities, caregivers are prone to greater physical, psychological, and relational strain as compared to their peers. The goal of this chapter is to spur interdisciplinary research to aid intergenerational family caregivers by integrating research from different disciplines and cultures. Three central communication challenges faced by caregivers (identity, attribution, and relationship) serve as reference points for this discussion.

Over the past few decades, improvements in sanitation and prevention of infectious disease have increased life expectancies in most developed countries.[1] Subsequently, more focus has been placed on reducing the number of years that individuals and families live with debilitating disease and injury due to chronic illness (Murray et al., 2012). The majority of individuals with serious impairments, such as those caused by heart disease, cancer, stroke, and age-related dementia, require sustained care in their activities of daily living. Informal family caregivers provide most of this care in the home voluntarily. For example, in 2009, approximately 43.5 million Americans (approximately 19% of all U.S. adults) were caregivers for older friends or relatives, and this number is expected to rise exponentially as the baby boomer generation nears retirement age (National Alliance for Caregiving, 2012). This demographic shift has substantially increased the length of time that people require a caregiver, as well as the number of individuals who will require care. In addition, birth rates are dropping in many developed nations, thereby reducing the number of younger family members available to provide care to older adults (Aldous, 1994; Suchy, 2013). Together, these developments have led to what the Rosalynn Carter Institute for Caregiving (2010) has termed a "caregiving crisis."

Social scientists have made great strides in describing how the stress and burden of informal family caregiving can affect both families and individuals (Walker, Pratt, & Eddy, 1995; Zarit, 1989). On one hand, caregivers are more likely than their non-caregiving peers to suffer depression, anxiety, and anger, as well as lost wages, marital and family conflict, and loss of identity (Zarit, 2006). Family caregivers are also more vulnerable to heart disease, high blood pressure, and diabetes (Vitaliano, Zhang, & Scanlan, 2003). On the other hand, providing care is also related to positive outcomes, such as emotional satisfaction and a closer relationship to the care receiver (Zarit, 2012). Although there is less research focusing on the effects of caregiving on care receivers (Lyons, Zarit, Sayer, & Whitlatch, 2002), negative effects for care receivers can include loss of identity, emotional strain, reduced self-esteem, and feelings of guilt and resentment (Newsom, 1999).

Much of the existing research on caregiving has focused on relieving the caregiver's burden (Young & Kahana, 1994), with scant attention paid to the effects of the communication between the family caregiver and care receiver (Edwards, 2001; Williams & Nussbaum, 2001). Providing care is fundamentally a communicative act (Giles, Coupland, & Wiemann, 1990), and the qualities of communication between caregiver and care receiver can have a great impact on the health of not only the care receiver but the caregiver as well. As one example, Edwards and Noller (1998) found that when caregivers communicate in a patronizing manner, receiving care is associated with depression, reduced morale, lower relational quality, and increased levels of pessimism. Perhaps more importantly, Edwards and Noller's research highlights how the dynamic process of communication between caregiver and care receiver holds more potential than do investigations of individual characteristics alone.

Nursing researchers have taken important steps toward the conceptualization of caregiving as a relational activity. Although there is ample research highlighting the physical responsibilities of caregivers in assisting with care receivers' activities of daily living (Walker et al., 1995), nursing scholars have argued that caregiving also involves "invisible" and communicative work in which caregivers communicate to anticipate future needs and decisions, actively monitor the care receiver's safety and well-being, check in with the care receiver, and protect the care receiver from threats to his or her self-image (Bowers, 1987). Overall, caregivers are devoting more hours to administrative tasks such as coordinating physician visits and managing finances, as well as engaging in companionship activities (averaging 5 hours per day; Mendes, 2011). These communication activities are a large part of what family caregivers do, but social scientists know too little about how caregivers engage in these activities, what their related challenges are, and how to help caregivers function optimally. To intervene effectively in these types of challenges, researchers need to know more about the actual communication between caregivers and care receivers (Edwards, 2001).

Communication researchers are especially well positioned to examine caregiving appropriately as the product of caregiver–care receiver interaction (Kahana & Young, 1990). Communication scholars have laid important theoretical groundwork that can be leveraged to assist care receivers and their family caregivers. These theories, along with several theories developed in psychology and nursing, provide important reference points in the landscape of social science research on family caregiving. This chapter draws on literature from disciplines such as nursing, social work, psychology, gerontology, sociology, and rehabilitation to integrate the disparate findings and approaches related to communication and intergenerational family caregiving.

The most recent Gallup poll reported that a large majority of American caregivers provide care for an aging parent (72%; Mendes, 2011). Despite this trend, the majority of studies on informal caregiving has focused on spousal caregivers (Harris et al., 2009), and more research on other caregiving dyads is sorely needed (Edwards, 2001; Newsom, 1999). Intergenerational family caregivers (adults who provide care for their aging parents or other older relatives) are typically employed outside of the home at least 15 hours per week and have been providing care for 3 years or more (Mendes, 2011). Mounting responsibilities leave little time for self-care, recreation, or rest, causing intergenerational caregivers to suffer both physically and mentally. The communication challenges of fulfilling these many roles are often augmented by challenges of communicating with the care receiver, who is a member of a different generation, perhaps at the same time as the caregiver is communicating with and providing care to his or her own child (Williams & Harwood, 2004). The impending "caregiving crisis," driven by shifting demographics, will likely result in an even larger proportion of intergenerational caregivers in need of communication tools that optimize quality care and reduce negative health outcomes.

The first goal of this chapter is to examine the literature of communication and related disciplines to take stock of what we know about conversations between intergenerational family caregivers and the older adult family members for whom they care. Three sizable challenges facing intergenerational family caregivers are addressed: identity and face issues, attribution and stereotype issues, and relational issues between caregiver and care receiver.[2] Issues of identity and face highlight the difficulty of being a care receiver and becoming dependent on others when one was previously autonomous. Attributions and stereotypes can become problematic for caregivers as they struggle through previously held perceptions of responsibility. Finally, the relationship between the caregiver and the care receiver is an essential variable in the caregiving equation because caregiving dyads are subject to the interdependent and shifting dynamics of relational history, context, and interaction.

The second goal of this chapter parallels the first in that these three core caregiver challenges can be points of similarity and distinction across culture. In this context, the caregiver and the care receiver represent different subcultures that are formed as a result of their unique perspectives and experiences as caregiver or care receiver (Levine & Murray, 2004). Additionally, caregivers and care receivers experience their roles and relationships within the larger context of their shared social and ethnic culture. Within these shared cultures, "each ethnic and minority group retains its own individual meaning of family structure and family caregiving" (Morycz, 1993, p. 68). However, culture is an enigmatic and multifaceted phenomenon that is difficult to capture in one definition or conceptualization (Ting-Toomey, 1999). To not bypass the importance of cultural considerations related to intergenerational family caregiving, this review considers Hofstede's (1983) dimensions of individualism and collectivism as a starting place for discussion. According to Hofstede, people from individualistic cultures live in loosely structured social networks and are expected to take care of their own needs. Conversely, in a collectivistic culture, social networks are more tightly knit, and network members are expected to depend on each other for resources and assistance. Providing a more integrated picture of intergenerational caregiving research can help coordinate the interdisciplinary efforts of researchers in developing effective and culturally relevant interventions and strategies.

Challenges of Identity and Face

Communication is pivotal in the social construction of face and identity, and both of these concepts are fundamental to understanding what it is like to provide or receive care from a family member. One tool that is particularly useful in examining the experiences of care receivers and caregivers is the idea of facework (Brown & Levinson, 1987). Individuals use facework strategically in relationships to preserve their own "face" as well as the face of the other person (Cupach & Metts, 1994). The two kinds of face that individuals aim to protect are positive face (the goal for others to see them in a positive way) and negative face (the goal of having their efforts not be hampered by others).

Whereas facework is what individuals use to negotiate how others see them, people see themselves as reflections of personal and social identities. Social identities (or cultural identities) include the aspects of being that we share only with other members of groups to which we feel we belong, such as professions, families, genders, and races. On the other hand, personal identities are those characteristics that we embrace as distinguishing us from other people (those characteristics that make us unique individuals; Tajfel & Turner, 1979). Communication makes it possible to discover and manage one's "emergent self," which is at the nexus of one's personal and social identity (Richey & Brown, 2007).

Major shifts in social and/or personal identities, such as those caused by becoming dependent on others because of illness or impairment, require care receivers to socially construct a new emergent self. Previously held roles, activities, and responsibilities must give way to adaptations, substitutions, and new visions of self. Physical changes such as reduced vision, hearing, cognition, and memory can constrain the communication required to engage in care receivers' identity transformation (Heine & Browning, 2002). Just as these changes may be very difficult to integrate as a part of one's personal identity, changes in social roles also challenge social identities. Retirement, relocation, and losses of friends, family members, and social groups (through death or other means) are all major life changes that can fundamentally alter one's social identity (Hansson & Carpenter, 1994).

In the best cases, care receivers' identity transformation will result in what Villagran, Fox, and O'Hair (2007) call an "agentic identity," a term that represents when a person takes control in synthesizing new social and personal aspects of identity. Villagran et al. argue that agency is the doorway of adaptive identity transformation. Increasing agency enhances one's quality of life through empowered communication. "Each word choice, each interaction, each relationship can be an opportunity to enact agentic identity. Illness of any kind can create a barrier to agency that must be consciously addressed in all psychosocial decision making" (Villagran et al., 2007, p. 139). The care receivers' agentic identity is continually constituted through communication, empowering people to "recontextualize their identity as co-equal participants in their own health care" (Villagran et al., 2007, p. 129).

Despite this potential, feeling empowered as a dependent care receiver is not easy. By accepting the role of "care receiver," one's personal and social identities are challenged. One of the caregivers' most difficult roles, therefore, is assisting the care receiver in the process of identity transformation toward achieving agentic identity. Bowers (1987) calls this "protective caregiving"— when the caregiver protects the care receiver's identity, such as trying to hide the fact that the care receiver is even receiving care. This type of care requires the caregiver to maintain contact with the care receiver, even when the care receiver may not even be aware the caregiver is doing it. Maintaining continuity of self (a sense of self even though changes are occurring) is crucial for care receivers, as well as for their communication and relationships with other people. Caregivers support care receivers' continuity of self by helping care receivers feel more independent and less like a burden (Aberg, Sidenvall, Hepworth, O'Reilly, & Lithell, 2004). In this way, family caregivers are somewhat uniquely tasked with protecting both the physical and social self of the care receiver (Aberg, et al., 2004).

Although health professionals and other social network members often assume that the work of caregiving consists primarily of the instrumental activities of helping, primary caregivers overwhelmingly reported in Bowers's (1987) benchmark study that protective caregiving was the most important and the most stressful. Protective caregiving requires the intergenerational family caregiver to maintain the care receiver's personal identity, as well as balance the relationship between them as parent and child. So, although the caregiver may feel that he or she is taking on a "parent" role because of the care provided, it is not a role reversal, because caregivers often must accomplish their caregiving duties in such a way as to make it look as if the previous parent–child relationship has been maintained, leading Bowers (1987) to state that "much of the stress associated with caregiving is related to the process of continually constructing and reconstructing the meanings of events" (p. 29). In this way, caregivers' communicative goal is often to "conceal the burden of care" from the care receivers to protect their personal identity and positive face (Gillespie, Murphy, & Place, 2010, p. 1571). For example, although forgetting things can seem like senility to caregivers, they may frame the forgetting as "the way it's always been" or provide some other acceptable excuse (Bowers, 1987).[3]

This process of "constructing and reconstructing the meanings of events" as they pertain to one's identity is akin to another communication concept that has been applied to intergenerational caregiving research—problematic integration, or "integrative dilemmas" (Hines, Babrow, Badzek, & Moss, 2001, p. 330). According to problematic integration theory, dilemmas occur when probabilistic orientations and evaluative orientations about an event (such as an illness) are difficult to integrate. For example, the likelihood that one will need to depend on one's child for a help with day-to-day needs can fluctuate based on many variables, one of which is one's health status following an event like a stroke. If the care receiver's identity is tightly bound to a career as a long-haul truck driver, for example, the care receiver might evaluate this potentiality as particularly bad and work to understand and possibly alter the characteristics of the probabilistic orientation (learn more about the nature of the stroke and possible outcomes). According to problematic integration theory, this is a divergent dilemma. Other types of problematic integration include ambivalence (having to choose from evaluative and/or probabilistic orientations that are equally unattractive) and ambiguity (not being able to form evaluative and/or probabilistic orientations due to complications or incomplete information; Babrow, 2001).

Becoming a caregiver or a care receiver will likely require some degree of problematic integration, which is also accomplished and experienced through communication. Ambivalence related to changing roles is one form of problematic integration that can be expected. In a recent study, Gill and Morgan (2011) used problematic integration theory to study older parents, adult daughters, and their changing roles related to moving the parents to a care-related facility. They found that although daughters were open about their ambivalence, older adults revealed their ambivalence indirectly through slippage (opposing feelings expressed later), vacillation (orientations not being resolved), and sarcasm. Care receivers' ambivalence was revealed when they talked about how their caregiver had control over a decision or consequence, although care receivers may struggle admitting to relinquishing control. Care receivers also expressed uncertainty about the future and divergence about more loss of independence (e.g., moving to a long-term care facility). Caregivers reported successful coping when they acknowledged and accepted impossible or divergent outcomes. Other methods of coping included focusing on the positive and remaining hopeful. In addition, reframing the situation as benevolence, or a good thing, helped with coping (e.g., they are giving their children a gift by making the choice to move, and the facility will allow them to be more—not less—independent). Thus, caregivers reported coping through changing evaluations rather than probabilities and through emotional regulation. In a related study, researchers argued that care receivers can experience ambivalence about treatment decisions, too. The interdisciplinary collaboration of Ohnsorge, Keller, Widdershoven, and

Rehmann-Sutter (2012) suggested that caregivers can best help care receivers by withholding judgment and supporting the care receivers' sometimes complex struggle between the ideal and the lived experience.

Cultural Differences Related to Identity and Face

Understanding cultural beliefs and values is crucial to grasping the reciprocal influences of identity and communication in any context, but especially in the context of intergenerational relationships, such as the one between an intergenerational family caregiver and care receiver. Similar to the idea of agentic identity, where care receivers take control of their identity transformation after becoming dependent, members of a culture exhibit their agency through their emergent selves when they decide how and when to express personal and cultural identities (Dutta & Basu, 2011). In both cases, identity is considered to be adaptive, evolving, flexible, and negotiated (Y. Kim, 2007). As culture is learned in the family and affects worldview, relationships, and communication, it is central to the study of family caregiving (Phillips et al., 1996).

For care receivers from individualistic cultures, maintaining independence is central to positive face, which is why caregivers in these societies endeavor to hide the assistance provided from the care receiver (Gillespie et al., 2010; Ussher, Wong, & Perz, 2010). The counterpoint to individualism and independence in non-Western cultures is an emphasis on collectivism and relationship to others. In these cultures "caregiving in an interdependent sociocultural context is focused on the goals of promoting emotional closeness and social harmony, and care recipients are encouraged to develop multiple social relationships and accommodate themselves to the larger social group" (Giesbrecht, 2009, p. 376). For example, in India, the focus on harmony and duty leads to the idea that depending on others is nothing to be ashamed about, especially within families (Iwakuma & Nussbaum, 2000). These caregiving relationships foster other-oriented feelings such as sympathy and respect and strive to avoid disagreement. Conversely, in cultures that value independence, having to depend on others can cause conflict in interpersonal relationships. For example, the need for the caregiver to perform medical-related tasks such as dressing wounds or changing a colostomy bag can cause a relational strain between caregiver and care receiver, as the care receiver feels a loss of personal and bodily autonomy (Ussher et al., 2010).

It is important to keep in mind that cultures themselves are not homogenous (Pecchioni, Ota, & Sparks, 2004). For example, cultural groups within the United States vary considerably in their orientations toward independence and interdependence. Specifically, Native American caregiving stresses interdependence over independence, and caregivers from Italian American and Irish American cultures emphasize the importance of respect for the elderly and the responsibility for providing care (Merrill, 1997). Mexican American families are likely to interact frequently and to live in close geographic proximity; however, many elders in this culture do not receive the daily assistance that they require in terms of help with transportation, meals, and finances (Dietz, 1995). Thus, researchers interested in studying caregiving must consider the unique characteristics of a population before intervening in what may be a complex web of cultural and individual factors related to aging.

A focus on problems of identity and face provides the foundation for this review to build outward to the social perception of others through attribution and stereotype, which is the second central challenge of intergenerational caregiving. Although both are perceptual processes occurring through communication, constructing identity tends to be a social process reflecting inward, whereas constructing attributions also reflects perceptions out to others.

Challenges of Attribution and Stereotype

The second set of central challenges for intergenerational caregivers builds on the concept of identity (how people view themselves) to how people view each other. The field of psychology introduced the concept of attributions, or inferences people make about other people and their behaviors. These explanatory mechanisms are the basis for how people interpret another person's behavior as intentional and/or a result of the other's personality (internal attribution), or non-intentional and/or a result of the other's environment (external attribution; Harvey & Weary, 1984; Heider, 1958). The fundamental attribution error occurs when people indiscriminately apply external attributions to their own negative behaviors while applying internal attributions to their positive behaviors. On the other hand, people also have the tendency to perceive that other people are responsible for their failures and others' successes are the result of luck or circumstances.

The concept of attribution is helpful for framing misperceptions such as these, especially when studying communication between caregivers and care receivers with dementia, because it can be particularly difficult for caregivers to make appropriate attributions; it is hard to determine what is due to the care receiver personally and what is due to the dementia (Martin-Cook, Ramakel-Davis, Svetlik, Hynan, & Weiner, 2003; Polk, 2005). Behaviors that the caregiver sees as difficult for the care receiver to control are not viewed as intentional and therefore not judged negatively (i.e., the behavior is given an external attribution—due to the illness, not the person). On the contrary, if the caregiver sees a behavior as controllable, intentional, or in keeping with the care receiver's character prior to illness, it may be judged more harshly (i.e., given an internal attribution—the care receiver is personally to blame).

In particular, family caregivers of people with Alzheimer's disease often struggle to remind themselves to attribute negative behaviors of the care receiver to the disease (Polk, 2005). Especially in stressful situations, caregivers report attributing the negative behavior at least partly to the care receivers' personality. Research from psychology has shown that when these (mis)attributions are made, caregivers are more likely to lash out in frustration with the care receivers. For example, caregivers of people with lung cancer who blamed the care receivers for their disease had higher depression scores than did caregivers who did not blame the care receivers (Siminoff, Wilson-Genderson, & Baker, 2010). Although negative interactions are reported less frequently than positive interactions, they have been related to lower care receiver morale and more psychiatric symptoms in elderly care receivers who had suffered a stroke (Stephens, Kinney, Norris, & Ritchie, 1987). Caregivers often regret this reaction and again struggle with their attributions, reminding themselves that it is the disease, not the person, causing the behavior. In the end, when caring for a care receiver with a cognitive impairment, it is not necessarily the disruptive behaviors of the care receiver that cause caregiver resentment, but the number of behaviors that the caregiver attributes to the care receiver being willfully manipulative or controlling (Williamson et al., 2005).

Although they can be somewhat difficult to grasp, Stewart (1989) warns that overlooking attributional processes could cause researchers to miss the "multidimensional nature of social support and help-seeking" (p. 1276). Martin-Cook et al. (2003) similarly concluded that "premorbid relationship factors, patient function, pattern of cognitive impairment, caregiver personality, and behavioral disturbance all play a key role in the attributions caregivers make regarding the care recipient and caregiving" (p. 372). The repercussions of caregivers' wrongful attributions are similarly multidimensional and interrelated, affect both the caregiver and the care receiver (Siminoff et al., 2010), and can lead to relationship dissatisfaction and distress (Hui, Elliott, Martin, & Uswatte, 2010).

In addition to the research on internal versus external attributions, attributions can be used to illuminate how ingroup and outgroup differences form the basis for stereotypes that affect communication (Stephan, 1977). Unfortunately, many times the most salient information available to an observer relates to the target's social groups. These groups may include such constructs as race, gender, occupation, physical attractiveness, and age, as well as more specific constructs such as membership in social clubs or participation in a particular hobby. When one indiscriminately applies a group's stereotypical attributes to the dispositions and/or future behavior of an individual person, stereotyping occurs.

Stereotypes for older adults that are based on the attributions of younger adults can be both positive and negative. Positive stereotypes of older adults include being the "perfect grandparent" (wise, generous, interesting), a "liberal matriarch/patriarch" (distinguished-looking, alert, patriotic), and the "John Wayne conservative" (tough, conservative, tells stories about the past; Hummert, 1990). Negative stereotypes include that older adults are inflexible, self-centered, reclusive, severely impaired, shrew- or curmudgeon-like, vulnerable, and despondent.

Negative stereotypes of dependent older adults are cued when younger adults interact with them and form the blanket attribution that older people are uniformly incompetent and dependent in all areas of their lives. Based on these stereotypes, they may assume that the older adults are impaired due to age and communicate more slowly, simply, loudly, and so on (called elderspeak; Ryan, Hummert & Boich, 1995). In elderspeak, these types of communication patterns combine to form an exaggerated, patronizing tone, almost as if the older adult is childlike. The caregiver's performance of elderspeak reduces the enjoyment of the communication for the care receiver and can result in feelings of low self-esteem and disrespect.

As family caregiving is an interactional and interdependent process, the negative effects of elderspeak can extend to both caregiver and care receiver. When observed by a third party,

> speakers using elderspeak are rated as disrespectful, patronizing, unprofessional, angry, frustrated, dislikable, unintelligent, and unable to communicate well. At the same time, targets of elderspeak are seen as incompetent and incapable, with poor memory and communication skills. They are also considered frustrated, angry, unhappy, and displeased . . . [T]hese negative effects of elderspeak occur regardless of the age of the speaker, the relationship of the speaker and target, and the age of the observer. (Balsis & Carpenter, 2005, p. 90)

According to communication accommodation theory (Coupland, Coupland, Giles, & Henwood, 1988), elderspeak (the exaggerated patterns of simplifying language, slowing vocal rate, and increasing volume) is over-accommodation. Although an older adult may speak more slowly, the performance of elderspeak that amplifies the stereotype of aging adults as incompetent and slow does not reduce the social distance between the younger and older adult; in essence, it communicates that the younger adult is dissimilar to, and wishes to disassociate with, the older adult.

The problem of stereotypes and elderspeak in intergenerational communication can be tied back to the issue of caregiver identity through the communication predicament model of aging (Ryan, Giles, Bartolucci, & Henwood, 1986). In this model, the recognition of cues that characterize old age (physiological, psychological, and sociocultural) trigger old age stereotypes such as those discussed above. These stereotypes, according to communication accommodation theory, can cause the caregiver to exaggerate his or her speech in ways that are patronizing in tone. If this pattern of communication occurs a great deal (such as in daily interaction between a caregiver and care receiver), it could reinforce the very types of behaviors that are indicative of the stereotype (incompetence, impairment, etc.). As discussed earlier, because identity is socially constructed through people's communication and relationships, the negative feedback occurring as a result of elderspeak can facilitate changes in the identity of the care receiver to be in keeping with the feedback. In time, these perceptions of identity can affect the care receiver's physiological, psychological, and sociocultural identities through a sense of loss of personal control and self-esteem (Barker, Giles, & Harwood, 2004). Thus, in the end, the stereotype becomes the reality.

To illustrate further how these negative patterns of communication may lead to changes in the care receiver's self-concept, psychology researchers Baltes and Wahl (1996) discovered two recurring patterns of negative repetitive discourse: the independence-ignore and the dependence-support script. The first script occurs when the care receiver's efforts toward independence and self-sufficiency fail to be noticed by the caregiver. This disconfirming reaction can discourage the care receiver from trying to be independent, a phenomenon called "learned helplessness." Simultaneously, the care receiver's dependent behaviors are met with the caregiver's attention and support, even when the caregiver has applied an internal attribution. Although the caregiver may become frustrated with the care receiver's lack of ability, the disability stereotype is applied broadly instead of taking into account what the individual care receiver *can do*. In essence, the dependence-support script becomes the default in old age, whereas for younger adults, independence is the status quo. This research arrives at similar conclusions as the communication predicament model of aging, although it builds on social cognitive theory instead of on communication accommodation theory (Baltes & Wahl, 1996).

It should be noted that care receivers' attributions of others can be problematic as well. A series of studies by psychologists Hess and Blanchard-Fields showed that older adults are more likely than younger adults to "make snap attributional judgments" in lieu of "conscious, deliberate, well-thought-out causal analyses" (Blanchard-Fields, 1999, p. 223). Particularly with regard to negative relational outcomes, older adults tend to default to "automatic, rule-based social schemas and/or beliefs relevant to how an actor should behave" (Blanchard-Fields, 1999, pp. 223–224). Possible reasons for this perspective include that declining cognitive functioning may lead older adults to utilize only the most salient, accessible information, such as stereotypes. Another explanation is that older adults are less likely than younger adults to alter their first impressions of others even when presented with new or inconsistent information. Regardless, Blanchard-Fields (1999) cautioned that the effects of individual differences should also be taken into account when comparing younger and older adults. Thus, just as in considerations of culture, variations both between and within groups of individuals must be continuously sorted out before arriving at specific recommendations.

Cultural Differences Related to Attributes and Stereotypes

Although attribution theory as a general process can be applied cross-culturally, the way in which a culture's worldview focuses responsibility on a person or on some external factor can differ considerably. This section reviews attribution processes related to illness and caregiving in cultures other than the dominant European American culture in the United States. Because the research on intergenerational family caregiving in countries other than the United States is less extensive, this section also reviews research findings regarding the role of attributions in minority cultures within the United States.

Similar to the cross-cultural distinctions regarding face and identity, attributions often differ with regard to Hofstede's (1983) spectrum of individualistic and collectivistic cultures. In a recent U.K. study in which minority groups were asked about their caregiving practices, respondents commonly referenced their culture, whereas nonminority caregivers were more likely to speak about their individual personality or family (Willis, 2012). Parveen, Morrison, and Robinson (2011) similarly noted that minority caregivers felt rewarded in fulfilling their duty, whereas nonminority caregivers benefitted by learning new skills and acquiring life experience. Taken together, these studies, mostly from psychology, suggest that in caregivers' motivations for providing care, culture is much more salient in the attributions of individuals from collectivist cultures, even if the behaviors are similar to those enacted by those from individualist cultures.

The significance of cultural values in collectivistic cultures shapes how the caregiving role is perceived and enacted. Even the term *caregiver* polarizes cultural perceptions; whereas European Americans may use this term, it is not used frequently among African Americans or Asian Americans. For these minority populations, being a caregiver is not a role that people can choose to accept or not accept, but is the normal and expected fulfillment of familial duty (Milne & Chryssanthopoulou, 2005). Samoan families living in Hawaii are similar in that their culture values cooperation and interdependence. Growing old in this culture is seen as a peaceful time of life where elders can count on family members to take care of them (Tauiliili, Delva, & Browne, 2001). Latino immigrants living in the United States also see old age as a time of reward and high status. In this culture, children are bound socially and morally to care for their elderly parents (Beyene, Becker, & Mayen, 2002). Thus, one of the major attributions that differs by culture is how younger members of the culture view older generations. The negative stereotypes of older adults that form the basis of the communication predicament model of aging are less common in collectivistic cultures such as these.

Unfortunately, however, cultural attributions of illness (as opposed to simply old age) can lead to the misperception that elders in collectivistic cultures are universally respected by younger adults. For older adults becoming less independent, loss of cognitive functioning due to dementia can be stigmatizing even in collectivistic cultures where mutual help in families is highly valued. For example, in Vietnamese culture, stigma is applied to an elder's behavior depending on whether it is attributed to normal aging or mental illness. In Vietnamese, the word *lân* means confused due to normal aging, whereas two other words, *dien* and *binh than kinh*, are derogatory terms meant to stigmatize the behavior and show a lack of respect for the care receiver. Interestingly, caregivers who used the more derogatory terms were observed to be more burdened and distressed than the other caregivers (Yeo, Tran, Hikoyeda, & Hinton, 2001). Similarly, in South Asian communities in the United Kingdom, dementia and mental illness are regarded as shameful, and families commonly try to deny the problem or to pass the symptoms off as a physical illness (Willis, 2012).

Although China and Vietnam are generally considered to be more collectivistic cultures, recent research undertaken with immigrant Chinese and Vietnamese populations in the United States has revealed that negative stigmas related to aging and mental illness take their toll on family caregivers and care receivers. In their interviews with these minority caregivers, the medical research team of Liu, Hinton, Tran, Hinton, and Barker (2008) discovered a mixed set of negative and positive attributions:

> The disability, cognitive decline, and even the behavioral changes of older persons with dementia were thus viewed as a less desired trajectory of aging, while simultaneously an understandable and normal part of the aging process. A growing dependence on others and difficult or strange behaviors of the person with dementia were thus attributed to their becoming "childish," "confused," "foolish," or just "difficult." (p. 293)

In line with the communication predicament model of aging, the negative stereotypes of aging amongst Asian immigrants in the United States can lead to care receivers seeing themselves as being less of a person or as even worthless.

In mainland China, the relationships between aging, stigma, and caregiving are similarly muddled. When families see dementia as a normal part of aging, stigma is not usually attached to the care receiver or the caregiving family. However, if the dementia is seen as mental illness, and especially when outward symptoms of the dementia are more obvious, the stigma is attached through the prejudiced views of the wider society (Ramsay, 2010). In these situations, the family assumes the responsibility of the negative behavior or stigma instead of attributing it to the illness. Similar to the South Asian immigrant families mentioned earlier, Chinese families often attempt to avoid these stigmatizing attributions by hiding or denying the behavior or symptom.

Japan offers an interesting counterpoint to these Asian cultures in that Japanese families feel fewer obligations to care for elderly parents than even U.S. families do (Asai & Kameoka, 2005). Surprisingly, elders in Japan are stigmatized when they exhibit a reduced ability to maintain their social roles and networks. In addition, illness and aging are given internal attributions because people are held responsible for their own actions and condition. Older adults experience shame and loss of face when behaviors and aging cues are made public, thus stirring prejudicial and negative attitudes of observers. Instead, the concept of *sekentei* is prioritized, which is the social pressure to maintain one's public appearance, reputation, or dignity (Asai & Kameoka, 2005).

We should not overlook that many cultures will attribute the responsibility for illness (and even aging) to God. Latino populations residing in the United States, for example, attribute both their blessings in life and their trials to God's will; both aging and death are part of nature and should be accepted as part of God's plan. In Thailand and Pakistan, however, illness and disability are attributed to God and are seen as punishment or bad karma (Iwakuma & Nussbaum, 2000). Therefore, just like internal attributions, external attributions can be seen as both protective and damaging to identity.

In all, these studies show that there are similarities, as well as differences, in the way that cultures make attributions about aging and intergenerational caregiving. Although the beliefs about aging and illness may vary, as well as the characteristics of social networks, some variables still apply across cultural lines. For example, Chappell (2003) argued that the receipt of social support, whether it is from a close-knit family or a wider network of friends, contributes to quality of life for care receiver and their caregivers. Similarly, the type and magnitude of illness and/or impairment that requires the caregiving will affect quality of life as well. Other factors such as available resources and socioeconomic status should also not be overlooked in any comparative discussion of culture.

Challenges Related to Caregiver–Care Receiver Relationship

One limitation in the caregiving research is that many studies do not include the perspective of the care receiver or do not focus on the relationship between the caregiver and care receiver (Lyons et al., 2002; Newsom, 1999). However, to develop appropriate interventions and support services, the holistic perspective of the caregiver–care receiver dyad must be considered (Hollis-Sawyer, 2003). Thus, the third set of intergenerational caregiving challenges deals with the relationship between caregiver and care receiver. As in the previous two sections, theory undergirds our understanding of core concepts, leading to the communication-related outcomes of intergenerational family caregiving.

Social exchange theory is a good place to begin this discussion because many disciplines consider it a staple theory for conceptualizing relationship dynamics (Cook & Rice, 2006). Social exchange theory explains relationships as the pragmatic computation of rewards and costs. Rewards received from a relationship partner can be affection, time, social network inclusion, or anything else that is valued. Conversely, costs are things that an individual feels are drawbacks to the relationship, such as "spending" time, energy, and money. When engaged in an exchange relationship, individuals consider if the rewards of the relationship outweigh the costs, and the comparison of the relationship's reward/cost ratio to that of other potential relationships. Relational researchers have turned often to this theory. For example, many studies on social support have cited Shumaker and Brownell's (1984) conceptualization of social support as "an exchange of resources between two individuals perceived by the provider or the recipient to be intended to enhance the well-being of the recipient" (p. 11).

Equity theory rests on the same premise as social exchange theory, yet it extends this idea to include perceptions of the other partner's reward/cost ratio. If one's relational partner appears to be profiting a great deal less or a great deal more from the relationship, one would consider the relationship to be unbalanced (Hatfield, Walster, & Berscheid, 1978). Equity theory includes the idea that inequitable relationships cause distress and that individuals in inequitable relationships will work to restore equity, not just to maximize their relational rewards and to minimize costs. Both equity theory and social exchange theory are useful tools due to their intuitive appeal and the heuristic metaphor of monetary gains and losses.

Applying these ideas, a major relational challenge created by becoming a caregiver or care receiver in a preestablished family relationship is that the existing system of rewards and costs becomes unbalanced. Becoming a caregiver alters the reward/cost ratio of participating in a relationship with a care receiver, in that the rewards one had received historically may no longer be accessible in the same way. In addition, the care receiver now requires increased attention, money, time, and other relational "costs" (Pecchioni, Wright, & Nussbaum, 2005). Not being able to "give back," or reciprocate as before, relational rewards due to illness or impairment can cause the care receiver to feel useless (Dyeson, 2000) and depressed (Wolff & Agree, 2004), which can have a negative impact on the care receiver's personal identity in general and as a relationship partner. Thus, the well-being of both members of a relationship is influenced by how the care receiver can give back to the caregiver (or the family) and if the care receiver feels like a burden (Dyeson, 2000). On a positive note, when care receivers are frail or otherwise marginalized, expressions of gratitude and thanks can be seen as reciprocity, and accomplishments and experiences that care receivers have accrued during a lifetime (reputation, identity, sense of self) can also be symbolic reciprocity. However, when reciprocity is seen to be lacking, care receivers are more likely to suffer from depression (Wolff & Agree, 2004).

Although the social exchange/equity framework is intuitive, not everyone agrees on its fundamental premise. Communal relationships theory, out of the discipline of psychology, illuminates the nature of relationships instead of the individuals who participate in them. According to communal relationships theory, communal relationships are characterized by responsive behavior designed to meet the recipient's needs and are most commonly made up of close friends, romantic partners, and family members (Clark & Mills, 1979). In communal relationships (as opposed to exchange relationships, in which individuals expect immediate and like reciprocity), people pay more attention to one another's needs, help out with these needs, and do not keep record of how many times each helps the other. In fact, even when the other partner cannot reciprocate, the helping partner does not feel used and may actually feel good about helping. Researchers speculate that if a relationship is considered communal before illness onset, there will be fewer symptoms of depression after dependency (Williamson & Schulz, 1995).

Alternative perspectives regarding the way that intergenerational caregiving relationships function have led to additional theorizing, such as the theory of intergenerational solidarity (Bengston, Olander, & Haddad, 1976).

Intergenerational solidarity is the product of communication between adult caregivers and their care receiver parents (Williams & Nussbaum, 2001). Gerontologist Bengston and colleagues (1976) argued that the three factors affecting solidarity in intergenerational relationships are association (interpersonal contact, proximity), affection (helping behavior, duty), and agreement (consensus, communication). Solidarity is associated with relational closeness and cohesion and is bolstered by these factors in intergenerational relationships. Solidarity is often threatened by competing demands from children and parents for autonomy and individuality; however, if the intergenerational communication between them is fostered, the two parties can negotiate these tensions successfully (Williams & Nussbaum, 2001).

Unfortunately, however, some amount of conflict is inevitable in any relationship (Cahn, 1994) and thus continues to be a factor in intergenerational family relationships after one member begins to be dependent on the other for ongoing care. For example, research has shown that, prior to dependency, mother–daughter dyads often do not report many instances of conflict or disagreement (Pecchioni & Nussbaum, 2001), suggesting that mothers and daughters "choose their battles" and typically do not argue over small issues. This finding supports other researchers' conclusions that most adult child-parent relationships are positive ones (Nussbaum, Pecchioni, Robinson, & Thompson, 2000). However, when conflict does occur, especially once the parent has become a care receiver and the adult child a caregiver, the ensuing communication can negatively affect the mental health of both individuals. Surprisingly, however, when conflict in the family is perceived by either the caregiver or the care receiver, caregivers are more likely than care receivers to become depressed (Siminoff et al., 2010). Some potential sources of conflict between care receiver and family caregivers include discrepancies regarding the care receiver's care preferences (Reamy, Kim, Zarit, & Whitlach, 2011) and the types and amount of social support exchanged between parent and child (K. Kim, Zarit, Eggebeen, Birditt, & Fingerman, 2011).

In addition to conflict, relationships between caregivers and care receivers are subject to issues of autonomy and paternalism (Pecchioni, 2000). When stripped of their autonomy, older adults are likely to experience powerlessness, or feel that they have no control over particular events (Onega & Larson, 2002). Feelings of powerlessness are significant because they are related to increases in impairment and physical symptoms, as well as deteriorating health and future health problems (Onega & Larson, 2002). Limited resources and illness uncertainty can contribute to actual or perceived powerlessness (Cicirelli, 1992). Unwittingly, caregivers may be causing care receivers' feelings of powerlessness through overprotection and paternalism (concern for a care receiver and a belief that the caregiver knows what is best and has a moral responsibility to intervene). In other studies, paternalism in caregivers was related to lower life satisfaction for both caregivers and care receivers (Edwards & Noller, 1998), and communication satisfaction was improved when the caregiver had a higher level of autonomy in the relationship (Semlak & Pearson, 2011). Research by communication scholars Pecchioni and Nussbaum (2000) found that even prior to dependency, mothers' and daughters' paternalism was positively related to daughters controlling the conversation between them.

In general, research on caregiver–care receiver relationships has revealed that relationship quality plays a significant role in depression, satisfaction with caregiving, and other key outcome variables for both the caregiver and the care receiver. There is some evidence that relationship quality is even more important to care receivers' well-being than is the care receivers' level of physical functioning (Parsons, Cox, & Kimboko, 1989). Pecchioni and Nussbaum's (2000) findings suggest that mothers and daughters develop attitudes about decision making, paternalism, and autonomy before the mothers become care receivers and that these patterns are likely to persist once the daughters assume more of a caregiving role. In the case of care receivers with dementia and their caregivers, research has confirmed that the prior relationship between the caregiver and the care receiver will affect the form of the relationship between the two individuals after dementia onset (Ablitt, Jones, & Muers, 2009).

Becoming a caregiver can precipitate both positive and negative changes in the caregiver's relationship with the care receiver (Stone, Mikucki-Enyart, Middleton, Caughlin, & Brown, 2012). For example, the caregiver, out of necessity, may seek and gain medical expertise on the care receiver's situation. Along with the other roles of caregiver, this new expertise can make the caregiver feel more in control and capable. Also, the emotional challenges of being both an adult child and a caregiver can bring about changes (e.g., the adult child, who is upset, must put on a brave face and take on the responsibility of difficult decisions, or the adult child, wanting to be supportive, must also be the caregiver who has to monitor challenging behavioral changes). The caregiver may feel resentful of other family members who can just be supportive but do not have to monitor or challenge the care receiver. Another relationship change reported by caregivers in Ussher et al.'s study (2010) was related to the protective caregiving role described earlier; family caregivers became less likely to express their needs and changed their communication patterns to avoid conflict with the care receiver.

In general, research across disciplines generally supports the conclusion that communication between caregivers and care receivers affects quality of care, feelings of burden, and relationship quality (Phillips et al., 1996). Understanding the process by which communication can facilitate or obstruct intergenerational caregiver–care receiver relationships is complicated by factors such as age, identity, attribution, prior relationship patterns, and socioeconomic status. The transition to a caregiver–care receiver relationship is one of the most challenging paths to navigate because "no clear-cut parameters exist for the roles of parent or child at this point in the life span" (Gill & Morgan, 2011, p. 333).

Cultural Differences Related to Caregiver–Care Receiver Relationships

Intergenerational family caregiving relationships are situated within the larger contexts of family and culture; they are bound inextricably to both family and cultural beliefs. In addition, culture and family are interlocking concepts, as culture is transmitted to younger generations via the family and families are cultures in and of themselves. This chapter now turns to consider the role of intergenerational caregiving relationships in different disciplines and cultures. One helpful tool that is used to analyze family relationships in cross-cultural comparisons is familism, or filial piety. Similar to intergenerational solidarity, familism is a cultural belief in lifetime loyalty, solidarity, and reciprocity among family members. Although family piety is present in all cultures, it is traditionally less characteristic of European Americans than of ethnic minorities in the United States, such as Korean Americans and Latino Americans (Crowther & Austin, 2009; Schwarz, Trommsdorff, Zheng, & Shi, 2010).

In cultures characterized by a strong belief in filial piety, there exists a stronger sense of reciprocity of care across generations. Older family members often look after young children while younger adults work, understanding that the younger adults will take care of the older family members when they age. In many collectivistic cultures, when there is no spouse able to provide care to a care receiver, an adult daughter usually takes responsibility automatically. Thus, as a rule, these families are much less likely to even consider utilizing care facilities or home-based professional health services (Olson, 2003). Although cultural beliefs about family responsibility affect decisions regarding professional care, socioeconomic status and racial discrimination also play a role. For many African American families, for example, the church adds to the social and psychological well-being of its elder members, but it does not directly provide sustained eldercare or health care services. In this culture, adult daughters fill in the gap as caregivers. Unfortunately, the negative ramifications for caregiving African American daughters is that they are more likely to be caring for both children and parents, more likely to be in poorer health themselves, and more dependent on lower paying jobs than are European American caregiving daughters (Olson, 2003).

In Japan, traditional views of family piety that have constrained women to family caregiving roles now compete with demographic and sociocultural shifts in the population (Tanaka & Johnson, 2008). Similar to the postindustrial United States, more Japanese women are seeking higher education and establishing their careers prior to starting a family. Because the Japanese population has one of the longest life expectancies in the world, coupled with one of the lowest birth rates, the shortage of family caregivers has ballooned, placing traditional views of filial piety at odds with modern conceptions of families that include small family size and dual-income households.

As with the earlier discussions of identity and attribution, the cultural differences aligning along Hofstede's individualism–collectivism continuum can be applied to caregiver–care receiver relationships. As intergenerational caregivers from more collectivistic cultures focus on relationships and social roles that bring people together, their caregiving relationships are characterized by harmony and connection. Family caregivers strive to avoid conflict and to develop intergenerational solidarity through empathy and respect. Similarly, care receivers are expected to continue to participate in their social networks and endeavor to fit in with the larger social group (Matsumoto & Juang, 2008). On the other hand, intergenerational caregivers from more individualistic cultures work hard to encourage the care receivers' independence and individual identity. As discussed in the first section, protective caregiving is a primary goal for individualistic caregivers. In this regard, caregivers hope to promote agency within the care receivers so that they can be advocates for their own needs, express themselves openly, and maintain their individuality for as long as possible (Giesbrecht, 2009).

Among collectivistic cultures, however, the expectations and practices of reciprocity in families differ. For example, Latino families are characterized by strong norms of reciprocity that emphasize interdependence among the various family members, especially those in the immediate family. Supportive behavior from children is expected out of respect for the functions their parents performed for them as children (Beyene et al., 2002). In a comparative analysis of German and Chinese adult daughters' (rural and urban) attitudes toward caring for their parents, the adult daughters from rural areas in China were higher on perceived support provided to parents, in line with the Confucian ethic of familism (Schwartz et al., 2010). The urban Chinese daughters, however, were more similar to the German sample, reflecting a shift from traditional Chinese models of reciprocity and filial piety. The "erosion" of Chinese filial piety in urban areas suggests that conceptualizations of family structure and eldercare are in need of continual revision (Ng, Phillips, & Lee, 2002). Thus caregiving relationships from individualistic and collectivistic cultures differ with regard to the emphasis placed on facilitating the care receiver's connectedness to the caregiver (and the family unit if one exists), or facilitating the care receiver's autonomy and individuality. Caregivers from individualistic cultures also strive to maintain their autonomy in the face of their changing role. For example, when European American caregivers from the United States perceive that they have more autonomy in their relationship to the care receiver, they are more satisfied (Semlak & Pearson, 2011).

One final difference that distinguishes different cultural viewpoints of intergenerational caregiving is time orientation (Bruneau, 1979). According to Hall (1976), cultures can be monochromic (time is inflexible, tangible, and separates personal and work tasks) or polychromic (time is fluid, flexible, and governed by interpersonal relationships). Time orientation further underlines how intergenerational communication can demonstrate an intercultural dimension. For example, socio-emotional selectivity theory, a life-span theory of motivation, introduces a "time orientation" factor for intergenerational relationships (Carstensen, 1998). According to socio-emotional selectivity theory, as individuals age, their socio-emotional goals shift from a future-orientation with a focus on securing information, experiences, and new social contacts, to a focus on developing a smaller number of close, familiar, and meaningful relationships (Lockenhoff & Carstensen, 2004). This goal shift occurs in later life when care receivers perceive that they have limited time left in their lives, so they focus on the present instead of the future and seek positive emotional experiences over acquiring additional knowledge or personal development. Thus, if a researcher is interested in understanding how time orientation relates to a problem in intergenerational caregiving, perspectives of both the care receiver and the caregiver should be considered. For example, the difficulty of encouraging care receivers from an older generation to participate in health-related support group meetings could be attributable to culture (the care receiver does not operate on the same time orientation as the support group) or to stage in the life span (the care receiver does not value expanding his or her social network and learning about new things).

This juxtaposition of time-related theories illustrates the overarching goal of this review—to overlay research from different disciplines and cultures using important problems or concepts as reference points. Not only is part of the picture missing when one fails to consider the impact of culture on family relationships and the aging process, but researchers are also constrained by cultural perspective when theorizing about their findings. In the same way, ignoring the research coming out of related academic disciplines can likewise lead to a myopic view of highly complex human experiences. Although gerontology and gerontology-related specializations in social science are historically more inclusive, diverse, and interdisciplinary than are most academic factions, continued efforts toward expanded integration of theory and research are needed to leverage the important advancements made by colleagues in other disciplines.

Conclusion

This chapter has outlined some of the central challenges for intergenerational caregivers as they relate to the individual (identity), the caregiver (attribution), and the relationship between the caregiver and care receiver. Although certainly not an exhaustive review of important factors, these three concepts provide a basis for the discussion of intergenerational caregiving in cultures both within and outside of the United States. This discussion is vital because the powerful relationships described in the previous paragraphs between such concepts as identity and attribution may vary significantly between different cultural groups. On the other hand, there are also fundamental similarities between and within cultures that should not be overlooked. Finally, as intergenerational interactions are themselves a form of intercultural communication (Coupland, Coupland, & Giles, 1991), the implications for communication research are substantial in both depth (level of sophistication and understanding) and breadth (applying to diverse areas of research).

This integrated approach, although lacking the precision of discipline-specific theories, allows researchers to not lose sight of the "forest" for the "trees" (so to speak). In the end, everything about intergenerational caregiving, from the motivations for assuming a caregiver role to how caregiving is enacted through communication, is culturally bound (Wallhagen & Yamamoto-Mitani, 2006). A word of caution is necessary, however, because even research taking a comparative cultural approach is vulnerable to "overly simplistic conclusions and to outcomes which are regarded as significant only as they relate to the majority experience" (Janevic & Connell, 2001). With this caveat in mind, this chapter aimed to demonstrate how contemporary research in intergenerational caregiving could be meaningfully integrated via the three challenges of identity, attribution, and relationship. These three concepts are central to many of the theories and research programs that focus on caregiving problems and can be used as reference points, or constellations, to guide researchers in identifying key issues across discipline and culture.

As an illustration, the idea of protective caregiving has emerged as a central goal for caregivers in the dominant U.S. culture. As the goal of protective caregiving is to obscure the work of caregiving from the care receiver to protect personal identity, it is cast as "invisible" labor and has been largely neglected by researchers. However, communication researchers, in particular, must better understand the nature of protective caregiving as a prerequisite to assisting caregivers who struggle to provide it. On the other hand, in more collectivistic cultures, personal identity goals are eclipsed by social identity goals. For members of these cultures, the "invisible" caregiving that protects the family, tribe, village, and so on from identity threats related to illness and aging may take a different form. In China and Vietnam, for example, where a care receiver's mental illness stigmatizes the entire family, effective caregiving includes identity protection for the family as well as the individual. Although recent research has begun to untangle the competing influences of filial piety and social stigma for Chinese caregivers (Liu et al., 2008; Ramsay, 2010), few theory-driven interventions have yet been developed. Several theories such as those identified in this chapter (problematic integration theory, communication predicament model of aging, attribution theory, etc.) may be applicable in their current form, adapted for cross-cultural study, or additional theorizing may be necessary. In any case, interdisciplinary teams of researchers will be best equipped to help intergenerational caregivers tackle the joint challenge of providing care and protecting identity (both personal and social). The most accurate picture of these processes is captured by layering the perspectives of fields such as social psychology, interpersonal communication, health communication, family communication, and sociology.

As a second illustration, the intersection of issues such as reciprocity, conflict, and stigma could provide an orientation for understanding elder abuse and neglect. The first worldwide survey of elder abuse identified intergenerational conflict and stigma as contributors to elder abuse (Podnieks, Anetzberger, Wilson, Teaster, & Wangmo, 2010). Specifically, family caregivers who hold rigid stereotypes about older adult care receivers are more likely to feel justified in committing abuse (Brandl, 2000). The importance of reciprocity is evident in that even in a population of Chinese caregivers and care receivers, both verbal and physical abuse by caregivers was related to the degree of inequity between the care receiver's dependence on the caregiver and the caregiver's lack of dependence on the care receiver (Yan & Tang, 2004). As discussed earlier, care receivers who feel they are not reciprocating often suffer from depression (Wolff & Agree, 2004). Conflict, stigma, and reciprocity are just three factors that have been recently related to elder abuse, and that vary cross-culturally. As such, they provide a starting place (perhaps one of many) for interdisciplinary theorizing about the dynamics at play. The problem of elder abuse is a complex and understudied issue. Even those who have begun to consider communication processes relating to elder abuse acknowledge that no single model or theory can adequately account for the complexities of this issue and much more empirical attention is needed (Giles & Helmle, 2010), especially in countries outside of the United States (Kaindl, 2009). As a precursor, mapping out potential factors related to elder abuse, such as those related to intergenerational caregiving, can provide a fresh perspective for researchers in generating theoretical tools.

In terms of thinking about communication interventions to assist intergenerational caregivers and care receivers, there are a multitude of possibilities to be drawn from the literature reviewed here. From the first challenge, identity, working with caregivers to facilitate the agentic identity of the care receiver could reduce feelings of powerlessness in the care receiver and burden for the caregiver. One way that this process could be approached is by encouraging care receivers to reminisce about their life experiences. If younger family members are interested in knowing more about their culture, this interest can increase the care receivers' self-esteem and allow them something to "give back." Unfortunately, many younger adults do not see the benefits of learning about their cultural heritage. Reminiscence as a type of life review is a way of seeing how care receivers view themselves, regardless of historical accuracy. Sharing information about cultural and ethnic history makes the care receiver a teacher and strengthens intergenerational relationships, thus creating a family legacy (Wykle, Whitehouse, & Morris, 2005).

With regard to attribution, a group of nursing researchers have demonstrated a program with potential for improving communication between nurses and patients that could be extended to the caregiver–care receiver relationship. Van Meijel et al.'s (2009) skills training program teaches professional caregivers and care receivers the vocabulary they need to describe how they felt about the communication between them. During the exercise, the caregiver and care receiver each take positions on a mat where green indicates they accept the other's behavior, and red indicates that they do not accept it. This activity makes caregivers and care receivers more reflective regarding their acceptance of the other person's behavior and their own problematic attitudes. Both parties can then better articulate how they perceive the other's behaviors and what attributions are driving their attitudes and reactions. Interventions such as this one have promise in that they assist in the actual communication process between caregiver and care receiver. However, an activity such as this one may have to be adapted for members of more collectivistic cultures in which direct conflict is typically avoided to protect the other person's positive face.

Improving the relationships between caregivers and care receivers may be the most powerful way that communication scholars can provide assistance. In many ways, caregiving is inseparable from the relationship itself; "the care IS the relationship" (Sparks, Bevan, & Rogers, 2012, p. 13). Interventions that enhance communication competence for both caregivers and care receivers may reduce stress and increase satisfaction with social support (Query & Wright, 2003). For example, communication theories such as the predicament of aging model suggest that caregivers who are trained to avoid paternalistic communication will experience less conflict in their relationships with the care receiver, and the care receiver will be more likely to report high life satisfaction (Edwards & Noller, 1998).

In conclusion, communication researchers and their peers in other disciplines have a great deal to offer to intergenerational caregivers and their care receivers. Education and training regarding what to expect as a new caregiver or care receiver can go a long way in equipping people for the often difficult journey in front of them. It is hoped that this integrated review will spur new interdisciplinary research programs that find commonalities of meaning and application through this perspective. Because the need for quality intergenerational family caregivers is evident in both the United States and worldwide, it will take the coordinated, united effort of researchers from a diverse array of academic disciplines to arrive at effective and culturally relevant interventions and strategies.

Notes

1. In sub-Saharan Africa, HIV remains the dominant cause of disease burden (Murray et al., 2012).
2. A similar organizational structure is found in the volume edited by Hess and Blanchard-Fields (1999), *Social cognition and aging*. San Diego, CA: Academic Press.
3. Roberts, Wise, and DuBenske (2009) found that care receivers also protected caregivers from stress by hiding symptoms or pain in an effort to reduce their burden.

References

Aberg, A. C., Sidenvall, B., Hepworth, M., O'Reilly, K., & Lithell, H. (2004). Continuity of self in later life: Perceptions of informal caregivers. *Qualitative Health Research*, *14*, 792–815.

Ablitt, A., Jones, G. V., & Muers, J. (2009). Living with dementia: A systematic review of the influence of relationship factors. *Aging & Mental Health*, *13*, 497–511. doi:10.1080/13607860902774436

Aldous, J. (1994). Someone to watch over me: Family responsibilities and their realization across family lives. In E. Kahana, D. E. Biegel, & M. L. Wykle (Eds.), *Family caregiving across the lifespan* (pp. 42–68). Thousand Oaks, CA: Sage.

Asai, M. O., & Kameoka, V. A. (2005). The influence of sekentei on family caregiving and underutilization of social services by Japanese caregivers. *Social Work, 50*, 111–118. doi:10.1093/sw/50.2.111

Babrow, A. S. (2001). Uncertainty, value, communication, and problematic integration. *Journal of Communication, 51,* 553–571. doi:10.1111/j.1460–2466.2001.tb02896.x

Balsis, S., & Carpenter, B. D. (2005). Evaluations of elderspeak in a caregiving context. *Clinical Gerontologist, 29,* 79–97. doi:10.1300/J018v29n01_07

Baltes, M. M., & Wahl, H.-W. (1996). Patterns of communication in old age: The dependence-support and independence-ignore script. *Health Communication, 8,* 217–231. doi:10.1207/s15327027hc0803_3

Barker, V., Giles, H., & Harwood, J. (2004). Inter- and intragroup perspectives on intergenerational communication. In J. Nussbaum & J. Coupland (Eds.), *Handbook of communication and aging research* (2nd ed., pp. 139–163). Hillsdale, NJ: Erlbaum.

Bengston, V. L., Olander, G., & Haddad, A. A. (1976). The generation gap and aging family members: Toward a conceptual model. In J. J. Gubrium (Ed.), *Time, roles and self in old age* (pp. 237–263). New York: Human Sciences.

Beyene, Y., Becker, G., & Mayen, N. (2002). Perception of aging and sense of well-being among Latino elderly. *Journal of Cross-Cultural Gerontology, 17,* 155–172.

Blanchard-Fields, F. (1999). Social schematicity and causal attributions. In T. M. Hess & F. Blanchard-Fields (Eds.), *Social cognition and aging* (pp. 219–236). San Diego, CA: Academic Press.

Bowers, B. J. (1987). Intergenerational caregiving: Adult caregivers and their aging parents. *Advances in Nursing Science, 9,* 20–31.

Brandl, B. (2000, Summer). Power and control: Understanding domestic abuse in later life. *Abuse and Neglect of Older People,* pp. 39–45.

Brown, P., & Levinson, S. C. (1987). *Politeness: Some universals in language usage.* Cambridge, England: Cambridge University Press.

Bruneau, T. (1979). The time dimension in intercultural communication. In D. Nimmo (Ed.), *Communication yearbook* (pp. 71–92). New Brunswick, NJ: Transaction Books.

Cahn, D. D. (1994). *Conflict in personal relationships.* Hillsdale, NJ: Erlbaum.

Carstensen, L. L. (1998). A life-span approach to social motivation. In J. Heckhausen & C. S. Dweck (Eds.), *Motivation and self-regulation across the life span* (pp. 341–364). New York: Cambridge University Press.

Chappell, N. L. (2003). Correcting cross-cultural stereotypes: Aging in Shanghai and Canada. *Journal of Cross Cultural Gerontology, 18*(2), 127–147.

Cicirelli, V. G. (1992). *Family caregiving: Autonomous and paternalistic decision making.* Newbury Park, CA: Sage.

Clark, M. S., & Mills, J. (1979). Interpersonal attraction in exchange and communal relationships. *Journal of Personality and Social Psychology, 37,* 12–24. doi:10.1037/0022–3514.37.1.12

Cook, K. S., & Rice, E. (2006). Social exchange theory. In J. Delamater (Ed.), *Handbook of social psychology* (pp. 53–75). New York: Kluwer.

Coupland, N., Coupland, J., & Giles, H. (1991). *Language, society, and the elderly.* Oxford, England: Blackwell.

Coupland, N., Coupland, J., Giles, H., & Henwood, K. (1988). Accommodating the elderly: Invoking and extending a theory. *Language in Society, 14,* 1–41. doi:10.1017/S0047404500012574

Crowther, M., & Austin, A. (2009). The cultural context of clinical work and aging caregivers. In S. H. Qualls & S. H. Zarit (Eds.), *Aging families and caregiving* (pp. 45–60). Hoboken, NJ: John Wiley & Sons.

Cupach, W. R., & Metts, S. (1994). *Facework*. Thousand Oaks, CA: Sage.

Dietz, T. L. (1995). Patterns of intergenerational assistance within the Mexican American family: Is the family taking care of the older generation's needs? *Journal of Family Issues*, *16*, 344–356.

Dutta, M. J., & Basu, A. (2011). Culture, communication, and health: A guiding framework. In T. L. Thompson, R. Parrott, & J. Nussbaum (Eds.), *The Routledge handbook of health communication* (2nd ed., pp. 320–334). New York: Routledge.

Dyeson, T. B. (2000). Burden self-image: A mediating variable of depressive symptoms among chronically ill care recipients. *Journal of Gerontological Social Work*, *33*, 17–33. doi:10.1300/J083v33n01_03

Edwards, H. (2001). Family caregiving, communication, and the health of care receivers. In M. L. Hummert and J. L. Nussbaum (Eds.), *Aging, communication, and health: Linking research and practice for successful aging* (pp. 207–228). Mahwah, NJ: Erlbaum.

Edwards, H., & Noller, P. (1998). Factors influencing caregiver-care receiver communication and its impact on the well-being of older care receivers. *Health Communication*, *10*, 317–341. doi:10.1207/s15327027hc1004_2

Giesbrecht, N. D. (2009). Caregiving in sociocultural context. In B. Fehr, S. Sprecher, & L. G. Underwood (Eds.), *The science of compassionate love: Theory, research, and applications* (pp. 373–401). Malden, MA: Wiley-Blackwell.

Giles, H., Coupland, N., & Wiemann, J. M. (1990). *Communication, health, and the elderly*. Manchester, England: Manchester University Press.

Giles, H., & Helmle, J. (2010). Elder abuse and neglect: A communication framework. In A. Duszak & U. Okulska (Eds.), *Language, culture and the dynamics of age* (pp. 223–252). New York: DeGruyter.

Gill, E. A., & Morgan, M. (2011). Home sweet home: Conceptualizing and coping with the challenges of aging and the move to a care facility. *Health Communication*, *26*, 332–342. doi:10.1080/10410236.2010.551579

Gillespie, A., Murphy, J., & Place, M. (2010). Divergences of perspective between people with aphasia and their family caregivers. *Aphasiology*, *24*, 1559–1575. doi:10.1080/02687038.2010.500810

Hall, E. T. (1976). *Beyond culture*. Garden City: Anchor Press.

Hansson, R. O., & Carpenter, B. N. (1994). *Relationships in old age: Coping with the challenge of transition*. New York: Guilford.

Harris, J., Bowen, D. J., Badr, H., Hannon, P., Hay, J., & Sterba, K. R. (2009). Family communication during the cancer experience. *Journal of Health Communication*, *14*(Suppl. 1), 76–84. doi:10.1080/10810730902806844

Harvey, J. H., & Weary, G. (1984). Current issues in attribution theory and research. *Annual Review of Psychology*, *35*, 427–459. doi:10.1146/annurev.ps.35.020184.002235

Hatfield, E., Walster, G. W., & Berscheid, E. (1978). *Equity: Theory and research*. Boston, MA: Allyn and Bacon.

Heider, F. (1958). *The psychology of interpersonal relations*. New York: Wiley.

Heine, C., & Browning, C. J. (2002). Communication and psychosocial consequences of sensory loss in older adults: Overview and rehabilitation directions. *Disability and Rehabilitation*, *24*, 763–773. doi:10.1080/09638280210129162

Hines, S. C., Babrow, A. S., Badzek, L., & Moss, A. (2001). From coping with life to coping with death: Problematic integration for the seriously ill elderly. *Health Communication*, *13*, 327–342. doi:10.1207/S15327027HC1303_6

Hofstede, G. (1983). The cultural relativity of organizational practices and theories. *Journal of International Business Studies*, *14*, 75–89.

Hollis-Sawyer, L. A. (2003). Mother-daughter eldercare and changing relationships: A path-analytic investigation of factors underlying positive, adaptive relationships. *Journal of Adult Development, 10*, 41–52.

Hui, A. S.-K., Elliott, T. R., Martin, R., & Uswatte, G. (2010). Family caregivers' attributions about care recipient behavior: Does caregiver relationship satisfaction mediate the attribution-distress relationship? *British Journal of Health Psychology, 16*, 642–659. doi:10.1348/2044-8287.002003

Hummert, M. L. (1990). Multiple stereotypes of elderly and young adults: A comparison of structure and evaluations. *Psychology and Aging, 5*, 182–193. doi:10.1037//0882-7974.5.2.182

Iwakuma, M., & Nussbaum, J. F. (2000). Intercultural views of people with disabilities in Asia and Africa. In D. O. Braithwaite & T. L. Thompson (Eds.), *Handbook of communication and people with disabilities: Research and application* (pp. 239–255). Mahwah, NJ: Erlbaum.

Janevic, M. R., & Connell, C. M. (2001). Racial, ethnic, and cultural differences in the dementia caregiving experience: Recent findings. *The Gerontologist, 41*, 334–347. doi:10.1093/geront/41.3.334

Kahana, E. F., & Young, R. (1990). Clarifying the caregiving paradigm: Challenges for the future. In D. E. Biegel & A. Blum (Eds.), *Aging and caregiving* (pp. 76–97). Newbury Park, CA: Sage.

Kaindl, K. (2009). *Cross-cultural perspectives on elder abuse and neglect.* Geneva, Switzerland: Centre interfacultaire de gérontologie.

Kim, K., Zarit, S. H., Eggebeen, D. J., Birditt, K. S., & Fingerman, K. L. (2011). Discrepancies in reports of support exchanges between aging parents and their middle-aged children. *The Journals of Gerontology: Series B: Psychological Sciences and Social Sciences, 66B*, 527–537. doi:10.1093/geronb/gbr029

Kim, Y. Y. (2007). Ideology, identity, and intercultural communication: An analysis of differing academic conceptions of cultural identity. *Journal of Intercultural Research, 36*, 237–254. doi:10.1080/17475750701737181

Levine, C., & Murray, T. H. (2004). Caregiving as a family affair: A new perspective on cultural diversity. In C. Levine & T. H. Murray (Eds.), *The cultures of caregiving* (pp. 1–12). Baltimore, MD: Johns Hopkins University Press.

Liu, D., Hinton, L., Tran, C., Hinton, D., & Barker, J. C. (2008). Reexamining the relationships among dementia, stigma, and aging in immigrant Chinese and Vietnamese family caregivers. *Journal of Cross Cultural Gerontology, 23*, 283–299. doi:10.1007/s10823-008-9075-5

Lockenhoff, C. E., & Carstensen, L. L. (2004). Socioemotional selectivity theory, aging, and health: The increasingly delicate balance between regulating emotions and making tough choices. *Journal of Personality, 72*, 1395–1423. doi:10.1111/j.1467-6494.2004.00301.x

Lyons, K. S., Zarit, S. H., Sayer, A. G., & Whitlatch, C. J. (2002). Caregiving as a dyadic process: Perspectives from caregiver and receiver. *Journal of Gerontology, 3*, P195-P204. doi:10.1093/geronb/57.3.P195

Martin-Cook, K., Remakel-Davis, B., Svetlik, D., Hynan, L. S., & Weiner, M. F. (2003). Caregiver attribution and resentment in dementia care. *American Journal of Alzheimer's Disease and Other Dementias, 18*, 366–374. doi:10.1177/153331750301800606

Matsumoto, D., & Juang, L. (2008). *Culture and psychology* (4th ed.). Belmont, CA: Thomson Wadsworth.

Mendes, E. (2011, January 28). Most caregivers look after elderly parent; Invest a lot of time. Retrieved from www.gallup.com/poll/148682/caregivers-look-elderly-parent-invest-lot-time.aspx

Merrill, D. M. (1997). *Caring for elderly parents: Juggling work, family, and caregiving in middle and working class families.* Westport, CT: Auburn House.

Milne, A., & Chryssanthopoulou, C. (2005). Dementia care-giving in black and Asian populations: Reviewing and refining the research agenda. *Journal of Community & Applied Social Psychology, 15,* 319–337. doi:10.1002/casp.830

Morycz, R. (1993). Caregiving families and cross-cultural perspectives. In S. H. Zarit, L. I. Pearlin, & K. W. Schaie (Eds.), *Caregiving systems: Informal and formal helpers* (pp. 67–73). Hillsdale, NJ: Erlbaum.

Murray, J. L., Vos, T., Lozano, R., Naghavi, M., Flaxman, A. D., Michaud, C., . . . Lopez, A. D. (2012). Disability-adjusted life years (DALYs) for 291 diseases and injuries in 21 regions, 1990–2010: A systematic analysis for the Global Burden of Disease Study 2010. *The Lancet, 380,* 2197–2223. doi:10.1016/S0140-6736(12)61689-4

National Alliance for Caregiving (2012). Fact sheet: Selected caregiver statistics. Retrieved from www.caregiver.org/caregiver/jsp/content_node.jsp?nodeid=439

Newsom, J. T. (1999). Another side to caregiving: Negative reactions to being helped. *Current Directions in Psychological Science, 8,* 183–187. doi:10.1111/1467-8721.00043

Ng, A.C.Y., Phillips, D. R., & Lee, W. K. (2002). Persistence and challenges to filial piety and informal support of older persons in a modern Chinese society. *Journal of Aging Studies, 16,* 135–153. doi:10.1016/S0890-4065(02)00040-3

Nussbaum, J. F., Pecchioni, L. L., Robinson, J. D., & Thompson, T. L. (2000). *Communication and aging* (2nd ed.). Mahwah, NJ: Erlbaum.

Ohnsorge, K., Keller, H.R.G., Widdershoven, G.A.M., Rehmann-Sutter, C. (2012). "Ambivalence" at the end of life: How to understand patients' wishes ethically. *Nursing Ethics, 19,* 629–641. doi:10.1177/0969733011436206

Olson, L. K. (2003). *The not-so-golden years.* London, England: Rowman & Littlefield Publishers.

Onega, L. L., & Larson, P. D. (2002). Powerlessness. In I. M. Lubkin & P. D. Larsen (Eds.), *Chronic illness: Impact and interventions* (5th ed., pp. 297–310). Sudbury, MA: Jones & Bartlett.

Parsons, R. J., Cox, E. O., & Kimboko, P. (1989). Satisfaction, communication and affection in caregiving. *Journal of Gerontological Social Work, 13,* 9–20. doi:10.1300/J083V13N03_02

Parveen, S., Morrison, V., & Robinson, C. A. (2011). Ethnic variations in the caregiver role: A qualitative study. *Health Psychology, 16,* 862–872. doi:10.1177/1359105310392416

Pecchioni, L. (2000). The influence of autonomy and paternalism on communicative behaviors in mother-daughter relationships prior to dependency. *Health Communication, 12,* 317–338. doi:10.1207/S15327027HC1204_1

Pecchioni, L. L., & Nussbaum, J. F. (2000). The influence of autonomy and paternalism on communicative behaviors in mother-daughter relationships prior to dependency. *Health Communication, 12, 317–338.* doi:10.1207/S15327027HC1204_1

Pecchioni, L. L., & Nussbaum, J. F. (2001). Mother-adult daughter discussions of caregiving prior to dependency: Exploring conflicts among European-American women. *Journal of Family Communication, 1,* 133–150. doi:10.1207/S15327698JFC0102_03

Pecchioni, L. L., Ota, H., & Sparks, L. (2004). Cultural issues in communication and aging. In J. F. Nussbaum & J. Coupland (Eds.), *Handbook of communication and aging research* (2nd ed., pp. 167–207). Hillsdale, NJ: Erlbaum.

Pecchioni, L. L., Wright, K. B., & Nussbaum, J. F. (2005). *Life-span communication.* Mahwah, NJ: Erlbaum.

Phillips, L. R., Luna, I., Russell, C. K., Baca, G., Lim, Y. L., & Cromwell, S. L. (1996). Toward a cross-cultural perspective of family caregiving. *Western Journal of Nursing Research, 18,* 236–251. doi:10.1177/019394599601800302

Podnieks, E., Anetzberger, G. J., Wilson, S. J., Teaster, P. B., & Wangmo, T. (2010). WorldView environmental scan on elder abuse. *Journal of Elder Abuse & Neglect, 22*(1–2), 164–179. doi:10.1080/08946560903445974

Polk, D. M. (2005). Communication and family caregiving for Alzheimer's dementia: Linking attributions and problematic integration. *Health Communication, 18,* 257–273. doi:10.1207/s15327027hc1803_4

Query, J. L., & Wright, K. (2003). Assessing communication competence in an online study: Toward informing subsequent interventions among older adults with cancer, their lay caregivers, and peers. *Health Communication, 15,* 203–218. doi:10.1207/S15327027HC1502_8

Ramsay, G. (2010). Mainland Chinese family caregiver narratives in mental illness: Disruption and continuity. *Asian Studies Review, 34,* 83–103. doi:10.1080/10357820903568219

Reamy, A. M., Kim, K., Zarit, S. H., & Whitlatch, C. J. (2011). Understanding discrepancy in perceptions of values: Individuals with mild to moderate dementia and their family caregivers. *The Gerontologist, 51*(4), 472–483. doi:10.1093/geront/gnr010

Richey, J., & Brown, J. (2007). Cancer, communication, and the social construction of self: Modeling the construction of self in survivorship. In H. D. O'Hair, G. L. Kreps, & L. Sparks (Eds.), *The handbook of communication and cancer care* (pp. 145–164). Cresskill, NJ: Hampton Press.

Roberts, L. J., Wise, M., & DuBenske, L. L. (2009). Caregiving in the light and shadow of death. In B. Fehr, S. Sprecher, & L. G. Underwood (Eds.), *The science of compassionate love: Theory, research, and applications* (pp. 311–344). Malden, MA: Blackwell.

Rosalynn Carter Institute for Caregiving. (2010). *Averting the caregiving crisis: Why we must act now.* Americus, GA: Author. Retrieved from www.rosalynncarter.org/UserFiles/File/RCI_Position_Paper100310_Final.pdf

Ryan, E. B., Giles, H., Bartolucci, G., & Henwood, K. (1986). Psycholinguistic and social psychological components of communication by and with the elderly. *Language and Communication, 6,* 1–24. doi:10.1016/0271–5309(86)90002–9

Ryan, E. B., Hummert, M. L., & Boich, L. H. (1995). Communication predicaments of aging: Patronizing behavior toward older adults. *Journal of Language and Social Psychology, 14,* 144–166. doi:10.1177/0261927X95141008

Schwartz, S. J., Weisskirch, R. S., Hurley, E. A., Zamboanga, B. L., Park, I. J., Kim, S. Y., . . . Catillo, L. G. (2010). Communalism, familism, and filial piety: Are they birds of a collectivist feather? *Cultural Diversity and Ethnic Minority Psychology, 16,* 548–560. doi:10.1037%2Fa0021370

Schwarz, B., Trommsdorff, G., Zheng, G., & Shi, S. (2010). Reciprocity in intergenerational support: A comparison of Chinese and German adult daughters. *Journal of Family Issues, 31,* 234–256. doi:10.1177/0192513X09347991

Semlak, J. L., & Pearson, J. C. (2011). Big Macs/peanut butter and jelly: An exploration of dialectical contradictions experienced by the sandwich generation. *Communication Research Reports*, *28*, 296–307. doi:10.1080/08824096.2011.616449

Shumaker, S. A., & Brownell, A. (1984). Toward a theory of social support: Closing conceptual gaps. *Journal of Social Issues*, *40*, 11–36. doi:10.1111/j.1540–4560.1984. tb01105.x

Siminoff, L. A., Wilson-Genderson, M., & Baker, S. (2010). Depressive symptoms in lung cancer patients and their family caregivers and the influence of family environment. *Psycho-Oncology*, *19*, 1285–1293. doi:10.1002/pon.1696

Sparks, L., Bevan, J. L., & Rogers, K. (2012). An intergroup communication approach to understanding the function of compliance, outgroup typicality, and honest explanations in distant caregiving relationships: Validation of a health-care communication scale. *Journal of Communication in Healthcare*, *5*, 12–22. doi:10.1179/17538 07612Y.0000000002

Stephan, W. G. (1977). Stereotyping: The role of ingroup-outgroup differences in causal attribution for behavior. *The Journal of Social Psychology*, *101*, 255–266. doi:10.10 80%2F00224545.1977.9924016

Stephens, M. A., Kinney, J. M., Norris, V. K., & Ritchie, S. W. (1987). Social networks as assets and liabilities in recovery from stroke by geriatric patients. *Psychology and Aging*, *2*, 125–129. doi:10.1037%2F%2F0882–7974.2.2.125

Stewart, M. J. (1989). Social support: Diverse theoretical perspectives. *Social Science & Medicine*, *28*, 1275–1282. doi:10.1016%2F0277–9536%2889%2990346–8

Stone, A. M., Mikucki-Enyart, S., Middleton, A., Caughlin, J. P., & Brown, L. E. (2012). Caring for a patient with lung cancer: Caregivers' perspectives on the role of communication. *Qualitative Health Research*, *22*, 957–970.

Suchy, S. (2013, January 29). *Low birth rates could become caregiving problem: A HealthCentral explainer.* Retrieved from www.healthcentral.com/alzheimers/c/ 795915/158832/healthcentral/

Tajfel, H., & Turner, J. C. (1979). An integrative theory of intergroup conflict. In W. G. Austin & S. Worchel (Eds.), *The social psychology of intergroup relations* (pp. 33–47). Monterey, CA: Brooks/Cole.

Tanaka, K., & Johnson, N. E. (2008). The shifting roles of women in intergenerational mutual caregiving in Japan: The importance of peace, population growth, and economic expansion. *Journal of Family History*, *33*, 96–120. doi:10.1177/036319 9007308600

Tauiliili, D., Delva, J., & Browne, C. (2001). A study of attitudes toward aging and caregiving patterns among Samoan families in Hawaii. *Journal of Family Social Work*, *6*, 1–14. doi:10.1300/J039v06n01_01

Ting-Toomey, S. (1999). *Communicating across cultures.* New York: Guilford.

Ussher, J. M., Wong, W.K.T., & Perz, J. (2010). A qualitative analysis of changes in relationship dynamics and roles between people with cancer and their primary informal caregiver. *Health*, *15*, 650–667.

Van Meijel, B., Megens, Y., Koekkoek, B., de Vogel, W., Kruitwagen, C., & Grypdonck, M. (2009). Effective interaction with patients with schizophrenia: Qualitative evaluation of the Interaction Skills Training Programme. *Perspectives in Psychiatric Care*, *45*, 254–261. doi:10.1111/j.1744–6163.2009.00228.x

Villagran, M. M., Fox, L. J., & O'Hair, D. (2007). Patient communication processes: An agency-identity model for cancer care. In H. D. O'Hair, G. L. Kreps, & L. Sparks

(Eds.), *The handbook of communication and cancer care* (pp. 127–143). Cresskill, NJ: Hampton Press.

Vitaliano, P. P., Zhang, J., & Scanlan, J. M. (2003). Is caregiving hazardous to one's physical health? A meta-analysis. *Psychological Bulletin, 129,* 946–972. doi:10.1037/0033-2909.129.6.946

Walker, A. J., Pratt, C. C., & Eddy, L. (1995). Informal caregiving to aging family members: A critical review. *Family Relations, 44,* 402–411. doi:10.2307%2F584996

Wallhagen, M. I., & Yamamoto-Mitani, N. (2006). The meaning of family caregiving in Japan and the United States: A qualitative comparative study. *Journal of Transcultural Nursing, 17,* 65–73. doi:10.1177/1043659605281979

Williams, A., & Harwood, J. (2004). Intergenerational communication: Intergroup, accommodation and family perspectives. In J. F. Nussbaum & J. Coupland (Eds.), *Handbook of communication and aging research* (2nd ed., pp. 115–137). Hillsdale, NJ: Erlbaum.

Williams, A., & Nussbaum, J. F. (2001). *Intergenerational communication across the life span.* Mahwah, NJ: Erlbaum.

Williamson, G. M., Martin-Cook, K., Weiner, M. F., Svetlik, D. A., Saine, K., Hynan, L., . . . Schulz, R. (2005). Caregiver resentment: Explaining why care recipients exhibit problem behavior. *Rehabilitation Psychology, 50,* 215–223. doi:10.1037/0090-5550.50.3.215

Williamson, G. M., & Schulz, R. (1995). Caring for a family member with cancer: Past communal behavior and affective reactions. *Journal of Applied Social Psychology, 25,* 93–116.

Willis, R. (2012). Individualism, collectivism and ethnic identity: Cultural assumptions in accounting for caregiving behaviour in Britain. *Journal of Cross-Cultural Gerontology, 27,* 201–216. doi:10.1007/s10823–012–9175–0

Wolff, J. L., & Agree, E. M. (2004). Depression among recipients of informal care: The effects of reciprocity, respect, and adequacy of support. *Journal of Gerontology, 59B,* S173-S180. doi:10.1093%2Fgeronb%2F59.3.S173

Wykle, M. L., Whitehouse, P. J., & Morris, D. L. (2005). *Successful aging through the life span: Intergenerational issues in health.* New York: Springer Publishing.

Yan, E. C., & Tang, C. S. (2004). Elder abuse by caregivers: A study of prevalence and risk factors in Hong Kong Chinese families. *Journal of Family Violence, 19,* 269–277. doi:0885-7482/04/1000-0269/0

Yeo, G., Tran, J., Hikoyeda, N., & Hinton, L. (2001). Conceptions of dementia among Vietnamese American caregivers. *Journal of Gerontological Social Work, 36,* 131–152. doi:10.1300/J083v36n01_08

Young, R., & Kahana, E. (1994). Caregiving issues after a heart attack: Perspectives on elderly patients and their families. In E. Kahana, D. E. Biegel, & M. L. Wykle (Eds.), *Family caregiving across the lifespan* (pp. 262–284). Thousand Oaks, CA: Sage.

Zarit, S. H. (1989). Do we need another "stress and caregiving" study? [Editorial]. *The Gerontologist, 29,* 147–148. doi:10.1093/geront/29.2.147

Zarit, S. (2006). Assessment of family caregivers: A research perspective in family caregiver Alliance (Eds.), *Caregiver assessment: Voices and views from the field. Report from a national consensus development conference* (Vol. 2, pp. 12–37). San Francisco, CA: Family Caregiver Alliance.

Zarit, S. H. (2012). Positive aspects of caregiving: More than looking on the bright side. *Aging & Mental Health, 16,* 673–674. doi:10.1080/13607863.2012.692768

Part IV

Theorizing Emerging Areas of Communication Research

CHAPTER CONTENTS

11 Net Neutrality and Communication Research

The Implications of Internet Infrastructure for the Public Sphere

Maria Löblich

Ludwig-Maximilians-Universität München

Francesca Musiani

MINES ParisTech/CNRS

The principle of net neutrality posits that packets circulating within the Internet should be treated equally, regardless of content, platform, source, recipient, or service. This chapter explores the implications of the net neutrality debate for communication research and the public sphere. First, the divergent disciplinary contexts of net neutrality-related research are introduced. Then, we adopt a public sphere framework to discuss areas of net neutrality that are relevant for communication studies, and the contributions of communication scholarship to their analysis are highlighted. Peter Dahlgren's three-dimensional framework—structure, representation, and interaction—serves as an entry point into the field.

The principle of net neutrality posits that data packets circulating in the "network of networks" should be treated equally regardless of content, platform, source, recipient, or service (Vogelsang, 2010, p. 5). It contains the idea that users should be allowed to access any web content and applications they choose without a priori restrictions. Factors such as advancements in technology, the increased usage of "bandwidth-hungry" services such as video downloading and streaming, and the changing landscape of Internet access providers' economic interests have spurred a number of controversies around net neutrality—which is, nonetheless, hardly a new issue in itself (Marsden, 2010, pp. 14–15). The debate is no longer limited to the United States, where it emerged. Net neutrality has become an issue in other parts of the world as well (Blevins & Shade, 2010; Musiani, Schafer & Le Crosnier, 2013; Powell & Cooper, 2011). Furthermore, the debate has made visible a number of diverse—and intertwined—political, economic, and social concerns, illustrating how the net neutrality debate goes deeper and further than "mere" technical matters. A multidisciplinary field of research reflects upon these concerns; actors in this field are sometimes actors in the political arena and can influence political debates as well. Net neutrality is located at the intersection of scholarship from engineering, computer science, law studies, and the social sciences (most prominently, economic science).

Within communication research, the handling of the "net neutrality" label seems, at times, problematic. The editor of the *International Encyclopedia of Communication* (Donsbach, 2008) chose not to include a net neutrality related entry—though perhaps unsurprisingly, as net neutrality was at that time a nascent political issue. Academic "information subsidizers" on the topic of net neutrality to the public and to legislators in the United States are primarily law professors, not communication scholars (Kim, Chung, & Kim, 2011, p. 320). In 2007, a special section of the *International Journal of Communication* assembled "19 preeminent thought leaders" on net neutrality, but only a small minority of them call themselves communication scholars (Peha, Lehr, & Wilkie, 2007, p. 710). However, the interest of communication researchers in the topic is increasingly lively (Blevins & Shade, 2010; Kim et al., 2011; Powell & Cooper, 2011; Schafer, Le Crosnier, & Musiani, 2011; Storsul, 2010), and most important, net neutrality affects and relates to a number of issues widely addressed in communication research, including freedom of expression, communication rights, user control, diversity of media ownership, and Internet governance. Despite its "inherently technical character" (Yoo, 2012), the debate on net neutrality has implications for users and content providers, be they bloggers, media organizations, or social networking sites. Net neutrality raises the question of who controls the Internet and "which modes of social communication develop" (Peha et al., 2007, p. 709; see also Marsden, 2010; Meinrath & Pickard, 2008; Mueller, 2007, 2010).

In this chapter, we explore and critically discuss the variety of issues around which net neutrality and communication research intersect. We provide an overview of the current state of research and suggest areas for future research. Although other disciplines, such as law and economics, have played a more active role in the net neutrality debate so far, this chapter demonstrates that communication scholars have fundamental contributions to offer in illuminating core issues in the net neutrality debate.

First, communication scholars can inform and advance the debate by means of the public sphere concept. The public sphere, which is increasingly shaped by the Internet, permits the circulation of information and ideas. It consists of communicative spaces where the shaping of political will, entertainment, commerce, and education takes place. According to Habermas (1989), a functioning public sphere should be easily accessible to all citizens. The net neutrality debate is directly tied to the issue of access to the public sphere, as it questions the extent to which the Internet, as a set of distribution channels, can be used to discriminate, control, and prevent access and communication. A public sphere perspective on the net neutrality debate sheds light on the effects of Internet infrastructure on online communication spaces. We apply Dahlgren's (1995, 2005) public sphere framework to the net neutrality debate in order to demonstrate how communication scholarship can provide a useful lens to understand the issues raised by net neutrality.

Second, some of the issues that are now regrouped under the pervasive label of net neutrality—such as the centralization vs. the decentralization of networks, the effect of network bottlenecks on freedom of speech, the extent of user control, the diversity of media ownership, and Internet governance—have been under consideration by communication scholars under different labels before the "net neutrality" label became so prominent. These cognate issues are now crystallized in new ways, thanks to evolutions in both technologies and power balances. As a result, the study of net neutrality may benefit from more effective connections between the research conducted on these cognate issues within communication scholarship—even if this research often does not explicitly refer to net neutrality—and those bodies of work that explicitly include research on net neutrality. We illustrate this by means of several examples.

Several criteria led to the selection of literature that this article draws upon. We could not rely on a single criterion, as net neutrality is studied by a heterogeneous field to which different disciplines contribute, and those disciplines do not necessarily follow the same publication strategies. Therefore, a selection based, for example, only on EBSCO databases would have excluded books that play an important role in law studies and in sociology. The literature search was conducted via HOLLIS (the Harvard Library catalogs) and the Academic Search Complete database; it was also based on cross-references within the net neutrality–related body of work thus obtained. By means of the latter strategy, for instance, we found the oft-cited article by Tim Wu (2003) that authors often refer to as a "key article," but it is not included in the Academic Search Complete database. Furthermore, we included literature with a global span. A certain U.S.-centrism persists nonetheless, because most research on the topic remains located there—as do the companies providing the search engines used to perform the search. A bias toward English-language literature should also be acknowledged, even if multilingual literature (French and German, in particular) is included. Exclusively technical publications, not referring to net neutrality as a political debate, were excluded. Finally, we restricted our search to authors who explicitly use the net neutrality label. Many of the issues relevant to the net neutrality debate are explored under headings and themes in the literature that do not employ this label.

Net Neutrality: From Technical Foundations to Economic and Political Implications

Net neutrality started as a debate related to the transport layer of the Internet's infrastructure. In the Open Systems Interconnection (OSI) model, the functions of the Internet as a communication system are characterized and standardized in terms of abstraction layers, with similar communication functions grouped into logical layers. A layer serves the layer above it and is served by the layer below it. The transport layer provides transparent transfer of data between end users, providing reliable data transfer services to the upper layers (Zimmermann, 1980). As the Internet has evolved, net neutrality become an articulate and inflamed economic debate on infrastructure funding, a political battlefield on the respective roles of actors in the "Internet ecology," and an arena for debating the nexus of fundamental rights, democracy, and online communication services.

As the Internet has become the central nervous system of our societies, it has undergone profound changes. Entire industrial sectors participate in the shaping of the "network of networks": computer networking industries, data centers, content industries (media, video producers), service companies (social networking, electronic commerce), telecommunication industries, and even companies providing the energy needed to materially run computing equipment. The number of Internet users is now greater than two billion (International Telecommunication Union [ITU], 2012), and these users are becoming central actors in the Internet value chain, both as content producers and participants to many services whose "value" and usefulness increases with the number of people using them. These evolutions of the network and its global economic value are transforming this network into a central actor in economic, political, and geopolitical relations. It is within the frame of these conflicts and negotiations that the net neutrality debates should be placed and the main issues at stake perceived. These debates are further compounded by nation states questioning their own status vis-à-vis the Internet, launching public consultations, and trying to implement law reforms. In addition, a number of regulatory bodies and authorities in the communication sector face often contradictory demands from stakeholders and need to implement comprehensive responses to these demands.

The term neutrality can itself be a source of ambiguity. In journalism, neutrality is related to the idea of neutral reporting, implying a balance of viewpoints surrounding a topic and, more generally, a balance of discourses in the public media. However, the neutrality that Tim Wu, a law professor at Columbia Law School, referred to in his 2003 seminal article "Network Neutrality, Broadband Discrimination," did not entail balanced viewpoints on Internet-hosted documents nor the relation between content producers and their readers or users. Wu was concerned with the underlying infrastructure of the Web, the so-called transport layer of the Internet, in particular the ways in which data packets circulate in the network and the preservation of the principle that these packets of information, regardless of their source and recipient, should be treated equally (Wu, 2003). The most direct antecedent to neutrality in this context is the concept of neutrality as it is applied in regulatory contexts, for example, in policies crafted by the Federal Communications Commission (FCC).

The term *Internet* encompasses a global system of interconnected computer networks and all the different layers that make them operational. Yet, for the general audience, the term has often been considered the same as the World Wide Web. In the post–Web 2.0 era, the Internet is often identified with the myriad applications based on our mobile devices. If those are indeed the primary access points to multiple services (social networking, e-mail, e-commerce, gaming, and access to audio and video content) for a majority of users, they are in fact building on the Internet's "lower layers," in particular, the Transmission Control Protocol/Internet Protocol (TCP/IP) that defines how data packets are transmitted, addressed, and received. The "network of networks" is based on a layered model, and the transport of information is a common foundation on top of which several services may be developed: from the Web and its multiple applications to television and voice over Internet Protocol (IP), peer-to-peer exchanges, the Domain Name System, software updates, and numerous other services. These services are often hidden to the user but are nonetheless crucial for the balance and the maintenance of a global network. Indeed, the Internet may be considered as the common basis on which a variety of services are built. Thus, the issue of the "neutrality of the Internet" is about the very foundations of the network, at the technical level but also in terms of the social *imaginaires* (Flichy, 2007)—the collective visions shaping the Internet—that can be built on it, as a shared commons and the Information Society's infrastructure.

Notwithstanding a number of critical voices (Faulhaber, 2007; Hahn & Litan, 2007), scholars often argue that the principles of Internet innovation and openness are based on a lack of concentration of data processing at the core of the network (van Schewick, 2011, 2012). Net neutrality corresponds to the will of maintaining the network's "intelligence" at the extremes of the chain (the so-called end-to-end principle) on servers and users' terminals (computers and, increasingly, mobile phones). Several measures and arrangements related to network management have, in recent years, breached net neutrality (Krämer, Wiewiorra, & Weinhardt, 2013, p. 6), often because of technical necessity: for instance, the incessant fight against spam; the set up of firewalls at the gates of several companies' or institutions' intranets; or the existence of services such as virtual private networks or television over IP, which "borrow" the Internet as a channel but remain independent from it. The core question is to know whether the deliberate choice to distinguish between different kinds of data packets and route them to their destination in a more or less rapid fashion should be entirely left to the different Internet operators and to the commercial negotiations between them or if active regulatory measures are needed to preserve the neutrality of the global Internet as much as possible. Thus, net neutrality concerns both "the extent to which providers of Internet services should be allowed to favor some traffic or users over others, perhaps affecting what content, applications, or devices are used on the providers network" (Peha et al., 2007, p. 709), and the equal treatment of content providers and users (Blevins & Shade, 2010, p. 1).

Telecoms and the Power of Access

Telecommunication companies have a peculiar role in this system. They are the structure that allows users to access content and services distributed on the different big servers of the Internet. A telecommunication company—as Internet Service Provider (ISP)—is generally the actor users turn to in order to obtain their access. Recent commercial strategies of these companies have emphasized their customers'/users' perception that they can enjoy the full benefits of the "ubiquity" allowed by the Internet: enjoy high-bandwidth access at their home, their office, and on their mobile phone, all in the same conditions of quality with the ability to access even the information that are most "bandwidth-hungry" in terms of computing power, such as videos, games, and real-time information. Users are often offered attractively priced bundled services that merge their access to different types of services (television, communication, music consumption, etc.). All this makes telecom operators important actors of the management of the Internet's architecture, both technical and economic. As a result, these companies have a lot of responsibility and a lot of power. As they seek to negotiate the sharing of the value produced by and within the network, they also claim that, in order to keep up to pace with innovation, they need to endlessly improve the quality of networks. This entails large, ongoing investments that are also problematic due to the risk of their rapid obsolescence because the technical choices can become outdated before they deliver financially.

Along the same lines, telecommunication companies have expressed fear that regulation would discourage investments in broadband expansion, traffic management, and innovation (Powell & Cooper, 2011, p. 311). At the same time, they have powerful technical capabilities at their disposal to condition Internet traffic patterns. In some cases, the same advances in technology that allow for a better user experience—such as Deep Packet Inspection (which we discuss later), traffic management systems, Next-Generation-Networks, and "intelligent network functions" (Yoo, 2012)—are those that enable prioritization and blocking of data packets based on the type of content (Peha et al., 2007, p. 710). These issues are at the core of the net neutrality debate.

As a result of a rapidly changing landscape of applications and infrastructures, the Internet's economic model and the distribution of revenue among the different providers of services and access seems to be in the process of reconfiguring the relations between Internet service providers and application/service providers. The crucial question is the repartition of costs. Telecom operators claim that they bear the cost of the extension and evolution of the network in its entirety, yet these improvements are strictly linked to the exponentially growing number of connections and applications that mostly benefit other actors. They also—and in an equally controversial way—express the wish to not remain confined to a role of provider for content and service companies while being the ones that assume the industrial risks and the users' complaints in case of congestion.

According to these claims, should regulators consider a limitation of the bandwidth destined to the most bandwidth-consuming services, such as television over IP? Should some content benefit from a priority treatment and according to which criteria? An increasing need of bandwidth and broadband usage (video download, streaming, etc.) has led to inflamed discussions about traffic congestion, network management practices, and conflict between end-to-end-principle and quality of service requirements (McKelvey, 2010). The spectacular financial success of some of the Internet's *pure players* (companies whose activities are carried out exclusively on the Internet, for example, Google, Amazon, and Facebook) is framed by telecoms as a reason that this thriving sector should participate in the telecoms' investment efforts. From this dynamic comes the will to undertake a private commercial negotiation between these two categories of actors. Telecoms, able to throttle the rapidity of access to services, are in a privileged position to negotiate with content producers about the extent to which such contents can be routed more or less rapidly. Around this crucial point plays the issue of net neutrality. If the "transporter" can identify the type of protocol used for every information packet and apply specific rules according to its source, it becomes the central actor in the value chain, able to impose its models and interests to the entire Internet (Krämer et al., 2012, p. 4).

But it is exactly in promoting a model opposed to this one—typical of telecommunications in the 1980s—that the Internet has thrived in the past few decades (Musiani & Schafer, 2011; van Schewick, 2011). For its founding fathers, the ability to innovate would be strongest if the transport and management infrastructure of the network was kept neutral—not intervening in the content and service operators' decisions and allowing for transparency vis-à-vis the user (Berners-Lee, 2010). For now, this bet has been won, and it is mostly thanks to this victory that the Internet's recent history is one of emerging services and platforms. From online search to video streaming, from payments to social networking, the longevity of these services is arbitrated by public success (Musiani & Schafer, 2011; van Schewick, 2011). However, the close-future stability of this tendency is not a given, especially considering some of the developments that will be described later in the chapter. The congestion threat has existed since the birth of the Internet as an interconnected system of local, regional, national, and international networks (Marsden, 2010, p. 32). It has been kept under control by the cooperative extension of the network and by the improvement of coding protocols. An example is the well-known mp4, born from the need to transmit massive quantities of musical information in reasonably sized files (Chiariglione & Magaudda, 2012).

An Economic Debate Becomes a Political Issue

The neutrality of the Internet involves thinking about protocols and technical architectures as the meeting of the technical, economic, social, and political factors (Musiani et al., 2013; Schafer et al., 2011). This concept emphasizes that changes in architectures and technical models also induce changes in the arrangement of power (DeNardis, 2012; Lessig, 2006) and vice versa. Net neutrality offers a snapshot of the present and future challenges, possible evolution paths of the "network of networks," and power relations at work. It addresses the broader issue of Internet governance and competing Internet imaginaires (Flichy, 2007; Mansell, 2012).

In the conflict of visions aimed at the regulation of Internet exchanges, states intervene. In the past few years, state-mandated regulatory bodies and authorities on communication matters have undertaken a number of steps that qualify them as primary actors in net neutrality debates. They have overseen or impeded monopolistic tendencies and alliances, acted so that control over the Internet's "plumbing" does not extend to contents and services (e.g., preventing mergers between infrastructure operators and service providers), and allowed newcomers to have their chance in the IT market by offering innovative or complementary services (Brito & Ellig, 2007).

Governments and intergovernmental organizations have entered the debate, as well. Soon after he was elected in 2008, U.S. President Barack Obama asked the FCC, the U.S. regulatory authority, for advice on the issue of net neutrality. The European Commission has inserted a statement on net neutrality, related to the transparency of information supplied by network operators and ISPs to their subscribers, within the proposed Third Telecom Reform package, the European directives regulating the telecommunications sector (Crocioni, 2011). However, there are only two nation states in the world where the principle of net neutrality has been enshrined in law, Chile and the Netherlands (Saldías, 2012; van Daalen, 2012).

Civil liberty groups have intervened in the debate, including La Quadrature du Net in France or Free Press and the American Civil Liberties Union in the United States. This demonstrates that long-term thinking about the future Internet's shape is not the exclusive domain of political and economic experts (Hart, 2011, p. 425). Large Internet-based companies such as Amazon, eBay, Google, and Yahoo! have lobbied in favor of net neutrality, which is widely perceived to benefit providers of online content and is associated with speech rights (Powell & Cooper, 2011, p. 316). However, the line between Internet-based service companies and the telecommunication industry is more blurred than it used to be. Google's position in the United States, originally strongly supporting net neutrality, has become ambivalent with its engagement in the wireless Internet business (Davidson & Tauke, 2010; Hart, 2011, p. 438). The standpoints of the different stakeholders demonstrate the plurality of visions and approaches related to the Internet's role in society.

Academics, in turn, have a peculiar role in this dynamic. Not only is the debate surrounding net neutrality a "highly politicized" and normative debate (Meinrath & Pickard, 2008; Peha et al., 2007, p. 710) but a scholarly debate. Political contentions shape academic research, and academic research shapes political and public discourse (Lessig, 2006; Lessig, Wendell, & Carlsmith 2006; Wu & Lessig, 2003).

The net neutrality controversy raises the question of data discrimination and regulation and questions issues such as "communication rights," "electronic rights," transparency, accountability, and the status of intangible common goods (Dakroury, Eid, & Kamalipour, 2009; Raboy & Shtern, 2010). It carries in itself the evolutions, present and past, of the Internet and interrogates the notion of a "technical democracy" (Callon, Lascoumes, & Barthe, 2001). Indeed, within a private commercial negotiation, two essential democratic elements are at play: transparency to the user, who needs a reliable and equitable network that treats established "giants" and newcomers equally; and the ability of new information and service producers to build upon an open network before their ideas, products, or services are put to the test by the public (Zittrain, 2008).

By providing information carriers with an even more central role, some academics and civil society representatives fear a worsening of control and censorship (by asking or allowing operators to inspect data packets, trace uses, and act as the Internet's "private police"). In that case, the risk would be that information carriers would create hubs of "social control" under the disguise of technical management measures. This is at odds with what is thought to be the technical and cultural strength of the Internet—the inscription, within the very code of the TCP/IP protocol, of free expression logic, decentralized contact, and social innovation. By authorizing a specific actor to compromise the transport layer's neutrality, there is also a risk of favoring vertical concentrations, from content production to distribution to the user, which may lead to a disruption of the network's unity and foster a small number of hyper-concentrated actors. The danger represented by these vertical concentrations is denounced not only from an industrial innovation perspective but from one of "communication democracy" as well. The in-depth immersion of networks in users' professional and personal everyday lives would lead to eventual monopolies that would be both economic and political, in terms of civil liberties, cultural influences, and political lobbying.

Alongside the "best effort" logic enabled by the TCP/IP protocol—the logic of the first Internet, in which operators "do their best" to deliver the service in an uncertain environment of connection peaks, different file sizes, and bottlenecks—a number of "quality of service" strategies start appearing, translating into a prioritization of packets that is both "conditional" and "active." The conditional prioritization becomes more widely and rapidly accepted, as it solves congestion problems: for example, when the network is overloaded, it slows down every connection seeking the optimal exchange rate without losing too many packets (Clark, 2007, p. 705; Wu, 2003). However, the active prioritization is more problematic as it allows a "multiple-speeds" Internet, where packets would be more or less rapidly circulated according to their transmission protocol, or private commercial agreements. The issue of traffic management is far from being restrained to technology and even to economy: It entails reconfigurations of the right to communicate, of investments in high bandwidth as a service to the public interest, and of the quality of the communicative experience.

Net neutrality might be one of the core questions for the present and the future of communication policy worldwide, since the evolution of the Internet affects countries and populations, promoting different economies and ecologies of the Internet. In particular, countries that are not yet fully equipped with prime Internet infrastructure—and for whom the first-time access to the "network of networks" could happen primarily via mobile phones—are directly affected in their development by net neutrality breaches (see related section below and Hahn & Litan, 2007).

A Meta-Perspective on Terminology and Research

Net neutrality is a relatively recent concept; however, the term is already the bearer of several meanings. These nuances can sometimes blur the underlying issues, and it is important to stabilize the boundaries of a complex concept before starting to debate it. Depending on different stakeholders—economic, political, or legal actors—the meaning of the term *net neutrality* changes, in part because of the history and traditions of the field or sector to which the stakeholders belong.

Several authors, for example, would privilege the expression "open Internet" rather than "neutral Internet." For these scholars, openness refers more accurately to a communicative space that is not under the control of any one specific actor, where individuals can freely create, participate in enterprise, and see their expressions, creations, and activities available to the whole Internet (Ghernaouti-Hélie & Dufour, 1999, p. 96). The discourse on the "open Internet" is thus invested with strong values (freedom of enterprise, freedom of expression). Other words used in this discourse—for instance, *discrimination* and *equity*—are also invested with a strong symbolic and normative charge. In particular, the word *discrimination* is endowed with a negative connotation in the context of net neutrality, while in the language of economy, or competition law, the term is not so weighted, as discriminating means differentiating—for example, proposing personalized products or diversified tariff options according to diverse categories of consumers (Curien & Maxwell, 2011, p. 108).

A debate on where the neutrality question starts and ends—should it encompass the whole Internet value chain or limit itself to data routing mechanisms only—is also currently ongoing. A collectively authored document issued by the French research program Vox Internet (2010) remarks that

> Net neutrality is at best a technical concept, at worst an economic alibi . . . As the definition of neutrality as a political, legal and economic objects—and that of the Internet itself—are heavily debated, the interests-hiding notion of neutrality should be abandoned and replaced by the notion of openness, more precise from an economic and legal viewpoint, and certainly more productive in political arenas for the joint pursuit of the common good. (p. 1.8)

Thus, several academic and civil society commentators underline the limits of the net neutrality notion. At the same time, others point out how it is made of negotiations between different actors with conflicting goals. These negotiations generate the terms and stakes of the debate in the context of a polysemous concept, invested with different meanings and values, according to different stakeholders.

Net Neutrality as a Research Field

As previously mentioned, the "highly politicized" character of the net neutrality debate is not independent from its link to research (Peha et al., 2007, p. 710). Net neutrality contentions have been shaping academic research, and, vice versa, research has been informing political and public discourse (Kim et al., 2011; Powell & Cooper, 2011). This section outlines the manifold research directions on net neutrality that are currently partly competing, partly running parallel to each other, according to their authors, their orientations, and their academic and nonacademic backgrounds. A large part of this section refers to research that originated in the United States, where net neutrality research has originated.

The field of net neutrality encompasses several research communities with divergent disciplinary backgrounds. The main dividing line, however, seems to be the legal and economic communities. The primary issue is whether a nondiscrimination regulatory regime ensuring net neutrality is necessary (Powell & Cooper, 2011, p. 313). Although the legal community largely supports this idea (Crawford, 2007; van Schewick, 2012) with a few exceptions (Yoo, 2005), the economic scholarly community tends to be more skeptical (Crocioni, 2011; Faulhaber, 2007; Hahn & Litan, 2007; Szoka & Thierer, 2009; Thierer, 2004). This community has reframed the debate asking under what conditions price and quality discrimination is beneficial or harmful (Vogelsang, 2010).

Many economic scholars probably refuse to label themselves as "net neutrality researchers." In general, a common identity of net neutrality research does not seem to exist. There are hardly any self-reflections or extensive literature reviews of the field (for exceptions, see Quail & Larabie, 2010, pp. 33–38; Krämer et al., 2013, p. 7). Thus, if we refer to a "field" of net neutrality research, we refer to a construct that we use in order to describe the different contributions. We see again, as anticipated in the introduction, how this is a strongly interdisciplinary field of inquiry, in need of insights from multiple perspectives—of which communication studies is a crucial one.

With respect to this constellation, it is hardly surprising that mutual references between the two communities, if they exist at all, are mostly attempts to weaken the opposition's arguments rather than to build on them—notwithstanding attempts to link both communities, to balance risks and benefits of discrimination, and to find a "third way" (Marsden, 2010; Peha et al., 2007; Wu & Yoo, 2007). In both communities, there are scholars who agree that a distinction can be made between "good" and "bad discrimination." However, in this context, Atkinson (2011, pp. 413, 418–419) points to the role of divergent economic doctrines ("deeply held views of how society and the economy should work and what goals are paramount") that influence the ways in which scholars view facts and formulate their research questions. Conservative and liberal neoclassical economics, neo-Keynesian, and innovation economics paradigms shape network policy research and tend to prevent "constructive dialog" (Atkinson, 2011, p. 424). Similarly, Blevins and Barrow (2009, pp. 32–33) point to two lines of opposing liberal-democratic philosophies that appear to be the central division within the current net neutrality debate.

There are connections between the academic sphere and other spheres of society involved in net neutrality contentions in the United States. Some scholars are personally connected to regulatory authorities (e.g., Jon M. Peha was chief technologist of the FCC), Internet engineering groups, and the telecommunication industry. Some have held positions there prior to their academic career (Gerald R. Faulhaber at AT&T). Others are supporting civil advocacy groups (Tim Wu was chair of the media reform group Free Press, and Barbara van Schewick is member of the advisory board of Public Knowledge), or they explicitly link activism and research (Meinrath & Pickard, 2008; Nunziato, 2009, p. xv). Testifying before the Federal Communications Commission, the Federal Trade Commission, and the U.S. Congress, filing complaints and amicus briefs, and writing white papers are common contributions for several leading scholars in the field, including Lawrence Lessig, Susan Crawford, and Christopher Yoo (Kim et al., 2011).

Net neutrality research, both in the United States and in Europe, has primarily dealt with legal and economic concerns (Powell & Cooper, 2011, p. 313), although more broadly, many of the issues relevant to net neutrality that will be raised in the second part of this chapter have been and continue to be addressed in other disciplines, including communication studies, in ways that are now relevant to the net neutrality debate. There are elaborations on principles seen as conducive for the further development of the Internet (Crawford, 2007; Lemley & Lessig, 2001; Palfrey & Rogoyski, 2006) and attempts at "demystifying" those principles and strengthening market power, competition, and network diversity (Faulhaber, 2007; Hahn & Litan, 2007; Vogelsang, 2010; Yoo, 2005, 2012). Furthermore, there are proposals of rhetoric frameworks and regulatory models (Crawford, 2007; Meinrath & Pickard, 2008; Marsden, 2010; Palfrey & Rogoyski, 2006; van Schewick, 2012; Wu, 2003). In addition to this policy focus, which is typical for many U.S.-centered publications, the literature includes a number of comparative and transnational studies (Ganley & Allgrove, 2006; Michalis, 2010; Musiani et al., 2013; Stevenson & Clement, 2010; Stover, 2010), political process, and media discourse studies. The latter group addresses topics such as the role of knowledge and experts (Kim et al., 2011; Shade, 2008), agenda setting and denial (Cherry, 2007), framing, and citizen views (Barratt & Shade, 2007; Powell & Cooper, 2011; Quail & Larabie, 2010). These contributions largely grew out of communication research. Unlike legal and economic science, communication scholars have focused more on the political processes than on the specific net neutrality policy issues and problem solutions. Although communication scholars seem to be hesitant to get involved in normative debates, a handful of scholars are engaged in net neutrality-related media and communication activism (Frey & Carragee, 2007; Mueller, Kuerbis, & Pagé, 2007; Napoli & Aslama, 2011).

Net neutrality research has been characterized as mainly operating within the boundaries of an economic discourse (Blevins & Barrow, 2009, p. 31). Even proponents of net neutrality legislation employ economic perspectives and values such as "economic growth," "innovation," and "competition" in order to justify their position (van Schewick, 2007; Wu, 2003; see also Crawford, 2007, p. 874). Claiming that net neutrality is a "debate about more than economics," some authors attempt to reframe the debate as a "consumer and media policy problem" (Marsden, 2010, p. 1) or as a problem of public interest and free speech (Barratt & Shade, 2007; McIver, 2010; Mueller, 2007, 2010; Nunziato,

2009; Palfrey & Rogoyski, 2006; Quail & Larabie, 2010). These definitions of net neutrality as a "problem" serve as a starting point to define the relevance of net neutrality debate for communication scholars, as these definitions point to social communication and the public sphere (Lunt & Livingstone, 2013). Communication scholars can situate themselves in the field of net neutrality research by addressing relevant debates from a public sphere perspective.

Net Neutrality from a Public Sphere Perspective

The Internet affects social communication and the public sphere, and this influence has consequences for the political shape of the communication order—therefore, for society as a whole. Two important questions in this regard are: Which regulatory framework is being developed for the Internet? How does this framework enable, and at the same time, restrict, communication in the public sphere? Net neutrality is at the very core of this question: As we have argued, distribution channels can be used as a means to discriminate, control, and prevent communication. In other words, content and user behavior can be controlled through the architecture of the physical layer and the "code" layer of the Internet. The discussion on net neutrality touches fundamental values (public interest, freedom of expression, freedom of the media, and free flow of information) that communications policy authorities in liberal democracies frequently appeal to in order to legitimize their interventions in media systems. The implementation of these values, from a normative point of view, is seen as the precondition for media to create the public sphere—be it online or offline—and thus fulfill its function in society (Napoli, 2001).

Differing concepts of the public sphere are present in the work of several authors. However, the concept developed by Jürgen Habermas (1989; Calhoun, 1992; Lunt & Livingstone, 2013; Splichal, 2012; Wendelin, 2011) is widely recognized as being the most influential. According to Habermas, the public sphere links citizens and power holders; it is "a realm of our social life in which something approaching public opinion can be formed." Habermas's concept of the public sphere centers on deliberation. Functioning deliberation requires that "access is guaranteed to all citizens" (Habermas, 1984, p. 49). This emphasis on access makes this concept of the public sphere particularly useful for an investigation of the net neutrality debate. Peter Dahlgren (1995, 2005, 2010) developed Habermas's notion of the public sphere into an analytic tool in order to study the role of the media and the Internet vis-à-vis the public sphere. According to Dahlgren (2005), the public sphere is "a constellation of communicative spaces in society that permit the circulation of information, ideas, debates—ideally in an unfettered manner—and also the formation of political will" (p. 148). Traditional media and online media play an important role in these spaces or "public spheres" (because there are distinct, sometimes overlapping social spaces that constitute different public spheres; Dahlgren, 2010, p. 21).

Dahlgren (1995) distinguishes three analytical dimensions of the public sphere: the structural, the representational, and the interactional. The structural dimension refers to the organization of communicative spaces "in terms of legal, social, economic, cultural, technical, and even Web-architectural features" (Dahlgren, 2005, p. 149). These patterns have an impact on Internet access. The representational dimension directs attention to media output and raises questions concerning fairness, pluralism of views, agenda setting, ideological biases, and other evaluation criteria for media content. According to Dahlgren, representation remains highly relevant for online contexts of the public sphere. The interactional dimension focuses on the ways users interact with the media and with each other in particular online sites and spaces. In these "micro-contexts of every-day life" users deliberate on meaning, identity, opinions, or entertain themselves (Dahlgren, 2005, p. 149).

We use these analytical dimensions as a heuristic framework to identify net neutrality areas that are relevant for communication studies; thus, each dimension serves as an entry point into a particular set of net neutrality issues. The structural dimension is an analytical starting point for examining the bundle of net neutrality issues that are related to access to the Internet infrastructure for individuals and collective entities. The representational dimension leads to the question of how net neutrality relates to online content. We refer to content "accessible in the public Internet," as opposed to secure or closed private networks (Marsden, 2010, p. 29). The related issues are content diversity, control, and censorship of social communication—although, of course, net neutrality is just one aspect of these debates. The interactional dimension directs attention to the modes, cultures, and spaces of social communication online and whether they are affected by net neutrality. Closed systems or "walled gardens" will illustrate the extent to which the potential benefits of online interaction and deliberation can be impeded or lost.

Dahlgren outlined these dimensions before the Internet became so widely diffused; thus, there is some overlapping when they are applied to online spaces. Content control carried out by Deep Packet Inspection (DPI)—packet filtering techniques examining the data and the header of a packet as it passes an inspection point in the network—may affect interacting users as much as media organizations. Although Dahlgren (2005, pp. 149–150) pointed to the blurring of the representation and interaction dimensions in relation to the Internet, traditional mass communication categories such as "one-to-many" versus "one-to-one" can no longer be separated as clearly. However, by distinguishing access to Internet infrastructure, diversity of content transmitted via Internet infrastructure, and user interaction enabled through Internet infrastructure, these dimensions provide important analytical tools.

Structural Dimension: Access to the Network for Content Producers

Architectural, economic, and other structures shape the organization of communicative spaces and constitute the framework for different actors' access to Internet infrastructure. Net neutrality bears technical implications and economic consequences for audiovisual content producers, news media outlets, and other corporate content providers. These implications influence the definition and the implementation of the quality of service principle. This principle is essential for audiovisual service providers because video on demand needs to be delivered by strict technical deadlines ("real-time" traffic). Delays severely and negatively affect the viewing experience (van Eijk, 2011, p. 9). By contrast, an e-mail "just needs to get there as soon as (and as fast as) possible (so-called 'best-effort' traffic)" (Clark, 2007, p. 705). Therefore, some authors make the point that network management can benefit content providers and consumers by making the flow of traffic more balanced or smoother (Yoo, 2012, p. 542).

In order to prevent network overload at times of peak usage, corporate content providers make quality of service one of their priorities. Google has built its own infrastructure of server farms and fiber-optic networks in order to store content and get it more quickly to end users (Levy, 2012). Economists have argued that producers of the next generation of online video, who depend "critically" on the prioritization of data, need a legal or quasi-legal assurance of their delivery (Hahn & Litan, 2007, p. 605). Proponents of net neutrality, however, emphasize that the priority should be to keep the costs of market entry as low as possible for the "lowest end market entrants—application companies" (Wu & Yoo, 2007, p. 591).

As the Internet becomes an increasingly important distribution channel for traditional media, the boundaries of old business models (television, telecommunication) blur. Problems arise with the interaction of content and networks (Vogelsang, 2010, pp. 8–9). In the view of many scholars, deviations from network neutrality do not necessarily harm users and media organizations. However, these scholars generally acknowledge that situations where Internet service providers become content providers may favor the implementation of network management techniques in order to discriminate against competitors. Providers can exclude competitor content, distribute it poorly, or make competitors pay for using high-speed networks (Marsden, 2010, p. 30; van Eijk, 2011, p. 10). Critics fear a similar model, derived from cable TV industry, where cable providers "charge a termination fee to those who wish to get access to the user" (Marsden, 2010, p. 18). In particular, this would mean a burden for new media businesses and noncommercial services, such as citizens' media and blogs. Whereas large content providers are able to negotiate free or even profitable access, smaller content providers with less contracting power are forced to pay cable TV operators for access. As a result, net neutrality might be easily circumvented both by large content providers and by ISPs (Marsden, 2010, pp. 18, 101). Although some scholars argue that antitrust and competition laws are sufficient to protect upstart content providers from negative consequences of vertical integration and concentration (Hahn & Litan, 2007, p. 606), others argue that there are limits to competition in the access network market due to high fixed costs that restrict market entry (Vogelsang, 2010, p. 7).

In Europe, a special concern is public service broadcasting. Many scholars demand an open and non-discriminatory access to distribution for this service. Several German authors, for instance, regard must-carry rules as a suitable instrument to secure the circulation of online services: They suggest introducing a classification of online services that fulfill indispensable functions for public sphere, contribute to the diversity of opinions, and, therefore, should enjoy the privilege of must-carry rules. They classify public service broadcasting as such an indispensable service (Holznagel, 2010, p. 95; Libertus & Wiesner, 2011, p. 88). The question remains, however, who decides which services should get this privilege and, in general, whether net neutrality will only apply to public service broadcasting (directing other content into the slow lane) or to all content providers (Marsden, 2010, pp. 83, 98).

Representational Dimension: Diversity and Control of Content

A functioning public sphere is based on the representation of the diversity of information, ideas, and opinions (Dahlgren, 2005, p. 149). Different technical practices of inspection or prioritization of data packets, for political or law enforcement purposes, shape net neutrality in various ways. They condition access and circulation of content and restrict the variety and diversity of such content.

A number of technical practices are currently available to governments and the information technology industry to control or restrict content. Examples are bandwidth throttling (the intentional slowing down of Internet service by an ISP), blocking of websites, prioritization of certain services to the detriment of others, and DPI. The latter has several implications, beyond net neutrality, for privacy, copyright, and other issues. DPI may be implemented for a variety of reasons, including the search for protocol noncompliance, virus, spam, intrusions; the setting of criteria to decide whether a packet may go through or if it needs to be routed to a different destination; and the collection of statistical information (Bendrath & Mueller, 2011; Mueller & Asghari, 2012).

As a technology capable of enabling advanced network management and user service and security functions potentially intrusive or harmful to user privacy—such as data mining, eavesdropping, and censorship—DPI has been framed in a predominantly negative way. This is because, even though this technology has been used for Internet management for many years already, some net neutrality proponents fear that the technology may be used to prevent economic competition and to reduce the openness of the Internet. Indeed, this has already happened. For example, in April 2008, Bell Canada was accused of using DPI technology to block peer-to-peer traffic generated not only by clients of its service Sympatico but also by other consumers relying on independent ISPs (Bendrath & Mueller, 2011, p. 1153). Thus, net neutrality proponents argue that the purpose of DPI deployment is crucial and should be made as transparent as possible (Ufer, 2010). Furthermore, emphasis is put on the need to further reflect on the extent to which the employment of filtering techniques is bound to specific cultures. Blocking of content sometimes takes place in specific contexts in which it is regarded to be harmful to the public or to some segment of the public, as is the case for hate speech. Some researchers warn that the role played by local values and cultures in the deployment of such measures should not be underestimated (Goldsmith & Wu, 2006; Palfrey & Rogoyski, 2006, p. 33). However, others emphasize instead that the implementation of these techniques, especially if bent to the requirements of political actors, may lead to biases in, blockings of, or censorship of the content of online communications. These scholars emphasize the power that ISPs have to "control access to vast expanse of information, entertainment and expression on the Internet" (Blevins & Barrow, 2009, p. 41; Elkin-Koren, 2006).

The intermediaries of the Internet economy have the technical means to implement traffic shaping practices, as well as a number of measures that are susceptible to affecting diversity of content on the Internet such as DPI or filtering. So far, the directive or mandate to shape traffic has often come from governments. The literature identifies two central motivations for political actors adopting these practices. First, they may be used by authorities as an investigation tool. ISPs are sometimes used as the "sheriffs" of the Internet, when they are placed in the position of enforcing the rules of the regime in which they are doing business (Palfrey & Rogoyski, 2006). The use of these measures is also attributed to security purposes such as the fight against terrorism, child pornography, online piracy—with all the controversies this raises in terms of setting critical precedents (Marsden, 2010, pp. 19, 67, 81)—or to allegedly protect largely shared values such as the protection of minors or the fight against hate speech (Marsden, 2010, p. 102). These techniques are also used for law enforcement in the area of intellectual property protection. For example, in the infamous Comcast controversy of 2007, one of the first controversies labeled as net neutrality related, the U.S. broadband Internet provider started blocking P2P applications, such as BitTorrent. The stated rationale was that P2P is used to share illegal content and the provider's infrastructure was not designed to deal with the high-bandwidth traffic caused by these exchanges. Accordingly, the cinema and music recording industry have repeatedly taken positions against net neutrality in their fight against "digital piracy" (Bendrath & Mueller, 2011, p. 1152; Palfrey & Rogoyski, 2006, p. 45). Civil society organizations and some political actors have vocally opposed both these sets of motivations, deemed as inadequate to justify an increased control of data and the invasion of freedom of speech rights (Libertus & Wiesner, 2011, p. 87).

Interactional Dimension: "Walled Gardens"

Net neutrality breaches also have effects on the interactional dimension of the public sphere. The formation, in the landscape of information and communication technologies, of so-called walled gardens—the carrier offers service without access to the wider Internet, controls applications, and restricts non-approved content—has important implications for online interaction and illustrates the extent to which the potential advantages leveraged through online interaction and deliberation can be short-circuited by restrictions on software and content (Marsden, 2010, p. 88).

The debate over the neutrality of the Internet is—perhaps surprisingly—often separated from a reflection on the attacks on the universality of the Web. However, the two largely overlap in the economic strategies of content providers and application designers on the Web and their effects on the network (Dulong de Rosnay, 2011). The tendency to create "walled gardens" is perhaps the best illustration of this phenomenon. For example, social networking services harness users' personal data to provide them with value-added services but exclusively and specifically on their own sites. In doing so, they contribute to the creation of sealed "silos" of information, and they do not allow users to export or recover data easily. The "giants" of digital services manifest, more and more frequently, their intention to become broad social platforms underpinning the entire spectrum of web services using these strategies. In fact, their goal is oftentimes to direct users to specific commercial services, to closed economic systems and stores that control not only the software that can be installed on users' devices but the content (Zittrain, 2008).

This is an issue of both application discrimination and content discrimination (Marsden, 2010, p. 88). The ways in which content providers rely on applications that depend on major social networking players reinforces this logic of partition and gatekeeping. The walled-gardens phenomenon has also been described as "balkanization" or "gilded cages." Hardware manufacturers also seek to ensure a "captive audience": The model proposed by Apple, notably, forbids providers of content and media to directly propose applications to users and prevents them from buying paid goods, such as music or digital books, outside of the Apple ecosystem (which includes, e.g., a partnership with Amazon).

Breaches of neutrality also affect the application layer itself. Carriers "offer exclusive, preferential treatment to one application provider," thereby creating walled gardens of preferred suppliers (Marsden, 2010, p. 88). Search engines choose their answers to queries based on advertising revenue, while endorsement systems such as "Like" on Facebook and "+1" on Google, and social networking/recommendation systems such as the now defunct Ping for iTunes, form a set of competing systems that affect the entire value chain of the Internet. The issue of "exclusivities"—especially in the mobile Internet—and of the mergers between communication operators and other stakeholders, such as Deezer and Orange, are further symptoms of the emergence of vertical conglomerates.

The walled gardens phenomenon, as an illustration of the interactional dimension of the public sphere, bridges the structural and representational dimensions by revealing the close connection between the diversity of content and the "diversity of stakeholders who have editorial control over that content" (Herman, 2006, p. 116). The policy implemented by Apple in relation to applications developed by external actors is seen as a possible way to downplay unwelcome political and cultural ideas. Preventing an application from running on Apple devices may have immediate implications for diversity of political views. Similarly, an ISP may or may not allow users to select some of the Web sites contained or barred from the garden, thus hindering expressions of political and social significance with network management choices (Nunziato, 2009, pp. 5–8). The isolation of content on specific networks or services from other content on the wider Internet, preventing broader interaction between them, is reinforced by the "cumulative effect" of walled gardens. If a sufficient number of people join a service and the service is able to reach a critical mass of users, the system becomes self-reinforcing. The companies managing them are able to move toward a quasi-monopoly (Marsden, 2010, pp. 67, 186–194).

Legal scholar Christopher Yoo (2005, pp. 47–48) argued that ISPs and companies such as Apple may be considered as editors, endowed with "editorial discretion" and equipped with "editorial filters," because of their *de facto* right to remove inappropriate content. He controversially points out that "the fact that telecommunications networks now serve as the conduit for mass communications and not just person-to-person communications greatly expands the justification for allowing them to exercise editorial control over the information they convey. In the process, it further weakens the case in favor of network neutrality" (Yoo, 2005, pp. 47–48). In this view, net neutrality measures would be counter-beneficial as they would prevent ISPs from providing some guarantee of quality of content when faced with information overload. For example, Blevins and Barrow (2009) stated that "certain ISPs may not want to carry speech that in their determination is indecent, pornographic, or related to hate groups or particular religious or political persuasions" (p. 38). However, the comparison made by Yoo (2005, pp. 46–47) with editorial rights of newsrooms appears inadequate, as journalism is a profession with its own logic, self-understanding, norms, rules, and programs, which do not apply to ISPs. Herman (2006) pointed out that broadband providers are not considered to be editors. In addition, giving editorial control to users of the Internet, rather than providers, best exemplifies democratic goals (Blevins & Barrow, 2009, p. 41).

The issue of walled gardens and net neutrality is further compounded (and complicated) by the advent of the mobile Internet, for which the allotted bandwidth remains scarce. At the same time, mobile networks increasingly constitute the first "entry point" into the Internet for several regions in the world—first and foremost, Africa. Access restrictions on mobiles to certain protocols, such as Voice over IP (VoIP), and other limits, are officially justified by a poor allocation of band frequency. But they are often attributable, behind the scenes, to industrial battles. The model fostered by Apple's iPhone (and its "cousins," such as Amazon's Kindle tablet) contributes to the change in the market's power relations by contributing to the shift of power from the operator to the hardware manufacturer (Curien & Maxwell, 2011, p. 64).

Many of the most recent attempts to circumvent net neutrality directly involve mobile telephony. In the summer of 2010, Google and Verizon were discussing the prices that the "giant" of search would have to pay to the operator for a "preferential treatment" given to the videos of Google's subsidiary YouTube. The reasons why Google—previously very much in favor of Internet providers' independence—changed its position are numerous, but the first and foremost is the ongoing battle between Google's Android and Apple's iPhone. By blocking some of Google's applications—notably a system allowing to telephone via the Internet rather than the mobile network and the applications for geo-localized advertisement—Apple has shown the force of a system installed behind a steely wall of exclusivity. Also, in order to be diffused on the iPhone, YouTube's videos need to be encoded in the H264 format, for which Apple has patents. Google has now replied with the WebM format, bought from On2 Technologies and transformed into an open web media project. The speed at which YouTube became the primary video streaming service on the Internet may reinforce this tendency to WebM, which has become the standard on all Chrome and Firefox navigators since April 2011. This battle between Google and Apple shows how, even if there is a diversity of applications serving the same end, the lack of openness of such applications limits interaction, at best, to within each of them, thereby greatly reducing interoperability and access.

The danger of these power plays has not gone unnoticed by scholars. Interviewed by the *New York Times* on November 14, 2010, Tim Wu—whose then recently published book *The Master Switch* described the rise-and-fall cycles of great "communication empires" (Wu, 2010)—gave a disenchanted view of the Cupertino firm and its now-deceased CEO Steve Jobs, noting that

> firms today, like Apple, make it unclear if the Internet is something lasting or just another cycle . . . The man who helped create the personal computer 40 years ago is probably the leading candidate to help exterminate it. His vision has an undeniable appeal, but he wants too much control. (Wu & Bilton, 2010)

Communication Research and the Net Neutrality Debate

In addition to providing a way to organize the net neutrality literature, a public sphere framework illuminates how other communication concepts can inform the net neutrality debate. Communication research on media and communication policy and Internet usage research contribute to the understanding of the net neutrality issues highlighted by the public sphere framework.

The issue of access to the network for content producers can be linked to the debate about "bottleneck regulation" in broadcasting. Standard setting and the resulting control over distribution platforms and facilities have been a constant concern in the processes of adjustment of broadcast regulation to new communication technologies, such as cable and satellite television. Digitization and the Internet have led to a new wave of research on *gatekeepers* of information flows and the potential of distribution system owners to restrict access to certain types of content (Gibbons & Humphreys, 2012; Michalis, 2007; Simpson, 2004). Systems of standardization, encryption techniques, and new selection interfaces could all be used as market control mechanisms (Storsul & Syvertsen, 2007, p. 283).

The discussion about bottleneck regulation in broadcasting and instruments used in the past to ensure diversity intersects with the net neutrality debate. The earlier mentioned must-carry rules in cable television are one such instrument in Europe, "whereby private cable operators have been obliged to transmit public television, licensed private channels, and local television" (Storsul & Syvertsen, 2007, p. 283). Media and communication policy research has examined this modification of regulatory structures and, in part, also developed justifications for a media regulation framework that aims at ensuring "that all programs are treated on equal, adequate, and non-discriminatory terms" (Schweizer, 2013, p. 3). The public interest has been a central normative reference (Aufderheide, 1999; van Cuilenburg & McQuail, 2003, p. 189).

Furthermore, studies about the particular philosophical roots and ideological transitions that have shaped regulatory frameworks in different regions and countries (Schejter, 2009) help understand current policy decisions on Internet infrastructure.

The net neutrality debate can also benefit from Internet usage research, which would place net neutrality in the context of the broader discussion on digital inclusion. Broader conceptualizations of access to communications go beyond technical infrastructures and understand access as multifaceted, "encompassing an overlapping mixture of technical, economic, and social infrastructures" (Shade, 2010, p. 137). Access to economic and social infrastructures includes having access to online resources related to jobs, education, entertainment, and health, as well as the ability to produce and use online content.

From this perspective, the use of a communication infrastructure in which data packages are not discriminated is one part of the issue of access. Specific sectors of the world's population do not access that infrastructure at all, for reasons of socioeconomic status, culture, or geographical location. As a result, the current net neutrality debate is limited to those who already *are* participating online; those who, in general, have higher incomes, higher education levels, and live in densely populated areas in the northern hemisphere (Ball-Rokeach & Jung, 2008; Shade, 2010; Tsatsou, 2011), broadening the concept of access points to what is excluded when net neutrality scholars discuss access.

Policy makers and stakeholders tend to emphasize an image of Internet users that serve their particular interests (Livingstone & Lunt, 2011). Therefore, research on online usage and participation helps assess the validity of statements made in the net neutrality debate. The ways in which ICTs and content are leveraged and modified by users, and their degree of involvement, depend on the motivations and gratifications sought. These, in turn, are shaped by the socioeconomic conditions and the particular situations of usage (Burnett, Consalvo, & Ess, 2010; Hargittai & Shaw, 2013; Lunn & Suman, 2008; Nightingale, 2011; Vishwanath & Barnett, 2011). Both the position that fears for the restrictions of walled gardens for online interaction and the position that excludes these concerns appear in a different light when these findings of online usage and participation are taken into account.

Conclusion

The debate on net neutrality is only one aspect of a broader reflection on the future of the "network of networks." It cannot be considered a mere ensemble of technical measures. Net neutrality is a social and economic issue. It is a political issue. It is an issue of communication. It is central to the concept of technical democracy and to the shape of communication spaces—in other words, the public sphere.

A public sphere perspective applied to net neutrality sheds light on the infrastructure of the online public sphere, as well as its contentions. It underlines the issue of access to communicative spaces and the conditions under which the circulation of information and opinions takes place on the Internet.

Net neutrality is concerned with the organization of the online public sphere infrastructure, in particular its technical and especially its economic and power structures. At the same time, net neutrality takes into account the interests of old and new content providers and of Internet users and Internet service providers. Large content providers such as Google and Facebook are not the only gatekeepers in the Internet. Internet service providers, perhaps more than any other entity, enable and constrain online communication as well. Net neutrality research takes their position into consideration, exploring how diverse interests can be balanced in the light of increased bandwidth usage, quality of service demands, and limited mobile Internet capacities.

A functioning public sphere is based on the representation of the diversity of information, ideas, and opinions. Traffic shaping and filtering measures are applied not only for economic reasons but also for political and law enforcement ones. These measures can be fostered by actors other than Internet service providers.

The existence of walled gardens points to the fact that interaction in the online public sphere can be impeded by restrictions on software and content. In closed platforms, providers decide which applications, content, and information are allowed and which are not allowed within the service. Proprietary, closed systems set limits for connecting to the Web and pose limits to the user's individual capacity to refine or develop new applications based on existing ones. Users, when confronted with the net neutrality debates, are equipped with diverse and uneven tools. Not all users have the technical knowledge enabling them to make informed choices; therefore, these are, out of necessity, often left outside the realm of political intervention and to the exclusive authority of the market. Thus, actors with large and multifaceted stakes in the Internet value chain are constantly on the verge of monopolizing a debate with underlying impacts on social architecture, fundamental freedoms, and the conditions for democratic expression.

There is some overlapping and interrelation between the dimensions, due to the blurring of categories in an online public sphere. However, the three analytical dimensions—access to Internet infrastructure, diversity of content transmitted via Internet infrastructure, and user interaction enabled through

Internet infrastructure—highlight how a perspective grounded in communication studies can complement the frameworks offered in the economic and legal traditions, thereby offering a more robust basis for an informed debate on the issues raised by the contested net neutrality terrain. The public sphere perspective connects, for example, scholars interested by freedom of expression and speech with those concerned by issues of economic advantage, monopoly, and concentration. Several fundamental issues central to communication studies, which have been relabeled as net neutrality—for example, network (de)centralization, bottleneck regulation, monopoly and competition, and public service values—reappear in new forms in the Internet environment.

Further research is needed to better understand net neutrality's implications for a diverse and lively public sphere. Research on the structural transformation of the public sphere should not exclude the *technical* structures of the online public sphere because online communication is shaped by Internet architecture. Net neutrality provides interesting examples for this connection, and further delving into this insight can provide communication scholars with new tools for reflection on some of its research fields, such as journalism and news organizations research. Research at the crossroads of net neutrality and communication needs to explore how a seemingly technical question, handled by all-empowered network operators and a variety of legal systems and institutions, can be dealt with in a world of global and international communication.

The exploration of what constitutes a functioning public sphere might also address the inclusion of civil society and of users. Users are not just consumers of products and services but also producers of collective knowledge, using the network for their social, communicative, and cultural activities. In doing so, users foster different visions of a "neutral Internet" and of the democratic balance of information markets which is at stake.

Furthermore, net neutrality is an important topic for research examining media and telecommunications policy. In particular, policies and instruments that are created and implemented with the justification that they build a thriving public sphere should be examined. Telecommunications policy, media policy, and Internet policy, however, have developed along paths that are to a large extent disconnected from one another, due to the development of different regulatory regimes. The Internet challenges the borders between them and raises questions about the future of political regulation and government intervention in Internet governance, about the role that should be played by regulatory authorities, and who contributes to define the "rules of the game." This, in turn, has an impact on innovation, competition, and cooperation between the various actors.

These are the questions posed by the neutrality of the Internet. This set of issues invites scholars to (re)consider the forms of regulation and collective intervention capabilities of a network that has become a nervous system for information and communication activities, exchanges and consumption patterns, autonomy protection, and identity configurations.

References

Atkinson, R. (2011). Economic doctrines and network policy. *Telecommunications Policy, 35*, 413–425. doi:10.1016/j.telpol.2011.03.003

Aufderheide, P. (1999). *Communications policy and the public interest: The Telecommunications Act of 1996.* New York: Guilford.

Ball-Rokeach, S. J., & Jung, J.-Y. (2008). Digital divide. In W. Donsbach (Ed.), *The international encyclopedia of communication.* Retrieved from www.communication encyclopedia.com

Barratt, N., & Shade, L. R. (2007). Net neutrality: Telecom policy and the public interest. *Canadian Journal of Communication, 32*, 295–305.

Bendrath, R., & Mueller, M. (2011). The end of the net as we know it? Deep packet inspection and Internet governance. *New Media & Society, 13*, 1142–1160. doi:10.1177/1461444811398031

Berners-Lee, T. (2010). Long live the web: A call for continued open standards and neutrality. *Scientific American, 303*(4), 56–61. Retrieved from www.scientificamerican. com

Blevins, J., & Barrow, S. (2009). The political economy of free speech and network neutrality: A critical analysis. *Journal of Media Law & Ethics, 1*(1/2), 27–48.

Blevins, J., & Shade, L. R. (2010). Editorial: International perspectives on network neutrality. Exploring the politics of Internet traffic management and policy implications for Canada and the U.S. *Global Media Journal: Canadian Edition, 3*(1), 1–8.

Brito, J., & Ellig, J. (2007). A tale of two commissions: Net neutrality and regulatory analysis. *CommLaw Conspectus: Journal of Communications Law and Policy, 16*, 1–52.

Burnett, R., Consalvo, M., & Ess, C. (Eds.). (2010). *The handbook of Internet studies.* Malden, MA, and Oxford, England: Wiley-Blackwell.

Calhoun, C. (Ed.). (1992). *Habermas and the public sphere.* Cambridge, MA: MIT Press.

Callon, M., Lascoumes, P., & Barthe, Y. (2001). *Agir dans un monde incertain. Essai sur la démocratie technique* [Acting in an uncertain world. An essay on technical democracy]. Paris, France: Seuil.

Cherry, B. (2007). Analyzing the net neutrality debate through awareness of agenda denial. *International Journal of Communication, 1*, 580–595.

Chiariglione, L., & Magaudda, P. (2012). Formatting culture. The MPEG group and the technoscientific innovation by digital formats. *Tecnoscienza, 3*(2), 125–146.

Clark, D. (2007). Network neutrality: Words of power and 800-pound gorillas. *International Journal of Communication, 1*, 701–708.

Crawford, S. (2007). Transporting communications. *Boston University Law Review, 89*, 871–936.

Crocioni, P. (2011). Net neutrality in Europe: Desperately seeking a market failure. *Telecommunications Policy, 35*, 1–11. doi:10.1016/j.telpol.2010.12.007

Curien, N., & Maxwell, W. (2011). *La neutralité d'Internet* [The neutrality of the Internet]. Paris, France: La Découverte.

Dahlgren, P. (1995). *Television and the public sphere.* London, England: Sage.

Dahlgren, P. (2005). The Internet, public spheres, and political communication: Dispersion and deliberation. *Political Communication, 22*, 147–162. doi:10.1080/10584 600590933160

Dahlgren, P. (2010). Public spheres, societal shifts and media modulations. In J. Gripsrud & L. Weibull (Eds.), *Media, markets & public spheres. European media at the crossroads* (pp. 17–36). Bristol, UK: Intellect.

Dakroury, A., Eid, M., & Kamalipour, K. (Eds.). (2009). *The right to communicate: Historical hopes, global debates, and future premises.* Dubuque, IA: Kendall Hunt.

Davidson, A., & Tauke, T. (2010, August 9). A joint policy proposal for an open Internet [Blog post]. Retrieved from http://googlepublicpolicy.blogspot.com/2010/08/joint-policy-proposal-for-open-internet.html

DeNardis, L. (2012, April 26). The turn to infrastructure for Internet governance [Web log post]. Retrieved from www.concurringopinions.com/archives/2012/04/the-turn-to-infrastructure-for-internet-governance.html

Donsbach, W. (Ed.). (2008). *The international encyclopedia of communication.* Malden, MA: Blackwell Publishing. Retrieved from www.communicationencyclopedia.com

Dulong de Rosnay, M. (2011). Réappropriation des données et droit à la rediffusion [Re-appropriation of data and right to re-diffusion]. *Hermès, 59,* 65–66.

Elkin-Koren, N. (2006). Making technology visible: Liability of internet service providers for peer-to-peer traffic. *New York University Journal of Legislation & Public Policy, 9*(15), 15–76.

Faulhaber, G. (2007). Network neutrality: The debate evolves. *International Journal of Communication, 1,* 680–700.

Flichy, P. (2007). *The Internet imaginaire.* Cambridge, MA: The MIT Press.

Frey, L. R., & Carragee, K. M. (2007). *Communication activism* (Vol. I & II). Cresskill, NJ: Hampton Press.

Ganley, P., & Allgrove, B. (2006). Net neutrality: A user's guide. *Computer Law and Security Report, 22,* 454–463. doi:10.1016/j.clsr.2006.09.005

Ghernaouti-Hélie, S., & Dufour, A. (1999). *De l'ordinateur à la société de l'information* (Collection Que sais-je?, n. 3541) [From the computer to the information society]. Paris, France: Presses Universitaires de France.

Gibbons, T., & Humphreys, P. (2012). *Audiovisual regulation under pressure: Comparative cases from North America and Europe.* London and New York: Taylor & Francis.

Goldsmith, J., & Wu, T. (2006). *Who controls the Internet? Illusions of a borderless world.* Oxford, England: Oxford University Press.

Habermas, J. (1984). *The theory of communicative action* (Vol. I & II). Cambridge, UK: Polity Press.

Habermas, J. (1989). *The structural transformation of the public sphere.* Boston, MA: MIT Press.

Hahn, R., & Litan, R. E. (2007). The myth of network neutrality and what we should do about it. *International Journal of Communication, 1,* 595–606.

Hargittai, E., & Shaw, A. (2013). Digitally savvy citizenship: The role of internet skills and engagement in young adults' political participation around the 2008 presidential elections. *Journal of Broadcasting and Electronic Media, 57,* 115–134. doi:10.108 0/08838151.2013.787079

Hart, J. (2011). The net neutrality debate in the United States. *Journal of Information Technology & Politics, 8,* 418–443. doi:10.1080/19331681.2011.577650

Herman, B. D. (2006): Opening bottlenecks: On behalf of mandated network neutrality. *Federal Communications Law Journal, 59,* 107–159.

Holznagel, B. (2010). Netzneutralität als Aufgabe der Vielfaltssicherung [Net neutrality as a mission to protect diversity]. *Kommunikation und Recht, 13,* 95–100.

International Telecommunication Union. (2012). Key statistical highlights: ITU data release June 2012. Retrieved from www.itu.int/ITU-D/ict/index.html

Kim, M., Chung, C. J., & Kim, J. H. (2011).Who shapes network neutrality policy debate? An examination of information subsidizers in the mainstream media and at Congressional and FCC hearings. *Telecommunications Policy, 35,* 314–324. doi:10.1016/j.telpol.2011.02

Krämer, J., Wiewiorra, L., & Weinhardt, C. (2013). Net neutrality: A progress report. *Telecommunications Policy, 37*(9), 794–813. Retrieved from http://dx.doi.org/10.1016/j.telpol.2012.08.005

Lemley, M., & Lessig, L. (2001). The end of end-to-end: Preserving the architecture of the Internet in the broadband era. *UCLA Law Review, 48,* 925–972.

Lessig, L. (2006). *Code and other laws of cyberspace, version 2.0.* New York: Basic Books.

Lessig, L., Wendell, C., & Carlsmith, E. M. (2006, February 7). Testimony. Network neutrality: Hearing before the Senate Committee on Commerce, Science and Transportation. Retrieved from http://cyberlaw.stanford.edu/files/publication/files/lessig-020706.pdf

Levy, S. (2012, November). Power House. Deep inside a Google data center. *Wired,* pp. 174–181.

Libertus, M., & Wiesner, J. (2011). Netzneutralität, offenes Internet und kommunikative Grundversorgung [Net neutrality, open Internet and provision of communication services]. *Media Perspektiven, 2,* 80–90.

Livingstone, S., & Lunt, P. (2011). The implied audience of communications policy making: Regulating media in the interests of citizens and consumers. In V. Nightingale (Ed.), *The handbook of media audiences* (pp. 169–189). Malden, MA, and Oxford, England: Wiley-Blackwell. doi:10.1002/9781444340525.ch8

Lunn, R. J., & Suman, M. W. (2008). Exposure to the internet. In W. Donsbach (Ed.), *The international encyclopedia of communication.* Retrieved from www.communicationencyclopedia.com

Lunt, P., & Livingstone, S. (2013). Media studies' fascination with the concept of the public sphere: Critical reflections and emerging debates. *Media Culture & Society, 35,* 87–96. doi:10.1177/0163443712464562

Mansell, R. (2012). *Imagining the Internet. Communication, innovation and governance.* Oxford, England: Oxford University Press.

Marsden, C. (2010). *Net neutrality. Towards a co-regulatory solution.* London, England: Bloomsbury Academy. doi:10.5040/9781849662192

McIver, W., Jr. (2010). Internet. In M. Raboy & J. Shtern (Eds.), *Media divides. Communication rights and the right to communicate in Canada* (pp. 145–174). Vancouver, British Columbia, Canada: UBC Press.

McKelvey, F. (2010). Ends and ways: The algorithmic politics of network neutrality. *Global Media Journal: Canadian Edition, 3*(1), 51–73.

Meinrath, S. D., & Pickard, V. W. (2008). Transcending net neutrality: Ten steps toward an open Internet. *Journal of Internet Law, 12*(6), 11–21.

Michalis, M. (2007). *Governing European communications: From unification to coordination.* Lanham, MD: Lexington Books

Michalis, M. (2010, July). *The network neutrality debate in the USA and Europe: Economic growth, citizenship, and regulatory responses.* Paper presented at IAMCR conference "Communication & Citizenship," Braga, Portugal.

Mueller, M. (2007, November 5). *Net neutrality as global principle for Internet governance.* Retrieved from the Internet Governance Project website: http://internetgovernance.org/pdf/NetNeutralityGlobalPrinciple.pdf

Mueller, M. (2010). *Networks and states: The global politics of internet governance.* Cambridge MA: MIT Press.

Mueller, M., & Asghari, H. (2012). Deep packet inspection and bandwidth management: Battles over BitTorrent in Canada and the United States. *Telecommunications Policy, 36*, 462–475. doi:10.1016/j.telpol.2012.04.003

Mueller, M., Kuerbis, B., & Pagé, C. (2007). Democratizing global communication? Global civil society and the campaign for communication rights in the information society. *International Journal of Communication, 1*, 267–296.

Musiani, F., & Schafer, V. (2011). Le modèle Internet en question (années 1970–2010) [The Internet model "on trial" (1970s–2010s)]. *Flux, 3–4*, 62–71.

Musiani, F., Schafer, V., & Le Crosnier, H. (2013). Net neutrality as an Internet governance issue: The globalization of an American-born debate. *Revue Française d'Etudes Américaines, 134*, 47–63.

Napoli, P. (2001). *Foundations of communications policy: Principles and process in the regulation of electronic media.* Cresskill, NJ: Hampton Press.

Napoli, P., & Aslama, M. (2011).*Communications research in action: Scholar-activist collaborations for a democratic public sphere.* New York: Fordham University Press.

Nightingale, V. (Ed.). (2011). *The handbook of media audiences.* Malden, MA, and Oxford, England: Wiley-Blackwell. doi:10.1002/9781444340525

Nunziato, D. (2009). *Virtual Freedom: Net neutrality and free speech in the Internet Age.* Stanford, CA: Stanford University Press.

Palfrey, J., & Rogoyski, R. (2006). The move to the middle: The enduring threat of "harmful" speech to network neutrality. *Washington University Journal of Law and Policy, 21*, 31–65.

Peha, J., Lehr, W., & Wilkie, S. (2007). Introduction: The state of the debate on network neutrality. *International Journal of Communication, 1*, 709–716.

Powell, A., & Cooper, A. (2011). Net neutrality discourses: Comparing advocacy and regulatory arguments in the US and the UK. *The Information Society, 27*(5), 311–325. doi:10.1080/01972243.2011.607034

Quail, C., & Larabie, C. (2010). Net neutrality: Media discourses and public perception. *Global Media Journal—Canadian Edition, 3*(1), 31–50.

Raboy, M., & Shtern, J. (2010). *Media divides: Communication rights and the right to communicate in Canada.* Vancouver, British Columbia, Canada: UBC Press.

Saldías, O. (2012). *Patterns of legalization in the Internet: Do we need a constitutional theory for Internet law?* (Alexander von Humboldt Institut für Internet und Gesellschaft, Discussion Paper 2012–08). Retrieved from http://berlinsymposium. org/sites/berlinsymposium.org/files/patterns_of_legalization.pdf

Schafer, V., Le Crosnier, H., & Musiani, F. (2011). *La neutralité de l'Internet, un enjeu de communication* [Net neutrality, an issue of communication]. Paris, France: CNRS Editions.

Schejter, A. (2009). "From all my teachers I have grown wise, and from my students more than anyone else": What lessons can the US learn from broadband policies in Europe? *International Communication Gazette, 71*(5), 429–445.

Schweizer, C. (2013). How to regulate new bottlenecks of digital television distribution? Media and infrastructure owners' interests in the reformation process of the Swiss Radio and Television Act. In M. Löblich & S. Pfaff-Rüdiger (Eds.), *Communication and media policy in the era of the Internet: Theories and processes* (pp. 107–118). Baden-Baden: Nomos.

Shade, L. R. (2008). Public interest activism in Canadian ICT policy. *Global Media Journal, 1*(1), 107–121.

Shade, L. R. (2010). Access. In M. Raboy & J. Shtern (Eds.), *Media divides: Communication rights and the right to communicate in Canada* (pp. 120–144). Vancouver, British Columbia, Canada: UBC Press.

Simpson, S. (2004). Universal service issues in converging communications environments: The case of the UK. *Telecommunications Policy, 28*, 233–248. doi:10.1016/j.telpol.2003.09.001

Splichal, S. (2012). *Transnationalization of the public sphere and the fate of the public.* New York: Hampton Press.

Stevenson, J. H., & Clement, A. (2010). Regulatory lessons for Internet traffic management from Japan, the European Union, and the United States: Toward equity, neutrality, and transparency. *Global Media Journal – Canadian Edition, 3*(1), 9–29.

Storsul, T. (2010). Television in cyberspace: The net neutrality tussle in Norway. In J. Gripsrud & H. Moe (Eds.), *The digital public sphere. Challenges for media policy* (pp. 83–96). Göteborg, Sweden: Nordicom.

Stover, C. (2010). Network neutrality: A thematic analysis of policy perspectives across the globe. *Global Media Journal – Canadian Edition, 3*(1), 75–86.

Szoka, B., & Thierer, A. (2009). *Net neutrality, slippery slopes & high-tech mutually assured destruction* (Progress Snapshot, 5.11). Washington, DC: The Progress & Freedom Foundation. Retrieved from www.pff.org/issues-pubs/ps/2009/ps5.11-net-neutrality-MAD-policy.html

Thierer, A. (2004). *Net neutrality: Digital discrimination or regulatory gamesmanship in cyberspace?* (Policy Analysis for the Cato Institute. No. 57). Washington, DC: Cato Institute. Retrieved from www.cato.org/pubs/pas/pa-507es.html

Tsatsou, P. (2011). Digital divides revisited: What is new about divides and their research? *Media, Culture & Society, 33*, 317–331. doi:10.1177/0163443710393865

Ufer, F. (2010). Der Kampf um die Netzneutralität oder die Frage, warum ein Netz neutral sein muss [The battle for net neutrality, or the question of why must a network be neutral]. *Kommunikation und Recht, 13*, 383–389.

van Cuilenburg, J., & McQuail, D. (2003). Media policy paradigm shifts: Toward a new communications policy paradigm. *European Journal of Communication, 18*, 181–206. doi:10.1177/0267323103018002002

van Daalen, O. (2012, May 8). Netherlands first country in Europe with net neutrality. Retrieved from Bits of Freedom website: www.bof.nl/2012/05/08/netherlands-first-country-in-europe-with-net-neutrality

van Eijk, N. (2011). Net neutrality and audiovisual services. *Iris plus*, pp. 5, 7–19.

van Schewick, B. (2011). *Internet architecture and innovation.* Cambridge, MA: MIT Press.

van Schewick, B. (2012). *Network neutrality and quality of service. What a non-discrimination rule should look like.* Stanford, CA: The Center for Internet & Society. Retrieved from http://cyberlaw.stanford.edu/downloads/20120611-NetworkNeutrality.pdf

Vishwanath, A., & Barnett, G.A. (Eds.). (2011). *The diffusion of innovations: A communication science perspective.* New York: Peter Lang.

Vogelsang, I. (2010). Die Debatte um Netzneutralität und Quality of Service [The debate on net neutrality and quality of service]. In D. Klumpp, H. Kubicek, A. Roßnagel, & W. Schulz (Eds.), *Netzwelt – Wege – Werte – Wandel* (pp. 5–14). Berlin, Germany: Springer. doi:10.1007/978-3-642-05054-1_1

Vox Internet (2010, May 17). Consultation publique sur la «neutralité du Net». Réponse collective du programme Vox Internet II [Public consultation on net neutrality.

Collective response of the Vox Internet II research program]. Retrieved from www. csi.ensmp.fr/voxinternet/www.voxinternet.org/spip0e99.html?article355&lang=fr

Wendelin, M. (2011). *Medialisierung der Öffentlichkeit. Kontinuität und Wandel einer normativen Kategorie der Moderne* [Mediatization of the public sphere. Continuity and change, a normative category of modernity]. Köln, Germany: Halem.

Wu, T. (2003). Network neutrality, broadband discrimination. *Journal of Telecommunications and High Technology Law*, 2, 141–179. doi:10.1007/BF02109855

Wu, T. (2010). *The master switch: The rise and fall of information empires*. New York: Knopf.

Wu, T., & Bilton, N. (2010, November 14). One on one: Tim Wu, author of "The Master Switch" [Blog post]. Retrieved from http://bits.blogs.nytimes.com/2010/11/14/one-on-one-tim-wu-author-of-the-master-switch/

Wu, T., & Lessig, L. (2003, August 22). Re: Ex parte submission in CS docket no. 02–52. Letter to the Federal Communications Commission. Retrieved from http://faculty.virginia.edu/timwu/wu_lessig_fcc.pdf

Wu, T., & Yoo, C. S. (2007). Keeping the Internet neutral? Tim Wu and Christopher Yoo debate. *Federal Communications Law Journal*, 59, 575–592.

Yoo, C. S. (2005). Beyond network neutrality. *Harvard Journal of Law & Technology*, 19, 1–77.

Yoo, C. S. (2012). Network neutrality and the need for a technological turn in Internet scholarship. In M. E. Price, S. G. Verhulst, & L. Morgan (Eds.), *Routledge handbook of media law* (pp. 539–555). New York, and Abingdon, England: Routledge.

Zimmermann, H. (1980). OSI reference model—The ISO model of architecture for open systems interconnection. *IEEE Transactions on Communications*, 28, 425–432. Retrieved from http://dx.doi.org/10.1109/TCOM.1980.1094702

Zittrain, J. (2008). *The future of the Internet and how to stop it*. New Haven & London: Yale University Press.

CHAPTER CONTENTS

12 Narbs

A Narrative Approach to the Use of Big Data

Ananda Mitra

Wake Forest University

There has been an increasing attention to "big data" as a source of information about individuals. Much of the focus has been on the structured data such as demographics and behavior. However, other unstructured data in the form of utterances from individuals could shed light on personal opinions and attitudes. These data are considered as tiny narrative bits—narbs—that offer insights into the life of the individual. This chapter offers a way of categorizing the unstructured component to offer an analytical starting point to answer questions that arise when big data are examined through the lens of narbs.

This chapter offers a way for communication scholars to engage with a specific technological moment that is emerging: the explosion of big data across numerous platforms of digital communication. I propose a specific strategy for making sense of big data by arguing that these data can be parsed into narrative bits—*narbs*—that become available for analysis and interpretation through the lens of narrative theories (Mitra, 2010, 2011, 2012a, 2012b, 2013, in press). Here I first suggest a way of categorizing the unstructured component of big data to offer an analytical starting point, which could be considered an alternative way of understanding people and groups, or audience analysis. This is done by examining these self-generated narbs. Finally, I raise a set of questions that arise when big data are examined through the lens of narbs. The notion of the narb was first suggested in 2010:

> There has been an exponential growth in the number of people who use digital social networking tools to stay connected with friends and family. The connections are built and sustained through numerous digital "posts" that include simple "status updates" to elaborate videos and pictures that are made available through these tools. This paper argues that every such digital imprint is indeed a small narrative bit (narb) that tells a tiny story about an individual. (Mitra, 2010, p. 4)

This preliminary description of the narb was further refined in the essay to include all the different digital discourses that a person or institution produces within the digital environment in which that person or institution resides (Mitra, 2010). Thus, a status update on Facebook becomes an example of a narb just as micro-blogs on Twitter would be considered narbs. With the increasing variety of digital data—from plain old text to complex combinations of video and texts—it is important to be able to offer a systematic analysis of narbs. In the end, what has been called "big data" is indeed a collection of narbs of millions of people and institutions. Before elaborating on the categories of narbs, it is useful to consider the notion of big data.

Big Data

There is some degree of confusion regarding the exact meaning and definition of the term *big data*. Some commentators have pointed out that the term first came into existence within the Silicon Graphics Corporation in the 1990s as an internal term (Diebold, 2012; Lohr, 2013). The term has also been used in discussions of large data set analysis in computer science. Weiss and Indurkhya (1998) used the term in their discussion of mining large data sets. In addition, the term has been discussed within the context of macroeconomic measurement and forecasting (Diebold, 2003). The term big data started to become commonplace in 2012 and has gained institutional status with interdisciplinary conversations about big data, as demonstrated in many different forums dedicated to advance a better understanding of the ways in which large amounts of data can be manipulated and then used for different purposes. This process has gone on, although the term *big data* has been adopted without an accepted definition that captures all the elements of what big data could stand for. It is, therefore, first important to consider a working description of big data such as the following:

> Data are flooding in at rates never seen before—doubling every 18 months—as a result of greater access to customer data from public, proprietary, and purchased sources, as well as new information gathered from Web communities and newly deployed smart assets. These trends are broadly known as "big data." (Bughin, Chui, & Manyika, 2010, Section 5, para. 1)

Key to the idea of big data is the fact that these are personalized data coming from people who are actively and voluntarily contributing to the compilation of these data sets (Schoeberger & Cukier, 2013). Much of the attention on big data has focused on the two key components: (a) gathering the large amounts of data and (b) quantitatively analyzing the data to obtain both personal-individualized information as well as information about different groups of people. For instance, the organizers of the 2013 conference called "Big Data TechCon!" claim that the greatest benefit of attending the conference is learning how to "collect, sort and store massive quantities of structured and unstructured data" (BZ Media, 2013, p. 1). Generally, the structured data refer to quantifiable elements of the data, which, for an individual, are things such as gender, age, education, income, and other stable, easily measured, and easily quantified attributes. Such data are amenable to numeric analysis, which is the forte of computers, to produce specific statistics about an individual or cluster of people. It is the unstructured data that becomes more challenging to analyze and interpret. There are only exploratory and proprietary numerical tools that can extract meaningful statistics from thousands of messages sent, for instance, via Twitter, or the millions of lines of status updates that are produced by the nearly one billion users of Facebook. This is what I call narbs, and, as I show in this chapter, it is possible to categorize narbs to begin a more careful analysis of big data. These unstructured data need to be considered more carefully if indeed the promises of big data are to be met. Narbs serve as the repository of personal and communal narratives that need to be extracted from the data to offer a better understanding of the persons and groups represented by big data. The premise here is not necessarily new; indeed, it has been argued that analysis of the material available on the Internet is indeed a process of discursive analysis (Mitra, 1999; Mitra & Cohen, 1998). The combination of the theory of narbs and the availability of narbs in big data offers the opportunity of developing the analytic protocol discussed in this essay. It is important now, with the explosion of the discourses, however, to have a specific theoretical framework that could inform the analysis of the unstructured component of big data. As such, I turn to Fisher's (1984, 1985a, 1985b, 1987) narrative theories that were developed long before the advent of big data.

Narrative Theories

Within Fisher's (1984) way of considering narratives, the notion of a *narrative paradigm* becomes particularly important. The notion of the narrative paradigm was proposed in the early 1980s and became a point of intense discussion by the mid-1980s. Fisher's premise was based on the work of earlier scholars who identified the importance of storytelling and narratives in the process of meaning making in everyday life, as people operate within the cultural and social spaces that they occupy (Andrews, 1982; Gadamer, 1982; MacIntyre, 1981; Ricouer, 1977, 1983, 1984; White, 1984). In setting forth the notion that human beings operate not only as a rational and rhetorical beings, Fisher suggested that people can also operate as a narrative being in which the act of creating and articulating a coherent and rational narrative becomes a part of being human. In doing this, the narrative paradigm offers a different way of analyzing and understanding communication and the way in which people act. The narrative paradigm of Fisher is best considered by examining Fisher's own description:

> The narrative paradigm is a fabric woven of threads of thought from both social sciences and humanities. It seeks, like any other theory of human action, to account for how persons come to believe and behave. It differs from social scientific and humanistic theories in that it projects narration not as an art, genre, or activity but as a paradigm. It goes beyond these theories in providing a "new" logic, the concept of narrative rationality, which is applicable to all forms of human communication (1985a, p. 357).

There are many aspects within this definition that merit examination of big data in the early 21st century, particularly when the analysis of big data seeks to provide an account of how persons come to believe and behave (Kosinski, Stillwell, & Graepel, 2013). This is especially true when big data include an element that is not amenable to the traditional modes of research offered by the social sciences, which have relied significantly on the understanding of how the quantified elements of being human become the source for understanding how humans believe and behave. The multibillion-dollar international polling industry stands testament to this belief. Much has been done through attitude, opinion, and interest research to measure the feelings, opinions, and beliefs of people to explain and predict how people might behave within different contexts—from voting for a candidate to buying a specific brand of toothpaste. Fisher, however, provided an opening to consider other forms of data—the narratives—as a way of understanding everyday life. The narrative paradigm suggests that it is possible to examine a story to seek its internal coherence and fidelity. Coherence refers to the internal logic of the story, the way all the elements connect, or do not connect, in a coherent fashion. Fidelity refers to the believability of the story in terms of its truth value. Stories that demonstrate high coherence and fidelity could become the components that supplement the structural part of any big data set by providing insights into the story and its author. Although these two components of a narrative analysis offer better insight into a story, Fisher (1985a) confessed that the paradigm does not offer a specific analytical method that can be applied to a specific narrative. As such, the paradigm is called into question because analysts are unable to bring a specific toolbox to a narrative. In such a notable test, Rowland (1989) attempted to apply the concepts of narrative coherence and fidelity to three texts and stated, "The analysis of the works, however, reveals that narrative approaches are of little use when applied to discourse that does not tell a story" (p. 39). For this test, the researcher had looked at a book attacking religious fundamentalism, a film attacking Pat Robertson, and an allegorical science fiction that tells a story from the Bible. In a similar manner, albeit with more favorable outcomes, others have applied the narrative paradigm to specific stories produced by authors who are in the business of writing—and thus, according to Fisher—telling stories. The presumption that remained true for both proponents of the narrative paradigm and opponents is that the stories were primarily authored by institutional authors. The objective of the analysis, even when couched in the narrative paradigm, was to somehow discover and expose the role that those specific stories by "professional authors" play in shaping human belief and behavior. This presumption was predicated by the fact that there were a limited number of stories limited by the number of authors. Only a few such as Hyde (1985) considered stories told by individuals who were not professional storytellers. Others looked at famous speeches (Bass, 1985) and famous novels (Bennett, 1978; Fisher & Filloy, 1982), stories with far reaching consequences on large portions of the global readers. The focus on institutional authors seemed sensible because there were few others.

By focusing on the institutional author, a key element went missing from the paradigm—the private individual author. If, indeed, stories offer a powerful means of understanding how humans believe and behave, then it is important to look at the stories of private individuals. Consider, for instance, the analysis that Fisher (1985a) provided of the conversation between Socrates and Callicles. Fisher offered conclusions that relate to the ways in which a narrative analysis of this conversation throws light on how societies operate and how the stories remain in fidelity with the reality of some societies. Only in passing did Fisher focus on precisely what the storyteller was thinking when telling the story. In this case, the storyteller would be Plato because Fisher used the works of Plato to draw conclusions about the role of the stories in society. At the end of the analysis, Fisher claimed, "There can be no doubt that Plato's concern about rhetoric was pervasive—how it distorted education, corrupted politics, and failed as philosophy and a way of life" (1985a, p. 364). In making these statements and insisting that Plato's position is intertextually supported, Fisher provided the opening to fill in the missing element related to the author of the story. Once that gap was filled, it could be possible to draw conclusions about any individual who chose to express himself or herself, just as Plato did, as long as the data about the individual are in the big database.

With the availability of access to big data as discussed earlier, it is now possible to consider every element that makes up the big data as data that throw light on the storytellers. These are stories that are voluntarily and involuntarily told by individuals whose information is contained in the databases. These stories, much like other stories, are made up of a set of immutable facts about the individual and the points of view the storyteller adopts in telling the story. The first part of these two components deals with the undeniable facts about the storyteller. For instance, in the case of Plato in Fisher's (1985a) analysis, there are certain facts about Plato one needs to know to be able to understand the story. The fact that Plato was a privileged male within the social system in which he lived had an impact on the stories he told. In the realm of literary analysis, it is commonplace to learn about the storyteller's life in order to understand the narrative qualities of the story being told. Those facts offer the context of the story and the story itself deals with the second component—the perspective from which the story is told. The fact that Plato believed in certain things shapes the story that is told, and analyzing the story, in turn, can offer insights into the mind of the storyteller. Narrative analysis is not only concerned with the aesthetics of storytelling but is also equally concerned with the attitudes, opinions, and beliefs of the author. In the digital world of big data, it is now possible to find both the components of every person who gains "authorship" by being a part of the big databases. It is now possible to know the exact context within which the storyteller operates, because the database contains information about the context, which is often called the demographic attributes of the author. Consider the fact that a social media database such as Facebook could contain more than 200 different attributes of the every dweller in the Facebook space. This gives a vast amount of information about the storyteller. At the same time, in databases such as Facebook, there is a vast amount of information about the mind of the author, as many members of the social media systems speak about themselves by using their own voice to tell things about themselves. In such spaces, each individual becomes a "storytelling being," in the manner suggested within the narrative paradigm. Consequently, using the paradigm, it is possible to understand how people believe and behave by systematically analyzing the stories that are being told. In the case of social media systems, these stories appear as a collection of narbs that are made up of the different ways people express themselves—from simple status updates to the elaborate process of offering visual information. These narbs provide the elements of the narrative. The next section offers a specific approach to understanding the personal stories by categorizing and analyzing the narbs produced by individuals and institutions.

Narbs

A starting point for narb categorization begins with the question of authorship: Who creates a narb? Generally there are two options. Either the narb is created by the person whose story is being told, or it is created by someone else but contributes to the creation of the story of a particular person distinct from the author. In the case of the former, it becomes a *self-narb*, in which the power of authorship is retained by the person whose narrative is being told. The other option produces the *other narb*, in which the person whose narrative is produced has marginal control on the narrative.

By placing narbs in these two primary categories, it is possible to consider both kinds of narbs from the perspective of the content of the narbs and the role that content plays in creating the story of an individual. To begin with, the content-based categorization offers a starting point for systematically classifying narbs that use specific symbolic strategies to create narrative content and meaning—the stuff that makes up the story. Each content category could require different kinds of analytic methods to extract the stories from the narbs.

The most common category of narb is the *text narb*. This is essentially a simple statement that tells a tiny story about a person. Independent of whether the narb is a self-narb or an other narb, these textual pieces are usually small in size. A good example of a text narb is a simple status update that a person might post to a social media site on the personal space. For instance, I would often make a simple statement such as "Just reached Calcutta" to let others know of a safe arrival. Much of the content of social media is made up of such narbs. These are relatively easy to produce and can be done with a variety of tools, from a computer to a smartphone. Many smartphones offer the option of converting a spoken sentence into text and then posting the statement on a social media site. Social media sites are increasingly making it simple to create this information. There is an implicit assumption that these narbs would be short. However, through such short narbs, the users are constantly able to voice themselves. The text narbs are also evident and popular on micro-blogging systems such as Twitter. Indeed a single tweeted narb is limited to a strict number of characters, and each narb can only be as long as allowed by the system.

After the text narb, perhaps the most common category of narbs is the *picture narb*. These narbs are made up of still pictures added to the profile page of a person's social media site. The picture could come from many different sources and could serve both as a self-narb and as an other narb. The most popular way of creating a picture narb is with a smartphone that has a built-in camera. Most cell phones now have picture taking as a standard function of the camera. Many such cell phones also allow access to social media sites and thus uploading a picture is not a difficult task at all. Most social media sites also allow for the uploading of pictures from galleries of pictures stored on a computer. For instance, in 2013 about 350 million picture narbs were uploaded on Facebook every day (Smith, 2013). One of the most interesting aspects of picture narbs is the ability to not only place a picture on the social media site but to also provide an accompanying text narb explaining the picture and providing qualifying information accompanying the picture. For instance, during a trip to Munich, Germany, I took a picture of a busy street near the old city center. I also added a comment on the picture narb, stating my assessment of the crowded narrow streets. A picture narb thus often works in conjunction with a text narb. The picture narb also allows for the addition of meta-information in the form of tags. As most users know, it is possible to annotate the picture with specific names of people who might be in the picture. Indeed, the process of naming the people in a picture has become a part of the technology offered by some social media sites such as Facebook. For example, starting in June 2011, the social media site developed a semiautomatic tagging option through which users would have their picture narbs tagged by the Facebook computing system based on the history of tagging.

Much in the way that the picture narb has become popular because of the existence of cameras on cell phones and applications such as Instagram, it is possible to use smartphones to also capture digital video and quickly place that on a social media site. The *video narb* is thus the third category of narb. The process of creating and using a video narb is not dissimilar to the way in which a picture narb is used—a caption and a description in text would accompany the video narb. Generally, the production of a video narb is a more computing-intensive process, and uploading a video to a social media site takes a little bit longer. However, that has not necessarily been a deterrent. For instance, in 2010, Facebook reported that nearly 20 million videos were being uploaded every month (Calderon, 2010). The number was significantly higher than in 2009, and it has continued to increase.

A discussion of the category of video narbs remains incomplete without the mention of the specific web-based systems that are built to share videos. Among these, the YouTube site is perhaps most popular. These sites operate a little bit differently from social media sites where many different kinds of narbs can be used. The video-sharing sites are only for videos with different kinds of textual annotations such as tags, keywords, and descriptions. These sites operate in a manner similar to social media sites, and there are ways of linking these video sites to social media sites. The same video narb can be found on both kinds of sites. Together, these different sites are making video narbs increasingly popular.

The category of narbs that deal with audio is perhaps the least popular kind of narb—the *audio narb*. This is a narb that only uses sound to tell the story. With the increasing popularity of video narbs, much of the sound element of a narb is accompanied by images. In some cases, an individual might use an audio narb, which simply does not have any images attached to it. In such cases, the audio narb would serve much like a video narb by shedding light on what the individual is thinking about based on the kind of audio narb the person has shared. These narbs are best analyzed by using the metadata that surround the narb, especially in the form of textual annotations.

These content-based categories are certainly not meant to be mutually exclusive and often work together in a single narb, in which a video becomes a part of a self-narb that also includes a certain amount of text and an audio component that accompanies the video image. Consider, for instance, a very popular kind of narb in which an individual would update a profile with a short video of a child performing at a school musical ceremony. Interestingly, there are no reliable statistics on the kind of videos posted on social media sites, but even a cursory look at what is uploaded, one is likely to find several personal videos placed on social media sites that deal with family activities and that are tagged with labels and descriptions. These narbs tell specific stories about individuals, and, over time, these composite narbs can build to tell the larger narrative of an individual. The identity of an individual is eventually constructed by the combination of narbs that are available on a social networking site where different kinds of narbs work together to produce the composite narrative of a person at any moment in time. The content-based categorization scheme offers an analytical perspective for those who are interested in understanding the different parts of the overall narrative. Those who are posting narbs are not consciously considering whether a specific narb belongs to the text category or picture category; they are interested in telling a story. Yet, for the purpose of analysis, it is important to be able to bring a specific framework to the understanding of narbs.

The content-based categorization has to be coupled with one more analytic criterion to complete the categorization of narbs: the functional categorization, through which narbs of all kinds can also be considered from the specific function they perform in creating the narrative of a particular individual. The idea of function is quite traditional to understanding narratives. Most stories have characters and segments of the story that serve different purposes. There has been extensive consideration of the way in which narratives can be analyzed in terms of the codes that can be discovered in every narrative, discourse, or text. Consider, for instance, the five narrative codes suggested by Barthes (1975),[1] in which he has also argued that all texts first fall into an open or closed category, referring to the openness of the text to multiple meanings, which then is contained within the five codes. Among Barthes's codes, there is the suggestion that a text contains codes referring to action, deeper meaning, and external bodies of knowledge. Analysis of text can be performed by seeking these codes in the text and then interpreting the way the codes are used and how they function to produce meaning. At the same time, scholars such as Tzvetan Todorov

(1977) and Vladimir Propp (1968) have suggested that different elements of a story can be analyzed based on predictable narrative structure and repeated function of different elements in advancing a narrative. In the case of Todorov (1977), the idea of a narrative structure is particularly important; he argues that most narratives go through the structured process, starting with a state of equilibrium, followed by a crisis, and then the reestablishment of a desirable equilibrium. Indeed, the analysis of narbs is well served by this approach since it is now possible to test the various stages of the narrative structure of the stories created by different combination of the categories of narbs. When the idea of narrative structure is combined with the notion of narrative function suggested by Propp (1968), it is possible to claim that a narrative is built through the 31 functions that Propp identifies. These functions are the most fundamental elements of a tale, and they tend to follow each other to help build the structure of the narrative. For instance, in the analysis of the folklore, which was the focus of the work of Propp, he suggested *trickery*, when a villain tries to deceive his victim, always precedes *complicity*, when the victim submits to the trickery. In this manner, Propp builds a lexicon of functions, which focus in on minute details of narratives. It is the case that Propp was working with the specific genre of folktales, but his identification of the functions have been found to be useful for analysis of other kinds of texts, particularly film narratives. As such, although the functions were based on a small corpus of texts, the notion of functions is useful for the categorization of narbs.

I use these approaches to narrative analysis to argue that narratives produced by narbs also follow a structure, albeit less systematic as in the case of fiction, and the structure is composed of codes and functions, again less elaborated than in the case of fiction. Consequently, in the analysis of narbs, it is possible to divide them into specific functional categories. The first set of functional categories considers the *spatial narb*, which offers specific information about the real-life spatial location or spatial attributes of an individual. In the case of narbs that are self-narbs, this could be an important indicator about the background of a specific developing narrative about an individual.

The second functional category can be referred to as the *temporal narb*, which offers specific chronological information about a person. Every narb has temporal information connected to it because the narb is usually stamped with time information. It is possible to extract information about the time of a posting from the temporal narb. This kind of information can allow an observer to get a better sense of the flow of the identity narrative of an individual. In this case, the narbs provide information that show when the person has been born, perhaps how old the person is, and how the person's narbs are dependent on the specific point in one's life.

A third functional category is the *causal narb*, which offer information about the fundamental attitudes and opinions of a person that shape the person's identity narrative. These could be text narbs, picture narbs, or video narbs and are most frequently self-narbs. These include moments when individuals update their status by making statements that specifically express an opinion about a matter. Many narbs serve this function, including narbs that an individual would share on a profile page to demonstrate his or her specific opinion about a matter. Sometimes these narbs can take on collective power as a narb used by one individual connects his or her opinion with thousands of other people who might feel the same way. First, these narbs, over time, can shed light on the opinions of a particular individual. Such information can be extremely useful in creating the identity narrative of a narb by understanding what a person feels about a range of issues. It does not matter what type of a narb it is, as long as a specific feeling is expressed. Second, the collection of narbs that serve the causal function can also tell the story of a collection of individuals. In this situation, entire groups of people who post the same narb express a unified opinion about a matter.

The fourth functional category focuses on the specific activities that a person does and is called the *activity narb*. In this case, a person explicitly states what the person is doing. The activity function can be served by both self-narbs and other narbs. An individual can state what she is doing, just as the friends of a person can state what he is doing.

As shown in Figure 12.1, it is therefore possible to consider any single narb and place it within a three-dimensional space where it occupies a unique place based on the three criteria discussed here. Such a placement offers the point of departure to analyze the narb, and what it says about the author, using a systematic process that can be standardized for many narbs and for many authors.

However, it should be clear that some narbs include a set of data that do not neatly fall into the self-narb and other narb categories. That information is made up of specific things a user can do with most social media sites. The first such activity is the process of "liking" a narb. Independent of who produces a narb and the type of narb, it is possible to click on a button on the screen

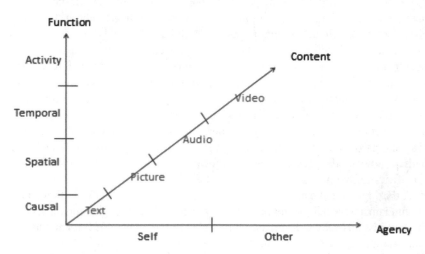

Figure 12.1 Placing a narb along the category axes

and simply express one's liking the narb. In that act, however, a person could also express an opinion, and, as a result, liking something could serve a causal function. Similar to the process of liking, a social media presence is also the process of becoming a fan of a company, a person, or a group. When people become fans, they are expressing a certain attitude as well. When constructing the identity narrative of an individual, it is useful to understand who or what the person is liking and becoming a fan of.

A second body of information that complements the self-narb is the comments one produces as other narbs. This is an extension of the liking process through which a person might express an opinion about another person's narb. Generally, these are text narbs that either support the opinion expressed in the narb of one person or set up a dialog with a person. When someone creates these comment narbs, he or she is also expressing an opinion. These comment narbs help to shed light on what he or she might be thinking about a matter that has been discussed by someone else's narb. These comment narbs need to be a part of an analysis to create the complete identity narrative of an individual.

In the end, every narb can be categorized in the ways described here. One simple way to consider the categorization is to think of each narb having at least three different values—agency, content, and function. It is possible to assign a number to each of these three aspects of the narb. For instance, a self-narb could have a value of 1, whereas an other narb has a value of 0, because the self-narb is considered to be more meaningful than the other narb. Similarly, it is possible to assign numbers to the content category, such as assign 1 for text narbs, 2 for picture narbs, 3 for audio narbs, and 4 for video narbs, because these categories represent progressively more complex forms of content. It is also logical to claim that a narb that fulfills either a spatial function or a temporal function gains a value of 1 in the function category, because these are basic functional aspects of the narrative as these aspects offer information about the location of the narrative and when the narrative happens. On the other hand, the activity function receives the value of 2, because knowledge of the activity offers greater insight into the narrative. Using this logic, the causal function earns the value of 3, because if offers greater depth of information, especially in terms of the reason that a person might have acted in a particular manner. This schema is useful because it allows us to examine the kinds of narbs individuals are producing. For instance, if one were to post a video of a political rally captured on a smartphone, it is a self-narb (1) that is made up of video content (4); because it was posted from a smartphone, it serves a temporal function (1) and probably has location information (1) and shows an activity (3) and an attitude (4). This narb would earn the value of 14, whereas a text narb about eating at a restaurant would earn a lower value (see Figure 12.2).

The tagging of narbs with specific values is of particular importance when narbs from a large number of individuals are being analyzed. By using the values, it would be possible to eliminate all narbs that have a value of 0 for the author component of the valence of the narb. Such screening based on specific valence numbers could allow the analyst to focus specifically on the narbs of interest. The

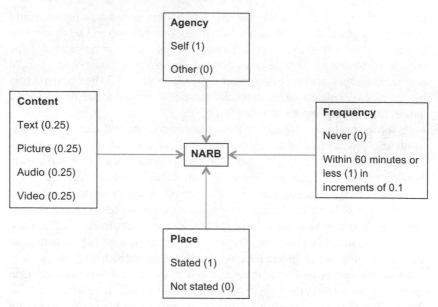

Figure 12.2 Computing narb weights

value-based screening of narbs can be done in an automated way in which only the relevant narbs are selected for analysis from billions of possible narbs. The addition of values to narbs essentially addresses one of the largest challenges of dealing with big data—that the data set is indeed big and that portions of it might be useless and would serve no analytic value. It is thus useful to attach values whenever possible to allow for more machine-based analysis.

Significance

The process of categorization of narbs is the starting point for a larger project where the narbs can eventually be gathered and analyzed. The categorization and coding offer a way of sifting through the extremely large number of narbs that are constantly being produced. A large number of these narbs are relatively useless from an analytic perspective. Consider for instance a situation where the analytic effort is to discover the specific ways in which people reported their behavior at a particular place and at a particular time, as in the case of a catastrophic event such as a natural disaster or a terrorist attack. The categorization helps to focus on self-narbs that have a spatial and temporal value as well as a value for activity function. By attaching the values to the entire domain of narbs gathered through *scraping* (Myllymaki, 2002), it is then possible to filter out the subset of narbs that have the specific numbers for each of the categorization criteria. This subset of narbs can then become a more manageable set of narbs for automated analysis. Without a categorization and coding process, the analytic process would be burdened with a large set of unusable narbs, which could slow the analytic process.

The analytic process itself could take on different forms. Some of the emergent forms of analysis are based in Natural Language Processing (NLP) technologies that use variants of Latent Semantic Analysis (LSA). These technologies allow for the extraction of themes from unstructured data. These themes could then be connected to create concept maps where a specific narrative would emerge from the numerous narbs that have been analyzed. For instance, using the narbs from public blogs of Arabists writing about Egypt and its neighbors, it was possible to create a concept map that showed the notion of war was strongly connected with Israel, Egypt, and Washington/the United States, whereas the narratives did not express similar connections with Tunisia, Palestine, or Saudi Arabia (Mitra, 2012c). Similar analysis can be conducted with any set of narbs in which the analytic process would extract the specific sentiments related to a large set of narbs and relate that to other elements ranging from political candidates to world events. All the analysis would be based on the filtered and codified narbs, which would be analyzed through the narrative lens provided by the narrative paradigm.

There are many implications for this analytic approach that first codes the narbs, filters them, and then passes them through NLP/LSA procedures. Consider, for instance, my argument that the access to big data can have the potential of *predictive policing*, allowing for better law enforcement practices (Mitra, in press). This is still a matter of speculation, but there are ongoing tests in the United States that clearly create a condition that has been described as "using big-data analysis to select what streets, groups, and individuals to subject to extra scrutiny, simply because an algorithm pointed to them as more likely to commit crime" (Mayer-Schönberger & Cukier, 2013, Section 5, para. 4). Indeed, as reported in 2013, it is clear that the PRISM program of the U.S. National Security Agency collects vast amounts of digital information, some of which could be narbs of individuals (Greenwald & Ball, 2013). There are different ways in which big data, made up of different kinds of narbs, are being analyzed to produce data about very small groups and individuals that have many different implications, from targeted marketing as in the case of warehouse stores in United States targeting products to specific individuals to the identification of specific profiles for law enforcement (Kelly, 2012). For scholars of human communication, the combination of availability of big data and its analysis from the narrative perspective provides ways of creating specific personal narratives, which can have an impact on many aspects of everyday life. However, the implications can only be best understood through a process of careful analysis, making the categorization process and method particularly important.

From the perspective of communication research, there are two critical points of significance. The first relates to the way in which audience research has been conducted within the broad areas of communication research (Delia, 1987). Much of the project of audience research has focused on understanding the attitudinal trends of audience segments. The presumption has been that the audience can be categorized into groups, however fragmented, and analysis of the overall attitudes of the groups would allow for an understanding of the individuals who belong to the group. This is, at best, a process of generalization with its inherent limitations, as is taught in every communication research methods class across the world. Within this project, the measurement of attitudes relied on research-defined statements of attitude, which become the yardstick for measuring attitudes. Traditional scales such as the Likert scale, the Semantic Differential scale, and other such scales offer the respondent the language of the researcher, which then is used to measure the attitude of the respondent. Although there are sophisticated and reliable techniques of reducing bias in this process, it still remains the case that it is through the language of the items in the scales that the final measurement of attitude takes place. Once the narbs have been appropriately identified and coded, they can be put through a systematic analysis, offering an alternative to the traditional approach.

Narbs offer user-generated information that can be categorized and analyzed to develop narrative patterns that speak about the attitude of the individual. Extrapolated to its logical end, the audience does not have to be treated as a mass that is looked at through generalizable data. Alternatively, the audience can logically be made of a single individual and a narrative of the individual can be developed based on the facts about the individual and attitudes of the individual—all of what can be obtained from the big data repositories that are potentially available for analysis. Indeed, as some of the examples mentioned earlier have demonstrated, this is already being attempted with some degrees of success. The narrative approach to narbs proposed in this chapter offers a more theoretically sound and analytically grounded way of single-audience analysis, in which narbs become the units of analysis.

This process of audience analysis leads to the second significance of the narbs analysis. If indeed the audience is an individual, within the free-market system, it is this audience that is the target for messages. So far, within the domain of persuasive message creation, much of the project has relied on generalizations about the audience based on survey audience research. If narb analysis begins to supplement traditional audience research, then the message creation strategy has to adjust to messaging for the individual. This also has started to happen to some degree where the behaviors of individuals, as recorded in the big databases, become the basis for individualized messaging. However, much of that targeting has been based on the "fact" portion of the database—things related to demographic attributes, self-reported behavior, and other such verifiable and measurable attributes. With narb analysis, it is now possible to create messages that draw not only on the facts about the individual but also on the attitudes of the individual as exposed through the narratives that they create about themselves. This additional component could change the way messages are designed so that the messages attain their persuasive appeal through identification with the audience about whom the messenger now has far more information than ever before.

These two aspects of narbs—audience analysis and message design—are fundamental to a free society. This potential is already being recognized as different industries are taking note of the potential of big data in changing how our everyday life could be organized in the future. Some, such as the CEO of IBM, have made the claim that big data is the next "natural resource," and the way it is used could alter the way we know the world (Frank, 2013). As is the case of many other resources that we have used and abused, we enter the new world of narbs without knowledge of what the stakes are or how to manage the resource. In the case of narbs, we can be more mindful and look at this resource through the lens of theory before plundering what it offers.

A set of issues comes up given the two consequences discussed here and the preliminary analysis of the narbs from the Arabist blogs. First, there needs to be more effort placed on the process of scraping. Although the process is usually automated, it would be more efficient to use the narb values to obtain more targeted scraping. Second, there needs to be further examination of the analytic process of narbs by attending to the various characteristics of narbs— the authorship, content type, and function. This analysis needs to be expanded to all kinds of narbs with appropriate algorithms, including the existing NLP/ LSA models. These two areas of research would allow for automation of some of the narb analysis process, which is essential because the number of narbs is always expanding and the size of big data is growing. Without specific systems of analysis, based on sound theory, the data would remain relatively unused.

Note

1. The five codes are those that offer a sense of mystery to a narrative (hermeneutic/enigmatic), those that describe action within the narrative (action), those that refer to additional material within the text (semantic), those that offer meanings through symbols (symbolic), and those that refer to larger bodies of information beyond the text (referential).

References

Andrews, J. D. (1982). The structuralist study of narrative: Its history, use and limits. In. P. Hernadi (Ed.), *The horizon of literature* (pp. 99–124). Lincoln: The University of Nebraska Press.

Barthes, R. (1975). *S/Z* (Richard Miller, Trans.). New York: Macmillan.

Bass, J. D. (1985). The appeal to efficiency as narrative closure: Lyndon Johnson and the Dominican crisis, 1965. *Southern Speech Communication Journal, 50*, 103–120. doi:10.1080/10417948509372626

Bennett, W. L. (1978). Storytelling and criminal trials: A model of social judgment. *Quarterly Journal of Speech, 64*, 1–22. doi:10.1080/00335637809383408

Bughin, J., Chui, M., & Manyika, J. (2010, September 22). Clouds, big data, and smart assets: Ten tech-enabled business trends to watch. *Financial Times*. Retrieved from www.mckinsey.com/insights/mgi/in_the_news/clouds_big_data_and_smart_assets

BZ Media. (2013). Big Data Tech Con. Retrieved from www.bigdatatechcon.com/ SanFrancisco2013/index.html

Calderon, S. I. (2010, June 10). Facebook's video stats show growth in uploads and views [Blog post]. Retrieved from www.insidefacebook.com/2010/06/10/ facebook%E2%80%99s-video-stats-show-growth-in-uploads-and-views/

Delia, J. G. (1987). Twentieth century communication research: An historical perspective. In C. E. Berger & S. H. Chaffee (Eds.), *Handbook of communication science* (pp. 20–89). Newbury Park, CA: Sage.

Diebold, F. X. (2003). "Big data" dynamic factor models for macroeconomic measurement and forecasting. In M. Dewatripont, L. P. Hansen, & S. Turnovsky (Eds.), *Advances in economics and econometrics, Eighth World Congress of the Econometric Society* (pp. 115–122). Cambridge, England: Cambridge University Press.

Diebold, F. X. (2012, September 21). On the origin(s) and development of the term "big data." PIER Working Paper No. 12-037. Retrieved from SSRN: http://ssrn.com/abstract=2152421 or http://dx.doi.org/10.2139/ssrn.2152421

Fisher, W. R. (1984). Narration as human communication paradigm: The case of public moral argument. *Communication Monographs, 51,* 1–22. doi:10.1080/03637758409390180

Fisher, W. R. (1985a). The narrative paradigm: An elaboration. *Communication Monographs, 52,* 347–367. doi:10.1080/03637758509376117

Fisher, W. R. (1985b). The narrative paradigm: In the beginning. *Journal of Communication, 35,* 74–89. doi:10.1111/j.1460–2466.1985.tb02974.x

Fisher, W. R. (1987). *Human communication as narration: Toward a philosophy of reason, value, and action.* Columbia: University of South Carolina Press.

Fisher, W. R., & Filloy, R. A. (1982). Argument in drama and literature: An exploration. In J. R. Cox & C. A. Willard (Eds.), *Advances in argument theory and research* (pp. 343–362). Carbondale: Southern Illinois University Press.

Frank, A. D. (2013, March 8). IBM CEO Rometty says big data are the next great natural resource. *The Daily Beast.* Retrieved from www.thedailybeast.com/articles/2013/03/08/ibm-ceo-rometty-says-big-data-is-the-next-great-natural-resource.html?account=thedailybeast&medium=twitter&source=socialflow

Gadamer, H. G. (1982). *Truth and method.* New York: Crossword Publishing.

Greenwald, G., & Ball, J. (2013, June 20). The top secret rules that allow NSA to use US data without a warrant. *The Guardian.* Retrieved from www.guardian.co.uk/world/2013/jun/20/fisa-court-nsa-without-warrant

Hyde, M. J. (1985). Storytelling and public moral argument: The case of medicine. In J. R. Cox, M. O. Sillars, & G. B. Walker (Eds.), *Argument and social practice: Proceedings of the fourth SCA-AFA conference on argumentation* (pp. 364–375). Annandale, VA: SCA.

Kelly, H. (2012, August 30). Police embrace social media as crime-fighting tool. *CNN.* Retrieved from www.cnn.com/2012/08/30/tech/social-media/fighting-crime-social-media

Kosinski, M., Stillwell, D. J., & Graepel, T. (2013). Private traits and attributes are predictable from digital records of human behavior. *Proceedings of the National Academy of Sciences, 110*(15), 5802–5805. doi:10.1073/pnas.1218772110

Lohr, S. (2013, June 19). Sizing up big data, broadening beyond the Internet. *The New York Times.* Retrieved from http://bits.blogs.nytimes.com/2013/06/19/sizing-up-big-data-broadening-beyond-the-internet/

MacIntyre, A. (1981). *After virtue: A study in moral theory* (2nd ed). Notre Dame, IN: The University of Notre Dame Press.

Mayer-Schönberger, V., & Cukier, K. (2013, March). Should we use big data to punish crimes before they're committed? *Popular Science.* Retrieved from www.popsci.com/science/article/2013–03/should-we-use-big-data-to-punish-crimes-before-theyre-committed?page=1

Mitra, A. (1999). Characteristics of the WWW Text: Tracing Discursive Strategies. *Journal of Computer Mediated Communication, 5.* doi:10.1111/j.1083–6101.1999. tb00330.x

Mitra, A. (2010). Creating a presence on social networks via narbs. *Global Media Journal, 9*(16), 1–18.

Mitra, A. (2011). Using narratives from social network to manage teacher-student interaction. In A. Méndez-Vilas (Ed.), *Education in a technological world: Communicating current and emerging research and technological efforts* (pp. 588–592). Badajoz, Spain: Formatex Research Center.

Mitra, A. (2012a). Collective narrative expertise and using the narbs of social media. In T. Takseva (Ed.), *Social software and the evolution of user expertise: Future trends in knowledge creation and dissemination* (pp. 1–20). Hershey, PA: IGI Global. doi:10.4018/978–1-4666–2178–7.ch001

Mitra, A. (2012b). Narbs as a measure and indicator of identity narratives. In A. Dudley, J. Braman, & G. Vicenti (Eds.), *Investigating cyber law and cyber ethics: Issues, impacts and practices* (pp. 132–140). Hershey, PA: IGI Global.

Mitra, A. (2012c, October). *Narbs of social media.* Paper presented at the second International Conference on Social Eco-Informatics, Venice, Italy.

Mitra, A. (2013). Mapping narbs. In G. Wise (Ed.), *New visualities, new technologies: The new ecstasy of communication* (pp. 23–45). New York: Ashgate Publishing Ltd.

Mitra, A. (in press). *Digital DNA: Managing identity in social networking sites.* New Delhi, India: Rupa Publications.

Mitra, A., & Cohen, E. (1998). Analyzing the Web: Directions and challenges. In S. Jones (Ed.), *Doing Internet research* (pp. 179–202). Newbury Park, CA: Sage.

Myllymaki, J. (2002). Effective Web data extraction with standard XML technologies. *Computer Networks, 39*(5), 635–644. doi:10.1016/S1389–1286(02)00214–1

Propp, V. (1968). *Morphology of the folktale: Second edition.* Austin: University of Texas Press.

Ricouer, P. (1977). The model of the text: Meaningful action considered as text. In F. R. Dallmayr & T. A. McCarthy (Eds.), *Understanding and social inquiry* (pp. 316–334). Notre Dame, IN: The University of Notre Dame Press.

Ricouer, P. (1983). The narrative function. In J. B. Thompson (Ed.), *Paul Ricouer, hermeneutics, and the human sciences: Essays on language, action, and interpretation* (pp. 274–296). Cambridge, England: Cambridge University Press.

Ricouer, P. (1984). *Time and narrative* (Vol. 1, K. McLaughlin & D. Pellaur, Trans.). Chicago, IL: The University of Chicago Press. doi:10.7208/chicago/9780226671 3519.001.0001

Rowland, R. C. (1989). On limiting the narrative paradigm: Three case studies. *Communication Monographs, 56*, 39–54. doi:10.1080/03637758909390248

Schoeberger, V. M., & Cukier, K. (2013). *Big data: A revolution that will transform how we live, work, and think.* New York: Eamon Dolan/Houghton Mifflin Harcourt.

Smith, C. (2013, September 18). Facebook users are uploading 350 million new photos each day. *Business Insider.* Retrieved from www.businessinsider.com/facebook-350-million-photos-each-day-2013-9

Todorov, T. (1977). *The poetics of prose.* Ithaca: Cornell University Press.

Weiss, S. M., & Indurkhya, N. (1998). *Predictive data mining: A practical guide.* New York: Morgan Kaufmann Publishers.

White, H. (1984). The question of narrative in contemporary historical theory. *History and Theory, 23*, 1–33. doi:10.2307/2504969

CHAPTER CONTENTS

13 Episodic, Network, and Intersectional Perspectives

Taking a Communicative Stance on Mentoring in the Workplace

Ziyu Long, Patrice M. Buzzanell,
Lindsey B. Anderson, Jennifer C. Batra,
Klod Kokini, and Robyn F. Wilson

Purdue University

We propose a research agenda to study mentoring as constituted communicatively from episodic, network, and intersectional perspectives. The episodic perspective highlights the everyday communicational events and moments of interactions where actions and meanings of mentoring are co-constructed. The network perspective encourages a holistic analysis of myriad agents, relationships, and evolutions for mentoring at different levels and stages in the form of communicative networks. Finally, the intersectional perspective enables researchers to view mentorship as comprised of complex, politically invested, and socially constructed intersections of identities. We call for communication research and practice on mentoring from these perspectives.

Mentoring, traditionally defined as "a communication relationship in which a senior person supports, tutors, guides, and facilitates a junior person's career development" (Hill, Bahniuk, & Dobos, 1989, p. 15), is considered to be one of the most important processes whereby individuals achieve success and well-being in the workplace (e.g., Ragins & Scandura, 1997; Zey, 1991). Whereas current research has explored diverse forms (formal and informal), functions (psychosocial, career, and role modeling), results (positive and negative), contexts (face-to-face dyadic, cluster, and online), and directions (downward, reverse, and peer) of mentoring (for a review, see T. Allen, Eby, O'Brien, & Lentz, 2008; Haggard, Dougherty, Turban, & Wilbanks, 2011; Ragins & Kram, 2007), relatively fewer studies have delved into how mentoring is communicatively constituted or organized in everyday life (for exceptions, see Bokeno & Gantt, 2000; Buell, 2004; Buzzanell, 2009; Buzzanell, Kokini, Long, Anderson, & Batra, 2012; Kalbfleisch, 2002, 2007; Kalbfleisch & Davies, 1991, 1993; Long, Buzzanell, Kokini, Wilson, Batra, et al., 2013).

To bridge mentoring and communication scholarship, we propose a communicative agenda guided by the constitutive approach (for constitutive rhetoric, see Charland, 1987; for a review of the communication-as-constitutive-of-organizing [CCO] approach, see Cooren, Kuhn, Cornelissen, & Clark, 2011; Kuhn, 2012;

Putnam & Nicotera, 2008). A CCO approach enables reconceptualizations of mentoring as constituted *in* and *through* communication, which opens the venues for innovative theoretical and empirical research to broaden and deepen current understandings of mentoring. This approach recognizes fundamentally that mentoring is not possible without communication and that language and interaction create both mentors' and mentees' identities as well as their relationships. The constitutive approach sees communication as the site of meaning production in mentoring, rather than a vehicle or strategy by which mentoring is accomplished. Thus, the constitutive approach offers a viable framework to engage in the interplays of (re)constructions of meanings and acts of mentoring at micro-, meso-, and macrolevels. Guided by the CCO approach, overarching discourses of mentoring, particularly the prototypical mentor–mentee story of career development and ascent, are made visible in routines and through examination of cultural formations of support and resistance (Buzzanell et al., 2013). Extending previous communication research on mentoring (Kalbfleisch, 2002, 2007), we articulate a processual and ontological view of mentoring (for ontological categorizations of organization, see Fairhurst & Putnam, 2004), that is, mentoring is viewed as a process constituted communicatively among parties. Furthermore, we argue that the constitutive approach has the potential to surface the situated and political nature of mentoring processes whereby power and authority are contested in day-to-day interactions of mentorship in sometimes straightforward but often ambiguous, fragmented, and paradoxical ways (Buzzanell & D'Enbeau, in press; Kuhn, 2012; Oglensky, 2008).

In taking a constitutive approach, we define mentoring as communicatively constituted in ongoing meaning making and interactional struggles for power and knowledge, and coproduced through layers of choice, interaction, and structure. This communicative process is then situated within and produces the oft-documented functions of career development, psychosocial support, and role modeling (T. Allen et al., 2008; Ragins & Kram, 2007). When actualized productively, mentoring is co-constructed through trust, respect, mutual learning, and co-discovery of knowledge (Bokeno & Gantt, 2000; Buzzanell, 2009). From this perspective, communication research uniquely contributes to expanding understandings about the breadth and depth of mentoring processes in different locales. Specifically, we argue that viewing mentoring through a communicative lens highlights the complexity and diversity of relational mentoring experiences coproduced within and across both mentee and mentor perspectives. It uncovers the nuances of mentoring in everyday mentoring interactions in formal, informal, and spontaneous mentoring relationships. Furthermore, mentoring, as an important part of organizational life, provides communication scholars with a different lens to engage in critical issues such as meaningful work and dignity (Buzzanell & Lucas, 2013; Cheney, Zorn, Planalp, & Lair, 2008), organizational and anticipatory socialization (B. Allen, 2000; Bokeno & Gantt, 2000; Jablin, 2001), leadership (Fairhurst, 2011; Fairhurst & Connaughton, 2014), difference and diversity (Mumby, 2011), and choices that can accomplish sustainable work and personal life intersections (Kirby & Buzzanell, 2014). Mentoring does so by offering a contested site for examination of the intertwined formations of everyday talk and cultural understandings through discourse (Phillips & Oswick, 2012) as well as the "overlooked core political concerns regarding equality, and reciprocity in constitutive processes and the difference between more and less generative forms of interaction" (Deetz & Eger, 2014).

The goal of this chapter is to build conceptual foundations, frameworks, and methods that appreciate the dynamics and complexities of mentoring as constituted communicatively and to inspire empirical and theoretical research from diverse perspectives in communication. To achieve this goal, we call for scholars to examine mentoring through three interrelated perspectives that we believe are of great value in bridging communication and the existing mentoring scholarship. We first offer the *episodic perspective* whereby everyday unstructured mentoring interactions are highlighted as integral but often unrecognized communicative units of mentoring. Different mentoring relationships including formal, informal, and episodic mentoring are mutually and communicatively constituted in face-to-face interactions and/or digital mentoring processes enabled by communication technology and the Internet. Second, we present the *network perspective* that conceptualizes mentoring structures in the form of networks with multiple mentoring agents—human, nonhuman, or the communicative episode itself—co-constructing the individual/organizational mentoring experience and processes in dynamic spatial, temporal, and cultural contexts. Finally, we articulate the *intersectional perspective* in which mentoring is viewed as communicative practice both shaped by and shaping the discursive (e.g., what counts as mentoring/a good mentor/mentee) and materialized (e.g., mentoring policy, structures, and procedures) aspects of mentoring. Guided by the intersectional perspective, interactions capitalizing on difference, including gender, race, ethnicity, culture, and nationality, are taken into consideration holistically. When different meanings and acts of mentoring are communicatively designed, translated, negotiated, and debated, mentoring can serve to increase individuals' feelings of belongingness, growth, and well-being and to promote institutional change toward more inclusive spaces. These three perspectives serve as communicative lenses with theoretical and methodological implications rather than a simple typology. Presented separately to explicate the layers and textures of mentoring, the lenses inform and intersect with each other to highlight mentoring as a communicative process. Taken together, the three perspectives foreground a communication research agenda to advance researchers' and practitioners' knowledge on mentoring and open up opportunities for interdisciplinary inquiry.

To elaborate on these mentoring perspectives, we situate our theoretical and methodological claims in the context of faculty mentoring, which has received less scholarly attention than employee mentoring in business organizations (Zellers, Howard, & Barcic, 2008). Mentoring plays an increasingly prominent role in faculty success as faculty are expected to engage in collaborative and multidisciplinary research, reach out to local and global communities, assist students in achieving learning and other outcomes, and foster a diverse and inclusive workplace (Chesler & Chesler, 2002; Jipson & Paley, 2000). In the past two decades, programs, workshops, online resources, policies, and procedures have begun to provide and promote mentoring in the academic context (Dominguez, 2012). A communicative lens to mentoring can unravel why and how such approaches have been more or less effective and can propose further insights into mentoring as fundamental to academe in ways not envisioned by current mentoring literature. In our discussion of faculty mentoring, our readers, many of whom have firsthand experience of mentoring in academe, are invited to not only intellectually engage with different theoretical perspectives but also take advantage of the practical insights generated from our illustrations to enhance their own mentoring experiences. In short, we view faculty mentoring as an area of research that deserves scholarly attention, a context to illustrate a communicative research agenda on mentoring, and a site to generate transferable practical implications of mentoring practices and processes.

To begin, we provide an overview of mentoring literature with a focus on faculty mentoring, outlining the values as well as the limitations in current scholarship. We then offer three communicative perspectives—episodic, network, and intersectional—to add to and reenvision the current mentoring research from a communicative constitution standpoint. For each perspective, we provide both theoretical and methodological propositions and illustrate the application of such perspective using our empirical data from a faculty mentoring project. Finally, we lay out a research agenda for communication scholars from various theoretical and methodological backgrounds to engage in this body of research. We conclude by addressing the practical implications of our approaches.

Traditional Approach to Mentoring

Different from other work relationships such as coaching or advising, mentoring relationships are traditionally characterized by reciprocity or mutuality of social exchange, developmental benefits linked to the mentees' work and career, and regular/consistent interactions between mentors and mentees over some period of time (Haggard et al., 2011). In this dyad arrangement, the mentors usually act as sponsors, coaches, helpers, and consultants in mentees' professional development. At the same time, they provide psychosocial support such as counseling, encouragement, and friendships, and assist the mentee in interpreting organizational realities (Bokeno & Gantt, 2000; Kram, 1983). The mentees usually assume the role of protégé, student, and inexperienced learner, and reap the majority of the relationship's benefits. In what follows, we tease out some major themes of existing mentoring literature and present how communicative perspectives to mentoring can extend this body of scholarship.

Themes in Existing Mentoring Research

The assessment of mentoring outcomes has been a major theme in existing mentoring scholarship. According to this line of research, mentors provided advice and assistance to their mentees with the potential benefit of achieving advanced social status and reciprocated support and aid; mentees tended to receive additional help, acquire skills more quickly than others, develop the ability to interpret unwritten rules of conduct, be integrated deeper into networks, and advance faster with associated benefits (T. Allen, Lentz, & Day, 2006; T. Allen, Poteet, Eby, Lentz, & Lima, 2004; Ibarra, Carter, & Silva, 2010; Kalbfleisch & Eckley, 2003; Long, Buzzanell, Kokini, Wilson, Anderson, et al., 2013). In addition to career advantages, mentoring also provided psychosocial support for mentees. Those who were mentored tended to become more productive workers/scholars, have more collegial relationships with other faculty, report higher career and job satisfaction, and possess greater senses of ownership in and attachment to their work unit (Cawyer & Friedrich, 1998; de Janasz & Sullivan, 2004; Lucas & Murry, 2002; Schrodt, Cawyer, & Sanders, 2003). Scholars have also investigated the ways gender and ethnicity entangled with mentoring experiences and outcomes. For instance, women were found to be less likely to engage in casual conversations about their career with colleagues, and often reported receiving more psychosocial benefits and less career support from the mentoring relationship than did men (Cunningham, 1999; Fox, 2010; Hill et al., 1989). Moreover, women were reported experiencing barriers to career advancement and feeling compelled to engage in masculine practices in the workplace, including accepted norms and standards related to mentoring (Faulkner, 2009; Nelson, 2005; O'Brien, Biga, Kessler, & Allen, 2010; Pawley, 2009). In addition to gender, research showed that individuals of color were more likely to suffer setbacks from lack of career guidance (Bowman, Kite, Branscombe, & Williams, 1999). Further, the underrepresentation of minority groups created challenges in finding mentors within their respective work settings who would understand their reported loneliness, isolation, and difficulties (Chubin, May, & Babco, 2005; O'Brien et al., 2010).

Current research provides useful but limited understandings about how mentoring partners make sense of and label their interactions as mentorship or how mentoring enacts and evolves in everyday communication. An outcome-driven orientation in mentoring, for instance, neglects the politicized ongoing production of mentorship, despite its importance in assessing effectiveness of various mentoring relationships and programs (for reviews of such programs in different organizational contexts, see Dominguez, 2012; Ragins & Kram, 2007). The focus on positive outcomes also obscures different ways of mentoring with multiple outcomes, including toxic and dysfunctional ones. Moreover, the traditional mentoring research tends to adopt the dyadic mentoring model and pays less attention to mentoring situated in individual social networks (e.g., professional networks), institutional contexts (e.g., departmental cultures), and the larger cultural settings (e.g., disciplinary and/or societal norms). Finally, existing mentoring research focuses on the influence of one identity anchor (e.g., being a woman/ethnic minority) on one's mentoring experience. Although we recognize the value of studying issues related to a single identity category (e.g., gender, race, or culture), we also caution that this approach might privilege one form of difference over others and not adequately capture the interplay of multiple identities and power relations in the mentoring processes. A more complex analysis examining how various forms of differences (e.g., different affiliations, personalities, and educational backgrounds) both privilege and marginalize in situ and are (re)produced, resisted, and changed over time in the mentoring process is needed to provide more realistic pictures of mentoring and suggestions for transformations that foreground differences and their political underpinnings.

Among the scholars who have studied mentoring from a communicative perspective, Kalbfleisch (2002) proposed the mentoring enactment theory (MET), which focused on the proactive communicative strategies that can be used by mentors and mentees to initiate, develop, maintain, and repair mentoring relationships. Kalbfleisch (2002) argued that the relational characteristics of mentoring relationships are enacted or carried out by strategic and routine communication between the partners. In addition, Buell (2004) developed four integrated communicative models of mentoring—cloning, nurturing, friendship, and apprentice—from faculty members' and students' understandings of how people mentor. Despite their significant contribution to the understanding of mentoring processes from a communicative lens, the existing studies have not fully explored the everyday communicative constitution of mentoring and the roles that gender, culture, and organizational context play in the mentoring processes.

To address the limitations of conventional mentoring theory and extend communication scholarship in the field, we present the constitutive approach to mentoring. The remainder of our paper uses the preceding review and critique as a springboard for suggesting three specific perspectives on mentoring informed by the CCO approach—episodic, network, and intersectional. We argue that these perspectives should be linked and expanded to privilege an understanding of mentoring that is contextual, complex, politicized, and fluid in nature. Our goal is not to replace the traditional mentoring models and theories with these alternatives. Nor do we claim that these three perspectives are the only or best ways to study mentoring. Instead, we propose these perspectives to initiate the dialogue about developing a constitutive approach to mentoring.

Episodic Perspective

An episodic perspective views mentoring as consisting of developmental interactions that occur at a specific point in time when two parties exchange knowledge, engage in relationship building, and enact social support (Fletcher & Ragins, 2007). These communication moments live in specific instances, occur at freely chosen times, and are agreed on explicitly or tacitly as mentoring by mentors and mentees (Parse, 2002). Constituted through talk-in-interaction, the episodic perspective not only highlights the everyday communication interactions where social practices and meanings of mentoring are co-constructed, but also has the potential to challenge institutionalized definitions and practices of mentoring and mentoring relations. Episodic mentoring is more about everyday moment-by-moment processes, that is, spontaneous teaching, advising, and connecting (Buzzanell, 2009). For example, mentoring may occur in the hallway between two colleagues during their conversation on work-related topics. We argue that episodic mentoring provides a more pragmatic way of framing mentoring in various work settings, in the sense that it offers a means of individual growth, participants' career development, and community contributions without burdening specific parties with long-term commitments or contractual obligations, as can occur in the case of formal mentoring programs.

Although an episodic perspective appreciates the potential life-changing effect of a singular mentoring interaction episode, we theorize episodic mentoring as situating these mentoring moments within ongoing streams and sequences of social-discursive practices, referred to as communicational events in CCO scholarship (Cooren et al., 2011). We argue that episodic mentoring viewed through a constitutive lens offers insight into how mentoring is enacted during these interrelated, generative, and co-constructed communicational events. Furthermore, although mentoring episodes may appear random to outsiders, the CCO lens allows us to envision how the turn of communicative actions and artifacts related to mentoring can be considered in its performative and/or transactional dimensions (Cooren et al., 2011). For instance, in a dyadic or group exchange, it is quite possible that particular mentors engage in spontaneous mentoring, or mentoring episodes, fairly routinely. This is because episodic mentoring is most likely to invoke mentoring as a core identity anchor, insofar as mentors who engage in episodic mentoring would have "a heart for mentoring" (Buzzanell et al., 2013), thereby gently reminding mentees of their commitments to work, linking them to communities of professionals, and recognizing occasions for celebration (Buzzanell, 2009; Parse, 2002). Mentoring episodes also offer possibilities on which potential mentees may act. The other actor in the episode may recognize and receive mentoring, thus assuming the role of mentee in that interactional moment, or may decline the "mentoring invitation." In this communicative process, we can see that episodic mentoring is not random but is authored more or less mindfully in ongoing negotiations where knowledge, roles, and status are made sense of, sustained, and/or contested (e.g., Brummans, Hwang, & Cheong, 2013; Cooren et al., 2011). As such, episodic mentoring does not reside in people but in awareness, naming, and/or enactment of mentoring as communicative accomplishment and process.

Although individuals can engage in mentoring episodes without such interactions being formalized as mentoring relationships, the cumulative experience of these episodes can yield similar outcomes to those documented by research on informal and formal mentoring relationships. For instance, a series of high quality relational mentoring episodes can result in the experience and consequences of positive mentoring relationships in career, work, and nonwork domains (Fletcher & Ragins, 2007). Highlighting the dynamic and fluid nature of relationship development, the notion of episodic mentoring provides a unique vantage point for studying how mentoring relationships from a constitutive perspective are enacted, developed, and transformed.

Additionally, taking an episodic perspective prescribes that mentoring can be constituted in face-to-face and technologically mediated communicative contexts. The computer-mediated, mutually beneficial relationships between mentoring parties are often referred to as e-mentoring/digital mentoring (Berema & Merriam, 2002; Ragins & Kram, 2007). Indeed, e-mentoring resources, which can be produced in video, interactive online forums, and even full-blown membership-based online mentoring programs, have been incorporated by increasing numbers of individuals and organizations into their mentoring processes (Booth, 2006; Haggard et al., 2011). Traditional mentoring relationships also have taken new forms and venues both online and off-line. For instance, mentors and mentees can interact with each other via emails, online collaboration platforms, social media sites, as well as videoconferencing technologies.

Theoretical Frameworks

Relational cultural theory (RCT) offers a viable theoretical framework for studying mentoring at the level of mentoring episodes. Emphasizing two-directional learning, interdependence of mentor and mentee and of the self, this theory explores the relational skills, conditions, and behaviors that influence these short-term mentoring interactions or episodes (Fletcher & Ragins, 2007). According to RCT, high-quality (mutually growth-fostering) mentoring relationships consist of a series of premium relational-mentoring episodes that occur over time. Uncovering how and why mentoring partners make sense of and characterize such mentoring moments as growth-fostering would be valuable in understanding how such episodes develop in situ and come to be understood as mentoring. However, it is important to note that even when the mentoring relationship is formed, mentoring is still realized, experienced, constructed, and named in episodes that are brief and fluid in nature.

In addition to RCT, Buzzanell (2009) theorized mentoring as positioned within overlapping relational processes "offering opportunities for development, engaging in spontaneous teaching and mentoring, enlarging and enriching resources, and encouraging continuous development" (p. 20). In these processes, mentors along with their mentees engage in co-learning and spiritual discovery of their whole selves and connections with others guided by spiritual values of compassion, simplicity, and humility. Spiritual mentoring is thus coproduced and politicized through ongoing meaning making and co-orientation toward inner and good work (Buzzanell, 2009). As such, mentoring takes place in an episodic format and serves as a site wherein multiple moments aid in mentoring partners' development.

In sum, mentoring is constituted through talk-in-interaction that is found in everyday moments. Mentoring theories that emphasize the communicative processes, multiple inputs, relational aspects, and individuals' agency in the communicative constitution of mentoring can be useful in capturing the tenets of the episodic perspective.

Methodological Approaches

Qualitative research methods are well suited to establish a contextual understanding of participants' perspectives and experiences (Weiss, 1994) and to uncover emergent political dynamics from the data (Lindlof & Taylor, 2002). Different "qualitative methods" have particular merits for the study of mentoring. In terms of data collection, semistructured in-depth interviews with mentors and/or mentees allow researchers to privilege participants' words, to mutually make sense of, and to probe responses to uncover the assumptions and nuanced understandings of mentoring (Lindlof & Taylor, 2002). Structured survey interviews may be used to retrieve the specifics of mentoring episodes (i.e., when, where, with whom, and how) that might be emergent and fragmented in nature. Ethnographic methods, including one-on-one ethnography such as shadowing/spect-acting and reflexive journaling (Gill, 2011), have unique potential for accessing the local episodic mentoring processes and experiences, and capturing the mentoring episodes as they are embedded in and evolve through everyday talks and narratives.

Mentoring research from the episodic perspective might also benefit from mixed methods or crystallized approaches (see Ellingson, 2009; Tracy, 2013). Ethnographic data that incorporate quantitative data (Bakeman & Gottman, 1997; Leonardi, 2009; Treem, 2012) or qualitative data that includes "thick description" (Caughlin et al., 2008; Kuhn & Corman, 2003) can be used to triangulate research findings (Kuhn & Nelson, 2002) and further tease out different dimensions and layers of mentoring episodes, factors that contribute to the enactment of these episodes, and the impact of episodic mentoring on relational partners' careers and psychological well-being. In terms of data analysis, a grounded theory approach (Charmaz, 2006; Glaser & Strauss, 1967) could yield insights for innovative/alternative mentoring constructs/models, and offer opportunities to integrate mentoring into existing frameworks to study communicative phenomena such as meanings of work, organizational sensemaking, leadership, socialization, and identity construction in the workplace.

Empirical Illustration

We completed an empirical study that examined the episodic mentoring experiences of engineering faculty members from a large midwestern U.S. university to understand how they provided and received episodic mentoring. Based on an inductive-deductive analysis of in-depth interviews, we found that this spontaneous form of mentoring contributed to the development of participants' careers, work/life balance issues, and ways to manage workplace politics (Buzzanell et al., 2013). Here we present insights from our empirical study to illustrate the theoretical and methodological approaches discussed earlier.

In our study, participants discussed three overlapping means of episodic mentoring: direct advice or information seeking, observation focused on learning, and engagement in serendipitous interactions. In direct advice or information seeking, our participants would tell us about times when they wanted to obtain information or advice from another person, so they would engage in conversations with that identified mentor. Many of our interviewees saw these episodic interactions as problem based, meaning that they sought counsel for a perceived need, problem, or question. Our participants reported observation as the second means of episodic mentoring and noted that observation occurred when they would watch and/or model the behavior of another colleague. This form of mentoring was described as direct (working on a research team with a possible mentor) or indirect (overheard advice given to another person). Finally, participants discussed episodic mentoring that occurred at serendipitous times. These interactions happened unexpectedly (in hallways, at airports, in coffee shops, and during social gatherings; see Buzzanell, 2009) and were facilitated through factors such as proximity, collegiality, and the organizational culture.

By engaging in an episodic mentoring perspective, we were able to identify instances of mentoring moments. The everydayness of episodic mentoring in both direct and mediated forms, can make it less visible and valued as "mentoring." However, in retrospect, many of these episodes became meaningful mentoring experiences. Our empirical findings also offer support for the cumulative nature of mentoring moments that may evolve into more structured and strategic mentoring processes.

In short, the episodic perspective allows us to unpack the theoretical and pragmatic importance of examining episodic mentoring as talk-in-interaction embedded within the everyday routines and structures of organizational life. Next, we explore how these episodes of mentoring may constitute and interact in communication networks.

Network Perspective

The network perspective views mentoring as constituted in the form of communication networks with multiple mentoring agents—human, nonhuman, or the communicative episode itself—and relationships among these agents at different levels and stages. This perspective is largely informed by network theories, which in essence enable researchers to "represent relational data and explore the nature and properties of those relations" (Monge & Contractor, 2003, p. 35). From the network perspective, mentoring is conceptualized as constantly (re)constructing networks that adapt to individual/organizational needs and preferences in changing spatial, temporal, institutional, and cultural contexts. This conceptualization offers a holistic and intricate view of mentoring, highlighting the interactions of its components and contextual influences.

The agents, typically represented as nodes in individuals' or organizations' mentoring networks, are not necessarily confined to only humans. Nonhuman agents, such as workshops and computer programs, can also be included in the mentoring network to provide a comprehensive account of the mentoring experiences under study. Additionally, mentoring that emerging from the dynamics of the group as a whole can also be counted as a group agent in the network (Dansky, 1996; see also Bozeman & Feeney, 2007).

In addition to recognizing multiple and diverse agents of mentoring, taking a network perspective highlights the relations, typically represented as links or ties connecting various nodes in the networks (Monge & Contractor, 2003). This perspective prescribes a shift of the unit of analysis from dyadic mentoring connection or single mentoring episode to the relationships of groups of mentoring agents and episodes. This shift of focus allows research guided by the network perspective to investigate the (dis)embeddedness of the mentoring network in larger social relationships and processes (Giddens, 2000; Granovetter, 1985). Informed by the network perspective, mentoring researchers also can study mentoring in relation to other types of network ties based on organizational charts, professional memberships, collaborations, information sharing, geographic locations, and so on. Multiple types of network ties, or multiplex ties, are usually interdependent and can influence the formation or dissolution of ties in each other's networks (Lee & Monge, 2011; Shumate et al., 2013). In the mentoring context, multiplexity may indicate that there are other relationships between mentor and mentee (e.g., leader–subordinate, collaboration, or friendship) in addition to mentorship itself. From this view, the network perspective can contribute to our understandings of the emergence and constitutive nature of mentoring ties and the coevolution of mentoring with other networks through communicative interactions.

Mentoring networks developed from self-report data can also display individuals' meaning making about their mentoring experiences over time. For instance, interview and career reflection data can situate mentoring within individuals' retrospective sensemaking, perceptions about current workplace experiences and exchanges, and career aspirations and linkages. Performing and co-orienting oneself to others in mentoring networks are communicatively constituted processes with the production of mentoring networks displaying effects of distanciation. That is, mentoring network becomes relatively "autonomous and de-contextualized from its condition of production" (Cooren et al., 2011, p. 1162). In other words, once mentoring is communicatively constructed in form of a network, the network then becomes the materialized structure or text. As noted by Cooren and colleagues (2011), "any subsequent talk relying on this text thus implies a work of recontextualization, which consists of actualizing its meaning in the current conversation" (p. 1162). Thus, reported networks not only situate mentoring experiences in specific spatio-temporal contexts but also, in turn, influence how individuals talk about their mentoring experience in the here and now as well as prospectively and strategically for their anticipated and aspirational mentoring networks. As such, mentoring networks can be considered as both the "organization" of mentoring resources, and the "organizing" processes for mentoring. Our approach aligns with the CCO perspective to consider how the ideational and material aspects of communication are "co-implicated and co-constituted in organizing" (Cooren et al., 2011, p. 1154).

Theoretical Frameworks

Existing mentoring research from a network perspective has not yet fully tapped into the theories of communication networks (Haggard et al., 2011; Ragins & Kram, 2007). In this section, we present a brief overview of the possible linkages between mentoring and communication network theories. The network approach to mentoring is useful because researchers can "map" and analyze individual as well as organizational mentoring configurations. Conducting longitudinal studies that capture the evolutions of individual and groups mentoring relationships over the span of their careers and communities of practice would enable researchers to explore various definitions, needs, and outcomes of mentoring at different stages.

At an individual level, one's mentoring experiences can be studied from egocentric networks, defined as networks that include "a focal persona or respondent (ego), a set of alters who have ties to ego, and measurements on the ties from ego to alters and on the ties between alters" (Wasserman & Faust, 1994, p. 53). In egocentric mentoring networks, the mentee serves as the "ego" or hub who reports linkages to identified mentoring agents, which are termed "alters" or nodes. Mentoring agents in networks include both human and nonhuman sources (e.g., books, websites, and blogs; Contractor, Monge, & Leonardi, 2011; Long, Buzzanell, Kokini, Wilson, Anderson, et al., 2013). When completing an analysis of egocentric mentoring network, the *size* (number of ties/mentoring agents linked to the mentee), *diversity* (number, type, and uniqueness of the mentors), and *strength* (emotion, reciprocity, and frequency of interactions between mentor and mentee) provide unique insights about mentoring experiences and structures that cannot be captured by traditional survey methods (McKeen & Bujaki, 2007; Van Emmerick, 2004). In addition to the egocentric networks, the network perspective can be extended to account for organizational level networks, or complete networks. This organizational level network can map mentoring relationships as well as other linkages between organizational members.

Multiple theoretical frameworks can be used to explain the constructions, configurations, and evolutions of individual and organizational mentoring networks (Monge & Contractor, 2003). For instance, the theory of homophily, when applied to a mentoring context, posits that mentees and mentors tend to select others who are similar to themselves (e.g., gender, race/ethnicity, prestige, and academic interests). These demographic features are seen as important factors in developing social networks because the relationships between and among individuals are based on social processes and personal preferences (McPherson, Smith-Lovin, & Cook, 2001). Moreover, the theory of social capital (structural holes) assumes that individuals try to develop outside connections (i.e., those who are not linked with each other) so that they can increase their autonomy and identify possible career development opportunities (Burt, 1992; Granovetter, 1985). Research related to social capital has demonstrated that the diverse networks developed by people can extend their exposure to novel information, more participation, and career mobility opportunities (Granovetter, 1985). When applied to mentoring contexts, mentees would attempt to connect with mentors/nodes that exist outside of their original professional networks with the hope of increasing their exposure, visibility, and career mobility (Dansky, 1996).

Methodological Approaches

Recognizing the versatility of network theories and methodologies (for a review of communication network theory and methodology, see Monge & Contractor, 2003), we propose a couple of network analysis techniques that are well suited to answer research questions guided by a network perspective to mentoring. We recommend a multidimensional mentoring network modeled after communication research recommendations by Contractor et al. (2011). The multidimensional network model acknowledges networks as constituted fundamentally in communication and aims to capture the complexity, diversity, and multiplicity of networks that are enacted communicatively. This model allows researchers to explore the networks consisting of multiple types of nodes (multimodal) and relationships (multiplex), which provide a more comprehensive picture of mentoring processes. Specifically, the multidimensional mentoring network captures both human and nonhuman sources of mentoring (e.g., individual mentor, group mentor, professional organizations, books, and technology), the relationships between mentor and mentee that occur in multiple social contexts (e.g., friendships and research collaborations), and communication in multiple media (e.g., virtual and/or face-to-face mentoring).

Expanding CCO-guided methodologies to study broader networks of communication episodes, Blaschke, Schoeneborn, and Seidl (2012) proposed a network analysis approach that situates communication at the center of the network analysis and turns the prevalent network perspective "inside out" insofar as network nodes represent communication episodes and network ties represent individuals. Researchers can thus create networks of mentoring episodes that provide data for explicating how these communicative interactions unfold in specific locales and how mentoring is mobilized by various agents.

In addition to capturing and depicting mentoring in network forms, statistical analysis of aggregated network data can predict potential causes and consequences of various mentoring network configurations and (co)evolutions (Monge & Contractor, 2003). For instance, exponential random graph models (ERGMs) can be used to statistically explore and explain network configurations including the parameters of a given network (Shumate & Palazzolo, 2010). These explanations and predictions can be valuable in understanding the mentoring process at a broader scale to facilitate decision and policy making related to mentoring. Further, agent-based simulations, which create hypotheses/models for empirical testing by giving agents simple rules and letting agents operate based on those rules over time, can be used to uncover the mechanisms influencing mentoring networks (Palazzolo, Serb, She, Su, & Contractor, 2006).

To collect empirical network data, researchers can employ data gathering techniques such as interviews or observations, or combine multiple databases related to mentoring in addition to the traditional network survey method. Multiple data points provide richer contextualized knowledge of the mentoring process and can increase validity of research findings via data triangulation (Tracy, 2013). When incorporated in a comprehensive research design, mentoring networks can display the manifestations of structures and routines that coproduce mentorship, which can help explain both the sensemaking about and the talk-in-interaction recognized as mentorship. Finally, semantic networks can be used to present individuals' shared interpretations or constructions of mentoring. In these semantic networks, linkages can be established between people who share similar interpretations (Monge & Eisenberg, 1987; Shumate et al., 2013). In the mentoring context, the resultant network can provide understandings of those who share common understandings of communicative messages or events about mentoring, those who have idiosyncratic meanings, and those who serve as boundary spanners between nodes (Monge & Contractor, 2003).

Empirical Illustration

In our study of the multidimensional mentoring network, we mapped the egocentric mentoring networks of male and female faculty members with different academic rankings in a midwestern university based on in-depth interview data (Long, Buzzanell, Kokini, Wilson, Anderson, et al., 2013). During the interviews, we asked participants to detail the linkages between themselves and mentoring nodes. We then analyzed the interview transcripts using inductive-deductive strategies (Charmaz, 2003, 2006), paying specific attention to the mentoring agents at different stages of their careers, their interactions with agents in various contexts, their feelings about such relationships, and their perceived outcomes to construct their respective egocentric mentoring network.

We noticed that the mentoring networks were primarily career based and informal, consisting of diverse mentoring agents serving different functions. In addition, mentees and mentors usually interacted in multiple contexts in addition to mentoring. In other words, the ties between mentoring agents were multiplex. These findings align with the theoretical claims that we proposed before. Furthermore, female and ethnic minority engineering faculty's mentoring networks indicated that they had larger and more diverse mentoring networks compared to those who belonged to the dominant gender and ethnic group. We found that untenured faculty, as opposed to tenured faculty, also had more expanded mentoring networks and were more motivated in constructing their mentoring networks. Furthermore, mentoring networks were not fixed but were constantly evolving as one's career advanced. We observed that faculty's mentoring network tended to shrink after tenure and that faculty shifted from the role of mentee to the role of mentor.

In short, the network approach depicts graphically the multiple mentoring relationships and agents that emerge in diverse circumstances. Such structural analysis can be combined with other data and analytic techniques to provide empirical understandings about individuals' sensemaking of emerging and highly politicized mentoring structures, retrospective interpretation of past mentorships, and prospective meaning making and/or strategic planning of future mentoring possibilities that may be formal, informal, and episodic. To further situate mentoring in the discourses of power, knowledge, empowerment, and social justice, we present our final communicative perspective—the intersectional perspective—on mentoring.

Intersectional Perspective

Mentoring has been emerging as a process essential to creating more inclusionary institutional cultures that appreciate intersections of differences (Buzzanell et al., 2013; Johannessen & Unterreiner, 2010). Intersectionality refers to "the complex, irreducible, varied, and variable effects which ensue when multiple axes of differentiation—economic, political, cultural, psychic, subjective, and experiential—intersect in historically specific contexts" (Brah & Phoenix, 2004, p. 76). Guided by the intersectional perspective, interactions capitalizing on difference, including gender, race, ethnicity, culture, and nationality, are taken into consideration as a whole when exploring individuals' and collectivities' mentoring processes and practices. The intersectional perspective views mentoring as communicative practice both shaped by and shaping the discursive and materialized aspects of mentoring, in which different meanings and acts of mentoring are communicatively constructed and used effectively/meaningfully. Thus, mentoring from the intersectional perspective can be analyzed as a contested site for the reproduction of both marginalization and privilege, which offers opportunities to increase individuals' feelings of growth, inclusiveness, and well-being and to promote institutional change toward more inclusionary spaces.

From an individual standpoint, mentoring from an intersectional perspective can be viewed as a communicative process that aims to empower individuals to become agents in their own worlds and create opportunities for them to envision the possible selves to which they aspire (Buzzanell et al., 2013). In this line of thought, mentoring can be constructed as mutual empowerment as exemplified in what Jipson and Paley (2000) called co-mentoring, a simultaneous and alternating mentoring practice based on collaboration, which constructs "a creative, democratic space for the formation of insights and understandings that help us search for and choose ourselves in the situation" (p. 37). In this dynamic and engaged process, both mentor and mentee at the moment gain knowledge, resources, and support to mobilize their agency. Whereas productive mentoring processes cultivate these agentic aspirational selves, toxic or dysfunctional mentoring (Feldman, 1999; Simon & Eby, 2003) can diminish the sense of confidence and inclusion one may experience. The individual at this point may search for better mentoring systems to disrupt unproductive mentoring patterns. Regardless, the mentoring processes are generative and intergenerational in that individuals' mentoring experiences or lack thereof as mentees shape how they approach mentoring when they become mentors. Taken together, the intersectional perspective contributes to mentoring as well as diversity and inclusion scholarship by providing in-depth understandings of how individuals seek and cultivate their aspirational selves in navigating the mentoring process in organizational settings. It also uncovers the tacit ways by which privilege and marginalization are produced and reproduced despite good intentions and efforts to create more inclusionary climates through workshops or formal mentoring programs.

At the community/organizational/societal level, the intersectional perspective of mentoring contextualizes mentoring in myriad social and organizational texts; it highlights mentoring's potential for transforming organizations through co-constructed communicative practice. Mentoring from the CCO perspective can be viewed as intertextual, which entails that "texts that are formed upon, within, in opposition to—and exist as conglomerations of—a myriad of social and organizational texts" (Kuhn, 2012, p. 554). Guided by examination of the interweaving relationships among interaction, linguistic choices, and text, mentoring is investigated in situ with text referring to organizational strategies, policies, values, operation procedures, and other forms and practices that provide deeper insights into how power and resistance are produced and reproduced in everyday mentoring processes. Indeed, researchers guided by the CCO perspective recognize that "organizational values, knowledge, or ideologies can be conveyed, incarnated, and constituted not only through what people say and write, but also through what they wear, how they look, and how they gesture or behave" as well as how they make sense of and use (or fail to use) text (Cooren et al., 2011, p. 1152).

We advocate a politically attentive lens to the constitutive processes of mentoring because attention to these processes would examine more fully the political formation of mentoring in its discourses and materialities (see Deetz & Eger, 2014). This lens would foreground organizational and, by extension, mentorship problematics and processes including identity and recognition, order, truth, life narratives, distribution (ethics and justice), relational claims, and change. In short, the intersectional perspective provides a site for communicative inquiry that helps scholars to (re)imagine mentoring's role in initiating change and building sustainable and inclusionary workplaces.

Theoretical Frameworks

The theoretical lens of intersectionality challenges fixed conceptualizations of and solitary attention to race, gender, age, sexuality, culture, and class by highlighting the complexity, multiplicity, and fluidity of differences in specific locales. As a result, intersectionality reinforces the notion that all individuals are constructions of multiple identities with each of these singular identities working together to create collective experiences. Each of these identities within context informs the ways in which people experience life. The intersectionality theoretical lens makes visible the multiple positionings that constitute one's mentoring experiences, and the gendered, racialized, sexualized, and international/cultural relations of power (Holvino, 2008). Considering that people experience life events through multiple positionings, mentoring relationships can be constructed in ways that allow appreciation for the various individual differences that exist and support new ways of knowing and experiencing. The intersectional perspective thus empowers researchers to unveil the everyday mentoring experiences of individuals, such as organizational members from underrepresented minority groups, both for how they are marginalized and for where they also experience privilege.

Stemming from the intersectionality theory, mentoring also can be theorized as a communicative process where emotions intersect and are layered with gender and other identity anchors in nuanced, complicated, and shifting patterns in particular contexts (Buzzanell, 1994, 1995; Buzzanell & Turner, 2003; Mumby & Putnam, 1992; Tracy, 2000, 2004; Tracy & Trethewey, 2005). As noted by Mumby and Putnam (1992), emotionality can be "an alternative mode of organizing in which nurturing, caring, community, supportiveness, and interrelatedness are fused with individual responsibility to shape organizational experiences" (p. 474). Thus, mentoring, as a way of organizing that is constituted in communication, can also be depicted as organizing and experiencing workplaces through emotionality (Anderson, Long, Buzzanell, Kokini, & Batra, 2013). The embodied emotionality of mentoring can be explored through attention to emotional labor, namely, the work through which feeling displays are managed to be situationally appropriate as dictated by the organization, profession, or larger society (Hochschild, 1983; Miller & Koesten, 2008; Yanay & Shahar, 1998). Within a mentoring context, each party constitutes mentorships through ongoing talk-in-interactions whereby emotions may be regulated to meet various expectations and strategically elicit responses from others (Metts & Planalp, 2003; Redden, 2012). Furthermore, people who are considered different from dominant groups can be disadvantaged and advantaged in complex ways depending on how identities come to bear on particular situations (Davis, 2008; Dhamoon, 2011; Holvino, 2008; Winkler & Degele, 2011). Construction of emotionality in mentoring might provide important insights into promoting more inclusionary and empowering institutional cultures.

Methodological Approaches

In terms of methodology, those that privilege the participants' words and bring to light their different needs, ambivalences, disjunctures, vulnerabilities, and frustrations in mentoring relationships are valuable for understanding mentoring from an intersectional perspective. Narrative analysis, for instance, offers useful means of accessing one's sensemaking and storytelling of mentoring over time and in various contexts (Fisher, 1987). Narratives at a local level can also serve as counternarratives to the grand narratives of mentoring as uniformly beneficial to career development and social support. In particular, feminist poststructural narratology allows researchers to analyze how the overarching stories of mentoring become actualized, shifted, and fragmented; it offers spaces for agency, voice, and the emergence of possible selves in faculty members' everyday discourses to better understand academic mentoring and its transformative potential (Buzzanell et al., 2013).

In narrative analysis, individuals are viewed as "homo narrans" (Fisher, 1984, 1987) as they are making sense of the meanings of the world and are telling stories based on their own interpretations. In these narratives, audiences and the storytellers themselves can explore how they have become who they are today. Additionally, through details told within and about particular contexts, researchers can situate these stories in rich detail about material and discursive constraints and opportunities where power, authority, structure, and agency are negotiated. Poststructuralist narratology illuminates such negotiations and tensions as mentors and mentees construct multiple and shifting stories to preserve voice, power, dignity, and agency (Bloom, 1996; Buzzanell & Liu, 2005; Mezei, 1996; Smith & Dougherty, 2012; Trethewey, 2001; Weedon, 1997). In short, a poststructuralist narratological methodology enables scholars to see mentoring as a contested site in which individuals develop agency and their own situated spaces for formal, informal, and/or episodic mentoring.

We also call for other critical and feminist approaches to study mentorship, such as Critical Discourse Analysis (Berger & Luckmann, 1966; Fairclough, 1992), which examines how texts shape and are shaped by social, political, and historical contexts at the micro- and macro-levels. Critical Discourse Analysis can assess how mentoring as text is strategically arranged and/or omitted to achieve specific goals and promote certain interpretation of narratives. Autoethnography also can be employed to theorize individuals' experiences and interpretations (Lindlof & Taylor, 2002). This method enables mentors and mentees to engage in reflexive theorizing and tease out the various manifestations, emotions, relations, and power dynamics in the mentoring processes. We illustrate some of our theoretical and methodological claims in the following empirical study.

Empirical Illustration

In our research, we investigated how women faculty of color in male-dominated academic environments, such as engineering, described various aspects of mentoring processes critical to their own well-being and that of their communities (Buzzanell et al., 2013). We analyzed their narratives of mentoring from in-depth interviews selected from our larger database on faculty mentoring. The poststructuralist narratological critique encouraged us to explicate shifting subject positions, ambivalences, contradictory and surprising emplotments, missing or forgotten voices, exigencies, everyday struggles, and the very nature of mentoring grand narratives themselves. Using poststructuralist narratology and intersectionality theory, we drew out key particularities of these women's mentoring experiences in situ to explore how these women engineering faculty of color perceived mentoring to be simultaneously enriching and constraining, inclusionary and exclusionary, obligatory and agentic, as well as bounded and boundaryless spatially, temporally, and personally. Guided by the intersectional perspective, we read between the lines of faculty members' narratives to understand how privilege and marginalization mutually informed formal, informal, as well as episodic mentoring processes and how these power dynamics influenced the career development as well as the personal well-being of these women. Further, our participants' stories highlighted women's meaning making about their resilience and agentic power in challenging the traditional mentoring model, creating meaningful mentoring structures, and (re)inventing their aspirational selves.

Toward a Communicative Research Agenda for Mentoring

We have proposed three perspectives—episodic, network, and intersectional—as valuable additions to the existing mentoring scholarship. We highlight and link these three, which have been underdeveloped theoretically in current mentoring scholarship, by extending their utility in our development of a comprehensive approach to mentoring as constituted communicatively through meaning making, relational coproductions, and structures. We emphasize their value in terms of studying mentoring, particularly from this multifaceted constitutive communicative approach. These three perspectives are mutually productive and informative in our mentorship model. For example, in our empirical studies of faculty mentoring, we investigated formal, informal, and episodic mentoring, meaning making about mentoring in particular contexts, and comparisons of mentoring networks across gender, race/ethnicities, and academic positions. Utilizing multiple perspectives offers insight into privilege, access, and structures for acquiring the needed resources and constructing productive identities to enhance success and well-being.

As a key communicative process that shapes organizational members' career, relationships, sense of inclusion, and overall well-being, we call for research from varying communication perspectives, contexts, and methodological approaches to unpack the intricacies of mentoring. Mentorship is not constructed simply as a tool for human resource management (HRM) in different organizational contexts but as an ongoing constitutive process that harbors potential for greater insight into human communication and for the transformation of current organizations (for revisiting communication in HRM, see Miller & Gordon, in press). Throughout our literature review and proposed extensions, we have acknowledged that there are multiple communication and interdisciplinary perspectives that add value to understanding the scholarship and practice of mentoring. Taking a lead from Deetz and Eger (2014), we begin with the premise that we need to study mentorship from multiple vantage points but also need to develop more fully what a mentoring-as-communicatively-constituted approach would look like. As Deetz and Eger put it, their organizational communication lens

> in no way denies the existence of things called structures, roles, norms, knowledge, networks, and information flow nor minimizes the benefits of temporarily holding them as stable and studying them as such; rather, it highlights the recognition that these areas were developed, deployed, and rendered significant in complex interaction systems. This recognition is core to communication studies, yet relatively few organizational communication scholars have approached research in this way.

In keeping with this sentiment, communication researchers can explore further the discursive, performative, and relational constructions of mentoring by individuals, developmental networks, and collectivities in context. CCO provides a metaperspective on mentoring in which episodic, network, and intersectional mentoring can be co-oriented. By approaching mentoring as constituted in and through communication, such an umbrella approach brings order to the seemingly disparate practices, theories, and methods in mentoring (Cooren et al., 2011) and guides the integration of the various perspectives articulated in this piece.

In the following section, we outline a research agenda that addresses the intersections of mentoring and communication research from a constitutive approach to mentoring. Research threads stemming from the three mentoring perspectives with proposed research questions are presented in Table 13.1.

Mentoring as Constituted and Manifest Complexly

Studying the discursive construction of mentoring can provide unique insights into individuals' career development and nuanced understanding of how mentoring processes (or substitutes) weave into their organizational lives. Guided by tenets of CCO, the constitutive approach to mentoring unveils the unstructured and spontaneous talk-in-interaction between mentors and mentees that has the potential to challenge the taken-for-granted dominant (dyadic) mentoring definitions and structures. A constitutive approach encourages investigation into how multiple stakeholders construct knowledge and practices about mentoring processes that may be fraught with paradox, uncertainty, and ambiguity because of difference. In this way, it can bring not only gender and race but also other differences into consideration by explicating the coproduction of mentoring processes. Moreover, such an approach looks to participants' sensemaking in situ to uncover the design processes whereby mentorship can become productive for all in diverse ways over the course of individuals', institutions', and communities' life span.

In addition to destabilizing mainstream conceptualizations of mentoring, this line of research also contributes to a meaning-centered communication research agenda on multiple levels (Dougherty, Kramer, Klatzke & Rogers,

Table 13.1 A Communicative Research Agenda for Mentoring

Perspective	Mentoring Conceptualization	Suggested Research Questions
Episodic Perspective	Mentoring is conceptualized as consisting of episodes that are constituted communicatively between mentors and mentees	Definitional issues of mentoring episodes: • How do the mentoring moments differ from other constructs such as advice giving/seeking, information gathering, and professional networking? • What part of knowledge transmission/relational interaction is considered as mentoring? • How are the beginnings and endings of mentoring episodes and relationships constituted communicatively and bracketed? Intentionality of the mentoring process: • How do agents enact roles of mentor and mentee in their dynamic mentoring interactions/communicative events? • Does mentoring need to be recognized as such to be mentoring? If the interaction is considered as mentoring only in hindsight, when and how would we call these interactions mentoring? • Do both parties need to recognize mentoring as such or only one party? What are the implications of one party offering mentoring that is not perceived as mentoring by the other party? • How do organizations foster an environment that encourages and appreciates the emergence of mentoring episodes? Impact of episodic mentoring: • How does mentoring as episodes cross/reinforce the boundaries between personal and professional, life and work, and friendship and collegiality? • How do communicative mentoring episodes constitute or supplement formal and informal mentoring in both online and offline settings?

(Continued)

Table 13.1 (Continued)

Perspective	Mentoring Conceptualization	Suggested Research Questions
Network Perspective	Mentoring is conceptualized as constantly (re)constructing communicative networks that adapt to individual/organizational needs and preferences in changing spatial, temporal, institutional, and cultural context.	Form and configurations of mentoring network: • What do individuals' or collectives' multi-dimensional mentoring networks look like? • How do individuals' mentoring networks differ from the existing mentoring structures (e.g., formal mentoring assignment)? • What are the relationships between mentoring and other types of network ties (e.g., professional membership, workplace friendship, collaboration, information sharing, and geographic locations)? (Co)evolution of mentoring network: • How do individuals use mentoring networks to make sense of their mentoring experiences retrospectively and strategically design their career networks? • What are the underlying mechanisms that influence the constructions, configurations, and evolutions of mentoring networks at both the individual and organizational level? • How do the organizational structure, professional community, and larger societal narratives of work and career influence one's construction of mentoring networks? • How is mentorship created, sustained, constrained, and contested in accordance with McPhee and Zaug's (2000) four-flow model?

| Intersectional Perspective | Mentoring is conceptualized as highly politicized and situated sites in which individuals perform complex and interconnected identities and communicative interactions capitalizing on difference, including gender, race, ethnicity, culture, and nationality. | Deconstruction of the grand narrative of positive mentoring:
• How do multiple stakeholders construct knowledge and practices about mentoring processes that may be fraught with paradox, uncertainty, and ambiguity?
• How are toxic or dysfunctional mentoring processes constructed? With what consequences?
• How do mentors and mentees deal with tensions in the communicative interactions, such as discontent, misunderstandings, or conflicts of interest?

Difference and power enacted in mentoring:
• How are gender, race, ethnicity, power structure, and other differentiating schemes constituted and enacted in mentoring interactions and relationships?
• What are the everyday mentoring experiences of those who are under-represented/socially marginalized? Where do privilege and marginalization intersect?
• How are power and resistance produced and reproduced in everyday mentoring processes?
• How is mentoring used to perpetuate or deconstruct the power dynamics and the taken-for-granted privileges in the workplace?
• How are structures of institutions shaping and being shaped by mentoring processes that influence the development and well-being of individuals and organizations?

Emotions in the mentoring process:
• How is emotionality constructed in mentoring that might provide insights into promoting more inclusionary and empowering institutional cultures?
• How do emotions and characters of caring and nurturing come into play in mentoring episodes in the workplace?
• To what extent do mentors take roles aligned with mentee nurturing, care, and growth? |

2009). From an interpersonal relational perspective, it would be promising to explore how mentors and mentees deal with tensions in the communicative interactions, such as discontent, misunderstandings, or conflicts of interest. Future research could also delve into the contextual variables (proximity of the office, organizational culture, or group membership) and personal aspects (personality, physical appearance, ethnicity, or academic interests) that influence the communicative interactions and strategies used by mentors and mentees. On the organizational level, scholars could examine how organizations define mentoring, identify how and through what qualities members want to enhance mentoring relationships, and situate mentoring within the organizational rhetoric related to growth and well-being. From a more structurational view, mentorship as constituted communicatively could pursue alignment with McPhee and Zaug's (2000) four-flow model in which membership negotiation, reflexive self-structuring, activity coordination, and institutional positioning intersect and contribute distinctly to mentorship processes and practices. How mentorship is created, sustained, constrained, and contested can be examined communicatively within and across these flows.

Furthermore, we call for critical, feminist, and postcolonial scholars to deconstruct the grand narratives of positive mentoring. These studies could display how mentoring is actually enacted within various contexts rather than relying on assumptions that mentoring is always a positive experience or yields beneficial outcomes for mentors and mentees. How mentoring relationships can be both productive and destructive with wide-ranging effects to current mentoring participants and other organizational members could be studied (Feldman, 1999; Ragins & Kram, 2007; Simon & Eby, 2003).

Mentoring as Episodic and Mediated

Mentoring, as constituted in and through communication, often occurs in episodic, discontinued, and fragmented fashion. A productive research line could stem from questions about when and where mentoring takes place and about who mentors and mentees are. Research questions might center on the parameters/boundaries of mentoring, which are constantly unfolding from the episodic perspective. We encourage mentoring scholars to explicate the episodic nature of mentoring through discussion of intentionality, evaluation, and conditions that prime the emergence of spontaneous mentoring episodes (for specific research questions, see Table 13.1).

Additionally, the effects of mentoring moments on formal and informal mentoring programs should be examined to better understand how these moments supplement existing organizational structures, create new opportunities, and gain legitimacy. Indeed, the mentoring episode offers a useful lens for distinguishing mentoring interactions from mentoring relationships. The concept of mentoring episode captures the dynamics of relationships and may provide insight into how spontaneous mentoring interactions in everyday organizational life transform and reconfigure the interactional parties into mentors and/

or mentees in formal or informal mentoring relationships. In addition, insights of how, when, where, and why mentoring is happening from individuals' perspectives provide valuable theoretical and pragmatic implications to foster a mentoring culture and improve the existing mentoring structures.

In addition to mentoring research based on face-to-face interactions and collective organizing in situ, we can expand the existing research to include the digital mentoring processes. Although previous research has investigated e-mentoring programs and the benefits associated with them (e.g., boundaryless, egalitarian, and interorganizational connections), the literature mostly focused on evaluating the large-scale, formal, online mentoring programs using primarily quantitative data (Berema & Merriam, 2002; Single & Single, 2005). Research has not yet unpacked how communication technology, especially social media in the Web 2.0 era, has shaped how we define mentorship, seek and/or receive mentoring, and engage in mentoring episodes. As the Internet and communication technology are permeating our daily life, it seems impossible to provide an accurate and comprehensive account of one's mentoring experience without considering the mentoring received/performed online and in other computer-mediated forms. Thus, an interesting research area would be to explore how mentoring unfolds in mediated communication spheres. Moreover, researchers could explore the impact of communication technology on the changing notions of mentoring. In today's context, blogs, podcasts, online forums, and anonymous online support groups provide "on the go" mentoring, and it is not uncommon for people to start seeking mentoring by searching a list of keywords online. As communication technology continues to develop and convey, it is critical to understand the (co)production of mentoring content generated by users online, and its impact on what scholars and organizational members consider as mentoring and on how mentoring is performed.

Researchers can also examine the structure of online mentoring using social network analysis. Previous research indicated that e-mentoring programs could provide mentoring opportunities for those who otherwise would be left out of important informal networks (Single & Single, 2005). It would be beneficial to explore the relationship between e-mentoring experience, use of communication technology, and individual's current and aspirational mentoring networks. Finally, we call for research efforts to explicate the overlapping boundaries between mentoring across different channels/venues. For instance, how do formal, informal, and episodic mentoring play out with multiple mentors in both online and off-line spheres? The increasingly connected nature of mentorship may also enable and/or constrain individuals' efforts to separate and/or integrate boundaries between work and life, professional and personal, and public and private.

Mentoring as Fundamental in Inclusion and Well-Being

In this call for mentorship as constituted communicatively, we look both at talk in which mentorship parties express their identities and their relational work. This work examines who they are and how mentorship coproduces the bases for inclusion and collaboration. Rather than focusing on mentorship as a means of creating a more inclusionary climate to foster belongingness, collaboration, and authenticity—important goals for researchers and practitioners—we situate mentorship as the fundamental process in inclusion. When mentors and mentees envision their relationships as sites in which they can give of their selves, they look outward rather than inward. They can take risks and engage in problem identification in multidisciplinary contexts such that they can get at the heart of collaborative interests. Moreover, research may seek to explore the embeddedness and politicized nature of mentoring in the existing organizational structural arrangements, which is played through the communicative constitution of mentoring. Another research line can look at the commodification of mentoring such as mentoring consulting, self-guided books, and computer software programs. Research can critically analyze these discourses distinctly and in combination with everyday talk of mentoring to answer questions about how mentors and mentees are portrayed, what notion of mentoring is privileged and/or silenced, and the social and political underpinning of these discourses.

Furthermore, as noted earlier, mentoring research can contribute to engaged scholarship to redress marginalization for particular groups and promote equality in the workplace. This role of mentorship in combating the isolation of (many) working lives is underdeveloped in current scholarship. Communication scholars could take a critical approach and explore how gender, race, ethnicity, power structure, and other differentiating schemes are constituted and enacted in the episodic mentoring interactions and in the formal/informal mentoring relationships. Mentoring research can serve as a unique entrée point to deconstruct the power dynamics within the workplace, challenge taken-for-granted privileges, and advocate for transformation. Communication scholars interested in this line of research can engage populations that have been ignored by traditional mentoring scholarship. These populations include but are not limited to unemployed workers, contract/temporary workers, labor-intensive workers, business owners, and others.

Practical Implications

In addition to theoretical contributions, integrating the episodic, network, and intersectional perspectives into mentoring offers pragmatic value. These perspectives can provide guidelines to create more productive mentorships—not from lists of dos and don'ts but from consideration of interactional, relational, and structural mentoring processes that are constituted communicatively.

Integrating these different perspectives within a constitutive approach means that mentorship may be dyadic but more often would form and reform based on different parties' interests and needs. Although parties would switch roles as mentor and mentee, when performing as mentees, these individuals and groups would benefit from strategically developing collaborative mentorships of multiple parties and recognizing the value of mentoring episodes for diverse viewpoints, innovative ideas, and just-in-time advice. Moreover, mentees can engage in building their multidimensional mentoring networks whereby they construct collaborative and diverse mentoring partnerships to leverage mentoring as a potential arena for empowerment and opportunity for personal thriving. Mentors can take on different mentoring styles to support mentees both emotionally and psychologically and serve as resources and sponsors to help mentees develop their careers and expand their professional networks (Buzzanell, 2009; Ibarra et al., 2010), knowing that they can also learn and benefit from mentorships. In terms of mentoring interactions, we suggest that mentors engage in dialogues, rather than reinforcing monologic interactions (Bokeno & Gantt, 2000), to construct organizational realities with mentees. Moreover, mentors should take the lead in constructing and maintaining mentoring cultures that value co-learning and see the politicized nature of mentoring as beneficial for revitalizing that which could be amplified and institutionalized throughout systems.

As communication plays a constitutive role in mentoring, training and guidelines focused on understanding meaningful mentoring, diversity and inclusion, and communication and dialogue skills of mentors and mentees could help to facilitate productive mentorship for all stakeholders. In the academic context, these stakeholders could include faculty, lecturers or instructors, administrators, staff, students, advisory boards, alums, and visitors in particular contexts. To develop well-defined, accountable, and transparent formal mentoring programs, decision makers should reject the one-size-fits-all model and listen to the needs of the mentors and mentees to constantly improve mentoring policies and procedures. The constitutive approach to mentoring distinguishes between and integrates formal, informal, and episodic mentoring as processes fulfilling different mentoring needs. How these processes occur in particular contexts and with what effects offer opportunities for best practices and nuanced engaged scholarship.

In addition, organizations can use the episodic, network, and intersectional perspectives to (re)articulate and (re)design their mentoring practices to foster a culture of mentoring that values well-being, co-learning, collaboration, growth, and inclusion of its members. Mentoring has the potential to transform institutions into cultures that are inclusive and supportive (Johannessen & Unterreiner, 2010; Maranto & Griffin, 2011). To build mentoring cultures, administrators and senior faculty members would need to take the lead in learning mentoring theories and techniques and in promoting mentoring. In the academic context, deconstructions of privilege are particularly important for international faculty, faculty of color, those from working-class backgrounds, and women faculty in traditionally male-dominated disciplines (Faulkner, 2009; Maranto & Griffin, 2011; Putnam, Jahn, & Baker, 2011; van den Brink & Benschop, 2012).

Finally, we suggest individuals and organizations embrace the network approach to mentoring. A network of mentors can offer mentees resources to address different needs, multiple supports, and diverse insights into one's professional and personal life (Higgins & Thomas, 2001). The benefits of having multiple sources of knowledge, support, and sponsorship contribute to an array of career outcomes, including promotion and career advancement (Ibarra et al., 2010; Singh, Ragins, & Tharenou, 2009), the establishment of professional identities (Dobrow & Higgins, 2005), and more impressive academic achievements (Lach, Hertz, Pomeroy, Resnick, & Buckwalter, 2013). In addition, the mentoring network approach can overcome some of the weaknesses and dissatisfactions associated with mentoring dyads and can contribute to the socialization of new organizational members, and cultivation of peer mentors and nonhierarchical, collaborative, cross-cultural partnerships (Buell, 2004; Cawyer & Friedrich, 1998; Dobrow, Chandler, Murphy & Kram, 2012; Mullen, 2005; Sorcinelli & Yun, 2007).

Conclusion

This chapter sets the groundwork to study mentoring from a constitutive communicative perspective, which provides a more nuanced understanding of mentoring experiences and their potential for inclusion, collaboration, and authenticity. The episodic mentoring approach directs attention to the everyday mentoring moments and the enactment of mentoring relationships embedded within and structuring communicative interactions. The network mentoring approach enables researchers to consider multiple, non/human, and reciprocal mentor–mentee relationships based on different needs at different times of these parties' lives. Finally, the intersectional mentoring approach encourages scholars and practitioners to view mentorship as highly politicized and situated sites of contestation and struggle. By legitimizing and extending under-researched areas in mentoring scholarship—episodic, network, and intersectional perspectives of mentoring—the richness, complexities, and political nature of mentoring can be explored more fully and embraced for institutional change. We call for more communication scholars to engage in this research.

Acknowledgments

We thank our reviewers for their insightful guidance throughout the revisions of this chapter.

References

Allen, B.J. (2000). "Learning the ropes": A black feminist standpoint analysis. In P.M. Buzzanell (Ed.), *Rethinking organizational and managerial communication from feminist perspectives* (pp. 177–208). Thousand Oaks, CA: Sage.
Allen, T., Eby, L., O'Brien, K., & Lentz, E. (2008). The state of mentoring research: A qualitative review of current research methods and future research implications. *Journal of Vocational Behavior, 73*, 343–357. doi:10.1016/j.jvb.2007.08.004
Allen, T., Lentz, E., & Day, R. (2006). Career success outcomes associated with mentoring others: A comparison of mentors and nonmentors. *Journal of Career Development, 32*, 272–285. doi:10.1177/0894845305282942

Allen, T., Poteet, M. L., Eby, L., Lentz, E., & Lima, L. (2004). Career benefits associated with mentoring for protégés: A meta-analysis. *Journal of Applied Psychology, 89*, 127–136. doi:10.1037/0021-9010.89.1.127

Anderson, L. B., Long, Z., Buzzanell, P. M., Kokini, K., & Batra, J. C. (2013, November). *Compartmentalizing feelings: Emotional labor in academic mentoring relationships.* Paper presented to the National Communication Association Conference, Washington, DC.

Bakeman, R., & Gottman, J. M. (1997). *Observing interaction: An introduction to sequential analysis.* Cambridge, England: Cambridge University Press.

Berema, L. L., & Merriam, S. B. (2002). E-mentoring using computer mediated communication to enhance the mentoring process. *Innovative Higher Education, 26*, 211–227. doi:10.1023/A:1017921023103

Berger, P., & Luckmann, K. (1966). *The social construction of reality.* London, England: Penguin.

Blaschke, S., Schoeneborn, D., & Seidl, D. (2012). Organizations as networks of communication episodes: Turning the network perspective inside out. *Organization Studies, 33*, 879–906. doi:10.1177/0170840612443459

Bloom, L. R. (1996). Stories of one's own: Nonunitary subjectivity in narrative representation. *Qualitative Inquiry, 2*, 176–197. doi:10.1177/107780049600200203

Bokeno, R. M., & Gantt, V. M. (2000). Dialogic mentoring: Core relationships for organizational learning. *Management Communication Quarterly, 14*, 237–270. doi:10.1177/0893318900142002

Booth, R. (2006). E-mentoring: Providing online careers advice and guidance. *Journal of Distance Learning, 10*, 6–14.

Bowman, S. R., Kite, M. E., Branscombe, N. R., & Williams, S. (1999). Developmental relationships of Black Americans in the academy. In A. J. Murrell, F. J. Crosby, & R. Ely (Eds.), *Mentoring dilemmas: Developmental relationships within multicultural organizations* (pp. 21–46). Mahwah, NJ: Erlbaum.

Bozeman, B., & Feeney, M. K. (2007). Toward a useful theory of mentoring: A conceptual analysis and critique. *Administration & Society, 39*, 719–739. doi:10.1177/0095399707304119

Brah, A., & Phoenix, A. (2004). Ain't I a woman? Revisiting intersectionality. *Journal of International Women's Studies, 5*, 75–86. doi:10.1177/1464700108086364

Brummans, B., Hwang, J., & Cheong, P. (2013). Mindful authoring through invocation: Leaders' constitution of a spiritual organization. *Management Communication Quarterly, 27*, 346–372. doi:10.1177/0893318913479176

Buell, C. (2004). Models of mentoring in communication. *Communication Education, 53*, 56–73. doi:10.1080/0363452032000135779

Burt, R. S. (1992). *Structural holes.* Cambridge, MA: Harvard University Press.

Buzzanell, P. M. (1994). Gaining a voice: Feminist organizational communication theorizing. *Management Communication Quarterly, 7*, 339–383. doi:10.1177/0893318994007004001

Buzzanell, P. M. (1995). Reframing the glass ceiling as a socially constructed process: Implications for understanding and change. *Communication Monographs, 62*, 327–354. doi:10.1080/03637759509376366

Buzzanell, P. M. (2009). Spiritual mentoring: Embracing the mentor⇅◊mentee relational process. *New Directions for Teaching and Learning, 120*, 17–24. doi:10.1002/tl.373

Buzzanell, P. M., & D'Enbeau, S. (in press). Intimate, ambivalent and erotic mentoring: Popular culture and mentor–mentee relational processes in Mad Men. *Human Relations.* doi:10.1177/0018726713503023

Buzzanell, P.M., Kokini, K., Long, Z., Anderson, L.B., & Batra, J.C. (2012). Episodic mentoring for engineering faculty. In N. Dominguez (Ed.), *Proceeding of the Fifth Annual Mentoring Conference: Facilitating developmental relationships for success* (pp. 59–68). Albuquerque, NM: Mentoring Institute.

Buzzanell, P.M., & Liu, M. (2005). Struggling with maternity leave policies and practices: A poststructuralist feminist analysis of gendered organizing. *Journal of Applied Communication Research, 33*, 1–25. doi:10.1080/0090988042000318495

Buzzanell, P.M., Long, Z., Kokini, K., Anderson, L.B., Batra, J.C., & Wilson, R. (2013, June). *Designing engineering mentoring cultures for the professoriate: Men and women faculty's stories of mentoring for diversity and inclusion.* Paper presented to the International Communication Association Conference, London, England.

Buzzanell, P.M., & Lucas, K. (2013). Constrained and constructed choices in career: An examination of communication pathways to dignity. In E.L. Cohen (Ed.), *Communication yearbook 37* (pp. 3–32). New York: Taylor & Francis.

Buzzanell, P.M., & Turner, L.H. (2003). Emotion work by job loss discourse: Backgrounding/Foregrounding of feelings, construction of normalcy, and (re) instituting of traditional masculinities. *Journal of Applied Communication Research, 31*, 27–57. doi:10.1080/00909880305375

Caughlin, J.P., Brashers, D.E., Ramey, M.E., Kosenko, K.A., Donovan-Kicken, E., & Bute, J. (2008). The message design logics of responses to HIV disclosures. *Human Communication Research, 34*, 655–684. doi:10.1111/j.1468-2958.2008.00336.x

Cawyer, C.S., & Friedrich, G.W. (1998). Organizational socialization: Processes for new communication faculty. *Communication Education, 47*, 234–245. doi:10.1080/03634529809379128

Charland, M. (1987). Constitutive rhetoric: The case of the *peuple québécois. Quarterly Journal of Speech, 73*, 133–150. doi:10.1080/00335638709383799

Charmaz, K. (2003). Qualitative interviewing and grounded theory analysis. In J.A. Holstein & J.F. Gubrium (Eds.), *Inside interviewing: New lenses, new concerns* (pp. 311–330). Thousand Oaks, CA: Sage.

Charmaz, K. (2006). *Constructing grounded theory: A practical guide through qualitative analysis.* London, England: Sage.

Cheney, G., Zorn, T., Planalp, S., & Lair, D. (2008). Meaningful work and personal/social well being. Organizational communication engages the meanings of work. In C.S. Beck (Ed.), *Communication yearbook* (Vol. 32, pp. 136–185). New York: Routledge.

Chesler, N.C., & Chesler, M.A. (2002). Gender-informed mentoring strategies for women engineering scholars: On establishing a caring community. *Journal of Engineering Education, 91*, 49–55. doi:10.1002/j.2168-9830.2002.tb00672.x

Chubin, D.E., May, G.S., & Babco, E.L. (2005). Diversifying the engineering workforce. *Journal of Engineering Education, 94*, 73–86. doi:10.1002/j.2168-9830.2005.tb00830.x

Contractor, N.S., Monge, P.R., & Leonardi, P.M. (2011). Multidimensional networks and the dynamics of sociomateriality: Bringing technology inside the network. *International Journal of Communication, 5*, 682–720. doi:1932–8036/20110682.

Cooren, F., Kuhn, T., Cornelissen, J.P., & Clark, T. (2011). Communication, organizing and organization: An overview and introduction to the special issue. *Organization Studies, 32*, 1149–1170. doi:10.1177/0170840611410836.

Cunningham, S. (1999). The nature of workplace mentoring relationships among faculty members in Christian higher education. *Journal of Higher Education, 70*, 441–463. Retrieved from www.jstor.org/stable/2649310

Dansky, K. H. (1996). The effect of group mentoring on career outcomes. *Group and Organization Management, 21*, 5–21. doi:10.1177/1059601196211002

Davis, K. (2008). Intersectionality as buzzword: A sociology of science perspective on what makes a feminist theory successful. *Feminist Theory, 9*, 67–85. doi:10.1177/1464700108086364

Deetz, S., & Eger, E. (2014). Developing a metatheoretical perspective for organizational communication studies. In L. L. Putnam & D. K. Mumby (Eds.), *The SAGE handbook of organizational communication: Advances in theory, research, and methods* (3rd ed., pp. 27–48). Thousand Oaks, CA: Sage.

de Janasz, S. C., & Sullivan, S. E. (2004). Multiple mentoring in academe: Developing the professional network. *Journal of Vocational Behavior, 64*, 263–283. doi:10.1016/j.jvb.2002.07.001

Dhamoon, R. K. (2011). Considerations on mainstreaming intersectionality. *Political Research Quarterly, 64*, 230–243. doi:10.1177/1065912910379227

Dobrow, S. R., & Higgins, M. C. (2005). Developmental networks and professional identity: A longitudinal study. *Career Development International, 10*, 567–583. doi:10.1108/13620430510620629

Dobrow, S., Chandler, D., Murphy, W., & Kram, K. (2012). A review of developmental networks: Incorporating a mutuality perspective. *Journal of Management, 38*, 210–242. doi:10.1177/0149206311415858

Dominguez, N. (Ed.). (2012). *Proceeding of the Fifth Annual Mentoring Conference: Facilitating developmental relationships for success.* Albuquerque, NM: Mentoring Institute.

Dougherty, D. S., Kramer, M. W., Klatzke, S. R., & Rogers, T. K. K. (2009). Language convergence and meaning divergence: A meaning centered communication theory. *Communication Monographs, 76*, 20–46. doi:10.1080/03637750802378799

Ellingson, L. L. (2009). *Engaging crystallization in qualitative research: An introduction.* Thousand Oaks, CA: Sage.

Fairclough, N. (1992). *Discourse and social change.* Cambridge, England: Polity.

Fairhurst, G. T. (2011). Discursive leadership. In A. Bryman, D. Collinson, K. Grint, B. Jackson, & M. Uhl-Bien (Eds.), *The Sage handbook of leadership* (pp. 493–505). London, England: Sage.

Fairhurst, G. T., & Connaughton, S. (2014). Leadership communication. In L. L. Putnam & D. K. Mumby (Eds.), *The SAGE handbook of organizational communication: Advances in theory, research, and methods* (3rd ed., pp. 401–424). Thousand Oaks, CA: Sage.

Fairhurst, G. T., & Putnam, L. (2004). Organizations as discursive constructions. *Communication Theory, 14*, 5–26. doi:10.1111/j.1468–2885.2004.tb00301.x

Faulkner, W. (2009). Doing gender in engineering workplace cultures. I. Observations from the field. *Engineering Studies, 1*, 3–18. doi:10.1080/19378620902721322

Feldman, D. (1999). Toxic mentors or toxic protégés? A critical re-examination of dysfunctional mentoring. *Human Resource Management Review, 9*, 247–278. doi:10.1016/S1053–4822(99)00021–2

Fisher, W. R. (1984). Narration as human communication paradigm: The case of public moral argument. *Communication Monographs, 51*, 1–22. doi:10.1080/03637758409390180

Fisher, W. R. (1987). *Human communication as narration: Toward a philosophy of reason, value and action.* Columbia: University of South Carolina Press.

Fletcher, J. K., & Ragins, B. R. (2007). Stone center relational cultural theory: A window on relational mentoring. In B. R. Ragins & K. E. Kram (Eds.), *The handbook of mentoring at work: Theory, research, and practice* (pp. 373–400). Thousand Oaks, CA: Sage.

Fox, M.F. (2010). Women and men faculty in academic science and engineering: Social-organizational indicators and implications. *American Behavioral Scientist, 53*, 997–1012. doi:10.1177/0002764209356234

Giddens, A. (2000). *Runaway world: How globalization is reshaping our lives.* New York: Routledge.

Gill, R. (2011). The shadow in organizational ethnography: Moving beyond shadowing to spect-acting. *Qualitative Research in Organizations and Management, 6*, 115–133. doi:10.1108/17465641111159116

Glaser, B., & Strauss, A. (1967). *The discovery of grounded theory.* Chicago, IL: Aldine.

Granovetter, M. (1985). Economic action and social structure: The problem of embeddedness. *American Journal of Sociology, 91*, 481–510. Retrieved from www.jstor.org/stable/2780199

Haggard, D.L., Dougherty, T.W., Turban, D.B., & Wilbanks, J.E. (2011). Who is a mentor? A review of evolving definitions and implications for research. *Journal of Management, 37*, 280–304. doi:10.1177/0149206310386227

Higgins, M.C., & Thomas, D.A. (2001). Constellations and careers: Toward understanding the effects of multiple developmental relationships. *Journal of Organizational Behavior, 22*, 223–247. doi:10.1002/job.66

Hill, S.E.K., Bahniuk, M.H., & Dobos, J. (1989). The impact of mentoring and collegial support on faculty success: An analysis of support behavior, information adequacy, and communication apprehension. *Communication Education, 38*, 15–31. doi:10.1080/03634528909378737

Hochschild, A.R. (1983). *The managed heart: Commercialization of human feeling.* Berkeley: University of California Press.

Holvino, E. (2008). Intersections: The simultaneity of race, gender and class in organization studies. *Gender, Work and Organization, 17*, 1–30. doi:10.1111/j.1468–0432.2008.00400.x

Ibarra, H., Carter, N.M., & Silva, C. (2010). Why men still get more promotions than women. *Harvard Business Review, 88*, 80–126.

Jablin, F.M. (2001). Organizational entry, assimilation, and disengagement/exit. In F.M. Jablin & L.L. Putnam (Eds.), *The new handbook of organizational communication: Advances in theory, research, and methods* (pp. 732–818). Thousand Oaks, CA: Sage

Jipson, J., & Paley, N. (2000). Because no one gets there alone: Collaboration as co-mentoring. *Theory into Practice, 39*, 36–42. doi:10.1207/s15430421tip3901_6

Johannessen, B.G.G., & Unterreiner, A. (2010). Formal and informal mentoring in academia for the 21st century. *Education and society, 28*, 31–49. doi:10.7459/es/28.3.03

Kalbfleisch, P.J. (2002). Communicating in mentoring relationships: A theory for enactment. *Communication Theory, 12*, 63–69. doi:10.1111/j.1468–2885.2002.tb00259.x

Kalbfleisch, P.J. (2007). Mentoring enactment theory: Describing, explaining, and predicting communication in mentoring relationship. In B.R. Ragins & K.E. Kram (Eds.), *The handbook of mentoring at work* (pp. 499–517). Thousand Oaks, CA: Sage.

Kalbfleisch, P.J., & Davies, A.B. (1991). Minorities and mentoring: Managing the multicultural institution. *Communication Education, 40*, 266–271. doi:10.1080/03634529109378850

Kalbfleisch, P.J., & Davies, A.B. (1993). An interpersonal model for participation in mentoring relationships. *Western Journal of Communication, 57*, 399–415. doi:10.1080/10570319309374464

Kalbfleisch, P. J., & Eckley, V. K. (2003). Facilitating mentoring relationships: The case for new technology, *Informing Science*, 1581–1590.

Kirby, E., & Buzzanell, P. M. (2014). Communicating work-life. In L. L. Putnam & D. K. Mumby (Eds.), *The SAGE handbook of organizational communication: Advances in theory, research, and methods* (3rd ed., pp. 351–373). Thousand Oaks, CA: Sage.

Kram, K. (1983). Phases in the mentor relationship. *Academy of Management Journal, 26,* 608–625. Retrieved from www.jstor.org/stable/255910

Kuhn, T. (2012). Negotiating the micro-macro divide: Thought leadership from organizational communication for theorizing organization. *Management Communication Quarterly, 26,* 543–584. doi:10.1177/0893318912462004

Kuhn, T., & Corman, S. R. (2003). The emergency of homogeneity and hetrogeneity in knowledge structures during a planned organizational change. *Communication Monographs, 70,* 198–229. doi:10.1080/0363775032000167406

Kuhn, T., & Nelson, N. (2002). Reengineering identity: A case study of multiplicity and duality in organizational identification. *Management Communication Quarterly, 16,* 5–38. doi:10.1177/0893318902161001

Lach, H. W., Hertz, J. E., Pomeroy, S., Resnick, B., & Buckwalter, K. C. (2013). The challenges and benefits of distance mentoring. *Journal of Professional Nursing, 19,* 39–48. doi:10.1016/j.profnurs.2012.04.007

Lee, S., & Monge, P. (2011). The coevolutation of multiplex communication networks in organizational communities. *Journal of Communication, 61,* 758–779. doi:10.1111/j.1460-2466.2011.01566.x

Leonardi, P. M. (2009). Why do people reject new technologies and stymie organizational changes of which they are in favor? Exploring misalignments between social interactions and materiality. *Human Communication Research, 35,* 407–441. doi:10.1111/j.14682958.2009.01357.x

Lindlof, T. R., & Taylor, B. C. (2002). *Qualitative communication research methods.* Thousand Oaks, CA: Sage.

Long, Z., Buzzanell, P. M., Kokini, K., Wilson, R., Anderson, L. B., & Batra, J.C. (2013, November). *Implications of women and men engineering faculty's mentoring networks.* Paper presented to the National Communication Association Conference, Washington, DC.

Long, Z., Buzzanell, P. M., Kokini, K., Wilson, R., Batra, J. C., & Anderson, L. B. (2013). Exploring women engineering faculty's mentoring networks. In *Proceedings of the 2013 American Society of Engineering Education (ASEE) Annual Conference,* Atlanta, GA, Session T571. Retrieved from www.asee.org/public/conferences/20/papers/6463/view

Lucas, C. J., & Murry, J. W., Jr. (2002). *New faculty: A practical guide for academic beginners.* New York: Palgrave.

Maranto, C. L., & Griffin, A. (2011). The antecedents of a "chilly climate" for women faculty in higher education. *Human Relations, 64,* 139–159. doi:10.1177/0018726710377932

McKeen, C., & Bujaki, M. (2007). Gender and mentoring: Issues, effects, and opportunities. In B. R. Ragins & K. E. Kram (Eds.), *The handbook of mentoring at work: Theory, research and practice* (pp. 197–222). Thousand Oaks, CA: Sage.

McPhee, R., & Zaug, P. (2000). The communicative constitution of organizations: A framework for explanation. *The Electronic Journal of Communication/La Revue Electronique de Communication, 10,* 1–2.

McPherson, M., Smith-Lovin, L., & Cook, J. (2001). Birds of a feather: Homophily in social networks. *Annual Review of Sociology, 27*, 415–444. doi:10.1146/annurev. soc.27.1.415

Metts, S., & Planalp, S. (2003). Emotional communication. In M. Knapp, J. Daly, & G. R. Miller (Eds.), *Handbook of interpersonal communication* (3rd ed., pp. 339–373). Newbury Park, CA: Sage.

Mezei, K. (1996). Introduction: Contextualizing feminist narratology. In K. Mezei (Ed.), *Ambiguous discourse: Feminist narratology and British women writers* (pp. 1–18). Chapel Hill: University of North Carolina Press.

Miller, V., & Gordon, M. (Eds.). (in press). *Meeting the challenge of Human Resource Management: A communication perspective.* New York: Routledge

Monge, P. R., & Contractor, N. S. (2003). *Theories of Communication Networks.* New York: Oxford University Press.

Monge, P. R., & Eisenberg, E. M. (1987). Emergent communication networks. In F. M. Jablin, L. L. Putnam, K. H. Roberts, & L. W. Porter (Eds.), *Handbook of organizational communication* (pp. 304–342). Newbury Park, CA: Sage.

Mullen, C. (2005). *Mentorship.* New York: Peter Lang.

Mumby, D. K. (1997). Modernism, postmodernism, and communication studies: A rereading of an ongoing debate. *Communication Theory, 7*, 1–28. doi:10.1111/ j.1468–2885.1997.tb00140.x

Mumby, D. K. (2011). Organizing difference: An introduction. In D. K. Mumby (Ed.), *Reframing difference in organizational communication studies: Research, pedagogy, practice* (pp. vii–xiii). Thousand Oaks, CA: Sage.

Mumby, D. K., & Putnam, L. L. (1992). The politics of emotion: A feminist reading of bounded rationality. *Academy of Management Review, 17*, 465–486. Retrieved from www.jstor.org/stable/258719

Nelson, D. (2005). *A national analysis of diversity in science and engineering faculties at research universities.* Washington, DC: National Organization for Women.

O'Brien, K. E., Biga, A., Kessler, S. R., & Allen, T. D. (2010). A meta-analytic investigation of gender differences in mentoring, *Journal of Management, 36*, 537–554. doi:10.1177/0149206308318619

Oglensky, B. (2008). The ambivalent dynamics of loyalty in mentorship. *Human Relations, 61*, 419–448. doi:10.1177/0018726708089000

Palazzolo, E. T., Serb, D., She, Y., Su, C., & Contractor, N. S. (2006). Co-evolution of communication and knowledge networks as transactive memory systems: Using computational models for theoretical development. *Communication Theory, 16*, 223–250. doi:10.1111/j.1468–2885.2006.00269.x

Parse, R. R. (2002). Mentoring moments. *Nursing Science Quarterly, 15*, 97. doi:10. 1177/08943180222108868

Pawley, A. (2009). Universalized narratives: Patterns in how faculty members define "engineering". *Journal of Engineering Education, 97*, 309–319. doi:10.1002/j. 2168–9830.2009.tb01029.x

Phillips, N., & Oswick, C. (2012). Organizational discourse: Domains, debates and directions. *Academy of Management Annals, 6*, 435–481. doi:10.1080/19416520.2 012.681558

Putnam, L. L., Jahn, J., & Baker, J. (2011). Intersecting difference: A dialectical perspective. In D. K. Mumby (Ed.), *Reframing difference in organizational communication studies: Research, pedagogy, and practice* (pp. 31–53). Thousand Oaks, CA: Sage.

Putnam, L. L., & Nicotera, A. M. (Eds.). (2008). *Building theories of organization: The constitutive role of communication.* New York: Routledge.

Ragins, B. R., & Kram, K. E. (Eds.). (2007). *The handbook of mentoring at work: Theory, research, and practice.* Thousand Oaks, CA: Sage.

Ragins, B. R., & Scandura, T. A. (1997). The way we were: Gender and the termination of mentoring relationships. *Journal of Applied Psychology, 82,* 945–953. doi:10.1037/0021–9010.82.6.945

Redden, S. M. (2012). How lines organize compulsory interaction, emotion management, and "emotional taxes": The implications of passenger emotion and expression in airport security lines. *Management Communication Quarterly, 27,* 121–149. doi:10.1177/0893318912458213

Schrodt, P., Cawyer, C. S., & Sanders, R. (2003). An examination of academic mentoring behaviors and new faculty members' satisfaction with socialization and tenure and promotion processes. *Communication Education, 52,* 17–29. doi:10.1080/03634520302461

Shumate, M., & Palazzolo, E. (2010). Exponential random graph (p*) models as a method for social network analysis in communication research. *Communication Methods and Measures, 4,* 341–371. doi:10.1080/19312458.2010.527869

Shumate, M., Pilny, A., Atouba, Y., Kim, J., Peña y Lillo, M., Cooper, K. R., . . . Yang, S. (2013). A taxonomy of communication network. In E. Cohen (Ed.), *Communication yearbook 37* (pp. 95–124). New York: Taylor & Francis.

Simon, S., & Eby, L. (2003). A typology of negative mentoring experiences: A multidimensional scaling study. *Human Relations, 56,* 1083–1106. doi:10.1177/0018726703569003

Singh, R., Ragins, B. R., Tharenou, P. (2009). What matters most? The relative role of mentoring and career capital in career success. *Journal of Vocational Behavior, 75,* 56–67. doi:10.1016/j.jvb.2009.03.003

Single, P. B., & Single, R. M. (2005). E-mentoring for social equity: Review of research to inform program development. *Mentoring and Tutoring, 13,* 301–320. doi:10.1080/13611260500107481

Smith, F., & Dougherty, D. (2012). Revealing a master narrative: Discourses of retirement throughout the working life cycle. *Management Communication Quarterly, 26,* 453–478. doi:10.1177/0893318912438687

Sorcinelli, M. D., & Yun, J. (2007). From mentor to mentoring network: Mentoring in the new academy. *Change: The Magazine of Higher Learning, 39,* 58–61. doi:10.3200/CHNG.39.6.58-C4

Tracy, S. J. (2000). Becoming a character for commerce: Emotion labor, self-subordination and discursive construction of identity in a total institution. *Management Communication Quarterly, 14,* 90–128. doi:10.1177/0893318900141004

Tracy, S. J. (2004). The construction of correctional officers: Layers of emotionality behind bars. *Qualitative Inquiry, 10,* 509–533. doi:10.1177/1077800403259716

Tracy, S. J. (2013). *Qualitative research methods: Collecting evidence, crafting analysis, communicating impact.* Oxford, England: Wiley-Blackwell.

Tracy, S. J., & Trethewey, A. (2005). Fracturing the real-self↔fake-self dichotomy: Moving toward "crystallized" organizational discourses and identities. *Communication Theory, 15,* 168–195. doi:10.1111/j.1468–2885.2005.tb00331.x

Treem, J. W. (2012). Communicating expertise: Knowledge performances in professional service firms. *Communication Monographs, 79,* 23–47. doi:10.1080/03637751.2011.646487

Trethewey, A. (2001). Reproducing and resisting the master narrative of decline: Midlife professional women's experiences of aging. *Management Communication Quarterly, 15,* 183–226. doi:10.1177/0893318901152002

van den Brink, M., & Benschop, Y. (2012). Gender practices in the construction of academic excellence: Sheep with five legs. *Organization, 19,* 507–524. doi:10.1177/1350508411414293

Van Emmerick, I.J.H. (2004). The more you can get the better: Mentoring constellations and intrinsic career success. *Career Development International, 9,* 578–594. doi:10.1108/13620430410559160

Wasserman, S., & Faust, K. (1994). *Social network analysis: Methods and applications.* New York: Cambridge University Press.

Weedon, C. (1997). *Feminist practice and poststructuralist theory.* Oxford, England: Basil Blackwell.

Weiss, R. S. (1994). *Learning from strangers: The art and method of qualitative interview studies.* New York: Free Press.

Winkler, G., & Degele, N. (2011). Intersectionality as multi-level analysis: Dealing with social inequality. *European Journal of Women's Studies, 18,* 51–66. doi:10.1177/1350506810386084

Yanay, N., & Shahar, G. (1998). Professional feelings as emotional labor. *Journal of Contemporary Ethnography, 27,* 346–373. doi:10.1177/089124198027003003

Zellers, D., Howard, V., & Barcic, M. (2008). Faculty mentoring programs: Reenvisioning rather than reinventing the wheel. *Review of Educational Research, 78,* 552–588. doi:10.3102/0034654308320966

Zey, M. G. (1991). *The mentoring connection.* Homewood, IL: Dow Jones-Irwin.

About the Editor

Elisia L. Cohen earned her PhD in communication from the University of Southern California and is Associate Professor of Communication and Director of the Health Communication Research Collaborative at the University of Kentucky. Today, she is Chair of the Department of Communication in the College of Communication and Information at the University of Kentucky. Her research has been supported by the Centers for Disease Control and Prevention, the National Institutes of Health, Merck Sharp & Dohme Corporation, and an unrestricted gift from GlaxoSmithKline. She is an investigator with the Rural Cancer Prevention Center, St. Louis Center for Excellence in Cancer Communication Research, and was past media coordinator for the Cervical Cancer-free Kentucky initiative. Her research on public communication, public opinion, and public health has appeared in such journals as *Health Communication*, *Health Education and Behavior*, *Journal of Applied Communication Research*, *Journal of Broadcasting and Electronic Media*, *Journal of Communication*, *Journal of Health Communication*, *Qualitative Health Research*, and *Prometheus*. She is married and has one daughter, Addison Lydia.

About the Contributors

Lindsey B. Anderson is a doctoral candidate in the Brian Lamb School of Communication at Purdue University, where she studies organizational communication. She earned her master's degree at Indiana University, Indianapolis. She is interested in examining the intersections of communication, age, and emotion in the workplace. Her research has appeared in or is in press with *Journal of Public Relations Review*, *Management Communication Quarterly*, *Communication Research Reports*, and the *Journal of Professional Communication.*

Analisa Arroyo is Assistant Professor at the University of Georgia in the Department of Communication Studies. She earned her PhD in communication at the University of Arizona. Her primary research interests rest at the junction of health and interpersonal communication in the realm of body image issues. Her research explores how both interpersonal skills and dynamics (e.g., family interactions, social skills, relationship outcomes) and what is explicitly said about weight (i.e., fat talk) are associated with health-related outcomes (e.g., self-perceptions, psychosocial well-being, and health maintenance behaviors). Her publications have appeared in *Communication Monographs*, *Journal of Applied Communication Research*, *Journal of Family Communication*, and *Personality and Individual Differences*, among others.

Jennifer C. Batra is a third-year doctoral student at Purdue University, Brain Lamb School of Communication. With more than 10 years work experience, Jennifer's research draws on her experiences in local, state, and national government and seeks to understand the dynamics between organization structures and team performance. As an outcome of her work, Jennifer hopes to increase job satisfaction and organizational awareness.

Patrice M. Buzzanell is Professor in the Brian Lamb School of Communication and the School of Engineering Education by courtesy at Purdue University. The coeditor of three books and author of 140 articles and chapters, her research centers on the everyday negotiations and structures that produce and are produced by the intersections of career, gender, and communication, particularly in STEM (science, technology, engineering, and math). Her research has appeared in such journals as *Communication Monographs, Management Communication Quarterly, Human Relations, Communication Theory, Human Communication Research,* and *Journal of Applied Communication Research,* as well as handbooks on professional, organizational, gender, applied, family, ethics, and conflict communication. A fellow of the International Communication Association, she has received awards for her research, teaching/mentoring, and engagement.

Ioana A. Cionea is Assistant Professor in the Department of Communication at the University of Oklahoma. She earned her PhD at the University of Oklahoma. She specializes in intercultural communication with a specific interest in arguing behaviors and conflict. Her work traces cultural factors that affect arguing and its functions within and across cultures. Some of the topics she has studied include cross-cultural comparisons of serial arguments, the functions of arguing in other cultures, and the factors that influence the decision to engage in arguments in interpersonal relationships. Her work has been presented at many national and international conferences and has been published in journals such as *International Journal of Intercultural Relations* and the *Journal of Argumentation in Context.*

Tina A. Coffelt is Assistant Professor in the Communication Studies Program at Iowa State University. She earned her PhD at the University of Missouri. She teaches courses in interpersonal communication. Her research examines sexual communication in marital and parent–child relationships. She is also interested in identity, crisis situations, and interpersonal communication in organizations. Her research has appeared in the *Journal of Family Communication,* the *Journal of Sex Research, Women's Studies in Communication,* and *Qualitative Research Reports in Communication* and will soon appear in the *Journal of Sex and Marital Therapy.*

Nichole Egbert is Associate Professor in the School of Communication Studies at Kent State University. Her research centers predominantly on social support in health contexts with a specific focus on family caregiving. Other research interests include spirituality/religiosity and health behavior and health literacy. She actively collaborates with a wide range of researchers, including those in the fields of nursing, public health, medicine, and communication. Her research can be found in outlets such as *Health Communication, Journal of Health Communication, Journal of Communication and Religion, Journal of American College Health,* and the 2011 *Routledge Handbook of Health Communication.*

Howard Giles is Professor of Communication at the University of California–Santa Barbara. He is founding Editor of the *Journal of Language and Social Psychology* and the *Journal of Asian Pacific Communication.* Giles is past president of International Communication Association and the International

Association of Language and Social Psychology. His research interests encompass interpersonal and intergroup communication processes in intergenerational, police–civilian, and other settings, and he is the editor of the *Handbook of Intergroup Communication.*

Dale Hample is Associate Professor in the Department of Communication at the University of Maryland, College Park. He earned his PhD at the University of Illinois. His primary specialization is the social scientific study of interpersonal arguing. He has published widely in the specialty argumentation journals, as well as the mainstream journals in the field of communication. He has been keynote speaker at meetings of both the Ontario Society for the Study of Argumentation and the National Communication Association/American Forensic Association Summer Conference on Argumentation. Among his major research topics are personalizing conflicts, editing one's own arguments, serial arguing, and deciding whether or not to engage in a possible argument. His *Arguing: Exchanging Reasons Face to Face* (2005, Erlbaum) is an analysis of interpersonal arguing that focuses mainly on social scientific research.

Jake Harwood is Professor of Communication at the University of Arizona. He earned his PhD at the University of California, Santa Barbara. He is the author of *Understanding Communication and Aging* (2007, Sage) and coeditor of *The Dynamics of Intergroup Communication* (2011, Peter Lang). His publications have appeared in *Personality and Social Psychology Bulletin*, *Journal of Applied Communication Research*, *Communication Monographs*, *Human Communication Research*, and the *British Journal of Social Psychology*, among others.

Amy Janan Johnson is Associate Professor in the Department of Communication at the University of Oklahoma. She earned her PhD at Michigan State University. Under the broad umbrella of interpersonal and relational communication, Dr. Johnson's research examines interpersonal argument, communication in long-distance relationships and friendships, and communication in stepfamilies. Her research has been published in such venues as *Communication Monographs*, *Journal of Social and Personal Relationships*, and *Argumentation and Advocacy.*

Jennifer A. Kam is Assistant Professor in the Department of Communication at the University of Illinois at Urbana–Champaign. Her research focuses on stressors that place Latino adolescents at risk for poor mental health and substance use outcomes. She also examines how communication with parents and friends affects substance use beliefs and behaviors, as well as attenuates the negative effects of stressors.

Vikki S. Katz is Assistant Professor of Communication in the School of Communication and Information at Rutgers University. She earned her PhD at the University of Southern California. Her research explores the communication challenges that immigrant families face as they integrate into U.S. society, with particular interest in the roles that children play in these learning processes. She is author of *Kids in the Middle: How Children of Immigrants Negotiate Community Interactions for their Families* (2014, Rutgers University Press) and coauthor of *Understanding Ethnic Media: Producers, Consumers, and Societies* (2011, Sage Publications). Her work has also been published in *Hispanic Journal of Behavioral Sciences*, the *Journal of Children and Media*, the *Journal of Communication*, *Journalism*, and the *Journal of Information Policy*.

Jeong-Nam Kim received his PhD in communication (public relations) from the University of Maryland, College Park, in 2006 and joined the faculty at Purdue in 2007. His specialties are communication theory, strategic management of public relations, public behavior and its social consequences, information behaviors, and problem solving. Jeong-Nam has constructed the situational theory of problem solving with James E. Grunig. The situational theory explains causes and processes of information behaviors in problematic life situations. He applies the situational theory to public relations, public diplomacy, health communication, risk communication, science communication, and employee communication. He also developed a new theoretical model that integrates the causes and processes of organizational relationships, reputation, and brand through the Behavioral, Strategic Management Paradigm in public relations.

Klod Kokini is Professor in the School of Mechanical Engineering and the Weldon School of Biomedical Engineering by courtesy. He is also Associate Dean for Academic Affairs in the College of Engineering at Purdue University. Kokini is a Fellow of American Society of Mechanical Engineers (ASME; 2002), a Fellow of the American Institute of Medical and Biological Engineering (2008), and a member of the Board of Directors of Women in Engineering ProActive Network. He earned a PhD from Syracuse University and a BSME from Bogazici University. He has initiated collaborations with faculty in social sciences to study issues related to gender in engineering and how mentoring can have an impact on faculty. He was the recipient of the Purdue Dreamer Award (2005), the Violet Haas Award (2007), and the ASME Johnson and Johnson Medal in recognition of his outstanding efforts on diversity.

Janice L. Krieger is Assistant Professor in the School of Communication at The Ohio State University, where she teaches and conducts research on social influence processes and health decision making. She is specifically interested in the relative contributions of health care providers and family members on patient decision making. She is an author or coauthor of more than 30 articles appearing in journals such as *Health Communication*, the *Journal of Health Communication*, *Human Communication Research*, and *Patient Education and Counseling*.

Arunima Krishna is a graduate student at the Brian Lamb School of Communication with an emphasis on public relations. Her research interests include the strategic management of public relations and public behavior, crisis management, and the management of internal communication. Her recent projects include an examination of an organization's informal social networks and how those contribute to organization–employee relationships, as well as a study of the linkages between risk-related issues and of how the risk perceptions held by publics may transfer between risks.

Vanja Lazarevic is a postdoctoral research fellow at the Refugee Trauma and Resilience Center, Boston Children's Hospital and Harvard Medical School, Boston, Massachusetts. Her research focuses on acculturation- and immigration-related factors and how those factors affect immigrant and refugee youth well-being, their relations with their parents, and overall family dynamics.

Maria Löblich is Assistant Professor in the Department of Communication Science and Media Research, Ludwig-Maximilians-Universität München. She was part of the fellowship class at the Berkman Center for Internet & Society at Harvard University in the 2012–2013 academic year. Her research focuses on Internet policy with a particular interest in political processes and actor-structure interactions.

Ziyu Long is a third-year doctoral student in Organizational Communication in the Brian Lamb School of Communication and a recipient of the Ross Fellowship (2011–2012) and the Bilsland Strategic Initiatives Fellowship (2012–2013) at Purdue University. Her research interests include entrepreneurship, career, and gender in the globalized and digitalized workplace. Her research has appeared in such outlets as *Journal of Business and Technical Communication* and conference proceedings of the American Society of Engineering Education.

Ananda Mitra is Professor of Communication at Wake Forest University, teaching courses on new media, research methodology, and India. His publications include a 10-volume series on digital technology and its social impact, a critical examination of the Indian TV series the *Mahabharat*, an examination of the portrayal of India in Western cinema, a book about the ways in which new digital technologies are increasingly alienated from the users, a book on the cultural issues surrounding the use of social media, and two books on research methodology. He has published nearly one hundred journal articles and presented papers at numerous conferences all over the world. He has consulted with many different industries and is the inventor of the concept of "narbs" that allows for a careful and systematic narrative analysis of the unstructured component of big data.

Francesca Musiani is a postdoctoral researcher at the Centre for the Sociology of Innovation, MINES ParisTech/CNRS. Recently, she was the 2012–2013 Yahoo! Fellow in Residence at Georgetown University and an affiliate of the Berkman Center for Internet & Society at Harvard University. She is the author of *Nains sans géants. Architecture décentralisée et services Internet* (2013, Presses des Mines). Her research explores Internet governance in an interdisciplinary perspective.

Loreen N. Olson is Associate Professor in the Department of Communication Studies at the University of North Carolina–Greensboro. She teaches courses in and conducts research on interpersonal, gender, and family communication. More specifically, her research focuses on the darker side of intimate and family relationships, including, for example, intimate partner violence, the luring communication of child sexual predators, relational aggression, and the communication of deviance. Dr. Olson has published numerous book chapters and articles that have appeared in academic journals such as *Communication Theory*, *Communication Monographs*, *Women's Studies in Communication*, *Sex Roles*, and the *Journal of Applied Communication*. She is the coauthor of a book titled the *Dark Side of Family Communication* and is the editor of the *Journal of Family Communication*.

Allison M. Scott is Assistant Professor in the Department of Communication at the University of Kentucky. She earned a PhD from the University of Illinois. Her research examines how people in close relationships manage illness experiences and make health-related decisions. Her work has appeared in outlets such as *Health Communication,* the *Journal of Communication*, the *Journal of Health Communication*, the *Journal of Social and Personal Relationships*, *Qualitative Health Research*, and *Research on Aging*. In 2011, she received the Gerald R. Miller Outstanding Doctoral Dissertation Award from the National Communication Association, and in 2012, she received the Award for the Analysis of Interpersonal Communication in Applied Settings from the International Communication Association.

Jordan Soliz is Associate Professor in the Department of Communication Studies at the University of Nebraska–Lincoln. His research investigates communication and intergroup processes primarily in personal and family relationships, with a current emphasis on multiethnic families, interfaith families, and grandparent-grandchild relationships. In addition to various edited volumes, his work has been published in *Communication Monographs*, *Communication Quarterly*, the *Journal of Family Communication*, the *Journal of Marriage and Family*, and the *Journal of Language and Social Psychology*.

Robyn F. Wilson is a second-year student in the College of Science at Purdue University, majoring in biology. She has participated in multidisciplinary research teams on mentoring (Colleges of Liberal Arts and Engineering) and is currently engaging in research on food and nutrition. She has had papers presented to the International Communication Association and National Communication Association as well as at university presentations.

About the Editorial Assistants

Sarah C. Vos is a doctoral student at the University of Kentucky, where she earned her master's degree. Her research examines the intersection of health and the mass media. Her current focus is on the relationship between media representations and health disparities. She has presented her research at national and regional conferences, and her work was recently published in *Health Communication*. Before turning to the study of communication, Sarah worked as a reporter at *The Lexington Herald-Leader* in Kentucky and at the *Concord Monitor* in New Hampshire. She was also an assistant editor at *Harper's Magazine* in New York City.

Laura E. Young is a doctoral candidate at the University of Kentucky. Her research examines internal and external communication processes in high-risk, high-consequence environments such as fire departments. Specifically, she explores how inevitable organizational change, such as budget cuts or change in leadership, influences communication satisfaction. She is interested in policy changes, updates, and everyday workplace information and the ways these messages are disseminated to organizational members who are constantly on the move. She concentrates on the intersection of interpersonal and organizational communication by examining how interpersonal relationships between superiors and subordinates during change can affect the organizational culture, satisfaction, structure, and performance as well as the external image and reputation of the organization. Her work has been presented at national and international conferences and has been published in journals such as *Communication Education* and *Qualitative Health Research*.

Author Index

Subject Index

Please note: page numbers in *italics* followed by an *f* indicate figures and by a *t* indicate tables